Learning and Development
Fifth edition

Rosemary Harrison is a Fellow of the CIPD and of the Royal Society of Arts, member of the Society of Authors, and a leading academic and author in the learning and development field. After graduating in history honours from King's College London she worked as a training officer in the National Health Service. She then became a lecturer in personnel management and organisational behaviour at Newcastle Polytechnic (later Northumbria University) and course leader of the Institute of Personnel Management's professional qualification programme there. She was subsequently appointed Lecturer in Human Resource Management at Durham University Business School, where she also became director of its Human Resource Development Research Centre. From 1996 to 2008 she was the CIPD's Chief Examiner, Employee/Learning and Development.

The Chartered Institute of Personnel and Development is the leading publisher of books and reports for personnel and training professionals, students, and all those concerned with the effective management and development of people at work. For details of all our titles, please contact the publishing department:

tel.: 020-8612 6204

email: publish@cipd.co.uk

The catalogue of all CIPD titles can be viewed on the CIPD website:

www.cipd.co.uk/bookstore

Learning and Development
Fifth edition

Rosemary Harrison

Chartered Institute of Personnel and Development

For Malcolm, Piers and Dominic

Published by the Chartered Institute of Personnel and Development,
151 The Broadway, London, SW19 1JQ

First edition published 1997
Reprinted 1998, 1999
Second edition published 2000
Reprinted 2000
Third edition published 2002
Reprinted 2002, 2003
Fourth edition published 2005
Reprinted 2006
This edition published 2009

Typeset by 4Word Ltd, Bristol
Printed in Great Britain by Short Run Press Limited, Exeter

British Library Cataloguing in Publication Data
A catalogue record of this book is available from the British Library

ISBN 978 1 84398 216 6

The views expressed in this publication are the author's own and may not necessarily reflect those of the CIPD.

The CIPD has made every effort to trace and acknowledge copyright-holders. If any source has been overlooked, CIPD Enterprises Ltd would be pleased to redress this in future editions.

Chartered Institute of Personnel and Development
151 The Broadway, London, SW19 1JQ

Tel.: 020 8612 6200   Fax: 020 8612
Email: cipd@cipd.co.uk Website: www.cipd.co.uk

Incorporated by Royal Charter Registered Charity No.1079797

Contents

Figures

Tables

Editor's Foreword

I am very pleased to have this opportunity to introduce the fifth edition of Rosemary Harrison's book on *Learning and Development*. As ever it offers a remarkable journey through this ever-expanding field, providing readers with a clear, systematic and comprehensive understanding of what has become a vast and increasingly complex area. Before writing this foreword, I looked through the contents of Rosemary's earlier editions and realised just how dramatically the learning and development agenda has changed even since 2005. Readers hoping to make do with the previous edition are in for a rude shock; this book contains so much new material, it is ordered differently, and it is written in an even more engaging way than previous editions. Anyone who wants to remain ahead of the field and feel confident in their knowledge and understanding of L&D needs to buy this book.

The book is organised into four parts. The first provides readers with an understanding of the field, introducing them to the main themes and issues, as well as providing analysis of the national frameworks and the education system. Without appreciating the mass of activity in these areas, it is impossible to see just how much has changed and its impact on employers and L&D professionals. The second part helps readers get to grips with practice and understand some of the theoretical and ethical considerations involved in embedding learning and development at work. This raises the key issue of how L&D may aid organisational performance. In addition, this edition goes much more deeply into an explanation and critique of learning theories and their application in learning technology and workplace skills and learning. In a break from the past, Chapter 8 is devoted totally to a single in-depth case study which acts as a learning vehicle throughout the book. Part 3 examines how L&D, both the specialist function and in general, can make a contribution to the business, not in terms of vague generalisations and exhortations to engage in training but from the perspective that a variety of solutions may work in the quite different circumstances faced by organisations of different sizes or in different sectors. Finally, the book turns to address how L&D can build for the future, in relation to careers, talent, leadership and management development. Typical of Rosemary, she ends with a series of challenges for the L&D profession and a reiteration that context is critically important, making reference to the 2008 financial crisis as a prime example. As ever, Rosemary's book is totally contemporary, but this is not at the expense of ignoring more deep-seated and enduring issues to do with ethics, wisdom and humility.

Over the years Rosemary Harrison has made a phenomenal contribution to the development of L&D as a field of inquiry, not just as a practical subject, and this book is one which CIPD students in particular need to read from cover to cover if they are to truly understand what the professional standards actually mean. The book is also eminently suited to other postgraduate and post-experience groups, including those who wish to reflect on their own contribution to the subject. In my view, the book succeeds in providing a wide-ranging yet very readable account of how L&D has developed, why its practice varies between contexts and where it might be going in the future. As such it will appeal to a much wider audience, both those on formal courses and people who want to know more about L&D as a corpus of knowledge. By the end of the book, readers will be desperate for the next edition to see how she addresses the challenges posed here.

Professor Mick Marchington
Professor of Human Resource Management,
Manchester Business School,
The University of Manchester

Preface to the fifth edition

THE AIMS OF THE FIFTH EDITION

This fifth edition has the same three aims as the fourth: to meet the needs of a postgraduate market, to encourage high professional standards in the learning and development (L&D) field and to update and enhance readers' understanding of that field. Its stronger research focus is a necessary reminder that in its organisational context L&D no longer constitutes an area of work for beginners. It is – or should be – a central contributor to the success of the business as well as to the growth of individuals.

The first aim means that although the book's content is relevant for CIPD students it is in no way dictated by their particular syllabi. I write, as I have always done, as an independent author. The text's primary focus is on the needs of postgraduate-level students whether studying for the CIPD's professional qualification (CIPD 2005a), on L&D/HRD modules within MBA or master's-level HRM programmes or on specialised L&D/HRD courses of some other kind. However, since it has also been written as a reflective contribution to the field of practice, I hope that it will also be of interest and use to professionals working there.

The second aim rests on an uncomfortable reality: that the L&D field can be too demanding for many. It is complex, challenging and dynamic. Its parameters are broad and its boundaries fuzzy. It offers no black and white prescriptions and its outcomes can be frustratingly difficult to measure. It is under constant public scrutiny as awareness increases about the key role that L&D processes have in aiding business performance, improving the nation's skills and knowledge base and providing help to a significant proportion of the UK's economically active population that lacks the education or training required to gain access to fulfilling jobs and careers. Yet an organisation's investment in L&D is often the first to be cut back at times of external or internal crisis. All of this explains why the L&D field demands of its practitioners exceptional levels of business and partnership skills and of professional expertise.

The need for more evidence-based practice is stressed throughout this book. However, L&D professionals must also innovate and therefore demonstrate the willingness and ability to take intelligently calculated risks and learn from failure. Without those qualities the profession will continue to deserve the judgement passed by two commentators quoted in the book's first chapter: one that fails to move with the times.

The third aim of the book explains why every chapter of the fourth edition has been revised to accommodate new material and integrate it with older but still relevant content. Each also contains textbook and internet-based reference sources to guide further study. I refer frequently to the CIPD's magazine, *People Management*, its research projects and other publications, not only with the needs of CIPD students in mind but to help all readers, because the Institute's website provides so much easily accessible information (see Appendix 2). The third aim has also required a balance to be struck between the book's breadth and depth of coverage. This has called for some hard choices and their outcomes may not please all readers. I hope, though, that most will find that their interests have been met.

THE STRUCTURE OF THE BOOK

The fifth edition of this core text has the same structure as the fourth, as follows:

Part 1 'Understanding the field' introduces L&D as an organisational process and locates it in an external context that sets the scene for all that follows.

Part 2 'Getting to grips with the practice' is concerned with how to achieve high-quality, ethical and professional L&D practice, convincingly linked to organisational as well as individual needs. It contains a real-life case study (Chapter 8) that forms the centrepiece of the book, illustrating in detail what is meant by 'translating theory into practice'.

Part 3 'Making a business contribution' again emphasises the importance of external as well as internal context. It explores L&D in different sectoral settings, major pressures in today's business environment on traditional ways of organising and managing the L&D function and the variety of responses to those pressures. It explores too what the demanding process of 'partnership' involves for L&D practitioners and ways of adding value through L&D activity.

Part 4 'Building for the future' focuses on change management processes and the tasks they raise for L&D practitioners (a new chapter), and on building future capacity and strategic capability through talent and career planning and the development of organisations' leaders and managers. The concluding chapter recalls some of the big issues that have emerged in the book and suggest key challenges now facing the L&D profession.

LEARNING MATERIALS

This fifth edition continues to incorporate learning aids to stimulate and support readers. They include:

- *a glossary of terms* that, although in frequent use in the literature, may be unfamiliar to some. L&D, like any other field, has its own language that is not always comprehensible to those outside it.

- *an introductory section* to each chapter explaining its purpose and the main issues with which it deals and a *concluding section* summarising main ground that it has covered

- *'reflection'* breaks within each chapter to encourage readers to step back from the text in order to consider material covered in the light of their own experience and learning needs

- *case examples* to highlight key issues covered in each chapter

- *review questions* (Appendix 3) relating to the content of each chapter, and advice on how to tackle similar questions in an examination context.

- *further information sources* listed at the end of each chapter, usually incorporating websites as well as books and articles. These and supporting references within the chapters provide readers with the opportunity to explore topics in greater depth. Tutors using the book also have access to a linked Tutors' Manual on the CIPD's website. This manual has been completely revised, restructured and updated, complementing and expanding on material in the book and now forming a major product in its own right.

TERMINOLOGY

Throughout the book terms like 'the firm', 'the business' and 'the company' are used loosely to refer to any kind of organisation, not just those in the private sector. Unless otherwise stated, the term 'HR professionals' should be understood to refer to professionals working in any HR field and therefore to L&D specialists also.

'BEING STRATEGIC'

The fifth edition focuses strongly on the strategic contribution that L&D activity could, and should, make to organisational as well as to individual performance and growth. Yet to those without influence on strategic players in the organisation or on 'strategy' in its more obvious guises such discussion may seem of only theoretical interest. That view is mistaken. In September 2008 the Institute of Employment Studies reported on its recent study of HR functions and their 'customers' in a wide range of UK-based organisations (Hirsh *et al* 2008). The researchers found that participants rarely used the word 'strategy' although they clearly wanted HR activity to have a strategic impact on the business and also saw training and development as an area of high potential value here. 'Strategic' for them meant proactive practitioners who, at no matter what organisational level they operate, have the professional expertise and business understanding to help solve key people problems faced by the business. In CIPD terminology, they wanted their HR professionals to be 'thinking performers'.

So even the most newly-qualified practitioner with L&D responsibilities can be 'strategic' by helping to introduce and embed initiatives that, however small-scale, fulfil the straightforward criteria identified in the IES report. Their influence will grow as people learn to trust and respect their knowledge and judgement. As they work effectively in partnerships, expand their expertise and demonstrate their value to the business and its people their credibility will increase. When the opportune moment comes they will be well placed to become players on the central strategic stage.

Rosemary Harrison
January 2009

Acknowledgements

All real-life material reported in the book relates only to situations current at the time. Unless otherwise indicated, comments on such material are my own and do not represent any official views within or by the organisations concerned.

I thank all the organisations that, through the years of this book's several editions, have allowed me to publish accounts of their business and human resource (HR) policies and practice and I am especially grateful to all those who gave me their time and help in researching and producing the 'Procon' case study recounted in Chapter 8. I acknowledge permission from the following to reproduce or summarise material in this edition:

- Brightwave and AOL for their case in Chapter 6

- The Chartered Institute of Personnel and Development, for material from its research reports

- Dr Carley Foster and Professor Lynette Harris for their Diversity case in Chapter 9

- Hemsley Fraser Group Limited for its case in Chapter 13

- Janice Leeming for her case in Chapter 15

- Palgrave Macmillan for Table 2 in Chapter 2 and the local government cook-freeze centre case in Chapter 6

- *People Management* journal and authors for material from articles as the basis for many case examples

- Sterling Selection Limited for Figure 1 in Chapter 1

- Taylor & Francis Books for Figure 7 in Chapter 5

My thanks also go to the anonymous reviewers of the book's draft text for their helpful suggestions, and to CIPD editorial staff Jenna, Kirsty, Caroline and Ruth for their excellent support. I am most grateful to four members of my CIPD examination marking team – Rona, Deb, Jim and Claire – who gave generous help with the time-consuming tail end of my chief examiner work

Glossary of terms

Adding value in a business context, achieving outcomes that significantly increase the organisation's capability to differentiate itself from other, similar organisations, and thereby enhance its progress; and achieving those outcomes in ways that more than offset the costs that they have incurred

Andragogy the art and science of teaching the adult

Affective engagement pride in the company to which one belongs (Maitland 2007). See also *cognitive engagement*

Assessment centre 'A systematic approach to identifying precisely what is required for success in a particular job and then labelling these requirements in terms of a short-list of tightly defined criteria' (Stevens 1985). Data collected in this way is used primarily to feed into decisions about promotion or some other form of employee redeployment

Asynchronous taking place after a time delay

Behaviourism also known as positivism – a mindset that rests on the assumption that the world is an objective reality 'out there'

Bite-sized learning popularised by the Learning and Skills Council – the approach described as 'light touch' or modular workplace learning by which subject matter is divided into short chunks (one- or two-hour blocks are common) in order to achieve speed, reduce learning time and costs, and increase ease and motivation for learners

'Black box' refers to the fact that although many studies have explored the link between HR practices and policies and organisational performance, few have sought to explain the nature of this connection. The Work and Employment Research Centre at the University of Bath has sought to remedy this by looking inside the 'box'. The resulting 'people and performance' model offers a way of examining and understanding the influence of HR practices on organisational performance (Purcell *et al* 2003)

Business partnership when applied to HR practitioners, the collaboration of those practitioners with key players in the business – especially managers – in order to achieve outcomes that will benefit that business

Career 'The total sequence of employment-related positions, roles, activities and experiences encountered by an individual' (Jackson 2000)

Cognitive engagement support for one's own company's strategy and the direction it is taking (Maitland 2007). See also *affective engagement*

Cognitive learning theories also known as positivist theories – theories that focus on the cognitive structures that enable the individual to make sense of events and situations

Cognitive structures theoretical concepts and knowledge of procedures (also known as 'representations') that become organised in the individual in particular patterns in their memory and are subsequently applied to solving new problems

Cognitive concerned with the psychological processes of perception, memory, thinking and learning (Coffield *et al* 2004)

Communities of practice people engaged in a common set of tasks, with its associated stories, traditions and ways of working (Tennant 1999: 173)

Competencies set of character features, knowledge and skills, attitudes, motives and traits that comprise the profile of a job-holder and enable him or her to perform effectively in his or her role

Competency framework framework of core competencies that provides a template against which individuals and teams can be developed

Computer-based training training through *e-learning* and computerised learning tools such as CD-ROMs

Constructivism mindset that rests on the assumption that there is no objective 'out there' reality. Individuals construct their world through an ongoing process of social interactions

Constructivist learning theories also known as humanist theories – theories that view learning as intimately shaped by the social relationships and culture that most directly influence the individual's values, beliefs and perceptions of the environment

Cybernetics the science of control and communication in animals and machines

Decentralised transferred from central to local control, as in 'decentralised training function'; or, in the case of educational institutions, from local authority control to self-government

Deregulated no longer subject to any direct Government restrictions, constraints or regulations

Develop to unfold more fully, bring out all that is contained (Onions 1973). To make or become bigger or fuller or achieve more elaborate or systematic advancement (Pearsall and Trumble 1996)

Development centre methodology by which participants take part in a variety of job simulations, tests and exercises in front of observers who assess their performance against a number of predetermined job-related dimensions. Data thus generated are used to diagnose individual training needs, facilitate self-development or provide part of an organisational development audit (Rodger and Mabey 1987)

Dialogic learning approach to learning that involves interacting with others in ways that produce a growing understanding of the culture of the organisation, and of how that organisation typically achieves its goals (Mezirow 1985)

Discretionary behaviour the exercise of initiative. In a work context, this refers to the extent to which the individual exercises control over the key parameters of his or her job, such as speed, care, innovation and style of job delivery

Double-loop learning concept formulated to describe the style of learning that involves questioning why certain problems occur in the first place and identifying and tackling root causes instead of only surface symptoms (Argyris 1977). Contrast with *single-loop learning*

Educate to bring up from childhood so as to form habits, manners, mental and physical aptitudes (Onions 1973); give intellectual, moral and social instruction to, especially as a formal and prolonged process (Pearsall and Trumble 1996)

E-learning electronically-based learning, whether enabled through wired or wire-free systems

Evaluation of learning identification of the total value of a learning event or process, thereby putting it into its organisational context and aiding future planning

Evidence-based practice used widely in medical work, also in social work, government policy-making and clinical psychology – in an L&D context 'the conscientious, explicit and judicious use of current best evidence in making decisions about the development of individuals, groups and organizations, integrating individual practitioner expertise with the best available external evidence derived from systematic research' (Hamlin 2002: 97–8)

Explicit knowledge knowledge that has been articulated and codified

External consistency applied to L&D activity: the commitment, shared purpose and perceptions of stakeholders that can be achieved through actively involving them in the planning, design, delivery and evaluation of learning events and processes (Kessels 1996)

Fordism/Fordist workplace system of mass production characteristic of private sector organisations during the 1940s to 1960s. Under Fordism, mass consumption combined with mass production to produce sustained economic growth and widespread material advancement

Function body of (for example, L&D) activity provided for an organisation and the personnel directly responsible for that provision

Green Paper consultation document issued by Government, containing policy proposals for debate and discussion. Usually followed by a *White Paper*

High-performance work organisation forms of HR policies and methods of work organisation that 'engender employee involvement, the maximisation of effort, initiative and commitment' (Lloyd and Payne 2005)

Holistic view looking at a system, situation, organisation or collection of activities as a whole that is greater than the mere sum of its parts – taking a helicopter view

Human capital the knowledge, skills, competencies and attributes embodied in individuals that facilitate the creation of personal, social and economic well-being (OECD 2001: 18). A view of people management by which people are assets to be deployed and managing them is a value-adding activity (CIPD 2003a)

Humanism/humanist see *constructivism*

Implementation putting something into practice. The process by which strategy or plans are converted into action

Instrumental learning learning how to do a job better once the basic standard of performance has been attained. It is helped particularly by learning on the job (Mezirow 1985)

Internal consistency applied to L&D activity: the outcome achieved by the effective application of a systematic approach to planning, design, delivery and evaluation tasks (Kessels 1996)

Internet 'massive network of networks, which connects millions of computers together globally' (Ahmed 2008). See *world-wide web*

Job training analysis process of identifying the purpose of a job and its component parts, and specifying what must be learned in order for there to be effective work performance

Job training specification a key outcome of job training analysis, a job training specification describes in overall terms the job for which training is to be given, or the key problem areas in a job which training will enable learners to tackle. It then specifies the kinds and levels of knowledge, skill and, where relevant, attitudes ('the KSA components') needed for effective performance, together with the performance standards for the job and the criteria for measuring achievement of the standards

'Key skills' six 'key skills' are identified in the UK Government's current (at time of writing) educational strategy: communication, use of IT, use of numbers, working with others, improving own learning and performance, and problem-solving

Knowledge knowledge can be viewed as a type of commodity – something 'out there' that can be searched out and acquired, assessed, codified and distributed across the organisation. In this sense, it is an intangible asset that can have unique competitive value for an organisation. Knowledge can also be viewed as a process, emerging from within the individual but intimately shaped by relations with others. In this sense knowledge is dynamic, changing as the individual's interpretation of the world around him or her changes.

Knowledge economy an economy in which 'knowledge' has become the key to wealth. In this kind of economy the application of knowledge adds more value than the traditional factors of capital, raw materials and labour, and the 'knowledge worker' has unique status

Knowledge management term often used to describe the capture and storage of information, usually by electronic means. In its broader sense it refers to 'using the ideas and experience of employees, customers and suppliers to improve the organisation's performance'. It has come into regular use for three reasons: the use of knowledge as a competitive weapon; the increasing awareness of how easy it is to lose knowledge; and new technology's facilitation of knowledge sharing (Skapinker 2002)

Knowledge productivity term coined by Professor Joseph Kessels (1996) to refer to an organisation's ability to generate, disseminate and apply knowledge to products, processes and services. Knowledge productivity should therefore enable an organisation to continuously adapt and improve and to regularly innovate

Knowledge workers Peter Drucker (1993) is thought to have been the first to use this term, to describe specialist workers such as management consultants, architects, lawyers, accountants and PR experts, whose market value lies in what they know. In its broader sense, the term applies to all organisational members who apply their knowledge (especially of the unique tacit kind) successfully to the improvement of operating procedures, products, services and processes and to innovate

KSA components see *job training specification*

Learning qualitative change in a person's way of seeing, experiencing, understanding and conceptualising something in the real world (Marton and Ramsden 1988); also the process whereby such change occurs

L&D function the way in which the whole body of L&D activity is structured in an organisation

Learning facilitator a person who helps and encourages others to take a self-directed approach to learning

Learning media routes or channels through which information is transmitted to the learner

Learning technology the way in which learning media and methods are incorporated into the design and delivery of a learning event and interact with those participating in the event.

Mission detailed (and usually written) articulation of *vision*, which acts as an inspiration and a guide for action. Sometimes a mission statement represents only a minority view, and mission statements also fall out of date. Many therefore regard missions as valueless, yet the process that produces them does have value if it brings together organisational members in ways that encourage informed reflection on crucial issues and that generate innovative thinking

Monitoring 'taking the temperature' (eg of a learning process) from time to time in order to check on progress and identify any issues needing action

Organising dynamic process needed if organisational design is to be effectively implemented and regularly renewed. The skills involved in how to organise and regularly re-organise are as important as knowing what organisational design to choose (Whittington and Mayer 2002)

Organisation 'Involves all the elements of organisational design; not only the formal structures of organisational charts but also the systems, processes and people dimensions that are essential to making these work' (CIPD 2003b)

Organisational context internal and external organisational circumstances that shape and help to explain the organisational situation being examined. Often, organisational context is defined by reference to culture and structure, but they themselves emerge from the interplay of more fundamental factors. Research indicates that three of the most powerful are: top management's vision and values, line management's style and actions at all organisational levels; and HR strategies and practices

Paradigm shift permanent change in an established pattern of thinking – for example, by organisational members about their work organisation; a radical shift in the way they understand their world

Pedagogy the art and science of teaching the child

Pluralist system the concept of an organisation as a system in which there are many and often conflicting interests, and therefore in which conflict itself is a natural occurrence. Contrast with *unitary system*

Positivism see *behaviourism*

Post-Fordism/post-Fordist workplace system in which the Fordist workplace has been dismantled in order to ensure more efficient operations and a more equal distribution of knowledge, authority and responsibility (Zuboff 1988). See *Fordism*

Psychological contract the social and emotional aspects of the contractual exchange between employer and employee (Sparrow 1999: 420). It refers to that aspect of the relationship binding individual and organisation that consists of felt and perceived expectations, wants and rights. It represents a dynamic and reciprocal deal, with new expectations being added over time

Reflective practice derived originally from the field of medicine – 'A conscious act … with the intention of finding out more about our own learning processes and how they affect our professional practice and working relationships' (Hunt 2005 : 234)

Reflexive practice the process of understanding what has been learned about one's own learning through reflection and then putting it into practice

Relational contract psychological contract based on mutual commitment. See *psychological contract*

Representations see *cognitive structures*

Self-managed learning term coined by Ian Cunningham to describe an approach he developed at the Anglian Regional Management Centre in the 1970s – it essentially refers to the individual taking charge of their own learning, whether through independent study or in a learning group in an organisation (eg an action learning set). In each case the individual negotiates a learning contract agreeing on learning goals and how he or she will achieve them

Self-reflective learning an approach whereby individuals redefine their current perspective in order to develop new patterns of understanding, thinking and behaving. It requires unlearning as well as new learning (Mezirow 1985). See also *double-loop learning*

Single-loop learning concept formulated to describe the style of learning involved in taking a problem at its face value and therefore tackling its surface symptoms but not its root causes (Argyris 1977). Contrast with *double-loop learning*

Situated learning learning grounded in the everyday situation of the individual or group

Skilled incompetence term coined by Aryris (1986) to describe the way in which once successful organisations rest on their laurels for too long, causing strategies and behavioural patterns to become increasingly inappropriate in the face of new challenges. The learning that once enabled them to become highly competent has become the biggest barrier to their survival

Social capital networks together with shared norms, values and understandings that facilitate co-operation within or among groups (OECD 2001: 41)

Strategic capability 'Strategic capability provides the vision, the rich and sustained learning and knowledge development, the integrity of purpose and the continuous direction and scope to the activities of the firm that are needed to secure long-term survival. It is based on a profound understanding of the competitive environment, of the resource-base, capacity and potential of the organisation, of the strategy process, and of the values that engender commitment from stakeholders to corporate goals' (Harrison and Miller 1999)

Strategising dynamic process by which a chosen strategy is continuously adapted and often changed to fit or exploit changes in the external and internal environment of the organisation (Whittington and Mayer 2002)

Strategy route chosen for a period of time in order to achieve organisational and business goals

Synchronous taking place in real time

Tacit knowledge term originally coined by Polanyi (1966) to describe knowledge that is embedded deep in the individual or the collective subconscious, expressing itself in habitual or intuitive ways of doing things that are exercised without conscious thought or effort (Nonaka 1991)

Technology the particular way in which, in a workplace, technical systems, machinery and processes are designed to interact with human skill and knowledge in order to convert inputs into outputs

Theories constructs that are the products of reflections on, testing of, and generalisations from, experience. Theories help to aid understanding, to give structure to ideas, to suggest explanations of actions and events, and to improve skill in problem-solving and practice

Thinking performers term used by the CIPD in its Professional Standards to describe practitioners who are knowledgeable and competent in their various fields, able to move beyond compliance to provide a critique of organisational policies and procedures, and to advise on how organisations should develop in the future (CIPD 2005b)

Train to instruct and discipline in or for some particular art, profession, occupation or practice; exercise, practise, drill (Onions 1973); teach a specified skill, especially by practice (Pearsall and Trumble 1996)

Transactional contract psychological contract representing a mainly functional relationship between employer and organisation: specified services in return for specified compensation. See *psychological contract*

Unitary system system in which there is one overriding goal or set of interests, and in which consensus, not conflict, is the expected norm. Contrasts with *pluralist system*

Validation of learning assessment of the extent to which learning objectives have been achieved

Vision in an organisational context, the picture that people hold in their minds about what kind of organisation theirs should be. Some believe the vision should be clear and shared across the organisation, in order to be an effective guide to action. Others see value in a vision that, while being compelling, also has sufficient ambiguity to cause searching questions to be asked about the organisation's direction, and to stimulate creativity in finding ways forward

White Paper document issued by a government department, containing detailed proposals for legislation. It is the final stage before Government introduces its proposals to Parliament in the form of a Bill.

World-wide web 'an information-sharing model built on top of the Internet which allows information to be accessed over the medium of the Internet (Ahmed 2008). See *internet*

Workforce development activity that increases the capacity of individuals to participate effectively in the workplace, thereby improving their productivity and employability (DfES 2003a)

'Zone of proximal development' context where learners are challenged near to, but slightly above, their current level of development (Vygotsky 1978)

PART 1
Understanding the field

CHAPTER 1

Learning and Development in Organisations Today

INTRODUCTION

In *Barnaby Rudge* Charles Dickens wrote:

> Chroniclers are privileged to enter where they list, to come and go through keyholes, to ride upon the wind, to overcome, in their soarings up and down, all obstacles of distance, time and place.

Most chroniclers find it hard to decide on exactly where to list as they begin their story. 'Begin at the beginning,' Alice in Wonderland would have said. But where is the beginning of learning and development (L&D)? As an organisational process it represents a multi-faceted field of study and practice. In the first two sections of this chapter I will open five gateways into its territory before introducing in the third some of the big issues that confront L&D professionals today.

GATEWAYS INTO LEARNING AND DEVELOPMENT TERRITORY

Figure 1 contains an advertisement picked from many that appeared in a single month in *People Management*.

What image does the Figure present of L&D in a progressive organisation today? That it is essentially about training? Not so. The advertisement does refer to operational training but it also emphasises senior management and leadership development, 'championing the Learning and Development agenda' and acting as a 'catalyst for change'. That the work takes place in a traditional HR or training department? No – it is located in a large shared services centre, a fast-growing trend in some of today's organisations. That it involves a cluster of functional tasks? Certainly, but that is only the starting point: this small L&D team has a broad-based mandate to achieve 'effective solutions' that will make an impact at all organisational levels.

FIGURE 1 The Sterling Selection advertisement

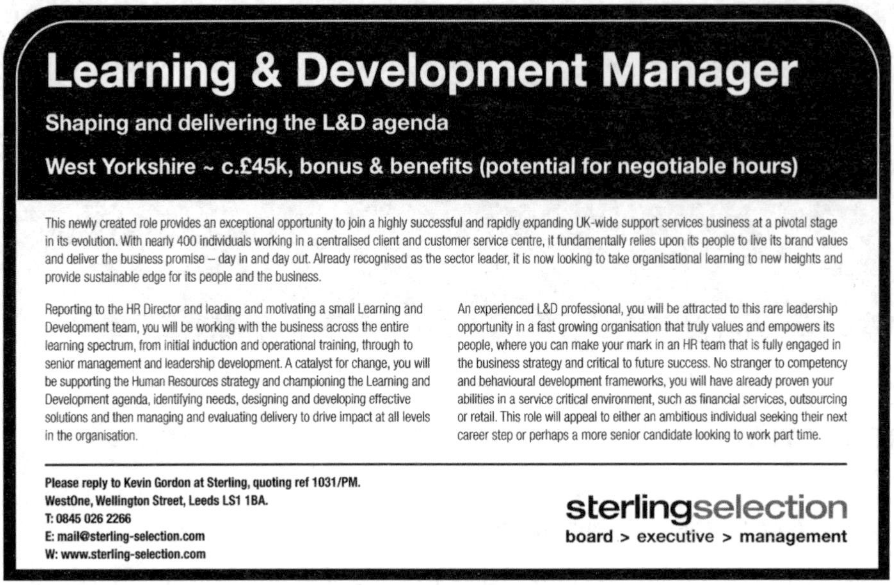

Learning & Development Manager

Shaping and delivering the L&D agenda

West Yorkshire ~ c.£45k, bonus & benefits (potential for negotiable hours)

This newly created role provides an exceptional opportunity to join a highly successful and rapidly expanding UK-wide support services business at a pivotal stage in its evolution. With nearly 400 individuals working in a centralised client and customer service centre, it fundamentally relies upon its people to live its brand values and deliver the business promise – day in and day out. Already recognised as the sector leader, it is now looking to take organisational learning to new heights and provide sustainable edge for its people and the business.

Reporting to the HR Director and leading and motivating a small Learning and Development team, you will be working with the business across the entire learning spectrum, from initial induction and operational training, through to senior management and leadership development. A catalyst for change, you will be supporting the Human Resources strategy and championing the Learning and Development agenda, identifying needs, designing and developing effective solutions and then managing and evaluating delivery to drive impact at all levels in the organisation.

An experienced L&D professional, you will be attracted to this rare leadership opportunity in a fast growing organisation that truly values and empowers its people, where you can make your mark in an HR team that is fully engaged in the business strategy and critical to future success. No stranger to competency and behavioural development frameworks, you will have already proven your abilities in a service critical environment, such as financial services, outsourcing or retail. This role will appeal to either an ambitious individual seeking their next career step or perhaps a more senior candidate looking to work part time.

Please reply to Kevin Gordon at Sterling, quoting ref 1031/PM.
WestOne, Wellington Street, Leeds LS1 1BA.
T: 0845 026 2266
E: mail@sterling-selection.com
W: www.sterling-selection.com

sterlingselection
board > executive > management

Source: Reproduced with the kind permission of Sterling Selection

Its members will require sophisticated business and partnership skills as well as high-level specialist expertise.

The message in all of this is that L&D in many of today's organisations has become recognised for its potential to be a major contributor to the business, and that its scope extends far beyond 'training' (see, for example, in Appendix 1 the 10 key areas of activity that the CIPD identifies for L&D generalists). This message is underlined by the fact that learning, training and development professionals are now earning more than the average human resource (HR) salary. The annual Croner-CIPD's 2007 pay survey revealed that in a single decade they have moved from being among the lowest-paid HR specialists to coming second-highest, earning on average £45,000 per annum (Croner Reward/CIPD 2007).

The section that follows opens four gateways into the L&D field: those of terminology, of purpose, of theories and of HR management. The final gateway, of history, is given a subsequent section of its own.

THE GATEWAY OF TERMINOLOGY

Terms for L&D as an organisational process

The terms that we choose to describe things matter. In the past, three have been widely used to describe the L&D field: 'training and development', 'employee development' and 'human resource development'. For a lengthy discussion of their derivation and meanings you should read Wilson (2005: 4–10). Here, I would simply make the following observations:

The traditional term *training and development* remains popular, particularly in official publications. However, training is only one way of achieving development and to give it this kind of prominence can be dangerous. It can imply that all that really counts in an organisation, or indeed in a country, is formal, accredited learning activity. Some national policy consequences of this view are discussed in Chapters 2 and 3.

The term *employee development* smacks too much of the old 'master–servant' relationship. It is no accident that it is falling out of use at a time when many organisations are referring to their members as associates or partners rather than as employees, and where 'equality' and 'inclusivity' are the aspirations of the day.

The term *human resource development* retains its popularity amongst academics but it has never been as attractive to practitioners. They tend to dislike it because they see its reference to people as a 'resource' to be demeaning. Putting people on a par with money, materials and equipment creates the impression of 'development' as an unfeeling, manipulative activity.

What then is left? During 1999 and 2000 the CIPD conducted an extensive consultation process to review the professional standards it had first produced in 1996. The issue of what to call the revised 'Employee Development' standard was endlessly debated. Many titles were rejected until only one remained: 'Learning and Development'. This term alone focused on what everyone agreed mattered most – the learning needed if organisational and individual development is to occur. It is an inclusive term too, and it came closer than any other to capturing the desired vision of shared endeavour. Like HRD, but without the pitfalls associated with that term, it conveys the scope of a process that can extend beyond those who work in the organisation to those who, although not legally its employees, make an essential contribution to its success – for example, voluntary and contracted-out workers and suppliers. Coincidentally the national occupational standards in 'Training and Development' that were being revised at the same time acquired the same title: 'Learning and Development'.

Terminology, then, has changed significantly over the years. But has the function changed with it – or is it really a case of old wine in a new bottle? For one commentator at least there has been little progress (Peter Critten, principal lecturer in HRD at Middlesex University Business School, quoted in Wain 2008a: 25):

> One senses little real movement over the past decade – worrying given the extraordinary developments that have happened in the wider business and economic world.

Wain (2008a: 25), an L&D consultant, tends to agree:

> If the past is indeed a foreign country, it is less because we did things differently there than because we used different terminology.

Later in this chapter I will return to these claims. Here, though, there is more to consider about terminology.

Meanings attached to 'learning'

In adopting the term 'learning and development' there is a danger that what is gained in scope is lost in generalisation. 'Learning' has so many meanings. A common view is to interpret it as a lifelong activity involving three processes (Onions 1973):

- *To develop*: to unfold more fully, bring out all that is contained in.

- *To educate:* to bring up from childhood, so as to form habits, manners and mental and physical aptitudes.

- *To train:* to instruct and discipline in or for some particular art, profession, occupation or practice; to exercise, practise, drill.

Combining these processes highlights conditioning and the gaining of competencies through planned instructional or coaching activity. As will be seen in Chapters 4 and 5 this perspective remains quite deeply embedded in many organisations, reflecting a perception of training as the most efficient and effective way to achieve changes sought by management in employees' behaviour and performance.

A very different way of understanding 'learning' is to perceive it as driven by the individual's curiosity, intelligence and desires and fundamentally shaped by their social interactions in the workplace. Such a definition focuses on the integration of work and learning as a major route to change, and to learning facilitation rather than training as the key requirement. This approach too will be explored in Chapters 4 and 5.

So the terms that we choose to describe things do matter. They bestow identity and they both reflect and influence perceptions. If in Figure 1 the advertisement had contained the word 'training' instead of 'learning and development' throughout, how differently might you have understood it?

 REFLECTION

Reflecting on the various meanings just discussed – and then on some organisations known to you that have a function dealing with training, learning and development – what do they call the function? How far do you think those titles correspond with the function's purpose and type of activity?

THE GATEWAY OF PURPOSE

Terminology cannot take us much further. What we need now is a statement of purpose that can provide a deeper level of insight into L&D as an organisational process.

L&D activity first acquired a specific organisational meaning in the USA in the 1970s. Termed 'human resource development' its purpose was regarded as primarily about short-term training, encompassing skills acquisition and behavioural change. It was defined by one of its most influential commentators (Nadler 1970) as:

> a series of organized activities conducted within a specified time and designed to produce behavioural change.

By the 1980s some commentators were moving towards a more strategic perspective. Hall (1984), another well-known American author, had this to say:

> Strategic human resource development is the identification of needed skills and active management of learning for the long-range future in relation to explicit corporate and business strategies.

By the early 1990s in the USA 'HRD' had developed into a recognisable profession. Many of its members emphasised their role as agents of organisational change, viewing HRD as less to do with training or with 'explicit strategies' than with a generalised task of renewal (Burack 1991):

> HRD people have been charged to blueprint and lead the way to organization and individual renewal.

However, there was still no universally accepted definition in the USA (Nadler 1992). The situation was no clearer in the UK, where in 1998 a survey commissioned by the Institute of Personnel and Development found that training and development practitioners were (Darling, Darling and Elliott 1999: *xii*):

> affected by the confusion of meanings and boundaries between such terms as human resource management, human resource development, training, learning and development.

In 2001 the Institute (by then chartered) produced an extensively revised set of professional standards that remain in place today (mid-2008). The explanation of the L&D Generalist Standard starts by identifying L&D's purpose as an organisational process, emphasising its significance for the business. It also recognises the need to obtain the active commitment of the learners by responding to their needs. You cannot force people to learn. All that you can do is excite, encourage and help them to do so. Central to the CIPD's definition is the following statement (CIPD 2005a: 81):

> The organisational process of developing people involves the integration of learning and development processes, operations and relationships. Its most powerful outcomes

for the business are to do with enhanced organisational effectiveness and sustainability. For the individual they are to do with enhanced personal competence, adaptability and employability. It is therefore a critical business process, whether in for-profit or not-for-profit organisations.

Throughout its professional standards the CIPD identifies two generic roles for people and development professionals: those of thinking performer and business partner. *Thinking performers* are knowledgeable and competent in their field, able to move beyond compliance to provide a critique of organisational policies and procedures and advice on how organisations should develop in the future. A *business partner* works with others at his or her level both within and outside the organisation in order to make a strong contribution to organisational performance. These roles underline the need for a clear business focus in L&D activity, no matter at what organisational level it is carried out.

My own definition of L&D's purpose is shorter than the CIPD's and has a rather different emphasis:

> The primary purpose of learning and development as an organisational process is to aid collective progress through the collaborative, expert and ethical stimulation and facilitation of learning and knowledge that support business goals, develop individual potential, and respect and build on diversity.

This definition emphasises partnership and ethical behaviour as central to L&D professional practice. In using learning to meet organisational ends we are intervening in a process that goes to the heart of human identity. We cannot expect individuals to use that process to benefit the organisation unless they believe that it will also benefit them. And we should not use learning processes in ways that exploit human vulnerability or that cause or increase damaging divisions between people. As employees, those with L&D roles should work to add value to the business, but as members of a wider professional community they must do so in ways that reflect that community's espoused ethical values.

My definition also highlights learning as the route to knowledge – and that is a central theme in this book. Knowledge creation enables an organisation to continuously improve and from time to time radically innovate in its products, services and processes. An organisation that invests in the learning of its members without understanding and putting to good use the knowledge that the investment generates is an organisation that courts failure. As one commentator pointed out (Coulson-Thomas 2001):

> For many years before its break-up, Rover had championed learning at all levels in the organisation. But what was learned did little to enhance the company's competitiveness, as events subsequently proved.

Today so many meanings have been claimed for L&D in the organisational context that it can be arbitrary to select any one definition. McGoldrick and his colleagues (2002: 10) found no consensus in their survey of research, concluding that what they termed 'HRD':

> can be seen to constitute multiple, shifting, competing and contingent identities.

They attributed this confusion to differing philosophical perspectives and research methodologies related to the field. Others stress its complex interdisciplinary nature, drawing as it does on psychology, sociology, educational theory, economics – the list goes on. I find any search for causes unsatisfactory because so many shifting factors are at work here, as our final gateway of history will reveal. First, though, the third gateway: that of 'theory'.

THE GATEWAY OF THEORY

This third gateway into L&D territory is provided by theoretical frameworks, or 'constructs' as they are often called in research studies:

- Theories are the products of a) reflections on experience, b) the testing of experience, and c) generalisations from experience. The experience may be taken from real life, or it may be artificially constructed before being tested in a real-life situation.

- Theories can aid our understanding, give structure to our ideas, suggest explanations for actions and events that we encounter and improve our skill in problem-solving, decision-making and practice.

- However, theories about L&D are not rules and should not be treated as such. There are no theories that explain beyond dispute how people think, learn and acquire knowledge, so there can never be black-and-white L&D prescriptions.

Theories can seem dry and academic. Stories, on the other hand, provide us with the *feel* of L&D. Without them we may study theory yet be unable to relate it to the real world. Even for the most experienced practitioner, narratives about unfamiliar situations and contexts can offer an emotional understanding of the L&D process. They also have a central role to play in developing a community's culture, bringing its members together as they reflect on their past and take pride in their unique identity.

The studies with which the following narrative is associated made a major contribution to L&D theory and the story was one of a number that gave birth to three central concepts related to workplace learning and knowledge in organisations. They will be explained and discussed in detail in Chapters 4 and 5.

- learning situated in workplace communities of practice (Vygotsky 1978; Brown and Duguid 1991; Lave and Wenger 1991)

- knowledge as a process that is significantly shaped by social interactions (Kelly 1955; Knowles 1973)

- knowledge that can be tacit or explicit (Polanyi 1966; Nonaka 1994).

CASE EXAMPLE

THE PHOTOCOPIER REPAIR TECHNICIANS

A group of technicians had to repair photocopier machines in customers' locations. They had been given detailed instructional manuals and training. However, it soon became clear to them that this formal knowledge was not enough. The people who had designed the machines had not understood the different social settings in which they had to be used, and so had ignored many of the everyday human errors that cause such machines to break down.

When the technicians realised this they got together to discuss the many repair problems that they were encountering. All they had to fall back on was their own experience and intuition. They had to draw on their 'tacit' knowledge – the kind of knowledge that is often buried deep in the subconscious, expressing itself in habitual ways of doing things that people often exercise without conscious thought or effort (Nonaka 1991).

The technicians shared this kind of knowledge as they exchanged stories of similar problems they had encountered in the past and of how they had dealt with them. By comparing what they knew from experience with the 'explicit' or formal knowledge contained in their training and repair manuals, they began to work out how to tackle the many repair problems they faced. Uncertainty, the need to know, experimentation and discovery finally gave them an unrivalled understanding of the machines. This understanding was developed as much through their social interactions and conversations as through any technical know-how. It enabled them to combine 'tacit' and 'explicit' knowledge in ways that produced innovative ideas and led to improved work methods.

Source: Orr, J. E. (1990)

What matters even in this brief version of Orr's story is to notice the way in which it breathes life into academic theory through the reassuringly commonplace setting in which it is located and its picture of a society in miniature, its identity developing through collective informal learning.

Evidence-based practice

Stories alone are not enough, of course. The methods by which research is undertaken, the values and assumptions held by the researchers, the research questions they pose, the samples they use, the reliance we can place on their data and its analysis – all these are critical factors in deciding which findings and theories to use as our guides. Even the most respected constructs can prove fallible. You will find throughout this book regular statements such as 'there is evidence to suggest', 'there are statistics to indicate', 'it is logical to conclude that', or 'it may seem that'. These are all marks of uncertainty concerning the crucial question 'What is really going on here?'

Centuries ago a revered theologian (St Augustine) wrote – naturally in a different context, but producing insights relevant to this discussion:

> The appearance of what we do is different from the intention with which we do it, and the circumstances at the time may not be clear.

Many commentators have found a major disconnect between what firms claim as their HR strategy and what happens in reality (Storey 1992; Truss and Gratton 1994; Becker and Gerhart 1996; Pettigrew *et al* 2002a). That kind of gap can be wide and littered with intervening variables. Strategy-makers often see only what they wish to see. Those who have to put plans into action may not always be aware, or may not wish to confess to, the many changes that those plans can go through once they reach the workplace. And those charged with strategy's implementation may be incompetent or unwilling to perform the task.

So too with theories: all should be challenged and tested, and many will ultimately be found wanting. But it is a sign of strength, not weakness, to admit that some need to be abandoned in the face of new findings. As L&D practitioners test out theories in an increasing range of organisational situations they should become more confident in their own views. It is one of the tasks of a professional to decide where theory works, where it does not, in what evidence it is grounded and how best to apply it in the particular situation.

EVIDENCE-BASED PRACTICE

CASE EXAMPLE

Lucia has just gained her CIPD diploma and is working as an L&D adviser – a fairly junior post – in a small HR unit that provides in-house HR services and advice to line management in an organisation. She has covered a lot of theory in her CIPD studies and wants to make best use of it, but often this is difficult – so few of the constructs she has learnt about seem to fit the real-life issues with which she has to deal. Yet at various HR conferences that she attends she hears regular mention of the importance of 'evidence-based practice' (EBP). Exactly what does that mean?

'I think it's something to do with using published research and theory to justify your advice and initiatives, isn't it?' says a colleague during coffee break as they skim the gossip columns of one of their favourite magazines for light relief from their pressured working day.

'But what does "published research" mean?', says Lucia. 'Could be anything, couldn't it? Look at all the surveys quoted here about how to lose weight, get rid of wrinkles, make new friends, bring up perfect kids … and then next week they'll be publishing another lot of surveys giving us quite different advice!'

Organisational psychologist Rob Briner clarifies things at this point by identifying the central challenge of EBP as the following (Pickard 2007):

> To what extent are we prepared to find relevant evidence, review it systematically, evaluate it and use it with other factors to help us make decisions?

American gurus Pfeffer and Sutton (2006a), like Briner, criticise HR practitioners for being dominated by 'fads and fashions' – the tendency to go by gut feel instead of adopting a reflective, evaluative approach. If Lucia had read their article she would understand that EBP is about a careful search for evidence drawn from theory, from practice and sometimes from experimentation. The kind of advice they provide is straightforward:

Collect enough sound, relevant and well-analysed information to convince yourself and others of where the greatest improvement opportunities lie for L&D to add value. Separate facts from assumptions and use a variety of reliable information sources.

Know what the literature says about ways in which L&D practices can help the organisation and its employees. Use theories as a major information source to help you in your search for understanding and in generating options for solutions. Have a good understanding of how research findings are building up through time, and use your own judgement to decide which conclusions you can safely rely on.

Run small-scale experiments and develop the right mindsets. EBP is a continuing process, not an ad hoc initiative. Lucia and her colleague should always be building on what has been shown to work well and to fit their organisational context best. They should also be constantly seeking new ideas and fresh ways forward – ways for which, by definition, there won't as yet be any adequate evidence base. They will have to generate evidence of their own, bringing to their work a spirit of enquiry and working with colleagues and learners in trying out new approaches on a small scale. They should embrace challenges to customary ways of thinking and doing and use failure – including their own – as a learning vehicle, not a cause for blame.

Act on findings from such experiments. Evaluate them to see what outcomes they produce and how feasible it would be to introduce them on a wider scale in their organisation. Regularly monitor new initiatives to ensure that they do no harm to those who use them or are affected by their use; ethical practice is crucial.

Sources: Pickard, J. (2007) *People Management*, 1 November; Pfeffer, J. and Sutton, R. I. (2006a) *People Management*, 28 September

THE HRM GATEWAY

Our fourth gateway offers a unique perspective on L&D – that of its membership of a family of HR processes. Traditionally the term 'human resource management' has been taken to mean the practices, formal policies and overarching philosophies whereby an organisation's employees are attracted, deployed, retained, rewarded, developed and nurtured (Jackson and Schuler 1995). Figure 2 shows this family of processes and their interaction in the form of a wheel.

There are many studies in the UK and the USA going back to the 1980s whose findings support the view that L&D should be linked in appropriate ways with wider HR practices in order to make its due organisational contribution. One important CIPD-sponsored research programme carried out at the University of

FIGURE 2 The wheel of HRM and the business

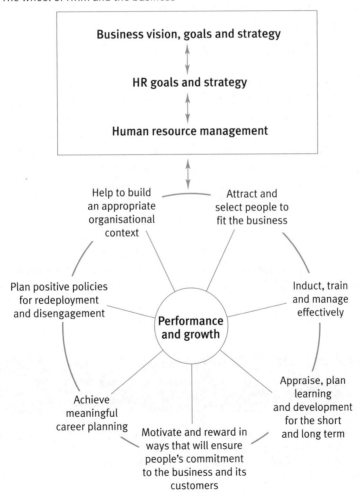

Bath has confirmed the need for this integrative approach (Purcell *et al* 2003), as I will explain in detail in Chapter 6. Its findings make abundantly clear the need for people management and development professionals to work together in a shared purpose. Not all trainers accept the logic of this argument. Some seek the separation rather than the integration of 'training' and 'personnel' so that training can make a unique impact on the business. This is to fly in the face of logic. Whatever the problems in HR professionals from different specialisms working in partnership – and there can be many – there is now a convincing weight of evidence to show that:

- L&D activity has a crucial part to play in raising the skills and commitment levels needed by high-performing organisations.

- This activity needs support from other HR practices if it is to be effective.

- This activity must link clearly and convincingly with organisational goals if the L&D function is to add value to the business and gain the support it needs from business leaders and managers.

INTRODUCTION TO THE FIFTH GATEWAY

The final L&D gateway is the biggest because it takes us into the history of L&D as a business process. Some say that history is unimportant. They claim that in a fast-changing world it can teach us little of relevance and that its narratives are in any case biased. I disagree. Historical accounts cannot be completely objective, since they are produced by fallible human beings, but they remain a vital key to the past. They cast light on the routes we have travelled to reach where we are today. They reveal values and mindsets that have coloured past views of the world and that explain past decisions. They show outcomes of strategies on which we have relied – often so different from those that were intended. This need to know, coupled with a willingness to take responsibility for the past and to learn from it, are vital to the healthy working of any society. My account of L&D's history is necessarily brief. The selection and analysis of data on which it rests are coloured by the lens through which I view the L&D world. But I hope that it can still provide some useful insights.

REFLECTION

Reflecting on your own organisation or one with which you are familiar, how effectively do you think that its L&D activity is linked to other HR practices and to the organisation's goals? Could you suggest any improvements to make the link stronger?

(Note: As the term 'Learning and Development' refers to a field that is more usually known in the literature as 'human resource development' (HRD), I use the latter term throughout most of this section.)

The study and practice of HRD will always be challenging because its boundaries are disputed and the needs it serves do not sit comfortably together. In organisations the demands made on it by the business and by the individual can never be completely reconciled. Often pressures upon it from different groups of stakeholders cause acute and sometimes destructive conflicts of interest.

THE FOUNDATION YEARS

During the twentieth century there were three distinct strands to HRD's development. I discuss them below.

The cusp of the twentieth century: scientific management and the psychological theories of learning

For many this is where HRD really began. The work of American organisational psychologists from the 1950s, discussed below, was essentially the continuation of pioneering activity in industrial management and in the psychology of learning that started at the onset of the industrial age.

The American engineer F. W. Taylor (1856–1915) and his colleagues produced in those early years a body of work that has continued to influence management theory and practice down to present times (Taylor 1947). That work, expanded subsequently, came to be known as Scientific Management. Taylor believed that the chaotic conditions that he often found in industrial settings must be tackled by the application of rational, fair and systematic forms of management and organisation. He saw in scientific method a way of ensuring the orderly design and structuring of work, improved conditions for employees and greatly enhanced efficiency and productivity for the business. It could help to build mutuality of interest and effort between management and workers (Taylor 1947).

Taylor saw a need for training to be a well designed systematic process so that operators could rapidly and with minimum stress achieve competent and consistent standards of performance in their tasks. His approach here was greatly influenced by early psychological studies into animal and human behaviour that proposed stimulus–response theory as the key to learning (see Chapter 4). It was also influenced by his desire to improve the health and welfare of industrial workers.

If we place the true origins of organisational HRD in the dawn of the industrial era when management science, health and safety research and psychological theories were beginning to converge, we can more easily understand the tensions that still bedevil the L&D process. Many of them arise from trying to combine a business imperative with a genuine concern for the well-being and development of the individual, from an over-reliance on scientific method to explain and control human behaviour and from an excessive preoccupation with training as the key to employees' learning (something I will discuss in Chapter 4).

World War II: the growth of industrial training

For those who see the HRD process as being essentially about training, its historical starting point is here. During World War II, training as a work field developed a business profile in both the USA and the UK. In the UK, training officers came into being as a distinct category of staff, and the influential author G. R. Moxon (1943) linked education with training to form one of the 'six categories' of personnel management work. By 1996 the professional field in the UK had broadened to incorporate HRD at levels 4 and 5 of the new national occupational standards in training and development.

As I will explain in Chapter 4, this training strand in the history of HRD continues to be enormously influential. Whatever its considerable virtues, it has led to an over-emphasis by government and employers on learning activity that is planned, formalised and measurable, underplaying the value of more informal learning processes. The lasting popularity of the systematic training model has much to do with this, and so deserves an explanation at this point.

I have already noted that the thrust to systematise training goes back to the days of Taylorism. It received a huge boost during the war years because of the need for thousands of inexperienced factory operators (many of them women entering employment for the first time) to quickly master tasks that were vital to the war effort. In the post-war reconstruction years much basic research was carried out in the UK by psychologists like Douglas Seymour (1959) and by institutions like the Department of Scientific and Industrial Research and the Industrial Training Council, all working to perfect techniques that would aid the speedy and accurate learning of industrial tasks. In the 1960s as the UK's industrial performance began to flag, the systematic approach to training was developed into a full-blown framework (Taylor 1991). It was widely publicised by the 23 Industrial Training Boards set up in 1964.

The framework's purpose is to make training methodology more rigorous, consistent and scientifically based. As shown in Figure 3 it represents an orderly, sequential cycle of functional training tasks. Specific instruments used include needs assessment techniques, instructional objectives, learning strategies, training materials, guidelines for trainers, and evaluation instruments.

Work continued to be carried out on the systematic cycle of training activity, especially by Tom Boydell (1971). In the late 1990s the cycle underpinned the development of national occupational standards in training and development, and in later years their revision. Its weaknesses as well as its strengths are reflected there.

FIGURE 3 The systematic training cycle

The major criticism of the cycle is that it presents training as operating in a free-standing closed system dominated by functional tasks. The underlying assumption is that these tasks should and can take place in a predetermined sequence, requiring only the application of specialist expertise to ensure their success. Real life, of course, is not so simple. In reality, training has to be carried out in contexts that can be messy, disorganised, and complicated by the interplay of powerful political forces. No matter how perfect its design and delivery, it can still fail if it does not pay enough attention to that context. When it does fail it is usually because it lacks the support of key stakeholders – especially front-line managers of learners and the learners themselves – whose buy-in is essential to its success (Kessels and Harrison 1998).

The post-war years: organisational psychology and systems theory

During the 1950s and 1960s in the USA organisational psychologists like Argyris (1957), McGregor (1960), Likert (1961) and Hertzberg (1966) were studying motivation at work. Their research drew attention to the needs of all employees for self-fulfilment, meaningful work and tasks that could engage their intelligence and develop their potential. The idea that all organisational members had a creative contribution to make and deserved the opportunity to do so no matter at what level they worked in the hierarchy became widely popularised. Coupled with a developing interest in Japanese notions of total quality management and a concern to find new ways of gaining competitive advantage, this led many organisations to innovate in their HRD practices as well as in other business processes.

Meanwhile in the UK, researchers at the Tavistock Institute of Human Relations were exploring organisations as systems, the interaction of whose human and technical elements determined the overall capability of an organisation to adapt to its environment (Trist and Bamforth 1951). This organic view stressed the need for as much attention to be paid to human as to technical needs in organisations. It highlighted learning as the means whereby organisations continuously adapt to their environment. This added a major perspective to HRD and both systems thinking and organisational psychology had a powerful impact on the subsequent development of 'learning organisation' theory (Senge 1990) and indeed of HR theory more widely. They provide a link to the current preoccupation with informal workplace learning and knowledge creation as sources of unique competitive capability – a topic we will touch on again towards the end of this chapter. They also reflect much of the thinking that informs the latest HR research today concerning the links between individual and organisational performance, as will be seen in Chapter 6. There is little, after all, that is new under the sun …

THE PUSH FOR BUSINESS RESULTS

As the HRD field expanded during the second half of the twentieth century the business imperative also grew stronger, particularly in the USA. Human capital theory (Schultz 1961) was by then widely known, largely due to the writings of the economist G. Becker (1975). This theory presents people as organisational assets whose economic value derives from their skills, competence, knowledge and experience. Intangibles such as intellectual property and customer equity are all derived from human capital and are regarded as the ultimate source of competitive advantage. Becker argued that investment in training and education leads to increased productivity and thence to increased wages and business earnings. This makes HRD a value-adding process for both for organisations and for individuals. Since education is a powerful means of creating a more numerate, literate and informed society, it can enable HRD to fulfil its wider social purpose.

There is a direct relationship here with the emphasis today in the HR literature and research on the building of human capital and the need for human capital reporting by businesses. I will return to this point later in this chapter.

The business imperative expressed itself in a strong drive for performance improvement that has continued to dominate HRD practice in the USA. In the UK, the same drive gained ground during the 1980s, notably in larger and multi-divisional organisations. A sustained period of recession had been accompanied by a collapse in manufacturing and by a rapid decline in the country's skill base as apprenticeship numbers were slashed. The outcomes of these crises highlighted the need for performance improvement and skills development. At the same time, much was being learnt about business-focused training strategies practised in successful competitor countries like Germany and Japan.

Throughout the last two decades of the twentieth century governments in the UK attempted to break the old pattern of a 'stop–go' approach to vocational education and training and put pressure on organisations to invest more in training their workforces. As Chapter 2 will show, their efforts were largely in vain.

Meanwhile, many in the HRD profession were becoming concerned at the extent to which the drive to improve short-term economic performance was dominating employers' HRD investment. In the USA in the early 1990s a group of HRD academics and practitioners established the Academy of Human Resource Development. It was not a physical institution but a body of people who felt that an undue preoccupation with the business drivers of HRD was undermining its potential to achieve individual and social benefits. The Academy's membership expanded over the years and it now has strong partnership ties with the more recently established University Forum for HRD in the UK. The Forum's network in this country consists of over 20 universities conducting research and providing postgraduate master's-level HRD programmes. It also links to EURESFORM, an international association for universities, reflective practitioners and learning-oriented organisations. Its aim is to achieve through improved research and practice a strong focus on lifelong learning that will expand the capabilities and creativity of individuals as well as of the business and the economy (http//www. ufhrd.com [accessed 24 July 2008]).

REFLECTION

This section has provided an overview of HRD's history, from its beginnings as a set of operational activities focused primarily on training to its current position as an organisational learning process with powerful but rarely realised strategic potential. Reflecting on practices to do with the development of people in your own organisation or one with which you are familiar, what new insights have you gained from reading this section?

TODAY'S BIG ISSUES FOR L&D PROFESSIONALS

A CRITICAL VIEW

Early in this chapter I mentioned the view of two informed commentators on L&D in organisations that, despite major changes in the world outside organisations, the world of L&D had not evolved in line with these. Problems in delegating its basic tasks to line managers, lack of strategic status of its practitioners, an inadequate focus on the business and its needs, failure to establish effective business partnerships, the unrealised promise of new learning technology – all these and many more weaknesses have been regularly recorded down through the years, not least in the CIPD's annual Training/Learning and Development reports. Comparing findings from the first (IPD 1999) with the ninth (CIPD 2007a), Daniel Wain noted little movement either in practitioners' preoccupations and type of practice or in barriers to a greater 'elevation in the HRD function's corporate remit and power' (Wain 2008b):

If the CIPD's surveys are to be believed, we're either irrepressible optimists or serial self-deceivers, always expecting more progress each year.

At the start of 2008 *People Management* ran an illuminating two-part series on the state of L&D in organisations today (Wain 2008a; O'Connell 2008). The authors identify some big challenges, but while they convey a sense of excitement at those facing professionals who have the skill and credibility to rise to them, there is also disappointment at opportunities missed and at a lack of any dramatic progress. In a separate article Wain (2008b) concluded with an urgent plea that 'learning and development should be transformational, proactive and future-focused ...'. As will be seen subsequently in this book, there is scant evidence as yet that in most organisations any such transformation has occurred. Furthermore, the focus and management of training continues to attract many criticisms. One of the most conspicuous recently was made by the regulator Ofcom who, in fining the BBC heavily for numerous industry code breaches, accused the Corporation of failing to have 'adequate management oversight' of its training procedures to ensure its audience was not misled (Block 2008).

And yet, and yet ... At the start of this chapter I also noted that L&D's potential to add value to the business as well as to individuals is now appreciated in a sufficient number of organisations to have boosted the average pay of L&D specialists by a remarkable degree over the past 10 years or so. Over the same period there have been radical reforms across the whole national vocational training and education system. Equally radical reforms are changing the face of HR functions in the public and voluntary sectors, whilst in the private sector a turbulent environment and the operation of a service-based knowledge economy have put increasing pressure on all HR professionals to either make a convincing contribution to the business or face downsizing, outsourcing or unemployment. Operating in such a dynamic context, many L&D practitioners have been found wanting. Many, though, have survived and prospered. Five of the challenges they are now tackling are outlined below. Many more will be discussed in detail later in this book.

ADAPTING TO CONTEXT

Today, although employers increasingly call for their L&D activity to be more convincingly tied to business needs, there are still many organisations where this is not happening. Often this is because L&D practitioners do not relate their activity sufficiently to context. Context has two dimensions:

The external context consists of the outer environment of the organisation, shaped by a wide variety of forces that have a powerful impact on the business and many of which have a direct direct relevance for L&D practice within the organisation.

The internal, organisational context is expressed most obviously in workplace culture and most directly shaped by:

* top management's vision and values, goals and leadership

- management (especially front-line management) style and actions

- HR strategies and practices.

Looking first at external context, the economic environment, the legislative and regulatory system and government policies and practices produce between them many opportunities from which employing organisations can benefit. However, as Chapters 2, 3 and 10 in particular demonstrate, they also give rise to many pressures that fundamentally shape and can often seriously constrain the direction of organisations' business and HR operations. These pressures are particularly acute in the UK's public sector, where, too, the training and development budget has always been the first to be cut at times of financial stringency. As I will explain in Chapter 10, it is therefore no accident that it is in the public sector that L&D practitioners face some of their biggest challenges in tailoring their activity to context.

Looking at internal context, it has always been the case that to ensure relevant activity that adds value to the business as well as to individuals HR practitioners, including those specialising in the L&D field, have had to form effective business partnerships, working at multiple organisational levels in order to integrate their operations with business activity (Ulrich 1987; Mohrman and Lawler III 1999). Too often, as will be seen subsequently in this book, the skills and business understanding that such partnerships require has been lacking.

Overall, the unique importance of 'adapting to context' for L&D functions today explains why so much of the book is concerned with exploring collaborative approaches to L&D activity in a variety of organisational settings, and with the need for L&D professionals to possess a deep understanding of the external environment of their organisations as well as of its key internal features.

REFLECTION

If you could change *one* aspect of organisational context in order to improve L&D's business impact in your organisation, which would you choose – and why?

BUILDING HUMAN AND SOCIAL CAPITAL

I referred earlier to the notion that an organisation's employees are a unique form of capital for development. Two kinds of capital are involved here.

Human capital is officially defined as (OECD 2001: 18):

> the knowledge, skills, competencies and attributes embodied in individuals that facilitate the creation of personal, social and economic well-being.

Social capital is defined as (OECD 2001: 41):

> networks together with shared norms, values and understandings that facilitate co-operation within or among groups. Trust may be viewed as both a source and an outcome of social capital.

There has been a resurgence of interest in the concept of building human capital. The US federal government's Office of Management and Budget insists that its agencies include human capital management in their performance plans, and there is no lack of HRD academics identifying the development of human capital as one of the profession's most urgent tasks (see, for example, Nafukho *et al* 2004). In the UK it is mandatory for all except the smaller UK organisations to report on their management of human capital. However, this requirement is far from rigorous, and the CIPD has produced its own reporting framework (http://www.cipd.co.uk/changeagendas). It focuses on all the ways in which an organisation can gain value through its people, and recommends as one of the core components of any annual report a section on how the company develops and manages employees. The Saratoga Institute, an arm of PricewaterhouseCoopers, has developed a range of metrics to facilitate this.

Despite such interest, research in the UK indicates that most organisations today are continuing to invest only or mainly in the short-term training of human capital. The typical training and career development investment also tends to be restricted to personnel seen to be 'key' to the business, mainly managers, professionals and specialist knowledge workers. Far fewer opportunities are available for the rest (Stevens and Ashton 1999; Stevens 2000). Yet in a knowledge economy it is essential to develop social capital, since it concerns human relationships that act as the glue for society. Putnam (2000), Professor of Public Policy at Harvard University, emphasised the dangers facing society when the sum of its social capital shrinks: communities fragment, trust and mutual commitment are lost, commonality of purpose disappears and society itself begins to break down.

Organisations failing to invest in social capital face a similar fate because without it they cannot generate the new knowledge upon which, in a knowledge economy, their survival depends. It is the development of an organisation's social capital that provides the conditions that nurture a willingness among individuals to connect and learn together and to apply the fruits of that learning to a shared organisational purpose (Huysman and De Wit 2002: 166). As will be seen in subsequent chapters, this has many implications for workplace learning, knowledge and diversity management and the building of organisational capacity for the future.

FIGHTING THE TALENT WAR

There is nothing new in competition between organisations to gain and retain scarce skills, but in recent years the so-called 'talent war' has intensified in the UK due to a toxic mix of factors including:

- a situation of near-full employment (although that is changing in the face of the recession caused by the US banking crises that developed during 2008)

- the emergence of a full-scale knowledge- and service-based economy where intellectual and relational rather than practical or manual skills offer the keys to prosperity

- the nation's continuing failure to build the kind of skills base that it needs to drive the economy forward

- a regular reorganising process by organisations across all sectors and countries in order to achieve greater cost efficiencies, a faster rate of innovation and enhanced competitive capability

- an accompanying need for the development of gifted corporate and front-line leaders in organisations.

The war for talent is being fought on many fronts – employer brand, the reward package, work–life balance, career planning and development. However, each organisation defines 'talent' in its own way and in consequence each adopts its own tactics for winning the war.

Traditionally 'talent' has been strongly associated with the young and high-fliers. That perspective needs adjustment in the face of a unique phenomenon: Europe's ageing workforce. It has been estimated that by 2050 'the number of workers for every individual of 65-plus will fall from more than three to fewer than two' (Duncan 2007). Retirement ages are set to rise accordingly. This, coupled with falling birth rates and increased longevity, is happening at a time when emerging market populations are producing a surplus of young talent, with twice as many university graduates as the West (Guthridge and Lawson 2008). Yet recent research by the McKinsey consultancy (*ibid*) has highlighted the fact that while some organisations have invested heavily in HR systems and processes and talent management has become a key issue on many boardroom agendas, very few organisations are getting it right. Short-termism, minimal collaboration or talent sharing between business units and lack of clarity about HR's role in managing talent are major obstacles to the process in many global corporations. In Chapter 16 challenges confronting talent management and their implications for L&D professionals will be explored in detail.

WORKING IN PARTNERSHIP

One issue that has always been central to the success of any effective training, learning or development yet remains problematic is the competence of L&D practitioners to form and sustain effective business partnerships. The whole of Chapter 13 concerns this issue but it underpins discussion throughout the book. 'Working in partnership' is a dominating theme in NVET strategy and its implementation. It is a key message in Government's extensive public sector reforms described in Chapter 10. It is essential to the so-called shift from training to learning discussed in Chapters 4 and 5, and it is the rock upon which major L&D programmes such as the one described in Chapter 8 rest.

In Chapter 13 reference is made to the CIPD's 'Partnership model of HRD' which suggests one way forward for L&D professionals as business partners (CIPD 2006a). Aspiration, though, is not enough. There has to be expertise also. Central to the success of L&D business partnerships is the ability of L&D professionals to gain the confidence and respect of leaders and managers in the business. They must be able to identify and understand the big challenges facing the organisation in order to convincingly propose where L&D investment should be focused. They must firmly tie the aims of their initiatives to business outcomes, and use business rather than training metrics and measures to assess subsequently whether those outcomes are being achieved. They must use business processes in their work as skilfully as they use training and L&D processes. They must engage partners not just in the delivery and evaluation of their activity but in its conception, planning and design.

SUPPORTING THE FRONT LINE

As far back as the early 1990s a major Cranfield European HRM survey indicated a growing awareness in organisations across Europe of the need for a greater synergy between the training and development of the individual employee, development of business strategies and plans, and development of the organisation (Larsen 1994: 121). Trends indicated an increased decentralisation of L&D responsibilities to line management to achieve this. In the UK this decentralisation has subsequently grown apace, but synergy lags far behind.

In recent years research has been conducted by Professor John Purcell and his team at the University of Bath in collaboration with other research institutions, exploring links between HR practices and organisational performance (Purcell *et al* 2003). I will discuss this research in detail in Chapter 6. Its relevance to this section is the attention it has drawn to the critical role played by front-line managers in enabling or hindering the implementation of L&D plans, and the concerns that exist around their commitment and competence in their L&D roles (Hutchinson and Purcell 2003). These concerns were underlined in the CIPD's 2007 annual L&D survey (CIPD 2007a), which pointed to two particularly worrying issues:

- Barely half of the respondents reported that their line managers were supporting staff development, despite the importance of those managers' L&D role.

- Only 40% of organisations covered trained all, or most, of their line managers to carry out that role.

The 2008 survey identified some progress, with respondents reporting a significant increase in the investment their organisations were now making in management development (CIPD 2008a). However, there is still a long road to be travelled. Purcell and Hutchinson (2007) stressed the need for L&D professionals to plan, design and deliver training and learning processes that will help to build a positive relationship between FLMs and their own managers, since this relationship is probably the biggest variable influencing FLMs' own levels of organisational commitment. The real-life case study that forms the bulk of Chapter 8 will demonstrate how seriously one major organisation is taking that task, and the expertise, commitment and partnership skills it requires to carry it out.

REFLECTION

What seem to be the most significant current trends in training and development in your own organisation? And what do you judge to be their biggest practical implications for those who carry L&D responsibilities there?

CONCLUSION

Having read this chapter you should by now be able to identify the kind of contribution that the L&D process can make to a business and to individuals. You should be able to confidently tackle the review questions for this chapter (Appendix 3). The rationale of the 10 L&D performance indicators shown in Appendix 1 should also now be apparent.

To summarise the main ground covered by the chapter's three sections:

- the variety of meanings attached to the L&D process and their implications for the purpose and scope of L&D activity in an organisation; the increasing value now being attached to 'learning and development' rather than simply to training in many organisations and the substantially higher financial and career rewards now on offer for those who have proven expertise in, and commitment to, that field

- the importance of 'evidence-based' L&D practice; tensions that exist between the need to build a convincing business case for proposed L&D initiatives and the need to experiment in order to develop the new knowledge essential to innovation and progress

- an outline history of what is commonly termed in the literature 'HRD' and the strong emphasis on performance improvement and the development of human capital that continues to characterise L&D practice in the USA and UK; the need, in

CONCLUSION CONT.

a service-based knowledge economy, for far more attention to be paid to the building of social capital

- evidence of a general failure of L&D functions to achieve a powerful business impact, and the need in this respect both for a greater integration between the functions in the 'HR wheel' and for a more business-focused and contextualised approach to all

HR activity, including that in the L&D field

- criticisms of the L&D profession for the slowness of its progress over the past decade or so, but recognition of the major issues that it continues to confront in a highly volatile external environment; an introduction to five of these, that alongside many others will be discussed subsequently in this book.

EXLPORE FURTHER

FURTHER INFORMATION SOURCES

Hamlin, B. (2002) 'Towards evidence-based HRD practice'. In McGoldrick J., Stewart J. and Watson S. (eds) *Understanding Human Resource Development: A research-based approach*. London: Routledge. pp93–121

Wilson, J. P. (ed) (2005) *Human Resource Development: Learning and training for individuals and organizations*, 2nd edition. London: Kogan Page

http://www.cipd.co.uk/onlinein fodocuments/?dropdown=sitem ap [accessed 26 July 2008]. The

CIPD's links to its wide range of information sources on HR issues of the day

http://www.trainingzone. co.uk [accessed 26 July 2008]. A lively and informative virtual community

http://www.ufhrd.com [accessed 26 July 2008]. Website of the UK University Forum for HRD, 'an international association for universities, reflective practitioners and learning-oriented organisations'

CHAPTER 2

National Skills Strategy

INTRODUCTION

Government in England since 1997 has followed a wide-ranging strategy related to skills and vocational education. The purpose of this and the following chapter is to outline and assess the current status of this strategy, and to identify key implications for employers, the L&D profession and individuals. This chapter's focus is national skills strategy and initiatives for workforce development, and in Chapter 3 is vocational education reforms.

Given their scope, these two chapters are bound to be quite lengthy. Therefore, in this chapter I cannot include assessment of national vocational education and training (NVET) policy in the UK during the greater part of the twentieth century. For those interested I recommend Cannell's (2007) online fact sheet. I have further simplified this chapter by focusing on government policy at the expense of opposition party policies, and by including only limited reference to skills strategies in the Devolved Administrations and in other countries. Relevant information sources for the two latter areas of interest are noted at the end of this chapter. Appendix 4 gives an introduction to Devolved strategies.

The chapter has six sections. In the first I discuss governments' and employers' differing views of the UK productivity and skills gap and implications for NVET policy. In the second I outline the (Labour) government's national skills strategy between 1997 and 2006 with particular reference to its plans for workforce development. The third and fourth sections cover the 2006 Leitch review of adult skills and implementation to date (mid-2008) of its recommendations. In the fifth section I assess the extent to which Britain seems any nearer to resolving its skills crisis, and in the final section I suggest priority tasks for L&D professionals in their organisations.

The chapter contains many abbreviations relating to government agencies and initiatives. It is a necessity that is also one of NVET policy's more irritating features.

THE LIFELONG LEARNING VISION

Tory and Labour governments' NVET policies in the UK since the 1970s have been driven by a vision of lifelong learning for all, leading to an 'interdependence of social justice and economic success' (DfES 2003a: 11). UNESCO adopted lifelong learning as its mission in the 1970s, and the European Community espoused it in the early 1990s. Global initiatives followed, including the World Initiative on Lifelong Learning and the European Lifelong Learning Initiative.

The Labour Government's vision is that (DfEE 1998: 1):

> Investment in human capital will be the foundation of success in the knowledge-based global economy of the twenty-first century. That is why the government has put learning at the heart of its ambition.

In line with this vision, its NVET policy has sought to transform the UK economy into a world leader that competes on the basis of capability for innovation, enterprise, quality and adding greater value through its products and services (DfES 2003a: 11).

By 2006 when Leitch produced his review of adult skills, that transformational vision seemed little nearer realisation despite nearly two decades of continuous reform in national training and educational systems. Why was this?

THE ECONOMIC CONTEXT

By the start of 2008 the UK's economy had sustained unbroken growth for 15 years and had achieved one of the highest employment rates in the G7. However, during 2008, worsening problems in the US sub-prime mortgage market and their implications for the US banking system began to seriously threaten economic stability across Europe. If the situation at the time of writing (mid-2008) continues to deteriorate, its impact on UK employment rates and on businesses will be increasingly adverse. This would bode ill for L&D functions, whose budgets are usually the first to be cut at time of financial crisis.

The UK economy's profile in recent years has already changed significantly in a different way that poses challenges for education and training policy at macro and micro levels. The service sector now accounts for around three quarters of the economy. Of the 29 million people employed in the UK, three million are self-employed, around a quarter work in small firms of less than 50 employees, over 20% work in the public sector and just under 50% work in large firms (Leitch 2006). Those without qualifications are increasingly disadvantaged. *Skills at Work*, the report on the fifth national survey on work skill in Britain since 1986 (Felstead *et al* 2007), revealed that the proportion of jobs requiring level 4 qualifications and above rose between 1986 and 2006 from 20% to 30%. There has been a marked increase in jobs requiring the use of influencing, technical and literacy skills, and jobs using automated or computerised equipment have increased dramatically with three quarters of the workforce using such equipment now (Sloman 2007a).

GETTING TO THE HEART OF THE MATTER: THE GOVERNMENT VIEWPOINT

The central thrust of most of the reports that have informed government's NVET policy over the years is that the UK economy is held back in its ambition to become a world leader because of a major weakness in national productivity levels, and that this problem has been compounded by employers' persistent failure to invest sufficiently in the training of their workforces. To be specific:

- Since the 1950s there has been a wide and stubborn productivity gap between the UK on the one hand, and comparator countries such as the USA, France and Germany on the other. By 2005 the UK was still low down in the league table, ranking around 12th among the 15 countries that made up the EU before 2004 (Mattin 2005). One fifth or more of that gap was estimated to be the result of its relatively poor skills base (Leitch 2006).

- While capital investment, research and development and information technology are all keys to differences in productivity levels between firms and between countries, a significant body of evidence now points to a direct link between accredited skills and business productivity, innovation, quality and sophistication of products (Tamkin 2005: 4). The proportion of the UK workforce with level 4 skills (degree equivalent or above) is comparable to that in France and Germany and has increased over the past 10 to 15 years in line with reforms to the UK's educational system. However, other countries have also been improving their skills over that period, often from a higher base. The net result is that the UK's overall skills base remains mediocre by international standards, with the greatest weaknesses being in its low-level and intermediate-level skills (PIU 2001; Leitch 2006). The UK is also weak in management and leadership skills and practices – a factor that helps to explain the closure of 37.5% of small start-ups within their first three years (SU 2002).

- The UK's skills gap has widened over the past decade, in an era of economic turbulence when skills have been depreciating ever more rapidly and global migration flows have been increasing. Like the rest of Europe, the UK has an ageing workforce whose skills must be upgraded if businesses are to gain the fullest advantage from technological advances. Accredited skills are key to employment and therefore serve crucial social as well as economic ends. Despite the UK's high employment rate, by 2006 more than 20% of its potentially economically active population was either not in work or was not seeking work. While only 10% of those with graduate-level qualifications was in this group, it contained over 50% of those with no qualifications, a situation made worse by the fact that the number of unskilled jobs in the UK is expected to fall from around 3.2 million in 2006 to only 600,000 by 2020 (Leitch 2006). Leitch feared this will lead to (*ibid*: 9):

> a lost generation, cut off permanently from labour market opportunity ... Where skills were once *a* key driver of prosperity and fairness, they are now *the* key driver. Achieving world class skills is *the* key to achieving economic success and social justice in the new global economy.

- Training is associated with greater productivity gains than wage gains and therefore should bring substantial rewards to employers and individuals as well as to the economy at large (PIU 2001). It can also improve employees' morale and engagement, as well as increase the likelihood of wage benefits, improved promotability and less likelihood of redundancy for individuals (Tamkin 2005: 5). Yet in the view of successive governments employers have consistently failed to make an adequate training investment (PIU 2001).

In a series of attempts to increase employers' investment in formal training of their employees, governments in the UK during post-war years have swung from a voluntary approach to one of regulation through Industrial Training Boards (Cannell 2007) and back again to voluntarism with the establishment of Training and Enterprise Councils (TECs). A clearer framework than hitherto of vision, policy and aims for NVET emerged during the Thatcher and Major years, and TECs formed some fruitful partnerships with employers. However the TECs did not produce their intended outcomes fast enough and in 2001 they were abolished. A major overhaul of the whole NVET system then took place, as I will explain shortly.

REFLECTION

Consider your own organisation, or one with which you are familiar. Where are its major proficiency gaps, and how far – and in what ways – do you think it is tackling them successfully?

GETTING TO THE HEART OF THE MATTER: THE EMPLOYER VIEWPOINT

Employers' perspective on the training-skills situation has been predictably different from that of governments. In outline:

- Employers' failure over the years to invest in the kind of training prioritised by successive governments has been in significant part due to increasingly unpredictable market conditions, reduced profit levels, the uncertain and often long-term returns on training and development investment and a fear of seeing trained talent walk out of the door. The small to medium-sized businesses (SMEs) which account for 52% of the UK's total turnover are particularly vulnerable here and it is their support for NVET policies and initiatives that has always proved the most difficult to obtain.

- Employers have been unable to acquire a strong voice to express their view on future skills, largely because mechanisms to do so have been ineffective and inefficient (Leitch 2006: 11). Partly as a result of this and partly in consequence of the usual political powerplay that has accompanied the coming and going of ministers and governments, NVET policy has been regularly revised and consistently dictated by governments', not by employers', definition of the skills gap problem and how to tackle it.

- Successive governments up to the end of the twentieth century assessed skill needs by reference to international and national, not local, economic criteria. They adopted a *supply-driven* policy, tying official skills initiatives and funding tightly to national learning and development targets that involve attainment of vocational qualifications (PIU 2001). Yet CIPD surveys indicate that 40% of total employer-provided training in the UK relates to non-accredited learning activity (Philpott 2004: 34) and it is clear from the *Skills at Work* survey (Felstead *et al* 2007) that workbased learning of the informal as well as accredited kind is now more central to upskilling the workforce as pressures increase to acquire new and more complex skills quickly in most jobs. What employers are most concerned about are specific gaps in proficiency in their own workplaces, threatening the profitability and sometimes the survival of their businesses. What they have always wanted is a *demand-led* NVET system driven largely by their specific needs.

Employers in the UK have tended to rely more on recruitment than training to solve their proficiency gaps, investing in formal training and development only when they see a powerful business case in their own organisation for doing so. This helps to explain why 'managers and professionals or those with a degree [are] up to five times more likely to receive work-based training than people with no qualification and/or in an unskilled job' (Westwood 2001: 19). These are the people who employers perceive to be the drivers of the business. This focus on a trained elite has intensified the economy's problem of lack of skills at the basic levels, yet has had little apparent impact in terms of improving leadership and management capability across the UK economy (SU 2002).

There have been genuine attempts by governments over the years to actively involve employers in the various bodies set up to inform and implement NVET policy. But each framework has proved inadequate and employers and individuals have continued to find NVET institutional structures and government funding overcomplicated, constantly changing, and lacking in clear, relevant and timely information and advice (Leitch 2006; Coffield 2007).

OTHER KEY PLAYERS

There are many other NVET stakeholders, often separated by more interests and needs than those that could unite them. These include unions, educational and training providers, and those government departments and official agencies at national, sectoral and local levels that have had to share responsibility for NVET policies and implementation. Of critical importance are the customers at the end of the line: employees, those out of work but seeking to gain employment, and new entrants to the world of work – especially, today, valuable specialist knowledge workers – who want well-paid jobs, meaningful career progression and education and training opportunities to match. Unions, in particular, had to wait until the advent of the Learning and Skills Councils in 2001 (see the next section) before being given any real voice in NVET planning.

REFLECTION

Consider an organisation with which you are familiar. Where does it target most of its training spend – both for accredited and non-accredited learning – and what is its rationale for that focus? What changes – if any – do you think it should make, and why?

A NEW ERA – ENGLAND'S FIRST NATIONAL SKILLS STRATEGY

DEMAND FOR A CHANGED STRATEGIC APPROACH

A comprehensive assessment of the productivity-skills problem and the NVET policies to have flowed from it over the years was contained in an influential independent report presented to Prime Minister Tony Blair in 2001, entitled *In Demand, Part 1*(PIU 2001). It identified the fundamental problem facing the UK's economy as one of competitive strategy: too many UK firms compete on the basis of low cost/low added value, and the 'low skill/low wage' cycle that this generates gives employers no incentive to upskill their workforces or to improve qualification rates in the workplace. The report's authors urged that it makes no sense for the UK's economy to continue with a competitive strategy already being pursued successfully by many other economies with cheap labour forces and high technological skills, notably China and India. If our economy is to become a world leader, the competitive strategy of its firms needs to move much further along the high-specification/high value-added route. The Netherlands and the USA were cited as evidence that the adoption of such a route automatically drives employers to invest more heavily in vocational education and in-company training, since only by doing that can they acquire the higher-level skills that are needed to make their competitive strategy viable (PIU 2001).

THE 2003 NATIONAL SKILLS STRATEGY

Blair's Government accepted the main arguments made in *In Demand, Part 1*. Following also commitments made in a series of Green and White Papers from 1998 onwards it published in 2003 a White Paper, *21st-Century Skills*, that announced a ground-breaking skills strategy for England (DfES 2003a). At the heart of this strategy, and in line with the thinking behind *In Demand, Part 1*, lies the belief that British firms need to be encouraged and supported in moving to a high-performance work organisation (HPWO) model. Definitions of quite what this model means vary greatly but its 'constituent practices … are meant to be forms of human resource management policies and methods of work organisation that engender employee involvement, the maximisation of effort, initiative and commitment' (Lloyd and Payne 2005). The belief is that those outcomes will ultimately generate above-average levels of firm performance defined in financial or economic terms.

The 2003 national skills strategy, the first ever formally articulated by a UK government, seeks to apply a demand-driven approach to the three primary tasks identified by *In Demand, Part 1*, namely (PIU 2001):

- to ensure through lifelong learning policies that all adults have basic employability skills

- to focus on helping employers to rethink their business and organisational strategies around more ambitious high-performance/high value-added goals that, to be achieved, will require them to invest in more highly skilled workforces

- alongside that, to adopt a far more demand-led approach to NVET provision, with employers and individual learners in the driving seat.

The 2003 skills strategy introduced a crowded agenda of proposals to pursue these three tasks along two major routes, each feeding into and supported by lifelong learning initiatives: workforce development and educational reform. In Chapter 3 I will outline the agenda being pursued for educational reform. Here, my focus is on workforce development.

THE 2003 STRATEGY FOR WORKFORCE DEVELOPMENT

Workforce development is defined officially as (SU 2002):

> Activities which increase the capacity of individuals to participate effectively in the workplace, thereby improving their productivity and employability.

In *21st-Century Skills* (DfES 2003a) the Government accepted one of the most important points made in the *In Demand, Part 1* report (PIU 2001): that skill needs do not exist in a vacuum. If people are to be motivated and enabled to use their skills to 'go the extra mile' in order to achieve exceptional performance, there must be a conducive context of business strategies, leadership and management, and HR practices. The White Paper announced actions to achieve the skills strategy's three targets (see Table 1 on p. 37) by 2010. Priority was given to efforts to involve low-skilled adults and small firms and to the public sector as employer and purchaser, in view of their unique importance to the economy. The actions had a threefold thrust (SU 2002, Annex 1):

- *Raising informed demand* through improving management, leadership and HR strategies in organisations, stimulating the development of HPWOs, encouraging innovative workplace learning and reforming the national qualifications framework.

- *Meeting demand* by promoting flexible funding mechanisms and quality assurance measures, and devolving more purchasing power to consumers of training and education notably through Sector Skills Councils (SSCs – see below), Investors in People (IiP) and new Employer Training Pilots offering firms free training advice and brokering of funding.

- *Ensuring effective delivery*, with a new deregulated structure that replaced the TEC system in England in 2001 and was intended to deliver NVET policy through 'working in partnership'. The web of partners set up in 2001 was large and complex, ultimately feeding into the regional labour market planning system and being supported by the Department of Trade and Industry (DTI).

In outline, the delivery framework consisted of:

- *At national level* a new single, non-departmental public body called the national Learning and Skills Council (LSC), introduced in 2001. At local level the LSC was to operate through 47 LSCs, working in partnership with regional employment and skills agencies and with employers. The single biggest representation (40%) on LSC boards at local as at national level was employers, joined by trade unions, government and other voluntary groups. Unions had no representation on the previous TECs, so this was a real advance for them.

- *At regional and sectoral levels* a Skills for Business Network, set up in 2001 to deliver skills-based productivity improvements in industry and the public services. It comprised Sector Skills Councils (SSCs) and a Sector Skills Development Agency (SSDA). SSCs took over the tasks of the 72 national training organisations (NTOs) that had been established in 1998 – themselves swallowing up the 170 Industry Training Organisations set up in 1981 – but that had never managed to fulfil their potential. Each SSC was intended to be the most authoritative source in the country of information and analysis about skills that its sector needed to drive up productivity and close skills gaps. To give SSCs regional influence, 'working in partnership' was again the key.

- *At organisational level*, employers to work closely with SSCs and regional development agencies to articulate organisational learning needs. Union learning representatives (ULRs) also had an important role to play. Following publication of *The Learning Age* Green Paper (DfES 1998) the Government had provided in 1998 a Union Learning Fund to help unions encourage and support workplace learning. In 2001 the TUC set up a ULR network with the task of encouraging the low skilled to engage in training, and further government funding enabled the network's rapid expansion.

IMPLEMENTATION OF WORKFORCE DEVELOPMENT STRATEGY, 2003–2006

Between 2003 and 2006 some major changes for the better in national Workforce Development Strategy (WfD) undoubtedly took place, among them the following:

- Government's acceptance of the importance of the organisational context in which skills are acquired and applied. This led it to focus its strategy on workplace development and organisational culture as well as on WfD, and in particular led to the successful *Employer Training Pilots* and to the further strengthening of the *Investors in People* initiative following its 2004 review (see a later section).

- Government's determination to achieve a more demand-led approach to WfD provision.

- Government's intention to ensure the delivery of the LSC's WfD strategy through a partnership process where employers and unions had a stronger voice.

Warning signs

Despite these improvents, in March 2005 a White Paper *Skills: Getting on in business, getting on at work* (DfES 2005a) reported that around one in five organisations was still experiencing a serious skills gap. It set out proposals to further develop the 2003 national skills strategy. These were intended to work alongside educational initiatives that had just been announced in the 14–19 *Education and Skills* White Paper (DfES 2005b – see Chapter 3). Proposals included the establishment of 12 Skills Academies, one for each major sector of the economy, to be developed by SSCs in collaboration with the LSC and with the aim of improving workplace skills. Employers were requested to provide half their funding, the rest to come from the LSC (35%) and other sources (15%) including education and training providers.

But in September 2006 EEF, Britain's manufacturers' organisation, published a further alarm call in a report claiming that (Phillips 2006):

> The learning and skills sector is beset by an array of market-muddlers, as organisations with overlapping responsibilities trip over each other to influence the system.

In 2004 Gordon Brown, then Chancellor of the Exchequer, had commissioned a major review on UK skills, headed by Sir Sandy Leitch. In December 2006 the

Leitch Review was published. It set out a raft of recommendations that now form the basis in England of the Government's revised NVET targets, plans and delivery framework to achieve the 2003 Skills Strategy, and to which the Devolved Administrations have also been asked to work (see Appendix 4). Because of the Review's importance, details follow in a separate section below.

REFLECTION

From your own desk research, find some organisational stories that illustrate both the ways in which the demand-led approach to NVET delivery is working in specific cases, and the barriers that prevent it working better. Then reflect on implications that these suggest to you for your own organisation. (I will return to this theme at the end of the chapter.)

THE 2006 LEITCH REVIEW

NEW TARGETS FOR 2020

Leitch forecast from an analysis of extensive data that by 2020 the UK would have sunk to near the bottom of the league of European economies unless radical actions were quickly taken. He called for (Leitch 2006: 14):

> a new shared national mission, moving beyond the old distinction between voluntarism and compulsion, forging a new compact between the Government, employers, trades unions and individuals.

He moved forward to 2020 the target date for the UK to become a world leader in skills, and produced new, more challenging skills and qualification targets (see Table 1). They will require more than double the 2006-projected rate of attainment in many cases.

As to who should pay the piper, Leitch recommended that:

* Government should provide the bulk of funding for basic skills and the platform of skills for employability, channeling its funds through *Train to Gain*, *Learning Accounts* and university tuition fees.

* employers and individuals should make a much higher contribution than currently for higher intermediate skills (level 3), and at level 4 and above they should pay the bulk of the additional costs because they will benefit most.

Leitch's key proposals were all accepted by Gordon Brown's Government. To relate them to the actions set out in the national skills strategy White Paper (DfES 2003a)

TABLE 1 National adult skills targets

> ### National education and training targets for foundation and lifelong learning, 1991
>
> 1 By 1997 at least 80% of all young people to hold by age 18 an NVQ/SVQ at level 2 or its academic equivalent.
>
> 2 All young people who can benefit should be given an entitlement to structured training, work experience or education leading to NVQ level 3 or its academic equivalent.
>
> 3 By 2000 at least 50% of that age group to be qualified to at least level 3 or equivalent.
>
> 4 By 2000 50% of the employed workforce to be qualified to at least level 3 or its academic equivalent.
>
> ### National skills objectives, 2003–2010
>
> 1 At least 28% of 16- to 17-year-olds to start on a *modern apprenticeship* in 2004 (tied to level 2 skills attainment).
>
> 2 Reduction by at least 40% of the estimated seven million adults lacking NVQ2 or equivalent level 2 qualifications.
>
> 3 Working toward this, at least one million adults already in the workforce to achieve level 2 between 2003 and 2006.
>
> ### Leitch Review national skills targets, 2006–2020
>
> By 2020:
>
> - 95% of adults to have achieved the basic skills of functional literacy and numeracy, from 2005 levels of 85% literacy and 79% numeracy.
>
> - Over 90% of adults to be qualified to at least level 2 , from 2005 level of 69%, with the aim of achieving 95% as soon as possible thereafter.
>
> - The balance of intermediate skills to have shifted from level 2 to level 3, requiring 1.9 million additional level 3 attainments over the period and a total of 500,000 apprentices per year.
>
> - Over 40% of adults to be qualified to level 4 and above, from 2005 level of 29%, with a commitment to continue progression thereafter.
>
> *Broad definitions:* 'Adults' means age 19 to state pension age. 'Basic' describes everyday literacy and numeracy skills. 'Level 2' equates to five good GCSEs; 'level 3' equates to two 'A' levels; 'level 4' equates to a degree or vocational equivalents.

Sources: Employment Department Group (1991); Department for Education and Skills (2003a); Leitch, S. (2006)

I will group them under the three headings used there. I will also identify those to be discussed in detail in Chapter 3.

RAISING INFORMED DEMAND

In line with the 2003 aim of encouraging organisation cultures fostering innovation, change and growth, Leitch urged Government to:

- launch a new 'Pledge' for employers to achieve 'mass' voluntary commitment to train all eligible employees up to level 2 in the workplace, working to a training plan based on their business needs. Currently employers focus their training investment 'disproportionately' on highly-skilled workers, and around one third of firms do no training at all, almost all of those being located in the less well performing sectors. If by 2010 upskilling has been insufficient, introduce a statutory entitlement to workplace training at level 2 in consultation with employers and unions and delivered in England through *Train to Gain.*

- increase employer investment in level 3 and 4 qualifications in the workplace by extending *Train to Gain* to higher levels, and by dramatically increasing *apprenticeships* numbers (see Chapter 3)

- make education or workplace training compulsory up to age 18. Increase people's aspirations and awareness of the value of skills to them and their families, creating high profile, sustained awareness programmes, rationalising existing 'information silos' and developing a new universal adult careers service

- significantly reduce by 2008 the thousands of vocational qualifications on offer, with the SSC to approve only those vocational and work-based learning qualifications that will deliver 'economically valuable skills' (see Chapter 3)

- use SSCs and skills brokers to drive up employer investment in leaderships and management skills by employers, extending the funding programme so that even very small firms can benefit from it.

MEETING DEMAND

In line with the 2003 aim of promoting flexible funding mechanisms and quality assurance measures that will engage employers and encourage a high-calibre provider market, Leitch urged Government to:

- introduce new *Learner Accounts* in England, as in Wales and Scotland, for individuals wanting to improve their basic and level 2 skills, in order to contribute towards accredited learning of their choice; target financial support at those who need it most (see Chapter 3)

- reform SSCs to give employers greater collective voice, and expand skills brokerage services in *Train to Gain* for both small and large employers

- in higher education (HE), improve engagement between employers and universities, increasing co-funded workplace degrees and the focus on level 5 and above skills (see Chapter 3).

ENSURING EFFECTIVE DELIVERY

To produce a more flexible, accessible and 'joined up' framework for delivering education and training at organisational and individual levels, Leitch recommended Government to:

- rationalise existing NVET bodies, strengthen the collective voice and better articulate employer views on skills by creating a new *Commission for Employment and Skills*, reporting to central Government and the Devolved Administrations

- create a new integrated *employment and skills service*, based upon existing structures, to increase sustainable employment and progression, delivery to be monitored by the new Commission. Leitch emphasised the need to resolve the confusion and demotivation experienced by individuals seeking to improve their skills but frustrated by misaligned skills and employment systems and by services with a short-term focus, differing aims and a multiplicity of agencies

- launch a new programme to improve basic skills for those out of work, with particular concern for the disadvantaged and for repeat claimants. Link services better together so that people are supported when they move into work, helping them to stay employed and to progress (see Chapter 3).

REFLECTION

Table 1 provides a comparison between national skills targets set by the Conservative Government in 1991, the Labour Government in 2003, and Leitch in 2006. Leitch claimed that his targets were more coherent than those set in 2003 because they focus on outcomes, measure attainment rather than participation and cover the whole adult population rather than subsets. Reflecting on all three sets of targets, what seem to you to be the most significant differences between them, and how far do you agree with Leitch's claim?

IMPLEMENTING LEITCH

2006–2008: THE PATH OF REFORM

Following Leitch and also a 2006 White Paper on further education reform (DfES 2006a) came the usual period of frantic activity at various national, regional and local levels induced by such reviews. The July 2007 White Paper *World Class Skills* (DIUS 2007) formally announced the adoption of Leitch's recommendations. Its major thrust was plans to make it easier for employers' training programmes to be accredited through the Qualifications and Credit framework and so give greater power to vocational training driven by employers (see Chapter 3).

Other main changes to implement Leitch's Review are as follows:

All change at the top

http://www.dius.gov.uk/press/ [accessed 14 April 2008]

In June 2007 Gordon Brown, newly created Prime Minister, announced the setting up of three new government departments in order to bring 'renewed energy to tackling the UK skills agenda' (Temple 2007). The Department for Education and Skills disappeared, giving way to a Department for Innovation, Universities and Skills (DIUS) and a Department for Children, Schools and Families (DCSF). What was left of the old DTI became the Department for Business, Enterprise and Regulatory Reform (DBERR).

On the way in: a new Commission

http://www.dfes.gov.uk/pns/pns/newslist.cgi [accessed 14 April 2008]

Other measures included the launch of the new *Skills Pledge*, the appointment of the Chair of the new *Commission for Employment and Skills* (Sir Michael Rake, International Chairman of KPMG) and the extension of the *National Skills Academies* network. The Commission, a new single employer-driven body, became operational in April 2008 when it replaced the SSDA and the National Employment Panel in order to achieve better integration of the current, 'disjointed' Employment and Skills services and to 'depoliticise' the skills agenda. Its main responsibilities are to:

- provide advice to ministers across the UK concerning progress of the reformed employment and skills systems in meeting competitive challenges faced by business, and in supporting changing employment trends

- fund and manage the performance and re-licensing of the 25 employer-led SSCs, taking the lead role in developing occupational standards, approving vocational qualifications, and collating and communicating sectoral labour market data

- raise employer engagement, demand and investment through its network of Employment and Skills Boards.

On the way out: Learning and Skills Council

http//www.lsc.gov.uk [accessed 11 April 2008]

At the time of writing (mid-2008) the LSC remains responsible for planning and funding education and training for everyone in England other than those in universities. However, it was announced in a White Paper in March 2008 (DCSF and DIUS 2008a) that it will be dissolved by 2010. Local LSCs were abolished by the 2007 Further Education and Training Act, which introduced instead 'committees', to be called regional learning and skills councils, for each area of England.

Key measures to be implemented under the 2008 White Paper are:

- Following abolition of the LSC local authorities will become responsible for the provision to all young people from ages 0 to 19 in their areas of a full menu of choices – both the new *diplomas* and *apprenticeships* (see Chapter 3) alongside GCSEs and A levels.

- Sponsorship of the FE service as a whole, and apprenticeships, to be the responsibility of the new Department for Innovation, Universities and Skills (DIUS).

- A new smaller *Skills Funding Agency* for employers and adult learners in order to streamline the funding process to colleges and training providers. The Agency will also manage by 2010 (DCSF & DIUS 2008a):

  - a newly formed *National Employer Service*, the single service for employers with 5,000+ employees

  - the creation and management of a new England-wide adult advancement and careers service, which will play a key role, with Jobcentre Plus, in boosting individual demand for skills and guiding people to the right training to meet their needs and help change their lives

  - a new *National Apprenticeships Service* (NAS) to take end-to-end responsibility for the apprenticeships programme. The NAS will be led by a director reporting to the Secretaries of State of DCSF and DIUS, although initially coming under the LSC.

- Overall planning and funding for 14–19 learners to be the responsibility of the new Department for Children, Schools and Families (DCSF).

- Local authorities and the new Skills Funding Agency to have substantial power over the planning and funding system for FE colleges and providers, and the Agency to become responsible for their performance management. It is to be 'the single point of intervention where either pre- or post-19 performance does not meet nationally agreed acceptable standards'.

- Funding for school sixth forms, sixth form colleges and the contribution of FE colleges to the 14–19 phase to be transferred from the LSC to local authorities' education budgets.

Reformed and performance-managed: Sector Skills Councils

http://www.sscalliance.org [accessed 11 April 2008]

Leitch found that the effectiveness of SSCs was impeded by a 'patchy' overall performance 'due to conflicting objectives, the lack of a clear remit, deficiencies in performance management and ineffective leadership'. Accordingly, in April 2008 the 25 SSCs then in place were reformed to become a collective body called

FIGURE 4 Delivery system for national skills strategy post-Leitch

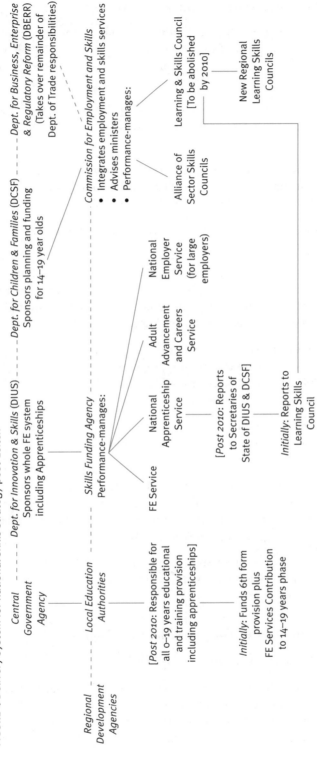

Key
- - - - Partnership working
———— Direct reporting lines

the *Alliance of Sector Skills Councils*, accountable to the new Commission for Employment and Skills. The Alliance has as its initial focus representing and co-ordinating the strategic work of SSCs to stakeholders across the four home nations.

Figure 4 shows in outline key components of the new education, employment and skills structure to deliver NVET policy covering those areas. As can be seen, the picture is a very complex one and the system is heavily criticised by commentators like Coffield (2007) for being excessively centralised, leaving local authorities too little power to ensure its democratic functioning. Others, by contrast, believe that local authorities have been given too much power, but they too fear that the confusing mix of centralised control and 'partnership' will prove unworkable.

On the way up: Unionlearn

http://www.unionlearn.org.uk/ [accessed 11.04.08]

By 2005 there were 8,000 ULRs, and there is a target of 22,000 by 2010. Since 2002 they have been legally entitled to 'reasonable' paid time off to be specially trained for their role and to undertake their duties. In 2005 the *Union Academy* was launched to further the aims of the 2005 White Paper *Skills: Getting on in Business, Getting on at Work* (DfES 2005a). The Academy is building on the work of ULRs, offering guidance on training for employers and employees, with courses ranging from basic to high-level skills.

In 2006 the Prime Minister launched *unionlearn*, which in 2007 was given responsibility for the Union Learning Fund, with an annual budget of £12.5 million mainly provided by the Department for Education and Skills. *unionlearn*'s strategic aims are:

- to help unions to become learning organisations, with programmes for union reps and regional officers and strategic support for national officers

- to help unions to broker learning opportunities for their members

- to research union priorities on learning and skills, identify and share good practice, promote learning agreements, support union members on learning and skills bodies, and help shape sector skills agreements.

By 2007 *unionlearn* had supported over 450 projects covering about 3,000 workplaces and accessed by over 67,000 learners per year. Research by the CIPD, the TUC and the LSC in 2004, and by Leeds University Business School in 2007 showed that union involvement significantly increases participation of shop floor workers and managers in learning activities and improves employment relations (Mahony 2007).

REFLECTION

In your own organisation, who are the 'learning champions' whose main activity is to help promote individual learning – especially at basic skills level – in the workplace? And how far do you think they work effectively with management and with any L&D staff in that activity?

TWO KEY INITIATIVES

Before assessing the progress being made in delivering the 2003 skills strategy (DfES 2003a) in the post-Leitch era, it is relevant to outline two initiatives that are central planks to ensure demand-led workforce and workplace development: Train to Gain, and the Investors in People Standard.

Train to Gain

http://www.traintogain.gov.uk [accessed 8 April 2008]

Train to Gain emerged in 2006 from the success of Employer Training Pilots. It offers a demand-led approach to training through the services of Skills Brokers who can:

- give free impartial and independent advice to businesses, helping them to identify the skills they need and to pinpoint the right training

- match any training needs identified with training providers

- ensure a tailored training package, delivered to meet business needs and utilising available funding (see http://www.learndirect-business.co.uk/traintogain/

CASE EXAMPLE

TRAIN TO GAIN AT CREWE ALEXANDRA FOOTBALL CLUB

Crewe Alexandra football club used Train to Gain to fund level 2 NVQs in spectator safety for its stewards. The training included a significant element of literacy, numeracy and communication skills to get people up to speed and proved hugely successful in raising stewards' performance and their confidence, said stadium operations manager Cliff Simpson. The reduction in fights and incidents helped the club to cut police costs by 40%. Simpson added:

> By the end of the year we will have trained nearly all our 110 stewards. We could have done it without the Train to Gain funding, but we could never have done it as quickly. It would have taken us several years to roll the training out to all stewards.

Source: Carrington, L. (2007a)
People Management, 23 August

[accessed 8 April 2008] to see how one training provider works with Train to Gain to offer clients a flexible training portfolio).

- help employers to review progress made by the training.

Train to Gain enables access to training mainly focused on NVQ level 2 (for employees aged 23 and above) and apprenticeships. Some of the training is subsidised by the Government, and some will need to be invested in by employers themselves. Almost all official funding is tied to formal qualifications.

In 2006 Leitch praised the initiative's success, with 30,000 employers and 250,000 employees having participated by March 2006. Its expansion, announced in November 2007, is intended to encourage businesses of all sizes to invest in training that will raise their capability base.

The Investors in People Standard

http://www.investorsinpeople.co.uk/ [accessed 10 April 2008]

Established in 1990 by the Conservative Government, and designed by a partnership of leading businesses and national organisations, this Standard is the most long standing, flexible and successful official initiative to date whereby to improve the planning and delivery of business-focused training and development in the UK. Alongside Train to Gain it has become the central plank of national workforce and workplace development and skills strategy and over 30,000 UK organisations covering a wide spectrum of UK industries have now achieved its kitemark. It is delivered through Business Link and LSCs to make it easily accessible, and further impetus is provided by the annual National Training Awards (NTA) that offer a framework for benchmarking the training of organisations and individuals and a sharing of 'success' stories.

IiP has been revamped regularly since its launch. At the time of writing (mid-2008) the last review was in 2004. That version of the IiP Standard continues to mirror the business planning cycle (Plan, Do, Review), making it clear for organisations to follow and implement in their own planning cycle, but it now uses a simplified structure, carries a new focus on management and leadership at work and has a new indicator to encourage organisations to involve employees in decision-making. IiP UK is also working with the Department of Health to develop a new indicator on health at work. The whole Standard is now more flexible, easier to administer, focuses on outputs and has a specially tailored version for small firms.

Leitch (2006) recommended that the Government review IiP's remit to consider how IiP UK and its products, including the Standard itself and the new 'profile' tool, could be reshaped to achieve further upskilling in the workplace.

REFLECTION

The IiP's website offers a free business support tool designed to guide the user through development activities designed to enhance the organisation's performance and help transform your performance. Built into the tool is a diagnostic to provide a snapshot of how current performance measures up. Try using the tool, then assess how accurate and helpful you consider the snapshot of your own organisation's performance to be.

My own outline of IiP is a brief description only. To probe more deeply you could read the fuller critique in Marchington and Wilkinson (2008: 327–31).

LIFE AFTER LEITCH?

Leitch's reforms were intended to deliver a simplified skills system driven by demand rather than central planning, with fewer bodies involved in skills delivery and a greater employer voice in articulating skill needs. As such, they have been accepted by Government and most are already being implemented. But is this progress – or just old wine in new bottles? Five questions raise particularly important issues here, and are therefore discussed below.

WAS LEITCH REALLY NECESSARY?

Peter Kingston, the *Guardian*'s FE editor, questioned the need for the whole Leitch Review, following so soon after the introduction in 2003 of a national skills strategy that made a significant break with the past in its more demand-led approach to the UK's skills policy. He suspected a primarily political agenda at work, since the commissioning and publication of Leitch coincided with Gordon Brown's final period as Chancellor and his accession to the position of UK Prime Minister (Kingston 2007a).

For the more cynical commentators – amongst whom, after 20 years spent assessing the tortuous pathways of the UK's NVET policies and their delivery, I count myself – that is a persuasive interpretation. Admittedly, though, Leitch's review did reinforce the main thrusts of the 2003 national Workforce Development Strategy.

Kingston also found Leitch's emphasis on skills as the increasing driver of productivity simplistic, when so many other elements make up the highly complex productivity equation. He concluded with severe doubts as to whether the bulk of employers will sign the Skills Pledge and whether Leitch's review will lead to any significant reduction in the UK's skills problem – or to any redefinition by Government of what that problem is.

Such doubts are shared to an extent by the Institute for Public Policy Research, *http//www.ippr.org/centreforcities/articles/archive* [accessed 14 April 2008]. It has welcomed the integration of skills and employment services and the 'streamlining' of the LSC, and feels that the Commission for Employment and Skills with its network of boards should strengthen employer engagement provided the Treasury grants enough resource for that work. What it doubts is whether employers will at last begin to invest more in accredited skills, since these are the ones most likely to be poached. It points to evaluation of Employer Training Pilots by the Institute for Fiscal Studies, which found little evidence of employers increasing their training investment, suggesting that many simply switch from using their own training funds to using government funding instead for the training that they provide. Also, some individuals receiving funding already possessed the skills and experience required at level 2, so although the initiative benefited them through accreditation, the outcome did not add to the organisational or national skills base (Coffield 2007).

HOW BAD *IS* THE UK's TRAINING RECORD?

At the heart of Leitch's review lies the contention that UK employers are far down the European training league in terms of training investment. Specifically, he claimed that our national skills gap will have widened to catastrophic proportions by 2020 unless that investment increases very significantly. Similar arguments have been made regularly through time in official reports on our NVET system.

It is undeniable that continental European countries' systems are more integrated in terms of the balance they achieve between vocational and academic pathways for young people, in the institutional and organisational partnerships that fund training and in the emphasis placed on workplace learning. Table 2 outlines some of the major differences.

However, generalised international comparisons can be misleading because we know from much research that VET systems vary widely from one country to the next due to different principles that drive the role of the state, and differences in the link between education and vocational training, the responsibility of organisations to fund training, the degree to which there is a training culture, and the depth of training provision (Sparrow and Hiltrop 1994: 425). Furthermore, while such comparisons focus heavily on qualifications, these measure only part of the skills spectrum. Keep (2006) identifies the lack of focus on generic and soft skills as particularly damaging in the UK economy, now dominated by the service industries.

Philpott (2004), the CIPD's Economic Adviser, found that the claim that employers in Britain lag far behind employers in Europe in the investment they make in training is not fully substantiated by the body of comparative data provided by employers and held at the EU's statistical office, Eurostat. His analysis revealed that in reality UK employers score highly on most indicators of adult training, and that based on a number of key measures the UK appears to 'sit comfortably in the top half of the EU spending league'. Where it slips right down the league table is in regard to intensity of training, with a picture of a little training spread across a lot of employees. Philpott concluded that UK employers' record of investment is better than it is often taken to be, but that one probable reason for UK employers investing more in adult training compared to France and Germany is that those

TABLE 2 A comparison of country NVET systems

Country, VET system and funding	Training provision	Workplace learning
The Netherlands Dual. Funding shared between state and employers.	Partnership approach between the state, employers and unions. Sectoral, sub-sectoral and company networks stimulate and help to deliver training.	Integral part of new ways of organising work. Managers are committed to and strongly interested in workplace learning.
Germany Dual. Funding shared between state and employers. The university system is being reformed to make it more responsive to the market and to share funding more equally between state and private sectors.	The dual system provides the framework for training and development at company level, and training provision is overseen by regional chambers of commerce and industry.	No particular emphasis on workplace learning as a separate system. Employers have to take most of the initiative, and a focus on informal workplace learning processes is hampered by the rigidity of the dual system.
France Dual but highly centralised. Funded by a training tax. Mutual funds at sectoral and multi-sectoral levels help training to meet specific industrial and cross-industrial needs.	Strong emphasis on partnership between state, employers and unions. Social partners specify training priorities and negotiate collectively for use of funds and advice from official agencies.	Strong emphasis on formal courses and vocational training. Other forms of workplace learning need more focus, but this is impeded by operation of the levy system and probably also by unique organisation and management of French firms.
The USA Market-driven system with federal funding to aid special groups. Recent federal legislation has attempted to stimulate training to better meet market needs.	Partnership between state-funded Workforce Investment Boards and local governments at federal state level, and between employers and labour unions at company level.	Left to the initiative of employers, but high-performance working practices and a historic culture of self-development stimulate innovation and some world-class best practice.

TABLE 2 A comparison of country NVET systems

Country, VET system and funding	Training provision	Workplace learning
The UK Market-driven system with state funding to aid special groups. Legislation has attempted to stimulate training to better meet market needs.	New attempt at partnership between state-funded Learning and Skills Council, employers, unions, educationalists and regional development agencies. Within companies, basically determined by employers, although unions have begun to claim a role.	Responsibility lies with employer and individuals. Recent emphasis has tended to focus on formal training and education and accredited competency schemes, whose quality and management national funding and standards are now trying to improve. The introduction of some high-performance working practices in organisations is leading to greater interest in work-based learning processes.
Japan The heavily centralised state educational system sets high standards of broad-based educational attainment upon which employers can build training and development tailored to company needs and goals.	Line management, not the training function, is the major partner in employee development. Japanese companies are nested in broader economic, structural and cultural systems. They are characterised internally by integration of all business and HR strategies and their subordination to a single corporate strategic goal. The preferred strategy is to recruit well-educated workers and develop an internal labour market and career system. Japan's deep economic recession now threatens that model.	Managers are responsible for creating a learning culture and employees are expected to be active in their own development (Tjepkema, ter Horst and Mulder 2002: 18). Strong emphasis on continuing training, and strategically-focused group learning and knowledge creation as an integral part of everyday work. 'Nested stability and the lack of labour mobility means that organizations are effective "social containers" for accumulated individual and collective tacit knowledge.' (Ray 2002: 102–3).

Source: Harrison, R. and Kessels, J. (2003) *Human Resource Development in a Knowledge Economy: An organisational view*, pp80–1. Reproduced with permission of Palgrave Macmillan.

countries have a superior basic education and initial vocational training system and so do not need to prioritise adult training in the same way.

Two conclusions follow from this kind of analysis:

- As *In Demand* (PIU 2001) urged, more attention should be paid to integrating skills policies with action on work organisation, job design and the wider economic development agenda (Keep 2006).

- It is pointless to require or expect employers to simply increase their training spend. What NVET policy should be seeking to achieve is improvement in the quality of general education and initial vocational education, including work-based apprenticeship, to raise the baseline of general employability skills on which employers can make better use of their training budgets (Philpott 2004).

WHAT DO EMPLOYERS THINK?

The CIPD's tenth annual L&D Survey (CIPD 2008a) revealed mixed reactions to the implementation of the Leitch Review. Senior HR/training personnel in over half (53%) of organisations covered by the survey said that their L&D work has not yet been influenced by Leitch and only 57% believed that employers have a role to play in raising standards within the workforce. Despite most expecting that a broader range of skills will be needed in their organisations in the next two years and 44% reporting that a higher level of skills would also be needed, only 13% had signed the Skills Pledge. However, nearly half were considering or would consider signing up either to that or to Train to Gain.

A 2007 CIPD/KPMG Labour Market Survey had produced similar findings. It also identified a very low level of awareness concerning Train to Gain, and that of those who had used it only 12% found that it met their needs 'to a great extent'. The LSC and SSCs were rated very badly, and only 23% of the 742 respondents across a wide range of UK organisations cited government agency officials as effective 'skills champions', compared to 32% citing ULRs and 79% citing other internal training champions.

Such findings provided the rationale for a CIPD Adviser's online comment that employers seem as yet unconvinced that the Government has the right answers to the problem, and that the drive to equip everyone with basic skills 'may be coming at the expense of the urgent need to develop higher level skills on a more selective basis' (*http://www.cipd.co.uk/pressoffice/_articles/* 07 April 2008 [accessed 16 April 2008]). Nothing new there, then ….

ACCREDITED SKILLS OR PROFICIENCY?

A critical test of the effectiveness of post-Leitch reforms will be how far they centre on proficiency rather than just qualifications as a measure of skills. The Leitch NVET targets are all qualification-driven as are most of the funded NVET initiatives, but there are some positive signs.

- First, as already explained, employers and unions now have a stronger voice in determining the focus and content of vocational qualifications. It remains to be seen how far their collaboration with SSCs in this respect proves effective enough to capture outcomes of workplace learning in the assessment mechanisms used in relation to those qualifications.

- Second, consultation began early in 2008 to explore the whole field of informal adult learning, as the following example details.

CASE EXAMPLE

CONSULTATION ON INFORMAL ADULT LEARNING

On 15 January 2008 a Government consultation, 'Informal Adult Learning – The way ahead' was launched, to run until 15 May 2008, the results to be made public later in the year on the DIUS website.

John Denham, Secretary of State for DIUS, observed on the website that while it was right for the Government to prioritise 'formal' education to enable people to develop their skills and gain better jobs, informal adult learning also had a vital role to play. Much of the innovation in the adult learning sector was now being driven and achieved by learners themselves: people adapting new technologies, not relying on support from local or national government to organise activities, but seeking out fellow enthusiasts through online communities and other channels besides. It was therefore important to decide how to build on 'the growing desire for people to come together and to organise their own learning'.

The aim of the consultation is to formulate new proposals to further expand learning and ensure that people have more control over the format and availability of courses. It is spearheaded by working groups made up of major organisations from broadcasting and new technologies, the voluntary sector, other government departments, families and older people.

Source: *http://www.dius.gov.uk* [accessed 14 April 2008], inviting members of the public to participate in the consultative process

This UK initiative reflects a wider European concern to promote the learning of older adults, one of the main target groups under the EU Lisbon process. In 2007 the European Commission launched a two-year Leonardo project TOP+ ('Training Older Persons – Pioneer model usable for older adult trainers') to identify and explore the competence of teachers and other facilitators of both formal and informal adult learning (see *http//www.trainingolderpeople.eu*).

There is scant documentation available in this area, so in support of the project the International Research Institute of Stavanger AS (IRIS) in Norway ran a survey in 2008 to map the terrain in Europe and beyond. Results (not available at the time of writing) can be obtained from the Institute (email: tarja.tikkanen@iris.no, or go to *http://www.iris.no*).

REFLECTION

The results of the IRIS survey will be important not only in informing the Leonardo Project but in enriching the European database on adult learning in both formal and informal modes. To gain more insight into this vital field you could obtain the survey results from IRIS, identify those of particular significance for the UK, and compare them with the findings of the UK's 2008 consultation exercise (on the DIUS website).

A MORE POWERFUL DEMAND-LED APPROACH?

Two further crucial tests of the effectiveness of post-Leitch reforms will be how effective the reformed SSCs prove to be in working with employers to reshape vocational qualifications in line with employers' needs (see Chapter 3); and how far the skills strategy delivery framework operates as intended.

One familiar and depressing consequence of the Leitch Review has been the playing out of that old game of musical chairs at the top that has recurred throughout NVET's history at times of UK Government or administration change. It is possible the three new departments and the Employment and Skills Commission may work the miracle that no previous reshuffles have managed to achieve. However, the signs are not too hopeful, since unlike Wales or Scotland (Appendix 4), England still lacks a single unitary authority to take responsibility for skills, education and economic policy. What is in danger of evolving instead is yet another dog's dinner preventing joined-up thinking and action and thwarting governments' oft-repeated aspiration of 'working in partnership' to tackle the UK's skills and productivity gaps.

There is another issue here. Politicians change the course of strategies and plans, too often for the worse, and so original strategic intent fails to materialise. Surveying in 2002 the many redrafts of national skills strategy and planning documents since the watershed created by *In Demand, Part 1* (PIU 2001), one of its authors concluded that policy proposals as they had changed from original intent to their form only a year later were unlikely to be able to deal adequately with the fundamental problems that underpinned the UK skills deficit (Coffield 2002). As Leitch found in his review, that prophecy proved correct.

Yet as I wrote here in 2005 it could equally be argued that what is remarkable is not the ground that has been lost since *In Demand*, but the ground retained. There is a more demand-driven system than before, and government is making real attempts at joined-up thinking by encouraging not only WfD but the building of new learning cultures in the workplace through promoting better leadership and management. So it is possible that this time things will get better …

At the organisational level, if the aspirations expressed in Leitch are to be realised, more attention must be paid to the business strategies followed by firms and their consequences for skill needs in the workforce. HR/L&D professionals may or may not have influence over that issue in their particular organisations, but they have a clear role to play in helping to achieve better managed workplaces where employees can put to good use the capabilities that at present so many feel they are not being enabled to apply to their work.

HPWOs – a red herring?

The HPWO argument that I explained in the second section of this chapter had a crucial influence on the 2003 national skills strategy and on the Leitch Review. It carries with it a particular emphasis on HR 'high involvement' practices as causally linked to levels of job satisfaction and organisational commitment that in turn should ultimately lead to above-average organisational performance. However, evidence to support these claims is thin and contested (see my discussion in Chapter 6). Lloyd and Payne (2005) concede that 'there is some evidence that HPWO can, in some circumstances, be linked with performance' but find that 'the mechanism through which such gains are achieved remains unclear' and that evidence that employees benefit in terms of skills or wider outcomes is 'very weak and inconclusive'.

Brown *et al* (2007) cast further doubt on the HPWO argument in a study drawing on data from the 1998 and 2004 Workplace Employment Relations surveys in Britain. They concluded that there was a relatively weak association between HR practices and reported increases in job satisfaction, the latter being more probably due to the existence of more benign labour market conditions during the period, which may have driven employers to make improvements in the quality of work.

The 2006 UK national Skill for Work survey (Felstead *et al* 2007) also showed that in the two decades to 2006 employees were increasingly recording the view that they were overqualified for the jobs they hold, with that figure by 2006 standing at 40%. The trend was particularly strong amongst those with 'high' qualifications. This carries worrying implications for engagement levels, job performance and ultimately organisations' capability to progress, especially if the high level of employment enjoyed in the UK for many years begins to slip under the pressure of strains comparable to those becoming evident in the US economy.

All in all the emphasis on HPWOs does threaten to distract from more important HR activity.

Making the demand-led strategy work

If HR professionals are well advised to spend little time in what may be a profitless search for a causal link between any particular bundle of HR practices and organisational performance, there is much else that they can do to enhance proficiency and accredited skills in the workplace through better use of the support offered by the NVET system.

Post-Leitch, the phrase 'demand-led' has taken on fresh meaning. Individuals can exercise their demand for learning by using the new Learner Accounts to help fund courses of their choice that fall within the official funding framework. Employers in even the smallest organisations now have access to more funded programmes for their employees, and employers and unions can drive demand beyond the doors of their own business by working with SSCs to produce qualifications and sector skills agreements relevant to the local and sectoral labour markets. At the least, therefore, L&D practitioners should be focusing on the following five tasks:

- Like all HR professionals they must become fully informed about funding streams and NVET provision locally. In the past, information and advice has been poorly communicated at national and local levels and it seems that even now levels of awareness remain disturbingly low amongst employers and individuals. L&D practitioners should therefore be raising awareness in their organisations of the many opportunities offered by government funding to improve workplace and workforce development. In the worsening economic climate now facing the country (mid-2008) all available sources of external funding should be used to support L&D activity that otherwise, no matter how great its value for some stakeholders, may struggle in the eyes of the business to maintain financial viability.

- Increasingly in a volatile economic environment they should be working with their business partners to identify exactly where key current and anticipated proficiency gaps lie, and using sectoral and local networks to find ways of closing those gaps. They should also be working on a wider front to aid the wider local economy (Pickard 2003a) and to help those who will be particularly vulnerable if unemployment rates begin to increase.

- Within organisations a vital area for analysis should be people management at first-line management level (Purcell and Hutchinson 2007). CIPD research with Kingston Business School and IPSOS MORI (Truss *et al* 2006) highlights the fact that almost a third of employees feel they are not managed well enough to enable or motivate them to make best use of their existing skills. The Leitch Review has resulted in a boost to the improvement of leadership and management skills through expanded funding for levels 4 and 5 training, while the IiP Standard aims to improve not just management and leadership capability but also management practices that impede employees' training and learning. Funding the acquisition of management qualifications in an organisation, however, will not be sufficient of itself, because what is at issue here is not simply functional managerial competence but managerial attitudes and practices, work processes and job design.

- L&D practitioners should also be identifying those who need help to enhance or change their skills, and should be encouraging them to come forward – often not an easy task – thereby acting as a resource for those needing support (Hope 2004).

- L&D practitioners should pay particular attention to ensuring that when the organisation uses external training and learning providers it selects those who can be relied on for high quality and customised service (Pickard 2003a).

REFLECTION

It will help your understanding of national skills strategy if you follow up some of the information sources shown in my endnote to this chapter. Then reflect on L&D practice in your own organisation today. How far does it seem to be in line with the five recommendations made at the end of this section, and where do you feel improvements are needed?

CONCLUSION

Having read this chapter you should by now be able to form your own views on the vision, goals and strategy of government related to national WfD. You should also be able to confidently tackle the review questions for this chapter (Appendix 3).

To summarise the main ground covered by the chapter's six sections, I have:

- outlined key issues relating to the UK's productivity, skills and training problems in post-war years, and have contrasted the viewpoints of governments and of employers on those issues

- explained the Labour Government's skills strategy, and discussed its plans and delivery framework for workplace and workforce development between 1999 and 2006

- outlined the main proposals made by the 2006 Leitch Review of national skills strategy, the NVET targets now set for 2020, and steps taken up to mid-2008 to implement the Review's proposals

- identified five critical issues that will influence how far real progress is made in developing the UK's workforce and base of skills for the economy

- proposed five key tasks for L&D practitioners in helping to drive a demand-led approach to workforce and workplace development within and beyond their organisations.

EXLPORE FURTHER

FURTHER INFORMATION SOURCES

Because of the amount and complexity of information on NVET it is best to keep to textbook and other sources that provide clear, regular updates and those offering an appropriate balance of factual and evaluative content. For example:

Coffield, F. (2007) 'Running ever faster down the wrong road: an alternative future for education and skills'. Inaugural Lecture to the Association of Colleges. Online version available at http//www.ioe.ac.uk/schools/leid/lss/FCInauguralLectureDec06.doc [accessed 4 May 2008]

Marchington, M. and Wilkinson, A. (2008) *Human Resource Management at Work: People management and development*, 4th edition. London: CIPD, pp309–41

European Journal of Vocational Training, published by CEDEFOP (European Agency that promotes the development of VET in the European Union). Website is at http://www.cedefop.europa.eu/ [accessed 12 October 2008]

CIPD podcasts, and webchats such as Webchats TV 26 March 2008: *The business benefits of investing in people* (about Train to Gain), available online at http://

www.webchats.tv/webchat.php?ID=509 [accessed 10 April 2008]

http//www.skope.ox.ac.uk [accessed 12 April 2008]. The website of the ESRC Centre on Skills, Knowledge and Organisational Performance (SKOPE) which provides a variety of research resources, including a series of Issues Papers evaluating key aspects of government's skills and education policies

http://www.dius.gov.uk/press/pressarchive.html [accessed 14 April 2008]. A useful information point tracking government consultative documents, strategies and initiatives related to national skills strategy

http://www.dius.gov.uk/publications/index.html [accessed 16 April 2008]. List of DIUS publications and links to these

International VET: http://www.b.shuttle.de/wifo/ [accessed 18 April 2008]. Provides basic information on VET and HRD research in 25 European countries

NVET in the Devolved Administrations: See Appendix 4 for an introduction and a list of websites

CHAPTER 3

Reforming Vocational Education and Training

INTRODUCTION

At the start of Chapter 2 I noted that in order to achieve its vision of lifelong learning the Government's NVET strategy since 1997 has had two broad strands, related to workforce development and educational reform. The purpose of this chapter is to explain and explore the latter and assess implications for L&D professionals.

Since the 1944 Butler Education Act no government has been able to carry through the integrated reform needed in England in order to approach the high quality vocational education and training systems that most European countries provide. The major changes under way have that aim. The Government's reforms cover the entire educational spectrum incorporating the schools, further and higher education systems and lifelong learning.

These reforms are heavily documented and hotly debated. Any attempt to cover them in a single chapter can only be partial. Especially to help those with no prior knowledge, I have adopted a narrative approach, treating each main area of reform as an unfolding story, shaped by past actions as well as present pressures. This approach leaves no space for more than limited international comparisons (a bulky literature in itself: some information sources are shown at the end of this chapter), or for discussion of policies in the Devolved Administrations (an introduction to those is provided in Appendix 4).

The chapter falls into six sections. In the first I identify and discuss key developments in reforms to the schools system and to the 14 to 19 pathways. The second and third offer a similar assessment of reforms to the further and higher education systems, and the fourth widens out to incorporate government's lifelong learning strategy. The fifth section moves into the workplace to consider key ways in which HR/L&D practitioners can promote productive educational partnerships. The sixth section offers a verdict on the government's skills strategy as covered both by this chapter and Chapter 2.

REFORMING SCHOOLS AND THE 14 TO 19 PATHWAYS

http://www.literacytrust.org.uk/database.secondary/Schoolstructure; http://www.dfes. gov.uk/14-19 [accessed 25 April 2008]

The primary and secondary educational systems in any country fundamentally influence the nature and quality of initial competence of school leavers and so lay the crucial groundwork for the subsequent distribution of competencies among the working population. These systems therefore form the starting point for this chapter.

MOVING TOWARDS THE TWENTY-FIRST CENTURY: OVERHAULING THE EDUCATIONAL SYSTEM

Nearly a decade of the most radical overhaul of the state educational system since 1944 began with the Thatcher Government's 1988 *Education Reform Act* (ERA 1988). This landmark legislation that applied to England, Wales and Northern Ireland increased the legal power of central government over the education system and reduced LEAs' policy-making discretion. From then until 1997 the Tories introduced a series of controversial changes to the primary and secondary educational systems, increasing their exposure to market forces and attempting to achieve more coherence and a greater parity of esteem between post-16 vocational and academic pathways. However, most of the vocational and semi-vocational qualifications that they introduced failed to gain the confidence of the market or of employers.

NEW LABOUR'S U-TURNS

The 1997 Blair Government introduced further centralisation into the schools system, but of a different kind. Under the Tories it had taken the form of nationalising the curriculum and introducing tests to regularly assess pupils across all age ranges. In the early days of the Blair administration (in the White Paper: *Excellence in Schools* (DfEE 1997) and the *School Standards and Framework Act* (STFA 1998), it took the form of returning to local education authorities (LEAs) a significant amount of the power that earlier Tory legislation had stripped from them. However, the year 2000 saw a U-turn in Blair's educational strategy when it was announced by the Secretary of State for Education that (Blunkett, 2000):

- Government would encourage the establishment of new foundation or voluntary-aided schools in areas where there was local demand.

- It would also allow more existing independent schools to become part of the publicly funded education system.

- Most radical of all, it would allow the replacement of failing schools with *city academies* – free schools catering for all abilities and located in the most disadvantaged areas. Generously resourced by a mix of private and public sector funding, they were similar to the city technology colleges set up in the 1980s by the Tory Government.

In 1998 grant-maintained schools had 'lost their status, autonomy and a sustained proportion of their funding' (Johnson 2000). Now, only two years later, the same government was giving a boost to what one critic called 'the creeping privatisation of education' (Gillard 2007).

2004: A NEW NATIONAL EDUCATION STRATEGY

In 2004 the government's *Five-Year Education Strategy for England* (DfES 2004) was launched, to cover the whole education system. It continued the 2000 policy U-turn with measures including the extension of specialist status to all 3,500 secondary schools and it encouraged good schools to apply for foundation status (a status that carried substantial release from LEA control). It also announced that the number of city academies in the most deprived areas was to increase to 200 by 2010. But although the Act put schools rather than LEAs in main charge of their funding, it required their admission policies to be approved by both local authorities and local forums.

More reforms

Following a dispiriting Ofsted report at the end of 2004 the White Paper *Higher Standards, Better Schools for All* (DfES 2005c) promised to open up an education 'market' with 'parent choice' as the 'powerful driver of improved standards'. It all looked at first sight like Blair's most complete U-turn to date. For example, schools could now opt out of local council control, set up as independent trusts run by private companies, charities, even parents, and set their own selection criteria. A new Schools Commissioner would advise parents and trust schools on how to make choice work.

But education policy in England has always been played out in a hall of mirrors where the reality hides behind many illusions. In fact the Act safeguarded LEAs' power over admission policies, insisted that all schools followed the national curriculum and blocked remaining grammar schools from growing any further. Subsequently LEAs were authorised to issue 'warning notices' to 'coasting' schools that were failing in various ways, and could ultimately take over their budgets, dismiss their governing boards and even compel such a school to join a federation so that it could be run by a more 'successful' neighbour. Since about one in four schools already fell into the 'coasting' category this decision threatened to affect a great number of schools (Halpin 2006a). In due course that threat became a reality.

14–19 VOCATIONAL EDUCATION: THE BLAIR ADMINISTRATION'S REFORMS

Alongside the schools reforms major changes were being set in train to overhaul the 14–19 years vocational education system.

The Continental dual system model

At this point, it is helpful to note the major differences that exist between the British vocational education system and that commonly found on the Continent. As I explained in Chapter 2, international comparisons must be treated with caution. Nevertheless a short discussion of the Continental dual system model as typified by the German system does provide some relevant insights.

THE GERMAN DUAL SYSTEM

CASE EXAMPLE

The German reverence for trade crafts is at the heart of its three-track high-school system, considered to be the best in the world. About one third of young people go on from *gymnasium* (high school) to university, the remaining two thirds to vocational and technical schools. There is a careers office in every town and city to help young people make decisions about their future education and employment.

Flexible

The education system is flexible, allowing qualified vocational and technical students to switch to the gymnasium at any point, while on the other hand some gymnasium students enrol in vocational programmes even after getting into university. It is illegal for a young person to begin their working life without vocational training and this is provided through a partnership approach in which that training takes place largely on the job with less, but complementary, provision in institutions of study away from the company. In this dual system the major emphasis is on the acquisition of practical competencies, with theoretical qualifications being primarily focused on the underpinning

knowledge they require. The interaction between academic and vocational pathways is co-ordinated so that both employers' and trainees' requirements and objectives are fulfilled. Training is only counted as at an end when a trainee passes final examinations and gains a vocational qualification (Sampson 1992).

Partnership-based

The dual system operates on a partnership basis. The German federal government is responsible for training regulations, the 11 Länder governments are responsible for schools, and regional chambers of commerce and industry are responsible for overseeing the dual system. Vocational colleges are funded by local and regional governments. Employers collaborate with unions and the authorities to provide a high-quality, rigorously administered and controlled dual system.

Strains in the system

There is a downside, however. As the German economy continues to experience severe pressures the partnership between union and employers is weakening and the dual system is proving increasingly inflexible and unaffordable, not least because of failed reunification policies pursued by the two main political parties. Germany also suffers from skills shortages because more 16-year-olds are now opting for an academic rather than a manual education. There is a major concern to reform the education system to make it more oriented to market needs, and to spread cost and control more evenly between the state and the private sector.

Research shows that the importance of the German VET system has been based in part on the fact that key competencies can often only be acquired within the firm and with practical experience. Employers' skill needs have therefore been met by that system (Sung *et al* 2006). However, it also suggests that the content of VET curricula no longer corresponds to the profile of employers' requirements (Dietrich *et al* 2004). The biggest learning point for the UK seems to be the importance of achieving an 'appropriate balance between the need for strong institutional ownership of the competency framework and the need for flexibility to cope with changing economic and individual needs' (Sung *et al* 2006: 102).

Sources: Harrison, R. and Kessels, J. (2003); Sampson, H. (1992); Sung, J. *et al* (2006)

The British full-time system

In Britain, the vocational education system since World War II has been basically of the full-time kind: vocational routes begin to open up in the school system from 14 years and thereafter most vocational education takes place at a state (or independent) institution of study, with least taking place in-company. The major emphasis is on obtaining theoretical qualifications. The system broadly resembles that in the United States but is severely weakened by disparities between academic and vocational pathways, poor standards, multiplicity of providers, resource constraints and a high proportion of underachievers. As one commentator wrote, 'A faultline has run through the English secondary education system at least as far back as the hallowed 1944 Education Act'. That Act unintentionally reinforced a division between academic and vocational education. Attempts since then to broaden the academic route by introducing GCSEs to replace O-levels and introducing GNVQs have never solved the problem (Kingston 2007b).

The 2004 Tomlinson Report: the diploma proposals

In 2004 Mike Tomlinson, former chief inspector of schools who had been heading a major review of the whole 14 to 19 educational system, presented his Report to Government (Tomlinson 2004). He identified four core problems:

- In Britain young people from 14 upwards become alienated from a curriculum too dominated by academic needs. Those whose skills are not academic often become uninterested in or disengaged from schooling. They perform so poorly in their GCSEs that they gain little from their education and leave school as soon as they can (Hames 2004).

- For those of 16 and over there is a 'confused and devalued qualifications system in which vocational studies are regarded as inferior' (Ward 2004) and an 'alphabet soup' of up to 5,000 vocational courses (*Guardian* 2004).

- A-levels do not stretch and stimulate the brightest students enough, and do not distinguish adequately between them (Hames 2004).

- There is a lack of key literacy and numeracy skills in students right across the ability range.

Tomlinson recommended that academic and vocational pathways be brought together in a type of dual system: a new two-track, four-tier diploma system replacing GCSEs and A-levels and incorporating vocational and academic learning. The system would make basic skill studies compulsory and would be tied to the levels of the national qualification framework.

It was an ambitious formula and the Blair Government decided not to take it on board. The White Paper *14–19 Education and Skills* (DfES 2005b) accepted the need for basic skills to be a compulsory component of 11- to 19-year-olds' education and training, but rejected Tomlinson's proposals for a new dual system. Instead, it proposed introducing 14 new vocational diplomas to run alongside A-levels and GCSEs and to be in place by 2015.

2007: A NEW PRIME MINISTER AND A NEW DIPLOMAS SYSTEM

By 2006 when the Leitch Review of adult skills was published (see Chapter 2), 1.24 million people in Britain aged between 15 and 24 were not in education, work or a training scheme – a 15% rise since 1997, with a particularly sharp increase of almost one third for 16- to 17-year-olds and men (Browne 2006). Leitch emphasised the vital need to ensure that the UK's educational reform programme delivered a fully integrated 14–19 phase, including curriculum, funding and financial support, if his proposals to improve adult skills were to have a chance of success.

In October 2007, four months after Gordon Brown became Prime Minister and at the end of a long consultation period, the first of many major educational reform surprises to be introduced during his administration was announced. The Government rejected the 2005 White Paper diploma proposals and instead announced its intention to adopt the original Tomlinson model. Two measures were key:

- Up to 2013 young people could choose either the academic or the diploma route to qualification, but in 2013 government would review the entire exam system.

- Three new diplomas – in sciences, languages and humanities – would come on stream in 2011. They would include A-level syllabi but in addition would contain 'more rigorous' academic material.

Up to this point the proposed new diplomas had been in subjects generally seen as a job-related, practical route for the less intellectually able (with the possible exception of the engineering diploma). But the three new diplomas are clearly aimed at high-flying academic students and they may well signal the eventual demise of GCSEs and A-levels as free-standing qualifications. Table 3 shows how the diplomas picture changed between 2005 and 2007, and its present status.

TABLE 3 Changes in plans for 14–19 Education and Skills diplomas

How many new diplomas will there be?	
2005: 14 diplomas in place by 2015	2007: 17 diplomas in place by 2015
When will they come on stream?	
2005: The first five in September 2008, the rest by 2015	2007: The first five in September 2008; the three new diplomas in 2011, the rest by 2015
Who will design, approve and implement their detailed content? Employers, working through SSCs	
What components will a diploma contain? Generic learning (functional skills in English, maths and ICT)	
A project, plus development of personal, learning and thinking skills	
At least 10 days of work experience	
Principal learning (specific knowledge and underpinning skills needed to progress in the student's chosen sector)	
Additional/specialist learning (a selection of options chosen from a range of qualifications)	
What must students do to gain a diploma? Reach a minimum standard in each component	
How will diplomas relate to GCSEs and A-levels?	
2005: GCSEs and A-levels can be taken either as part of or as well as a diploma course	2007: Until 2013 GCSEs and A-levels can be taken either as part of or as well as a diploma course. In 2013 the entire exam system will be reviewed by Government
At what levels will diplomas be set, and how graded? Graded in the same way as GCSEs and A-levels, and set at three levels:	
2005:	2007:
Level 1 (equivalent to 4 or 5 GCSE passes)	*Foundation* (equivalent to 5 GCSEs at grades D to G)
Level 2 (equivalent to 5 or 6 GCSEs at grades A* to C)	*Higher* (equivalent to 7 GCSEs at grades A* to C)
Level 3 (equivalent to 3 A-levels)	*Advanced* (equivalent to 3½ A-levels)

Sources: Department for Education and Skills (2005b); October 2007 announcement to Parliament

Further radical reforms have followed.

Raising the school-leaving age

In January 2008, responding to a Leitch recommendation and also taking forward proposals in the consultative Green Paper *Raising Expectations: Staying in education and training post-16* (DfES 2007) the Education Secretary announced that the school leaving age in England will be raised by 2015 for the first time in nearly 50 years from 16 to 18. Scotland (where the rate of those aged 16 to 19 not in employment education or training is one of the highest in the world) is likely to follow a similar path.

2008: The Secondary National Strategy

Around the same time a *Secondary National Strategy* (DCSF 2008) for school improvement was launched. It incorporates a new secondary curriculum at key stage 3 – the biggest such change in 20 years – and *Renewed Secondary Frameworks* based on programmes of study for the new secondary curriculum and to be introduced in May 2008 in order to help teachers increase pupils' learning and attainment in the three functional skills that are central to the 14–19 reforms. There will also be new numeracy and literacy frameworks in the primary sector, the biggest change there in a decade. All this, together with other measures including schools workforce remodelling, is part of 'a broader vision to develop a modern world-class curriculum that will inspire and challenge learners and prepare them for the future' (*http://www.qca.org.uk/* [accessed 20 April 2008]).

2008: LEAs take charge of 0–19 educational delivery

Table 4 shows the routes that, with the introduction of the new diploma system, will be open to children from 11 to 19 to move from school to employment or further or higher education.

By 2010 when the LSC will be abolished, LEAs will become the drivers of education and training delivery to all children and young people aged 0–19. They will have full power to commission provision to meet demand from young people and employers, and to work with national agencies and the Regional Development Agency to provide a 'coherent planning and funding system' for educational providers.

The speed with which so many major educational reforms have been introduced since 2006, the changing political and ideological forces that have driven them and the complex partnerships required to make them work have all provoked fears for their delivery. For those who saw in every failed educational

TABLE 4 Proposed routes for entry to employment, further or higher education from late 2008

18/19 years and over

Entry to employment, further or higher education

16 to 19 years: Level 3/Advanced-level learning tier

Advanced apprenticeships/apprenticeships leading to technical certificate (equivalent to one NVQ level 3)

NVQ level 3, whether taken as part of apprenticeship or at school

Advanced diploma – equivalent to 3½ A-levels

A-levels: now more demanding, and to be equivalent to a level 3 diploma must include a new extended project

IB multi-disciplinary diploma – broad two-year programme in six subjects, equivalent to 6½ A-grade A-levels

Pre-U diploma

14 to 16 years: Level 2/Higher-level learning tier

Young apprenticeship leading to a technical certificate (equivalent to one NVQ level 2)

NVQ level 2, whether taken as part of apprenticeship or at school

Other work-based qualifications such as a general NVQ (phased out after 2007), Btecs and OCR Nationals

Higher diploma (equivalent to 7 GCSEs at grades A* to C)

GCSEs

14 to 16 years: Level 1/Foundation learning tier

For those needing extra support in personal and social development, key and basic skills, and vocational subject-based learning, to prepare them for entry to level 2: Young apprenticeships or Foundation Diploma (equivalent to 5 GCSEs at grades D to G)

11 to 14 years: Key stage 3 curriculum

To strengthen teaching and learning across the curriculum for all pupils, with more emphasis on developing general skills such as initiative, enterprise and capacity to learn independently. Teachers to have more power to help children master the basics while retaining core elements of the national curriculum.

initiative of the last two decades of the twentieth century the dead hand of LEA bureaucracy, the power now vested in LEAs by the Brown administration is likely to prove the most damaging obstacle to government's attempts to ensure better educational standards, a more joined-up NVET system and the closing of the UK's skills gap.

In April 2008 the concerns of many about the excessively speedy introduction of the new diplomas came home to roost with a vengeance when the head of Edexcel, one of the UK's leading exam boards, revealed a 'huge educational risk to this country' in a chaotic situation rapidly unfolding around the introduction of the first five, with inadequately trained teachers and examiners, concerns about the IT management systems and a general climate of ignorance and doubt about the new diplomas' features and value (Curtis 2008).

The CIPD had warned from the start that if diplomas did not succeed in gaining parity with A-levels they could become 'a dumping ground for weak pupils' or 'give employers the signal that it's a second-class qualification' (Chynoweth 2008). Now, an educational journalist summed up the whole diplomas initiative as 'a hurried and ill-thought through mess, offering little more than the fictional claim that pupils are being better prepared for the world of work' (White 2008). There is the additional danger that if a flawed diploma system goes ahead, alongside GCSEs and A-levels now heavily criticised for their lack of academic rigour, unitisation and heavy dependence on coursework assessment, this will drive more parents out of the state system altogether (by mid-2008 private schools, despite their high fees, were at a peak of popularity) and will encourage more independent schools to introduce the International Baccalaureate or the Pre-U diploma developed by the University of Cambridge International Examinations Board.

The raising of the school leaving age in 2015 to 18 is the Government's biggest gamble. A *Times* leader identified two conditions as essential if the move is to be 'little more than repackaging a longstanding social dilemma that has defeated successive governments – how to harness the potential of the least academically able 10% of teenagers rather than abandoning them to a dispiriting, dysfunctional and often destructive life on benefits' (The *Times* 2007):

- a vocational curriculum that can meet the needs of business

- properly funded plans to enable teenagers to split their training between schools or FE colleges and the workplace.

Both these conditions are the subject of current government plans (see next sections) but one big challenge will be to ensure the provision of suitable work experience for learners. The National Audit Office has found that more than two thirds of local educational partnerships report problems in engaging enough employers to meet current work experience requirements, let alone the number and range required in the future (Chynoweth 2008).

REFLECTION

Government's educational reforms between 1997 and 2008 have had innumerable twists and turns. Reflect at this point in the chapter on the educational strategy and plans that are currently in place, and on how they seem likely to fare, updating your knowledge by checking on articles and news items in the press and in journals like *People Management*, and by going to websites like *http://education.guardian. co.uk/1419education/story/0,,2257981* [accessed 25 April 2008].

STRATEGY FOR FURTHER EDUCATION

http//www.dfes.gov.uk/learning&skills [accessed 1 May 2008]

THE FURTHER EDUCATION (FE) SECTOR IN ENGLAND

Components of the English FE sector are shown in Figure 5.

FIGURE 5 Main components of the FE sector in England

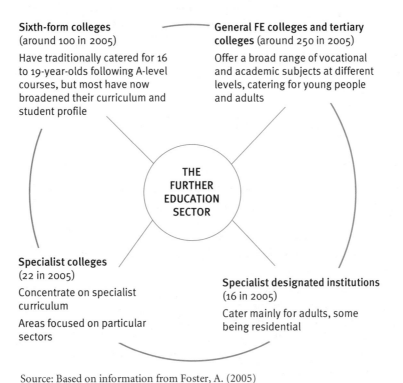

Source: Based on information from Foster, A. (2005)

In 1993 under the Tories FE colleges were removed from local authority control to become independent institutions, fully exposed to market forces. 460 were created at incorporation, but in the ongoing 'rollercoaster of change' (Whittaker 2003) many either merged or failed to survive. The remainder were responsible between them for providing more than two thirds of all vocational qualifications.

When the Labour Government came to power in 1997 70% of companies, notably small firms, were failing to use the FE system, mainly for the following reasons:

- the tying of colleges' government funding primarily to courses leading to national vocational qualifications (NVQs) and skills levels related to them. This put a severe constraint on the extent to which colleges' courses could be truly led by what employers and individuals wanted

- the way colleges traditionally had to deliver learning. Government funding was tied to whole, not part, qualifications, while allowances for students heavily favoured full-time courses. This meant that colleges could not respond meaningfully to employers' and individuals' preference for bite-sized chunks and for portable part-qualifications that were easier for users to finance.

- poor-quality teaching and low completion rates of students on courses. These were predictable outcomes of colleges' lack of ability to respond adequately to learners' needs, and of the staffing problems that had become endemic in the FE system. From 2002, greatly increased numbers of students put an impossible strain on college resources and the national targets to which FE funding was tied were far from being achieved. The effects on staff recruitment and retention rates were disastrous, with lecturers taking strike action in 2002.

1997: NEW LABOUR'S STRATEGY FOR FE REFORM

The Dearing Report

In 1997 during the last year of the Tory Government's life, Lord Dearing's Report, *Higher Education in the Learning Society* (Dearing 1997), was published. It provides the backcloth to the overhaul of the FE as well as the HE systems that has taken place since then. Dearing revealed how greatly complicated the higher and FE sectors are by an interplay of powerful stakeholders, each with their own view about appropriate goals for the post-16 system and their own perceptions of what they stand to lose or gain by responding to government's vision of lifelong learning. He identified those stakeholders – individuals, the state, employers and providers of education and training – and called for a new contract between them so that historic boundaries between vocational and academic education could disappear and active partnerships involving sets of mutual obligations could be forged in their place.

2002 – Success for All?

Blair's Government took a series of measures to tackle the problems that Dearing had identified, notably through its strategy paper *Success for All* (DfES 2002), its national skills strategy (DfES 2003a, see Chapter 2) and its *Five-Year Education Strategy* (DfES 2004 and see previous section) all of which pledged to build broader and deeper links between further and higher education and employers in the future. However, it was the *Foster Review* (2005) that gave the most powerful kick-start to reform.

2005: The Foster Review

In his independent review of the future role of FE colleges, published in November 2005 after wide-ranging consultation and research, Sir Andrew Foster identified both strengths and major weaknesses in the FE system and provided illuminating comparisons with FE in other European countries. He stressed that government must adopt a 'crystal clear' focus on skills if the FE sector was to make the necessary greatly improved contribution to tackling Britain's education and skills gap. His main recommendations centred on building better partnerships with employers, and on improving colleges' image and reputation, clarity of purpose, focus on individual learners, leadership, management and funding systems and infrastructure. He warned that there was no single 'magic bullet' to solve FE's problems. What was needed was a comprehensive and continuing set of reforms across the whole of the FE system (Foster 2005: 8).

Outcomes of the Foster Review

His recommendations were taken forward in March 2006 by the White Paper*: Further Education Reform: Raising skills, Improving life chances* (DfES 2006a). It set out the five-year FE strategy now being followed by government in order to end the situation where Britain had fallen to 24th out of 29 developed nations in the proportion of 16-year-olds in education or training. The strategy is set in the context of the new 'Model for Public Services Reform' and has four components:

- the Framework for Excellence

- the LSC Intervention Programme

- the national Improvement Strategy

- the self-regulation project.

Its seven areas are shown in Table 5, and the full action plan to achieve targets set for 2008 can be found at the website identified in that Table. Further information on the crucially important Framework for Excellence follows below.

TABLE 5 Seven areas of national strategy for the FE sector

---

1 **Focusing on employability**
– including the setting up of national skills academies, the first three to open in 2006

2 **Meeting the needs of learners and employers**
– mainly through a National Learner Panel, a Learner Involvement Strategy, and a trial of Learner Accounts – see the case example overleaf

3 **Improving teaching and learning**
– through a Workforce Strategy including national mandatory CPD framework, leadership qualifications for college principals, Learner Engagement strategies to be developed by all providers, the national Improvement Strategy, and a national Teaching and Learning Programme. There would be an £11 million investment in the recruitment and retention of the FE workforce, with a focus on attracting top graduates and managers into the sector (Halpin 2006b)

4 **Spreading success and eliminating failure**
– through piloting of the Framework for Excellence plus an Intervention Strategy to tackle poor FE provision

5 **Funding to support national objectives**
– key to which would be a national Capital Strategy, plus authority given to the LSC to end funding for failing colleges and to use a competitive tendering process to attract alternative providers including private companies

6 **Building a new relationship with colleges and providers**
– including a new FE Information Standards Authority, advice on the formation of college federations and trusts, a single integrated FE Inspectorate, and a National Learning Model

7 **Achieving impact and outcomes**
– including impact on race equality, and a Reputation Strategy

---

Sources: Department for Education and Skills (2006a); *http//www.dfes.gov.uk/furthereducation/*, links to 'FE Reform White Paper Update November 2006' [accessed 27 April 2008]

THE IMPLEMENTATION OF 2006 FE STRATEGY

In December 2006 Leitch endorsed the White Paper's FE proposals in his review of adult skills and in the targets he set to close the UK's skills gap by 2020 (see Chapter 2). The *FE and Training Act* of October 2007 (FETA 2007) enabled aspects of his recommendations to be implemented. They were mainly to do with the LSC's new responsibilities, but also – and controversially – granted power to specific FE institutions in England to award their own foundation degrees.

In March 2008 the White Paper, *Raising Expectations: Enabling the system to deliver* (DCSF and DIUS 2008a), completed the infrastructure announced in 2006 to support NVET reforms in England (see Chapter 2, Figure 4).

FOUNDATION DEGREES

Foundation degrees (FDs) provide an HE route not only for those entering vocational education after leaving school or college but also for those already in employment and those considering a return to the labour market. The qualification is broadly equivalent to the first two years of a bachelor's degree and is positioned at level 4 (Intermediate) on the English Framework for Higher Education Qualifications.

It takes around two years to complete a full-time FD, or three to four years part-time. It is an HE qualification in its own right, but the intention is that FD graduates should also be able to proceed to a relevant honours degree in a further 12–15 months, or progress towards a professional qualification or licence to practise. Currently FDs are developed by partnerships that include a degree-awarding HE institution, an employer representative (typically an L&D professional) and a delivery institution, typically an FE college. What attractions do they hold?

- They promote work-based skills, key skills and generic skills like management.

- They present an opportunity for raising the organisational commitment and the motivation to learn of employees, especially those in low-level work and who currently lack educational attainments to access career routes.

- They offer educational institutions a unique chance to engage more actively with business.

- They involve an imaginative blend of learning methods, especially through use of e-technology combined with workplace learning and attendance at college or university, with credit given for relevant prior learning or experience.

FDs are being used to open up routes to being a 'semi-professional' in the NHS, the biggest spender on learning among British employers. They form part of its 'skills escalator' strategy for staff development (see Chapter 10). Given the variegated nature of the NHS workforce they have required the operation of an intricate partnership of stakeholders. Unsurprisingly, therefore, there have been problems during their development, many to do with the difficulty of finding, funding, operating and assessing work placements for non-NHS students.

Case studies, including Tesco and Young's Sea Foods, appear on the FD website.

Sources: Hiscock, D. (2004) *People Management*, 15 July; *http://www.foundationdegree.org.uk/* [accessed 1 May 2008]

2008: THE NEW FE FRAMEWORK FOR EXCELLENCE

In June 2008 the Minister for Lifelong Learning, Further and Higher Education announced details of the new *Framework for Excellence* developed by the LSC in consultation with colleges and work-based learning providers, DIUS, Ofsted and the Learning and Skills Improvement Service. The Framework, operating from September 2008, allows colleges and work-based learning providers to self regulate and provides a consistent set of measures for this purpose. By 2010 all providers must publish their assessment rating publicly, allowing prospective students and employers to compare results. The main aims of the Framework and self-regulation system are (Scott 2008a):

- a single framework for assessing performance, giving colleges and training providers a consistent set of measures on which to base continual improvements in the quality and responsiveness of their provision

- the provision to every prospective student and employer wanting to access FE of clear information that will enable them to choose providers best suited to their needs.

WILL IT ALL WORK?

FE reform is part of an overall plan for the whole 0 to 19 years and adult education system. Once again, as with all previous reforms, two crucial determinants of success will be whether a complex delivery system will prove capable of implementing the new, partnership-driven and demand-driven strategies, and whether – given political and ideological chopping and changing – those strategies will be given the time to settle in and prove their worth. There are two major concerns here:

A split system?

At the time of writing (mid-2008) the LSC is reviewing whether further fundamental changes to the FE system are needed. There are indications that Gordon Brown intends an ultimate splitting of the FE sector into two: one part to educate young people up to 19 years, the other for those over that age (Kingston 2007c). Such a split is common in most countries, and adults could gain by attending a local college uniquely devoted to meeting their skills and development needs – rather like the community colleges in the United States which are particularly valuable in providing second-chance opportunities for adults (Kingston 2007c). However, there is no compelling evidence that advantage would be gained in the UK by separating the two age groups. Also it can be motivating for young people to work alongside older learners, and a split at 19 would be in any case inconsistent with the fact that in the UK many young people leave education after retaking GCSEs or completing other one-year courses only to pick up again in their early twenties, having benefited from a year out (*ibid*).

Will many adult learners miss out?

Government spending projections have predicted a loss of 500,000 FE places by 2008 and a possible further 500,000 by 2010, but those totals matter less than how they will be made up. Government intends that by 2010 education will remain free for the under-19s and for those under 25 without level 3 qualifications, but will have fallen to 50% for those studying other courses 'valued by employers'. For recreational courses funding 'will depend on local choice'. After 2010 provision for the under-25 groups will continue to expand at the expense of other adult learners (Halpin 2006b).

The White Paper *Further Education: Raising skills, Improving life chances* (DfES 2006a) started the funding switch. While a *Times* leader agreed with the strategic sense of replacing non-accredited 'pleasure and leisure' courses in order to help fund job training for the one third of working-age adults who lack a basic school leaving qualification, it also pointed out that this would exclude many older adults trying to improve themselves for the sake of the economy (The *Times* 2006a). Has access by those adults to lifelong learning opportunities been driven off the Government's agenda? I will return to that issue later in the chapter.

 REFLECTION

Foundation degrees are central to Government's mission to substantially expand participation in FE and HE. L&D professionals have a key part to play in partnerships to develop FDs, helping to ensure 'the right fit between an individual, the right qualification at the right time and the skills needed by the organisation' (Hiscock 2004). They must also ensure that their organisations have the resources and the expertise needed to provide effective, well monitored and well assessed workplace experience. Can you identify any examples where L&D practitioners have made, or are making, a significant contribution to the introduction of FDs in an organisation?

STRATEGY FOR HIGHER EDUCATION

http://www.dfes.gov.uk/hegateway/hereform/index [accessed 28 April 2008]

THE 1997 DEARING REPORT: START OF RADICAL REFORM

The Government's aims for the higher education (HE) system are to:

- open up access even more, moving towards participation by 2010 of 50% of all 19- to 30-year-olds, and ending the HE social class divide

- promote research, giving British universities the chance to match the best in the world in an increasingly competitive market

- promote excellence in teaching

- improve links with employers.

In 1997 the Dearing Report into HE identified deep-rooted problems across the whole system. HE, like FE, had been plunged into confusion after the 1988 reforms, particularly when the polytechnics lost their unique vocational status and became 'new universities', forced to compete with the old universities in a challenging and expanding marketplace. In January 2003 most of Dearing's recommendations were endorsed by the White Paper on *The Future of Higher Education* (DfES 2003b), and they were taken forward by the *Higher Education Act* (HEA 2004) setting out Government's detailed plans for radical reform and investment in universities and HE colleges. These are still being implemented.

The 2004 Act introduced measures in six key areas, intended to improve HE leadership, management and human resource strategies in HE institutions, drive up the quality of HE teaching and research, give universities more freedom to raise and use their own funds, and build more productive partnerships with Sector Skills Councils and Regional Development Agencies. There was a major focus on links with employers, with two measures particularly important here:

- a big funded expansion of two-year foundation degrees

- establishment of a new category of universities by private companies or public bodies engaged heavily in training, with a minimum requirement to take 4,000 full-time students or equivalent.

Finally, a new *Office for Fair Access* (Offa) was created to assess how far 'top' universities meet their own planned milestones for opening up access to students from 'non-traditional' and 'disadvantaged' backgrounds.

LEITCH REVIEW AND SUBSEQUENT 'WIDENING PARTICIPATION' MEASURES

Leitch (2006) noted that participation in HE had increased significantly since 1997, covering around 42% of young people age 18–30 and driving a welcome increase in the proportion of highly skilled workers. However, he found access to university was still 'extremely inequitable' and urged firm government action to tackle this alongside continuing schools reform until standards in schools in the poorest areas matched those in the richest.

The Leitch target for HE is to equip 40% of the workforce with level 4 and 5 skills by 2020. By then, it is estimated that the potential home student population will have fallen by 100,000, or around 16%. The target can only be met if tens of thousands of the existing workforce achieve tertiary education (Wintour

2008a and b). Leitch emphasised the need to change the targets for 'high' skills away from the sole focus on young people aged 18–30 in order to achieve a step change in liaison between employers and higher education institutions. To further embed these incentives, he recommended that a portion of HE funding be delivered through a similar demand-led mechanism as Train to Gain in England, contributing to both young and adult HE attainment levels. He also urged the use of government funding to stimulate greater private investment in HE.

Late in 2006 the DfES in its *Widening Participation* paper (DfES 2006b) announced that government would expand its HE reforms by:

- developing ways to further engage HE institutions with the new 14–19 education reforms (see the first section of this chapter)

- improving immediately the targeting of *Aimhigher*, a national programme to widen participation in HE by raising the aspirations and developing the abilities of young people from under-represented groups (*http// www.aimhigher.ac.uk/ practitioner* [accessed 30 April 2008])

- supporting the development of 10 partnerships of schools, HE institutions and other providers to work with gifted young people from disadvantaged backgrounds

- investigating the need to improve HE provision in some areas of the country

- encouraging SSCs, HE institutions and employers to explore *Earn to Learn* models to boost HE participation by 18- to 30-year-olds (a type of Train to Gain programme aimed at enabling employees to work for 50% of the time and carry out HE studies for the other 50%.)

Further reform is on the way. In April 2008 DIUS launched an online consultation process proposing radical reshaping of universities with 30,000 new places to be co-funded by employers in order to help refocus HE's culture and purpose (DIUS 2008). In addition undergraduates on the new business-focused courses should complete work experience as part of their degree, and English undergraduates should study for two intensive years rather than the present three. In 2009 the Government, working with Offa, will establish an independent review of HE funding arrangements that were introduced in 2006.

HE REFORM: WHAT IS IT LIKELY TO ACHIEVE?

Once again it is impossible at this early stage of the latest radical reforms (mid-2008) to make an informed assessment of where they are likely to lead. What is clear is that with only 6% of employers' spending on training going to universities, the HE system in future must engage far more closely and effectively with employers. To be specific (Wintour 2008a and b):

- There must be a major cultural shift in universities, with all the changes in leadership, management and workforce profile that this will involve, as the traditional timetable pattern is altered and the typical student becomes older, in work, studying part-time and living away from campus. Some universities will welcome the opportunity to make a more direct contribution to the local community, but others may not see it as their job to do so.

• Likewise, the university system will have to meet very different demands for study, with students who will need and expect education directly relevant to their job or career route. Qualification systems will have to change too, so that individuals can build up credits from more than one institution (reforms to these systems are covered in the next section).

Two issues drive to the heart of the matter. The first, identified by John Denham, head of DIUS, is that in the Government's determination to reach the Leitch HE target there is a danger that 'widening participation' comes to be seen purely in terms of helping the poorest into higher education, and therefore as a minority issue that distorts universities' rightful image and purpose. To avoid this he advises the incorporation of a wider range of criteria, including the contribution a university makes to the local economy through breaking down barriers caused by low aspiration and inspiring greater confidence in the admissions system (Wintour 2008a).

The second issue goes deeper, taking the form of a question: is the entire basis of government's insistence on the need to raise to 50% by 2010 participation rates for graduate level qualifications misconceived? The UK is now primarily a service economy, and research in its dominating service sector suggests that (Mason 2002):

• the push towards the 50% target may result in an excess of young people qualified at level 4, many of whom will therefore have to take jobs more appropriate for non-graduates with good-quality technical skills

• if that happens, expansion of mass higher education will not have the intended impact on economic performance, unless far more British employers than at present can be encouraged to adopt a high-skill, high value-added product or service strategy – something that, as yet, is far from happening (see Chapter 2).

So once again the verdict is out. It will be vital in tracking the progress of HE reform to identify credible research findings that should inform government's, employers' and our own views on the contentious issues surrounding HE reform.

REFLECTION

Reflecting on an HE institution with which you are familiar, what strategy does it seem to be using to strengthen its links with employers, and what part is its HR function playing in that process?

OPENING UP ACCESS TO SKILLS FOR LIFE

LIFELONG LEARNING: A FRUSTRATED MISSION

In its *Widening Adult Participation Strategy* (LSC 2004), the LSC revealed that over a third of adults were still not participating in learning once they left compulsory education. Lifelong learning is vital in a knowledge-based society but it needs new mindsets. It will not happen by itself. Union learning representatives are helping to achieve mutual trust related to learning in the workplace, but the education and training of adults in employment have historically received little attention by national skills strategies. The old priorities were the unemployed and young people, while for employers the focus tended to be on managers and professionals, leaving low-skilled adults 'in a twilight zone with no career prospects' (Pickard 2003b).

Since 2003 that has changed. National skills strategy has shone a powerful spotlight on the low-skilled and unskilled adults in work and the Brown administration has made it a priority to target groups that are at most disadvantage in the labour market and in society at large. As one example, the *Apprenticeships* scheme has been extended to adults over 25. As another, in January 2008 the Government outlined proposals to help the unemployed to obtain the skills they need, including a 'skills check' for every unemployed person, one in five under-21s who are unemployed being steered towards an apprenticeship, and private and voluntary sectors being used to create the necessary training posts. These are carrot-and-stick measures because the unemployed who refuse to participate will lose benefit, initially for two weeks and ultimately for up to 26 weeks. However the Work and Pensions Secretary James Purnell has announced the intention to accelerate the Government's welfare reforms and deepen their reach, aiming to move one million people off incapacity benefit and help another 300,000 single parents to find work (Webster 2008).

By mid-2008 as problems in the US and UK banking systems worsen, the threat of recession increases and unemployment rates have begun to rise, all these measure have begun to seem ambitious, but the Brown administration continues to invest heavily in Labour's 2001 *Skills for Life* strategic framework for improving employability and lifelong learning skills in England (DfEE 2001). The framework incorporates a commitment to introduce new national standards for adult literacy, numeracy and language learning together with a national curriculum within each major strand, new entry level qualifications and national tests. One initiative to help all adults, whether in or out of work, to gain full level 3 qualifications, including NCQs, A-levels or BTEC National Diplomas basic skills, is *Learner Accounts*.

Before looking in more detail at the end of this section at the ongoing overhaul of the national vocational qualifications system, it is relevant to outline two other important ways in which government is trying to open up routes to lifelong learning for all are through *Local Employment Partnerships* and *Apprenticeships*.

CASE EXAMPLE

LEARNER ACCOUNTS

Learner Accounts aim to help learners over 19 by giving them greater choice and control over their learning. Learners receive independent advice on training options up-front. The value of each voucher varies depending upon the learning programme the individual chooses and whether they are expected to pay fees or not.

Once learners have signed up for a course they should receive a written statement confirming the cost of the course and the amount that the state and individual or employer will be expected to pay for it. As they progress through their learning journey, they will receive regular updated statements.

Trials to test the accounts began in September 2007, with the aim of ultimately making up to 4,000 available. The trials focused on economic growth areas in the south east and the East Midlands and will be evaluated as they progress, expanding in scale in the second year (2008/09).

Source: *http://www.lsc.gov.uk/ adultlearneraccounts* [accessed 11 April 2008]

LOCAL EMPLOYMENT PARTNERSHIPS

The Local Employment Partnership (LEP) scheme was launched in 2007 as part of the Blair Government's drive to raise skills levels. It made rapid progress in encouraging businesses to provide work placements and educational support for unemployed people in ways that will make a secure connection between 'work' and 'skills' (Fennell 2008). All SSCs are examining what LEPs can do for their particular industries and by the end of 2007 250 employers had already made a commitment to be involved (Fennell 2007). They included big names like Asda, John Lewis, B&Q and the Royal Bank of Scotland, and also small firms (a vital target because they are the source of most UK employment).

Agreements typically offer either guaranteed interviews for permanent jobs or 'work trials' for up to six weeks to recruits referred from Jobcentre Plus. In return employers get candidates who have been prepared by relevant pre-training and are motivated to work (Brockett 2008a). What employers and individuals find attractive is the initiative's flexibility, in sharp contrast to the rule-bound prescriptive approach that has caused many such measures in the past to fail. LEP programmes are designed to respond to a wide variety of individual needs in order to help people acquire the necessary skills or experience through pre-employment training and support them in getting and staying in work thereafter (Fennell 2008). Leitch identified as essential that official schemes and the government departments responsible for them must in future give far better support to individuals in moving from 'out of work' to 'in work' and staying there. Recognising this, LEPs ensure that throughout their work trials LEP candidates can continue to receive

CASE EXAMPLE

THE SOUTHWARK WORKS PROJECT

Southwark Works was established in 2005 by the London Borough of Southwark's local strategic partnership's multi-agency employment taskforce. The aim of the project was to help around 50,000 unemployed people whom government initiatives had failed to get back into work. They constituted about 27% of the borough's working-age population and so represented a major potential skills resource. The project targets single parents, those on health-related benefits, young people leaving care, refugees, and others who cannot find work for other reasons. It is funded by the Government's neighbourhood renewal fund and the London Development agency.

Its unique feature is that its 17 advisers are 'embedded' in a range of different public and private sector organisations. Those organisations employ them, but their salaries are paid by the project. Each adviser works individually with a client to create an action plan to get them back to work, including identifying training needed and also any practical assistance needed – for example with childcare, travel expenses or buying clothes for work. The adviser also helps to arrange company placements.

In its first two years the project helped 1,500 back to work, with 400 supported through training to boost their skills. 60 employers including Asda quickly signed up, finding clients to be hard-working and highly motivated. The project works because it successfully obtained buy-in from a partnership of statutory, community and voluntary organisations who host the advisers and provide the necessary resources to help clients get into work and back into the community. You can read stories of some of the many whose lives have been transformed by Southwark Works by going to its website (below).

Sources: Andalo, D. (2007) *Guardian*, 21 March; *http://www. southwark.gov.uk/BusinessCentre/ EmploymentandEnterprise/ Southwarkworks/* [accessed 29 April 2008]

benefits and support, for example with childcare, and employers can liaise with the Jobcentre contact to discuss progress.

LEPs grew out of the kind of scheme exemplified by Southwark Works.

APPRENTICESHIPS

http//www.apprenticeships.org.uk [accessed 28 April 2008]

Since 2004 apprenticeships have provided the major funded route for young people into vocational training and thence into skilled employment. They cover the three levels shown in Table 4 earlier in the chapter.

Apprenticeships involve a mix of on-the-job and off-the-job training and education, and on average take two years to complete (although those at advanced levels can take up to four). All apprenticeships frameworks designed by SSCs have a requirement to develop key skills through NVQs, and employers are subsidised for the costs involved in apprentices attending education courses. Apprenticeships can benefit employers where skilled staff are hard to recruit or where upgrade training cannot provide sufficient vocational knowledge. They can also improve the selection and socialisation of young people who are prospective long-term employees, and promote linkages between educational programmes and career advancement within the organisation (CIPD 2006b).

The Apprenticeships Strategy (2008)

In 2007 the Secretary of State for Innovation, Universities and Skills admitted to Parliament that 'apprenticeship has an unfortunate history of initiatives announced but not implemented and of decisions taken and then changed or reversed'(Cm 7228, 2007: paragraph 15). Early in 2008 the Government published its new strategy, *World Class Apprenticeships: Unlocking Talent, Building Skills* (DCSF & DIUS 2008b) to ensure that apprenticeships become a mainstream option for young people, running in parallel with a suite of qualifications to ensure that all have access to education and training post-16. The strategy responds to Leitch's (2006) recommendations with a commitment incorporating significant growth in apprenticeships for older learners as well as young people. It sets out how government intends to work with business and employers to raise the skills of the country through the funded apprenticeships system.

To simplify the overall control and funding of the apprenticeships system, DIUS now leads on the scheme overall, sharing policy responsibility with the DCSF (DCSF and DIUS 2008a). SSCs design apprenticeship frameworks for their sectors, in line with a blueprint produced by the Learning and Skills Council in 2005. In 2010 local authorities will take over from the LSC the management of the scheme, the processing of funding and ensuring effective provider competition. A national vacancy-matching system for apprenticeships will begin in England by the end of 2008 in order to simplify the recruitment process for employers and provide a single point of entry for potential apprentices (Phillips 2008). Again responding to Leitch's recommendations, government has also opened apprenticeships to adults over 25 and is committed to ensuring by 2013 an apprenticeship entitlement to all aged 16 to 18.

Issues for employers

Since Labour came into power in 1997 apprenticeships in England has made undeniable progress, with over 250,000 participants in 2007 compared to 75,000 at the start of the decade. By 2008 over 130,000 employers were offering apprenticeship places across 80 sectors and in more than 180 different types of business (Cm 7228, 2007; DCSF and DIUS 2008c). The CIPD's 2008 Annual

L&D survey showed that 30% of respondents were involved in operating apprenticeships in their organisations and 36% more were considering the scheme (CIPD 2008a). Completion rates have begun at last to rise, averaging around 63% for levels 2 and 3 and so coming much closer than before to those in Germany, where apprenticeship places seem to be declining – partly on grounds of cost, partly because of their inflexibility in the face of technological change (Cm 7228, 2007: 4).

All of this, however, is less promising than it seems. Much of the increased participation since 1997 has been due to existing training schemes being converted into apprenticeships, and in reality too few employers support apprenticeships; most of the programmes are located in a small number of big firms like BT and British Gas (Smedley 2008). There is also the fear that with the increasing threat of recession in the UK economy many organisations currently employing apprentices will cut back on their number or cease to offer places at all. One way or another there is a great deal of ground to make up if the Leitch target of 400,000 apprenticeships in place in England by 2020 is to be achieved. Why do more employers not support the apprenticeships scheme?

- Many lack understanding of how to become involved. They are confused by the series of changes made to the scheme over the years and by the alleged poor quality of many external training and educational providers.

- While the benefits of investing in apprenticeships become more powerful in the long term, employers are most concerned with immediate outcomes and often fear that their expensively trained products will be poached (Phillips 2007a).

- Many employers do not want the complete apprenticeship package, querying the need for every trainee to complete a full NVQ, or to cover all the key skills.

- Many employers run small or medium-sized firms facing an uncertain future, and so feel unable to commit to keeping apprentices on for two or three years after they enter training (Kingston 2007d). For the apprentice this creates significant problems, because NVQs are the official outcomes of apprenticeship and they must be completed in a workplace or the individual cannot claim to be fully qualified and competent.

- Many employers find the funding system excessively bureaucratic and inflexible. Their participation could improve significantly if, as the Secretary of State for DIUS has urged (Cm 7228, 2007), employers were to be placed firmly at the centre of all apprenticeship provision, with all funding being re-routed directly to them. They could then choose either to provide or subcontract off-the-job training or other services. Tax incentives or direct subsidies for firms to engage in apprenticeships would also encourage a greater take-up by employers.

Often those who start their apprenticeship education in FE colleges have serious problems to face. Colleges receive funding because like all providers they are paid per apprentice taken on. However, there is a significant mismatch between supply and demand, so many 'partly-trained hopefuls' (File On 4 2007) flood into the marketplace only to become unemployed. Train to Gain (see Chapter 2) is the Government's big national initiative to tackle the problem but it only goes up to NVQ level 2. It therefore excludes many wanting apprenticeship training, particularly adults with existing experience who are qualified above level 2 but who have been made redundant or are trying to return to employment after a period away for other reasons.

The next case study example outlines one initiative that offers help here.

A major sign of a more flexible national approach to apprenticeships emerged in July 2008, when it was announced that Government had accepted proposals

PROGRAMME-LED APPRENTICESHIPS

CASE EXAMPLE

The SSC ConstructionSkills announced in 2007 that it was going to create 3,000 'programme-led' apprenticeships (PLAs). PLAs started in September 2004, in order to find a new way of combining academic and vocational education into a package of learning that meets employers' and learners' needs alike. They are at the forefront of a drive for sixth form colleges in particular to develop their provision in the field of work-based learning.

PLAs enable employers who may not be able to support apprentices through a whole apprenticeship framework to offer training opportunities incorporating at least one of the major qualifications that are included in an approved apprenticeship or advanced apprenticeship framework – that is to say an NVQ or the Technical Certificate.

The idea behind the Construction skills initiative is that since not

all apprentices can be employed at the start of their training, attempts should be made as soon as possible after anyone starts a training programme based in a college or a private training firm to get them onto an 'employer-led' apprenticeship. The time in college provides a confidence often not possible for those starting work with an employer 'cold' and also ensures through the two-year college period a sound starting base of knowledge leading to the same qualification as apprentices so that when the college-leavers do gain employment they are already well on their way to final technical and NVQ qualification (Kingston 2007d).

Sources: Kingston, P. (2007d)
Guardian, 8 May;
*http://www.lsc.gov.uk/largonbuster/
Programme+Led+Apprenticeship.htm*
[accessed 28 April 2008];
*http//www.sussexlearningnetwork.
org.uk/documents/4B.ppt*
[accessed 28 April 2008]

made by Tesco – the supermarket chain whose successful apprenticeship scheme provides a strong base for internal promotion – to simplify procedures for certification, assessment, quality assurance and inspection (Gribben 2008). In the same month a new *Apprenticeships Bill* established for the first time a statutory basis for Apprenticeships, ensuring a statutory definition of the term, the arrangements to apply to determining the content of apprenticeship frameworks, a right to public funding for apprenticeship programmes and a compulsion on public bodies to offer apprenticeships. It also set out how the new *National Apprenticeship Service* will deliver an expanded programme and provide a single point of contact for employers (DCSF and DIUS 2008c).

These substantial reforms, together with the overhaul of the national vocational qualification system detailed below, offered at last the hope of greatly improved access for all young people and adult learners to lifelong learning routes that recognise both formally and informally acquired knowledge and skills.

REFORMING THE NATIONAL VOCATIONAL QUALIFICATION SYSTEM

By 2008 there were still around 500 national vocational qualifications (NVQs, or SNVQs in Scotland) in a wide range of subjects. They are identified on a National Database of Accredited Qualifications (*http://www.accreditedqualifications.org. uk/ index.aspx* [accessed 1 May 2008]). Commenting on their complexity, the Qualifications and Curriculum Authority has observed (QCA 2004):

> Today's qualification system is a series of mini-frameworks that have developed in different sectors or through different awarding body conventions. Many qualifications in the national qualification framework are valued, while others are duplicated, confusing or have no obvious pathways for progression to employment or learning.

Perhaps, therefore, it is unsurprising that although employers invest £33 billion in staff training annually, only a third of this leads to a qualification (Brockett 2008b). In the past they have never greatly valued NVQs, largely because of their perceived bureaucracy, jargon and inflexibility, but research indicates that amongst those who do use them there is a general recognition of their positive features (Roe *et al* 2006):

- They engage staff in skills development who would not otherwise have been engaged.

- They are motivating for staff.

- They are flexible, improve skills and are relevant to the work situation.

- They deliver a range of identifiable benefits to the organisation.

The new qualifications framework

A new eight-level Qualifications and Credit Framework (QCF) was introduced in 2006 for testing and trial until June 2008, involving stakeholders including learners, employers, awarding bodies, sector skills councils, colleges and training providers. A final report for ministers followed, evaluating evidence and exploring options for the implementation of the new framework across England, Wales and Northern Ireland. QCA was then asked by DIUS to carry develop a full and specific business case, including a detailed delivery model for QCF, by the end of September 2008. Further information is provided at the QCA website (*http://www. qca.org.uk/qca_19674.aspx* [accessed 16 September 2008]).

The framework, intended to be in place by 2010, is designed to support a more flexible and responsive approach to both the development and accreditation of qualifications. It will break down qualifications into small pieces of learning, or 'units', allowing learners to accumulate 'credit' as they learn over time. The qualifications themselves will have simple titles, to avoid confusion and overlapping names, and could include both whole qualifications and smaller 'parcels' of training, which are focused on specific areas of business. All these reforms are not just about reorganising existing qualifications. They reflect the aim of bringing into the framework the best learning and training, wherever it exists and whoever provides it.

2007: Accreditation of in-house training

In September 2007 government took NVQ reforms yet further along the road by announcing plans for accrediting the in-house training schemes of major companies, thus honouring its promise in the earlier report, *World Class Skills* (DIUS 2007), to make the vocational qualifications system easy and attractive for employers to have their own training programmes accredited within a national qualifications framework. Already the initiative has attracted the interest of some big employers. Those involved in LEPs, who will be among the first to have access to fast-tracked accreditation of their training programmes, include Vodafone, McDonald's, Network Rail, Sainsbury's, De Vere and Transport for London.

The main fear is of dumbing down, an outcome that would further weaken the credibility of the whole vocational qualification system. For some, this fear has been reinforced by the announcement in December 2007 that the QCA was to be split in two to form on the one hand an independent regulator of exam standards, and on the other a body responsible for curriculum and national test matters. The aim is to develop high exam standards and assessment expertise. The concern is that power over the exam system will become concentrated in the hands of a few individuals chosen for their administrative rather than assessment expertise, leading to 'a bureaucracy that cannot answer the big questions' (Baird 2007). L&D professionals should be making their voices heard in relevant arenas to protect the rigour and integrity of vocational qualifications and their assessment in the workplace.

McDonald's leads the way

CASE EXAMPLE

In January 2008 McDonald's, along with the Ministry of Defence, Flybe and Network Rail, became the first employers to have their in-house training schemes accredited by the QCA. McDonald's Director of People said that the scheme would enable people to better themselves, and those who left after gaining a qualification would also become 'brand ambassadors for life'. The aim of the course is not staff retention, since that is not a major problem for McDonald's, but to improve staff service (Brockett 2008b).

The course is for basic shift managers, will be equivalent to an A-level, includes 80 hours of classroom study and will provide a grounding for promotion. Modules cover customer service, health and safety, food hygiene, finance and HR. HR staff will be amongst those who participate, and will be supported to take CIPD qualifications as their subsequent step.

McDonald's has around 60% of employees aged under 21 and expects many to leave after the chain has become their first stepping-stone. A company spokesman said that this was not a problem for McDonald's, because the old model of keeping people for life was no longer relevant. What mattered for the company was that staff were loyal, engaged, and provided good customer service. The new NVQ-accredited course is targeting all those outcomes (Frean 2008a).

Overall McDonald's expects around 3,000 of its 67,000-strong workforce to achieve the new qualification annually. One example is an employee who started working part-time in York at the age of 16, enrolled with his manager's help on an online maths course offered by the company to all employees, and quickly passed a GCSE equivalent in maths (a subject he had failed when at school) to add to the eight GCSEs that he already possessed. That pass enabled him ultimately to gain a place at university to study paediatric nursing – an achievement he attributed to McDonald's online educational facility. He also became a fully qualified shift manager and will continue working at the chain part-time during his time at university – one of 10,000 university students working for McDonald's (Frean 2008a).

Sources: Brockett, J. (2008b) *People Management*, 24 January; Frean, A. (2008a) *Times*, 28 January

REFLECTION

Are NVQs used in your own organisation? If so, for which staff, and how successfully? If not, why not – and what could your L&D practitioners do to make them more relevant and attractive to your employer?

KEY TASKS FOR L&D PRACTITIONERS

It is essential to the success of all the reforms covered in this chapter that there is a far stronger relationship between education and learning providers on the one hand and employers on the other. The task is formidable and L&D practitioners have a crucial role to play. They must become active in raising the levels of basic skills in their workforces, reducing rigid divisions in their internal labour market, and opening up more access to educational opportunities and career development paths.

Within organisations, fairer recruitment and selection policies and career development planning for all employees would go a considerable way towards encouraging more participation in apprenticeships and other qualification-linked training. The website *http://www.dfes.gov.uk/skillsforemployers/* [accessed 27 April 2008] provides on its home page links that identify the areas of national policy and initiatives most relevant to help employers in the recruitment, training and development of their staff, and to give them a 'key role' in supporting a workable national system for education and skills. As just one example, by 2020 it is estimated that the UK will need 4.5 million extra graduates, so more young people must be helped to progress to higher levels of skill. HR/L&D professionals should be raising awareness in their organisations of the opportunities offered by SSCs to employers to take a lead role here and should be ready to work with universities and SSCs to provide higher-level skills development (Hirst 2008).

IMPROVING WORKPLACE-BASED LEARNING

If accredited workplace learning is to become more attractive for employers to invest in, its provision must be improved. In 2000 L&D practitioners involved in funded work-based learning in the workplace numbered between 95,000 and 110,000 in England. They included:

- managers, supervisors, resource and programme co-ordinators

- tutors/occupational trainers and assessors, mentors and coaches

- administrators and other support staff.

In research undertaken by the Institute of Employment Studies (IES) for the DfES the researchers were 'appalled' to find how little understanding was demonstrated by training providers at the most basic level of how NVQs should work and how few providers were assessing needs on an individual basis. Much of the training was still menu-based (Smethurst 2005). One problem is the wide range, varying levels and skewed focus of their qualifications to practise, most of which centre on work-based assessment and verification. Other qualifications, in particular those focused on the management of training and quality and related planning activities, are much less widespread. Workplace learning practitioners need to be properly developed and tested as fit to practise, preferably by external experts, with testing rigorously linked to the needs and characteristics of the workplace. Assessment should relate both to the standards to be reached by the practitioners and to their reliability, punctuality and quality in performing their tasks.

Similar problems exist in relation to external providers, including FE colleges. By mid-2004 LSCs in England had issued contracts to around 800 – a reduction of over half the number previously and an indictment of the very poor standards revealed by the Adult Learning Inspectorate's (ALI) annual reports in 2002 and 2003. The 2004 ALI annual report concluded that 34% of adult learning and work-based learning provided in colleges was still inadequate. Those in greatest need suffered most from this, including the disabled, those with low basic skills levels and those with learning disabilities. The report urged more training for FE teachers as a priority.

The delivery of learning in many schools is also being severely impeded by poor management and performance. In May 2008 (Frean 2008b), the Chief Executive of the General Teaching Council (GTC) for England estimated that up to 24,000 out of the 530,000 teachers registered with the Council are incompetent and in need, at the very least, of intensive retraining. Many questioned that estimate and in any case put most blame on any critical failure to deliver even adequate teaching to young people on the accumulating pressures piled on the teaching profession by the pace and demands of educational reform. Be that as it may, it is clear that government plans, local partnerships and the opening up of access to high-quality lifelong learning from cradle to grave will all come to nothing if those who deliver the goods on the ground are found wanting.

A new *Ofsted* (the Office for Standards in Education, Children's Services and Skills) was established in 2007. It brought together four former inspectorates, including the ALI, to inspect and regulate care for children and young people, and education and training for learners of all ages. Its aim is to be instrumental in achieving a rapid improvement in standards related to the provision, management and assessment of workplace learning. Certainly L&D practitioners in the workplace learning field need to take a lead in such improvement, particularly by:

- sharing responsibility with funding bodies for raising work-based learning schemes' profile and demonstrating their value to businesses

- improving their own expertise and partnership skills, for example by getting centrally involved in the design of apprenticeship programmes via their SSCs

- helping line managers and mentors to develop skills and attitudes that will improve the quality and outcomes of work-based learning in their organisations.

In summary, HR and L&D professionals need to consider with great care the employee relations, performance management and development implications of underperformance in their workplaces, because at the end of this particular line the consequences of failure to deliver could hardly be more serious.

REFLECTION

Reflecting on this chapter's coverage, it should by now be clear to you that HR professionals have a crucial role to play in improving access to lifelong learning for those within and outside their organisations. How far and how effectively do you think those professionals are carrying out these tasks in or for your organisation?

THE VERDICT?

NATIONAL SKILLS STRATEGY

Having reviewed in this and the preceding chapter the Government's entire strategy covering workforce development and education reform, how optimistic should we be about its chances of success?

Running through both chapters is the dominating theme of making that strategy truly demand-driven. There are two problematic issues here. First, what employers want will not always coincide with what learners want. Second, if government funding is provided for an initiative, then that funding must bring benefits not only for the employer but for individual learners and for the economy at large. To tackle these issues government reforms currently seek to provide:

- a primary and secondary education system where key functional skills – English, maths and CIT – are consistently developed, leaving employers freer to decide on whether and how to build on those basic skills to meet their particular proficiency needs

- an appropriate vocational education, centred on a new diploma system that can integrate academic and vocational pathways

- a flexible and inclusive framework of qualifications, with its design and the approval of qualifications largely in the hands of employers working with SSCs.

The intention of strategy is clear but the crucial test, as ever, will be delivery. As Figure 4 in Chapter 2 shows, 'working in partnership', governments' mantra over the years, remains challenging to achieve. Also, by 2010 at latest, LEAs will have direct authority over all education of 0- to 19-year-olds. They will have regained thereby the dominating influence over the whole NVET system that they held throughout much of the twentieth-century post-war period. Some applaud this as the rightful working of local democracy. Others believe that it will operate to the detriment of the educational system.

On another front, there have long been concerns about the Government's reliance on a voluntary approach to achieve its national skills strategy and fears that this approach will never be enough to pull down the formidable barriers still faced by adults – especially the most disadvantaged – seeking full access to lifelong learning opportunities. With the review of the NVET system that is due to take place in 2013 and the warning that government will seek to introduce an element of compulsion if the skills gap remains too great by then, regulation seems likely to return in some form. Whether that will achieve more than did the unsuccessful regulatory regime of the Industrial Training Boards in the 1970s remains to be seen.

A major question mark must also hang over the Government's preoccupation with tackling the skills gap through an increase in qualifications. To balance against this, there are the current re-modelling of vocational qualifications via diplomas and vocational in-house training and all the apprenticeships measures to put more control over funding and provision into employers' hands. The new Diplomas system is intended to be highly attractive to young people and to employers and the new diplomas are already gaining UCAS points similar to three or more good A-levels because they are grounded in core basic skills (*People Management* 2008a).

At the end of the day, though, the doubts remain. As Coffield (2007) observed, since 1997 the Labour Government has taken post-16 education more to its heart than any previously, pouring money into it, pulling down old structures and agencies and putting others in their place, and giving England, Wales and Northern Ireland their first national skills strategy (DfES 2003a). Yet in a damning and influential indictment of the mass of reforms since 1997 he concluded that England 'does not have an educational system, but instead three badly co-ordinated sectors – Schools, Post Compulsory Education and HE'. He identified the main tensions as (*ibid*: 24):

> those between competition and collaboration, between standardisation and innovation, between centralisation and local flexibility, between enabling and controlling strategies, and between long-term sustainability and short-term goals and targets.

Caulkin, another seasoned observer, holds essentially the same view, pointing the finger of blame at central planning and 'the toxic interplay of vested interests' that has led managers and policy-makers to try ever harder 'to make something come right that they shouldn't be doing in the first place' and so producing ever more targets, prescriptions, incentives and sanctions to shore up 'the crumbling management edifice even as it buckles under their increasing weight' (Caulkin 2007: 39).

Commenting on national skills strategy in the light of findings from the CIPD's 2008 L&D Annual Survey and of the Leitch Review, Opie (2008) stressed the need for a serious commitment from education, business and government to work purposefully together in ensuring that by 2020 young people will have the necessary functional, generic and sector-specific skills. He divides education and business, in this respect, into four self-explanatory camps: cynics, dinosaurs, spectators and players. It will be interesting to see, in two or three years' time, whether the players have succeeded in converting the rest, or whether by then the game and its rules have changed yet again.

REFLECTION

The website *http://www.dfes.gov. uk/skillsforemployers/*[accessed 27 April 2008] provides links on its home page to help and encourage employers to play a 'key role' in supporting a workable national system for education and skills. Reflecting on these, and taking a specific organisation with which you are familiar – a firm, a hospital, a school, perhaps – what do you think L&D professionals should be doing to ensure that opportunities offered by national educational initiatives are put to good use there?

CONCLUSION

Having mastered the material in this chapter, you should now understand the aims, scope and progress of key reforms taking place in schools and in the further and higher education sectors, and some of their major implications for employers, individuals and L&D professionals. You should also be confident in tackling the review questions relating to this chapter, contained in Appendix 3.

In summary, the chapter's six sections have covered the following ground:

- key stages in reforms since 1997 to the schools system and to 14 to 19 years vocational and educational pathways, setting them in an overall context of earlier Tory reforms. They have seen important U-turns in policy as each administration, under the influence of political and ideological pressures, has tried to meet the imperatives of the 2003 national skills strategy: a demand-led and partnership-based approach to educational provision, and improved institutional, sectoral and organisational contexts for development and provision

- radical changes in the FE and HE systems that have called for a new emphasis on funding tied to improved performance and provision, for stronger partnerships with employers and learners, and for greatly expanded participation rates by learners whose profile now differs fundamentally from that of the traditional full-time, campus-based 18- to 21-year-old student

CONCLUSION CONT.

- issues and initiatives to do with opening up wider access for all, both in and out of work, to lifelong educational opportunities, and their key implications for employers and L&D professionals

- doubts about the chances of success for the Government's lifelong learning mission and for its national skills strategy overall, given the basically centralised approach that it continues to apply to the planning and management of the whole NVET system

- recognition of the breaks that current reforms are attempting to make with a past littered with structural, strategic and implementation failures. Future success will depend largely on the successful remodelling of vocational qualifications via diplomas and vocational in-house training, on improved delivery and, not least, on L&D professionals taking a decisive lead in enhancing workplace learning and in promoting VET partnerships within and across organisational boundaries.

EXLPORE FURTHER

FURTHER INFORMATION SOURCES

Gillard, D. (2007) *Education in England: A brief history*. Available at http//www.dg.dial.pipex.com/history/ [accessed 26 April 2008]. Strong anti-New Labour bias but a stimulating critique of the English education system up to 2007

Foster, A. (2005) *Realising the Potential: A review of the future role of further education colleges*. Online version also available at http//www.dfes.gov.uk/furthereducation/index [accessed 26 April 2008]. Vital reading for its analysis of international practice in post-16 education and training

Marchington, M. and Wilkinson, A. (2008) *Human Resource Management at Work: People management and development*, 4th edition. London: CIPD, pp309–41

Sung, J., Raddon, A. and Ashton, D. (2006) *Skills Abroad: A comparative assessment of international policy approaches to skills leading to the development of policy recommendations for the UK*. Research Report 16, May. South Yorkshire: Sector Skills Development Agency. Also available at http//www.skillsforbusiness.org.uk [accessed 29 April 2008]

You should also regularly read:

- the CIPD's publication *People Management*, which contains updates on NVET policy and

FURTHER INFORMATION SOURCES

initiatives plus useful case studies illustrating take-up

- the quality press for a range of informed views about education reform.

Useful websites to add to those provided in the chapter

Acts of Parliament, plus Green and White Papers on educational and skills reform

http://www.opsi.gov.uk/acts.htm [accessed 4 May 2008]

http://www.dcsf.gov.uk/ publications/keydocuments. shtml [accessed 20 April 2008]. Provides links to Government Green and White Papers, strategy documents and so on, plus articles, reviews, etc on educational reform

Schools reform
http://www.teachernet.gov.uk/ educationoverview/ [accessed 26 April 2008]. Key updates on Government's strategy for education in England

UK NVET reform: general
http://www/dfes.go.uk/research [accessed 29 April 2008]. Details of all DCSF/DIUS-funded research projects as well as previous DfES projects

http://www.dfes.gov.uk/ readwriteplus/Workplace [accessed 25 April 2008]. Summaries of government policy and strategies across

the education and workforce development fields

Further education reform
http://www.dfes.gov.uk/ furthereducation/index [accessed 27 April 2008]

http://excellence.qia.org.uk/ page.aspx?o=home [accessed 25 April 2008]. Overview of FE government policy and initiatives plus useful links

http://www.dius.gov.uk/ press/23-10-07.html [accessed 25 April 2008]

Basic skills and workplace initiatives
http://www.lancs.ac.uk/wbsnet [accessed 27 April 2008]. Provides information to support good practice delivery of workplace learning

http://www.unionlearn.org.uk/ [accessed 27 April 2008]. How to set up basic skills training in an organisation, and other ways in which *unionlearn* can support workplace learning

http://www.cipd.co.uk/ onlineinfodocuments [accessed 8 May 2008]. Investors in People Factsheet

International VET systems
http://www.teachernet. gov.uk/educationoverview/ international/ [accessed 22 July 2008]. Highlights key sources of information about international education systems and policies

PART 2

Getting to grips with the practice

CHAPTER 4

Understanding Learning and the Learners

INTRODUCTION

Part 2 of the book explores ways in which L&D practitioners can ensure high quality and ethical learning and development practice, linked to organisational as well as individual performance and responsive to changing needs and challenges. The focus in this chapter is on learning and the learners.

Traditionally learning in organisations has been defined as (Bass and Vaughan 1967: 8):

> A relatively permanent change in behaviour that occurs as a result of practice or experience.

Here, though, is a rather different view (Marton and Ramsden, 1988: 271):

> A qualitative change in a person's way of seeing, experiencing, understanding, conceptualising something in the real world.

And here is one that takes 'learning' into a new terrain altogether, defining it as (Zuboff 1988: 395):

> The heart of productive activity. To put it simply, learning is the new form of labor.

How can three definitions be so different? And what do their differences signify for the individual, the work organisation and the L&D profession?

To find answers to these questions the first three sections of this chapter explore traditional and more recent approaches in learning theory. Each section ends by identifying practical challenges for L&D practitioners. The fourth section traces parallel advances in training and learning technology, concluding with implications for a potential 'age of the universal knowledge worker'. The final section reviews the evidence to assess whether in reality a 'shift' to a learning and knowledge age is occurring in work organisations.

REFLECTION

This Introduction outlines three notions of learning in organisations. In what ways do you find these three notions differ – and what do you find most significant about each? Drawing on your previous reading and/or experience, try to identify factors that might explain these differing notions. It will be helpful to keep a note of your observations by you as you read through this chapter.

THE AGE OF THE TRAINER

As we saw in Chapter 1, throughout most of the twentieth century training was the main approach to employee development in which employers invested. After World War II, the need to rapidly rebuild the UK's skills base increased its popularity, which was reinforced by the advent of Industrial Training Boards in the 1960s, then of the Training Services Agency and, in the 1980s, of the Training and Enterprise Councils.

Throughout this era the dominance of training was underpinned by the development of psychological learning theories based on the assumption that individuals learn as the result of conditioning and of information processing.

LEARNING AS CONDITIONING: BEHAVIOURIST THEORIES

Behaviourist learning theories are known as 'positivist' approaches. This is because they rest on the assumptions that the world is an objective external reality, and that the aim of learning is to acquire accurate knowledge from 'out there' to transfer to individuals 'in here' so that they can engage with that world successfully. Behaviourist theories emerged initially from Pavlov's (1927) work with dogs, which led to his 'classical' theory that all behaviour can be explained by reference to learnt patterns of stimulus and response. Skinner's (1953) pioneering work with pigeons and rats led to a broader understanding of the learning process: one that took into account the part played in the learning process not only by instinct but by reinforcement from social and environmental factors.

This latter strand of 'radical behaviourism' focused on the role of 'operant conditioning' in the modification of behaviour. Described in simple terms, operant conditioning proposes that learning is an interaction of four core processes in the individual:

- *drive* – Human beings have a fundamental need to seek new knowledge, skills, or attitudes when confronted with an unfamiliar problem, challenge or scenario. They are instinctively driven to close gaps in their existing learning so that they can continue to perceive their world as one that is meaningful and over which they have control.

- *stimulation* – An individual must experience a specific trigger that activates and sustains their drive to learn in a particular situation – when, for example, they have to perform a new task, work in a changed way, or acquire changed values and beliefs. That trigger may occur naturally, or it may be engineered by another party.

- *response* – Learning involves the acquisition by the individual of some new or reorganised set of responses – 'behaviours'.

- *reinforcement* – The key to the acquisition of appropriate behaviours (behaviours that enable a learner to solve a problem and thereby move forward) lies in reinforcing such behaviours and in ensuring that inappropriate behaviours are eliminated before they can become habit-forming.

In the US behaviourist learning theories were introduced into industry during the first half of the twentieth century by Scientific Management theorists and practitioners, for whom the concepts of operant conditioning fitted well within the 'command–control' model of management. The approach put trainers firmly in the driving seat of the learning process. Its rationality and efficiency led to its widespread popularity and ultimately to the development of the systematic training model described in Chapter 1. It still exerts a powerful influence on training practice.

LEARNING AS INFORMATION-PROCESSING: THE TRADITIONAL COGNITIVIST VIEW

Cognitivism became a dominant force in psychology during the 1950s. The term 'cognitive' refers to the interacting psychological processes of perception, memory, thinking and learning. In cognitive psychology, learning is understood as a process to do with the acquisition and application of knowledge, and problem-solving as its major vehicle (Garrick 1999: 222). The individual's knowledge base expands, alters or is transformed as they apply their representations – whether or not successfully – to similar and not-so-similar situations to those in which they were originally acquired.

Traditional cognitivist theories of learning emerged from behaviourism and reinforce the notion of 'trainer as driver'. They focus on the cognitive structures that enable the individual to make sense of events and situations, and that inform the ways in which they interpret and respond to their environments. 'Cognitive structures' are representations – theoretical concepts and knowledge of procedures – that, once acquired by an individual, become organised in particular patterns in their memory and are subsequently applied to solving new problems (Gioia and Poole 1984; Porac *et al* 1989; Harris 1994; von Krogh *et al* 1994).

Cybernetics has made a significant contribution to the cognitive approach to learning. It concerns the information and feedback channels that should be used to stimulate and help people to learn. Which senses to make most use of – sight, touch, taste, sound and kinaesthetics (or the 'feel' and positioning of muscles) – all come into the equation. So do the perceptual process and the ways in which attention will shift and sharpen during a learning programme as some tasks are mastered, leaving the conscious mind freer to focus on others that are more demanding. Integral to cybernetics theory is the idea of breaking down a whole task into parts, or elements (part and whole learning), in order to design a stepped learning process.

Here is a personal case that illustrates an information-processing approach to learning:

THE SELF-INSTRUCTION MANUAL

CASE EXAMPLE

In the 1960s I used a manual called *Principles of Management – A program for self-instruction*, written by American guru Leonard Kazmier, to guide me at my own pace through essentials of management theory in preparation for the Institute of Personnel Management's business administration exam. It was designed to be completed in anything from seven to 14 hours, and could be used as an adjunct to various management textbooks and other coursework materials, thus encouraging the individual learner to take the learning at their own pace, seeking out information from other sources as and when they needed to expand their understanding of particular sections of the text.

The book divided management theory into bite-sized units, each of which commenced with a small chunk of theory, then took the reader through a series of self-test statements to ensure their understanding of it, then moved on to the next chunk. That cycle of explain, test, provide feedback and reinforcement was repeated for every element of the unit until all had been mastered and a grasp of the entire body of theory covered in the manual had been acquired.

In the final unit of the book, entitled 'Learning and employee development' (which I confess I never reached, having abandoned the manual at an earlier point where mathematics had entered too heavily for me into a unit on management control systems), the author explained the factors on which he relied in designing this learning programme (Kazmier 1964: 225):

These factors, called principles of learning by psychologists, include the need to maximize the individual's motivation to learn, providing feedback during learning, appropriately sequencing the materials to be learned, providing for active participation during training, and considering the individual differences among trainees.

As this example illustrates, traditional cognitivism reflects, like behaviourism, a positivist view of the world. It therefore assumes that filling learning gaps is a rational process whereby the learner seeks access to and mastery of a theoretically perfect body of knowledge 'out there', provided by experts. However, the example hints at ways in which cognitive psychology moves away from behaviourist principles in recognising that learning cannot be acquired solely through conditioning. It owes much also to differences in individuals' cognitive structures and to the operation of the brain as an information processing system that enables adults to intelligently search for information to solve problems and challenges.

Traditional cognitive theories have been influenced particularly by Piaget's (1950) research into child development which led him to form the view that knowledge grows as the result of continual individual construction and reorganisation of experience through time. He produced a threefold classification of responses to explain how adults resolve tensions between their instinctive desire to learn and their preference to do so by keeping within their customary frameworks of thought (Wiltshire 2005):

- *assimilation*: where we accept new information because it is consistent with our existing cognitive framework

- *accommodation*: where we experience some tension but manage to adapt the new information so that it fits into our existing framework without radically changing it

- *rejection*: where the new information challenges our existing framework to such a degree that we are not prepared to make the necessary changes to accept it.

Piaget's theories also influenced later approaches in learning theory that are very different from 'traditional' cognitive approaches. As such I will return to them shortly.

POSITIVIST APPROACHES TO LEARNING: THE ROLE OF THE TRAINER

Behaviourist and early cognitivist theories led to the 'empty vessels' model of training in organisations, rooted in the old command–control paradigm: one party – the expert – is the fount of knowledge that the other party – the learner – receives in order to fill the gaps in their learning. No matter how imaginative, sensitive and participative may be the organisation, design, delivery and evaluation of learning events and assessment of learners, it is the trainer who remains firmly in the driving seat.

Key tasks for the trainer as driver are:

- Identify and analyse the tasks that the learner must master, breaking each down into core elements of knowledge, skill and attitudes (KSA). Then analyse each core element in detail to identify the set of responses that its effective and efficient performance requires.

- Design the curriculum so that sets of desired responses are arranged in a sequence, from simplest to more complex. Once the first set has been mastered by the learner it must be combined with the next, and so on, until through this cumulative learning process all sets have been mastered and a whole new pattern of behaviour emerges.

- Set concise KSA objectives for each stage of the learning programme and determine appropriate methods of assessment for the trainer to be applied, related to those objectives, both during (formative) and at the end of (summative) the learning event.

- When the learner achieves 'correct' responses, ensure that these are reinforced in order to embed them, using practice, feedback and other forms of reward.

- When the learner produces 'incorrect' responses, ensure either that these are 'punished' before they have a chance of becoming habitual (for example, by withholding rewards) or that they are 'negatively reinforced' through supportive actions that encourage the individual to abandon them and try harder to learn the correct responses.

Is it here, then, in positivist theories, that the first definition at the start of this chapter fits in?

> Learning – a relatively permanent change in behaviour that occurs as a result of practice or experience.

In its emphasis on practice, yes. But its equal emphasis on experience provides the link to learning theories that differ profoundly from positivist approaches, as the next section will show.

REFLECTION

Consider a training or other formal learning event that you have experienced, based on 'trainer as driver' principles. How far did it succeed in achieving its stated objectives, and what do you think were both its strengths and its weaknesses as a learning vehicle?

THE AGE OF THE LEARNER

CHALLENGES TO POSITIVIST THEORIES OF LEARNING

Throughout the second half of the twentieth century, research into adult education and into the psychology and sociology of learning in the workplace began to place big question marks against the view, held both by behavioural and traditional cognitive theorists, that there is a separation between knowing and doing. This questioning in the academic and educational domains also made itself felt at practitioner level in industry, drawing attention to the fact that to train or teach is not necessarily to achieve learning. Only the learner can learn.

In the view of later cognitive theorists adults are not merely information processors. Their learning cannot be understood simply by reference to a type of 'input, conversion, output' system, largely or wholly governed by the application of reason. Making new information available to people – no matter how skilfully – will not necessarily change their base of knowledge, because each individual's learning process, mindset and perceptions of the world are unique and are also shaped by experience. Therefore people will always differ to some extent – and sometimes radically – in their responses to new information. Some will accept it, some disregard it; some will distort or misinterpret its intended meaning, some will not even notice it because their attention is elsewhere.

Most fundamentally of all, according to the body of theory called 'social constructivism', individuals construct their own learning through a social process.

THE LEARNER IN CONTEXT: SOCIAL CONSTRUCTIVISM THEORIES

The constructivist approach is often described as 'humanist' because it places the individual in the driving seat of learning, which it views as intimately shaped by the social relationships and culture that most directly influence the individual's values, beliefs and perceptions of the environment.

Knowles (1973), one of the leading experts in the field of adult learning, was a major influence on this new approach. He acknowledged the contribution that Piaget's theories made to constructivist learning theory, but because their base lay in research into child development he questioned their relevance for adult learning. His argument was that andragogy (the art and science of teaching the adult) differs significantly from pedagogy (the art and science of teaching the child) because adults have more to contribute to the learning of others and a richer foundation of experience to which to relate new experiences. They also possess a larger number of fixed habits and patterns of thought, and therefore tend to be less open-minded (Parr 2005).

Constructivist theories also owe much to the work of Kelly (1955), who proposed that we each create our own model of the world – our personal construct – and of others in it and our relationship to them; and that the construct is shaped as much by feelings, beliefs and values as by experience. Other leading researchers include Lave and Wenger (1991), who popularised the concept of 'situated learning' (see below), Sternberg (1994) and Vygotsky (1978), one of the first to direct attention in research away from a preoccupation with what is learnt to the ways in which learning capability can be developed through the learning process (Matthews and Candy 1999: 51). By proposing that learning is 'a collective activity in which the focus is on asking questions and engaging in dialogue' (Schuck 1996: 200) researchers like these have extended definitions of learning to include group and organisational levels. I will discuss those levels further in the next chapter.

A central concept in constructivism is what Vygotsky (1978) has called the 'zone of proximal development'. This refers to a context where learners are challenged near to, but slightly above, their current level of development. The successful completion of each challenging task gives them the self-confidence and motivation to move on to the next, more complex challenge. Lave and Wenger (1991) produced a similar concept of 'legitimate peripheral participation'.

It is not only learning but also expertise that, when viewed through constructivist eyes, has a 'relational, embedded, competent, reciprocal and pertinent nature' (Garrick 1999: 224, drawing on Billett 1998). 'Pertinent' here means knowing what problem solutions are feasible and acceptable in the particular circumstances.

So it is here, then, in constructivist theory, that the second of this chapter's initial definitions of learning fits in:

> Learning: a qualitative change in a person's way of seeing, experiencing, understanding, conceptualising something in the real world.

COMMUNITIES OF PRACTICE

The 'situational' approach (another way in which theories of social constructivism are described) reflects the belief of the educationalist John Dewey (1916) that individual experience is the core of knowledge. Reflection on past experience in the light of new experience is the means whereby new understanding develops and new knowledge is formed. Competency, in this light, is the capacity to perform in a context, and 'reflective practice' (to which I will return in the next chapter) is crucial to its development. Such practice, derived from Schon's (1983) work on professional practice has been defined as (Hunt 2005: 234, 235):

> A conscious act ... with the intention of finding out more about our own learning processes and how they affect our professional practice and working relationships.

The situational approach stresses the significance of learning in authentic settings like workplaces where learning is also social in orientation. In Chapter 1 I referred to 'communities of practice' and their role in building social capital and organisationally valuable knowledge. That concept too is central to the situational approach (Lave and Wenger 1991; Greeno 1997). It represents (Tennant 1999: 173).

> A community engaged in a common set of tasks, with its associated stories, traditions and ways of working.

Two influential studies that supported this view of learning were reported by Eraut *et al* (1998) and by Zemke (1985), both quoted by Stern and Sommerlad (1999: 69) in their important review:

- Zemke in a study in the Honeywell company found that 50% of the ways in which managers learnt to manage came from challenging job experiences, 30% from relationships with others in the organisation, and only 20% from training.

- In similar vein, Eraut's researchers found that the two modes of non-formal learning reported as important by nearly all respondents in their study of technical and professional personnel were learning from the challenge of the work itself, and learning from other people.

An expanding body of literature now points to the crucial importance of the social basis of learning. Whereas psychological investigations of learning that have produced positivist learning theories focus largely on the individual as the unit of analysis (Matthews and Candy 1999: 50), humanist approaches rest on social sciences research focused primarily on the social relationships that influence individual learning. This focus has many educational implications. For example, whereas traditional learning theories point to the need to teach learners abstract concepts before, and distinct from, the context in which they are to be applied, situational theories emphasise the opposite: training, education and practical learning that is fully integrated (Gonczi 1999: 184).

CASE EXAMPLE

WORK-BASED LEARNING METHODS AT BIRMINGHAM CITY COUNCIL

A senior management development programme run by Birmingham City Council for some years involved a range of established learning methods including visits to other organisations, work shadowing and mentoring. What was unusual, however, was the lack of any classroom-based component. Instead, participants had to set their own goals for learning and then find largely work-based ways to meet them. The MD centre manager explained:

> Had we gone for a more traditional approach, the content would already be out of date. By using a self-managed learning approach, each senior manager creates their

own programme that responds to needs that are relevant to both them and the Council.

Not all participants welcomed the idea, which was met with a degree of uncertainty and scepticism. However the results of the course showed 'dramatic improvement in their ability to influence others, manage change, work in teams and think strategically (Cunningham 2004: 38). It also enabled deep learning that helped participants better understand and cope with the current complexity and uncertainty in local government.

Source: Cunningham, I. (2004)
People Management, 8 April

Such an approach calls, of course, for very skilful facilitation and support by L&D practitioners. It is a form of what is called 'cognitive apprenticeship' which I will explain in the next chapter.

The close association of constructivist theories with a 'learning by doing' approach does not exclude the classroom (actual or virtual) as an effective learning domain. As a Korean case shows (Kim 2005), that approach can be followed there by gearing the learning environment and process closely to the required real-life context. The facilitator's role involves agreeing a goal-oriented learning contract with the learners, providing sufficient structure, direction and expertise to give them confidence and ensuring challenging learning activities that will help them take increasing control over the learning process. The facilitator must also provide regularly throughout the classroom period and at its end clear routes for effective transfer of learning.

CHALLENGES TO SITUATIONAL THEORIES OF LEARNING

Let us stop at this point to critically examine assumptions that lie at the heart of constructivist learning theory.

REFLECTION

Situational theory rests on the belief that (Boud *et al* 1993: 8–14):

- Experience is the foundation of, and stimulus for, learning.

- Learners actively construct their own experience.

- Learning is a holistic experience.

- Learning is socially and culturally constructed.

- Learning is influenced by the socio-emotional context in which it occurs.

Before reading on, what tensions can you identify between some of these assumptions?

There are powerful inherent tensions between several of the assumptions shown above – particularly between the second and the fourth (Garrick 1999: 220). Consider the following:

- What if the individual learner's 'experience' referred to in the first assumption is one that has led to their reduced trust in their 'community of practice' and to lack of commitment to its goals?

- In many learning situations it is impossible to let learners move entirely at their own pace, or to determine what the content of learning should be, if they have not yet gained the knowledge or experience to do so (Wiltshire 2005).

- There are many different types of knowledge. Some concern specific procedures, formulae, routines and techniques required to solve a problem or act appropriately in a situation; others relate to academic theory and conceptual models; others are about values, behaviours and practical competencies of various kinds. Not all are equally easily or effectively developed along the lines suggested by the five assumptions.

- What about failure to learn? It can leave learners blaming themselves, or being blamed by others (Wiltshire 2005).

- How can assessment of learning in the workplace be organised so that it incorporates inputs from the learners but also remains rigorous and valid?

These tensions increase when learning is located in a workplace community of practice, and today in many organisations a variety of workplace training and learning processes are being put in place to resolve them. I will expand on these in the next chapter. Suffice to say here that there are no easy or clear answers to the questions posed above because in its fundamental premise constructivist theory hits the nail on the head: it all comes back to context. After a review of relevant research Harrison and Kessels (2003: 225) concluded:

> Study after study points to the impact of organisational context. Where top management's vision and values ... and ... management actions, work practices and HR processes at all organisational levels ... recognise the new importance of workplace learning, then a culture of learning is likely to develop and be sustained.

SITUATED LEARNING: THE TRAINER/FACILITATOR

The need for workplace learning to bring benefits for the business as well as individuals and groups draws attention once again to the skills, behaviours and values that trainers need to acquire if they are to become effective facilitators of learning. Pickard (2006a: 36–7) describes the case of the UK's Department for Work and Pensions where, as the first step in a 'revolution' from training to learning, an experiential learning project was designed to develop the trainers, in order through that process to ensure a change in their function's culture. The project was successful in building a community of practice in that function, transforming its practitioners into agents of change. Their experience of a learner-centred approach stimulated and enabled them to cascade it to line managers who, in turn, began to adopt it in their workplaces.

In situated learning the facilitator's role calls for a demanding skill set because:

- The facilitator's own culture, values and background will become part of the learners' context and so will have a significant influence on the learning process. That influence must be a positive one, developing trust between facilitator and learners.

- Since learning is a social process, facilitator and learners must tackle challenging activities together and engage in reflective practice that leads to a mutual development of learning capability.

- The facilitator must strike a balance between directing the learning process sufficiently to ensure that it serves the goals of the business, and focusing on learning activities that will help learners to gain the confidence, ability and autonomy to increasingly direct and manage their own learning. Such facilitation should be assessed and rewarded (Schuck 1996: 267).

- When assessing learning, there should be a shift away from formal measurement dominated by the trainer to assessment as a continuous and interactive process, built into the learning process (Gredler 1997). It must be supportive and confidence-building so that it stimulates learners' further development (Holt and Willard-Holt 2000).

THE AGE OF THE UNIVERSAL KNOWLEDGE WORKER?

LEARNING IN A KNOWLEDGE ECONOMY

So far in this chapter the discussion has focused on the nature of the learning process. This section raises the implications for learning and the learners of the emergence of a knowledge economy: a theme that will be taken further in the next chapter.

The consequences of the 'dizzying pace' of technological change in the past few decades have included an information-rich, computation-rich, and communications-rich organisational environment (Bettis and Hitt 1995) and, alongside and interacting with it, a heightened level of knowledge intensity. In the new economy knowledge unlocks wealth, because its application adds more value than the traditional factors of capital, raw materials and labour.

Globalisation is a key factor here. In the context of this discussion it is a process directly linked with the Internet and the pricing and information revolution that the net has made possible. Through the World Wide Web buyers and sellers can come together naturally, speedily and continuously. Companies must quickly learn how to co-create value with customers who have access to information on a global scale and who can rapidly and easily compare experiences. They can experiment with and develop products, and so have an unprecedented influence on value creation (Prahalad and Ramaswamy 2002). Sometimes through their purchasing power they can force fundamental changes in organisations' choice of suppliers and in their ethical stance. Consider, for example, the growing success of the Fair Trade movement, or the extent to which retailers like Marks & Spencer, Tesco and Sainsbury's have 'gone green' in order to keep and expand their customer base.

To make progress in a knowledge economy, organisations must regularly innovate as old knowledge that is vested in current products, processes, services and brands falls quickly out of date. Organisational boundaries become blurred through the development of new cross-boundary webs of alliances, partnerships, supply chains and joint ventures that provide access to far greater resource and knowledge than any single organisation can hope to acquire (Whittington *et al* 2002: 483).

In 2005, in this book's 4th edition, I commented that restructuring was no longer an infrequent activity whose outcome was a stable form of organisation design. It was a recurrent process, in which most organisations were involved around once every three years, sometimes more often. Now, for many organisations that process has become almost continuous. In like manner business strategy can no longer be cast in stone. Organisations must be able to produce new strategic responses as soon as old recipes become obsolete. 'Continuous strategising' rather than 'producing the strategy' is the appropriate way of describing the process whereby they regularly have to find new ways of doing new things, adapt with little warning to the complex and the unfamiliar and sometimes adopt quite new business goals (Whittington and Mayer 2002).

The two-fold flexibility that organising and strategising involves rests on organisations' ability to guide and facilitate continuous individual and collective learning and knowledge creation (Sanchez 1995; Eisenhardt and Santos 2002). And this is where the third definition of learning given at the start of this chapter comes in:

> Learning – the heart of productive activity. To put it simply, learning is the new form of labor.

Zuboff was referring here to learning as the source of knowledge that can enable organisations to continually do new things in new ways, as well as customary things better, to continuously improve and also to radically innovate in goods, processes and services. One term for such organisations is that they are knowledge-productive (Kessels 1996). In other words they have the capability to rapidly generate, disseminate and apply knowledge that ensures continuous improvement and regular innovation throughout their value chains. (For more discussion of the organisation's value chain, see Chapter 14.)

This focus on knowledge productivity requires all employees to become knowledge-creative. In knowledge-intensive firms such as consultancies, R&D institutions and software businesses, employers give unique status to their specialist knowledge workers, described by Peter Drucker in 1993 as those with high levels of education and specialist skills combined with the ability to apply these skills to identify and solve problems. But in an economy where knowledge creation is a task for all organisations, all organisational members possess uniquely valuable knowledge – especially of the tacit kind. Given the opportunity and incentive, all can become valuable knowledge workers. That is why I call the final age covered in this chapter that of the universal knowledge worker.

CONSTRUCTIVIST THEORY AND NOTIONS OF KNOWLEDGE

I have already explained that in the constructivist view knowledge is not a type of commodity to be captured 'out there' and brought 'in here' to transfer from experts to learners in a systematic way. Rather, 'knowing' is both a product and a process. It is an ever-changing outcome of learning and is itself a stimulus to ongoing learning as our past and present knowledge interacts with that held by others with whom we associate. It is about relational and emotional as well as rational processes, and is influenced by social as well as psychological factors (Daft and Weick 1984; Gioia and Sims 1986). Both practical and social competencies are crucial in explaining intelligence and 'contextually appropriate behaviour' (Ginsberg 1994: 155). The basic principles here are by no means new. They go back at least to Kant (1781), if not further (Kim 2005).

The following definition summarises this interrelationship of learning and knowledge processes (Greeno *et al* 1993: 100, cited by Tennant: 174):

> Knowing is the ability to interact with things and other people in a situation, and learning is an improvement in that ability … that is getting better at participating in a situated activity.

THE EMPLOYEE AS KNOWLEDGE WORKER: TASKS FOR THE L&D PROFESSIONAL

Any transition from an 'age of the learner' to an 'age of the universal knowledge worker' will involve a transformational change for most organisations in their vision and values, structure, culture and core competencies. In Chapter 6 I will discuss in greater detail the issues that raises for learners, management and leadership in an organisation. At this point, it is relevant simply to note that L&D professionals will need to help their organisations and individual learners to make that shift by:

- raising awareness across their organisations of the need for a learning culture that promotes knowledge productivity

- identifying and advising on barriers to the development of such a culture and how they can be tackled

- helping to develop social capital through expanding learning capacity within small groups in the workplace, and through contributing to policies and practices that build organisational commitment, trust and engagement amongst employees

- developing the competence and motivation of leaders, managers and team leaders to promote learning that leads to knowledge creation in the workplace

- working to ensure that L&D resources are focused not just on 'key' personnel but also on all an organisation's knowledge workers, especially those at the lower-skilled levels who in the past have customarily received little support from managers in their learning and development

- harnessing new information and communication technologies (ICT) to the knowledge process.

The next section expands on that last and vital point.

REFLECTION

Reflecting on this section of the chapter, how far do you think it is important for your organisation to invest in learning approaches that could start to transform its employees into 'universal knowledge workers'? And what aids and barriers might there be to the success of such an investment?

ADVANCES IN LEARNING TECHNOLOGY

THE IMPACT OF NEW INFORMATION AND COMMUNICATION TECHNOLOGY

Learning technology has changed out of all recognition since the pioneering days of the early twentieth century, but before outlining how that has happened it is important to clarify the meaning of that word 'technology'. I define it as:

> Technology – the particular way in which, in a workplace, technical systems, machinery and processes are designed to interact with human skill and knowledge in order to convert inputs into outputs.

From the 1960s on, computers played an increasingly important part in the technology of training. Initially, designers moved from a dependence on paper-bound materials such as the Kazmier manual I mentioned earlier in this chapter to the production of computerised programs that offered the individual control over a greater variety of simulated learning situations, more rapid and involving feedback systems and an altogether more imaginative self-paced learning experience. The basic principle that drove the technology was still that of stimulus-response theory, but expressed in a more subtle and user-friendly mode.

Today, in the so-called post-Fordist workplace, new ICT has brought together electronically-based hardware, human skills and knowledge in unique ways that enable individuals to quickly and easily access information as and when they need it. Since being opened up to the public in 1992, the World Wide Web has developed into an extraordinary powerful vehicle for learning and knowledge. As Lymer (1996) observed, it is not just a tool to provide access to existing data in more flexible, user-friendly, timely ways. It changes the way new information is generated by offering users a new medium through which to exchange ideas, formulate proposals and generate solutions in ways not previously possible. Joy Matthews *et al* (2004: 126–7) identified five examples:

- *synchronous communication* – takes place in real time and relies on the use of bandwidth to carry images and sound – eg chatrooms and webcam conferences

- *asynchronous communication* – takes place with a time delay – eg emails, bulletin boards

- *use of learning objects* – bite-sized chunks of learning material

- *web-based training* – learning packages available on the Web

- *support from a learning management system* – a system that enables the management of the process of learning and development, from skills analysis to learner assessment and feedback.

An ICT-enhanced workplace offers an environment for thinking and problem-solving in which the employee's role can be (Schuck 1996: 199):

> not only to push buttons to control processes, but also to use the information generated by the technology to 'push the business' – to redefine process variables, to improve quality, and to reduce costs.

In such an environment, the intelligence of employees can expand until it exceeds that of the software with which they interact. These smart workers can become knowledge workers by applying knowledge gained in the course of their work and through ICT-aided self-directed learning to continuous improvement and to innovation.

USING ICT AS A LEARNING DRIVER

Given its dominance, the crucial question now is not whether, but how, we make best use of ICT to drive learning in our own organisation (Harrison and Kessels 2003: Chapter 11). The following are essential guidelines:

- There must be the shared vision and purpose, the leadership and management, the workplace environment and the human resource strategies that recognise and support the change.

- E-learning must be driven by learning needs rather than by any technological imperative. It should be delivered in support of needs recognised across the organisation, with appropriate structures to support it, learners who are motivated to learn and who have good IT skills (CIPD 2004a).

- There must be adequate capital expenditure and the operational infrastructure to support ICT applications.

- A one-size fits all approach will not be successful. Research evidence suggests that the best way forward is to have a series of small-scale experiments, frequently reviewed, in a structure in which success is followed up and failure is used to aid future design (CIPD 2004a).

- Research also points to the need for blended learning solutions that include varying levels of e-learning adapted to suit a variety of learning contexts. The real challenge here is to give more control to the learners over the whole learning process while ensuring that they are equipped to handle that shift and are motivated to do so (CIPD 2004a).

- Online learning involves accessing much wider groups of people than is customary in traditional training situations. E-learning facilitators must therefore be competent in working cross-culturally and in building on diversity.

- Facilitators and managers must be skilled in motivating learners and have an informed knowledge of what stimulates or hinders them in an e-learning process. In the late 1990s Lloyds TSB had 450 learning centres in the UK. Researchers found some regions much better than others in achieving enthusiasm among employees for computer-based training. This was mainly because local training administrators and line managers were supportive, proactive and imaginative in their approach to learners and the learning experience (Hills and Francis 1999). It is particularly important that e-learning does not carry the image of a solitary and demotivating experience. More sophisticated technology can avoid the problems that led in early days to such an image.

BP is one company that has invested heavily to meet these requirements as the example overleaf shows. Yet we must be cautious here. BP is a leader in the field of L&D practice but there is a long way to go before any such transformation occurs in most organisations. The CIPD's 2008 annual L&D Survey (CIPD 2008a) raised even more doubts than its 2007 survey concerning the effective practice of e-learning in organisations. Over half of the 729 respondents reported that their organisations used it but only 7% ranked it in their top three most effective training practices. Coaching by line managers and in-house development programmes were rated much higher. Nearly all the respondents believed that e-learning is more effective when combined with other forms of learning. This raises the question, why is it not being so combined in their organisations?

In his travels to explore L&D practice in a variety of contexts across the world, Sloman (2007b) concluded that the progress of e-learning has been 'gradual rather than spectacular' in organisations, with the greatest advances being made in the USA. He sees its current state as one concerned with developing best practice after initial stages of excessive hype followed by the identification of critical issues (Sloman 2007b: 177). His concern following the CIPD's 2008 L&D Survey is that far too much e-learning is driven by IT departments, far too little specifically tailored by HR staff to meet the needs of learners (Sloman 2008a).

CASE EXAMPLE

ICT-DRIVEN LEARNING AT BP

In his article, Reynolds (2002) describes one of BP's goals as being the introduction of services that allow the individual, group or network of employees in a workplace to take charge of their own learning through 'an appropriate mix of inputs and outputs, individual and collaborative study, formal and informal processes, and a blend of face-to-face and virtual contact'. The idea is to provide a 'rich set of options' in terms not only of the ways in which individuals choose to learn, but of what and why they wish to learn.

Reynolds clarifies the spectrum that can be involved here for employees, extending from fully supported learning with clear learning objectives at one extreme to a self-initiated knowledge-creating process at the other. The three applications of e-learning that he identifies as aiding this are:

- *web-based training*, where content is delivered to the learner without significant interaction or support – a throwback, in other words, to the age of the trainer and to what is basically a stimulus-response conditioning process although still useful for certain purposes

- *supported online learning*, where the learner 'interacts intensively, supported by content as appropriate' – typifying the kind of activity involved in an age where control over the pace, place and timing of the learning process is moving significantly from trainers to learners, but where trainers still play leading albeit more design-focused, facilitative and supportive roles in the learning process

- *informal e-learning*, where learning occurs through self-directed communication, information retrieval and co-operation between peers during the normal course of work. It is this type of learning that has the potential to transform learners into their organisation's knowledge workers. In Reynolds' words, it marks a 'move beyond the replacement of conventional courses into richer and more fertile learning domains'.

Source: Reynolds, J. (2002)
People Management, 4 April

SHIFT OR NO SHIFT?

FINDING THE EVIDENCE

Within the space of a few generations we seem to have moved from an age where, in organisations, 'learning' was treated as a *planned event*, dominated by training, through an age where attention shifted to learning as a *social process* dominated by

TABLE 6 Summary of some key findings from the CIPD 2008 annual Learning and Development Survey

---

- For the first time in three years on-the-job training was not identified by respondents as the most effective way to learn, but it remained widely popular (43%). Its lower rating was probably caused more by the introduction of new items into the questionnaire than by any reduced shift in preference.

- In-house programmes were rated highest (55%) with 61% of respondents also saying that they used these types of programmes more regularly than two years ago.

- Coaching came second (53%), thereby regaining almost all the ground it had temporarily lost in the 2007 survey. It 'appears to be the shining star of the portfolio, with seven in ten believing it to be an effective tool' (CIPD 2008a: 27).

- 62% of respondents identified efforts to develop an L&D culture in their organisations. 60% recorded new approaches to identifying individual training needs, with some evidence of rather more involvement now of employees/learners in determining L&D needs of the organisation as a whole.

- Management development approaches were placing greater emphasis on learning through projects, and with and from peers.

- 72% of respondents reported that over the past two years there had been a growth in new programmes to develop the role of line managers – the most significant new practice to emerge from the survey.

Source: Chartered Institute of Personnel and Development (2008a)

workplace context, to a potentially transformative new age where learning, work and knowledge can become an *integrated activity*.

But is this really the case? 729 out of 5,000 CIPD members in senior L&D-related positions in organisations across all sectors responded to the CIPD's 2008 annual survey of current and emerging trends and issues in the L&D field. Some of their comments have a particular relevance to claims of a shift from planned to learner-led approaches to learning in organisations today, amongst them those outlined in Table 6.

The findings outlined in Table 6 could be interpreted as signs of a real shift from a trainer-led to a more learner-led approach to learning. But they are ambiguous, because they could equally be symptomatic of what respondents to the 2008 survey forecast as the most important change likely to affect L&D in organisations in the coming five years – the drive for a closer integration of L&D activity and business strategy (68%). In-house, tailored training and coaching all aid such integration without necessarily bringing with them any real attempt to put learners in the driving seat of an organisation's L&D process, let alone transforming them into a community of knowledge workers.

Finally, the sustained popularity of coaching does not appear to reflect any genuine recognition of the importance of reflective practice or of learning located in communities of practice. On the contrary, most coaching reported in the 2008 survey was carried out by line managers coaching those reporting to them – thereby setting up potentially powerful tensions at the heart of the coaching relationship that Howe explains in detail (Howe 2008a: 18); and a high proportion used it for remedial purposes (74% overall, rising to 80% in the private sector). Furthermore a quarter of respondents said that coaching had no link with the overall L&D strategy in their organisation, being considered as a stand-alone process, and only 12% found coaching 'very effective' (*ibid*). Such data suggest that if there is any 'shift to learners' in UK-based organisations it is slow and conservative.

In this chapter I have examined from a variety of perspectives the claim that in the past decade or so organisations have been experiencing a significant shift from an age of the trainer to one of the learner – possibly, even, of the learner as knowledge worker. At its end there remain many unanswered questions. That also reflects the state of research into the psychology and sociology of learning, and into notions of learning, knowing and knowledge creation in the workplace. No clear consensus on any of the big issues has yet emerged. Perhaps it can never be achieved. With each scientific advance we seem to know more yet understand less about the human condition. What are the roots of human learning and knowledge? How far and in what ways can that learning be managed, directed, made productive for the organisation? What part does it play in determining an individual's performance at work? Is there such a thing as collective or organisational learning? And how far might that link to organisational performance?

In the next chapter I will explore further issues to do with the workplace as a source of individual and collective learning, with the development of knowledge-creating organisations, and with challenges that these issues raise for the L&D profession.

 REFLECTION

How far, if at all, in your own organisation, do you see evidence of a shift from 'the age of the trainer' either to 'the age of the learner' or to 'the age of the universal knowledge worker'? Reflecting on concepts and issues in this chapter, what reasons do they suggest for this shift, or for the lack of it?

CONCLUSION

This chapter has sought to identify whether a gradual shift has been occurring in recent years from trainers to learners as prime controllers of learning and knowledge in the workplace. You will find review questions related to the chapter's content in Appendix 3.

Main themes covered in the chapter's five sections have related to:

- an increased awareness now in organisations of theories of learning that emphasise the role of experience and of social interactions in the learning process, and that cast doubt on the validity of the traditional trainer-dominated approach to planned learning

- alongside this, a changing business environment featuring rapid technological advance, the emergence of a new and globalising knowledge economy, and a growing emphasis on organising and strategising as key processes for business organisations. It is only through these processes that an organisation can learn faster, more regularly create and apply new knowledge to continuous improvement and innovation, and quickly redeploy its internal resources in order to collaborate and compete effectively in turbulent conditions

- a consequent possible but very gradual shift in most organisations to pass more control over the learning process to the individual learner, and a parallel need for trainers and managers to take on facilitative learning roles

- the powerful potential – not yet realised – for ICT to accelerate a shift from trainers to learners, and beyond that to enable the transformation of learners into knowledge workers, and the tasks here for L&D professionals

- the requirement this raises for e-learning strategy to become an integral part of business strategy and to be fully supported by people management and development and ICT strategies and practices.

FURTHER INFORMATION SOURCES

Harrison, R. and Kessels, J. (2003) *HRD in a Knowledge Economy: An organisational view*. Basingstoke: Palgrave Macmillan

Holmes, B., Tangney, B., Fitzgibbon, A. and Savage, T. (2001) 'Communal Constructivism: Students constructing learning *for* as well as *with* others'. In *Proceedings of 12th Society for Information Technology and Teacher Education International Conference*. Orlando, Florida, 5–10 March. Case-based account proposing a new kind of educational theory that moves beyond social constructivism, building on the contribution advanced ICTs can make to teaching and learning environments

Sloman, M. (2007b) *The Changing World of the Trainer: Emerging good practice*. London: CIPD. Essential reading to complement this chapter, with case examples drawn from across the world

http://www.cipd.co.uk/tools/ [accessed 14 March 2008]. Online tool: *Training to Learning: Supporting, accelerating and directing learning in your organisation*

http://www.trainingzone.co.uk/ [accessed 13 March 2008]. Online community of practice of 35,000 training and HR professionals

CIPD podcast, 1 May 2007: *Learning and Development*. Available online at: http://www.cipd.co.uk/podcasts [accessed 25 March 2008]

EXPLORE FURTHER

CHAPTER 5

Promoting Workplace Learning and Knowledge

INTRODUCTION

> The [truly successful] organization is a learning institution, and one of its principal purposes is the expansion of knowledge ... that comes to reside at the core of what it means to be productive. Learning is the heart of productive activity. To put it simply, learning is the new form of labor.

> (Zuboff 1998: 395)

This completion of the quote that came at the start of Chapter 4 makes it highly relevant for this chapter. In a knowledge economy the learning employees achieve in the workplace, the knowledge that flows from that, and the extent to which that knowledge is shared across the organisation to be successfully applied to continuous improvement and radical innovation can build unique organisational capabilities.

However, behind these apparently straightforward statements lies uncertainty. In the previous chapter I noted the concept of knowledge as both a product and a process of learning. But that is only one view. In reality notions of knowledge and its links to individual and collective learning are widely debated and emerge from a bewildering variety of theories. There are innumerable classification systems, models and concepts, many of which overlap or are interpreted in differing ways whether by theorists or by practitioners. Workplace learning and knowledge theory has a multi-disciplinary base and there are no clear-cut boundaries between the various schools of thought, nor is it invariably the case that the most meaningful theories are those produced most recently. We may have more information about 'knowledge' now, but that does not necessarily mean that we understand it any better than we did decades ago.

Within the constraints of a single five-part chapter all that I can attempt is an overview. My starting point is a more detailed look at workplace learning, some problematic issues that are raised by its theory and practice, and a new framework to aid its analysis and improvement in an organisation. The second section queries concepts of 'organisational learning' and the 'learning organisation' and suggests practical starting points for building a learning culture. The third links workplace learning to knowledge creation that adds individual and organisational value, and the fourth and fifth draw on international research to identify 'knowledge management' challenges and tasks for organisational leaders, managers and HR/ L&D professionals.

ISSUES IN WORKPLACE LEARNING

HELPING THE NOVICE LEARNER

As we saw in Chapter 4, one of the values of workplace learning is the way it can shift the locus of control over the learning process from the trainer to the learner. One issue here is how best, in a workplace setting, to help those new to a task, job or role to develop learning strategies that will enable them to reach the required standard of competence and also to enhance their personal learning capability. Coaching and mentoring are two examples of the kind of help that can be provided, and I will discuss each in more detail in the next chapter.

Smith and Sadler-Smith (2006: 45) refer to the use of 'cognitive apprenticeship' for all novice learners, not just those in a formal apprenticeship role. This term refers to giving the novice the tasks that he or she needs to learn, with experts supplying the 'scaffolding' needed to carry out those tasks. Scaffolding in this sense refers to the facilitation, encouragement, feedback and assessment needed by novices as they move successfully through the learning process. Scaffolding can be gradually reduced and finally withdrawn as the learner gains mastery over the tasks.

The experiential learning cycle

Cognitive apprenticeship revolves around learning from experience, a concept derived most directly from the work of Kolb (1984) whose 'learning cycle' is outlined in Figure 6. Its true roots lie in the work of John Dewey, the American philosopher and educationalist and in his time the foremost exponent of 'experiential education' programmes and experiments.

FIGURE 6 The experiential cycle of learning (based on Kolb, Rubin and McIntyre, 1974)

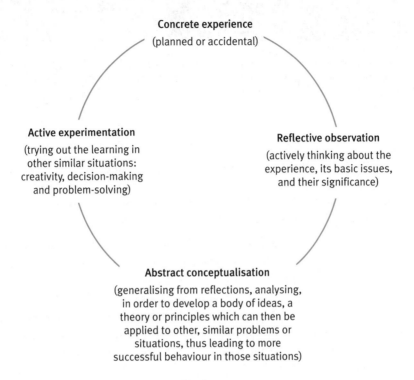

Concrete experience
(planned or accidental)

Active experimentation
(trying out the learning in
other similar situations:
creativity, decision-making
and problem-solving)

Reflective observation
(actively thinking about the
experience, its basic issues,
and their significance)

Abstract conceptualisation
(generalising from reflections, analysing,
in order to develop a body of ideas, a
theory or principles which can then be
applied to other, similar problems or
situations, thus leading to more
successful behaviour in those situations)

Honey and Mumford (1992) are among many who have built on this theory to inform training and learning design. Their learning styles inventory (LSI) identifies four main types of learner and of learning style – activist, reflector, analyst and pragmatist – and links them to the four stages of Kolb's learning cycle.

Despite the popularity of LSIs their validity has been disputed. Researchers at Newcastle University in the UK have reported on 13 (Coffield *et al* 2004). They found only one (by Allinson and Hayes 1996) gave statistically meaningful and consistent results. Amongst the researchers' concerns was the presentation of learning styles as relatively stable and genetically fixed, when there is much to suggest that individuals learn in quite flexible ways and may deliberately alter learning style to suit context. They advise that rather than being wedded to any one inventory it is better to encourage individuals to reflect on what they do, why they do it, how they see their learning and how they plan and monitor it.

Experiential learning theory has made a major contribution to training and learning practice, but it can lead to an overemphasis on the individual at the expense of the wider workplace, organisational and institutional contexts that powerfully shape their everyday experience at work and the knowledge that they seek to acquire through their learning.

REFLECTION

How useful or otherwise in practice do you think (or have you found) the concept of the experiential learning cycle to be? And how far do you support or reject criticisms of LSIs?

PROMOTING COMMUNITIES OF PRACTICE

We saw in Chapter 4 that through a process of 'asking questions and engaging in dialogue' within a community of practice individuals and teams can expand their own knowledge and also the knowledge base of the organisation (Schuck 1996: 200). Wenger *et al* (2002: 4) define communities of practice as:

> Groups of people who share a concern, a set of problems or a passion about a topic, and who deepen their knowledge and expertise in this area by interacting on an ongoing basis.

Such communities may evolve naturally through shared work activities, processes or workspace or they may be deliberately constructed. They will be 'composed of different people at different times, the interests of the [members] will change over time and the degree of peripherality of its members will also change' (Joy-Matthews *et al* 2004: 105).

The central learning process to enable a community of practice to fulfil the potential indicated in Wenger's description is reflective practice – a concept briefly mentioned in the previous chapter but which now needs to be examined in more detail.

Reflective practice

Reflective practice is 'a conscious act … with the intention of finding out more about our own learning processes and how they affect our professional practice and working relationships' (Hunt 2005: 234). The understanding gained from this should enable our practice to be 'simultaneously informed by and freed from what we have learnt so far' (*ibid*: 235). In other words, reflective practice is a way of ensuring that people become willing and motivated to subject their own 'taken for granted' and activities to serious scrutiny in order to learn from them and if necessary change (Johnston and Badley 1996: 10).

The concept of experiential learning is often thought to equate with that of 'reflective practice', but it is important to distinguish between reflection as a form of individual development and reflective practice in the wider sense of Hunt's definition. In that sense, Gray (2007) claims that it can stimulate collective learning and action and also become a component of organisational learning and change.

Hunt (2005: 241–3) points out that the historical roots of the reflective practice concept go back at least to the ideas and traditions of the Enlightenment – the eighteenth-century cultural movement that applied the insights of the seventeenth century Scientific Revolution in Europe to the broader fields of politics, science and the arts. Hunt summarises its core belief:

> human beings have the capacity to reflect rationally upon their own actions and to use the understanding thus derived as a basis for the personal change which is an importance element in social change.

However, the concept of 'reflective practice' applied to workplace learning is most strongly linked to Donald Schon's work on professional practice (Argyris and Schon 1974; Schon 1983). Schon, a philosopher by training, became famous for his contribution to the literature and practice of learning in organisations. He observed that in exhibiting skilful action people often appear to be drawing on information that they are subsequently unable to put into words, and that reflective practice, when implemented skilfully, can help to bring their 'tacit knowing' (Polanyi 1966) to the surface where it can be shared with others. Nonaka (1991) developed Polanyi's concept into the now well-known notion of knowledge as a two-dimensional process:

- *Tacit knowledge:* the knowledge that is embedded deep in the individual or collective subconscious, expressing itself in habitual or intuitive ways of doing things that are exercised without conscious thought or effort.

- *Explicit knowledge:* the knowledge that, once articulated, is written down, codified in protocols, guidelines, checklists, reports, memoranda, files, training courses or other tangible forms. At that point, it becomes a type of commodity, to be protected in patents and other legal formulae.

Schon researched the type of reflective practice now termed 'reflection-in-action' – that which takes place while work is ongoing. Beckett (1999: 90) suggests four straightforward questions (exemplified in Orr's 1990 study, already described in Chapter 1) that can aid this kind of reflection, helping to spread learning across a group or team by integrating thinking, feeling and doing in ways that lead from, and back into, actions:

- What are we doing?

- Why?

- What should we do next?

- How can we/I do better?

On the other hand 'reflection-on-action' takes place once work has been completed. In work organisations and particularly within management development programmes action learning has become the most widely known approach here (Revans 1982). It is a process of mutual learning within a small 'set' of individuals drawn either from the same or a number of different organisations. They come together to question and reflect on their perceptions of and reactions to complex work-based problems in order to aid action in the workplace and to develop self-knowledge and learning capability in the individual. A skilled facilitator aids the process for novices.

Reflective practice has become highly influential in some professions, especially nurse and teacher education, with a systematic approach being taken to its incorporation into all levels of training. However, Bright (1996) found its implementation to be fairly superficial, lacking evidence of any deep understanding of what it is, the processes and skills it involves, and its implications for practice. Hunt (2005) expressed a similar view, and found it hard to uncover any common practices related to the approach although some processes and techniques seem to have a generalised relevance. These include:

- critical incident technique, as used in job analysis

- reflective writing and journal-keeping

- story-telling

- auditing good practices

- reflective and reflexive conversation (reflexive practice is the process of understanding what has been learned about one's own learning through reflection and then putting it into practice)

- repertory grids

- concept mapping.

Critical reflection is not a process that comes naturally to many (Hunt 2005). Skilled practitioners in any field are unlikely to reflect in action through the medium of words and most of the time the majority do not question what they do. Therefore they may have to be taught or helped to reflect, whether in a formal classroom context or through processes such as coaching, mentoring and action learning (Gray 2007). Hunt concluded that because there are no clear working definitions, main objectives, processes or competencies for reflective practice there are difficulties in pursuing it with peers, in facilitating it for others and in assessing it.

There are also concerns about action learning, despite its many enthusiastic adherents across the world. Wallace (1990) observed from his review that:

> The approach has rarely been examined for the coherence of its principles, rigorously evaluated, or compared with evidence from elsewhere about how professionals learn to improve their job performance.

My own literature review led to a similar conclusion. I found the concept to have a poorly tested evidence base, and identified wide variations in the way it is interpreted and implemented, as well as high costs associated with the practice that are rarely identified in the literature or in the field (Harrison 1996).

REFLECTION

Can you call to mind any managers or HR professionals in your own organisation who understand and promote reflective practice in their teams? If so, what value seems to flow from it?

WORKPLACE LEARNING: A PROBLEMATIC TERRAIN?

I have noted in Chapter 2 that a Government consultation on informal adult learning was launched in January 2008 in England. The outcome will be of particular importance to a field judged by Clarke (2005) to suffer conceptually from a literature that fails to specify clearly the nature of workplace learning, and to lack any unified body of evidence to support claims for conditions constituting an effective learning climate. His research in the healthcare sector suggests that aspects of the workplace environment likely to be important in fostering such a climate will vary according to the types of learning outcomes that are desired. However, he found it hard if not impossible to determine from the literature how or why differing aspects of an organisation's learning environment should influence particular learning outcomes.

In Chapter 4 I noted that the tensions inherent in constructivist learning principles increase when that learning is located in a workplace community of practice. Garrick (1999: 226) identified various attempts often made to resolve these, including the development of on-site mentors, coaches and supervisors with educational skills. He recommended new approaches to performance appraisal and employee development together with:

- infrastructure support

- clearer 'educative' links between workplace supervisors and staff

- more 'educative' leadership roles

- more 'developmental' supervisory and managerial functions.

Whatever remedies are attempted, the tensions that can exist between 'learning for work' and 'work for learning' may remain, given the 'sheer complexity and diversity of factors that directly (and indirectly) shape one's learning including what counts in the workplace' (Garrick 1999: 226). Certainly in an organisation where those styled workers, managers, supervisors and educators all have different, sometimes conflicting, perceptions, power, values and focus related to 'what counts', it will be hard to develop any shared purpose relating to workplace learning goals and practice.

Tensions encompassing a range of philosophical, political, gender and ethical issues often surface within communities of practice, leading Solomon (1999) to describe the workplace as a 'problematic terrain' for learning. I will return to such views in Chapter 9, but the following are key points:

• Not all communities of practice will recognise that they have a collective responsibility towards the learning of all their members and potential members (Joy-Matthews *et al* 2004: 105).

• Some communities 'can harbour various kinds of conflict, especially as members compete for power' (*ibid*).

The knowledge secured through learning that is situated in one community of practice may not be transferable into other workplaces whether within the same organisation or across its boundaries, because of differences in workplace cultures and social relationships.

REFLECTION

Reflecting on your own workplace – or one with which you are familiar – can you identify any tensions of the kind just described that make it a 'problematic terrain' for learning? If not, why do you think they are absent?

UNLEARNING, ADAPTIVE AND GENERATIVE LEARNING

Looking beyond tensions in the workplace setting to barriers that certain kinds of workplace learning can place in the path of organisational progress, one is of major significance in an external environment that increasingly requires organisations to be fast-adaptive and creative. It is that the learning that emerges from communities of practice in the workplace can bring success initially but after a time can lead to complacency. The development of increasing narrowness and rigidity in the ways in which organisational members see their world and make decisions about it then fosters 'skilled incompetence' (Argyris 1986). This describes a situation where once successful work teams or entire organisations rest on their success for too long, causing their strategies, skills, ways of thinking and behaving to become ever less appropriate in the face of new challenges. When failures start to occur, defensive behaviours can cause people to cling even more tenaciously to past routines and recipes, so that skills fall further out of date and creativity is blocked. The firm then loses competitive edge, dragged down by the weight of its past learning. The case example provides an illustration.

NORTHERN ROCK BUILDING SOCIETY, UK

In the summer of 2007 Northern Rock plc (NR), one of the UK's biggest banks and building societies, with its headquarters in Newcastle upon Tyne, still enjoyed its long-held reputation of outstanding success. Its young chief executive (CE) – Adam Applegarth, a local man and an MBA graduate from Durham University Business School – was widely held to be one of the banking system's brightest and best and its largely local board of directors included some of the most influential names in north east business and local society. By September 2007 its reputation was in ruins, and early in 2008 it was nationalised.

The full story is a complex one but in large part it concerns a once-successful business strategy that ultimately bred a fatal skilled incompetence at the top of the organisation.

Like many other high-street lenders, in an age of stable world financial markets NR had borrowed billions of pounds to expand its mortgage portfolio. Its decades of success, however, rested on a strategy that had one potentially fatal flaw: a borrowing at six times its own reserves, proportionately more than any other UK bank. So remote, however, did the CE and board of directors consider the likelihood of any external event that could fundamentally undermine this strategy that they kept it firmly in place long after they should have been reviewing its validity. So throughout most of 2007, when signs of cracks had begun

to appear in the world lending markets and other UK banks who had been pursuing a similar lending policy began to pull in their horns or change track, NR continued to offer mortgages of up to 125% of income on a wide scale.

In August 2007 the unthinkable occurred. As a result of the US sub-prime mortgage crisis, banks across the world began to reduce or stop their lending to each other and almost overnight NR was faced with a huge cash-flow problem. Its directors concluded that the way out would be a takeover, but early in September, following a week of complex negotiations behind the scenes between government, the Bank of England, NR and potential buyers, the society was left with only one way forward – to apply to the Bank of England for a £13 billion facility as lender of last resort.

Word immediately leaked out and over a single weekend caused panic amongst thousands of NR savers who, fearing their investments were at risk, began queuing outside the bank's branches across the UK to withdraw their money. The panic was on such an unprecedented scale that after a few days the Chancellor of the Exchequer had to announce that the Government would guarantee 100% of all deposits in the bank. By November the Bank of England had bailed out £24 billion of taxpayers' money to keep NR going and finally, early in 2008, NR was nationalised, bringing with it the likelihood that 144,000 small shareholders would see their investment wiped out and around 6,000 NR staff would lose their jobs following wholesale closure of NR branches across the country.

NR's outstanding record of past success and the city's praise for its 'whizz kid' leader had bred a fatal complacency in its chief executive and board of directors, causing them to become blind to any need for change until it was too late. Their skilled incompetence played a major part in a crisis whose ripple effects have extended far

beyond the bank's boundaries. Yet the incompetence was an institutional one as well, for the Financial Services Authority was to be criticised many months later for its own failure to adequately oversee NR's affairs and to draw the attention of the NR's board to the dangers of continuing with its lending strategy. Just over a year later, of course, exactly the same skilled incompetence largely explained the disastrous collapse of Lehman Brothers, one of the biggest, oldest and most prestigious of US banks, and the global economic crisis that swiftly followed.

This case raises a key concept: that of unlearning. 'Relearning' is a familiar term that refers to the need to transfer old learning to new contexts, and to make the necessary physical, mental and social adjustments that this process involves. Its significance in relation to all types of change situation is clear and in consequence it receives much attention in organisational change programmes. Yet in the achievement of such change 'unlearning' is often of much greater importance. The process involves the removal of barriers to relearning and to new learning that are presented by previously acquired knowledge, skills, attitudes and cognitions. It can be one of exceptional difficulty when skilled incompetence is deeply embedded not only in the organisation but in its institutional context.

Double-loop learning is one way to achieve unlearning. It is a concept first formulated, along with single-loop learning, by Chris Argyris (1977) who subsequently developed it with Donald Schon in 1978. Single-loop learning only tackles the surface or stated symptoms of a problem. It is 'adaptive' (Senge 1990) or 'exploitive' (Snell 2005) in that it involves individuals and groups in responding to feedback, adjusting their behaviour continuously in relation to fixed goals, norms and assumptions so that the organisation becomes increasingly efficient and effective at achieving its current goals. Behaviour steadily improves in relation to required performance standards, without, however, fundamentally changing. Single-loop learning therefore has relevance for groups and organisations that can survive through time without any fundamental change of direction. Snell (2005: 41) provides the example of Toyota's continuous improvement and capability enhancement in automotive production, based on the capability to 'more deeply refine and manipulate' the firm's existing knowledge.

Double-loop learning, by contrast, is the outcome of probing to establish the fundamental causes of the problem – why did it arise in the first place? It represents a generative learning process (Senge 1990), known also as 'exploratory' learning (Snell 2005) whereby ultimately the very goals, norms and assumptions of the organisation itself must be open to questioning and the possibility of radical change. It is therefore essential where there is a need for creativity, innovation and transformation. Again, Snell (2005: 41) provides a useful example: Kodak's move beyond its traditional base in silver halide photography to pursue digital technology.

Not all researchers in the field of individual and organisational learning are convinced by the concepts of single- and double-loop learning. Some see them as too simplistic, ignoring the possibility of discontinuous, non-linear learning to explain the sudden leaps in understanding that result in people breaking out of customary ways of thinking and perceiving. However, the concepts undeniably have strong face validity – in simple terms, they 'feel right'!

A FRAMEWORK FOR IMPROVING WORKPLACE LEARNING

I have devoted considerable space to outlining the lack of a convincing evidence base to support many of the claims made in relation to workplace learning. What then is the way forward?

Many frameworks have been developed to improve workplace learning (see in particular Smith and Sadler-Smith 2006) but one carries particular conviction. It is the 'expansive-restrictive' framework designed by Evans and colleagues (2006) as one of over 60 projects supported by the UK's largest ever co-ordinated educational research initiative: the ESRCC's Teaching and Learning Research Programme. The Programme has enabled many of the UK's best researchers to work on the direct improvement of policy and practice to support learning, and so any project that it has sponsored carries real weight in the field.

The expansive-restrictive framework is explained in a small handbook (Evans *et al* 2006). Here, it is sufficient to outline the principles on which it is based and its key features.

The focus of the expansive-restrictive framework

The focus of the framework is workforce development, its specific aim being to enable the identification of features of the environment or work situation that influence the extent to which the workplace as a whole creates opportunities for, or barriers to, apprentice learning – that is to say, the learning of novices. However, 'all employees would … benefit from and contribute to [an] expansive environment' which will enhance the extent to which employees at all levels share their skills and knowledge and have access to learning opportunities within and beyond the workplace (*ibid*: 36).

The framework involves analysing the institutional as well as organisational and individual levels of activity that influence workplace learning and using the insights thus gained to inform subsequent decisions on action. This integrated, holistic approach remedies a fundamental weakness in much of the existing literature: its preoccupation with the characteristics of workplace learning as experienced by the learner. Some researchers do place emphasis on internal organisational context (see, for example, Ashton 2004; Billet *et al* 2004; Hodkinson and Hodkinson 2004) but generally there is a marked tendency to ignore or underplay the nature of the employment relationship and the external institutional context that contribute to its shape. We have just seen in the Northern Rock case the importance of that context. Key influences such as government politics, union pressure, and advances in the professional field are hardly considered, and tensions caused by plurality of interests and of powerplay between key actors within and outside the organisation are rarely explored (Poell and Tijmensen 1998).

A multi-level analytical approach

The starting point in the application of the expansive-restrictive framework is analysis of three 'scales' or levels of context that influence learning in the workplace (Evans *et al* 2006: 163):

- *The first level of context* is provided by macro-level social structures and social institutions, where the 'collective actors' include government, unions, professional bodies, sectoral and local level training and learning agencies and so on. I explained in Chapters 2 and 3 the importance for L&D in organisations of this level of context and will focus on it again, particularly in Chapter 10.

- *The second level of context* is that of the organisation. The researchers note that in most UK-based organisations workers' learning is not a priority and represents a 'third-order decision', usually with a short time-frame, following on from markets and competitive strategy (first) and strategies relating to work organisation and job design (second). Where it is a higher and longer-term priority there is more likelihood that HR professionals, managers and internal learning champions such as union learning representatives will be able to implement expansive learning principles in the workplace. Even in such cases, however, difficulties still exist, not least where, within an organisation, 'similar units may have very different cultures of learning'.

- *At the individual level* it is the immediate social context and personal characteristics, past experiences and dispositions of individuals that will influence the extent to which they take advantage of the opportunities afforded by their immediate work environment (ibid: 165).

Following analysis, decisions on action proceed by reference to key features whose presence signifies the existence of an expansive workplace learning environment or of one that restricts learning (see Figure 7). One conclusion reached by the research team is that while analysis will often identify a range of areas where action can

FIGURE 7 The expansive-restrictive continuum (applied to an 'Apprenticeship' context)

Approaches to Apprenticeship

EXPANSIVE	RESTRICTIVE
Participation in multiple communities of practice inside and outside the workplace	Restricted participation in multiple communities of practice
Primary community of practice has shared 'participative memory': Cultural inheritance of apprenticeship	Primary community of practice has little or no 'participative memory': no or little tradition of apprenticeship
Breadth: access to learning fostered by cross-company experiences built into programme	Narrow: access to learning restricted in terms of tasks/knowledge/location
Access to range of qualifications including knowledge-based vocational qualifications	Access to competence-based qualifications only
Planned time off the job including for college attendance and for reflection	Virtually all on the job; limited opportunities for reflection
Gradual transition to full participation	Fast: transition as quick as possible
Apprenticeship aim: rounded expert/full participant	Apprenticeship aim: partial expert/full participant
Post-apprenticeship vision: progression for career	Post-apprenticeship vision; static for job
Explicit institutional recognition of, and support for, apprentice's status as learner	Ambivalent institutional recognition of, and support for, apprentice's status as learner
Apprenticeship is used as a vehicle for aligning the goals of developing the individual and organisational capability	Apprenticeship is used to tailor individual capability to organisational need
Apprenticeship design fosters opportunities to extend identity through boundary-crossing	Apprenticeship design limits opportunity to extend identity; little boundary-crossing experienced
Reification of apprenticeship highly developed (eg, through documents, symbols, language, tools) and accessible to apprentices	Limited reification of apprenticeship, patchy access to reificatory aspects of practice

Reproduced from Evans, K., Hodkinson, P., Rainbird, H. and Unwin, L. (2006) *Improving Workplace Learning.* Abingdon:Taylor and Francis Books. Figure 2.1, p 34. With permission of the publishers.

fruitfully be carried out to enhance workplace learning, this will not always be the case. Sometimes it may reveal too many unfavourable features of wider context to make local action feasible or advisable at the particular point in time.

REFLECTION

Consider your own workplace – or one with which you are familiar – in the light of the expansive-restrictive framework of analysis. What insights does that exercise provide for you, and what practical recommendations about workplace learning would you make?

NOTIONS OF COLLECTIVE AND ORGANISATIONAL LEARNING

COLLECTIVE LEARNING: THE LITERATURE

A focus on learning as a social process has led to an increasing preoccupation in a wide range of literatures – notably those of business strategy, of learning theory, of organisational behaviour, of workplace learning and of knowledge management – with the firm as a complex social institution that enables collective or 'organisational' learning to occur both within and beyond its boundaries. Here are five of the most well-known views on such learning:

- For researchers Brown and Duguid (1991) it is the integration of working, learning and innovation that links workplace and organisational levels of knowledge so that an organisation evolves through the outcomes of 'competing perspectives of different communities of practice'. Much workplace knowledge is generated, held and applied collectively within these communities and their network within an organisation helps to produce the organisational capability to quickly make sense of and act upon a complex mass of data – an ability that is a vital key to competitive advantage.

- Victoria Marsick, well-known US academic in the field of organisational learning, equates it with an organisational capacity for growth, change and transformation. As a constructivist, she stresses team learning as the key 'since teams provide a minimum critical mass for more widely shared learning' (Marsick 1994: 16).

- For strategy authors Ghoshal and Bartlett (1994) as well as for many other constructivist theorists the interactive development of workplace context and management action is a key influence on collective learning and company performance, and general managers have the central responsibility for shaping workplace context. Ghoshal and Bartlett's model features discipline, stretch, trust and support as the primary dimensions of context which in turn influences the levels of individual initiative, mutual cooperation and collective learning within an organisation. This kind of model has appeared frequently throughout the years and the concepts it embodies have been reflected strongly in recent UK research, including that carried out by a team of researchers at

Bath University which I will be discussing in the next chapter (Purcell *et al* 2003).

- In systems thinking and in the business strategy literature, organisational routines are often seen as the basis of collective learning (Cyert and March 1963; Nelson and Winter 1982) because they capture knowledge from the organisation's past to guide individual and group behaviour and action in the present. In this view, organisational learning is 'an adaptive change process that is influenced by past experience, focused on developing and modifying routines, and supported by organizational memory' (Eisenhardt and Santos 2002: 141, drawing on Nonaka and Takeuchi 1995). That process represents an 'absorptive capacity' that enables the organisation to 'recognise the value of external information, assimilate it and apply it to commercial ends' (Cohen and Levinthal 1990). The capacity is largely a function of the level of the firm's prior knowledge which, in turn, has been shaped in unique ways not only by internal channels of communication, but by the pattern of the firm's R&D investment decisions and the way knowledge is distributed in the firm's environment as well as internally (Eisenhardt and Santos 2002: 142).

- In the mainly British 'relational' school of strategy research, the vital context is provided by the employment relationship. The whole organisation is nested in an institutional context that includes professional and sectoral networks (Scarbrough 1998: 227). These allow or hinder transfer of knowledge across sectors, and so fundamentally influence learning and knowledge within the organisation (DiMaggio and Powell 1991). Firm-level change is based on shared knowledge and 'recipes' as much as on unique organisational competencies (Huff 1982; Child 1988) because the more organisations interact with one another, the stronger the tendency to adopt shared belief systems and common frames of reference (Scarbrough 1998: 228). Again this phenomenon has been strikingly illustrated by the American banking crisis that developed over a single week in September 2008, throwing the global economy into potential chaos. It is this viewpoint – not a universal one, but certainly influential – that explains why Evans *et al* (2006) place so much stress in their 'expansive-restrictive' framework on the need to take as the starting point for any changes to workplace learning an analysis of the organisation's institutional context.

Underlying such propositions about 'organisational learning' lies more than a hint that organisations have a life of their own and are themselves capable of learning (Matthews and Candy 1999: 52). This is not the case. Only people learn. Spreading the learning of individuals to teams, and from teams to the whole organisation in order to develop some kind of organisational learning capability requires at the very least skilfully planned processes, systems and strategies. It cannot happen of its own accord and even when new technology is drafted in to aid the process any semblance of it may still fail to occur. Organisations comprise many and often conflicting human needs and interests, and are themselves influenced by a wider context. Diverse interests and influences do not conveniently converge in common pursuit of mutual learning that will benefit the organisation. Sometimes their reconciliation is impossible.

THE LEARNING ORGANISATION: MYTH, MAGIC OR REALITY?

The literature on organisational learning falls into two basic categories – the scholarly and the practitioner-oriented. The former has been 'predominantly skeptical' about the concept of organisational learning (Argyris and Schon, 1996: 180) and displays as yet little integration, leaving crucial conceptual and practical questions unanswered. For example, we know that the individual's cognitive structure is a key influence on how, why and what they learn, but quite what that structure comprises and exactly how it operates is still the subject of complex scientific enquiry. And how far and how much learning must be shared for it to become collective? What would be the likely content and form of a collective cognitive structure? How is an organisation's knowledge structure constructed and made manifest? Is it stable or a dynamic (Laukkanen 1996)?

The practitioner-focused literature on the 'learning organisation' (LO) at first sight seems to offer more certainties. However, on analysis these begin to unravel. Three of the most popular writers and researchers, Pedler, Burgoyne and Boydell (1997: 3), define the LO as 'an organization that facilitates the learning of all its members and consciously transforms itself and its context'. Burgoyne (1999) in his reformulation of that model established the following as key principles (Miller and Stewart 1999: 43):

- Learning and business strategy are closely linked.

- The organisation consciously learns from business opportunities and threats.

- Individuals, groups and the whole organisation are not only learning, but continually learning how to learn.

- Information systems and technology serve to support learning rather than to control it.

- There are well-developed processes for defining, creating, capturing, sharing and acting on knowledge.

- These various systems and dimensions are balanced and managed as a whole.

This prescription does not lend itself easily to implementation or measurement and the extent to which the LO is a genuine possibility offering new ways forward for collective learning is questionable. In the words of two scholars 'magic would be nice, but it is not easy to find' (Levinthal and March 1993). Consider the following points:

- The concept's underpinning philosophy tends to ignore or underplay issues of who controls that organisation and the uses to which new learning will be put and the concept itself reflects an essentially managerialist perspective. There are parallels here with the fundamental weakness already noted in much of the theorising about 'communities of practice'.

- Change in organisations is rarely a linear, rationally-based activity and much of it involves making radical breaks with the past rather than a process of continuous improvement, yet leading exponents of the LO continue to put the main emphasis on the finding of better ways of tackling existing problems and of rationally reorganising work (Morris 1991; Pedler and Boutall 1992).

- The LO concept is based on the expectation that individuals are willing to learn continuously, be innovative and engaged permanently in double-loop learning, be responsible for their own development, and be able to learn together with colleagues. But not all are able or disposed to do any of this, especially if it means that the everyday learning activities they undertake by themselves are ignored or undervalued (Poell and Tijmensen 1998).

- The LO practitioner literature focuses on the internal organisational context and is mainly about workers, managers and training consultants, whose interests it assumes are fundamentally the same. Once again, in other words, the preoccupation is with the lowest level of the activity scale – the workplace and actors within it – instead of adopting a holistic approach that starts with analysis at the macro level.

For reasons such as these it is unclear whether or how the LO concept can be satisfactorily put into practice, not least when so much depends on team learning and its transference to the learning of the entire organisation. Even the answer to the most basic question here is unclear: how, in an LO, should work be organised? The practitioner literature emphasises the value of multi-functional team-based working where thinking and doing are integrated into jobs, and workers are empowered to participate in team decision-making processes (Tjepkema 2003). But this is a partial and optimistic notion. Bringing the LO to life in most organisations would be likely to require major redesign of jobs and a radical change in management style. It would also require a deep understanding of learning processes and of the skilful balance needed between formal systems and informal features in the workplace that few L&D practitioners seem likely to possess.

Despite such concerns the notion of the LO continues to exercise a strong appeal in the field. Its emphasis on openness, support, a climate of trust and challenge and a commitment to continuous learning and knowledge creation from a base of individual and team reflection and experience all hold out the promise of achieving high-commitment organisations and solving hitherto intractable organisational problems.

PRACTICAL STARTING POINT: THE 'THINKING ORGANISATION'?

Does lack of a convincing evidence base and doubts about the validity as well as practicality of the LO concept mean it should be abandoned? Or should we turn

CASE EXAMPLE

HYDRO POLYMERS: A THINKING ORGANISATION

In an earlier book I described how, at Hydro Polymers, Aycliffe, Co. Durham in the UK, the aim in the last two decades of the twentieth century was 'to educate, not just train, the workforce in order to create a thinking culture – one where everyone thinks strategically, looking out into the environment for new challenges and ideas, and thinking for the future as well as for immediate improvements' (Harrison 1997).

The aim at Hydro Polymers was not to become a 'learning organisation' (a phrase which was thought hard to express in any practical way) but rather to develop a 'thinking organisation'. 'This quite simply means a workplace where, stimulated and focused in their learning by the vision and long-term aspirations of the business, people are encouraged to import new information, and are enabled by the structure,

business processes, routines and culture of the firm to disseminate it widely in order to create new insights and knowledge, and influence strategic as well as operational decision-making. [...] In this thinking organisation it is essential to achieve a style of relationships that produces trust, partnership and involvement.'

Employees at Hydro Polymers did not receive special payments for attaining qualifications, yet there was a high level of vocational qualification because they were encouraged to seek accredited learning by the nature of their work and the opportunities offered for self-learning – for example, through access to the Open College, MBA courses and the Open University (with on-site tutorials for OU students). There was an important focus on mentoring, and everyone had a self-development plan.

Source: Harrison, R. (1997)

instead to the notion of a 'thinking organisation' in much the same spirit as the CIPD has used its concept of the 'thinking performer' to inform its professional standards (CIPD 2005b)?

Most LO definitions emphasise such notions as (Poell 2005: 108):

- shared vision and values

- collective learning

- continuous improvement

- making tacit knowledge explicit

- entering into dialogue.

What the Hydro Polymers example suggests is that the concept of the 'thinking organisation' embodies such notions and does have practical value. It directs attention to the vital role of workplace learning in helping to build unique organisational capacity and human capabilities and to regenerate and expand the organisation's knowledge base. It emphasises the centrality of management's role in building and sustaining a climate and environment in the workplace where such learning will be stimulated and supported.

Poell (2005: 108) concludes that if there is such a thing as an LO it represents a process rather than a fixed state, and that the answers to three questions can suggest where to start in that process. The questions suggest the same kind of logic as that underpinning Evans *et al*'s (2006) 'expansive-restrictive' framework discussed earlier:

- What learning is already going on? For example, how do people solve problems in their work? Which individual or private learning efforts could bring benefit to the organisation?

- Who organises learning? For example, what learning initiatives have managers and workers already taken? Are there any outside influences on the corporate learning system and are these positive or negative in their impact?

- How do people cope with tensions in organising learning? For example, how are conflicts resolved? Who is a dominant influence on what learning goes on? How do other organisational members exert their influence?

The CIPD's (2006a) interactive tool 'The changing role of the trainer: building a learning culture in your organisation, which can be downloaded from its website likewise employs a diagnostic approach. It avoids use of the term 'learning organisation', referring instead to an aspirational learning culture that, like the culture at Hydro Polymers, aims for an environment where 'learning is seen as relevant to the needs of the business and of the learners and is integrated in day-to-day activities'. Its practical recommendations, while modest in scope and depth and tending to a managerialist perspective, provide useful advice for trainers who are only at the very start of the challenging tasks involved in promoting and helping to build a culture of learning in their organisations. As we saw in the previous chapter, this may well be the majority.

REFLECTION

Having downloaded the CIPD's tool from *http://www.cipd.co.uk/subjects/ training/general/_chngrltrnr.htm*, take the sections of it that concern skills and priorities for the L&D professional. Looking at the questions posed there, what gaps do they suggest in your own knowledge and skills related to building a workplace learning culture? And what kind of action plan would it be feasible for you to follow in the coming year if you wanted to tackle those gaps?

KNOWLEDGE MANAGEMENT?

In his famous article in the *Harvard Business Review* Nonaka (1991) unified the concept of knowledge as a process (the tacit dimension) with knowledge as a commodity or resource (the explicit dimension) by viewing tacit and explicit knowledge as combining in a learning spiral to form new knowledge. While there are innumerable other notions of knowledge, how it is formed and how it can influence organisational progress, his concept is probably the best known in the practitioner field. He cited companies like Honda, Canon, Matshushita, NEW, Sharp and Kao as typifying continuously innovative, dominating emergent technologies. They treated the creation of knowledge as not simply about information processing but about 'tapping the tacit … insights, intuitions and hunches of individual employees and making those insights available for testing and use by the company as a whole' (*ibid*: 97). In such companies:

> inventing new knowledge is not a specialized activity … It is a way of behaving, indeed a way of being, in which everyone is a knowledge worker – that is to say, an entrepreneur … [there is] a shared understanding of what the company stands for, where it is going, what kind of world it wants to live in, and … how to make that world a reality.

Such a view of the knowledge process poses challenges for management. On the one hand, in a knowledge economy it is the case that (Sharkie 2003: 31):

> An organizations's success will finally depend on the speed at which it can generate, capture and disseminate knowledge and then use this knowledge to develop capabilities that cannot easily be copied by rivals.

On the other hand, knowledge as process cannot be owned by the company, as tangible assets can. Individuals own it and have to want and agree to put it at the service of others. Therefore it cannot be 'managed'. It can only be encouraged, facilitated and rewarded.

What then is meant by knowledge management (KM)? In a practical sense the answer to that question depends on notions of knowledge held within the particular organisation. In some, especially financial institutions, knowledge is valued as intellectual capital. In some, it is exploited as intellectual property essential to competitive strategy. Some codified, explicit knowledge is of such value to an organisation that it has to be managed as a legal entity, often with property rights (for example, patents, copyright and licences). Other again may relate to particular jobs, positions, tasks or functions and so may need to be recorded in training and personnel manuals (Hall 1996).

All such notions revolve around knowledge as a commodity or resource – a view that is reflected strongly in the literature of the resource-based view of the firm. In this view the focus of KM should be capturing, protecting and deploying that resource to the benefit of the business. Since tacit knowledge is by definition impossible to observe or classify, the emphasis of this kind of KM is primarily on the management of explicit knowledge and on the attraction, retention and engagement of those human containers of uniquely valuable knowledge – specialist knowledge workers.

But for organisations like Hydro Polymers KM's focus is rather on 'knowing' as a process that takes place continuously in individual and team-based projects and in everyday work activity. Its outcomes (knowledge as commodity) benefit individuals, and also spread across the organisation to inform continuous improvement and innovation, thereby adding organisational value. This constructivist view leads to a different approach to KM, which Wilson and Cattell (2005) describe as:

> the systematic process that supports the continuous development of individual, group and organizational learning, and involves the creation, acquisition, gathering, transforming, transfer and application of knowledge to achieve organizational objectives.

Reflecting on these two different approaches to KM, it should come as no surprise that in their literature review Eisenhardt and Sanson (2002) found the conceptualisation and measurement of knowledge to be inconsistent across research studies, and saw a need for more work on organisational context and its impact on knowledge flows.

Focusing knowledge management in the organisation

Sharkie (2003: 31, cited by Wilson and Cattell (2005), suggested the following questions to supply the necessary focus for KM in an organisation:

- What knowledge must we have to be unique and superior to others?

- What should we do to eliminate any gaps between that and the knowledge we currently possess?

- What explicit knowledge seems to be available to rivals but not to us – and how can we acquire it?

- Do we have an excess of knowledge compared to that which we need?

- How do we leverage our knowledge to our benefit?

At one level these questions may all appear to relate purely to knowledge as commodity, not to knowing as a process. Yet at another they offer helpful guidelines in both senses, since even knowing as process needs some overall direction, some ultimate purpose for the business as well as for individuals and teams. The answers to such questions can help to identify 'what matters most' at each of those levels, revealing where perceptions and ideas converge and where they differ, thus indicating issues requiring shared attention and action.

Such enquiry matters greatly because in the KM literature a surprising number of fundamental assumptions remain relatively untested. In particular, the notion that knowledge is the most important competitive resource rests on little if any empirical evidence. There is no significant use of actual measures of performance that can yield insights into the nature of the competitive advantage it might bestow, the source of that advantage, or whether that advantage exists at all (Eisenhardt and Santos, 2002: 159). Studies also reveal that sometimes the benefits of knowledge creation go to the individual or team, not to the firm. This raises the possibility that increasing the amount of knowledge sourcing, transfer, and even integration in an organisation may not always be to the organisation's advantage unless there is clear evidence that the knowledge in question is or could become strategically valuable (*ibid*: 152).

THE IMPACT OF NEW TECHNOLOGY

In Chapter 4 I noted ways in which new information and communication technologies (ICT) are shifting office work increasingly away from data-processing towards various forms of knowledge work. At this point it is relevant to consider ICT advance in rather more detail in order to reflect on some implications for the 'management' of learning and knowledge in organisations.

Such reflection may perhaps raise at least a small warning flag to those who wax lyrical about the new age of Learning 2.0. The technological advances of the past couple of decades, with all their promise of redefining what work is and fulfilling that claim by Zuboff that I reproduced at the start of Chapter 4, are not necessarily leading all organisations to become more knowledge-creative. Often individuals are simply becoming smarter in how they perform. Their new knowledge produces no real impact at any other level.

Furthermore, as we have already seen, knowledge is viewed by many organisational leaders as a resource to be captured and put at the service of the business. That can give rise to a purely transactional relationship with the workforce in general and with the firm's scarce specialist knowledge workers in particular. When, in addition, an organisation has a highly segmented labour force to which management applies differentiated HR practices, work communities will be disposed to hoard rather than share knowledge or apply it to the benefit of the business. Indeed, members of such communities will often be unaware of, or disinterested in, any wider quest for knowledge than that likely to improve their own earnings, job-retention prospects or bargaining strengths.

REFLECTION

Consider first the 'new office': smaller but with huge scope through its virtual private networks and VoIP telephony, its hot-desking area, its office-wide wireless network, its remote access for home and mobile workers, its boardroom with video-conference equipment. All of this can transform work and learning, and offer 'spectacularly fast returns on cash invested in the technology involved' (Stone 2006).

Consider too Web 2.0, otherwise known as 'Learning 2.0' or second-generation learning. As Shepherd (2008) explained, the web has moved on from being a 'top-down and essentially one-way publishing medium' to become, potentially, a fully collaborative mode of communication and mutual learning, enabling every web user to become a contributor as well as a consumer. The tools to achieve this transformation include online journals – including, for example, learning journals (blogs), databases created and edited by users (wikis), and social networking sites enabling users to build and maintain their own networks of contacts – LinkedIn being the most widely used to date by the business and professional world.

At last, then, we seem to be entering a true new age made possible by a more knowledge-based economy and advances in ICT: an age when all an organisation's employees can become genuinely self-managing learners and creative knowledge workers. An age where (Shepherd 2008):

With the many new sources of information, advice and support, traditional learning interventions may soon become marginalised. If learning professionals are not to be marginalised too, they must be seen to engage with the new social tools.

But is a new age really dawning? What does your own reflection on experience and practice in organisations with which you are familiar suggest?

KM tools: answer to a problem?

It is out of a concern to prevent hoarding, and also to protect the loss of valuable knowledge when employees leave – especially in the wake of downsizing, mergers and acquisitions – that companies are making increasing use of 'knowledge management tools'. Three of the most common objectives here are (Merali 1999):

- to provide banks of information that enable employers to record and access explicit knowledge across the organisation

- to provide access to data across boundaries

- to allow groups of people to interact and create new knowledge, through virtual communities where they can share expertise and tacit knowledge.

But – and it is here that the previous **Reflection** is particularly relevant – that third area of use remains the most problematic. One obvious reason is the frequent lack of a company culture that favours the development of all an organisation's employees – not just its professional specialists – into knowledge workers. Another reason, only now beginning to attract the attention from employers that it deserves, is that to open portals into a virtual world of infinite information, available anytime, anywhere, for the shared construction of new knowledge, can overwhelm or distort instead of enhance an organisation's search for valuable knowledge. People can become lost in a sea of unmanageable data, unable finally to make sense of what they discover. Equally, they can become ever more distracted as their attention is caught first by one enticing interactive byway, then by another, and then by yet another.

The advent of social networking sites does offer the potential to take learning into quite new territory. It also provides a vehicle for increasing employee voice, and consequently suggests a way of enhancing employees' commitment and engagement levels. But free use of such sites in the workplace also carries risks – for the business and also for some individuals: risks of misuse, abuse or overuse. The fact that organisations are adopting widely contrasting policies related to the use of Facebook and YouTube by their employees is just one example of how sensitive are the issues involved here, and of their strategic significance.

We can conclude, therefore, that most organisations now need to produce not just knowledge management tools but a robust, well-communicated, innovative and equitable strategy for creativity and knowledge creation – one that is aligned with business goals yet also offers benefit to employees in their own right. Here is an example of a well-known commercial organisation that is attempting to do just that.

'IMAGINE' – INNOVATION AT ITV PLC

CASE EXAMPLE

In 2004 Carlton and Granada merged to form ITV plc. Since then it has become vital for the company to expand capacity for creativity and knowledge creation in order to survive and progress in a highly competitive environment. It also has to increase its capability to cope with the scale of change facing the media industry, and to enable it to actively shape the transformed landscape in which all media organisations now operate.

In 2004 the new HR director at ITV established a small innovation unit called ITV Imagine, to work as an internal consultancy to all parts of the company – an unusual initiative for an HR professional to introduce, but well in line with pleas from gurus like Gary Hamel that innovation is something HR should make a priority. The unit was reshaped following a 2005 ITV-wide cultural audit and in December 2006 it was officially launched. Its stated aim on its official website is 'to contribute to and enhance the creative processes as well as to identify new opportunities for the company'. Its remit is to incubate ideas or concepts from staff and to gather external knowledge and expertise in order to anticipate future thinking and develop content ideas. It is not put in the sole charge of R&D nor is it isolated from the rest of the business, since its purpose is to unlock silos of creativity so that they serve the whole organisation (Evans 2007).

Imagine offers a knowledge pool of latest thinking through a team of 11 full-time staff from a wide variety of skill-sets, life-stages and backgrounds, joined on a partnership basis by creatives from related industries. There are three or four six-month secondment positions for ITV senior managers, and a culture change programme was launched in 2007 to inspire and embed 'creative spirit' among staff and line managers.

The culture change programme includes a change initiative called Create – reinventing the company's ideas scheme – accompanied by training sessions to support and enhance creative abilities of people from all parts of the business. When an idea is accepted, whoever suggested it is invited to work on it. Central to culture change is another programme, Realise, that targets senior managers with whom the unit's staff will work on a one-to-one basis and in workshops to help them understand their own leadership role and how they can contribute to the creativity of the company. By October 2007 300 people had already taken part. The Imagine centre is also a resource for all staff, with drop-in facilities such as screens, private pod areas for thinking time, interactive media and presentation facilities.

For the HR director it made sense for HR to lead on the whole Imagine initiative because the culture and environment of an organisation are areas that are directly linked to the psychological contract and are therefore areas where HR should be at the forefront of activity.

Source: Evans, R. (2007)
People Management, 22 March; *http//
www.theandvsinsteadofexperiment.
com/2007/10/it-started-with-wish.html*
[accessed 24 March 2008]

The information in Evans' article and the Imagine website make it clear that the unit is trying to strike a feasible balance between focusing on knowledge as product and knowing as social process. It has followed classic principles for an innovative organisation by establishing four critical roles (Tushman and Nadler 1996):

- Idea generators – people who creatively link diverse ideas and see new approaches.

- Champions or internal entrepreneurs who take creative ideas and bring them to life: they produce tangible innovations.

- Gatekeepers or boundary-spanners who link their more local colleagues to external information sources. They bring external information into the organisation or steer colleagues to the right sources.

- Sponsors, coaches or mentors – senior managers who provide informal support, access to resources, and protection as new ventures emerge.

What remains to be seen is how far ITV will manage to strike the necessary balance between fostering innovation through the generative learning that the Imagine unit is there to stimulate, and facilitating and rewarding adaptive learning across the organisation that is also essential to its survival. Much research has shown the difficulty of getting that balance right. It requires the capability for bilateral learning (Snell 2005: 41–2):

> Bilateral learning requires executives to pay particular attention to the design of their HR architectures in order to integrate employee skills and knowledge (human capital), internal and external relationships (social capital) and organisational processes, structures and systems (organisational capital) to acquire and integrate knowledge.

Much will therefore depend on the kind of organisational structure and work design context in which the Imagine unit is embedded and on the HR systems and practices that support it – especially in relation to performance management and development, reward and employee relations. Only time will tell whether the Imagine unit will succeed in its ambitious aim.

LESSONS FROM INTERNATIONAL RESEARCH

WORKPLACE LEARNING CULTURES

International research studies repeatedly show that an organisation's investment in workplace learning is most directly influenced by organisational leadership, management actions, and HR strategies and practice (Harrison and Kessels 2003: 225). In the UK, workplace learning and innovative learning processes are receiving increasing attention in organisations that are introducing new high-performance work practices which in turn change the nature and organisation of work. The extent to which this is happening in competitor countries is generally more marked, although practices vary across organisations and across countries due to variations in national education and training policies, skill gaps, labour market trends and so on.

A major case-based European research project has examined L&D practice in nearly 200 self-styled learning-oriented organisations across Europe, including in the UK (Tjepkema *et al* 2002). The researchers rarely found signs of a strong workplace learning culture, but where they did, its development could be traced to the interaction through time of number of contextual factors (Tjepkema 2002):

- a strong push to innovation in the workplace

- new structures that provide employees with new possibilities for linking work and learning, for example through increased contact with customers, through teamworking and through learning networks

- top management that is active in establishing and communicating new organisational vision and values

- clarity on L&D's new role related to learning, plus positive results of new L&D initiatives.

However, the combination of such a culture with the above four contextual factors usually seemed accidental. Learning cultures appeared to have been introduced as a result of blind faith, not of any reasoned business case. Also, although knowledge management, knowledge sharing and creating a favourable learning culture were all in reality big issues for the participating companies, the researchers found that (Tjepkema 2002):

- despite considerable innovation in L&D practice, there was a generalised failure of its professionals to actively promote a learning culture in the workplace or to promote high-quality workplace learning whether in informal or formal modes

- when they used the term 'knowledge management', L&D professionals were referring mainly to sharing knowledge more widely across the organisation. They rarely if ever used it to signify creating opportunities for knowledge-productive learning and development for all organisational members.

- Most L&D activity was concentrated at the individual level.

The picture seems in some ways more encouraging now in the UK, where the CIPD's 2007 and 2008 Learning and Development surveys both revealed efforts to develop an L&D culture as one of the main reported changes in organisations covered (CIPD 2007a; CIPD 2008a). The introduction of new programmes to develop the roles of line managers was the most significant change reported in the 2008 survey, which also revealed that internal knowledge-sharing events were being used in more than 40% of respondents' organisations. However, job rotation, secondments and shadowing – all important methods of informal learning and knowledge development – saw much smaller increases in 2008. Action learning sets too were no longer in use by nearly half the organisations covered. Here too, then, the story is an ambiguous one.

KNOWLEDGE MANAGEMENT CHALLENGES FOR HR PROFESSIONALS

Companies that 'manage' knowledge most effectively – ie stimulate people to continuously share and apply their knowledge in ways useful to the business – are those where (Skapinker 2002: 3):

- their knowledge management programmes are an intrinsic part of their overall business strategy

- their HR and IT policies support information-sharing but work to an organisational knowledge-management policy that is clear and regularly communicated to all organisational members. That policy should ensure that a clear distinction is made between 'sharing' that ensures a value-adding knowledge process at different organisational levels, and 'sharing' that runs counter to business interests and/or creates unacceptable levels of stress for employees

- they have a corporate culture that encourages people to share what they know – a difficult task if employees tend to feel insecure in the present business climate.

In a knowledge economy HR professionals should be working with management, project leaders and external partners to carry out the tasks that Skapinker's principles involve, but research suggests that as yet few are doing so (Scarbrough and Swan 1999; Stewart and Tansley 2002; Tjepkema *et al* 2002; Harrison and Kessels 2003). Worryingly, most seem unaware of the need to do so. Many appear unfamiliar with the KM field and have no language for entering it. General management is often hampered by a similar lack of understanding. Key features of organisational context often restrict the rapid and effective mobilisation of knowledge by all employees as and when it is most needed, and there still appears to be a preoccupation with ICT systems to process and spread information.

TASKS FOR L&D PRACTITIONERS

EIGHT KEY TASKS

Concluding their survey of research findings and of practice both good and poor in the area of workplace learning and knowledge, Harrison and Kessels propose eight key tasks for L&D practitioners (2003: 234–5):

- Raise awareness across the organisation of the value of a workplace learning culture that taps into and shares explicit and tacit knowledge of organisational members, applying it to continuous improvement and innovation in goods, services and processes.

- Work in partnerships to implement business processes and developmental activity that will equip managers and team leaders at all organisational levels to fulfil their knowledge-creating roles.

- Produce well-contextualised processes and initiatives that can foster a workplace learning culture that is conducive to knowledge creation, knowledge sharing and the development of new dynamic capabilities for the organisation.

- Ensure an inclusive and ethical approach to learning in the workplace (I will return to this in Chapter 9).

- Stimulate and support self-managed learning at all organisational levels, utilising relevant social, occupational and professional networks to achieve this.

- Incorporate into training, learning and developmental processes opportunities for individuals to explore and invest in their personal domains of interest while also adding value through their work for the organisation. This is particularly important if the organisation is to get best value out of scarce talent that may otherwise move elsewhere or lose commitment to its goals.

- Facilitate those involved in learning and knowledge processes in virtual environments, and help disperse team members to connect and align their interests and priorities.

- Ensure their own continuing professional and personal development.

EVIDENCE-BASED PRACTICE AND EXPERIMENTATION

In this chapter the case examples have featured large organisations, some with complex, high-cost knowledge-management and learning systems. It should not be forgotten, though, that smaller enterprises can also provide effective environments for workplace learning and knowledge creation. While some show little concern for their human or social capital (as will be seen in Chapter 10), there are others that are fast-reactive, well-informed about their external and internal environments, and foster a climate of continuous learning that promotes innovation. They operate like this not necessarily because there has been any conscious decision to do so, but because they have learnt intuitively that it enables them to gain a leading edge. In the new knowledge economy most organisations no matter what their size or type have to find unique ways of organising and strategising precisely because they are in a novel and increasingly turbulent environment where learning through doing is often the only reliable way to make progress.

Sometimes, then, it is intuition, accident and experimentation that lead to productive ways forward for organisations. This suggests an important message for those L&D practitioners who are struggling to make progress in the fields of workplace learning and knowledge, where there is no clear evidence base to support many of the theories and practices that are so popular in the field.

REFLECTION

Evidence-based practice or experimentation – how best to combine the two in L&D work? What would you suggest, and why?

CONCLUSION

You should by now understand the kinds of contribution that L&D professionals should be making to promote workplace learning and the creation of organisationally-valuable knowledge, and feel confident to tackle the review questions in Appendix 3 that relate to this chapter.

The main issues discussed in the chapter's five sections have been:

- the potential value of the workplace as an integrated domain of work and learning, both for novice learners and for established communities of practice, but the problematic nature of that terrain given its contested evidence base and the practical tensions that can exist when stakeholders' goals, power and values are highly divergent

- the utility of a research-based framework focused on institutional, organisational and workplace levels of activity, that can aid analysis of workplace learning's context and guide action to achieve the best balance of advantage for its stakeholders (Evans *et al* 2006)

- concerns about the validity of theories of collective learning and the 'learning organisation'

and suggested starting-points for building a learning culture in the workplace

- the differing notions and treatment of 'knowledge' that exist in organisations, and the implications of this for those responsible for 'knowledge management'

- people-centred principles to develop creativity and innovation in an organisation; reliance for their successful implementation on top leadership's vision and support, line management and team leaders' co-operation, an appropriate infrastructure of HR practices and ICT, and high-calibre L&D expertise.

- European research findings identifying major challenges for the L&D profession in achieving the planning and culture change needed if the workplace is to become a powerfully integrated domain of learning, work and knowledge

- eight key tasks for L&D practitioners related to promoting workplace learning and knowledge; the importance of balancing evidence-based practice with experimentation and innovation.

EXLPORE FURTHER

FURTHER INFORMATION SOURCES

Evans, K., Hodkinson, P., Rainbird, H. and Unwin, L. (2006) *Improving Workplace Learning*. London: Routledge. Details the expansive-restrictive framework

Harrison, R. and Kessels, J. (2003) *Human Resource Development in a Knowledge Economy: An organisational view*. Basingstoke: Palgrave Macmillan. Chapter 3 is particularly relevant to this chapter

Smith, P. J. and Sadler-Smith, E. (2006) *Learning in Organizations: Complexities and diversities*. London: Routledge. Detailed analysis and practical advice on learning cultures and communities of practice; pp31–51

Stern, E. and Sommerlad, E. (1999) *Workplace Learning, Culture and Performance*. London: IPD. Important account of international, UK and organisational contexts of workplace learning, incorporating review of research evidence

http://www.knowledge-nurture. com [accessed 24 March 2008]. Buckman Laboratories' informative website whose goal is 'to establish a resource to help people learn about knowledge sharing. Our audience is not only our customers and our associates within Buckman Laboratories, but also the worldwide knowledge management community – practitioners, newcomers, academics, students, and thinkers'. For related reading see Pan (1999).

CHAPTER 6

Enhancing Performance Management

INTRODUCTION

The focus of this chapter is the organisation's performance management process (PMP). That process has a twofold purpose: to enable, support and reward all organisational members in achieving good performance, and to retain and develop able and committed people who will help the organisation to achieve both its immediate and its longer-term goals. Specifically, the PMP involves:

- setting individual targets linked to business goals, and establishing desired performance levels

- appraising and improving performance

- ensuring continuous learning and development

- giving recognition and rewards.

In the current economic environment the importance of enhancing the productivity of British industry is emphasised by government, employers and trade unions alike (Bryson *et al* 2005: 451). It is therefore unsurprising that the PMP is under increasing scrutiny. 87% of HR practitioners responding to the CIPD's 2004 survey confirmed that a formal PMP was in place in their organisations (Armstrong and Baron 2004). Another large-scale survey two years later showed that of 400 managers involved in the process in over 200 public and private sector organisations nearly 70% valued their PMP for keeping people focused on work goals and organisational strategy (Houldsworth and Jirasinghe 2006). However, whereas in the CIPD's 2004 survey 83% of respondents agreed that the PMP's focus should be developmental, evidence now indicates a distinct trend away from such an emphasis.

This chapter has five sections. The first explores issues around individual motivation, attitudes and performance. In the second I review the uncertain research base for claims that a 'causal chain' links HR practices and organisational performance and in the third I discuss current and more promising research that is moving forward in a rather different direction. The fourth section covers the stages of the PMP cycle and looks at two widely-used 'helping' activities – coaching and mentoring. The fifth and final section summarises the pressures on performance management in organisations today and the challenges they pose for L&D professionals.

REFLECTION

How far does there seem to be a formal performance management system in your organisation? And who do you think is/are primarily responsible for ensuring effective performance management there, whether or not on a formalised basis?

MOTIVATION AND PERFORMANCE

UNDERSTANDING MOTIVATION

It is not my intention to attempt a learned discussion of motivation theory. There is a mass of literature on that subject, impossible to summarise in the space available here. My purpose is to take one particular theory about motivation that, despite its surface simplicity, has much of relevance to suggest for those responsible for the conduct of the PMP in their organisations.

In 1985 Charles Handy produced his concept of 'the motivation calculus' to explain the links between motivation and individual performance. He presented performance as the outcome of an ongoing interaction within the individual of felt needs, perceived and expected results and rewards, and 'e-factors':

● *Needs* – How far does the performance required or requested of the individual promise to satisfy the needs that he or she brings to work? If little satisfaction seems likely, then it is unsurprising if the individual's motivation to perform is low. But what are the individual's needs? Clues will lie in the expectations they were led to form when they were offered the job initially. What deal did they think was put on the table then?

- *Results* – How far does the individual fully understand what is wanted from him or her, and why? Have they had the opportunity to set work targets jointly with their manager, or have targets been unilaterally imposed? Do managers and team leaders act as good role models, give timely and accurate feedback, reinforce effective performance and deal fairly and appropriately with poor performance?

- *Rewards* – What rewards does the individual perceive to be on offer for the performance required? Rewards can take many forms, financial and non-financial, and they take on different meanings in different contexts. In the particular situation, what rewards are actually available, and does the individual expect to receive them, find them worthwhile, or regard them with scepticism? Do some rewards conflict with others that the individual also values – acceptance within the workplace community of practice, for example, or those to do with their life outside the organisation? And what has the individual's experience in the organisation thus far led them to expect – that the employer's promises of rewards will be honoured? Or that management cannot be trusted to deliver?

- *'E-factors'* – Looking at the above, how far does the individual calculate it to be worthwhile to expend effort, energy, excitement and expertise in their work? What level of those 'e-factors' does the individual actually possess, and has that level been over- or under-estimated by others?

This stripped-down account may give the impression that concept of the motivation calculus is simplistic. It is not. It has a strong underpinning base of psychological theory, particularly expectancy theory (Vroom and Deci 1970; Machin 1981). Even in outline it clearly highlights the unique interplay of internal and external factors that shape and continuously change each individual's motivation, and the powerful effects on performance of past learning (not just of skills, but learning from life experience) and of the individual's expectations of, and interactions with, others in the workplace and in the organisation more widely.

You may find it helpful to identify the main messages that the following fictional case suggests about the links between motivation and individual performance. Comments follow at its end.

LINDA, THE DISILLUSIONED RECRUIT

CASE EXAMPLE

Pyrotem is a light engineering company employing 1,000 people and is located in an industrial conurbation in the Midlands. It is struggling to retain its leading edge, and is continuously driving down costs whilst also trying to achieve innovation and high quality in its products and excellence in its supplier and customer relationships.

Linda, who has an impressive school and university CV, was recruited immediately on her graduation two years ago to a trainee supervisory post at Pyrotem. Pyrotem's management boasts of the company's human resource practices and of its refusal to recruit any but 'the best' to work there. Starting pay, terms and conditions for supervisors and managers are above local norms. Throughout her selection process (which involved two days at an assessment centre) Linda was told that they were looking for someone with the potential to become an excellent performer and teamworker, who would be encouraged to develop by being given challenging work and a significant amount of discretion. She was delighted when she was selected.

Alas, during her induction and basic training programme Linda was given little clarification of targets and little guidance or support from managers. After six months she moved into a supervisory position where she found that her manager gave her no real discretion, expecting her to adopt his own controlling style of management. Linda's preferred approach to team leadership was very different and this caused considerable tension. Try as she might to bridge the gap between them, she found it impossible both to please her boss and to achieve the best out of those working for her.

Linda soon realised that her prospects at Pyrotem were not impressive. Few promotion openings existed. When they occurred, success seemed to depend on the subjective views of a small group of senior managers. There was no objective or meaningful performance review or staff development scheme – just a formal appraisal system to which managers gave minimal attention other than filling in annual forms in an offhand fashion. Morale and performance levels were unsurprisingly poor. Those who got out, did so. Those who could not had little commitment to the organisation, and infected new recruits with their negative attitudes.

Linda left halfway through her second year at Pyrotem, seizing an unexpected opportunity to take a post with a well-known competitor firm with an excellent reputation as an employer. People were proud to work there. It lived up to Linda's expectations. Although management made no pretence that there would be any prospect of fast promotion the financial rewards were as good as at Pyrotem, and her work provided the stimulation, development and discretionary opportunities that she had never been able to find at Pyrotem.

What light does this kind of case throw on motivation and performance at work?

- Linda had the skills needed to perform well in her job. She also had the initial motivation, but that declined as she realised that she had no chance to use her skills meaningfully, whether as an individual or as a workgroup member and leader. It was this lack of opportunity and of discretion to do her job as she thought it should be done that led to Linda's loss of commitment to Pyrotem, and so to her eventual departure from the firm.

- Leadership, management and HR practices were all at fault here: what they promised at recruitment and selection stages they never delivered. The frustrated expectations that this produced in Linda and other new recruits proved damaging to their subsequent employment relationship with the firm. The deal that seemed to be on the table initially was very different from the reality that they encountered in the workplace. The outcomes were inevitable: depreciation and then the loss to the firm of valuable human assets.

THE CONTESTED 'HR CAUSAL CHAIN'

Linda's case highlights the important effects of contextual factors – leadership, front-line management (FLM) and HR practices – on employee motivation, attitudes and commitment to the organisation. In this, and in pointing to discretion as a significant influence on employees' performance, the case takes us to a large body of research into a so-called 'causal chain' linking HR practices to business performance. This research has been conducted worldwide over the past 15 or so years, so it should by now have produced invaluable insights, especially for those responsible for the PMP in their organisations. Yet recent reviews indicate that it has largely failed to do so. Why? And what is the way forward?

RESEARCH ASSUMPTIONS AND PROPOSITIONS

First, to clarify the main notions that have underpinned most of the research into the 'causal chain' to date. A number of literature reviews point to a general assumption in the research studies that, taken together, flexible work practices (FWPs) and supporting HR practices form a work system that leads to above-average organisational performance. This system is often described as a 'high-performance work system' (HPWS), a term roughly equivalent to a number of others also widely used, including (Bryson et al 2005):

- 'high-performance management'– implying that a particular configuration of management practices enhances organisational performance

- 'high-commitment management' – implying that there is a positive relationship between high employee commitment and enhanced organisational performance

- 'high-involvement management' – implying that task-related practices intended to maximise employees' sense of involvement in their work combined with HRM practices that aim to maximise their commitment to the wider organisation will result in high organisational performance.

A HPWS is widely taken to have three dimensions (Bailey 1993; Bryson et al 2005; de Menezes and Wood 2006):

1 At its core are organisational structures associated with flexibility and high worker involvement, together with job autonomy that expands employees' opportunity to contribute to the organisation (Bailey 1993: 6, quoted by de Menezes and Wood 2006: 111). Providing employees with more involvement in

the design of work processes and encouraging them to share their task-specific knowledge of how these processes may be improved are key to the HPWS (Bryson *et al* 2005).

Six FWPs are commonly associated with the HPWS (de Menezes and Wood 2006):

– worker teams, whether or not autonomous

– total quality management (TQM)

– 'on line' or 'in work' practices like functional flexibility and self-inspection

– 'off-line' or 'out of work' practices like suggestions programmes and quality circles

– employee involvement in the firm's technology

– equipment purchase decisions.

2 Two sets of HR practices are commonly regarded as supporting the successful implementation of these FWPs. The first set is task-related. It overlaps with TQM methods that provide individuals and teams with operational management tools to help them as they are engaged in FWPs. These HR practices relate to:

– training

– appraisal

– disclosure of information (especially regarding strategic issues).

3 The second set of HR practices is motivational, aimed at recruiting and retaining people who will work in a highly engaged manner. These HR practices relate to:

– incentive pay systems

– job security guarantees

– internal recruitment and promotion based on merit.

WHAT DO THE 'CAUSAL CHAIN' STUDIES TELL US?

Recent reviews of all the major studies concerning the 'causal chain' linking HR practices to HPWSs (which I will term from now on the *HR causal chain*) have produced the following findings:

● that some researchers, especially in the USA (including Huselid 1995; MacDuffie 1995; Applebaum 2000), claim to have found a clear link between HR systems supporting FPWs and organisational performance, but that most of these studies have not obtained consistently strong effects across all outcome variables (de Menezes and Wood 2006). A major study drawing on the US 1993 Survey of Employer Provided Training (SEPT) did identify a link between some HR practices – training, incentive-based compensation and generous benefits – and some use of flexible practices. But in each case it was *only* some. Overall, the diversity of practices and their inconsistency across establishments even in the same industry was so great that it was impossible to reach any firm conclusions (Gittleman *et al* 1998)

● that another cluster of well-known studies (including those by Capelli and Neumark 2001; Guest *et al* 2003) revealed little or no link (de Menezes and Wood 2006). Whether judged by impact on labour productivity or on financial performance of the firm, the evidence regarding the economic impact in British-based organisations of high involvement management – the type that is at the heart of the HR system – is mixed and inconclusive (Bryson *et al* 2005)

● that because different researchers use widely different measures and concepts there is little or no agreement on which HR practices make up an HR system. In fact 'as the number of studies increases there is growing uncertainty about the underlying concepts that are being measured' (de Menezes and Wood 2006)

● that because HR systems themselves are measured in different ways, entail different assumptions and are researched using a variety of methodologies they, and the findings related to them, are unlikely to be equivalent. For example, research like Gittleman *et al*'s (1998) was carried out in the UK by Wood and de Menezes (1998) using data from the 1990 Workplace Employment Relations Survey (WERS). WER surveys, conducted five times between 1980 and 2004, provide the most nationally representative account we possess of the state of employment relations and working life inside British workplaces (see *http://www.statistics.gov.uk/STATBASE/Source.asp?vlnk=1328* [accessed 26 March 2008]). The researchers reported rather more positive findings than those from Gittleman *et al*'s study (1998). Although they felt that in part this could have been due to the fact that the WERS database covered a more comprehensive set of HR practices than the SEPT database, they thought it was more probably explained by the different methodology that they themselves had used to identify types of organisations (de Menezes and Wood 2006).

Frustrated by the 'very mixed and ambiguous' evidence relating to the HR causal chain, de Menezes and Wood took research one major step further by investigating the use of FWPs and HR practices as documented in WERS 1998. Its data covered not only most of the practices included in the HR system-performance studies to date, but also operational management methods associated with TQM and lean production. Those methods overlap with FWPs and also are often treated as part of the high-performance model. The results of this review further underlined the weaknesses in the HR causal chain's evidence base. Main findings were as follows (de Menezes and Wood 2006: 130–1, 134):

- Flexible working and TQM in British workplaces form a single coherent system reflecting an underlying high-involvement management centred on enhanced participation in work processes.

- The core elements in HR systems in Britain are HR practices associated with working flexibly and producing innovations, and with the ways in which employees are given training or information to work successfully in a high-involvement manner. However, these are highly related to TQM and appear to form a single approach within it.

- Although HR motivational practices (such as variable pay and job security guarantees) are somewhat more likely to be used in flexible workplaces, they are not distinctive to them. They are also found in non-flexible workplaces, where their use is determined by factors other than a high involvement or total quality orientation.

- Likewise the use of FPWs is not limited to contexts where jobs have high levels of autonomy or variety but seems to be part of TQM. As such, FPWs are as likely to be found in the context of largely Taylorist jobs where they have no effect on the level of autonomy or variety that employees possess when actually carrying out their work, as in a context of 'high-involvement' jobs.

- High involvement does not seem to be associated particularly strongly with non-unionised workplaces [Bryson *et al* 2005 in their review of WERS 1998 data had reached a similar conclusion: they found HI's impact there to be at best marginal].

Finally, in another important study Brown and colleagues (2007) researched data from the WERS 1998 and 2004 surveys and found significant increases over that period in employee satisfaction derived from a sense of achievement from work and overall. Yet during the same period the incidence of many HR and 'high-involvement' approaches to management appeared to have declined, and the researchers found a relatively weak association between HR practices and reported job satisfaction. The latter correlated more closely with improvements in job security and in the climate of employment relations.

Thus at the end of this section we have to conclude that, as yet, there is no reliable research evidence to substantiate the claim that there is a causal chain linking HR practices to HPWs (Bryson *et al* 2005: 485).

REFLECTION

Before reading on, it will be helpful to pause at this stage. Looking back over this section of the chapter, consider carefully the conclusions reached by authors who have reviewed the literature and research on the HR causal chain. Then reflect on the big theory-based issues that came to the fore in Chapters 4 and

5. What do those issues suggest to you as a possible way forward for future research into ways in which HR practice (including that related to L&D) can contribute to effective performance management in the workplace? My own comments follow in the next section.

A WAY FORWARD FOR RESEARCH?

THE PROBLEM OF THEORY

We have just seen that since the early 1990s a substantial volume of research has been carried out on the relationship between HR practices and organisational performance, to little apparent practical use. That is not to say that there is a lack of theories. Quite the reverse. Fleetwood and Hesketh (2006: 1986) uncovered:

> a bewildering array of theories, not to mention approaches, perspectives, models and maps, at various levels of abstraction, generality, universality, particularity and concreteness, exist in the HRM-P literature. ... This embarrassment of riches should alert us to the fact that the theoretical base of the HRM-P link is, to say the least, in rather a parlous state.

What is at issue is a lack of *useful* theories and it is at this point that research philosophy comes into the picture (Fleetwood and Hesketh 2006). Chapters 4 and 5 explored learning theories that stemmed from two contrasting views of the world – the positivist, with its scientific management approach to learning, and the humanist (or 'constructivist'), with its focus on learning, behaviour and performance in the workplace as substantially the outcome of a social process. Most of the research carried out so far into the HR causal chain reflects a positivist approach. Its aim is to find 'the truth' out there. It seeks to uncover the facts that will 'prove' that HR and management practices, organisation structures and work design working in combination can ensure levels of employee commitment and discretionary behaviour producing outstanding business performance. It is assumed that obtaining this knowledge is just a matter of time, requiring a systematic and continuous testing of hypotheses until the 'right' answers are found.

In contrast to this positivist approach, the rarer 'explanatory' research, which has its roots in a constructivist approach to learning, seeks to illuminate rather than predict. Its aim is to provide an understanding of the ways in which employees make sense of and react to their organisational world and the reasons for the views and attitudes that they form, since those strongly shape their behaviour and performance in the workplace. The explanatory approach then leaves it to us – the managers and HR practitioners in the field – to decide on the basis of that understanding what action to take when performance needs to be changed in some way.

It is this kind of thinking that explains why, in the **Reflection** leading into this section, I drew attention to the big issues raised in Chapters 4 and 5. They suggest a need for research into workplace behaviour and performance to take a pluralist, not a unitary, view of the organisation. Instead of measuring organisational 'success' by reference to a single type of goal – economic or financial – set by the employer at corporate level and superseding all others, research should start from a zero base. Its aim should be to take no specific goal for granted, but instead to explore each organisation as a unique set of human relationships that shift and change through time, producing a variety of goals at different levels that reflect non-economic as well as economic interests. Research that uncovers those goals and how the behaviours associated with them by the actors in the particular case will go further than any purely economic or financial measurement of performance to explain why an organisation is, or is not, 'effective' – that is to say, achieves a sufficient commonality of purpose amongst its many different interest groups to make progress in its environment while also responding to the wants and needs of stakeholders.

Over half a century ago one of the wisest of management thinkers wrote that human beings are motivated by many different interests but will tend to respond positively to organisational strategies that can inspire co-operative personal decisions by creating faith in the integrity of common purpose (Barnard 1938: 259). The most valuable HR research today is that which, in the particular case, illuminates how that common purpose has been achieved.

THE BLACK BOX STUDIES: A WAY FORWARD?

One set of research studies that is now moving in a strong 'explanatory' direction is the so-called 'Black box' research, sponsored by the CIPD and undertaken since 2001 by a team under Professor John Purcell at the University of Bath, working at various points in time in partnership with other research institutions.

The studies originally centred on 12 organisations in the UK that are recognised for their commitment to HR practices thought to have a strong positive link to organisational performance. The first cluster of findings led the researchers to conclude that where employees are consistently performing above and beyond the minimum required of them, at a level ultimately likely to lead to business success, three conditions are necessary (CIPD 2001):

- they have the *ability* to do so because they have the necessary knowledge and skills, including skills of working with others (A)

- they are *motivated* to do so (M)

- they are given the *opportunity* to use their skills both in their jobs and in contributing to their work groups and organisational success (O).

This AMO model interprets performance as a function of ability, motivation and opportunity. But what is it that brings such a model to life? Opening up that 'Black box' remains the purpose of the Bath team's ongoing research, and Figure 8 shows the initial 'people and performance' framework that they produced as the context for the AMO model.

Purcell and Hutchinson (2007) still believe that a causal chain of some kind does connect an organisation's HR practices to organisational effectiveness and therefore also to its financial or economic performance. However, their main preoccupation now is not to find 'evidence' from which to produce complex statistical or financial predictions of the kind favoured in several US and UK studies (for example Huselid 1995; Patterson *et al* 1997). It is to find explanations of why and how such a wide and negative gap exists in so many organisations between the intention of HR practices and their impact on the ground.

Their core assumption is that it is not so much the kind and number of HR practices that matter in explaining employees' attitudes to work and performance, but the perception that employees form of whatever HR practices are in place. Their research is therefore focused on the ways in which employees experience HR practices in their particular context, and on the impact of that experience on their attitudes and performance at work. To gain this understanding the researchers use a methodology designed to obtain both managers' and workers' perceptions of HR practices. Their findings have lead them to conclude that (Purcell and Hutchinson 2007):

- A significant gap exists in many organisations today between intended HR practices and those actually experienced by employees.

- The gap is explained mainly by problems experienced by front-line managers (FLMs) in applying those practices in their workplace. FLMs are those who are are accountable to a higher level of management for the performance of a work group of approximately 10 to 25 people.

- FLMs are critically important in helping to create, or transmit, impressions of the organisation as a whole (commitment) and in making jobs satisfying by influencing how demanding the job is, how much autonomy the employee has in the job and the sense of achievement that comes from doing the job. They therefore largely determine how effectively the AMO model operates in the particular situation.

- The body of an organisation's HR practices communicates to employees the nature of that organisation, their value to it and the type of behaviours expected from them. However, if those practices are to be successfully applied, FLMs must be effective in people management. In turn, if FLMs are to be effective people managers they must have appropriate HR policies to work with. It is to this

FIGURE 8 The people and performance framework

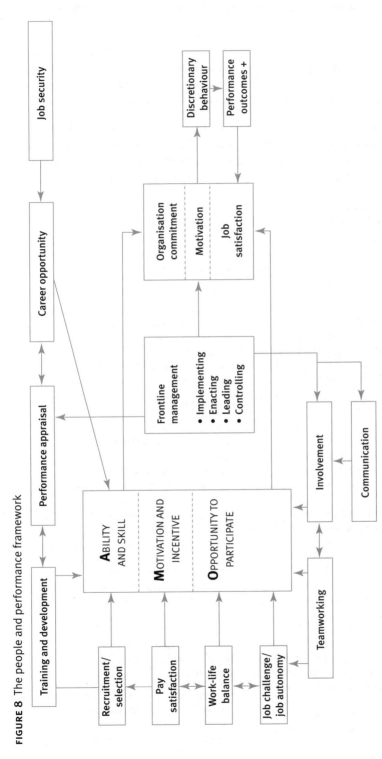

Source: Hutchinson, S. and Purcell, J. (2003) *Bringing Policies to Life: The vital role of front line managers in people management.* London: CIPD, p.2. With permission of the publisher.

interactive relationship that employees respond. It fundamentally influences their own attitudes and behaviour.

- Ultimately, it is the quality of people management in the workplace that is the crucial factor, since poorly designed or inadequate HR policies can be 'rescued' by good management behaviour in much the same way as 'good' HR practices can be negated by poor management behaviour or weak leadership.

- Therefore it is people management (PM) as a whole, not just specific kinds of HR practices or the extent of their coverage in the organisation, that makes the crucial impact on organisational performance. By PM the researchers mean a combination of leadership behaviour, HR practices and organisational culture.

Here is an outline of one of the studies in the Black box research that helped to produce these conclusions.

CASE EXAMPLE

PEOPLE MANAGEMENT AND BUSINESS PERFORMANCE AT TESCO STORES

Tesco is one of the organisations featured in the 'Black box' studies. By the start of the twenty-first century it had been way ahead of its rivals for years, yet in the late 1980s no city analyst would have predicted its extraordinary and sustained rise.

HR practices

The Bath University researchers tracked the progress of HR practices at four Tesco stores. All had been carefully standardised across Tesco and yet there were marked variations in the way they were applied by store managers and in the employee responses and perceptions they evoked. These variations were reflected in variations in the business performance of each store, and some of those variations had negative effects. The HR practices in the best-performing stores were flexible, and were implemented by FLMs who gave their teams significant opportunity for discretionary behaviour in their

jobs, supporting them in using that discretion to improve store performance, and constantly making an explicit link between that performance and Tesco's 'Big Idea'.

The Big Idea

The 'Every little helps' campaign credited to Terry Leahy, now Tesco's chief executive, is often thought to have kick-started Tesco's turnaround. It represents what the researchers have called the 'Big Idea' that acts across Tesco as the primary source of shared organisational purpose. Their studies suggest that in any organisation a Big Idea can have a similar power, provided that it has five attributes, each dependent on leadership and management actions and style, particularly at the organisation's front line (in Tesco's case, its stores). The Big Idea must be:

- *embedded* – Tesco's mission is well communicated, and the values related to it are spread throughout the organisation, becoming deeply rooted in policies and their local application.

- *connected* – The values behind the Big Idea must link together internal and external customers, organisational culture and behaviour. By acting as this kind of glue the Big Idea can give a collective focus to individuals' work and learning and to the application of their skills.

- *enduring* – Those values must remain clear and strong through time, helped by organisational routines and practices – especially training and career development – that managers and team leaders apply to gain commitment to them.

- *collective* – In every workplace across the organisation there must be 'the creation and continuous refinement of excellent routines so that everyone knows what to do and how to do it, time and again' in the local context.

- *measured and managed* – The balanced scorecard approach

(to be discussed in Chapter 14) is used at Tesco to make an explicit link between individuals' goals and those of the organisation. Selfridges expresses its own Big Idea in three goals: to be the place where people want to shop, invest and work. Performance against each of these is measured regularly.

While Tesco's success continues to be remarkable in terms of financial profitability, popularity right across the customer spectrum and a loyal workforce, influential community groups and 'ethical' investors have voiced new interests and goals related to Tesco's performance. Some of these arise from fair trading and environmental concerns and some from a high-street dominance that threatens the livelihood of smaller traders as well as raising fears of a monopoly. So this success story, like all others, is not written in stone. But the Bath studies of Tesco, its front-line managers and their application of the store's HR practices have unique value as an example of explanatory research.

Sources: Purcell, J. *et al* (2003: 28–31);
Rankine, K. (2004)

The overall thrust of the Bath research findings to date is in line with a number of much earlier 'explanatory' research studies carried out elsewhere. For example, the importance of FLMs in embedding and sustaining a cohering organisational purpose was the key feature of Ghoshal and Bartlett's (1994) longitudinal study of Semco (the pseudonym given to an electronics-based industrial products company owned by a diversified group). Two other American researchers, Floyd and Wooldridge (1992, 1994) explored the vital part played by middle-level FLMs in informing and implementing corporate strategy. And Bartel's (2000) study undertaken in Canadian banks showed the importance of site managers in creating an HR environment that had a positive impact on site performance.

REFLECTION

Reflecting on the content of this section of the chapter, what insights does it give you into HR practices in your own organisation? Should there be any changes in their type or in the way in which they are implemented in the workplace?

THE PERFORMANCE MANAGEMENT PROCESS

THE PERFORMANCE MANAGEMENT CYCLE

Performance management is both a process and a cycle of activity whose developmental and control elements need to be in balance to ensure its smooth functioning. The earlier discussion of motivation and of insights provided by the Black Box research and other studies points to the importance of a developmental thrust at those stages in the cycle where individuals' motivation and commitment to the organisation are most prone to dip. Figure 9 identifies induction, skills training, appraisal and continuing personal and professional development as key activities at those points.

INDUCTION

The purpose of induction, whether for the newcomer to the organisation or for the employee who is moving into a new job, role or organisational level, is twofold:

FIGURE 9 The performance management cycle and related L&D activity

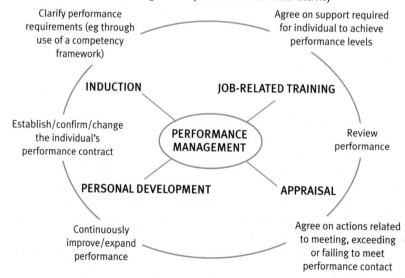

- to introduce newcomers to their job, their team, and the workplace and organisational context

- to establish a positive relationship between the new recruit and the organisation, building his or her commitment to its vision and goals – its 'Big Idea'.

Induction represents the final stage of the recruitment process and the first stage of the performance management process, so by contributing to the design and delivery of effective induction L&D practitioners are aiding both those processes.

Individuals at this stage need to understand more about the organisation's values and belief systems in order to identify any conflicts with their own and how to tackle these. They need to consider the mutual expectations that seem to bind them and their employer (I will discuss this 'psychological contract' in Chapter 9), and where a gap seems to be opening up they may need help in learning how to function confidently in their new context. Whatever the form and content of induction, it should lead to personal development plans that will contribute to work performance and personal growth.

Mentoring is a popular aid to induction. At McDonald's, new entrants go through a three-hour induction and are then partnered with a 'buddy' who comes from a 'training squad' of specially trained employees belonging to their work team.

SKILLS TRAINING

Skills training is the next stage to support the performance management cycle. Sometimes the need for it may be slight and can be met within the induction period, but more usually it follows on from induction. The term is a broad one, since it can encompass the development of any special skills, attitudes or knowledge that are an essential part of the job or task the employee has to perform, and that he or she currently lacks.

Training on or near the job can be carried out by a skilled member of the workteam or by a high-performing member of a workgroup who has proven training skills and the disposition to foster job-related learning – using the kind of 'cognitive apprenticeship' approach discussed in Chapter 5 as a way of also helping the novice to become a full member of the work team that constitutes their community of practice. Other widely used skills training approaches include:

- individual and team-based coaching to develop specific skills and capability (see below)

- short training events, special assignments, projects and visits to other organisations or departments

- educational programmes to achieve an enhanced level of professional knowledge or a broadening of business or functional awareness

- flexible learning methods that blend the use of e-technology with more traditional face to face approaches (see below).

Whatever the methods or combination of methods chosen, they must be based on a sound business case if they are to get the full support needed from management and other key parties. Typical objectives might be to attract and retain the calibre of people needed by the organisation, to provide training that is standards-based and related to national vocational qualifications, to establish a cost-effective way of reinforcing company culture, to build a base for flexibility of skills and for employability – and so on.

While numerical data about training can only indicate a generalised picture, saying nothing about quality, relevance or effectiveness, they do provide valuable insights when gathered through time. The 2004 WERS indicated an improving picture related to the provision of training in UK organisations in that 84% of workplace managers reported off-the-job training had been provided for some of their experienced core employees over the previous year – a significant increase since 1998 when the equivalent figure was only 73%.

Of course it is not only at the first stage of the employment cycle when employees need to acquire new or updated skills, and that is where the continuing development process becomes of such importance – as will be seen below.

APPRAISAL

In the 2004 WERS survey (WERS 2004) 73% of managers in UK workplaces reported that appraisals were undertaken in their organisations, with two-thirds of all workplaces conducting regular appraisals for most non-managerial employees compared with only 48% in 1998.

Appraisal, then, constitutes one of the main tools for managing performance, serving various purposes including the identification of training needs. In the Bath studies, as in many others, it was found to have the potential to raise motivation, commitment and the extent to which employees make positive use of any discretionary power they possess. Broadening the coverage and scope for the appraisal discussion can have particularly positive outcomes (Purcell *et al* 2003). However, when it is misused the appraisal process can produce highly damaging effects on individuals and on the organisation. Four factors are of major importance here:

- *Organisational context* – For example, it is fruitless to try to introduce a developmental appraisal process into an organisation that has a rigid, divisive role structure and a controlling management style that discourage openness, the use of individual discretion and the development of potential.

- *Relationship between the parties* – This, which is itself significantly shaped by organisational context, is the single most powerful influence on the conduct and outcomes of an appraisal discussion, and constitutes one of the key areas of difficulty related to it. If the appraiser–appraisee relationship is not open and supportive it is virtually impossible for a formalised appraisal system to make it so.

- *Methods* – Some methods used during the appraisal process are more likely to produce valid information than others. A popular method (Armstrong and Baron 2004) is 360-degree appraisal: it expands the number of sources involved in reviewing the individual's performance and if handled skilfully it can be a more effective way of helping the individual to gain a balanced perspective on their performance. However, it is not always appropriate or successful (see below).

- *Scope* – Three core principles are stressed in the literature in order to achieve an effective appraisal scheme:

  - A scheme should avoid performance ratings that use structured forms. It is also best to avoid direct and immediate links to pay and promotion, since while such linkage may motivate the relatively rare high achiever, the tensions it can introduce for average and poor performers are likely to have an adverse effect on their motivation and thereby compound the difficulties involved in improving their performance.

  - A scheme's scope should not be restricted to review, planning and control of the appraisee's performance, since this too is likely to have an adverse effect on the appraisee's motivation and their commitment to the organisation.

  - For a scheme to be motivating for appraisees it must have the active commitment of management, the opportunity for mutual learning by appraiser and appraisee, and an emphasis on future-oriented action-planning and continuing development for the appraisee.

The basic problem in appraisal can be an assumption that an organisation is a unitary system rather than one in which there is (and it is natural that there should be) a multiplicity of interests, power groups, perceptions and expectations – the same problem that I have suggested earlier also bedevils much of the research into the HR causal chain. The problem is aggravated where an organisation applies a rigid standardised appraisal scheme to a highly differentiated workforce. What is needed is an appraisal system that, while grounded in a set of core principles that all appraisers must observe, allows business unit leaders to adapt the appraisal process to the specialised characteristics of their local workforce. The balance to be struck here is a difficult one and represents another big challenge for those responsible for designing and overseeing the appraisal system in organisations – usually, HR professionals.

Cultural problems represent another obstacle to effective appraisal, as the following case example illustrates.

CASE EXAMPLE

360-DEGREE APPRAISAL

Although 360-degree appraisal is popular in many organisations it should always be treated with caution.

One issue, esssential to consider where there is an ethnically-mixed workforce, is that for some cultures this form of appraisal represents an unacceptable intrusion on personal dignity. Another is that while those closest to the appraisee are likely to have information that the appraiser would otherwise lack and so can contribute to a fully balanced view of the appraisee's performance, the opposite can occur: some informants may for whatever reason provide biased information that distorts the picture for the appraisee.

Of more relevance than all of this, perhaps, is that at the end of the day while the views of peers, customers, functional bosses and other parties will all carry weight, those of the line manager are still likely to be the most powerful in determining the outcomes of appraisal. If the manager is inept and/or ill-disposed towards the appraisee, then introducing 360-degree appraisal will almost certainly make little difference to a fundamental bias in the appraisal discussion's outcome.

Happily, few difficulties in appraisal should be intractable. Provided that there is the will within the organisation to develop a system that is appropriate, flexible and fair, together with the commitment to make it work, a way can always be found to overcome operational problems. Once again it all goes back to context and to the vision, values and leadership both at the top of the organisation and within each workplace.

CONTINUING DEVELOPMENT

The appraisal discussion should trigger a process of personal development planning, action and review to aid every employee's continuing personal and professional development during their time in the organisation. Again this is not a trouble-free process, as there may be conflicting views between appraiser and appraisee about what constitutes appropriate development. As will be seen in Chapter 7 it requires a genuine collaboration between managers, any HR professionals and individuals to produce personal development plans that are feasible, that meet the needs of individuals in ways that the organisation can, and is willing to, afford, and that will have the active support of line management and team leaders. Continuing personal development can be powerfully aided through day-to-day work activity, but that too has costs attached and must be carefully thought through.

REFLECTION

How far do you think performance management in your own organisation strikes an acceptable balance between a focus on business targets and achieving a motivating and developmental process for the individual? And what suggestions – if any are needed – would you make for its improvement?

TYPES OF LEARNING AND 'HELPING' ACTIVITY TO AID PERFORMANCE MANAGEMENT

For the purpose of this section I will use Mezirow's (1985) classification of three types of learning, since these fit well into a performance management context:

- *Instrumental learning* – This means learning how to perform a job or role better once the basic standard of performance has been attained. A key method here is learning on the job. This can be highly effective, provided that there is someone to encourage learners in the course of their daily tasks to identify problems, to formulate appropriate action and try it out, to observe the effects and learn from them.

- *Dialogic learning* – Dialogic learning involves interacting with others in ways that will produce a growing understanding of the culture of the organisation and of how it typically achieves its goals. Dialogic learning is particularly valuable at induction stage or when people are promoted into unfamiliar areas of the organisation. It can help individuals to quickly make sense of the organisational world they have entered and develop the confidence to operate competently in it. Mentoring is a powerful dialogic learning process.

- *Self-reflective learning* – This is the kind of learning that leads individuals to develop new patterns of understanding, thinking and behaving. It is needed when people have to operate in ways that are unfamiliar to them. Self-reflective learning, as I explained in Chapter 5, involves unlearning and new learning and so is only possible in an environment that enables people to see error as a positive learning vehicle (Argyris 1982). Depending on their design, educational and training programmes can generate self-reflective learning. So can work-based learning processes that expose people to new ways of thinking and new situations.

Coaching and mentoring are important processes that can support the PMP. To take each in turn:

Coaching

Coaching is defined by one expert, Anthony Grant at the University of Sydney, as (*http://www.psych.usyd.edu.au/coach* [accessed 28 March 2008]):

> Coaching: The research, theory and practice of the application of the behavioural science of psychology to the enhancement of life experience, work performance and personal growth of normal, non-clinical populations.

Coaching, like counselling and mentoring, is about helping the individual to gain self-awareness, but it is goal-focused and action is required so that the individual can move forward. The goal-setting process has two components: skill development and psychological development. The outcome sought is that coachees (to use the technical if clumsy term) will achieve the goals set, and will thereafter feel able and confident to set personal goals for themselves (Passmore 2003: 31).

Many managers see coaching as simply a training tool. There is an equally mistaken view that coaching is a highly directive and supportive style only appropriate with relatively inexperienced people of moderate competence (*ibid*). In fact in business organisations coaching is widely used to develop leadership potential, to promote team effectiveness, to enhance individuals' influence and improve interpersonal skills, and to support people during career transitions (Lee and Pick 2004). Styhre and Josephson (2007) reviewed a year-long action research coaching project in the Swedish construction industry. It showed that by participating in a coaching programme site managers developed skills for reflecting on their work–life situation, improved their communication and became better equipped for seeing a broader range of perspectives in their work. In addition, the programme opened up new discussions in the construction projects which benefited further communication. The authors noted the costs and effort that coaching involves but also its potential as an effective approach to leadership development.

Coaching in the UK has seen explosive growth within a short period of time. Findings from the CIPD's 2008 annual L&D survey suggest that almost three-quarters of UK employers now use it in their organisations (CIPD 2008a). Two fifths of respondents' organisations offered coaching to all employees, although 39% provided it for directors and senior management only and a third restricted it to senior managers and line managers/supervisors. Its purpose varied likewise. When offered to all employees the aim was usually general personal development and improvement of poor performance, whereas 61% of those offering it only to managers used the process more strategically, as part of a wider management and leadership development programme.

However, there are still wide variations in practice and in standards. Critical issues include:

- whether to 'tack coaching on to an ever-growing list of line manager responsibilities' or to develop a 'clear, embedded, fully aligned strategy that deploys dedicated coaches to impregnate the engire organisational culture' (Howe 2008b: 34)

- how best to structure and measure the coaching process in order to ensure that it adds organisational as well as individual value

- how to ensure high, ethical and consistent coaching standards across the organisation.

Investment in internal coaching often derives from a belief that an internally-run process is cheaper. Skilled and well supervised internal coaching can bring important benefits including a deeper understanding of the business and its culture than external coaches often possess, and the development in senior HR managers of skills as internal consultants. Coaching by leaders and managers, when available to all employees, can also make a positive impact on organisational climate, on motivation and on performance (Goleman 2000). As Arney observed (2006), managers who acquire coaching skills in order to improve their all-round managerial capability can use them in many areas of their management role, not least that part of it relating to staff development.

Yet caution must be exercised here. Internal coaching can involve high costs of training, of supervising the coaching process and of ensuring workloads are freed to devote the time needed to coaching activity. And as Arney (2006) also stressed, coach and manager, like mentor and manager, are two quite different roles. For a manager to combine the two in relation to those who report directly to him or her can set up tensions that ultimately destroy the coaching process.

The CIPD's 2008 L&D annual survey revealed that the bulk of the responsibility for delivering coaching in respondents' organisations was held by line managers coaching those who report to them (36%) and by HR staff or L&D specialists (30%). Nearly half the respondents anticipated an even greater coaching responsibility would fall to line managers in the coming five years. It also revealed serious concerns that led one expert to remark on (Howe 2008b: 34):

> the murky picture painted by organisations undertaking coaching. There is still no great clarity emerging around its purpose … It would seem that coaching is still the least understood learning intervention.

Despite the fact that 80% of respondents reported that line managers were using coaching methods for some of their staff, only some of those managers had received 'some' basic coaching training. For such a complex and demanding process, that is no guarantee of high standards of quality, ethicality and consistency. Equally worrying, although 72% of respondents judged coaching to be an effective tool, half the respondents were satisfied with assessing coaching's value through informal reviews with line managers, coaches and coachees. Only 8% reported that coaching's organisational results were evaluated regularly and through a formal process. This failure to even attempt to link coaching to the business by more than an informal approach is a weakness that had also been identified in the CIPD's surveys in the previous two years. It suggests that L&D practitioners have still much to learn about the importance of making a business case for what has become one of their major fields of activity.

To end on a positive note: it seems from the CIPD's 2008 survey that more coaches do now appreciate the value of supervision for the development of their expertise and for the support it provides in what can be an isolating and demanding activity. From the organisation's point of view valuable information about how employees perceive the implementation of business strategies or change initiatives can be gathered from the supervisory process, provided that full client confidentiality is observed. This, then, is another area where L&D professionals should be taking a lead in bringing about improvements to the whole coaching process.

REFLECTION

Reflecting on the observations made in this section about coaching as a 'helping' process for performance management, how beneficial might it be – or is it – in your own organisation, and what reliable evidence is there to support your assessment here?

Mentoring

Garvey (2004: 8) defines mentoring as:

> [a] process whereby one person acts as counsellor and friend to another, usually to support them as they enter an organisation and have to familiarise themselves with its culture and processes, or as they take on new responsibilities in an unfamiliar part or level of an organisation. … The agenda is the mentee's and mentoring may have both an organisational and an individual focus.

Mentoring is usually a face-to-face process, although it can also be delivered through a virtual medium, when it becomes 'a learning dialogue conducted electronically' (Clutterbuck, quoted by Hall 2005: 34). It is closely associated with induction, career and personal development and change. Mentors can facilitate instrumental, dialogic and self-reflective learning. They should be both role models and guides, but they must be able to challenge their mentees and make them think. For mentoring to succeed as a helping activity it must be founded on a close, supportive and trusting relationship. In order to avoid conflict of interests it should never be carried out by mentees' managers or by anyone else who is in direct authority over the mentees.

There are many mentoring models. Microsoft, for example, uses the 'five Cs', which focuses individuals on the challenges they face and achievable results, the choices open to them, the consequences of each choice and creative solutions or conclusions. It makes use of both internal and external mentors, valuing the fresh perspectives that the latter can bring (Glover 2002a). Team mentoring is also practised and is of particular value in helping to build a close-knit community of practice.

Standards in 'helping' activity

If these 'helping' processes are to benefit the organisation as well as individuals there needs to be:

- an understanding of coaching and mentoring as processes that involve reciprocal learning, not a situation in which the coaches and mentors should be assuming a dominating or manipulative role

- a clear business case for their introduction, with an agreed process for supervising mentors and coaches and for monitoring and evaluating organisational as well as individual outcomes

- an adequate resource base, adjustment in the workloads of the involved, and support for mentees and coachees in their continuing development

- an up-to-date database of potential suitable mentors and coaches, and a skilled selection and training process against clear and relevant criteria

- careful piloting of initiatives, and the highlighting of their benefits across the organisation to ensure understanding of the way in which the processes operate and of their value.

Given the number of agencies and individuals in the open market offering coaching and mentoring services, it is essential that only those adequately trained and bound by a high-standard code of conduct are employed. The industry is very fragmented but five key bodies including the CIPD and the European Mentoring and Coaching Council (EMCC) are co-operating to develop and disseminate standards that should gain widespread acceptance. In 2006 the EMCC rolled out across European organisations the first Quality Award, linked to a competency framework which is now being further developed to fit with cultures in different countries. Coaching qualifications providers (including universities) and organisations' in-house coaching departments can be accredited under the scheme (*http://www.emccouncil. org* [accessed 28 March 2008]).

E-learning and performance management

Finally, e-learning can also be a helping activity. Currently there is little sign that it is achieving its full potential here, but the example on page 172 provides a benchmark in several respects.

WHAT CAN L&D PRACTITIONERS CONTRIBUTE?

PRESSURES ON PERFORMANCE MANAGEMENT

As we have seen, recent research has re-emphasised managers' and team leaders' powerful influence over employee commitment and performance. It has also

CASE EXAMPLE

USING E-LEARNING TO AID PERFORMANCE MANAGEMENT

In 2006 AOL UK, the world's leading Internet service provider, used Brightwave – a UK-based specialist in integrating communications, learning and performance in the workplace – to develop an e-learning programme designed to train staff in the company's new performance management processes. The programme covered communication, learning and performance support. It aimed to develop a blend of communication and learning to ensure successful adoption of the PM processes over a period of time rather than providing merely a one-off training experience.

'We are a fast-growing company and it is important that our HR processes keep up with this growth, which is why we are introducing new processes for personal development and performance management,' said Denise Cording, HR Business Partner for Learning and Development, for AOL UK. 'The first step is to educate our employees about the processes, why we are introducing them and how they will affect individuals.'

In AOL's fast-changing environment it was essential to ensure that the programme did not focus solely on provision of an e-learning course but was well contextualised. It incorporated several elements designed to appeal to the specific needs of AOL staff: a short multimedia trailer to raise awareness, a 30-minute e-learning course using a storyline to cover the key topics, a quiz to check knowledge, an evaluation questionnaire, and an interactive process map as a performance support tool. Brightwave gave careful thought to how to best position and support the training before and after its launch and completion, and created interactive process maps as a performance support tool to bridge the learning–doing gap.

Source: *http://www.brightwave. co.uk/05_00_34.htm.* With acknowledgements to Brightwave and AOL

demonstrated the importance to employees of receiving recognition and respect for their contribution to the organisation and of enjoying good relationships with colleagues and supervisors in the workplace (Rainbird *et al* 2004; Pass 2005).

Set against this is the fact that in today's increasingly unstable economic conditions pressures are building on managers to achieve ever tougher performance targets in their workplaces. Surveys such as those by Henley-Hay 2006 (Houldsworth and Jirasinghe 2006) and the Novations Group (Pfeffer and Sutton 2006b, and *http// www.novations.com* [accessed 30 March 2008]) show that measurement-based approaches are now widely used in organisations, with a particular emphasis on forced distribution (the allocation of predetermined quotas of managers' staff into categories such as above average, average and below average). The latter method has become particularly prevalent in the public sector where it is seen as a tough but effective way of helping to achieve the stringent performance and downsizing targets imposed by government (Arkin 2007a, and also Chapter 10). The same surveys reveal the damaging outcomes of such an approach in organisations where trust is already low and/or where employees do not clearly understand from performance criteria exactly what is expected of them.

So has the developmental approach reported by Armstrong and Baron (2004) been largely abandoned? It is hard to be certain. It seems that in some organisations, while the performance management system is strongly focused on measures related to achievement of business targets that will make a direct and positive impact on business performance, a variety of practices are being employed to enhance the motivation and engagement of employees (something I will discuss in detail in Chapter 14), especially through the reward system, effective communication and 'good' management. Despite concerns related to findings from the Henley-Hay survey 71% of its 400 respondents said that their performance management system was primarily about motivation, with only 29% seeing it as being about measurement despite the heavy emphasis on metrics; and three quarters reported that they had regular discussions with their manager about their development. Take the following example:

CASE EXAMPLE

MEASUREMENT AT BELRON

Belron is a global organisation trading under names such as Carglass and Autoglass. It has a strong measurement culture, using key measures such as windscreen repair rates and customer satisfaction scores in its performance management process. However, in managing the performance of its leaders it combines hard with soft measures, especially through use of a climate survey that provides data on the climate that managers have created in their workplace.

Each manager in their performance review is presented with results of the survey relating to their own workplace, based on a gap analysis that identifies the difference between perceptions of 'what it is like to work here' and 'what we would like it to feel like'. By focusing not only on quantitative but also on this kind of broader qualitative measures Belron believes it has achieved an appropriate balance between a hard and soft focus for performance management. By incorporating into its measurement process analysis of managers' influence on organisational climate as a key variable that influences business performance, it reports that it has achieved a 66% increase in managerial capability.

Source: Houldsworth, E. G. (2007)
People Management, 25 January

REWARD ISSUES

One point made consistently in the HR literature is that if L&D practices are to be effective they must be horizontally aligned – that is to say, linked with other HR practices and supported by them. In the PMP this is particularly true of the relationship between L&D and the organisation's reward strategies. The reward package should act as tangible evidence of recognition and respect for employees' levels of performance and commitment to the organisation. Therefore it has a key part to play in ensuring that the AMO model springs into life. However in the CIPD's 2008 Reward Management Survey (CIPD 2008b) only about one third of the 603 organisations covered had formally aligned their strategy for success with a reward strategy, and most of those who in the 2007 survey (CIPD 2007c) had noted their intent to introduce a reward strategy had not succeeded. Furthermore a smaller proportion of employers in 2008 (21%) than in 2007 (29%) had adopted a 'total reward' approach where the benefits package incorporates recognition of a range of features related to performance such as L&D and aspects of company culture and values.

Responding to the CIPD's 2008 Reward Survey, 73% of employers said that their line managers communicated the pay message. 68% of those line managers had been charged with the formal responsibility to do so (CIPD 2008b). Yet the employers also expressed doubts about the capabilities of their line managers to deliver the appropriate messages, and about whether their managers had received appropriate coaching and development. Too often reward seemed to be designed in isolation from a proper consideration of those expected to implement it.

Even when managers cannot play a significant part in decisions made about the total reward package for those who report to them, we have seen throughout this chapter the difference that they can make to the commitment and performance of those reporting to them through the quality of relationship that they develop. Yet here again there is also uncertainty. Where trust, co-operative behaviour and openness are all high, it is to be expected that both parties will perceive the relationship between them in very much the same way. Data from WERS 2004 revealed a confusing picture here. Managerial perceptions of management–employee relations indicated real progress had been made between 1998 and 2004, with 30% of managers believing that they had 'improved a lot', 30% reporting they had 'improved a little', and only 4% feeling that they had deteriorated. Yet their employees had perceived little improvement during the same period (Kersley *et al* 2006). Also, in half of all cases employees' perceptions of relations with their managers were worse than those held by the managers themselves, whereas management ratings were worse than employees' in only 13% of cases.

Reflection on reward issues and employees' perceptions related to them thus gives further weight to the points made by the Bath University researchers following their 'Black Box' research that (Purcell and Hutchinson 2007):

- It is the body of an organisation's HR practices, taken together, that most strongly communicates to employees the nature of that organisation, their value to it and the type of behaviours expected from them.

- If those practices are to be successfully applied, front-line managers must be effective in people management.

- But if FLMs are to be effective people managers they must have appropriate HR policies to work with.

L&D PRACTICES TO ENHANCE COMMITMENT AND DEVELOPMENT IN THE WORKPLACE

In the Bath University studies two L&D practices have been shown consistently to have a powerful influence over employee attitudes that lead to positive discretionary behaviour: careers (in the sense of a 'developing future') and training. These seem to derive their value for employees from the promise they hold 'of learning to do things better, or doing new things. It is the sense of progression and purpose that is important, especially in linking to organisational commitment' (Purcell *et al* 2003: 73).

L&D of such kinds may enhance levels of employee commitment, but they do not always need to be formalised or complex types of activity. Raising commitment is primarily about understanding what employees value most, given their work situation, and introducing managerial and developmental approaches that show recognition of and responsiveness to those needs. Many employees, especially those with low skills and poor educational attainment, are isolated in monotonous and unfulfilling jobs. As the following case example shows, they are not always motivated by the classic government strategy of promoting basic skills accreditation. L&D interventions of a different and simpler kind can improve the quality of their work environment and enable job mobility within and beyond the organisation.

CASE EXAMPLE

THE LOCAL GOVERNMENT COOK-FREEZE CENTRE

Research carried out under the Economic and Social Research Council's Future of Work programme to explore skills development amongst low-paid workers in the public sector involved in-depth case studies of six large public sector organisations. In a paper on the concept of 'employer demand for skill' Rainbird and colleagues (2004) discuss three small workplaces within these larger organisations, analysing the implications of different types of training interventions for performance management.

One finding was that the possession of skills demotivated workers who had no opportunity to practise them. Many of the workers studied had formal qualifications in excess of those needed for the job. Job redesign had no relevance for them, since they wanted career progression opportunities which for many did not exist. Where training was not accredited but tied tightly to a specific job, this was also demotivating because it reduced low-paid workers' employability yet further. Training was also often used to implement strategies involving new work arrangements, but this put more pressure on staff where it legitimised already unrealistic workloads. Used in this way training was not viewed as an opportunity but as an unwelcome necessity and a source of increased stress.

However, in one of the three studies, the least promising at first glance, a more positive picture emerged. It centred on a small, relatively stable workforce working on a production line in the cook-freeze centre employing 14 staff, who were part of a much larger functional department of the City Council. It was the central production unit for a 'meals on wheels' service and the customer was the Social Services Department. The work was monotonous – for example, using an ice-cream scoop for an hour – and job rotation was used less as a means of making work more interesting (because there was little scope for this), more to reduce the risk of repetitive strain injury.

Despite the limited and poorly-paid nature of the work, some of the staff mentioned their pride in doing a job which was socially useful and gave them a sense of responsibility and progression. The production supervisor identified a range of mechanisms for learning about the work. These included shadowing the manager, attending meetings and receiving training on new equipment from the suppliers. Part of her status derived from her recognition of the value of her own problem-solving skills and the fact that the workforce knew their own jobs extremely well: she perceived that she had a crucial role to play in building their self-confidence, especially by providing reassurance in relation to off-the-job training programmes, facilitating learning opportunities for the workforce even if those opportunities did not directly relate to their jobs.

Some workers felt they had developed as a result of learning opportunities provided through the workplace or external to it, and had gained self-confidence and an enhanced potential. Some were attending courses in their own time, and some were even paying for these themselves. Not all the courses were relevant to their work, but they were valued for having a utility in their personal lives or for contributing to their future employability. Levels of labour turnover were extremely low and the workers had a commitment to their workplace. Its mainly female members lived locally and considered that the working hours and the jobs they held were good.

Lack of resources restricted the demand for skills in the organisation of production and job design, but this had not prevented staff's access to broader development opportunities. Learning went wider than participation in formal training events and they could point to a number of ways in which it was facilitated in the work environment, both by their supervisor and by a culture where they felt they could learn from others and ask for help if they needed it. The supervisory style also contributed to the quality of the work environment and thence to the employees' commitment to their work.

Source: Rainbird, H., Munro, A. and Holly, L. (2004). With permission of the publishers, Palgrave Macmillan

The case shows once again that to be effective L&D processes need to operate in a context of good leadership and management. Looking back at the case of Linda the disillusioned recruit earlier in the chapter, her job satisfaction might have improved if she had been offered a clear career path and relevant opportunities for training at Pyrotem. But if the firm's leadership and management had remained unchanged her commitment to Pyrotem would almost certainly have reduced. In the end, therefore, she would probably still have left the firm.

TASKS FOR L&D PRACTITIONERS

In many organisations L&D practitioners will have little say in how the performance management process is designed to operate, in what kind of 'deal', new, old or indifferent, is put on the table for new recruits, or in how the motivation, attitudes and performance of people in the workplace are understood and treated. What, then, are the main contributions that they can make to ensuring a mutually beneficial PMP for employees and the organisation? Drawing on a variety of research studies and good practice in the field, the following should be priorities for action in most contexts:

- Raise awareness at all levels of management through L&D activity of the negative impact of low commitment on their organisation's performance and competitive capability and of the positive effects that can be gained when employees enjoy good relationships, respect and recognition (Pass 2005).

- Promote and deliver leadership and management training that develops not only functional performance management skills but also capability to understand and respond positively to people's experience and expectations of the PMP.

- Promote L&D that can encourage and aid discretionary behaviour in all employees, not just those judged to be key workers.

- Ensure appropriate L&D opportunities for line managers so that their capabilities will allow more sophisticated reward approaches to be implemented effectively in organisations (CIPD 2008b).

- Pay particular attention to FLMs as an occupational group with numerous responsibilities and often competing priorities. Respond to their needs for career development and training in leadership behaviours as well as technical skills and knowledge. Ensure that they have access to further development, coaching and guidance (Purcell and Hutchinson 2007).

- Work with FLMs to produce and apply straightforward, consistent and appropriate people management and development practices for their teams and to lead thinking on how to make the best of teamworking, whether or not autonomous (Purcell and Hutchinson 2007).

- Through the planning, design and delivery of training and learning processes, help to build a positive relationship between FLMs and their own managers, since this relationship is the biggest variable explaining FLMs' own levels of affective commitment (Purcell and Hutchinson 2007).

REFLECTION

Reflecting on this list of priorities that I have just suggested for L&D professionals, how many do you think apply in the context of your own organisation – and how well do you feel they are being put into practice?

CONCLUSION

The purpose of this chapter has been to explore research and practice relating to the performance management process in organisations, in order to clarify the kind of contribution that L&D professional can make to that process. You should by now understand the operation of the performance management cycle and the ways in which L&D activity can give it a strong developmental thrust. You can test yourself against the review questions for this chapter, in Appendix 3.

The chapter's five sections have covered the following main ground:

- Handy's (1985) motivation model as an aid to understanding the dynamic nature of the human motivational process and its links to workplace performance

- conclusions from reviews of 15 years of research studies into the 'HR causal chain', revealing an unreliable evidence base for claims that certain types and configuration of HR practices link to enhanced business performance as measured by economic or financial yardsticks

- the need for an HR research philosophy focused on explanatory rather than predictive studies, and the utility here of longitudinal research using national databases such as WERS in the UK to identify, compare and contrast managers' and employees' perceptions of employment relationships, job satisfaction levels and HR practices and values

- the need to achieve an effective balance of control and developmental elements in the PMP, and the contribution made here by induction, skills training, appraisal and continuing development processes

- types of learning – instrumental, dialogic and self-reflective – that can aid the effective operation of the PMP, together with helping activity – particularly mentoring and coaching – that can underpin it. Such activity must rest on a sound business case, be well understood across the organisation and be performed by those who are trained to a high professional standard

- the importance of consistency between all HR policies and practices that support the PMP, with particular attention needing to be paid to the total reward package and to the capability of line managers to convey the reward message effectively to employees

- seven priorities for action by L&D practitioners in order to enhance the PMP in their organisations.

The key message of this chapter has been that effective performance of individuals and teams in the workplace depends on a favourable organisational context. As one chief executive commented (Bajer 2001), personnel and development professionals may work hard with their business partners to create a well-organised performance management system, manage a network of coaching and mentor relationships, generate a mass of appraisal, feedback and PDP documentation and produce accurate training plans for the coming year. The organisation may pride itself that in these ways it is being transparently people-centred. Yet all will go for nothing without the appropriate vision, leadership, management and workplace climate.

EXLPORE FURTHER

FURTHER INFORMATION SOURCES

Chartered Institute of Personnel And Development (2005c) *People and Performance: Designing the HR processes for maximum performance delivery*. Online tool based on the CIPD's research project *Understanding the People and Performance Link*. Available at: http://www.cipd.co.uk/tools [accessed 30 March 2008]

Chartered Institute of Personnel And Development (2007b) *Coaching in Organisations*. Research Insight. London: CIPD. Online version also available at: http://www.cipd.co.uk/research/ [accessed 28 March 2008]

Garvey, B., Stokes, P. and Megginson, D. (2008) *Coaching and Mentoring: Theory and practice*. London: Sage. The first research-based book of its type

Hutchinson, S. and Purcell, J. (2007) *Line Managers in Reward, Learning and Development: Research into practice*. London: CIPD

Valentin, C. (2006) 'Researching human resource development: emergence of a critical approach to HRD enquiry', *International Journal of Training and Development*, Vol.10, No.1: 17–29. Concerns the need for more 'explanatory' research in the L&D field

CIPD podcast, 6 March 2007. *Reward*. Available online at: http://www.cipd.co.uk/podcasts [accessed 3 April 2008]

http://www.statistics.gov.uk/ STATBASE/Source.asp?vlnk=1328 [accessed 26 March 2008]. Workplace Employee Relations Survey website

CHAPTER 7

A Six-stage Training Cycle for Co-creating Value

INTRODUCTION

L&D professionals must be able to organise learning events that provide benefits for the business as well as for individuals, whether those events are of a formal kind or consist of more informal activity such as quality circles, coaching and team briefings. Training remains a highly popular approach to learning, but research across the world indicates that, despite the many 'success' stories published regularly in popular journals, training programmes too often fail to make a significant organisational impact.

In previous editions of this book I have recommended an eight-stage cycle to give a processual emphasis to the interlinked tasks of planning, designing, delivering and evaluating training events. I have now produced a revised version of the cycle in order to give an equally strong emphasis to collaborative value-creation. In Chapter 8 its practical application will be demonstrated through a real-life case study.

The chapter deals with the processes involved in organising and ensuring the successful outcomes of training whose purpose is to create major value for the business as well as for individual employees. However, its content is equally relevant for any kind of business-focused planned learning activity. There is no scope in the chapter to go into the operational detail of functional training tasks, so readers will need to consult specialist sources for that kind of information. Some useful starting-points are given at the end of the chapter.

The first section of this chapter outlines evidence pointing to the continuing lack of convincing links between training and the business, suggests the main reasons for this failure, and introduces the six-stage processual cycle whose purpose is to ensure that the training investment creates value for the business as well as for the learners. The subsequent six sections explain each stage of the cycle in turn.

WHAT IS GOING WRONG?

As seen in Chapter 6, in the UK the CIPD's 2008 Learning and Development (L&D) survey confirmed organisations' continuing preference for formal training events whether in or out of house as a way of achieving key organisational outcomes (CIPD 2008a). Research across the world produces a similar picture, with organisations' training investment rising steadily over the years (Bober and Bartlett 2004; Holton III and Naquin 2005). However, in the UK, going by the 2008 CIPD survey, that investment is very strongly influenced by line management's performance of its L&D role. To look at some key findings here:

- The bulk of responsibility for the tasks involved in the training cycle described in this chapter continued to lie with L&D specialists (CIPD 2008a: 13). However, 72% of the 2008 survey's respondents identified the biggest change in their organisations as far as L&D was concerned was new programmes to develop the line manager's role.

- Nearly 50% predicted that line managers would have greater responsibility for L&D in the coming five years.

- Only 21% identified monitoring and evaluation of training as the activity on which they spent most of their time, compared with 46% who spent most of their time delivering training, and 36% who spent most of it managing delivery by external providers.

- Despite that, 56% believed that the second most important change likely to affect L&D in their organisations in the coming five years was more emphasis on monitoring, measurement and evaluation of training effectiveness.

So no matter who holds the main responsibility for training in organisations, evaluation of its outcomes does not seem to be a priority in many. It is therefore unsurprising that training rarely provides convincing evidence of its business value. Key weaknesses are poor planning and a dearth of evaluation at unit and corporate organisational levels (Santos and Stuart 2003; Russ-Eft and Preskill 2005; CIPD 2007a).

What causes such weaknesses? Apart from lack of competence, one reason lies in many organisations' failure to provide line managers with adequate support and incentives to perform their training tasks effectively. Another is pressure on training managers to focus on hard budgetary and performance targets, coupled with a drive for cost containment that can lead to fluctuating training budgets and consequently complicate training planning and evaluation (Aragon-Sanchez et al 2003). Yet none of this is enough to explain the widespread disconnect between the business imperative and training activity.

I suggest that a major reason is the continuing influence of the 'systematic training cycle' on L&D practitioners' thinking and activity. I have indicated in Chapter 1 the weaknesses of that cycle and they are worth expansion here:

- the emphasis it places on functional knowledge and skills and the encouragement it thereby gives to an 'inside-out mindset' (Wright *et al* 2004). For any training to add value at the organisational level L&D practitioners should identify as their first priority the business outcomes that it is designed to achieve, and be able to make a tight link between business and training outcomes. However, research suggests that this focus on working 'outside-in' from the starting point of the business is rarely to be found. In training as in the wider HR arena 'inside-out' mindsets predominate (*ibid*)

- lack of attention to processes as distinct from functional tasks, and therefore failure to adequately involve key stakeholders in the entire cycle of training activity. The most expertly designed training can fail where such engagement is lacking (Kessels and Harrison 1998)

- the grounding of the systematic training cycle in a simplistic rational-economic view of the business universe (Pfeffer 2005). The training profession worldwide still relies overmuch on the logical, structured methods and tools of analysis and decision-making (Holton III and Naquin 2005). Too few training professionals speak the language of the business, or use business rather than training metrics to measure the value to the organisation of formal learning activity. It is unsurprising that in the UK at least they are not considered key business partners (CIPD 2007a).

A VALUE-ADDING TRAINING CYCLE

The six-stage training cycle proposed in this chapter is driven not by functional tasks but by a partnership process, as shown in Figure 10. The primary emphasis throughout is on collaboration to ensure that training tasks add value to the business, its L&D function and the learners. The cycle thus retains the former eight-stage cycle's reliance on achieving external as well as internal consistency – terms coined by Kessels (1996):

> *Internal consistency* refers to the outcome achieved by the effective application of a systematic approach to planning, design, delivery and evaluation tasks.

> *External consistency* refers to the commitment, shared purpose and perceptions of stakeholders that can be gained through actively involving them in the operation of the whole training cycle.

The six-stage cycle will rarely if ever operate in an entirely sequential fashion. Several stages may have to be conducted in parallel and some may fall out of sequence. Operating under time and other pressures, others will be subject to a variety of errors and omissions. In all these respects L&D professionals must be able to reconcile the neatness of textbook theory with the messiness of real life. A key

FIGURE 10 The six-stage value-adding training cycle

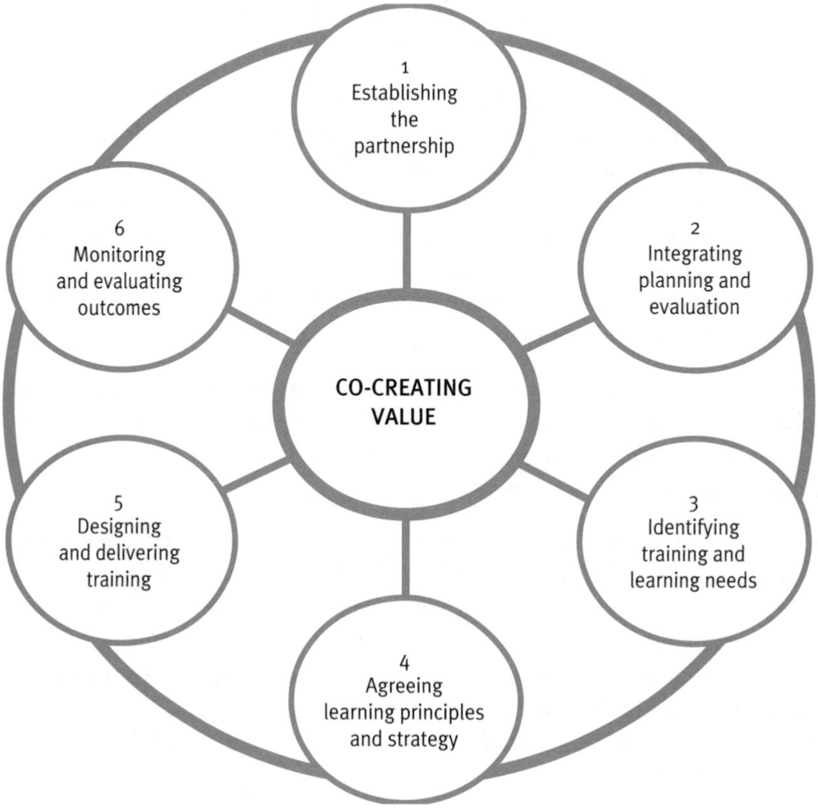

1
Establishing
the
partnership

6
Monitoring
and evaluating
outcomes

2
Integrating
planning and
evaluation

CO-CREATING
VALUE

5
Designing
and delivering
training

3
Identifying
training and
learning needs

4
Agreeing
learning principles
and strategy

message of this chapter, however, is that when they forge an effective partnership with sponsors, providers and customers that is based on a shared determination to achieve value through sharing expertise and insights, they will be able to resolve most difficulties. Such partnership can also produce innovative solutions that far exceed any they are likely to produce working alone in their functional silos. Prahalad and Ramaswamy (2002) observed that in an age of advanced technology and rapid change companies must quickly learn how to co-create value with customers who have access to information on a global scale and who can rapidly and easily compare experiences, giving them an unprecedented influence on value creation. The six-stage cycle rests on that same principle – of co-creating value.

REFLECTION

Consider whether a particular training programme with which you are familiar was generally judged to have been a 'success'. What did 'success' mean in that context, and what factors of the kind discussed in this section either helped it or prevented it from being achieved?

STAGE 1: ESTABLISHING THE PARTNERSHIP

This first stage of the six-stage training cycle creates value in two ways:

- by leading to the creation of a strong business case for the event, working in partnership with stakeholders

- by providing, through its processes, a vehicle to develop the project team's in-house skills relating to business partnership, project management and membership and business planning.

IDENTIFYING DRIVERS AND PURPOSE

As will be seen from the case study that follows in Chapter 8, the initial idea of investing in a training programme does not always come from human resource (HR) professionals. However, once L&D staff do become involved they must work with the originators to produce answers to two critically important questions. Their purpose is to clarify whether the proposed training will, in fact, generate added organisational value and therefore justify investment (Brooks and Hulme 2007):

- What are the organisational drivers for training? Identifying these will help to determine precisely where and why organisational performance has most to gain from investing in a training intervention – and whether such an investment will be worthwhile at all.

- What key business outcomes will such an intervention produce, and how? Agreeing on these in broad terms will enable the identification of a convincing organisational purpose for the proposed intervention.

If it is decided to go ahead with a training intervention, a partnership must be formed in order to drive the whole training cycle from that point on.

ESTABLISHING THE BUSINESS PARTNERSHIP

As will be seen in more detail in Chapter 13, training partnerships are rarely non-problematic. Once the initial decision to invest in training is made and more parties have to be brought in to help in its planning, design and delivery, 'added value' can become a contested term. It can raise the need for expert leadership of a complex cluster of stakeholders to reconcile conflicting interests and build shared perceptions of exactly what 'value' means, together with the commitment to strive for that value at every stage of the training cycle.

The partnership for any major training event operates at two levels – the overall partnership of sponsors and stakeholders and, within that overall group, the team that is given responsibility for the management of the project.

Gaining sponsorship

Sponsors are responsible for authorising a project's planning, design and budget, and for ensuring its effective delivery and evaluation. Their importance lies in their ability to ensure a high level of attention and buy-in for the project across the organisation, using their status and authority to give visible and active support to it through every stage of its cycle. With a corporate training programme, the business sponsors are likely to be the chief executive officer (CEO) or equivalent and the HR or L&D director. With more localised learning events they will probably be the equivalents of the organisation's L&D manager and its HR director.

Establishing the project team

A major training programme will often require the formation of a team consisting of relevant personnel within an organisation and some external experts, whereas smaller-scale events may be managed by a team consisting purely of internal personnel (including support staff). Team membership may increase or reduce over time as contingencies arise.

No matter what the size or fluidity of the project team may be, its members must be able to manage the training event effectively through all its stages, from planning to final evaluation. Building an effective team is thus not only about skilful project management. It is also about ensuring a powerful collective learning experience. A considerable front-end investment in time and expertise is needed in order to generate amongst team members a sufficiency of shared mental maps together with a mix of viewpoints and expertise that will produce innovative and flexible training design and delivery. Every significant problem, every emerging need before and during a programme for some change of focus, content or delivery, some rethinking of interim objectives or the resolution of problems at the individual learners' level – all will fall to the team to tackle. The more complex the training, the steeper will be the team's learning curve. Lack of attention to building an effective partnership both between members of that team and between team and wider stakeholder group explains why many training programmes have no lasting organisational impact (Kessels 1993; Stead 2004).

AGREEING THE BUSINESS CASE

I have already stressed in Chapter 6 the importance of making a convincing business case for any proposed L&D initiative. Authorisation of the case by the business sponsors puts the full business partnership for the training project on a firm footing. It marks the agreement between stakeholders of the ground rules by which it is to be conducted, its resource base, its core processes and the value-creating outcomes that it is designed to achieve for the organisation and for the individual learners involved. It must therefore clarify:

- the business drivers for the initiative, and its corporate purpose. If the organisation has a formal L&D strategy and plan, it should explain how the proposed initiative fits into those. It should also identify the initiative's link to wider HR and business policies, processs and practices and what kind of support from them it will require

- the value-adding organisational and individual outcomes proposed for the initiative

- the learning population to be targeted by the event and the kind of learning strategy likely to ensure both effective learning and flexibility in the face of workload and workplace demands (strategy will have to be considered in detail in a subsequent stage of the training cycle and so may change when all options have been fully explored)

- the resource base – financial, material and human – required for the initiative. It is particularly important to allow for any pre-event activity that may be needed, including any training of project team members and of team, line and top management and the introduction or revision of any HR practices or systems. This is necessary in order to ensure that the event's intended outcomes can be achieved and sustained in the workplace

- the evaluation process and types of metrics to be used in monitoring the event and identifying its actual against its originally intended outcomes

- the work schedule for planning and designing the event, and the deadline for commencing its delivery.

REFLECTION

Consider the following example as the starting point for a training proposal's business case (Brooks and Hulme 2007):

We are facing this business issue/ challenge. Having investigated, there are some key issues which relate to knowledge/skills and behaviours in the following groups of people. The penalty/cost to the business is £x ...

and the value of addressing them is estimated at £y ... We would like to develop a learning solution which is directly targeted at relevant key performance indicators.

Can you identify any examples of such an 'outside-in' approach to producing a training proposal in your own organisation? If not, what do you think is the reason for its absence?

Many learning events are planned informally, in a rush and without much supporting documentation of the kind described here. Sometimes those who identified and analysed needs for the event are not involved in its design or delivery or do not have full control over the selection of its participants. Sometimes although needs have been clarified and the purpose and resourcing of the event have been agreed, little else has been settled. Unsurprisingly such scenarios threaten the extent to which the event can achieve its desired purpose. While it may never be possible to achieve the ideal scenario, it is essential that the project team produces a well crafted business case and obtains sign-off for it at this stage by the business sponsors. The case must be carefully recorded, since it must be constantly referred to during planning, monitoring and evaluation of the event.

STAGE 2: INTEGRATING PLANNING AND EVALUATION

FORGING A CAUSAL CHAIN

Nearly four decades ago the British authors Warr, Bird and Rackham (1970) stressed the need for evaluation to be a continuous process, planned at the outset and continuing throughout the learning cycle, not merely used as a post-training activity. So this core principle that gives the training cycle a value-adding focus at its second stage is far from new, even though it is often ignored in training practice. A 'causal chain' must link organisational level outcomes, through specific business metrics and key performance indicators, to the core activities of the training cycle (Spitzer 2005). Informal as well as formal evaluation should be used to continually develop a training intervention, heighten its perceived credibility, and influence decision-making beyond the training sphere, thereby ensuring its wider business thrust.

COLLECTING THE BASELINE DATA

The whole training cycle must be grounded in a comprehensive baseline of data. For a major training programme collection will require much work with key stakeholders in the business to fully engage them in the project from its start. Success at this stage will prove invaluable as the programme is rolled out, since it will ensure its highly visible sponsorship and practical support from business leaders and line managers. The various stakeholder groups, including a sample of the intended learning population, will provide unique insights into organisational context and training needs. Their involvement in the data collection process should also clarify for them the added value that training can contribute to the business and to individuals, and this should enhance their commitment to the training project.

Two types of data should be collected, relating to the workplace environment and to training and learning needs.

Data on the workplace environment

These data will subsequently be analysed to clarify precisely how to link business goals to training. This can be a surprisingly neglected area. Many training initiatives are set in motion without the gathering of any clear baseline data against which to measure training's organisational outcomes (Audit Scotland 2005; Spitzer 2005; CIPD 2007a; CIPD 2008a). Such data, many of which will also have informed the business case for the training event, concern:

- the exact nature of the business goals

- the key business metrics used to report on them

- target conditions that the intended learning population must reach in the workplace, and how those conditions are measured

- the current performance of the intended learning population in relation to target conditions, and how it is measured

- contextual factors influencing workplace performance that may either help or hinder the success of training to improve that performance.

Data on training and learning needs

A number of different taxonomies (or classifications) of learning needs exist to guide data collection and analysis (see for example Gagne 1967). The simplest classification system refers to the skills, knowledge and attitudes (SKA) required in a job or role, and the level of these currently possessed by the intended learning population. A more sophisticated version of this is Bloom's taxonomy where learning needs are classified as (Bloom *et al* 1956):

- *cognitive*, covering knowledge-related skills, in ascending order of complexity (knowledge, comprehension, application, analysis, synthesis and evaluation)

- *psychomotor*, covering motor skills (abilities, techniques and competencies)

- *affective*, covering feelings and attitudes plus activities such as responding, valuing and judging.

However, with the rapid rate of change in organisations now it is as important to collect data on learners' and their managers' training expectations as on their training needs (Fairbairns 1991; Anderson 2007). Specific needs can quickly become outdated, whereas expectations exercise a lasting influence on motivation to train and to release staff for training, as well as on the extent to which individuals develop vital skills of 'learning to learn'.

STAGE 3: IDENTIFYING TRAINING AND LEARNING NEEDS

Analysis of data collected in Stage 2 enables identification of training needs in the job and in the job-holders, and of mediating influences between individuals' skills and the extent to which, post-training, they are likely to use them to the benefit of the organisation. It is one of the most time-consuming stages of the training cycle but it carries unique value-creating potential. This is because it requires the project team and the wider business partnership to look critically at barriers and aids to the commitment and performance of employees in the workplace and to take action now in order to improve the workplace in ways that will aid performance to target conditions. Even if no training subsequently takes place, such action will of itself produce workplace changes that will benefit the business and its employees.

Only an outline of key issues can be attempted here. For technical detail readers need to consult specialist texts.

ANALYSING WORKPLACE CONTEXT

The purpose of this analysis is to capture the essence of the current workplace environment, and to create a picture of what that environment is intended to look like when managed to the desired standard. This picture will help training planners to decide exactly what workplace outcomes must be linked to the programme, to integrate measurement strategy with planning from the outset and to identify potential or existing barriers to the success of the programme.

Typical causes of such barriers lie in HR policies and practices – often related to the design or operation of the performance management system – management style and actions, workloads, work targets, and business processes, procedures and routines. Many relate to cultural issues. Take, for example, the following comments made in 1989 by Manchester Airport's personnel director concerning an attempt to introduce an innovative management development programme into the organisation (Jackson 1989):

> If anything we underestimated the level of inertia and opposition which faced us in this. … Throughout the process, it was noticeable that the psychological barriers were more daunting than the administrative and technical ones. Because the Company had

no history of formalised and systematic Management Development, there was a degree of scepticism that the exercise would get off the ground successfully. At various stages, serious doubts were expressed as to whether we would see it through.

They did see it through, but only after spending much time at this early stage building a good working relationship with the key parties.

ANALYSING TRAINING AND LEARNING NEEDS

Training needs analysis (TNA) is a generic term used to cover the processes of identifying what successful task, job or role performance looks like, and what is needed from individuals in order to achieve those results. It therefore involves:

- analysing the tasks, job or role for which training is to be given

- identifying what constitutes good and poor performance and the consequences of each for the business

- identifying the extent and nature of the current performance gap and, relatedly, of the generic and specialised training needs of the intended learning population.

Job training analysis

In this sub-section space allows me to do no more than outline four of the most well-known methods of JTA and identify where each can be used to most advantage: comprehensive, key task, problem-centred and competency-based analysis.

Often it will be appropriate to use some of these methods in combination. For example problem-centred and key task analysis can work effectively together when people take up new jobs and already have most of the competence needed to perform them well, or again when new job-holders must quickly gain a firm grasp of key tasks and be able to overcome typical difficulties that they involve.

Comprehensive analysis

This approach requires a detailed examination in which every task in a job is broken down into SKA components. It must also be described by reference to its objectives, its frequency of performance, its standards of performance, and ways of measuring that performance. Analysis is very time-consuming and requires specialist expertise. Because it is resource-intensive it should only be used when absolutely necessary. Most commonly it is applied to jobs consisting of simple, usually manual, repetitive and unchanging tasks.

Comprehensive analysis leads to two typical outcomes: a job description to guide selection of learners; and a job training specification showing the skill, knowledge and (if relevant) attitudes required, the standards of performance to be reached and how performance against those standards is measured in the workplace. The specification guides training/learning design.

Key task analysis

This involves analysis only of those tasks whose effective performance is of central importance to the success of the job-holder's role. A brief job description must be produced, but this time the job training specification should only cover these 'key' tasks. Key task analysis is appropriate both for jobs or roles involving a variety of tasks only some of which have to be performed to a high standards, and those whose core tasks are changing in some way and so raise a need for training.

Problem-centred analysis

This approach identifies any major performance problems that a particular job or role typically involves. Analysis focuses on training implications and uses a sample of job-holders to provide the necessary insights. It has two benefits: it can achieve speedy resolution of problems for which training is the best solution; and it can gain the commitment of job-holders through involving them in analysis and in training design (Warr and Bird 1968). It is most appropriately used when:

- training is urgent, but analytical resources limited

- the job-holders' work is satisfactory except in one or two 'problem' areas

- it is important to gain job-holders' commitment to training.

The problem-centred approach involves recording a description of agreed problems, their typical causes and how they can best be tackled in training.

Competency-based analysis

The word 'competency' refers to a set of related but differing sets of behaviour that are believed to lie behind competent performance in a range of jobs or roles (Boyatzis 2008: 6). A competency framework therefore comprises (Pilbeam and Corbridge 2002: 499):

> A list of skills and competencies which identify and describe the behaviours necessary to perform a particular role or task at a particular level within an organisation.

Such frameworks are in common use, especially in management development schemes. They are the subject of more detailed discussion in Chapter 17.

Competency-based analysis is a lengthy, highly skilled activity and so does not come cheap. Continuing debate about how far it can adequately explain job performance and about the costs associated with it mean that any decision to use it must rest on a particularly sound rationale.

Like problem-centred analysis, competency-based analysis is both job- and person-related. It produces:

- a statement of the role or purpose of the general category of job being studied in the organisation

- a breakdown of that role into discrete areas of competence

- statements of the behavioural competencies needed to perform satisfactorily in each of those areas and criteria for measuring those competencies. Behavioural competencies 'look at the way people behave or go about their work. They describe "softer" attributes and traits' (Pilbeam and Corbridge 2002: 500).

Competency-based analysis is most often used:

- when core behavioural attributes and related performance standards must be identified in order to ensure consistent standardised performance across a family of jobs or the entire workforce (Shields 2007: 185)

  and/or

- when training has to link to a competency framework (that may sometimes itself be linked to national vocational qualifications for accreditation purposes).

Learning needs analysis

As indicated in Stage 2, this analysis must identify the core skills, knowledge and behaviours together with any specialist skills that the learning population possess and need to acquire, and its training expectations. These expectations can come from any source but research by Facteau and colleagues (1995) indicated that it is not any single variable but the 'big picture' – the overall organisational context – that shapes expectations most strongly. This picture can extend to the strategic plans for the business, layoff policies, emphasis on employee development and continual learning, creation of self-managed work teams, and organisation culture.

Facteau highlighted three kinds of incentive to train that suggest the particular importance of analysing the 'reward' factor related to a specific training proposal:

- intrinsic incentives (how far training is expected to meet internal needs and provide learners with growth opportunities)

- extrinsic incentives (the extent to which training results in tangible external rewards such as pay, promotion)

- compliance (the extent to which learners attend training because they are given no choice but to do so).

Here is a case, based on real life but with the identity of the organisation withheld. What do you think explains the ultimate failure of training to achieve its business purpose? Comments follow its conclusion.

CASE EXAMPLE

REWARDING TRAINING OR PERFORMANCE?

Training staff in a recently restructured company planned a series of modular skills training courses related to different areas of skill, in order to promote multi-skilling in the workforce. Appropriate training of supervisors to fill new team leader roles was already taking place.

The training staff carried out a thorough TNA exercise and as a result they focused training design on improving the supervisors' management knowledge and skills. However, they identified that training in new skills would not work unless most employees were better motivated to undergo it. They therefore persuaded management to introduce a financial reward system tied to successful completion of each skills module, with a final extra payment for those who went through the entire skills matrix relevant to their area of the business.

The new training matrix proved popular with trainees and training completion rates were excellent but the training subsequently proved to have far less impact on workforce performance than had been hoped. Few of the supervisors' newly acquired skills were put to significant use in the workplace.

After further analysis a new system was introduced whereby successful completion of each skills module was recognised by a small financial increase, but the main rewards were attached to effective post-training teamworking in the new organisational structure. This resulted in greatly enhancing the motivation of trainees to apply their new skills and behaviours in the workplace.

Why was there such a weak link between training outcomes and trainees' subsequent performance? One obvious reason is that the initial analysis of workplace environment data was inadequate, explaining why it took the training staff so long to realise that a training-related reward system was not likely to motivate trainees to put newly learnt skills into practice.

The focus of training on managerial rather than on leadership skills was the other major reason. It meant that, after training, most of the supervisors remained weak in the interpersonal skills needed to lead, inspire and support their teams, to encourage them to be more self-managing, and to work to a high standard with shared purpose. That problem was only resolved after the training staff devised a more appropriate type of team leadership programme, and new selection and financial reward criteria were introduced for team leader roles.

STAGE 4: AGREEING LEARNING PRINCIPLES AND STRATEGY

PUTTING LEARNING AT THE HEART OF THE TRAINING CYCLE

Strategy is the route to be followed in order to achieve a goal, or goals. Producing a learning strategy therefore involves looking at alternative ways in which the goal (purpose) for a learning event can best be achieved and selecting an option that is likely to create most value for organisation and individuals.

Putting learning, as distinct from instructional, design at the heart of the training cycle is a unique value-creating feature of the outside-in process (Brooks and Hulme 2007). In Stage 2 the need is to establish a system whereby there is a skilful integration of training planning, design, delivery and evaluation. This integration also requires the articulation of core learning principles on which a learning strategy for the programme will rest, and that is the focus of Stage 4 – which, in reality, will probably coincide with rather than follow Stage 3.

Learning principles will suggest a learning strategy for the programme. Both strategy and principles must then be linked to the intended outcomes of training and translated into a customised measurement strategy, with metrics at every stage. As far as possible, business rather than training metrics should be used. Ensuring a stronger link between training activity and workplace routines will make the programme more accessible for the learners, and increase its business credibility for all stakeholders.

The decisions to be made at this stage are threefold:

- to agree the most feasible and appropriate learning principles to underpin the programme's learning strategy and design

- to link those principles to the organisational as well as individual outcomes that the programme must achieve

- to suggest any new or improved business metrics that will be useful in the workplace as well as in the training programme.

As explained earlier in this chapter and in Chapters 4 and 5, there are many learning 'taxonomies' or classification systems. It is for the project team to decide which best suits their purpose. Consider the following case. What questions would you put to the team to ensure that the learning principles and strategy they propose are fully feasible? Comments follow at the end of the case.

THE LOCAL AUTHORITY TRAINING PROGRAMME

A training project team proposes to use a work-based learning strategy for a basic skills training programme for new administrative officers in a local authority. The trainees will enter the programme as novices and must reach a uniform standard of competence by its end. Their work goals will be identified before the programme starts, and the ability and motivation to achieve them will constitute its targeted outcomes. During the programme trainees will be set the tasks that they need to master in order to achieve those goals, together with a 'scaffolding' of competencies and learning support that will build their skills and knowledge in those tasks.

The project team feels that the most appropriate learning principles to underpin the strategy and inform the programmes design will be Collins' (1997: 9) six principles of 'cognitive apprenticeship', already discussed briefly in Chapter 5. The aim of these is to ensure that conceptual understanding and the ability to apply theory to real-life situations are developed in parallel by learners.

The team has linked each of Collins' six core learning principles to individual and workplace training outcomes as follows:

- *Authenticity* – Material to be learned should be embedded in tasks and settings that relate to the learners' real world. This will ensure that all learning is perceived to be fully relevant by trainees, and leads to continuous improvement in their real-life job performance.
- *Interweaving* – Learners should go back and forth between a focus on accomplishing tasks and the gaining of specific competencies related to those tasks. This will ensure that each competency achieved by trainees becomes the stepping stone for the next stage of task mastery, until finally they have acquired a fully co-ordinated set of competencies that enable skilful task performance.
- *Learning through the learning cycle* – Learning should occur through repeated cycles of planning, doing and reflecting. This will ensure that the core processes underpinning successful performance in the workplace are practised and improved regularly throughout training.
- *Articulating* – Trainees should be enabled to articulate their thinking and what they have learned. This will reinforce their understanding, and their ability to explain their progress to others.
- *Reflecting* – Trainees should regularly reflect on and compare their performance with that of others. This will help to ensure continuous feedback on their learning, and through building a community of practice amongst the trainees will support all of them in reaching the necessary performance levels.
- *Learning through multimedia* – The programme should utilise a blend of learning media. This will ensure that the learning experience appeals to all learning styles, thus enhancing trainees' motivation and ensuring more rapid and effective learning.

In this case example the project team has concentrated on appropriateness of learning principles to the programme's purpose and learning population. But what about feasibility? How effectively can each learning principle be applied in practice, given contextual factors? Questions that must be answered at the planning stage include the following:

- Will workplace culture and HR policies and practices adequately support a work-based learning strategy?

- Will senior and line management be able and willing to give learning strategy and each of its underpinning learning principles their active support?

- Will there be the necessary technical infrastructure and expertise to facilitate a blended learning system? And will training, management and IT staff work well enough together to ensure that it can be effectively piloted, introduced, embedded and monitored?

- Will strategy and principles fit with the profile of the specific type of learners likely to enter the programme? Does the team have any detailed information on that profile?

- Who will provide the skills training on the one hand and the knowledge-based elements of the programme on the other? If internal staff have to work in partnership with external providers, what will this involve, and what will be the main financial and other implications?

- Will the programme be accredited? If so, will that call for the training of workplace assessors or assessment by an external agency? And will conditions to be met for accreditation purposes support or conflict with the programme's intended purpose, principles and strategy?

PROFILING THE LEARNING POPULATION

The fourth point on the above list raises further questions. These include: how many learners are there likely to be? Who will select them? What are the implications if selection is not in the team's hands? What kind of variations can be expected in individual performance levels and the skills, knowledge and attitudes related to them?

There is also the matter of learning styles – something with which, as noted in Chapter 5, it is possible to become over-preoccupied (Coffield *et al* 2004). If a learning style inventory is used to aid strategy and design of training, it is important to realise that people can usually develop learning styles in more than one mode and that many may need to do so because of the nature of their present or intended future job or role. Suppose, for example, that prior to attending a 'Training the trainers' course a group of delegates have completed the Honey and Mumford (1992) inventory and have shown a marked activist profile (and those authors have encountered this). Since trainers have to organise training for all types of learners they themselves should be exposed to learning experiences that develop their strengths in all styles instead of those increasing their dependency on one.

The following example couples the process of job training analysis with the collection and application of precisely this kind of more individualised information. It is not a method to suit all learning situations but it proved relevant in this scenario.

CASE EXAMPLE

ELECTRONIC LEARNER PROFILING

The project manager and technical developer in the Learning and Development Department of Transport for London described how training needs analysis produced through using an electronic questionnaire threw up a variety of learning gaps to be filled in a programme that had to ensure the competence of 1,000 staff needing to use SAP, a new database and reporting system.

This electronic process enabled the L&D team to identify individuals' exact needs and to meet them not by the customary training course but in a more flexible manner which proved timely, efficient and motivating. They used a combination of tailored workshops, email tips and one-to-one coaching.

The success of this initiative led to the introduction of a new process for all IT training. Generic IT courses had been taking people away from their work stations for up to two days and

not always giving them adequate practice time. Using an expanded electronic questionnaire that checked each learner's current knowledge of a particular IT package and identified learning gaps, the L&D team was now able to group together people with similar needs and create tailored courses for them. These were designed around a single module, a combination of modules or elements of the modules – an example of bite-sized learning that reduced learning time while providing a well-tailored learning strategy for groups and individuals.

In describing this initiative the authors of the article concluded that the overall dynamic and pace of delivery of the training was greatly aided by rigorous training needs analysis which ensured that participants on each course were at a similar skills level.

Source: Harlow, T. and Smith, A. (2003) *People Management*, 20 November

STAGE 5: DESIGNING AND DELIVERING TRAINING

THE DESIGN PROCESS

If the first four stages of the training cycle have been tackled thoroughly the groundwork for design will already have been laid. There must now be agreement on the programme's structure, learning objectives and content, identification of programme enablers to be put in place, and agreement on how and by whom training will be delivered.

Programme structure and learning objectives

Programme vision and strategy together with a tight linkage to workplace outcomes and business results will provide a disciplined foundation for the programme's structure. Looking again at the case of the local authority training programme earlier in the chapter, three of the most obvious questions to ask would be:

- Given the programme's overall purpose, its learning strategy and principles and the profile of its learning population, what will be the most appropriate blend of knowledge, skills and behavioural change to achieve in the programme, and what kind of structure does that blend suggest? Perhaps a modular structure would be best, since that would allow regular intervals for application of learning in the workplace, and for reflection and articulation of learning by the trainees.

- What kind of structure will work best when learners' work schedules and workloads are taken into account?

- If accreditation of all or part of the programme is involved, does that have any practical implications for programme structure and content?

Specific learning objectives for the event should make clear the attitudinal, behavioural and performance outcomes needed in participants if the organisational-level outcomes set for the event are to be achieved. Except in very simple events it is helpful to formulate objectives at two levels: interim and final.

- *Interim behavioural objectives* – Sometimes known as 'intermediate', 'formative' or 'specific' objectives, these identify the outcomes that the learner should have achieved at each key stages of the learning process.

- *Final behavioural objectives* – Sometimes known as 'ultimate', 'criterion', 'summative' or 'overall' objectives, these identify the outcomes that the learner should have achieved once the learning event is completed.

You may have noted the use of the phrase 'behavioural objectives' in the above definitions; also the reference to 'outcomes'. The clearest guide to design can be obtained not so much by stating what the learning event aims to do in general terms but in specifying how the learner should be able to act or perform at various stages. By describing the kinds of behaviour and performance to be achieved at its conclusion, final objectives give a clear focus to that event and link it back to its purpose. All objectives must have contextual relevance and therefore should take into careful account the specific conditions in whic̲h̲ ̲ ̲n̲ers will have to perform once the learning event has concluded (Mager 198

REFLECTION

Imagine a customer care training course for staff whose work has not so far put them in any direct contact with the public. Its purpose is to equip them with the skills, knowledge and behaviours needed to ensure a high standard of customer service, and its delivery involves a combination of classroom-based training and on-the-job coaching. What kind of interim and final behavioural objectives would you suggest for such a course, and how would you justify them?

Programme enablers

Enablers should be put into place before the programme – and others may have to be added during its progress as well as after, as the case study in Chapter 8 will demonstrate. In addition to any new or revised HR and L&D policies and practices, new partners involved in programme delivery entering or being trained by the project team and so on, decisions must be made about any pre-course training, workshops or other preparatory activity for programme participants, their managers, top management or other stakeholders.

The importance of using business metrics in setting and evaluating workplace outcomes has already been stressed, but it is equally important to make good use of business metrics, targets and processes in the programme's design and delivery. This will improve the transparency and ease of access for participants to company information where that is relevant. The work that they have to do on the programme will also increase their competence in using those metrics, processes and procedures, to the benefit of their subsequent performance in the workplace.

The organisation's performance management system will be of critical significance, since unless there is consistency between that and the performance standards participants are being trained to achieve, much of their learning on the programme will fall away once they re-enter their workplace. Personal development plans set up before training, used as one of the guides during training and upgraded after training constitute a key enabler.

'Learning technology' is another important enabler. The phrase is commonly used to describe the way in which learning media (the routes, or channels, through which learning is transmitted to the learner) and methods (the ways in which learning is transmitted) are incorporated into the design and delivery of a learning event. I have already devoted much of Chapter 4 to a discussion of the importance of learner-centred approaches, and many texts contain specialist advice and examples. Decisions on what approach, or mix of approaches, to use in the particular case will depend on a range of contextual factors and on the learning principles that the project team has agreed must drive the training. There is no further space to discuss learning technology here but Table 7 provides a prompt for ideas.

TABLE 7 Designing effective learning events

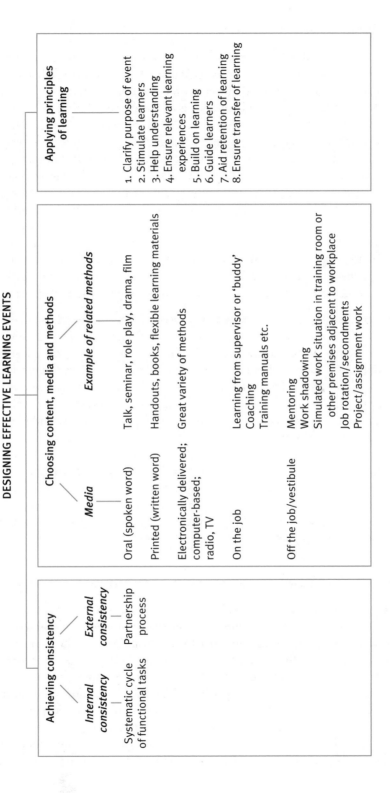

DESIGNING EFFECTIVE LEARNING EVENTS

Achieving consistency

Internal consistency	*External consistency*
Systematic cycle of functional tasks	Partnership process

Choosing content, media and methods

Media	*Example of related methods*
Oral (spoken word)	Talk, seminar, role play, drama, film
Printed (written word)	Handouts, books, flexible learning materials
Electronically delivered; computer-based; radio, TV	Great variety of methods
On the job	Learning from supervisor or 'buddy' Coaching Training manuals etc.
Off the job/vestibule	Mentoring Work shadowing Simulated work situation in training room or other premises adjacent to workplace Job rotation/secondments Project/assignment work

Applying principles of learning

1. Clarify purpose of event
2. Stimulate learners
3. Help understanding
4. Ensure relevant learning experiences
5. Build on learning
6. Guide learners
7. Aid retention of learning
8. Ensure transfer of learning

DELIVERING TRAINING

All the stages until now have been a preparation for delivery, so if they have been carried out effectively delivery itself should not pose intractable problems. However, flexibility is essential, both in order to cope effectively with contingencies and to adapt to changing skills and needs of the learners during the training programme. Smith and Sadler-Smith (2006: 38) propose that, in accordance with principles of cognitive apprenticeship discussed in Chapter 5, as learners move through various stages of mastering a new skill, body of knowledge or set of behaviours, learning design and delivery should reflect their progression from being a passive recipient of information to a more reflective and autonomous learner. It would be appropriate to shift gradually from training to coaching and mentoring, in line with that progress, during a programme. Once learners reach a yet higher level where they achieve a significant grasp of the intellectual dimensions of skill to be understood, knowledge becomes more internalised and more integrated and complete. At that point there should be less need for 'scaffolding' to support their learning, more for a push to increasingly self-directed learning.

Delivery, like design, has the potential to become transformed through e-learning. One point of relevance here is the importance of skills related to training and developing virtual teams and facilitating and monitoring online learning communities. Many traditional trainers and tutors are unlikely to possess these skills but they are vital when a programme is delivered mainly or entirely through e-learning media and methods. Take, for example, the Global Communities MBA, a blended programme launched by Spain's Instituto de Empresa and pitched at young professionals unwilling to interrupt their careers. It uses virtual teaching communities comprising programme alumni and executives from the corporate world, focusing on specific regions, sectors, functions or other areas of interest. Students can join as many communities as they wish and benefit from mentors and advisers from around the world (Anderson 2006). Such programmes produce a genuine shift from 'training' to 'learning'. They also demand a transformation in the skill sets of learning designers, tutors and support staff.

CREATING ADDED VALUE THROUGH TRAINING DESIGN AND DELIVERY

If Stage 5 is to achieve its full value-adding potential, it is important for the training team to research not only the most appropriate learning methods and solutions but also those that are innovative in the field. This will produce a high-quality training experience while at the same time expanding the skills, knowledge and expertise of members of that team. For example, it is well-known that, used in a relevant context, e-technology can help to achieve high-quality learning more cheaply and conveniently than a conventional course. However, there is less awareness of its potential to provide certain kinds of assessment of learning in a motivating way. In the UK, the former Polymer National Training Organisation (subsequently Cogent Sector Skills Council) delivered and assessed level 2 vocational training knowledge through web-based technology in an approach that was both robust and popular with learners. Learners found that the technology was used in a way that made the questions interesting, and felt that the assessment results fairly reflected their strengths and weaknesses (Mackinnon 2004).

In such ways as these, Stage 5 of the training cycle becomes the catalyst for the training team to acquire and practise new knowledge and skills. Their expanded expertise can subsequently be applied to producing other innovative learning designs for the organisation and, often, for external clients. In these ways design and delivery can be transformed from mere functional training tasks to value-adding processes for the business.

STAGE 6: MONITORING AND EVALUATING OUTCOMES

RESEARCH FINDINGS

First, it is important to distinguish between the processes of monitoring, validation and evaluation:

- *Monitoring* takes the temperature of a learning event or process from time to time, picking up problems or emerging needs.

- *Validation* measures the achievement of learning objectives set for a learning initiative or process.

- *Evaluation* assesses the total value of the outcomes of that event or process, thereby placing it into its organisational context and aiding future planning.

Over 40 years ago Kirkpatrick observed that training evaluation was 'still in its infancy' with most organisations doing little except measuring trainees' immediate reactions to the training experience (Catalanello and Kirkpatrick 1967). For him, the answer was simple: trainers must learn 'how to do it'. Since 1975 the four-level Kirkpatrick framework has dominated thinking and practice. Its simplistic and prescriptive appeal has often been criticised by academics (Santos and Stuart 2003), but this has not prevented its extraordinary popularity in the field, where there is a consistent and damaging preoccupation with the framework's lowest level of evaluation (of learners' reactions to training) and little – often, no – attempt to assess the impact of training at higher and especially corporate levels of the organisation.

Reviewing training evaluation practices worldwide, Russ-Eft and Preskill (2005: 71) concluded that evaluation has become 'stuck in a quagmire'. They found little formal evaluation of training, less that had rigour, and less still that focused on the organisational/corporate level. Whatever the reasons for this sorry situation, it seems puzzling that nevertheless, as noted at the start of this chapter, organisations' training spend continues to rise. Holton III and Naquin (2005: 258) conclude that: 'Either there are many organizations that have been incredibly naïve in spending huge amounts of money, or they are using different decision-making processes.' They opted for the latter explanation.

Skinner's research (2004) suggests that 'different decision-making processes' could indeed be the answer here. She found that many change management initiatives 'continued to follow one after the other with little evaluation of their impact being made before organisations progress to the next …'. Most of the reasons for this lay in the internal social structure of the firm, highlighted in HR literature as having a mediating role in relation to high-performance work systems and organisational performance (Evans and Davis 2005). Yet she found too that despite the virtual or complete absence of a formal evaluation process, below the surface much assessment still went on and that sometimes it was 'more acceptable and productive' than formal evaluation, significantly influencing strategic decision-making (Skinner 2004: 1). Case-based research like Skinner's is relatively rare but invaluable. Clarke's (2004) survey of the evaluation of formal and informal learning in UK hospices is one example.

In the six-stage training cycle the evaluation system and the planning system are integrated from the start. This demands as the first priority the identification and assessment of organisational-level outcomes for training, with a causal chain linking those outcomes through specific measurement and metrics to every stage of the cycle. The same business metrics, key performance indicators and other data used to forge that chain are used to monitor business outcomes during training and to measure their value on its completion. Most of the organisations in Purcell's 'Black box' studies (2003) used the HR balanced scorecard (Kaplan and Norton 1996) to guide measurement and evaluation of HR activity, including training. Because its methodology constitutes an ongoing strategic process it requires the linking of training to the business. Only after it has identified training outcomes at corporate level does the evaluation process work down through departmental/unit and job levels until it reaches the final, individual level.

L&D professionals and line managers often blame lack of time for their failure to carry out all their L&D tasks adequately. While in some cases this is an excuse rather than a valid reason, it does raise an important question: how can evaluation capture the key outcomes of a training event adequately but also efficiently? It is important not to opt for technical detail at the expense of common sense. A simple, pragmatic 'outside-in' approach designed by in-house staff can often be perfectly satisfactory. If it has been produced in collaboration with key partners, that should give it the credibility that any evaluation process needs if its results are to lead to useful future action. The most sophisticated and well-known cycles, on the other hand, will have no value if their findings fail to gain the acceptance in the organisation.

What is vital is to do enough evaluation of a training event to assess the value it has created for the business, for the programme team and for the learners, and the likely durability of its outcomes. Long-term evaluation can be particularly significant here, since it will often identify key 'sleeper' effects – outcomes that only become fully apparent many months after the completion of training, if not longer. That said, to evaluate at several different points in time will always be costly, and so the matter of 'when and how?' must be carefully considered.

Some of the most useful work on evaluation was done in the 1970s in the UK (Warr *et al* 1970; Hamblin 1974). Warr's fourfold 'CIRO' evaluation framework can be used to assess activity throughout the entire training cycle, should that be necessary. It is described in Harrison 2005 (pp143–6).

REFLECTION

Reflect on a training programme with which you are familiar, to identify how far the cycle of activity that produced it covered the six stages explained in this chapter. At which stage, or stages, of that cycle do you think greatest value was created, and for whom?

CONCLUSION

In this chapter I have presented a value-creating approach to the cycle of planning, designing, delivering and evaluating training events. You should by now have a sound understanding of its six stages and be able to tackle the review questions contained in Appendix 3.

The chapter's seven sections have demonstrated the ways in which the cycle of training activity, operated through effective business and learning partnerships, can co-create value at every stage:

- *Stage 1: Establishing the partnership* – The collaborative creation of value begins at this first stage, with the identification of the drivers and purpose of the proposed learning event so that its potential organisational and individual benefits can be assessed. The core business partnership for the event must be established, including its business sponsors and its project team. That team must work closely with key stakeholders in producing a business case that must gain sponsors' approval.

- *Stage 2: Integrating planning and evaluation* – This stage creates value by beginning the process of forging a causal chain to link organisational level outcomes, through specific business metrics and key performance indicators, to the core activities of the training cycle. The integration of planning with evaluation from start to finish of the cycle requires at this stage the collection of baseline data on the workplace environment and on training and learning needs. Involving the whole business partnership in the data collection process will yield uniquely valuable information about organisational context and training needs, and will also enhance their commitment to the training project.

- *Stage 3: Identifying needs* – This is the stage during which analysis of data collected in Stage 2 identifies where and what kind of job and learner-related training needs exist, and constraints and aids to meeting those needs. This analysis can add value in two ways: by revealing how to link training tightly to desired workplace outcomes, and by stimulating action before training begins to tackle workplace barriers to employees' performance and organisational commitment. Such action will not just aid transfer of training. It can lead to changes in the workplace that will produce lasting benefits for the business and employees.

- *Stage 4: Agreeing learning principles and strategy* – This stage creates value by putting learning, as distinct from instructional, design at the heart of the training cycle. A set of learning principles must underpin learning strategy and these must be customised to

enhance individual learning and the achievement of training's organisational outcomes. Business rather than training metrics should be used wherever possible to link learning to business outcomes, thus ensuring and demonstrating to stakeholders the programme's business relevance. Further value will be created if this exercise leads to the introduction of some new or improved business metrics that will aid management of the workplace to target conditions.

- *Stage 5: Designing and delivering the event* – This stage involves reaching agreement on the programme's structure and learning objectives, on programme enablers to put in place before, during and after training, and on content, mode(s) and methods of delivery. It will achieve its fullest potential to create value if the training team incorporates in design and delivery not only the most appropriate learning methods and solutions but also those that are innovative in the field. This will produce a high-quality training experience while at the same time expanding the skills, knowledge and expertise of members of that team.

- *Stage 6: Monitoring and evaluating outcomes* – Because the evaluation system and the planning system have been integrated from the start, what remains at this stage is to conduct monitoring and

CONCLUSION *CONT.*

evaluation using an agreed combination of informal and formal methods in order to capture the most meaningful data. These data should be used to enhance the ongoing operation of training, to identify and assess the value of training outcomes, and to influence decisions both about future training and more widely – as relevant – in the business. To gain organisastional value from this stage there must be an outside-in approach, with evaluation starting at the corporate not the individual level.

EXLPORE FURTHER

FURTHER INFORMATION SOURCES

McPherson, M. (2005) 'E-learning: a guide to principles and practice'. In J. P. Wilson (ed.) *Human Resource Development: Learning and training for individuals and organizations*. London: Kogan Page. Table 17.2, pp331–9 assesses from trainees' and trainers' perspectives many learning and teaching methods for use in conventional and web-based group and individual training

Palmer, R. (2005) 'The identification of learning needs'. In J. Wilson (ed.) *Human Resource Development: Learning and training for individuals and organizations*. London: Kogan Page, pp138–55. Contains helpful company examples

http://reviewing.co.uk/_links.htm [accessed 25 May 2008]. A lively, informative site about learning processes, activities and aids

CHAPTER 8

The Six-stage Cycle in Action: A Case Study

INTRODUCTION

This chapter describes a large-scale development programme for front-line managers (FLMs) which, together with the article by Brooks and Hulme (2007) referred to in the previous chapter, exercised a strong influence on my thinking when I was creating the six-stage training cycle described in Chapter 7. The case demonstrates how that cycle can operate in a real-life situation. The company where the programme was carried out wishes to remain anonymous, but I have only needed to make marginal changes to facts in order to respect that wish.

The programme is important not only in itself but because it covered around 1,000 FLMs – a group whose role in workforces in recent years has significantly expanded and which, as the case study will illustrate, has now become of critical importance to the effective delivery of both human resource (HR) and business strategies. The widely observed gap that is frequently found between espoused and actual HR practice – one that I will discuss in Chapter 12 – is 'often explained by FLMs' lack of training, lack of interest, work overload, conflicting priorities and self-serving behaviour' (Purcell and Hutchinson 2006).

The chapter has eight sections. The first provides the context of the case and the following six link the case to each stage of the value-creating training cycle. The chapter concludes with a reflection on the main issues arising from the case and lessons it suggests for L&D professionals.

PROCON MANUFACTURING, UK

Procon Manufacturing, UK (not its real name) is part of a multi-national conglomerate whose headquarters are in Germany. It employs about 15,000 across its four UK sites, one of which is the focus of this account and which I will call 'Birmingham'. That site employs around 6,000 people, most in manufacturing, the rest in support functions.

The EXCEL programme

The conglomerate that owns Procon Manufacturing, UK has no overall formal, integrated HR or L&D strategy. Instead there is a lean central HR function that operates its L&D activity mainly through projects and internal and external partnerships.

In 2002 Procon Manufacturing, UK introduced a programme of structural change and cost-reduction across all its sites. The aim was to differentiate the company from competitors by producing a leaner organisation while maintaining its world-class standards of customer service, continuous improvement and quality. The deadline to achieve the programme's targets was 2006.

Early in 2003 the Birmingham site introduced its own Excelling through Excellence (EXCEL) programme to support Procon's wider initiatives by building a high-performance work system that could achieve both culture change and cost-reduction targets. The EXCEL vision, still ongoing, was 'To make Birmingham a great place to work where people feel proud, valued and are able to give their best'. The EXCEL programme incorporated three major developmental initiatives:

- *The Lean Manufacturing Programme* (LMP)
  The LMP, held in Birmingham's learning resource centre, was a modular four-week training course for middle managers, introduced in 2003 and focused on lean manufacturing principles. It was managed by specially trained in-house personnel.

- *The Leadership Programme* (LP)
  The LP, designed and run by external providers, was also introduced in 2003 and consisted of a five-day workshop for the senior management team, two days for all team leaders, and one day for all other employees. The content focused on an exploration of leadership, with particular importance being given to the 'image' that leaders gave of themselves to their teams. The workshops were reflective in their nature and therefore very different from the LMP programme.

- *The Front-Line Managers' Programme* (FLMP)
  The FLMP was a set of linked and sequential training courses, modular in structure, and delivered over an 18-month period between 2004 and 2006 by

a project team of internal and external partners who also designed it. It is this programme that is the subject of this chapter.

Procon Manufacturing, UK: Birmingham Site

Birmingham's top management team consists of the heads of the business areas and the chief executive (CE). There are 200 middle managers and around 1,000 FLMs. The latter come from a number of different workplace and business unit cultures and have a pivotal role in functional and operational terms, but situated as they are between middle managers and their own work teams they are in a constantly pressured position. They are appointed at three levels:

* production unit managers (PUMs are the most senior level, and report to middle managers who in turn report to the business heads)

* shift leaders (intermediate level)

* production team leaders (lowest level).

Functional policies (for HR, finance, manufacturing, and so on) are set at Procon Manufacturing, UK's headquarters. Each local business function in its four UK sites then sets the standards and policies on how activities should be undertaken at their level, but must also implement transnational policies and standards originating from Germany. These policies and standards are all signed off by the senior management team at each of the UK sites to ensure that they are in adequate alignment before being cascaded down to functional teams working in site business areas.

The Birmingham site has a number of business areas, each structured around a major manufacturing process. Another important contextual feature is Birmingham's five *Key Values*:

* Safety

* Quality Assurance

* Efficiency

* Customer Delight

    and

* Our People.

Each business area has a matrix plotted against these values, with time-bound targets set against each. The matrix operates at five levels and scoring is from 1 (unsatisfactory) to 5 (world-class). Every workplace in a business area has a 'team board' in prominent display, updated daily, to plot the current status of that workplace in relation to each value and provide supporting business information. Reaching Level 3 means that the workplace is being managed to standard in relation to all five areas of value.

THE PROCON PROGRAMME, STAGE 1: ESTABLISHING THE PARTNERSHIP

DRIVERS AND PURPOSE

The drivers

The two fundamental drivers for the FLMP were:

- the need to drive down costs

- problems identified in a 2003 in-house survey of FLMs. At that time Birmingham employed around 950 FLMs. Most were loyal, long-serving and hard-working, appreciative of employment at Procon Manufacturing, UK which offered stability and work–life balance opportunities, and proud when the product went out in time and at cost. Early in 2003 the HR function carried out a survey of a sample group of FLMs and found that although most FLMs performed adequately in their functional tasks (and there were traditional programmes to develop them in that respect), most were also stressed, reluctant to make decisions, and lacked confidence and competence in their management roles. Few demonstrated appropriate leadership behaviour and their teams were often fractured. Most serious of all for the company, few FLMs were managing their workplace to Level 3 standard.

The survey results were not entirely surprising, because production numbers had just had an exceptional rate increase and there had been an influx of new team leaders, many of whom had been promoted virtually overnight. The survey convinced Birmingham's CE of the need for all FLMs to undergo a transformational learning experience incorporating LMP's lean manufacturing principles and the LP's values. He saw that dovetailing the three programmes would be essential in order to achieve the necessary synergies.

The purpose

Following the survey, the CE and his senior managers carried out external benchmarking in order to identify what a Birmingham world-class FLM should look like. This convinced them that their own FLMs would have to move through four levels of development if they were to achieve the world-class leadership standard required to turn the Birmingham site into a consistently high-performing organisation:

- *Level 1* – FLMs consistently managing their workplace to 'standard conditions' and fostering continuous improvement

- *Levels 2 and 3* – FLMs satisfactorily meeting new challenges and targets to do with task performance and role behaviours, and adapting effectively to the start of organisational and job restructuring

- *Level 4* – FLMs contributing effectively to a high-performing organisation where a coaching style of leadership at all levels inspires and enables teams to achieve their and the organisation's goals on a continuing basis.

The group agreed on the need to start by investing in a major FLM training programme linked to Birmingham's EXCEL project. Its purpose would be to lift all FLMs to Level 1. This meant that by the end of the programme FLMs must have acquired:

- a clear concept of the framework for managing across the site

- the competence, commitment and discretion to use the tools and techniques acquired during the programme to put the framework into practice, working to a clear set of standard conditions for all FLMs

- appropriate managerial and leadership behaviours and a common language related to Birmingham's five Key Values.

EXCEL would be the 'Big Idea' (Purcell *et al* 2003) to give the programme its guiding vision and the FLMs' existing performance management system would be changed in order to reinforce the workplace outcomes targeted by the programme. It would incorporate a new personal development process (PDP) and would be introduced in the workplace to coincide with the launch of the FLMP.

The CE was determined that the programme would produce a fundamental shift to a strong organisational climate – that is to say, one in which FLMs would have 'a *shared* perception of what the organization is like in terms of practices, policies, procedures, routines, and rewards – and what is important and what behaviours are expected and rewarded' (Bowen and Ostroff 2004: 205).

The decision to target the FLMP only at development Level 1 – stability and standardisation of processes and behaviours – was crucial. The CE and his colleagues recognised that the road to be travelled by FLMs before they could become 'super leaders' would involve years, not months, of development. They realised that it would probably have to encompass not only skills and behavioural change in individuals but also, at some stage, job redesign and organisational restructuring.

ESTABLISHING THE BUSINESS PARTNERSHIP

The sponsors

The CE was the programme's business sponsor and the Birmingham HR director was its HR and L&D sponsor. These sponsors ensured a high level of attention and buy-in for the programme by their visible and active support for it at every stage of its development. A particularly powerful aid to the programme's impact and credibility was their willingness to make all business metrics and data bases available for use in establishing and measuring organisational outcomes for the programme.

The project team

Late in 2003 the senior management group set up an FLMP project team to carry out detailed programme planning, design and delivery, giving the HR manager the combined role of project manager and leader. Following a rigorous selection process, an international training and consultancy firm was appointed the programme's service provider. Five of Birmingham's operations managers were made its 'programme champions', with therefore a vital part to play in programme design and in engaging other stakeholders. Five 'Procon experts', including the project manager, contributed their deep functional and commercial knowledge of Procon Manufacturing, UK's business, its core values and culture, and the organisational context for training. The consultancy provided high-level learning design expertise backed up by a quality-assured design process; this and the consultants' business partnership approach and project management skill were to prove critical in ensuring that the programme had the support of stakeholders, was designed to the requisite world-class standard, and was translated into reliable delivery by the internal team.

In all, 26 stakeholders (including the project team) were involved in the programme's overall business partnership. Those outside the team required regular briefings and consultation from the consultants and project team manager. The high number of interdependent work streams related to the FLMP necessitated careful alignment in order to link it and other EXCEL-related activity consistently to the business.

With only five months between the entry of the consultants to the project team and the planned launch date for the programme in mid-2004, the amount of work to be done was formidable. Table 8 shows the work schedule after the consultancy contract was awarded.

The complexity of up front factors created the need for in-depth discussions between the CE and the consultants to determine an appropriate ratio of front-end time to design time for the programme. They agreed on a 60/40 ratio – unusually high on up front time, but an acknowledgement of the vital importance of that work if the whole training investment was ultimately to pay off. It was a crucial decision for the project team. It enabled the collection of a wide range of baseline data and gave time for the team's work-based development from a group of heterogeneous individuals into a close-knit, efficient and expert community of practice.

The business case

Phase 1 (in Table 8) generated a detailed business case for the programme. It was signed off by the five programme champions, then presented to the business sponsors who approved it. It incorporated:

- costs relating to direct training time

TABLE 8 FLM Programme Project team's work schedule, from entry of consultancy firm to final programme evaluation

Phase 1: *November 2003 to end January 2004*
Full scoping of the programme, including resource base, design, administration, IT systems, management information and evaluation processes needed. Business case sign-off.

Phase 2: *February to early April 2004*
Detailed learning design and sign off; development of knowledge, skills and systems needed to deliver the programme. Phase 2 sign-off.

Phase 3: *April to end May 2004*
Piloting of key modules and of associated administration and IT systems. Phase 3 sign-off.

Phase 4: *June 2004 to April 2006*
Delivery roll-out to whole population of FLMs. Phase 4 sign-off.

Phase 5: *May to October 2006*
Evaluation of Programme's impact on the business, and of its planning, design and delivery standards.

- details of the other resources required to support programme planning, delivery and evaluation

- a risk-assessment to cover contingencies that could threaten the success of the programme at individual and organisational levels

- a communication strategy to raise workforce awareness and commitment to its goals.

The case identified considerable benefits in terms of cost savings and efficiencies to be gained through creating a consistency in FLMs' knowledge and skills. It identified even more benefits if their management behaviours in the workplace improved to the point where they linked everything they did to the overall strategy of the business, communicated clearly and confidently to their teams (with consequential benefits in raised morale and attendance and reduced turnover), and improved their teams' understanding of the impact of individual actions on commercial performance.

The business case thus had a powerful pay-forward focus. 'Pay-forward' assessment involves exploring how far and in what ways a proposed L&D investment is likely to make a real and positive difference to future organisational performance (Lee 1996). This focus made clear on the one hand the cost and scale of the investment that the FLMP would involve, and on the other the added value that its targeted outcomes would bring to the business and to individuals. Sign-off meant that thereafter there was no need for evaluation of the programme to centre on 'What did it cost, and was it worth it?' since those questions had been answered in the business case. Instead it would centre on 'Are the outcomes targeted in the business case being achieved? If so, what next? If not, what are the barriers and how should we tackle them?'

FORGING THE CAUSAL CHAIN

The 'outside-in' strategy taken by the project team ensured that programme planning, design and evaluation were fully integrated processes. The evaluation framework was loosely based on Kirkpatrick's (1975), but identified that outcome evaluation would start at the fourth (corporate) level, not at the first (individual) level. Programme results would be reported against a business context and linked where possible to business reporting cycles. The evaluation process began at Stage 2 when it involved the collection of baseline data from key stakeholders. More would be collected during and after training.

REFLECTION

Before reading on, consider what the implementation of the evaluation framework used for the FLMP involved. It required the project team to set and measure outcomes at four levels: corporate (organisational) Level 4, workplace Level 3, job Level 2, and learner (individual) reaction Level 1. What key question would you expect the team to ask at each level in order to focus evaluation on the most appropriate outcomes? And how should measurement at each level be carried out?

The project team agreed that the key questions to be asked at each level, and their associated measurement methods, would be:

- Level 4: '*Did the programme add value to the business?*'
  The balanced scorecard principle of linked metrics with leading and lagging measures was used to tie organisational outcomes to the programme, drawing for this purpose on the company's comprehensive and accessible knowledge bank including commercial and employee data and organisational and functional key performance indicators (KPIs). Throughout the evaluation system every opportunity was explored to use existing rather than specially created organisational measures and KPIs in order to create efficiencies and credibility with programme participants and other stakeholders.

- Level 3: '*Did they use it?*'
  This level involved a wide variety of measurement methods including post-programme interviews of delegates and their managers and a behavioural

template to gather views from colleagues and managers on participants' behavioural changes. Other measures related to the development of consistency of practices – for example in shift briefings and return to work interviews – and to evidence of where the workplace was now being managed to standard conditions. Critical return on investment (ROI) measures to do with reduction of waste, reduced absenteeism and so on were also used at this level.

- Level 2: '*Did they learn from it?*'
  This level involved using a combination of formal and informal information sources from participants and programme facilitators, with data collected before, during and after the course in order to determine how far interim and final behavioural learning objectives set for participants had been achieved.

- Level 1: '*Did they like it?*'
  This evaluation level incorporated the use of closed questions, verbatim comments, and anecdotal evidence from programme facilitators, participants and their managers in order to identify their reactions to the quality, relevance, design and delivery of the programme.

Participants' assignments were planned to provide an important measure of the outcomes of the programme. They were to be used for evaluation purposes in different ways at different levels. At Level 2 the measure to be used was 'Did the delegate pass or fail the assignment?', whereas at Level 4 it was 'Has the assignment been implemented?' Another powerful source of evaluative data was 'Look and Learn' a structured process to take place daily across the Birmingham site to observe in each workplace evidence of significant differences in the behaviours and attitudes of FLMs after the programme and their practical impact.

The project team then collected baseline data for analysis at the next stage of the cycle.

STAGE 3: IDENTIFYING NEEDS

ANALYSIS OF THE WORKPLACE ENVIRONMENT

Much discussion with senior management centred on the part the FLMP would play in improving achievement of business goals. These discussions fed into a detailed analysis of the FLMs' workplace environment. The need to get fully involved in this analytical process caused senior management and HR staff to question their own expectations of their team leaders, to dig deep in order to uncover the fundamental reasons for those leaders' underperformance, and to begin to tackle before the programme began the performance barriers they identified. The value of this time-consuming analysis of work processes, procedures and tools was that it ensured clarity about the target of 'creating the right environment' for learning to be transferred from the programme into the workplace.

Many work and HR processes were changed at this point in order to ensure that environment would be in place, one notable example being the redesigned performance management system to be launched during the programme. Thus not only did the FLMP constitute a major organisational change in itself: its planning and delivery also stimulated major changes to business processes, procedures and tools.

ANALYSIS OF LEARNING NEEDS

Analysis of training and learning needs used data gathered from the business partnership and a sample of the FLM population. This analysis ensured that:

- the programme was tightly linked to realistic and relevant workplace outcomes

- there was an appropriate balance in the programme between learning related to core generic skills and learning related to more specialised skills. All Birmingham's FLMs required a ratio of approximately 70/30 generic/specialised (per business area) skills to perform their roles. This high ratio of transferable skills facilitated transfer of labour across the site so that team leaders could move quickly from one business area to another when needed to cover production peaks, etc. It should have also produced a high level of common language and culture but in the 2003 FLM survey both had been found to be largely negative – a deep-rooted problem that the workplace and learning needs analyses now confirmed.

A key need for FLMs that emerged from this analysis was to acquire not just the functional knowledge but the self-confidence, interpersonal skills, motivation and holistic understanding to challenge everything in their workplaces, looking constructively at what to change and improve in order to reach required performance standards and identifying any site rules that could be counterproductive in relation to the company's five Key Values. In doing this, they would be speaking a new and appropriate managerial language and acting as catalysts for cultural as well as work process change.

STAGE 4: AGREEING LEARNING PRINCIPLES AND STRATEGY

LINKING LEARNING PRINCIPLES TO STRATEGY AND OUTCOMES

Following the analysis of baseline data, and guided by the purpose that top management had originally proposed for the programme together with EXCEL's wider strategic vision, the project team now developed a learning strategy for the programme. After identifying a number of benchmark learning practices and principles, it was agreed that the strategy would rest on six interrelated learning principles suggested by the consultants:

- Create value for the organisation and the individual.

- Combine action and reflection.

- Balance challenge and support.

- Learn through teaching and role modelling.

- Ensure that learning addresses attitudes and beliefs as well as behaviours.

- Support learning with other organisational levers.

The point of these principles was that all six must be applied in order to ensure the necessary speed, visibility and measurability of the programme's training and learning. If even one were to be wholly or partly ignored that would prejudice the value-adding impact of all the rest.

The first learning principle translated into 'headline measures' that must provide the organisational outcomes for the programme. It also required individual needs to be carefully considered. Too much focus on business needs would make it unlikely that the programme would achieve individual commitment; too much focus on individual needs would run the risk of making a negative impact on participants' engagement with business goals and priorities.

The next four learning principles provided a bridge between creating value and subsequent decisions about the precise nature of the learning solution. They required the team to undertake an in-depth analysis of how learning in the programme should be focused, designed and achieved. Key decisions included ensuring that:

- individuals would receive an appropriate balance of challenge and support in their learning experience, but that the learning programme would also create a stimulating level of challenge for the organisation to manage and implement

- learning would be directed towards behaviour change but also address underlying attitudes and beliefs, in order to deliver the necessary sustained change in the FLM climate

- learning would give adequate weight to action and reflection, in order to be accessible to all learning styles and to ensure the necessary focus on application in the workplace.

The sixth principle translated into organisational measures needed to ensure a workplace environment conducive to transfer and impact of learning once FLMs had been through the programme.

REFLECTION

Consider the implications of using innovative learning design as a way of helping an organisation's L&D staff to become progressively more skilled and creative with every major training programme that they organise. Is design treated as this kind of value-adding process in your own organisation? If not, why do you think that is?

STAGE 5: DESIGNING AND DELIVERING TRAINING

DESIGNING THE PROGRAMME

Although some generic management and leadership concepts were relevant for the FLMs, it was the way in which they were applied at Birmingham that determined the effectiveness of FLM performance. The programme's content therefore had to be highly customised and achieve an appropriate balance between theoretical and practical components. The crucial message of 'managing to standard conditions' was carried down to every detail of design to ensure the requisite blend of knowledge, skills and behavioural change.

The programme also had to meet the certification requirements of the Institute of Leadership and Management (ILM). The award of its diploma was an important feature intended to give participants individual recognition and reward and to link the training to their personal development.

Programme structure

Programme structure had to ensure delivery of training in short chunks that would provide regular intervals for reflection and application of learning and respond to the fact that FLMs could not be absent from their workplace for any prolonged periods of time. The finalised structure combined short classroom-based modules with inter-module work-based assignments to test and apply the knowledge element of the programme which would then be enhanced through skills development in the classroom. There were seven modules in all. A central core of five focused on the Birmingham site's five Key Values. These were fronted by a 'Context' module (which focused on the FLM task and behavioural role at Birmingham, putting it in its wider business and change management context) and completed by a 'Move on' module (which prepared participants for the transfer and application of their learning to their workplaces). Every module had its own behavioural learning objectives, all modules were mandatory, and they had to be attended in sequence.

In its entirety the FLMP was timed to run from mid-2004 to mid-2006 in seven overlapping individual programmes. Including time back in the workplace between each module, each of those programmes was designed to stretch across approximately 14 weeks, taking in ten cohorts of up to 15 delegates each and with a maximum of two days' delivery per module.

Programme enablers

An FLM training centre was built to house the programme. It role-modelled the high-technology standards and practices of the FLM workplace, providing a visual reminder throughout training of the relevance of participants' learning to their real-life work environment.

Much work was done before, during and after the programme to put in place other enablers to facilitate application of participants' learning. Preparation for the launch of the programme in 2004 included the piloting of key modules, coaching training for the FLMs' line managers, and a familiarisation workshop for all middle and senior managers. Preparation of programme participants covered the setting up of their ILM work-based assignments, pre-course briefing by their managers, and self-assessed behavioural assessments that would be compared with similar assessments completed on their emergence from the programme in order to measure behavioural change.

After completing the programme each participant was to enter a performance management process where, in a one-to-one developmental review with their line manager that normally must take place three times annually, every FLM's performance in relation to each of Birmingham's five Key Values would be measured against a clear standard. If any failed to achieve the required standard against each Value within six months of the 'Move on' module, performance gaps must be identified and a personal development plan (PDP) must be agreed to tackle them. This redesigned PDP process was vital to the success of the programme. Its role was to ensure that skills learnt were transferred to the workplace, assisting business units to meet site conditions and helping and motivating FLMs to identify their further development needs.

DELIVERING THE PROGRAMME

Each programme module was delivered by one of the consultancy's trainers supported by a consultancy-trained Procon facilitator. Meticulous programme planning, a quality-assured design process, adherence to the six learning principles that underpinned the programme's strategy, and regular monitoring of the programme with adjustments where needed all helped to ensure that delivery was widely judged by stakeholders to provide the intended 'transformational' learning experience for most FLMs, even those who had entered the programme reluctantly or with low expectations.

STAGE 6: MONITORING AND EVALUATING OUTCOMES

MONITORING AND POST-PROGRAMME EVALUATION

By the time the first cohorts had completed their training, all leading KPIs for the programme were on target and participant reactions were generally very positive. Informal assessments indicated the start of a shift to a stronger workplace climate as FLMs developed more accurate and shared perceptions of their managerial roles, tasks and competence. Attendance on the programme had inevitably suffered from work and personal disruptions, but the programme occupancy rates had increased rapidly after the first cohort, influenced primarily by the publicity given to positive informal assessments and to improved standards of FLM performance. It remained high thereafter, averaging around 80%.

The FLM project team manager regularly discussed ongoing evaluation data with senior management. The perceived effectiveness of the programme was a major factor in the management's decision to roll out the programme, adapted to new needs and context, across Procon Manufacturing, UK's other sites, using the same external provider.

It was central to the FLMP's evaluation process that it made use of a flow of informal as well as formal assessments. Anecdotal feedback was especially encouraged during the programme and was captured on whiteboards around the training centre's walls in the form of stories, metaphors, symbols and cartoons about the FLMP experience. The project team used positive informal assessments to create and increase momentum and demand for the programme across the Birmingham site, and to encourage the desired shift in workplace culture. Formal evaluation data were used to recognise and reward participants' success and to share best practice, notably at the major celebratory event held after every programme where senior managers presented ILM diploma awards.

LONGER-TERM EVALUATION

The informal process

By April 2006 the entire FLMP was nearing its end and preparation was in place for a comprehensive formal evaluation of its outcomes later in the year. I had been following the programme's fortunes from a distance for over a year, and during a two-day visit to the Birmingham site that summer I was offered the opportunity to talk individually with some of the key members of the programme's business partnership, together with two FLMs who had been through the programme.

For the CE, the programme had been very successful because FLMs across the whole plant now spoke to him using a common language and by reference to a set of shared workplace performance standards. This degree of consistency and standardisation was a major advance. The views of the other senior managers were typified more by a remark made by one of the driving forces behind the whole concept and development of the programme:

> There's been an excellent learning approach.... There's been partial progress on a common language and references relating to standards. Most previous training ... had been too abstract, too irrelevant, case-study-based. There was a need to create clarity about workplace outcomes – how the workplace of the FLMs would look at the end of the Programme. [But] we started the journey – that's all we've done.

Unsurprisingly it seemed that the most effective outcomes of the FLMP had occurred on those rare occasions where entire teams had been able to come onto it at the same time, alongside a cross-section of those in support functions for a team. Amongst barriers identified as currently preventing fully effective transfer of learning to the workplace three stood out:

- lack of time for FLMs to put the programme's learning fully into practice. '*They're used to fire-fighting, not steady maintenance*'

- the fact that some FLMs did not feel comfortable using the new tools and techniques they had learnt on the programme, the real difficulty here being with the FLMs' operators. They had not been on the programme themselves and indeed knew little about it. They often failed to understand why such changed approaches were necessary

- the fact that every workplace at the Birmingham site was different, not just operationally but culturally.

One of the five programme champions thought that the FLM role still wasn't working as it should:

> Perhaps we could roll it and the shift leader role into one [something that was subsequently considered by management]. Also, the leaders don't have targets to work to, and they should have. So it could be a mix of a role problem and a problem of transfer of learning from the Programme.

The performance management system

One of the biggest barriers to the effective transfer of learning from the FLMP to the workplace was the operation of the redesigned FLM performance management system. A particular example quoted by a number of discussants concerned the programme's work-based assignments, intended to be important measures of participants' skills and knowledge development and also a major motivating force for each individual. However:

- Some participants did not complete their assignments, seeing no point in doing so.

- Some middle managers (MMs) showed no interest in the assignments completed by their FLMs, and clearly did not perceive assignments to be important for the business.

- There was no formal procedure to ensure that assignments would be scrutinised for their business value and utilised where relevant.

These outcomes were demotivating for most FLMs, and also meant that considerable potential for continuous improvement and innovation in the workplace was in danger of being lost to the business. The view was expressed that if completion of assignments had been a compulsory feature of the programme, the assignments could then have been used as a lever to get them all up to a higher level of competence.

Evidently, too, the PDP process was not always working effectively. It had been launched at the same time as the programme in order to explicitly express required FLM standards and performance outcomes and use those as the basis for FLMs' continuing personal development. Participants had been told that during their first year following their completion of the programme they would each have a monthly one-to-one discussion with their production manager to agree on how to apply their learning in the workplace and on any further personal development they might need, related to that. Often, however, this had not happened and – as one senior manager said – in consequence a lot of the FLMs had subsequently 'fallen back into their old ways'.

A big issue here related to recognition and reward – an issue that the 2003 workplace survey at Birmingham had revealed as the cause of widespread discontent amongst FLMs. By mid-2006 it was clear that although the FLMP had been a major motivating experience for its participants, boosting their self-confidence, role clarity and self-esteem, once they had completed it there was no financial incentive for them to connect with leaders and management. Some senior managers felt that there was in fact nothing to induce FLMs to improve except the relatively rare prospect of promotion.

One, however, took the view that the real need did not concern pay, but engagement:

> We need to achieve real engagement… Our real vision at present is … based on products and services, and technology-driven, not on what we represent as a company in the way we treat our people. We don't have a 'Big Idea' … If we can make a connection between what's important and the barriers to it with the workforce, and connect that with what matters to the business, 60% of our problems would disappear.

The reference to the 'Big Idea' calls to mind findings from the 'Black box' studies reported in Chapter 6 (Purcell *et al* 2003). One of the main conclusions from those studies, of course, was that in addition to a Big Idea to draw people together in shared endeavour, individuals also need discretionary power over their work. Without that, their skills cannot be put fully to use and any motivation built up by their participation in a learning event to 'go the extra mile' to support company goals may be lost. On that issue, one of the FLMP's programme champions remarked that there were significant constraints on the degree of discretionary power that any FLM could exercise at Birmingham. Creativity could be exercised in discretionary areas such as reduction of waste and recycling, but any change to processes was bound to be difficult because it was a highly regulated business and standard operations had to be followed.

Another senior manager made a different point. He was enthusiastic about the LMP he had been through, calling it 'the best learning of my life'. It had given him permission to 'Look and Learn', and he could see that this is what the FLMP had achieved for its participants too: it had allowed them to challenge in a positive way. What he wanted now was support to go out and challenge things across the whole site, not just in his own business area, in order to boost standards everywhere to target level. However, he felt that this kind of change would never happen until there was also a change in middle management's mindset – and that, he believed, would only be brought about by 'a structured, disciplined performance management process'.

The middle management problem

There was a striking degree of consensus about the negative impact and behaviours of some middle managers (MMs) related to the FLMP but the problem was complex. To quote one senior manager:

> The biggest problem was and is how to get the right infrastructure to support the programme. There are two organisational levels above FLMs and the biggest disappointment of Programme delegates has been about leadership support that they've had during and after the Programme: it's there right at the top, but patchy at the middle level. The LMP focused on the top level, the FLMP at the bottom level – and that leaves the middle level. … We need to get their full understanding of the positive and negative consequences of their actions for the Programme. They need to understand what a fully supported FLM workplace would look like.

Views about the roots of 'the problem' differed and so, in consequence, did suggested solutions to it. For the CE the crucial issue was one of work pressures on MMs, and in his view the solution was coaching plus, ultimately, some organisational redesign:

> MMs are like a funnel, and at its neck is the constraint, the pressure point … where there is the most tension between issues pushed down from above and those pushed up from below.

> What we're missing here is some high-impact coaching, regularly done, with real lean leadership – leadership as it's done at Toyota: Fensei – so that it's totally understood from every point of view what leaders ought to do and how they ought to behave. So we're designing and trialing … a coaching programme, initially run by [an] external coach, and subsequently passed over to three or four of the senior leadership team, who would do the coaching as part of their daily full-time role.

> We're also looking at our organisational design… We may need to critically assess and modify the structure to release capability and capacity to do some things differently.

However, this ignored two salient facts:

- In reality less than half the PUMs (the most senior level of FLMs) had ultimately gone through the FLMP.

- The LMP, which most of Birmingham's MMs had attended, was only about lean manufacturing processes and therefore not as broad in scope as the FLMP.

REFLECTION

Reflecting on the middle management problems described above, what suggestions would you make to ensure that the value-adding outcomes of the FLMP were fully realised? (Suggestions made by some of the senior managers in this case follow below.)

Overall, it was clear that the CE's original intention to gain value-adding synergies by a careful overlap of the LMP and the FLMP had been frustrated. It was also clear that despite all the pre-programme preparation, the MMs had still not been fully committed to the programme when it was rolled out. The warning signs had been there in 2003 when the in-house FLM survey had shown many of them to be out of touch with FLMs' feelings and concerns. Now, adverse longer-term consequences of failing to achieve their full engagement before the programme began were becoming evident.

Yet although in theory more should have been done to actively involve MMs in planning as well as delivering the programme, in reality that was never going to be entirely possible when the FLM project planning team had to operate to such an unforgiving time-scale. More important now was to decide how to move forward.

So, how to do that? The fundamental need on which all senior managers agreed was to get a critical mass of FLMs *and* MMs through the FLMP and to engage all support functions and their heads in moving the whole organisational culture forward at Birmingham. Other suggestions included:

- coaching and support of other kinds for MMs so that they in turn would give the necessary support to their FLMs who had completed the programme

- once all FLMs had been through the programme, the allocation of a group of FLMs to each MM in order to follow up the programme with action in the workplace. Each MM should identify with the FLMs future actions and issues to address, including whether they needed any further learning

- every senior manager to be given explicit responsibility for supporting all the MMs in their business area in ways that would enable and encourage MMs to manage their workplace to specified standards and would ensure that the FLMP achieved its intended impact in that workplace.

Participants' views

What of the programme participants themselves? Both of those I talked with came from the same business area but what was striking was the degree of consistency between the views that they expressed and those voiced in the separate discussions I had with senior managers.

Regarding the delivery of the programme, they had found the course 'fantastic', skilfully designed and engaging. They felt that its major positive impact had been the standardisation of the site. They found that they could now go from one business area to another and find the same procedures in place – a view echoing that held by the CE, noted above. However, each had also encountered problems with MMs, as one of them explained:

> Currently there's a gap between the middle managers and the team leaders – there's a need to close that gap. There were some very good ideas in the assignments done for the Programme, but these weren't always put into practice; they could have had a big impact on efficiency and so on. Why doesn't management look at all the ideas and decide which can be used? Also, we've got the tools now but we're not using them …

They too stressed that behind these problems lay more fundamental issues. The main danger was that the FLMP's outcomes would be lost or delayed because there was virtually no 'give' in the system: production delays and restructuring of the business meant that there was a huge drive for cost efficiency and delivery to target. They concluded that if the FLMP was to achieve anything durable there must be better support in the workplace for FLMs, including more time for them to put their learning into practice.

DESIGN AS A VALUE-ADDING PROCESS

One final issue emerged from my discussions. There was unanimous praise for the programme as a major learning experience. For the HR manager who had headed up the project team the key factor here was the design standards that had been applied. The programme's learning strategy developed around the consultancy's 'Six Learning Principles' had been tested to the limit and had borne the strain. The major lesson from that, in his view, was that learning design itself can and should be a value-adding process for the whole business.

THE FINAL, FORMAL EVALUATION

At the time of my visit to the Birmingham site in 2006 the organisational impact of the FLMP in quantitative terms was already evident. Some of the achievements against KPIs are shown in Table 9.

Following the immediate success of the FLMP, longer-term assessment late in 2006 confirmed the need for a range of actions along the lines of those identified by stakeholders with whom I spoke that summer. However, fate subsequently

TABLE 9 Organisational outcomes of the Birmingham site's FLM programme

97% of the Birmingham site's FLMs have been trained
55% of all FLMs at Birmingham now have a nationally recognised management qualification
155 quality assurance proposals have been implemented
56 cost/waste reduction initiatives have been set up/completed
40 error reduction plans have been implemented
29 customer service improvement projects have been started

threw several spanners in the works. A few months later, developments in the conglomerate that owns Procon Manufacturing, UK resulted in significant restructuring of the UK business. In that process some senior managers left the Birmingham site, many MMs and FLMs there were moved into new roles, and actions that were to have been taken after the programme to improve transfer of its outcomes to the workplace were abandoned.

LESSONS FOR L&D PROFESSIONALS

What are the key issues highlighted by the Procon case, and what insights does it suggest for HR/L&D professionals?

BUSINESS PARTNERSHIP

Key to the success of the FLMP in meeting the expectations of its business sponsors was the business partnership that supported it at the macro level, and that at the micro level had the responsibility for its planning and delivery. The challenge here, was to ensure from the start that the programme had not only internal but also external consistency. Although the project team did not manage to secure the full engagement of all the stakeholders – middle management remaining the major area of concern – what was achieved was remarkable, given the size and complexity of the overall business partnership and the aggressive time-scale for planning and launching the programme. Crucial here was the 60/40 ratio of up front planning to design time for the programme, approved at the start by the CE. It ensured transformational learning for the project team members through an intensive individual and collective learning experience.

Pfeffer (2005) claims that one of HR professionals' most important roles is to influence the mindsets of the big organisational players. The Procon story demonstrates that working effectively in business partnerships to link organisational outcomes through planning, evaluation and learning principles to L&D activity can achieve that influence. In so doing it can offer a primary route out of the functional bunker and onto the strategic stage.

AN OUTSIDE-IN PLANNING, DESIGN AND EVALUATION SYSTEM

The outside-in approach adopted by the FLM project team to the whole planning cycle kept attention firmly on achieving an appropriate balance between the needs of learners and those of the business. Putting learning instead of instructional design at the heart of the programme raised the status and impact of the programme from one of a 'training course' to an integrated learning and business process. Evaluation, by utilising both formal and informal data at regular intervals and by being fully integrated into programme planning, played a key role in ensuring that programme outcomes influenced decision-making both in and beyond the training domain. As I explained in Chapter 7, research indicates that the power of informal assessments of training events is rarely understood or harnessed by L&D practitioners.

The FLMP itself represents in microcosm the company's approach to linking training to the business. The approach is strategic, driven by top management's clarity about business goals, its belief in the need to invest in its people, and a flexible partnering processes. The lack of any overall L&D strategy for the company, however, has the potential to produce weak links between the many L&D initiatives ongoing across the company, with a consequent loss of coherency and consistency – something of which there were signs in the concluding stages of the FLMP at Birmingham. This again emphasises the importance of an effective business partnership and a sustained focus on a 'Big Idea' to act as a guiding vision for clusters of interrelated projects and for each programme within those projects.

THE 'PEOPLE AND PERFORMANCE' LINK

The Procon case illustrates the vital importance to a business and to its employees of committed and engaged leaders at all organisational levels.

The whole programme was driven by the EXCEL vision, and by the CE's expressed belief that this training was a more important investment than any he could make in capital equipment or materials. It also demonstrated the value of taking a pay-forward rather than a pay-back approach to a major training investment, since once the programme's business case had been signed off, and given a continuing satisfactory state of leading KPIs related to the programme, the business sponsors' attention was focused not on 'How can you prove the programme's worth?' but on 'What should we do next to maximise its asset value?'

The narrative in this chapter confirms the validity of findings reported by Purcell and Hutchinson (2007: 16–17) in their 'Black box' research. To quote:

Paying particular attention to FLMs as an occupational group with numerous responsibilities and often competing priorities is necessary. This can include building involvement and problem-solving activities to allow access to decision-makers and provide means for mutual support, better selection with greater emphasis given to leadership behaviours as well as technical skills and knowledge, access to further development, coaching and guidance and career management.

The relationship between FLMs and their own managers is important and we have shown elsewhere how this was the biggest variable explaining FLMs' own levels of affective commitment and job satisfaction.

It also follows that since FLMs have a major role in 'bringing HR policies to life', the design of these policies should include consideration of how FLMs can apply them: to be as 'user-friendly' as possible.

THE IMPACT OF CONTEXT

Above all, the Procon FLM case demonstrates the central part played by the external environment, internal organisational context and workplace culture in determining how far learning interventions can achieve their intended outcomes. Three points are of fundamental importance here:

- The organisational purpose, value and workplace implications of an intervention must be recognised, supported and facilitated by key organisational players, by business processes and by HR policies and practices.

- Knowledge acquired by learners through that intervention must be enabled to connect with knowledge already held by other groups in the organisation – in the Procon case, those at the same level, at operator level below the FLMs, and at middle management level above them. Only when there is such a connection can collective learning and continuous improvement occur, together with the development of a 'unifying language' and 'appropriate relationships' across the organisation (von Krogh et al 1994).

- Just as events in an organisation's business environment can provide a powerful trigger for its investment in major L&D initiatives, so can unexpected changes in that environment subsequently shape their outcomes whether for better or for worse. Risk assessment must therefore form a central feature of the business case for all such initiatives.

To expand on that last point: sudden reversals such as the one that overtook Procon Manufacturing, UK after the FLMP ended are quite common in companies whose fortunes are intricately tied in with those of the conglomerates that own them. They are also experienced by many less complex organisations across all sectors as economic conditions in the West are worsening (mid-2008). Does that make such an expensive training investment by a company operating in a turbulent global business environment unwise? In my own view the answer is 'no', for the following reasons:

- When they first conceived the idea of an FLMP at the Birmingham site that site's CE and his small team weighed up the risks involved in making such a substantial training investment at uncertain business times against the risks of either failing to tackle the deeply unsatisfactory performance and workplace culture of FLMs at Birmingham, or of tackling it in some other way. The risks were reassessed in detail by the programme's project team when putting together its formal business case. Finally, they were given careful scrutiny by the business sponsors before they signed off that case. At each stage there was unanimous agreement that the benefits to be achieved by the programme significantly outweighed the risks it could involve.

- All value is time-bound and has to be set in a context. On the evidence, I believe that the FLMP delivered value in its own right, through savings that were real and whose beneficial impact on the company and on programme participants was also real. Certainly if more had been done at Procon's Birmingham site to engage middle managers from the start in the whole FLM project, problems that subsequently prevented the programme's outcomes making their fullest impact on the workplace would have been reduced. However the restructuring of the company and the job changes experienced by some of the programme's participants would still have occurred; without the benefits produced by the programme it is probable that their organisational and individual impact would have been considerably worse.

I believe that the changes in competence, confidence, values and behaviours that the programme produced in its participants, in the members of its project team and in its wider business partnership will have helped all of those stakeholders to respond more positively and creatively – both in a work and a personal capacity – than they could otherwise have done to the challenges that have subsequently faced the company.

REFLECTION

What are the most important lessons that you feel you have learnt from the Procon Manufacturing, UK FLMP narrative – and what questions, if any, does it leave unanswered in your mind?

CONCLUSION

In this chapter I have applied a real-life case study to the theory of the six-stage training cycle described in Chapter 7. You should by now have a sound understanding of how that cycle can operate in practice and be able to tackle the review questions contained in Appendix 3.

EXLPORE FURTHER

FURTHER INFORMATION SOURCES

Anderson, V. (2007) *The Value of Learning: A new model of value and evaluation*. Change Agenda. London: CIPD. Online version also available at http://www. cipd.co.uk/subjects/lrnanddev/ evaluation [accessed 25 May 2008]

CIPD podcast, 29 August 2007. *The Value of Learning*. Available at: http://www.cipd.co.uk/ podcasts [accessed 25 May 2008]

http://www. nationaltrainingawards.com/ [accessed 14 August 2008]. Awards to celebrate organisations and individuals demonstrating outstanding business and personal success through investment in training

CHAPTER 9

Achieving Ethical Practice

INTRODUCTION

> Ethical values shape the search for opportunities, the design of organizational systems, and the decision-making process used by individuals and groups. They provide a common frame of reference and serve as a unifying force across different functions, lines of business, and employee groups. Organizational ethics helps define what a company is and what it stands for.

> (Paine 1994: 111)

In today's service-based economy organisations in no matter what sector are faced with increasing demands from government, from investors and from the public to be socially and ethically responsible. In 2007 Business in the Community found that over 80% of FTSE-100 companies and 60% of FTSE-250 companies claimed to have ethical policies (BITC 2007). But policies are no longer enough. Environmental and community responsibilities, equality, inclusion, diversity, are all areas in which business leaders are having to demonstrate how they put into practice the values that they preach.

The purpose of this chapter is to explain and explore the two kinds of responsibility that L&D professionals hold in relation to ethics: to ensure that they themselves are ethical practitioners, and to work with others to build fairness and trust into the organisation's relations with its members and external stakeholders. For reasons explained in its first section, I have adopted the following definition of what is meant by 'ethical behaviour' in a business context:

> behaviour continuously striving to ensure that its consequences bring the greatest benefit and least harm to the greatest number in society (both within and beyond the organisation).

The first of the chapter's six sections sets the scene by reviewing various definitions of 'ethical behaviour' and the 'good' organisation. The second explores six powerful forces that are shaping organisations' approach to corporate social responsibility and ethics.

This leads in the third section to the importance of the psychological contract in building trust and commitment to a shared 'moral purpose'. The fourth section takes the discussion into the L&D field, examining what being an 'ethical' L&D practitioner can involve. Helping to achieve equality and the valuing of diversity are two key tasks here, and are the focus of the final two sections.

ETHICS AND CORPORATE SOCIAL RESPONSIBILITY

WHAT IS 'ETHICAL BEHAVIOUR'?

Ethics is concerned with rules or principles that help us to distinguish between right and wrong (Hamlin *et al* 2001: 98). It has been likened by John Gray (Cartwright 2007) to a 'hidden moral grammar that evaluates the causes and consequences of our own and others' actions'.

Such statements make it clear that any discussion of ethics can quickly plunge us into complex human territory. There are various codes offering ethical guidelines for HR professionals, including those established by professional bodies such as the CIPD (2008c). There are also codes of practice related to UK and European legislation. Yet conforming to a code does not of itself guarantee ethical practice. There is always a gap that only the individual can close, using as the reference points his or her own judgement and values. And here lies the difficulty in business ethics, because although being 'ethical' may be generally understood to mean 'morally correct' or 'honourable' (Pearsall and Trumble 1996), that raises the question – morally correct by whose standards? Honourable in whose eyes? Whose values should prevail here?

In considering ethics in a business context it is common to focus not on definitions of behaviour itself – since these inevitably drag insoluble philosophical debates in their train – but on behaviour's consequences for others. The rationale here is that any organisation has the potential to bring benefits and harms, both directly and indirectly, to human beings, and that the bigger the organisation and its scale of operations, the greater both benefits and harms can be (Ostapski *et al* 1996). 'Ethical behaviour' in a business context can therefore be interpreted to mean behaviour of an organisation, group or individual that brings the greatest benefit and least harm to the greatest number. At the practical level this raises the question of how far an organisation should go in attempts to distribute benefits and harms fairly – what does it, or should it, mean today to be a 'good' organisation?

WHAT IS THE 'GOOD' ORGANISATION?

Some argue that the wealth and power that many – especially international – businesses and their shareholders amass from their operations in free and open markets places on their owners a moral obligation to use at least part of those assets to improve the lot of the disadvantaged in society. Others, like the economist John Kay, take the view that the business of an organisation is to succeed as a business (Lye and Kay 2006). In this he is echoing the fundamental point made by Adam Smith who in *The Wealth of Nations* urged the practice of self-interest not because he saw human beings as essentially selfish, but because he saw the need for all of us to make 'rational efforts to further our material well-being'. Without 'prudence' there could be no 'benevolence' (or in our terminology, charity) since unless resources are first accumulated there is nothing for the benevolent to give away. By an extension of this logic the purpose of business organisations is to generate wealth – whether through its products or services – that contributes to the economic growth upon which society depends for its stability and progress. It is for society's members and their rulers or legislators to decide how best to use that wealth. 'Benevolence' is a personal virtue not a business competence.

Of course this bare-bones outline ignores the depth and complexity that make Adam Smith's reasoning so compelling. It also misses the compassion and wisdom that shine out of his philosophical treatise, *The Theory of Moral Sentiments*. But it does indicate why there can be no black and white answers to those who ask the difficult question 'What is the good organisation?' It is for an organisation's leaders to come to a view on the moral principles they believe should guide their particular organisation, and to achieve as best they can the commitment of stakeholders to those principles. Collier and Estaban (2007) describe how a business can become 'values-driven as well as finance-driven': in such a business (*ibid* 2007: 25)

> Ethics language becomes part of the 'culture of openness': moral awareness grows as words such as 'right', 'moral' and 'unethical' enter everyday usage.

They conclude that (*ibid*: 30)

> It is not enough to have mission statements and codes of ethics. It is necessary for ethics to become embedded in the cultural fabric of the business as well as in the hearts and minds of its members.

Business management authors like Barnard (1938), Simon (1945), Schendel and Hofer (1979) and Freeman and Gilbert (1988) emphasised the moral obligations of management as necessary components in the strategic planning process. However, Hosmer (1994) found little attention paid subsequently to this theme in the strategic literature. Today, that is changing, as the next section explains.

REFLECTION

Consider any organisation that is regarded as a 'good employer'. What forces do you think drove the organisation's owners or corporate management to seek that status, and how far in today's difficult economic conditions do you think the status is likely to prove durable?

FORCES INFLUENCING ORGANISATIONS' CSR AND ETHICS AGENDA

Many forces are interacting to produce a strong focus both on companies' corporate social responsibility (CSR) and on ethical business behaviour. Six of the most powerful are shown in Figure 11 and are discussed in this section.

THE MEDIA

Following the collapse of communism in the 1970s, the 'liberation' of market forces was at first widely welcomed as offering benefits both to businesses and to society at

FIGURE 11 Forces influencing organisations' definitions of CSR, moral purpose and bottom line

large. But as the corruption at the heart of powerful organisations including Enron, WorldCom, Arthur Andersen and Union Carbide (the company responsible for the Bhopal disaster in 1984) began to come to light a 'shameful' reality was revealed behind many impressive-sounding CSR policy statements (Partridge 2006). The ensuing publicity caused a wave of public revulsion and a heightened awareness of the damaging impact that business organisations can have on individuals, communities and their environment.

Today hidden TV cameras regularly record footage that can reveal to millions the fraudulent, exploitive or just downright incompetent practices of organisations ranging from NHS hospitals to big high-street retail stores. Campaigning websites, Internet search engines and other sources of scrutiny and exposure make it 'no longer possible to hide … Customers are demanding ethical behaviour, and companies that refuse to listen are likely to face severe punishment whenever they are caught acting wrongly' (Partridge 2006).

GLOBALISATION OF BUSINESSES

'Public morality must consist in the attempt to act with a view to consequences that will be for the common good' (Warnock 2006). 'Common good' has traditionally been defined by reference to the laws of the nation state, but globalisation in all its forms is now giving it a much wider and more complex scope. Collier and Estaban (2007) in their informative article observe that 'externalities' (defined as 'the costs of business activity that fall upon society as opposed to those that fall upon businesses themselves') now pose far greater threats – particularly environmental – to global society, with no framework of global governance able to impose the kinds of sanctions on business available to national governments in the past.

Such considerations lead some to propose the abandonment of the traditional concept of the single (economic) bottom line in favour of a triple bottom line that (Lye and Kay 2006: 56):

> embraces economic accountability, affordability, diversity and equity, which together represent corporate economic responsibility.

The triple bottom line concept has the appeal of being applicable not just to businesses with global scope but to all organisations, of no matter what size, type or sector. At the practical level, it can lead to ethically responsible business practice becoming part of managers' job descriptions and rewards systems, to training and educating managers in how to integrate CSR into companies, and to ensuring that CSR issues are reflected in internal and external training provision and in employee target setting, appraisal, incentives and rewards – an approach followed by Adidas in the appraisal of their national managers' performance (Glover 2002b: 39).

The Adidas example has its dangers, given the difficulty of making any direct link between individual behaviour and organisational performance. Yet an organisation that explicitly espouses some moral as well as economic purpose must ensure that its intentions are put into practice. Companies like KPMG with a high profile in relation to community and environmental initiatives seek to achieve this through closely aligning their CSR and HR strategies (Chynoweth 2007). The UK Government for its part regards CSR as a mainstream issue for all managers, urging that its principles be built into the education, training and development of staff throughout all organisations. Business in the Community launched a CSR Academy in 2004 as a resource for organisations wanting to develop their corporate social responsibility (CSR) skills. It was due to be re-launched in 2008 as a 'one-stop shop' on CSR training and as promoter of the 2004 national CSR Competency Framework which will be integrated into existing professional bodies (*http://www.bitc.org.uk/resources/training/csr_academy/ index.html* [accessed 5 July 2008]).

ENVIRONMENTAL CONCERNS

Research is showing a direct link between environmentally friendly organisations and employer brand. For example, a company adopting a strategy of reducing carbon emissions and 'greening' the business can thereby acknowledge both its social responsibility to limit the damage it causes to the environment and its recognition of customer concerns. Going 'green' also links to companies' economic bottom line, since with energy costs rising at unprecedented rates energy-efficiency is a business 'must'.

HSBC's CLIMATE PARTNERSHIP

CASE EXAMPLE

HSBC initiates partnership programmes with environmental charities and non-government organisations to carry out work of environmental benefit that draws on its core business and HR competencies. It launched a five-year HSBC Climate Partnership in 2007. It is a £50 million venture carried out in collaboration with four charities – the Climate Group, Earthwatch, the WWF and the Smithsonian Tropical Research Institute. It involves employees in two stages: learning about climate change, then getting involved in local environmental projects. 'Climate champions' have been created to observe projects around the world and bring ideas back into the business.

A CSR Forum has also been set up, developed from the Environment and Travel Group created in 2005 in response to staff's and customers' growing interest in first direct's environmental policies and record. Its members were briefed to propose ideas for 'greening' the business and to suggest how they could be implemented. The CSR Forum embraces a wider range of charitable and community activities and involves a wider group of volunteers.

HSBC's 2006 employee focus survey found that 75% of its

employees believed that the bank operated ethically and that 64% thought it was environmentally responsible. There also appeared to be a positive impact on employee retention figures. Its Climate Partnership projects benefit wider society while also resulting in benefits for the business. They help to bring together a global HSBC workforce and to forge an ethical company brand that can attract new talent as well as expand its customer and shareholder base.

Source: Simms, J. (2007)
People Management, 26 July

THE TALENT WAR

While many corporate leaders are coming to realise that establishing a strong ethical purpose for their organisations is 'integral to the long-term viability of their businesses, and in many cases as a series of opportunities to be embraced' (Stone 2007), one important business advantage is an enhanced ability to attract and retain talent. HSBC has been strongly influenced by research it has carried out in recent years showing that over 10% of recent graduates identified CSR as one of the top three factors influencing their choice of employer (Simms 2007). Generation Y (today's young people in their twenties) is the most strongly associated yet with environmental awareness and a preference to work in companies that are committed to 'giving something back'. Supporting community projects both at home and across the world, funding environmental improvement and setting up charitable foundations are all ways through which an increasing number of organisations are signalling their ethical purpose in order to attract young talent.

Early in 2008 OnePoll.com conducted an online survey covering over 1,500 employees working across sectors in organisations with 500 or more staff (CHA 2008). The survey revealed that many employees, especially at the younger end of the workforce, want to make a noticeable impact on major issues in society such as climate change and community improvement. Over 40% of 18- to 25-year-olds and 38% of 26- to 35-year-olds in its sample were considering a move from the private to public or charity sectors in order to find a more worthwhile job. On a broader front more than 70% of respondents said that private companies' efforts on climate change and social responsibility helped to strengthen those companies' reputation (CHA 2008).

LEGISLATION, BENCHMARKING AND CODES

Under pressure from the European Framework Directive for Equal Treatment in Employment and Occupation, the UK in 2006 produced sweeping changes in its anti-discrimination law, and this has direct implications for organisations' handling of workforce diversity as well as for its overall ethical code. The law's extensive coverage now protects employees against discrimination in employment and vocational training on the grounds not only of race, ethnic origin, gender, disability, religion, age or sexual orientation but of any strongly held belief that affects an employee's lifestyle. This opens up the possibility, for example, that employees concerned about their organisation's carbon footprint could pressurise their employer to introduce green policies, with an employer's refusal to do so without good reason constituting discrimination (Guianan 2008). In anticipation of such pressures some employers are already introducing a 'green policy'.

The 2007 Corporate Manslaughter and Corporate Homicide Act also has big implications for corporate and managerial ethics because of the heavy duty of care that it places on employers for the health and safety of those who work for them. It is now easier to prosecute employers when fatalities occur at work, and all employees potentially face criminal charges if it can be shown that their acts or omissions have caused or contributed to a failure resulting in a death (Leckie 2005). Any corporate manslaughter investigation will look particularly for a 'safety culture' in the organisation. One aspect of such a culture is evidence of an open attitude to the raising of concerns by employees so a clear whistle-blowing policy is essential (Leckie and Fraser 2007). Policy, though, will not be enough: there must be proof that staff are aware of it, that those handling disclosures are appropriately trained, and that management systems, records and practices across the organisation ensure that the policy is handled fairly, consistently and effectively.

Cooper (2003) refers to 'the maze of benchmarks, directives and guidelines' to CSR and business ethics. He noted that although no single standard or cluster of standards has gained common acceptance this variety of advice means that organisations can pick and choose according to their specific concerns, whether those relate to pay policies, general employee issues and industrial relations, pension guidelines, or discrimination (*ibid*).

Business in the Community's Corporate Social Responsibility Index, for example, was launched in 2002 to help businesses assess how well their CSR policies are embedded in their business operations and enables them to benchmark their performance against their peers (BITC 2007). The results, published annually each May, show that core business activities are becoming increasingly linked to the corporate responsibility activities of organisations. Some key findings from the 2006 survey are outlined in Table 10.

The contents of Table 10 show that the task of ensuring that an organisation is ethical in its goals, strategies, leadership and management does not always sit easily with business objectives, or with the diverse demands of stakeholders. Caught between business imperatives, a need to ensure legal compliance on all employment-related matters and a desire both to achieve good practice in CSR generally, an organisation can go 'horribly wrong' (Cooper 2003), ending up with a disconnected hotchpotch of policies and practices. Furthermore employees are often unaware that their organisation has an ethical code, let alone know what it contains (Drummond 2004). Codes will have little or no practical impact unless

TABLE 10 Some findings from BITC's Corporate Social Responsibility Index Report 2006

Positive findings from the 2006 survey include:	Concerns emerging from the 2006 survey include:
Board-level ownership of the various aspects of corporate responsibility is more prevalent and increasingly visible. Participating companies are placing growing emphasis on responsible business as a source of competitive advantage as they move beyond minimising risk to creating opportunities.	Evidence of social and environmental issues influencing decision-making around new investments and the development of new products and services is often limited to isolated examples.
Companies are doing more to integrate their systems and programmes in order to motivate, train and communicate with employees.	More needs to be done to embed values and engage employees.
More companies (now 92% of participants) are actively involving stakeholders in identifying key risks, opportunities and performance indicators for the business.	A major area for improvement is supply-chain management.
More companies report on policies, targets and performance.	Future-focused commitments and targets rarely tend to look more than a year ahead. This is particularly true in the 'hugely complex area of social and environmental impact'. For example, although climate change is now a mainstream business issue, most companies are still only focusing on making incremental yearly improvements instead of committing to major, long-term strategies.
The distinction between marketplace and community issues is blurring as companies develop a greater understanding of the gains to be made by addressing social issues through marketplace activities and behaviours.	Information available to the public about what organisations actually do is not always independently assured so may not always be accurate or reliable.

Source: Business in the Community's Corporate Social Responsibility Index, information drawn from Report on 2006 Survey, available online at *http://www.bitc.org.uk/what_we_do/* [accessed 19 June 2008]

they are an integral part of business strategy, are well communicated, and are supported by clear guidelines to their implementation and measures to ensure their effective implementation. Accenture's code, explained overleaf, is an example of one that seeks to achieve all these aims.

STAKEHOLDER POWER

John Philpott, the CIPD's chief economist, believes that the combined power of the forces already discussed in this section means that the prime goal of organisations should no longer be solely to maximise shareholder value. It should be to balance

CASE EXAMPLE

ACCENTURE'S CODE OF BUSINESS ETHICS

In 2006 Accenture, the global outsourcing firm, produced a substantially revised version of 'The Accenture Code of Business Ethics', which has to be read and followed by all its employees across the world. The Code has four distinguishing features:

- It places emphasis on Accenture's six core values.

- It gives practical examples for its employees of what those values mean in relation to their everyday work life.

- It incorporates new legal and regulatory developments.

- It aims to be user-friendly.

As explained on the Accenture website, the Code lies at the heart of the company's Ethics and Compliance programme, whose purpose is to ensure not only legal compliance in all its activity, but also the highest ethical standards in its employees. Periodically all who work for Accenture across the world must certify their compliance with the Code:

'The Code emphasizes critical areas particular to our organization and business model while highlighting aspects of conduct that are imperative for all employees. Our Code does not incorporate or refer to all policies, but acts as a synthesis of the key policies and principles that should govern all employees' conduct.'

Source: *http://www.accenture.com/ Global/About_Accenture/Corporate_ Governance/CodeProgram.htm* [accessed 16 July 2008], where the full Code can also be viewed

the interests of all stakeholders who are directly or indirectly affected by the organisation's activities. He stresses that 'simply implementing lots of stakeholder initiatives won't do' since it is unlikely to improve the way organisations perform – and performing effectively is their primary responsibility. What is needed is a strategic approach that stresses underlying performance improvement (Philpott 2003).

Shareholders and customers constitute stakeholder groups whose power has increased particularly strongly over the past two decades, both in the USA and the UK. In some companies shareholders' influence has led to unprecedented changes in the boardroom and is sometimes beginning to interfere in the legitimate role of management (Durman 2003). In the increasingly volatile economic climate that is confronting institutional investors worldwide, shareholders are more anxious than ever to get quick returns on their investment in businesses yet at the same time many want the companies in which they invest to have a clean ethical record, some because they have become genuinely ethically-minded, others because they perceive that 'ethics is good for business'. The steady growth in ethical investing is exemplified in the development of investment indices such as FTSE4Good and the Dow Jones Sustainability Indexes (sic) which offer an alternative to the mainstream stock market benchmarks. Pension funds are also legally obliged to make a statement of their ethical principles in their investment strategy (Cooper 2003).

As explained in Chapter 7 customers now exercise unprecedented influence over companies through the rapidity and ease with which, through the Internet, they can gain access to information, compare experiences and rapidly switch their loyalties. Many are strongly influenced by ethical and environmental considerations and expect to see these reflected in the conduct, products and services of the organisations with which they deal. However, in increasingly uncertain financial times it remains to be seen how far those considerations continue to exercise a real influence over customer choice.

BUILDING TRUST

A PROBLEMATIC PROCESS

'Trust' appears on many corporate value statements, and the building of trust and the commitment that it engenders is one of the core elements of the 'People and Performance' framework (Purcell *et al* 2003). However, ways of building it can differ widely according to the parties involved, especially in cross-cultural situations. Banu Golesorkhi, Director of the Research Centre for Pharos International in Brussels, cites the example of Asian managers who expect their colleagues to show 'benevolence' towards others. Those who do not are unable to gain trust no matter how expert or powerful they may be. On the other hand northern Europeans tend to distinguish between work and personal life 'so they don't expect their co-workers to behave like their friends' (Smethurst 2007: 34). Similar difficulties are involved in building trust between an organisation and stakeholders whose interests and expectations may be as varied as are cultural differences in a multicultural organisation.

Here is a very brief outline of one international organisation's trust-building strategy.

CASE EXAMPLE

TOSCA CONSULTING GROUP

The Tosca Consulting Group, whose participants include the United Nations Refugee Agency and Dave Ulrich, regards trust as a currency that an organisation must build up through:

- meeting its commitments
- effectively managing expectations
- keeping people informed
- giving them an opportunity to have their say.

It finds that discussions on ethics, on the company's code of conduct, and on related managerial and leadership issues can be built into learning materials and management training, giving a language and a vocabulary with which to talk about trust and business ethics to non-HR specialists.

Source: Smethurst, T. (2007)
People Management, 22 February

THE PSYCHOLOGICAL CONTRACT

In any discussion of trust-building in organisations it is inevitable that the concept of the psychological contract comes to the fore. It does not concern the legal contract that binds the individual to the employer by specifying their duties, terms and conditions, and material rewards. It concerns the perceived expectations, wants and rights that bind those parties at a deeper psychological level. Its basic proposition is that in order to motivate and retain employees, employers have to treat them properly, and that if they do, this will produce trust and help to build the commitment that can lead to improved organisational performance (CIPD 2008d).

The psychological contract is dynamic, with new expectations being added over time as contexts and needs change. In a world where long-term job security is rare and the pace of job and organisational change can be frenetic, some refer to a 'new deal' in the employment relationship: one in which the diversity management, work–life balance, flexibility and the redefinition of traditional working arrangements are all central as employers seek to attract and retain the human capital they need for their organisations. In reality, however, findings from the Economic and Social Research Council's five-year programme, completed in 2003, on the future of work in Britain did not provide any such picture. What they did highlight is the importance of the workplace and of building commitment to the organisation there through relational rather than transactional psychological contracts (Sparrow and Cooper 2003):

- *Transactional psychological contracts* are those that represent little more than a functional relationship: the employee offers services in exchange for compensation by the employer. Such highly specific contracts typify some short-term employment relationships where work is project-driven and/or involves outsourcing arrangements. By no means all, however. Many relatively short-term relationships still want more than a purely functional bond.

- *Relational psychological contracts* are those that are based on mutual commitment. They may be less specific where they are grounded in an expectation of a relatively long-term relationship – but whatever the anticipated duration of the legal contract, the psychological one seeks a shared purpose that can be achieved through an open, trusting partnership that is there for the long haul – however 'long' is defined.

Working towards a shared purpose will not happen by itself. Organisations are pluralist, not unitary systems. That is to say they comprise individuals and groups who have multiple goals stemming from differing values, beliefs and needs. A pluralist system is not dominated by any single logic. It is driven by a variety of non-economic as well as economic interests. Recognising that any organisation is pluralist means recognising that all value systems of its stakeholders matter and should be reflected in the type of psychological contract established not only between employer and employee, but in a more generalised sense between the organisation and its external stakeholders. There must be a mutually acceptable 'deal' and a genuine agreement to honour it. Such an approach is consistent with the advice given 70 years ago by one of the great management writers, Chester Barnard (1938: 259): that although an organisation's members are motivated by many individual interests, they will tend to respond positively to organisational strategies that can inspire co-operation by creating faith in the 'integrity of common purpose'.

REFLECTION

What kind of psychological contract do you perceive to exist between your employer and yourself? And how far (if at all) do you feel that it has achieved your trust and commitment to any shared ethical purpose?

ETHICS AND L&D PRACTICE

THE 'ETHICAL' L&D PROFESSIONAL

The starting-point in becoming an 'ethical' professional is for the individual to be clear about his or her own values. Here, they may have to face an uncomfortable reality: one where they may not be able to endorse corporate practices and conduct because these conflict with their personal ethical beliefs or with their profession's code of conduct. As one reader of the CIPD magazine *People Management* wrote (*People Management* 2002):

> If HR professionals want to be taken seriously, we need to be able to determine for ourselves whether the organisations in which we work are actually having a benign effect on society and to take action accordingly.

But what if such action is likely to be opposed by the employer or by senior management? To take it could alienate colleagues, superiors and work teams. It could open the individual to accusations of disloyalty. It could threaten their career progression. Ultimately it could even put their job at risk. Yet it is part of any L&D practitioner's professional responsibility to genuinely commit to the ethical standards and values that they are required by their organisation to communicate and to embed in training and development processes and initiatives. If they cannot give that commitment, and if they are unable to influence those standards and values in ways that they consider to be essential, the decision they then face is a harsh one: either to compromise their own values or to leave the organisation.

The risk of job loss makes it unsurprising that the path of compromise is often taken, despite the damaging consequences for others that can follow in its train. As I have pointed out in past editions of this book, in cases of bad practice in the L&D field the failures of L&D practitioners are often due in part to others, usually those who plan and provide the practitioners' education and training and/or those those who manage and are ultimately accountable for their performance. But the individual cannot entirely pass the ethical buck. No professional, HR or otherwise, should venture into areas of work where they are uncertain of their own competence, if in so doing they are likely to jeopardise the duty of care they have for others. Nor should they stand silently by in situations where that duty of care is jeopardised by the incompetent, discriminatory or harassing behaviour of others.

A fundamental conflict between an L&D practitioner's personal or professional code and the values he or she perceives to be the dominant values in the organisation may be rare. There is, though, a wide range of ethical issues that these practitioners confront in their daily activity. What would help them here are a framework to guide their practice, diagnostic tools and aids to problem-solving, and access to wise advice. One simple framework could be that suggested by Alred *et al* (1998) to help mentors in their relationships with their mentees – mentoring being a process that can bring with it some thorny ethical dilemmas:

- *explore* (identifying all the critical aspects of a situation that point to its having an ethical dimension)

- *reflect* (considering options in order to decide what course of action would bring the greatest benefit and the least adverse outcomes to those involved in the situation and to the organisation)

- *act* (taking that action, and monitoring its outcome).

Some urge detailed standards for the L&D profession. However, by their very comprehensiveness such standards tend to exclude from consideration any situation falling outside their boundaries and any values but the ones they espouse. They can also overload the individual with information. The National School of Government, launched by the Cabinet Office in 2005 to develop civil service leadership skills, has produced a code of ethical practice for L&D practitioners that strikes a healthy balance between a generalised framework and guidelines to aid problem-solving in the specific instance. It is available online at *http://www.nationalschool.gov.uk/about_us/jobs/ associate_working/ CodeOfEthics.pdf* [accessed 25 August 2008] and appears in full in my tutors' online manual.

Codes, professional standards and qualifications can clarify and support ethical practice but they can never guarantee it. The final decision on how to act depends on the individual's judgement. Each L&D professional must therefore develop their own well-grounded understanding of what is ethical behaviour in the particular situation and be guided by that understanding when facing ethical dilemmas. To do that, as Adam Smith explained in his great philosophical work *The Theory of Moral Sentiments*, the individual must put himself or herself in the shoes of an 'impartial spectator'. His reasoning is deceptively simple (Prowse 1995):

> When ethically perplexed, the question we should always ask is: would a disinterested observer, in full possession of the relevant facts, approve or disapprove of our actions?

SUPPORTING THE ORGANISATION'S ETHICAL CODE

One vital task for trainers, mentors and coaches is to communicate their company's ethical code and help leaders and managers understand how to put it into practice across their organisation. Ethics training programmes are now widespread, a common reason being that many employees now work unsupervised in jobs that are less precisely defined than before, and so have to rely more on their own discretion in dealing with ethical issues. Another, allied to this, is that there are now more opportunities for them 'to engage in covert actions that have the potential to subvert or harm the organization and its goals' (Trevino and Weaver 2001: 651).

Drummond (2004), head of a consultancy specialising in business ethics training, has found that a targeted process is by far the most effective to raise employees' understanding of ethical issues and gain support for the organisation's ethical code:

- *Start at the top*
  Ethics is a leadership issue, so the ideal starting point is workshops for senior management, preferably using a dilemma-based training approach. This involves shared problem-solving between trainers and participants focusing on real-life situations, captured in a variety of learning methods such as role play, case studies and interactive videos. It challenges and helps the managers to put theory into practice.

- *Cascade the training throughout the organisation*
  Following the success of the workshops, senior managers can then co-ordinate training for all other employees. They can appoint champions for each major business unit – preferably talented line managers since these are best placed to understand their front-line staff and the kind of ethical dilemmas they commonly face. Again the most effective approach to training is likely to be dilemma-based, supplemented by a blend of e-learning and face-to-face methods.

- *Carry out specialised training where relevant*
  Specialised training may be needed for those in high-risk areas such as procurement, marketing, health and safety. If this is followed by e-learning

exercises to test understanding and application of learning it will enable L&D staff and senior management to gauge the effectiveness of the training.

TRAINING FOR COMPLIANCE OR COMMITMENT?

Before designing and delivering any ethics training L&D practitioners need to agree with the organisation's management the kind of culture that the programme should support. If it is one focused simply on legal compliance, training should centre on clarifying the law, the consequences of breaking it, and responsibilities and controls needed to ensure that it is observed by employer and employees. In 2007 a new Commission for Equality and Human Rights was established, absorbing the three previous commissions for gender, race and disability and adding new responsibilities arising from the Employment Equality Directive, as well as those flowing from the 1997 Human Rights Act. As Overell (2005) had forecast, 'its purview is colossal'. With equal opportunities a 'notoriously disputatious field' where infringement of the law carries the risk for the employer of uncapped compensation payouts, and with health and safety also a minefield, some compliance-based training is essential in all organisations to ensure that at every level there is full understanding of legal responsibilities and how to carry them out.

However, as the Chair of the Equality and Human Rights Commission has warned, the Equalities Bill underlines the importance of going beyond compliance to achieving a profound culture change. He explained (*People Management* 2008b):

> Everything about equality and diversity in the workplace has been focused purely on employment targets rather than what it means to the service an employer is providing.

He was referring here to the need for employers to adopt what Paine in her illuminating article described as an 'integrity strategy', very different from one based merely on compliance (Paine 1994: 111):

> Broader in that it seeks to enable responsible conduct. Deeper in that it cuts to the ethos and operating systems of the organization and its members, their guiding values and patterns of thought and action. And more demanding in that it requires an active effort to define the responsibilities and aspirations that constitute an organization's ethical compass.

Training to support such a strategy needs to be based on commitment to values rather than merely compliance with the law. Compliance-based and values-based programmes can of course be complementary, but to succeed in their aims each requires a favourable organisational context including reinforcement from other HR programmes and practices. Trevino and Weaver's (2001) empirical research illustrated the importance for the success of any kind of equality programme of employees perceiving that they are treated in a generally fair way and that management follows through on the ethical problems that employees raise in the workplace. It is therefore essential to establish what those perceptions are (*ibid*: 651):

> Management may intend that an ethics program operates in a fair manner with consistent follow-through, but if employees perceive otherwise, unethical behavior and failures to report ethical problems may be more likely.

The following case example outlines training practice that apparently ignored all such principles.

CASE EXAMPLE

FAILURES IN RACE AWARENESS TRAINING

In 2000, a 'damning report' was published by Her Majesty's Inspectorate of Constabulary on the Metropolitan Police Force's efforts to erase racism. The race awareness training introduced following the Macpherson Report on the Stephen Lawrence murder investigation was found to be particularly inadequate. One reason was that senior personnel chiefs did not exercise enough influence and lacked the necessary power and organisational credibility to ensure wider support for the training; another was serious deficiencies in training expertise at strategic and operational levels, resulting in:

- lack of clarity on overall training strategy and how it fitted with wider HR functions

- lack of clarity about where responsibility lay for training at a senior level

- lack of rigorous training needs analysis

- lack of understanding as to who would be trained to what standard, and when

- failure to undertake effective long-term evaluation of training.

On a wider front, it was revealed in 2004 by a Commission for Racial Equality investigation that despite continuous high investment in police diversity training following the Lawrence Inquiry more than 90% of police race-equality schemes in England and Wales had failed to meet the minimum legal requirements of the Race Relations Act.

Sources: Cooper, C. (2000a)
People Management, 10 July;
People Management (2004) 30 June

In the light of such findings it is unsurprising that the accusation of 'institutionalised racism', whether or not justified, is still so frequently levelled at police forces in Britain.

AIDING EQUALITY: TASKS FOR L&D PRACTITIONERS

CLARIFYING THE TERMINOLOGY

When discussing ethics there are four terms that 'people in the organisation, including senior leadership, often use … loosely and interchangeably, without pausing for much thought as to what it all means' (Brook and Graham 2005). It is important here to differentiate them in order to give clarity to the discussion of equality in this section, and of diversity and inclusivity in the next:

- *Equity* is the overall concept. It is to do with achieving general fairness and justice and in that respect can complement, correct or go further than the law. It is what 'ethical behaviour' seeks to achieve.

- *Equality* is a narrower concept which in this context is to do with all employees enjoying their due rights and opportunities under the law. The law, however, cannot guarantee equity in an organisation – it can only create a common baseline to protect aspects of difference and sometimes that baseline is confused. To take one example: in Britain in 2006 age was added to the list of equality laws, yet in 2004 a new legal concept of a 'national default retirement age' had also been introduced, with the result that once an employee reaches 65 'an employer [is] entitled to offload him or her' (Overell 2005). The two laws do not sit easily together. Furthermore, when it is estimated that in 2050 the dependency ratio of 65+-year-olds to 20- to 64-year-olds in Britain will have reached 47%, the 2004 law seems increasingly perverse (*ibid*).

- *Diversity* is an approach to equity and equality that involves harnessing and valuing a wide range of visible and invisible differences in employees (Kersten 2000).

- *Inclusivity* concerns 'behaviours, processes and environmental factors that either facilitate or impede people feeling valued' (Brook and Graham 2005).

AIDING EQUALITY IN THE WORKPLACE: THREE L&D TASKS

L&D professionals can help the cause of equality at work in three ways: by raising awareness in order to improve practice, by ensuring equality of access to training and development opportunities and by contributing to affirmative action.

Their first step must be to review the HR and business policy contexts in which managers have to operate. A context unfavourable to achieving equality in the workplace will prevent training achieving its intended outcomes. It will also create negative employee perceptions of fairness in the organisation at large and so is likely to lower their commitment to training. Yet again context is all, but trying to influence it is not easy for the L&D practitioner who lacks influence over powerful organisational players. This helps to explain why many trainers, whether based in the organisation or working as its consultants, accept training briefs that in reality they should argue against or reject. This in itself is an ethical dilemma, although often not recognised as such.

Raising awareness about equality

To ensure understanding of the importance of legal compliance training needs to achieve a set of key outcomes:

- a sound practical understanding of what inequality, direct and indirect discrimination mean, both in legal and practical terms. This is essential for all employees, but should be a priority for managers since legislation makes them particularly exposed to employment tribunal claims

- a similar understanding of the organisation's equal opportunity policy, and the competence and commitment of those charged with its implementation to carry out the responsibilities that it involves

- commitment of all organisational members to reporting to relevant personnel any discriminatory attitudes that may affect decision-making and action at various organisational levels

- managerial commitment to keeping records of how recruitment, selection, promotion and reward processes are handled, and of their outcomes. Claims of unlawful treatment can be won on a failure by the employer to provide records demonstrating that all reasonable practical steps have been taken to avoid discrimination occurring.

There should be regular monitoring of progress towards these outcomes. There should also be organisational follow-up of any discrimination issues raised during the programme since it is essential to prevent the persistence of a culture in which discrimination is deeply embedded (although the trainer must raise such issues with management in ways that do not break confidence with the programme's participants). Remedial action is essential, particularly to ensure positive employee perceptions related to fairness both within the training itself and in the organisation generally. This, of course, calls for an effective partnership between training staff and management throughout the entire training cycle described in Chapters 7 and 8.

Ensuring equality of treatment and opportunity

It is easy to state that everyone in an organisation should have equal access to training and development related to their and the organisation's needs, but it is harder to achieve that aim. As discussed in Chapters 2 and 3 there is still a deep training divide in many organisations, making it a key responsibility of L&D professionals to ensure that:

- their own specialist staff, managers, and all others with L&D responsibilities, fully understand the law relating to ensuring access to opportunities for training, promotion and other forms of development

- policies for selection for training and development, succession planning and career development all incorporate equality issues

- policies are effectively implemented, so that there is no direct or indirect discrimination in selecting people for training and development. There should be regular monitoring to see whether, through time, people from a particular group or gender are failing to apply for certain kinds of training or assessment for promotion; are not trained, assessed or promoted at all; or are trained, assessed or promoted, but in significantly lower proportions than their rate of application or their representation in the workforce suggest should be the case. If such checks show that problems are occurring, causes must be established and remedial action taken

- all employees know how to access information about training, educational and other developmental opportunities, and how to apply for them. Such opportunities must not be communicated to employees in ways that could exclude or disproportionately reduce the numbers of applicants from any particular type, group or sector.

Contributing to positive action

It is unlawful to discriminate against some groups in order to improve the position of others previously disadvantaged (except in the case of disabled candidates for a position – there, under disability discrimination law, employers can discriminate in favour of individuals by making 'reasonable adjustments' in order to compensate for their disadvantages). However, legislation does allow an organisation to provide training for minority groups in order to encourage under-represented candidates, thereby increasing the diversity of the candidate pool. For example, where in a previous 12-month period there have been no or proportionately few employees of a particular sex or racial group in certain jobs, areas, or level of work when compared to the population at large, the following positive action is lawful:

- the employer to provide access to training facilities that will help to fit those minority group members for such work or responsibilities

- the employer to encourage them to apply for training or education, whether it is provided internally or externally

- the training manager to design training schemes for school-leavers designed to reach members of such groups; and to arrange training for promotion or skills training for those who lack particular expertise but show potential.

Reflecting on any organisation with which you are familiar, how far do you think training has helped to achieve 'equality' in the workplace, and in what ways? What evidence could you produce to support your assessment, whether or not it is a positive one?

DIVERSITY AND INCLUSIVITY: THE CHALLENGES

VALUING DIVERSITY AND INCLUSIVITY

Organisations employ a diverse workforce for reasons that can include maximising the available labour market talent, creating business opportunities by drawing on wider perspectives and thriving in different cultures, and better serving an increasingly diverse customer base. Being known as an inclusive place to work where diversity is valued can also bring reputational benefits, including becoming an employer of choice.

Recent legislation has highlighted the importance of effective diversity management. Early in 2007 a 'root and branch' Equalities Review that had been set up to 'investigate the causes of persistent discrimination and inequality in British society' produced its final report. It aimed to inform both the modernisation of equality legislation towards a Single Equality Act and the development of a new Commission for Equality and Human Rights (*http// www.theequalitiesreview.org. uk* [accessed 10 July 2008]). By mid-2008 a Bill was in progress through Parliament to bring all grounds of discrimination within one piece of legislation, uniting more than 100 existing pieces of anti-discrimination legislation, placing a single duty on public bodies to ensure equality across all strands of diversity and making diversity a key factor in awarding public procurement contracts (Brockett 2008c).

Perversely such a weight of legislation is likely to make it more, not less, difficult to ensure equality at work while also trying to build on diversity and achieve inclusivity. The next case example identifies some of the problematic issues.

MANAGING DIVERSITY AND EQUAL OPPORTUNITIES IN A RETAIL STORE

Research in a retail organisation showed that fear of legal consequences prompted managers to opt for a compliance-based approach to equality issues, at the expense of effective management of diversity. Organisational context was a powerful influence over their behaviour: the nature of this context in many situations led to management favouring a policy of 'sameness' rather than a more positive approach of building on differences.

Extending a compliance-based approach to the management of diversity in this way created particular inconsistencies where in the same organisation there were progressive HR diversity policies. Whereas training favouring 'sameness' tended to focus heavily on conforming with the law and therefore on 'what not to do', the HR policies emphasised the need to identify, value and build on individual differences in order to achieve a culture where every employee's contribution and potential was fully recognised and developed.

Source: Foster, C. and Harris, L. (2004)

PROBLEMS OF 'DIFFERENCE'

One big issue affecting diversity in the labour market at large and with specific consequences for an organisation's workplace is the impact of the knowledge economy. It can intensify old labour market divisions in countries like the UK where most new jobs are in the low-skill, low-paid sector and where knowledge workers form as yet only a small minority of the labour force. In the UK (as discussed in Chapters 2 and 3) there are wide income and job opportunity disparities between the better trained and educated and those who lack those advantages. The skilled continue to get the good jobs, while the unskilled either fall out of work or adapt by taking on the low-paid work that is often all that remains. Despite all the rhetoric of the learning organisation, the breakdown of hierarchy and the benefits of diversity, in the service-based knowledge economy 'difference' for many employees means an experience of continued subordination (Field 2000: 84).

There are many other differences in workplaces today that receive no legal protection but that can produce more harms than benefits for those experiencing them. Take, for example, the quite common situation where people who work side by side are contracted to different employers. They may be separated by significant differences – in pay, in terms and conditions, in the ways in which they are treated by their employers. When they are brought together in training or other forms of learning experience, such differences, unless identified and responded to effectively by L&D staff, can undermine the learning process.

Other examples of differences with significant implications for training and learning processes are those related to individuals' learning style, skills and preferences, to their ability to fit into the culture of the workplace and to their attitudes to change. Each type can lead to some participants in training feeling or becoming isolated, particularly if they are put under pressure to conform to values they do not share, or confronted by a learning approach that they see as threatening or that does not enable them to play to their strengths.

The sources of many difficulties associated with diversity go back to organisational context and are unlikely to disappear unless and until aspects of that context change. Consider, as a primary example, today's so-called post-Fordist workplace. Its emphasis is on collaboration, trust, self-managing teams, abolition of hierarchy, self-development and a 'learning organisation' – an attractive vision, but as Butler persuasively argues, it can result in new forms of control replacing the old, and new inequalities emerging (Butler 1999: 144–5). Four of the features that are most commonly held to characterise high-performing organisations can have particularly divisive effects:

- behavioural competency frameworks

- team structures

- group-based reward systems

- appraisal systems to monitor and measure performance.

The benefits that this cluster of HR practices can bring to a business have often been argued in research (Terry and Purcell 1997), yet those who cannot adjust easily to them can be sidelined, their 'difference' in this respect leading to them being regarded as 'difficult'. Difference then becomes a disability rather than a benefit, creating problems for individuals and for the business.

Competency frameworks

Competency frameworks comprise 'a list of skills and competencies which identify and describe the behaviours necessary to perform a particular role or task at a particular level within an organisation (Pilbeam and Corbridge 2002: 499). As I will explain in Chapter 17 there is a widespread use across Europe of national training systems focused on such frameworks. These systems aim to liberate learners in the workplace in three ways:

- by giving them, through competency-focused training, a sense of control over their learning

- by using learner-centred approaches that emphasise collaboration, participation and negotiation in the learning process.

- by supporting equality of treatment through a consistent approach to performance standards.

Yet by its very preoccupation with a particular set of learning processes and a particular approach to workplace learning, competency-based training can socialise people to become certain types of learners, and so can introduce new divisions (Solomon 1999: 123). Even training systems offering accreditation of prior learning often focus on particular kinds of knowledge and experience, excluding others. In other words competency frameworks and the training related to them can become yet another reinforcer of 'sameness' rather than building fruitfully on 'difference'.

Team structures and group-based reward systems

High-performing teams bring obvious benefits for the business and can offer their members social support, clarity of role and a buffer from the wider organisation. Yet not everyone can work well in a team, particularly one that is self-managing and internally controlled. A 2004 NHS staff survey of 200,000 NHS employees showed that 89% worked in a team but that only 41% of such teams were perceived by their members to be well-structured and effective (Griffiths 2004). In some teams certain individuals can find themselves marginalised, singled out as being unacceptably different from other team members. The stress on those who fail to conform is reinforced by group-based reward systems and by team training to achieve common behavioural norms.

Appraisal

Appraisal can be a divisive process if it is used in order to achieve strict conformity of all employees to centralised norms relating to performance and learning, or if it is administered with a discriminatory bias. A report on local government warning that the sector stood in danger of breaking race equality laws (Rana 2003) revealed, for example, that superiors' performance ratings of ethnic-minority senior and middle managers were lower than ratings given by peers and direct reports. Superiors also often failed to give ethnic-minority managers feedback on performance – sometimes possibly out of fear that if they gave any negative feedback they would be seen as racist. Because they were not getting a balanced feedback from their superiors on their performance strengths and weaknesses, the ethnic-minority managers then tended to rate themselves higher than they were rated by their colleagues (Rana 2003).

New organisational structures and HR processes can thus sometimes intensify old patterns of difference between people or create new ones. Such patterns can lead to employee perceptions of lack of fairness in the organisation and thence to lack of commitment to outcomes sought by diversity training. A dispiriting downward spiral can then occur, as Figure 12 shows.

Such a spiral, however, is avoidable, since sensitively organised workplace learning can be liberating for individuals. At BT and BP, for example, self-managed career development policies and flexible working policies signal to their employees a belief that they are mature enough to make their own decisions about how they develop, how they organise their work, and how they express their diverse qualities. Organisational leadership creates a sense of purpose and of a just organisation, while HR professionals have key roles in building an understanding of individuals that acknowledges the variety of individual potential and motivation (Gratton 2003a). Self-managed learning in such organisations draws benefits from diversity by allowing participants to design their own learning agenda and curriculum to suit their specific needs. In recognising the strengths and potential of each individual it encourages innovation and helps to build a culture that values diversity.

FIGURE 12 The downward spiral of 'difference' in workplace learning

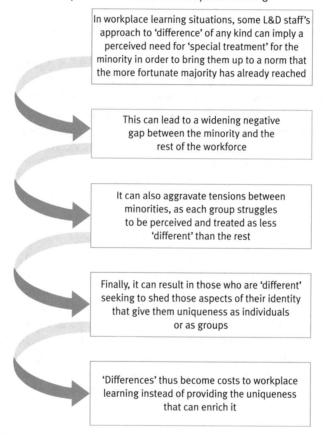

In workplace learning situations, some L&D staff's approach to 'difference' of any kind can imply a perceived need for 'special treatment' for the minority in order to bring them up to a norm that the more fortunate majority has already reached

This can lead to a widening negative gap between the minority and the rest of the workforce

It can also aggravate tensions between minorities, as each group struggles to be perceived and treated as less 'different' than the rest

Finally, it can result in those who are 'different' seeking to shed those aspects of their identity that give them uniqueness as individuals or as groups

'Differences' thus become costs to workplace learning instead of providing the uniqueness that can enrich it

VALUES-BASED TRAINING AND LEARNING

What, then, should be the guiding principles for L&D practitioners who seek to adopt a values-based approach to diversity?

- They must gain valid insights into the preferences and perceptions of learners regarding diversity issues and problems.

- They must work with other HR colleagues and with line managers to ensure that across the organisation there is an active commitment to good diversity practices, and that front-line managers especially understand how to achieve this and are enabled to do so.

- They must review policies for selection for training and development, for 'helping' processes such as mentoring and coaching, for succession planning and for career development, all of which should demonstrate that diversity is valued because of the benefits it offers to individuals and to the business.

- They should harness diversity in stimulating ways to the pursuit of learning goals. For example, Ely and Thomas (2001), researching race and culture in professional service organisations, found that linking diversity with the way employees work can encourage better relations between work groups, make employees feel more valued and produce more efficient functioning (especially through bringing many different perspectives to bear on problem-solving). Achieving a similar kind of integration in a training programme, perhaps where feasible having representatives from suppliers, customers and outsource partners all learning alongside the organisation's core employees in relevant training situations, is likely to have similar outcomes.

Achieving inclusivity is a long-haul journey and training initiatives can never be more than stages in its progress. But even the shortest programme that is based on a sound business partnership, is well designed, expertly delivered and followed up appropriately can make a useful contribution. Here is one example.

CASE EXAMPLE

DIVERSITY TRAINING: A VALUES-BASED STARTING POINT FOR CULTURAL CHANGE

Douglas, a training consultant, describes how he worked with a national police force on a short developmental initiative to promote changed behaviours related to diversity. Its aims were:

- to achieve a shift in participants' perception of diversity both within the force and in the local community in order to enable differences to be celebrated. Sensitivity to multi-cultural differences was crucial because of the profile of the workforce and of the local community

- to focus on meeting customer needs and improving service delivery, with a particular concern to accord dignity and respect to all local community groups

- to use ethical principles that guided the programme's design as key behavioural learning points for participants.

Approximately 350 police and civilian staff in diversified cohorts of 16 attended one-day workshops run by two facilitators, each of whom came from a different cultural or ethnic background. Although restricted to one day for the training, the trainers saw the need to ensure some in-depth work on difference. Dilemma-based exercises mirroring issues that participants encountered in the course of their jobs were devised to lead to a different outcome every time they were run. They dealt with issues around diversity, dignity and respect and required participants to choose from a range of behavioural options those responses that they felt best fitted the circumstances. They were encouraged to identify and reflect on changes in their behaviour that occurred through the day.

Influenced especially by Lewin's work on field force analysis (which will also feature in Chapter 15), the following principles guided the training:

- *Safety and mutual support* – The workshop provided a non-judgemental, open and supportive environment where all views were treated with equal respect and interest, and mistakes became vehicles for learning.

- *Reality testing* – Audit findings were used to test responses to scenarios.

- *Experiential learning* – In dealing with issues and scenarios during the workshop participants were asked to replicate their normal, in-role behaviour. They were also asked to give and receive feedback that would generate insights into the nature of that behaviour and its impact on others – in other words, to try to put themselves into the shoes of that 'impartial spectator' whose view (as I explained earlier in the chapter) Adam Smith saw to be vital in helping individuals decide on ethicality of their behaviour.

- *Building a bridge* – This was a process of transferring the sensitive and supportive ways in which participants were encouraged to behave in the workshop to their subsequent interactions with others in the force and the local community.

- *Closure and walking the talk* – Participants were required to work together on action plans based on their new self-awareness, and focused particularly on process.

In the early stages of the workshop participants typically resisted looking at self and taking responsibility for their own behaviour, trying instead to shift that responsibility to others whether management, leaders or the community. Some were openly hostile to the programme, angry and suspicious at having been 'sent' on it. During the day, though, a critical mass of those stimulated by the change process and willing to support it began to develop, and with it an increase in positive attitudes and the sharing of personal experiences and concerns.

Follow-up of outcomes by a questionnaire two months later showed that of the 19% of those who responded, around three quarters felt that 'a shift of some degree had occurred'.

Source: Douglas, D. (2004)

The principles on which Douglas' training design was based are similar to those applied by Barbara Walker (1994) in her 'valuing differences' training at Digital Equipment Corporation:

- Strip away stereotypes.

- Learn to listen and probe for the differences in people's assumptions.

- Build strong relationships with people one regards as 'different'.

- Empower oneself in order to become more open to learning from 'differences'.

- Explore and identify group differences.

Walker's training has proved a powerful adjunct to the company's Affirmative Action and Equal Employment Opportunity work, achieving consistency between employees' perceptions of a positive approach to diversity both within the training situation and in the workplace context. In a similar way the type of training intervention that Douglas describes needs to be supported by appropriate HR policies and practices, by role modelling by leaders and managers, and by a performance management and development system that has inclusivity and the valuing of diversity at its heart.

REFLECTION

Consider a learning event or educational programme with which you are familiar (whether directly or indirectly). How far do you think that it managed to change – or begin to change – participants' values related to diversity, and what do you think should be done to build on that change?

CONCLUSION

You should now have a sound understanding of the two kinds of responsibility that L&D professionals hold in relation to ethics: to ensure that they themselves are ethical as well as professional practitioners, and to work with others to build trust, fairness and inclusivity into the organisation's relations with its members and other stakeholders. You should also feel confident to tackle the review questions related to this chapter that are shown in Appendix 3.

The main themes covered by this chapter's six sections have been the following:

- varying interpretations of 'ethical behaviour' and the 'good' organisation; six forces powerfully influencing organisations' approach to corporate social responsibility and business ethics

- the concept of a triple rather than a single bottom line for the business, to embrace not only economic accountability but affordability, diversity and equity; the need for the 'good' organisation to embed a concern for ethics in its culture, practices and core behaviours

- the importance of achieving trust in order to engage

CONCLUSION CONT.

organisational members in a shared purpose and gain their commitment to enacting values associated with it; the value of relational psychological contracts in building trust

- the role of L&D practitioners in communicating and enacting their organisation's social and ethical values, and the moral conflict that, for some, this may involve; the need for them to recognise and respond appropriately to ethical dilemmas encountered in their daily work; the value of codes of conduct, but the need ultimately to act in accordance with their own personal and professional judgement

- L&D tasks related to equality, diversity and inclusivity in the organisation; the difference between compliance-based and values-based training and learning initiatives and the complementary benefits they can bring

- the need for a conducive organisational and workplace context if diversity is to be genuinely valued and inclusivity achieved; the importance of employees forming positive perceptions of 'fairness' in the organisation

- working in partnership with stakeholders – especially management – as the vital key to L&D practitioners' success, whether in trying to change negative aspects of context or in planning and organising learning events as part of a long-haul process to communicate, enact and embed the organisation's social and ethical values.

EXLPORE FURTHER

FURTHER INFORMATION SOURCES

Chartered Institute Of Personnel and Development (2008e) *Managing Diversity and the Business Case*. Research Report. London: CIPD. Summary available online at http://www.cipd.co.uk/Bookstore/reasearch.htm [accessed 7 August 2008]

Kitson, A. and Campbell, R. (2008) *The Ethical Organisation*, 2nd edition. Basingstoke: Palgrave Macmillan

Pinnington, A. H. and Bayraktaroglu, S. (2007) 'Ethical leadership in employee development'. In Pinnington, A., Macklin T. and Campbell T. (eds) *Human Resource Management:*

Ethics and employment. Oxford: Oxford University Press; pp190–208

Steare, R. (2006) 'How to create an ethical culture', *People Management*, Vol.12, No.3, 9 February: 46–7

http://www.cipd.co.uk/subjects/corpstrtgy/corpsocres/ Area of the CIPD's website providing information about corporate environmental and social responsibility

CIPD podcast, 1 June 2007. *Diversity*. Available at: http://www.cipd.co.uk/podcasts [accessed 7 July 2008]

PART 3

Making a business contribution

CHAPTER 10

The L&D Agenda in Different Sectoral Settings

INTRODUCTION

In Part 2 of the book I explored the basics of good practice in L&D activity. In Part 3 the concern is with ways in which L&D activity can be organised, managed and strategically focused to make a value-adding contribution to the business, and with the business partnerships on which those processes depend for success.

The location of the organisation in a wider world has a significant influence on its L&D agenda. This explains why, in this chapter, I explore different organisational settings that currently have powerful implications for that agenda. Having mainly referred to private sector organisations of the larger kind up to now, in this chapter I look at other types and sectors.

In the first of the chapter's three sections I review the L&D agenda in small to medium-size enterprises. The focus of the second section is the public sector, which is the UK's major employer. The final section deals with the not-for-profit sector upon whose workforce the public sector increasingly relies for provision of community services.

SECTORAL SETTINGS: SMALL AND MEDIUM-SIZED ENTERPRISES

DEFINITION AND STATISTICS

Using European Union definitions the SME sector comprises (EUC 2003):

- micro firms (0 to 1 person, and from two to nine staff)

- small enterprises (from 10 to 49 staff)

- medium enterprises (between 50 and 249 staff).

According to official statistics SMEs account for just over 99% of UK firms (Hall 2004). They generate 52% of the UK's total turnover, employ over half the private sector workforce, and about one third of their employees work in firms with fewer than 10 staff. SMEs also lose the greatest number of jobs (Small Business Service 2001: 6). In view of such statistics it is unsurprising that, as we have seen in Chapters 2 and 3, the UK Government regards workplace development and the enhancing of skills in SMEs as a key priority, targeted especially by Train to Gain, Investors in People (IiP) and apprenticeships.

LIFE IN SMES

It used to be the case that the HR literature on SMEs drew mainly on studies in larger organisations, despite lack of evidence that the conclusions reached in that context apply to managing people in smaller organisations. Although over the past decade the SME sector has attracted significant research interest, the HR literature is at present 'overwhelmingly qualitative in nature, ably depicting the complexities and subtleties of particular cases and situations, but limited in its ability to generalize to the wider population' (Forth *et al* 2006: 91). Quantitative studies are quite rare, research by Forth and his colleagues being one of the exceptions. They analysed data from the national 2004 Workplace Employment Relations Survey (WERS) covering employment practices in private sector workplaces belonging to SMEs. The survey was representative of 76% of all employees in SMEs and the researchers obtained views of both managers and employees within those workplaces, making their findings particularly persuasive.

Forth *et al*'s (2006) research cast a rather different light on the 'bleak house' small firm scenario that qualitative research often paints. In contrast to employees in medium-sized and large firms covered by WERS 2004, the majority of employees in small firms reported that managers at their workplace were good or very good at keeping employees informed about changes to the running of the organisation, changes in staffing and changes to their job. The level of trust between managers and employees and the rating of management–employee relations also appeared to be highest in the smallest firms (Forth *et al* 2006: xi). The data indicated that managers in small firms were more likely than those in large firms to involve employees in decision-making when making changes at the workplace. The researchers also found that SME employees were 'more likely to believe that they had job autonomy, influence and security, and reported lower work intensity and higher general well-being than employees who worked for larger firms. In addition, they were more likely to feel committed to the organization' (*ibid*: xii).

However – and here is where a 'bleak house' scenario does become evident – a significant minority of employees in smaller firms recorded a very different and negative view on decision-making (*ibid*: 93). Also Bacon and Hoque (2005) had found in their analysis of WERS 1998 data that in many SME workplaces managers considered workers easily replaceable and lacking value. Such employees were likely to remain 'skills-poor' and therefore disadvantaged in the employment market.

THE CONTEXT FOR EMPLOYMENT PRACTICES

Research shows that in planning employment practices for SMEs, including those related to L&D, four key issues need to be analysed (Hendry *et al* 1991):

* the history of the firm, that has shaped its employment practices to date

* its survival and growth strategies, that will significantly determine the kind of employees it needs

* the external factors that influence its skills strategies. For example, WERS 1998 data suggested that SMEs often feel compelled to seek IiP recognition to satisfy dominant customers, and through that process often adopt a training strategy (Bacon and Hoque 2005). But there is also evidence to indicate that such firms often view IiP as merely 'a procedural requirement that has no subsequent impact on training or employment practice once recognition has been secured' (Ram 2000)

* the stage reached by the firm in its life cycle.

The final point needs an explanation:

* *In start-up ventures* there is a need for labour flexibility and loosely defined tasks. Recruitment takes place in that context, and training will tend to be informal and on-the-job, restricted to teaching or showing people how to reach required performance levels.

* *During the period of initial growth*, other pressures make it inevitable that any except the most obviously necessary training will tend to receive little attention. In the early stages of the SME's life cycle the factors most likely to influence people management policies are the values and style of the entrepreneur and an interacting range of product market structure and industry structure factors. In so far as human resource (HR) processes are recognised as being important, most attention will usually be paid to recruitment, pay and termination.

* *As the firm becomes more mature*, it often undergoes change of ownership, organisational structure and managerial style. At this point, the need to develop

people for the future is likely to become more apparent. However, this will not always be the case, especially because at the time no one may be aware of what stage of development a firm is entering or leaving – such stages are easier to identify once they have taken place. Also, progress through stages of the life cycle is not a neat linear process. In transitional and terminal stages of the firm's growth owner-managers have to cope with demanding financial and market pressures, and some make the deliberate decision not to go for growth, or to close the firm down prematurely. Sometimes, too, an owner-manager may choose for no apparent reason to let the firm be acquired at some stage.

REFLECTION

The owner-manager of a small but fast-growing firm wonders whether the time is coming when he should take a more strategic approach to training. Reflecting on material in this section so far, what issues would you draw to his attention as a priority for his consideration?

TRAINING AND LEARNING IN SMES

The planned training investment

Maximising productivity is crucial to SMEs' survival, so a skilled and continuously developing workforce is essential to their success, but although training is the most common form of L&D activity reported by SMEs it is not necessarily a priority for their investment. Research shows that this is particularly true of the smaller organisations within the SME sector (Fitzgerald *et al* 2003; Forth *et al* 2006; Kitching 2007: 43). However, Forth and colleagues found that where SMEs did invest in training, the number of days provided was similar to the amount provided by larger firms, a finding confirmed in the CIPD's 2008 L&D survey. They also found that although teamworking arrangements, problem-solving groups and functional flexibility were less developed in SMEs than in large firms this seemed to be largely a factor of workplace size.

Overall, in fact, the training picture in SMEs is more encouraging than is often assumed. In 2001 SMEs were spending £5.8 billion each year on training, with 53% offering training of some kind to their employees and 15% being involved in IiP (Bacon and Hoque 2005: 1978). SME organisations covered by the 2008 CIPD annual L&D survey spent far more annually per head on training (£375) than those with over 5,000 employees (£108), and SME respondents were much more optimistic than their peers in large organisations that their funding levels would be sustained in the future (CIPD 2008a: 25, 26).

Issues that influence whether and when an SME will adopt a planned approach to L&D are not just money but time, the difficulty of releasing people for off-the-job training, and the people management experience of the employer. Research suggests that owner-managers are unlikely to be able to relate their fragmented and unfocused experience of managing people to the formal systems and procedures involved in national initiatives such as IiP. What matters most to them is to see the relevance to the business of any initiative that may eat into their time (Harrison and Lord 1992: 6).

'High' and 'low' training

National surveys and reports tend to treat 'high' (planned, strategic) training as superior to 'low' (informal, fragmented) training, but that can be a particularly misleading distinction when applied to SMEs. There, 'low' training is widely used and can be very relevant, effective and efficient (Jones and Goss 1991: 25). For example in the free house, restaurant and wine bar sector informal training prevails for obvious reasons to do with the nature of the job, the small workforces and the wide geographical distribution of the sites. Because such learning is often unrecognised as 'training' by researchers or by SME employers themselves, it is likely to be under reported especially in research studies relying heavily on quantitative survey data (Kitching 2007: 44).

Learning in the SME workplace

Informal training occurs not only through on-the-job and workplace-based practices, but also through interacting with co-workers and with external actors such as customers and suppliers and then sharing the learning with co-workers within the organisation (Gibb, 1997). 'Low' training can also be the best option for developing and sharing the tacit skills that are particularly important to smaller businesses (Manwaring and Wood 1985: 172–3). Many of their jobs are genuinely unique, leading to a 'desire of SMEs to hang on to and keep hidden specific skills and competences developed within the firm' (Hendry *et al* 1991: 84). Loss of valuable tacit skills represents a loss of strategic assets that SMEs can ill afford.

For all these reasons Kitching (2007) suggests that it may be more appropriate to describe the role of small firm employers as 'enablers of employee learning' rather than just training providers. Some SMEs are close to being natural 'learning organisations', being fast-reactive, well-informed about their external and internal environments, and fostering a climate of continuous learning, improvement and innovation. Stone and colleagues (2006) concluded from their research that:

- efforts should be made to embed training within the normal working practices of SMEs, alongside the development of standard training provision along more innovative lines

- Government should understand skills development in SMEs as a means to an end rather than a matter of compliance with outside standards, and therefore should allow a greater variety of forms of training to be eligible for funding support – something that is now happening (Chapters 2 and 3).

TRAINING AND LEARNING IN 'THE BEST' SMES

CASE EXAMPLE

Stone *et al* (2006) researched 19 firms appearing in the *Sunday Times*' list of the 'Best 50 Small and Medium Enterprises to Work For' in order to discover how they trained, promoted learning internally, and rated the importance of skills, knowledge and qualifications to the business. They found that in those firms the key drivers for skills development, in order of priority, appeared to be to:

- improve quality of service to clients, plus career development of individuals

- achieve competitive advantage

- exploit new market opportunities

- retain staff and aid business growth

- develop skills not available externally.

Most of the firms had a long-term approach to business development that led them to take a relatively long-term view of the development of people. Employers therefore viewed most forms of learning as potentially beneficial for the company, although favouring different kinds of training for non-management as distinct from management staff. For the former, they tended to prefer short non-accredited in-house events, specifically focused on the firm's requirements, either taking the form of on-the-job training by experienced workers/mentors or demonstration by an expert colleague or supervisor. For managers the in-house approach was also preferred but demonstration was seen as far less relevant and there was a big emphasis on self-directed and experiential learning.

Many of the employers aimed to create a work environment conducive to continuous learning by employees, and to do so as part of the routine work pattern so that skills development and training were 'a deeply embedded and valued part of what the firm does' rather than being externally designed or imposed (*ibid*: 24). Kitching (2007: 53) reported similar findings.

Over 60% of the firms reported having in place an HR strategy integrated with the business. The rest either had one in the planning stage or reported that they accepted HR's link with business need and that HR issues informed their decisions on training. Not all HR policies included formally planned or systematic training. Attitudes to costing also varied, but this reflected 'not so much a lack of awareness as a highly integrated and informal approach to training, one that does not especially lend itself to quantification and costing' (Stone *et al* 2006: 20).

Formal training programmes were used to develop certain technical skills, but firms recognised that training can also help to motivate staff by enhancing their job satisfaction, their sense of empowerment and their career prospects. It was therefore also used to 'reproduce the culture' (*ibid*: 22) and norms of behaviour desired in the firm, and to encourage loyalty and commitment. Supporting and creating opportunities for career progression within the firm had a similar purpose.

Source: Stone *et al* (2006)

EXTERNAL L&D PROVISION FOR SMES

We have seen in earlier chapters the effort devoted by the Labour Government to the training and workplace development needs of SMEs since the publication of its first national skills strategy in 2003 (DfES 2003a). However, take-up of national initiatives remains problematic in SMEs. In 2007 a survey conducted by the independent Small Business Research Trust found that almost 70% of smaller businesses that it covered were not aware of the training role of Sector Skills Councils or of Train to Gain (*BizHelp News* 24 2007). Awareness of Government training schemes was particularly low among micro firms, whereas among small firms about a third of the respondents were aware of one or both of these initiatives, and in medium-sized firms almost 29% knew about the Sector Skills Councils and over 40% about Train to Gain.

Lack of information on skills initiatives was one factor cited as a reason – although not the primary reason – for not undertaking formal/external training. For micro firms (but not for the great majority of larger SMEs) a more significant reason was a perceived lack of staff in need of training. The findings suggest that many owners of micro firms do not appreciate the benefits of formal training and that the smaller the business, the less likely it is to offer any, whether external or internal. Another significant concern is the difficulty of replacing employees during their absence on training (*BizHelp News* 24 2008).

SMEs can get training support from outside the firm in a number of ways other than through Government initiatives. For example:

- They can combine economies of scale with increased training through joining 'training clusters', working together in business parks or retail malls.

- Some larger firms open up their training facilities to smaller firms in the supply chain or in their area.

- Small companies can learn from best practice case studies available at the National Training Awards (NTA). They can also apply for these awards, and many are now reaching the NTA finals.

- L&D consultants with a good record of working with SMEs can help them to assess the cost, relevance and value of external provision.

PRIORITY TASKS FOR L&D PROFESSIONALS IN SMES

It follows from the discussion so far that L&D professionals working in or for SMEs should measure the L&D investment made, or proposed, against three key criteria (Pettigrew *et al* 1990: 25):

- *How far will it enhance organisational performance,* as indicated by a range of measures? This will be *the* vital consideration for firms at the early stage of their life cycle.

- *How far will it enhance employees' ability to cope effectively with internal and external change?* Small firms tend to be characterised by 'activity, energy, pace and having to find ways out of problems rather than planning for them to happen' (Hill 2002). Learning how to cope with that kind of pressure is therefore important for all who lead, manage and work in such environments.

- *How far will it contribute to the organisation's overall ability to achieve longer-term goals?* The impact of L&D interventions here will be to do with helping the firm to deal better with crises and to make the big strategic leap forward at the opportune time.

It is important to stress again the importance in SMEs of using the workplace as a powerful site of learning. I have explained in Chapter 5 that an 'expansive' environment is one that enhances the extent to which employees at all levels share their skills and knowledge and have access to learning opportunities within and beyond the workplace (Evans *et al* 2006: 36). L&D professionals should raise awareness of where and how such an environment can bring benefit for their SME and its employees, and be able to help construct and sustain one.

REFLECTION

Imagine that you have to write a management research report on the factors influencing training in small firms in your area. What methodology do you think you should use, and what size and type of sample? (There is more about how to research small firms in Hill 2002, 2004.)

SECTORAL SETTINGS: THE PUBLIC SECTOR

AN INTRODUCTION

A radical reform programme has now been in place for over a decade across the UK public sector. In this section I will first outline and assess the programme's rationale and key features, and then discuss two areas of the sector that employ a substantial proportion of its workforce: the National Health Service (NHS) and local government. Central government, of course, is another major site for modernisation, with a long-term programme of renewal and reform that was heralded in 1999 by the White Paper *Modernising Government* (Cabinet Office 1999), focused on a customer-facing service. Sir Peter Gershon's 2004 review of government efficiency emphasised the need for civil servants to be more professional, be given better developmental opportunities and be subject to more rigorous performance management. All of this, together with extensive central government restructuring, has resulted in a demanding L&D agenda, both in terms of culture change issues and service delivery.

THE PUBLIC SECTOR MODERNISATION PROGRAMME

In the 1980s and 1990s the public services were cash-starved and poorly managed. Key objectives set by the Labour Government that came to power in 1997 were (Cabinet Office 2007: 78):

- to rebuild public services

- to expand opportunity for all

- to create a fairer society.

Those objectives continue to drive the public sector reform agenda, which is currently concerned with four critical issues raised by the UK's changing demographic, economic and skills profile, people's demand for greater choice and control over their lives and the enhanced expectations they now have of public services (Cabinet Office 2007: 41):

- how to balance rights and responsibilities more effectively

- how to tailor public services better to individual needs – particularly for disadvantaged groups

- how to facilitate greater innovation, diversity and responsiveness in public service provision

- how to further adapt public services to exploit the opportunities and challenges posed by global economic and other changes.

The national model for the public services

After its election to power in 1997 New Labour injected a massive amount of public funding into the public sector, but at the same time it set targets for efficiency savings in excess of £20 billion (HM Treasury 2004). In 2005 Government introduced a model for achieving 'citizen-centred public services'(Cabinet Office 2007). The model can be seen in full on the Cabinet Office website, but in brief:

- It revolves around a hub of 'better public services for all'.

- Market forces and public service users drive the need for greater efficiency and quality of service.

- Workforce development plus 'top-down performance management' are the drivers to expand the sector's capability and capacity to respond to those demands.

A critical view of public sector reform

In 2007 the Prime Minister's Strategy Unit identified improvements in public sector management and delivery since 1997 but urged further reform in order to ensure that the 2005 model works to its fullest potential rather than becoming over-reliant on top-down performance management and funding alone (Cabinet Office 2007).

Many commentators take issue with its largely optimistic interpretation of public sector reform. Like Caulkin in 2003 they believe that there must be a fundamental shift from traditional command-and-control styles of management in order to achieve the customer-facing high-performance and people-centred organisations that the public sector needs. They see the sector's centralised targets, regulators and auditing regimes as the causes of 'Tayloristic, mass production systems in which employees face the wrong way, focusing on what their managers want (the targets) rather than what the customer or citizen wants' (Caulkin 2003). Since the Gershon Review (2004), and also heavily influenced by Ulrich's (1997) 'three-legged stool' model for HRM (business partners, service centres and a centre of functional excellence, to be discussed in the next chapter) there has been an unprecedented overhaul of work practices, incentives and rewards, leadership and management, job design, HR functions and training and development across the sector. As yet, though, the projected workforce transformation is proving slow to achieve. To take three sets of research findings:

- A CIPD research project reported in 2005 identified major problems in levels of trust and satisfaction across the sector. It revealed a continued focus on target-setting and budgetary control at the expense of an adequate understanding of the big people management issues that need to be tackled (CIPD 2005d).

- In 2007 findings from a study of 10 public sector organisations including local authorities, the NHS and the civil service, pointed to a similar conclusion. The researchers found that despite certain structural changes, older functional lines of authority still exist and that claims of significant 'post-bureaucratic' organisational forms in the UK public sector are not justified (Morris and Farrell 2007). Managers are working now in a more complex and harsh working environment, where old certainties such as job security, a safe career path and seniority-based pay have all been eroded.

- Research by the charity Roffey Park in 2008 found that public sector managers rate their organisations as poorer in almost every aspect than managers in other sectors rate theirs, and that morale is far worse than in the private or voluntary sectors. The only area to score highly was flexible working. Managers identified low morale, widespread bullying, and a failure to tackle under performance as major problem areas, caused primarily by bureaucracy, with poor management and lack of recognition as key factors also (Sinclair *et al* 2008).

'People centred organisations' are those that put effective people management at the heart of the business. They are government's vision for the public sector, but the reality is still lagging far behind.

THE NATIONAL HEALTH SERVICE

The HR agenda

1.3 million people currently work in the NHS and since 1997 there has been a heavy and continuing investment in reforms to refocus the whole system on patient-centred and patient-led services. Under the umbrella of the national model

TABLE 11 Ten high-impact HR changes for the NHS

Improving organisational efficiency	Improving quality and the patient experience
1 Supporting and leading effective change management	6 Job and service redesign
2 Establishing effective recruitment, good induction and supportive management	7 Appraisal policy development and implementation
3 Developing shared service models and effective use of IT	8 Staff involvement, partnership working, good employee relations
4 Managing temporary staffing costs as a major source of efficiency	9 Championing good people management practices
5 Promoting staff health and managing sickness absence	10 Effective training and development

LEADING TO

- Integrated workforce planning
- Capacity developed through working differently
- Staff provided with rewarding and satisfying careers
- Model employment practices

LEADING TO

The transformation of the NHS workforce's culture, values, capability and capacity

PRODUCING

Patient-centred and patient-led services

Source: Based on information drawn from the NHS *National Framework to Support Local Workforce Strategy Development*, Department of Health Workforce Directorate (2006)

for public sector reform the NHS *National Framework to Support Local Workforce Strategy Development* (DH Workforce Directorate 2006) aims to:

- integrate workforce planning

- develop capacity through working differently

- provide staff with rewarding and satisfying careers

- implement model employment practices.

In Table 11 I have shown how 10 'high-impact HR practices' identified and explained in the Framework documents are intended to help to produce a transformed NHS workforce (see DH Workforce Directorate/NHS Partners/ Manchester University 2006 for a detailed explanation and supporting case studies).

The NHS Agenda for Change (AfC) was launched at the end of 2004 in order to implement much of the strategy and to produce a new way of partnership working between NHS staff, employers and unions (Simms 2006).

THE NHS AGENDA FOR CHANGE

CASE EXAMPLE

Harmonisation of the workforce

AfC has involved shifting all directly employed NHS staff except doctors, dentists and very senior managers from the old Whitley Council system covering a myriad different staff grades and allowances to a single structure with only nine national pay bands and standardised terms and conditions. It has been underpinned by an often controversial job evaluation scheme intended to inject greater fairness into the reward system. AfC's first stage – shifting employees onto the new pay structure – was almost entirely completed in England over nine months in 2005, a remarkable achievement by employers and unions working in close partnership. Assimilation of staff into the new grading system, however, has taken much longer.

The Skills Escalator

Critical to the long-term success of AfC is a workforce Skills Escalator that links competency assessment to a national knowledge and skills framework. This in turn is supported by annual development reviews and personal development plans. The intended outcome is to ensure a clearer system for career progression through continuous development of professional staff, through enabling those without professional qualifications to access an NHS Learning Account or NVQ training, and through identifying and addressing adult literacy, numeracy and language gaps.

AfC – core purpose

The core purpose of the whole new structure is to get rid of outdated job demarcations and allow jobs to be designed around patient and staff needs in order to improve job satisfaction, productivity and patient care. The system should give employers far more flexibility to define the core skills and knowledge that they want staff to develop in each job, and to pay extra when they face recruitment or retention problems.

Source: Simms, J. (2006) *People Management*, 23 February

Strains in the system

The high costs involved in AfC's implementation have put enormous strain on the finances of NHS Trusts and heavy hidden costs also arose from the extra workloads related to introducing the new system. Implementing a raft of parallel initiatives to improve patient care is greatly increasing that strain, not least because of their complexity and frequent mismanagement. In 2007 came the first major financial crisis. It emerged that 174 of the 600 or so organisations that make up the NHS had huge deficits, resulting in a £536 million total overspend by the service. In addition new independent foundation trusts (a status awarded to high-performing organisations) had overspent by £24 million.

A Commons Health Select Committee put the main blame for the fiasco on lack of strategic planning by the Department of Health (DH) which had led to a 'reckless and uncontrolled' expansion of the workforce (quoted in *People Management* 2007a) – an expansion that according to an earlier report from the independent think-tank Reform had failed to produce the flexibility, quality and teamworking needed by the modern system (*People Management* 2006a). Sir Nigel Crisp, NHS Chief Executive, subsequently resigned.

The changing psychological contract

The continuing financial pressures on Trusts threaten to undermine AfC's early success in partnership working, as NHS workforce morale continues to deteriorate. According to Caulkin (2007) doctors have already become alienated, seeing the conjunction of centrally defined targets and individual financial incentives to achieve them as 'crude bribes' that are completely at odds with their professional values and mission. The biggest issue for staff is not the goal of getting better value for money and helping people to use the best service from different providers; it is the relentless pace of change, the lack of coherence between different policy strands, and the workforce's limited capacity to deal with so many pressures crowding in on it at once (Pickard 2006b).

Before he resigned in 2006 as director of workforce at the DH, Andrew Foster had warned that there was a 'mountain' to be scaled in order to design new roles, reorganise skill mixes and create better services, and that the strategy for modernisation would have to switch from transactional to transformational mode (Simms 2006). As Keep (2001) found in her research in a reorganised NHS Healthcare Trust, successful reform is achieved less by a constant moving around of the structural furniture, more by sustained culture change. In the NHS that is proving a major difficulty because of the weakened psychological contract between NHS employees and their employer. A 2008 survey of employees across all 391 NHS Trusts, carried out by the Healthcare Commission, showed that only 22% of staff think communication between staff and senior management in their organisations is effective, that only 26% feel valued in their work, and that some feel physically unsafe in their job. However, overall job satisfaction levels are high, indicating that although staff are dissatisfied with their employer they have more positive feelings about their jobs and supervisors (*People Management* 2008c).

In a House of Commons debate, 7 February 2008 (*www.parliament.the-stationery-office.co.uk/pa/cm200708/cmhansrd/cm080207/* [accessed 12 May 2008]), Greg Mulholland (LibDem MP for Leeds, North-West) observed that the Government sought to control everything from Whitehall, creating a paradox:

> Too often, they employ a one-size-fits-all approach, yet at the same time they seem to have something of a feudal, divide-and-rule attitude to NHS staff. Their running battles and regular and increasingly bloody skirmishes with different sectors of the NHS are causing resentment, disillusionment and anger among the people on whom we rely for the delivery of health services in this country.

Performance management

The real paradox at the heart of the NHS is the political pressure to improve productivity and quality of service at local level while at the same time meeting national standards and reducing costs – especially staffing costs (Rainbird *et al* 2004). It is unsurprising that there is no agreed definition across the NHS on what constitutes 'good performance' (Boaden *et al* 2008). Formal performance management from a national perspective is relatively new within the service, and the national framework for its assessment changed substantially in 2005 (CIPD 2006c: 2). The current (as at 2008) performance management system attempts to make measures patient-focused, but the ambiguity about performance goals and values remains at its heart, and research has highlighted the divide staff are experiencing in consequence (Boaden *et al* 2008). A fundamental flaw is that the national measures used to assess the performance of NHS Trusts make few links between critical elements of HRM and performance outcomes within individual trusts (CIPD 2006c: 3). Yet as the national HR framework document (DH Workforce Directorate 2006) itself emphasises, a series of studies have confirmed the impact that effective HRM can have on key NHS outcomes. Major findings are that (Hyde *et al* 2006):

- There can be a strong association between HR practices and patient mortality (West *et al* 2002).

- The impact of HR practices is mediated by front-line managers (Purcell *et al* 2003).

- Good people management makes a critical and positive difference to employee attitudes and behaviours, which in turn affect performance outcomes (Guest *et al* 2000; Purcell *et al* 2003).

- Teamworking is linked to healthcare effectiveness (Borrill *et al* 2000).

L&D in the NHS – an embattled agenda

It should be clear from this contextual analysis that the L&D agenda in the NHS is highly demanding because it encompasses not only workforce development on a major scale, but also the transformation of HR (including L&D) staff's capability so that they can play a leading role in driving forward the NHS cultural and structural reform programme.

At first, the outlook for delivering the L&D agenda was promising. From 1997 onwards the DH and the NHS put in place important initiatives and frameworks to increase the investment in staff learning and development. In addition to those already mentioned they included the Sector Skills Council 'Skills for Health', an HR Capacity Unit (in 2003) to support improvements in people management and a Leadership Centre for NHS senior leaders. All of this raised employee morale, as did the success of *Improving Working Lives* – a type of IiP kitemark focusing on organisations' commitment to improving the working lives of their employees through demonstrating model HR practices including training and development.

Political strains

One of the most promising ideas to open up access to lifelong learning for all NHS staff – a much-quoted aim of the DH – was the NHS corporate university, launched in 2003 with the aim of becoming a full degree-awarding university open to those outside the NHS as well as to its employees, and intended to offer staff access to foundation degree pathways within five years of their employment. However, in another of those negative twists that has characterised the NHS modernisation programme through time, the DH announced late in 2004 that the university was to be dissolved, along with the NHS Modernisation Agency and the NHS Leadership Centre. Instead, a new NHS Institute for Learning, Skills and Innovation (incorporating the new Innovation Board) was to be established. It was explained by the Health Minister as (*htttp://www.egovmonitor.com/node/344* [accessed 10 May 2008]):

> a much leaner organisation that is focused on innovation and change – not a provider of large-scale training programmes. Others are already doing the training or are well placed to do so. Instead, the new Institute will identify the opportunities for learning to ensure that all staff reach their full potential and are able to acquire the competences to implement new ways of working.

By the time the Institute was officially launched in mid-2005 as a Special Health Authority it had acquired a new title – *Innovation and Improvement* – although the DH stressed its commitment to increasing and widening participation of all NHS employees, especially those in the lowest grades, to lifelong learning and development. Yet by 2006 Professor Bob Fryer, National Director for Widening Participation in Learning, was robustly criticising the NHS for treating learning as 'an afterthought of an afterthought' run by a 'bunch of eggheads who talk a different language, never deliver on time and would rather work to their own agenda'. He observed that half of the NHS's staff had not received any training during 2005, and that of those who had, about half had only received only two days' or less. He complained that training was essentially the preserve of those high up the ladder, not of the workers on the ground (Brockett 2006).

Current tensions

At the time of writing (mid-2008) the future for the L&D reform agenda in the NHS remains uncertain. On the plus side, the research that made strong associations between HR practices and rates of patient mortality identified as particularly critical in this respect the extent and sophistication of appraisal systems, the quality and sophistication of training, and the number of staff trained to work in teams (West and Johnson 2002). These findings have given a high profile to training in the NHS and it is officially encouraged as one of the 'high-impact' HR measures.

On the downside, national funding for training continues to be regularly reduced. The disastrous financial failure in the NHS in 2007 was widely attributed to poor management and leadership, sending out a clear message about major training needs – but that crisis too was swiftly followed by yet another training budget cut.

The partnership imperative

There are few contexts within which L&D professionals need to be more effective in partnership working than in the NHS. The number and variety of stakeholders is formidable, each with their own agenda to pursue and many with powerful vested interests behind them – governmental, institutional, regional, professional, local and organisational. In the face of this array of often conflicting interests, 'working in partnership' hardly begins to describe the challenges awaiting L&D professionals who try to negotiate a path towards L&D solutions that will meet vital individual and corporate needs in their particular organisation.

Partnership is made even more demanding where – as is so often the case across all sectors of employment – managers at local level lack competence or commitment in fulfilling their L&D roles. Under increasing pressure from above to achieve cost-cutting and improve productivity rates they are likely to reduce their training budgets yet further, leaving L&D staff able to do little more than provide mandatory staff training, education and development.

Ways forward for L&D at local level

In 2007 there was a severe blow to one of the central planks of Agenda for Change: the Skills Escalator (SE). However, the following case shows that there are also SE success stories and that their underlying principles suggest the way forward for L&D professionals in the NHS.

CASE EXAMPLE

THE SKILLS ESCALATOR — GOING UP, COMING DOWN, OR 'BREAKING IN THE MIDDLE'?

In England researchers evaluating the operation of the NHS' Skills Escalator (SE) have found that funding problems are already beginning to threaten the integrity of the SE. Funding for intermediate qualifications that made employees eligible for entry to professional training has been reduced or cut altogether in some sites, thus 'breaking the escalator halfway up' (Cox and McBride 2007). They fear that in future more trusts will focus on skills development only when it relates to role redesign projects intended to produce immediate cost savings in service delivery, and that they will invest in career development only for the few. This would threaten many areas of critical need, especially as more care is pushed out into the community and groups of people working in public, voluntary and private sectors have to learn how to work effectively together in order to deliver a single seamless service.

However, the researchers also found some successful SE projects, and identified three factors that lay behind their success. These can also stand as principles to guide L&D practitioners working at local level in the NHS:

- effective coalitions between operational managers and staff development/HR managers

- dynamic L&D managers who are both visionaries for Trust-wide projects and are skilled negotiators, 'navigating their way through a maze of funding sources to create "funding cocktails". They form strong relationships with local learning providers to ensure that they get the best deal in terms of content, price and form of delivery'. They are also able to convince both prospective learners and line managers that the projects will be mutually beneficial.

- supportive colleagues and line managers who respect learners' needs both during and after participation in an SE project. This again emphasises the importance of L&D practitioners working in active partnership with these stakeholders throughout a project and thereafter to ensure that its ultimate outcomes can be achieved.

Source: Cox, A. and McBride, A. (2007) *People Management*, 17 May

TABLE 12 Achieving the L&D agenda at the local level in the NHS

Working in partnership
Commitment to the NHS cannot be assumed of all those providing services, especially those who are not directly employed, but L&D professionals should build on the commitment most are likely to have to the core values of the NHS – improving patient services and providing access for all to high-quality patient care. They should be careful to ensure that the initiatives they introduce, and the way they implement them, support the 'professional instincts' of NHS staff for good patient care.

Putting the national PMS into context
L&D professionals should work with other HR staff to clarify to organisational members the way in which NHS key indicators and targets used in the new PM framework link to performance at local and individual level. L&D processes, especially those related to induction, appraisal, mentoring and coaching, can be particularly effective in helping staff to understand why they are required to do and measure certain things.

Demonstrating improvement
Monitoring the implementation of any element of L&D should use a methodology that takes local context into particular account. Methods and measures that capture that context will help to provide stronger evidence of the beneficial impact of L&D at local level.

Source: Adapted from Chartered Institute of Personnel and Development (2006c) p.12

In addition to the positive factors noted in this case example there are two more on which L&D professionals should build at local level:

- Despite all the tensions, most NHS staff share core values related to patient care and 'derive their motivation from feeling that they make a difference locally' (CIPD 2006c: 4).

- The HR Capacity Unit recognises the importance of adapting people management and development in the service to the local context (CIPD 2006c: 11). Also within Trust and Foundation hospitals there is more freedom than formerly for local management to manage and and finance health care provision, and to exercise considerable discretion in their employment practices, including L&D (Sambrook and Stewart 2007: 5).

L&D staff should therefore introduce strategies and solutions that strike an adequate balance between helping their organisation and staff within them to 'make a difference locally' and enabling them to link what they do in L&D to key performance indicators used in the national PMS. Research into HRM in the NHS has produced many proposals to improve local HR functions (CIPD 2006c). In Table 12 I have adapted some that have a clear bearing for L&D work.

LOCAL GOVERNMENT

In this section I will briefly outline the local government (LG) modernisation programme, which is similar in essentials to that in the NHS, and suggest priorities for the L&D function.

The modernisation programme

Two million people work for the 467 local councils throughout the UK, and every council has dozens of different departments. Local authorities are increasingly promoting themselves as progressive employers, offering flexitime, part-time work, job sharing, career breaks, training and career development. However, there are the same acute pressures operating here as elsewhere in the public sector.

The local government modernisation programme at the time of writing (mid-2008) has two large and complex work and project areas:

- strengthening the way LG works in order to deliver accountable citizen-centred services

- improving the way in which LG delivers its services and ensures value for money.

In 2002 the Government introduced a comprehensive performance assessment (CPA) regime imposing statutory performance reviews on all councils and putting these in the public domain. In 2008 after consultation on a wide-ranging 2006 White Paper on local government reform (DCLG 2006, Vols. 1 and 2) CPA was replaced by a new regime called Comprehensive Area Assessment (CAA). This reduced the number of national indicators from over 1,200 to under 200, and gave freedom to local strategic partnerships to prioritise up to 35 of those for their area. The much simplified performance framework aims to be tailored to local needs and includes user-satisfaction and -perception measures.

As a result of CPA and CAA local government continues to go through radical organisational change in which HR must play a leading role. The 2002 CPA produced a highly critical picture of HR functions in LG, praising only 10%. Most have subsequently undergone a fundamental overhaul. The CAA framework has major implications for the focus of HR strategies and practices, as a paper jointly produced by the Improvement and Development Agency and Local Government Employers explains (IDEA and LGE 2008). The paper identifies some key national indicators for HRM at local level and suggests the kind of initiatives that could be associated with these. In the L&D area there is explicit reference to little beyond 'skills' and 'training' but the implications for the area go considerably wider, as Table 13 shows.

Priorities for L&D professionals in local government

Reflection on Table 13 suggests that the overall L&D agenda for local government organisations should prioritise:

- the embedding of cultural and structural change

- leadership and management development. Key issues here relate to senior management's competence, the quality and style of managerial leadership,

TABLE 13 Some key national indicators related to learning and development

- Aiding more transferability of employees, increasing need for relationship management skills
- Finding more creative and flexible ways of working to engage effectively with the community and partners
- Producing good workforce data on key indicators, to aid efficient performance management
- Reducing skills shortages, particularly by piloting new schemes on issues like improving basic skills in the council's workforce
- Benchmarking staff costs
- Involving the workforce in change
- Engaging employees with the new national indicators in order to create innovative thinking on how to improve outcomes for the local area
- Tackling skills gaps in the current workforce (for example by signing up to the Skills Pledge, working with the LSC at local level to access funding to help skills development and opening up workplace opportunities for workforce to gain accredited qualifications at levels 2, 3 and 4) – and so on
- Conducting a skills audit of the organisation (for example to establish a baseline level on skills, act as a good practice model, provide data that can be aggregated into local survey, and identify key current and future skills shortages to address through developing the existing workforce including providing skills pathways to open up career routes)

NOTE by the author:
In the overall indicator on 'performing well' there is no direct reference to anything beyond training that responds to identified gaps in skills and is resourced to deal with these and 'develop staff'. However, there is reference to the need for 'a strong improvement culture evidenced by managers and staff', also to 'Major organisational change (that) is supported by the leadership' and change that is 'well managed, achieves good workforce involvement and is effectively supported by IT services'. R.H.

Source: IDEA and LGE (2008)

and councillors' strategic awareness and skills. Time and again performance indicators and CPA results have shown that where these are lacking, the whole modernisation programme is at risk

- supporting the modernised PMS and the new CAA, especially through the appraisal and continuing development processes

- the rapid upgrading of the functional skills and business capability of those charged with delivering the PMS, especially HR staff

- an integrated, not silo-driven, approach so that all L&D activity is consistent with the wider workforce development strategy at local level and is founded on effective business partnerships.

CAMBRIDGESHIRE COUNTY COUNCIL – A STRATEGIC APPROACH TO PEOPLE MANAGEMENT AND DEVELOPMENT

Cambridgeshire County Council has 18,000 staff and was one of the first of those few councils in England to complete the switch to a single-status workforce by the official deadline of 2007. It used that achievement as the lever to harmonise terms and conditions for staff and streamline management. Following the restructuring needed in order to bring education and social services together – another national initiative – a major cultural change programme was set in motion in 2005. It started with an externally-run culture audit of its employees, which revealed that most staff found the Council bureaucratic and silo-driven. The Council therefore created an 'Inspire' project to change the way people worked and communicated.

'Inspire' has led to the Council now delivering through performance management and project management, cross-cutting on different themes. The biggest change has been a new framework defining 17 core behaviours expected of all staff and embedded in the PMS. The framework is aligned with other HR policies including L&D and reward, and has shaped leadership development from the Chief Executive down.

Working in partnership is of fundamental importance at the Council. An employee charter has made the psychological contract between staff and employer explicit, and there is a written partnership agreement with the three recognised unions. A more robust people management strategy introduced by the Council was produced through close collaboration with the unions, and they and a new Business Users Support Group within the Council have a major role in decision-making. Already in 2005 employee engagement levels as measured in the annual staff survey had risen to a high point, and recorded customer satisfaction levels were also increasing.

Source: Johnson, R. (2006) *People Management*, 14 September

CONCLUSION: CHALLENGES IN THE PUBLIC SECTOR FOR L&D PRACTITIONERS

The public sector modernisation programme is intended to provide all parts of the sector with a clear signal regarding how it should develop, allowing individual organisations to develop initiatives of their own that accord with the Government's aims. In reality, though, analysis of its progress in the NHS and LG uncovers a destructive tension in the sector between the pull to achieve demanding centralised targets and drive down costs and the push to build high-skill, high-performing organisations that provide a citizen-based service. The L&D agenda is therefore challenging, raising a set of core tasks for those charged with its implementation:

- *Finding the right balance*

  The continued dominance of the public sector's command-control management model leads to the possibility of a 'nightmare scenario' where Government takes resistance to its reforms as requiring yet more reform, and therefore tightens the 'sanctions' screw still further, every time (Caulkin 2007: 47). Few L&D professionals can influence the centralised planning system. However, at local level they should be agents of change, working with stakeholders to craft innovative solutions to meet local needs and raising understanding of how those solutions can be linked to national performance measures.

- *Building learning cultures*

  In some public sector workplaces a drive to enhance accredited skill levels – the focus of most nationally funded initiatives – can be not only irrelevant for employees but add to their frustration and demotivation when they are trapped in jobs where they cannot use many of the skills they already possess (Rainbird *et al* 2004). Working to develop expansive rather than restrictive workplace learning environments can be an effective way forward here (see Chapter 5).

- *Improving leadership and management capability*

  A report from Ernst & Young in 2006 (The *Times* 2006b) identified a lack of strategic capability in public service leaders and inexperience of most managers in new areas like implementing mergers, converting to shared services or managing joint ventures. Particular attention needs to be paid to L&D for front-line managers. They carry heavy people management responsibilities under the modernisation programme, particularly in relation to new national performance management systems that are being undermined by continuing low morale of employees, including managers themselves (Sinclair *et al* 2008).

- *Managing the budget*

  Nearly half of the public sector respondents to the CIPD's 2008 annual L&D Survey (CIPD 2008a) felt that funds for L&D had been cut during the past year, due to deteriorating economic circumstances, and only 16% anticipated any increase in funds in the coming year. These responses were in sharp and unfavourable contrast to those from the private sector. However, the survey also showed that 89% of respondents' public sector organisations allocated specific budgets to L&D – far ahead of the 71% of private sector organisations to do so. Furthermore, the public sector training budget per employee was very similar to that in the private sector (£222 compared to £296), and the number of training days per employee was virtually the same. These findings demonstrate the need for L&D managers in the public sector to be highly skilled in the management of their budgets, prioritising their activity and tailoring it to both current and predicted future needs. It is particularly important that they are fully informed about external NVET funding that can support key skills initiatives.

REFLECTION

Reflecting on the material in this section and on any experience you may have of L&D in a public sector organisation – be it a hospital, a school, a government agency or department, a police force or a branch of the armed services, for example – what conclusions do you yourself come to about key tasks for L&D professionals in aiding the Government's mission of building 'citizen-centred public services'?

SECTORAL SETTINGS: THE VOLUNTARY AND COMMUNITY SECTOR

AN INTRODUCTION

Little is said in research or textbooks about L&D in the voluntary and community 'third sector' (VCS), yet it contributes £21 billion to the economy (Richards 2006), employs around 1.5 million people and has 20 million volunteers regularly contributing (Carrington 2005). Voluntary organisations make £9 billion from selling goods and services and government funding now accounts for 37% of their revenue, most of it in the form of contract funding. The sector is complex and fragmented, with five main types of VCS organisation in addition to all the individual charities in the voluntary area (Richards 2006):

- umbrella or national bodies such as the National Council of Voluntary Organisations

- local groups, such as housing associations

- volunteer bureaus which hold details about the not-for-profit organisations in their locality

- social enterprises, a mix of a business and a voluntary organisation providing commercial services in a sector

- international organisations like Oxfam which place workers in the field.

Since 1997 the Government has focused strongly on wider service delivery in its voluntary sector agenda, leading to not-for-profit organisations now providing most social housing and 40% of social care. The third sector's ability to help provide services in the community was boosted by the establishment in 2004 of the *ChangeUp* programme, a collaborative initiative produced by the Home Office and the sector to aid capacity building and infrastructure development. Its management was taken over in 2006 by a non-departmental public body (NDPB) working with other funders (*http://capacitybuilders.org.uk/* [accessed 14 May 2008]). There is also an 'Investors in Communities' (IiC) scheme based on IiP principles to aid flexible demand-led provision of training and development.

The emphasis of public policy on social enterprise as a major thrust for the third sector, and the associated expansion of the sector's workforce, means that charities must professionalise their operations and develop a more corporate focus in their HR practice – for example, by using competency frameworks for selection and performance review (Carrington 2005). Yet people management in the third sector has a poor record, even in the larger organisations. Research by Lee and Brewster (*People Management* 2006b) into over 60 international non-government organisations (NGOs) found a lack of HR involvement in strategic planning and that HR had no presence on trustee boards. HR issues were often overlooked in favour of campaigning programmes and HR specialists, if existing at all, were rarely represented at senior levels. Performance management was inconsistent in its design, implementation and management.

THE FUNDING PROBLEM

Funding is an ongoing problem. In 2004 the Association of Chief Executives of Voluntary Organisations (Acevo) found the funding system to be inefficient and bureaucratic, causing chronic financial insecurity for charities delivering services contracted out to them by councils and health authorities. 92% of charities were found to be on contracts of a year or less, with many facing draconian short-term deals (Plummer 2004). Late in 2007, following official initiatives to enhance the sector's capacity, the Chancellor's pre-Budget report was accompanied by official offers of cash support for training the staff of non-profit organisations, and assurances that their public sector contracts are to be longer in duration and more secure (Walker 2007). However, alongside these promising signs there are plans to 'create a new apparatus of supervision' (*ibid*: 58). The Health Secretary wants social enterprises to provide primary care, even hospital services, and the current (2008) fast-deteriorating economic climate plus the heavy public sector overspend makes it likely that ministers will turn increasingly to the voluntary sector to provide cost-effective service provision (Walker 2007: 59).

The danger in expansion of social enterprise organisations is a restriction of charities' freedom of action. In 2007 a Charity Commission survey found that almost half of the charities it contacted felt that their activities were significantly determined by funding priorities, risking 'mission drift' (Moore 2007). There is also the risk issue, which has the potential to be far more damaging for the voluntary sector than the public sector when things go wrong. Take the following example.

FUTUREBUILDERS ENGLAND LOSES ITS GOVERNMENT CONTRACT

In 2008, to the dismay of Navca, the organisation which represents small charities, the Cabinet Office stripped Futurebuilders England (FE) of its contract to run a £215 million programme to help charities deliver more public services.

The Futurebuilders Fund was set up in 2005 to provide loans and grants to voluntary organisations and around 250 third sector organisations had received funding from it. Government decided that a different organisation, the Adventure Capital Fund (ACF), was to control its second phase starting in April 2008. FE staff were assured that their jobs were secure, but Navca fears that Government now wants to achieve its social enterprise aim by cutting back on grants and issuing more loans instead. It also doubts that ACF has adequate grant-giving experience.

Source: *The Times* (2008a)

As more charities worry about rigorous grant conditions and an overdependence on government funding, they are rethinking their funding strategy and in some cases seeing loans for the first time as a serious alternative (Bennett 2007). In 2002 the country's only not-for-profit bank – Charity Bank – was launched and grew steadily, making small, cheap loans to charities and community projects. Suddenly during 2006 it was inundated with loan enquiries from voluntary organisations in consequence of sweeping changes in the world of grant-making. The bank has subsequently considered more than doubling its size. Other options being tried especially by small and medium-sized voluntary and community organisations include alliances, mergers and joint projects with business.

PERFORMANCE MANAGEMENT

A unique feature of charities is that they have no equivalent to the private sector's bottom line, so making a clear link from what they do to what they achieve is difficult – in fact one commentator believes that 'analysing them is beyond any available methodology' (Brookes 2007). Yet because of the extent to which they are now being drawn into the social enterprise system, it is inevitable that there will and must be greater public scrutiny of how they do what they do, and to what end. Such scrutiny is also, for commentators like Brookes, a 'moral imperative' when they also now benefit from more than £1 billion of taxpayers' money and deal with many social problems that are an 'affront' to any civilised society. Brookes recommends that there should be a new non-departmental public body to help assess and improve charities' performance, independent but acting 'under the auspices' of the Cabinet Office. One way or another it is likely that before long the voluntary sector will be brought under much closer official scrutiny, and that will have clear implications for all its HR practices.

IMPLEMENTING THE L&D AGENDA IN THE THIRD SECTOR

In 2005 research by the University of Strathclyde indicated that two-thirds of voluntary organisations did not have a specialist dedicated HR staff member, despite the complexity of employment legislation (Czerny 2005). Most charities are still at the beginning of the road in trying to move from traditional personnel management to an HR business partnership approach (Carrington 2005).

Given this lack of even basic HR expertise in so many third sector organisations, few specialist L&D professionals are likely to be employed there full-time, or even part-time, except in the larger organisations. The main burden of L&D work is likely to fall on the shoulders of HR generalists where they exist, and on partnerships of various kinds. A unique characteristic of the sector is that its organisations co-operate and share resources and ideas, drawn together by a common purpose focused on their beneficiaries. Thus a Social Care Employers' Consortium was established by eight HR directors and now lobbies central government for increased resources to help the sector recruit, retain and train the professional staff it needs and that legislation expects (Zacharias 2003). Another organisation, People in Aid, also helps with HRM in the sector.

Bruce (2004) identified four core needs for charities, and these seem relevant even if not comprehensive as a basic L&D agenda for most of the third sector:

- enhancing performance
- management
- staff development
- governance (with board-level leadership training as an urgent priority).

The most likely sources of support to meet L&D needs in most of the sector at present seem to be innovative partnerships like those already mentioned and others like the two described in the following case examples.

A VCO FOUNDATION DEGREE

A partnership between four colleges of further/adult education originally produced the part-time work-based Foundation Degree in VCO Development aimed specifically at managers and aspiring managers in the voluntary, community and public sectors, and now run by Newman University College, Birmingham. Its content is designed to develop the required skills as an existing or aspiring manager in the voluntary sector. The degree is organised flexibly, using blended learning and a mix of classroom and independent learning modes. Accreditation is achieved through coursework and practical projects.

TRAINING THIRD-SECTOR MANAGERS

Health and social service charities piloted in 2005 a CIPD certificate in personnel practice aimed solely at the third sector and co-funded by the DH and the Home Office. It arose out of recognition by government and a voluntary sector working party that effective management of volunteers is central to the success of voluntary organisations, and that managers of volunteers need development opportunities and support. The aim was to create 100 volunteer managers qualified in the people management field. Most participants in the pilot scheme were unfamiliar with study at the CIPD certificate level, so the course used blended learning methods and a language and content tailored to the voluntary sector context. Following the pilot's success, the plan is to offer the CIPD Leadership and Management course.

Sources: Cottee, P. (2006) *People Management*, 12 January; *http://www.newman.ac.uk/Courses/Foundation/*[accessed 13 May 2008]

CONCLUSION

In this chapter the purpose has been to explore the L&D agenda in a range of organisational settings. By now you should have a broad-based understanding of the pressures, challenges and expectations that are shaping that agenda in smaller businesses, in the public sector, and in the voluntary and community sector. You should also be confident in tackling the review questions for this chapter, contained in Appendix 3.

The main ground covered by the chapter's three sections has been:

• the variegated L&D agenda across the small and medium-sized enterprise sector, where the crucial skill required of L&D practitioners is that of promoting highly tailored strategies and initiatives that can enhance performance at different stages of the SME's growth cycle

- the wide-ranging and demanding L&D agenda across the whole of the public sector, created by the Government's modernisation programme. In every area of that sector the same drive is aiming to transform outmoded, hierarchical and bureaucratic structures into customer-facing partnerships characterised by high quality, flexibility and adaptability to change. Wherever they work in the sector, HR professionals are having to rapidly learn new skills and values in order to implement the modernisation programme while at the same time trying to reduce the human tensions between the push to achieve centralised targets and reduce costs, and the pull to respond adequately and innovatively to local needs

- the unique L&D agenda in the fragmented but rapidly expanding voluntary and community sector where, despite increased public funding, the main need at organisational level is still for enough resources to produce tailored, partnership-based L&D initiatives that can meet current and projected strategic and capability needs.

FURTHER INFORMATION SOURCES

Sambrook, S. and Stewart, J. (eds) (2007) *Human Resource Development in the Public Sector: The case of health and social care*. London: Routledge

Stewart, J. and Beaver, G. (eds) (2004) *HRD in Small Organisations: Research and practice*. London: Routledge

Vere, D. (2005) *Fit for Business: Building a strategic HR function in the public sector*. Research Report. London: CIPD. Online summary also available at http://www.cipd.co.uk/research/ [accessed 13 May 2008]

Vere, D. and Butler, L. (2007) *Fit for Business:Transforming HR in the public sector*. Research Report. London: CIPD. Online summary also available at http://www.cipd.co.uk/research/ [accessed 13 May 2008]

Useful websites

SMEs
http://www.businesslink.gov.uk/bdotg/action/home [accessed 13 May 2008]. Provides information and advice for SMEs, including a free PDF download of case studies

The public sector
http://www.dh.gov.uk/PolicyAndGuidance/HumanResourcesAndTraining/fs/en [accessed 13 May 2008]. HR and training policies and initiatives to help the implementation of the NHS modernisation programme

http://www.dh.gov.uk/en/Managingyourorganisation/Humanresourcesandtraining/Modelcareer/index.htm [accessed 13 May 2008]. NHS Skills Escalator website

http//www.doeni.gov.uk/index/local_government/lgr_modernisation_of_local_government [accessed 13 May 2008]. Information about local government modernisation programme

The voluntary sector
http://www.prospects.ac.uk/cms/ShowPage/Home_page/Explore_job_sectors/Voluntary/overview/p!ejFagm [accessed 13 May 2008]. Provides overview of the voluntary sector, with statistical data

CHAPTER 11

Shaping and Managing the L&D Function

INTRODUCTION

In Chapter 4 I drew attention to the fact that in today's rapidly changing business environment restructuring is becoming a more or less continuous process for many organisations. A global study carried out by the RBL Group and the Ross School of Business at the University of Michigan suggests that it is the way in which HR departments are organised rather than the individual skills of HR professionals that have the greatest impact on the business (Arkin 2007b), and other research indicates that over 80% of HR functions have undergone some form of reorganisation since 2003 (Gifford 2007).

The purpose of this chapter is to explore ways in which an L&D function can be organised, the changing roles of L&D practitioners, and principles related to the leadership and management of the L&D function. By 'function' I do not imply a specialist unit. I simply mean the body of L&D activity provided for an organisation, and those who are responsible for that provision. The chapter is not intended as a technical guide. Detail concerning the routine management of L&D resources (including staff and budgets) is readily accessible in short texts and through specialist websites and online training communities. Some information sources are noted at the end of the chapter.

The first of the chapter's four sections looks at key issues related to organising and re-organising in turbulent times. The second explores ways of structuring the L&D function in organisations, examining tensions facing the function as it struggles between a push to fragmentation and a pull towards centralisation. In the third section I review old, changing and proposed new roles for L&D practitioners. The final section covers key issues to do with the leadership, management and professional development of those carrying L&D responsibilities.

STRUCTURE AS AN ORGANISING PROCESS

SOME KEY ISSUES

The aim of organising is (Harrison and Kessels 2003: 42):

> to achieve a continuous alignment of people, other resources, tasks and routines with strategic requirements in order to maximise current performance and generate options whereby to best position the organisation for the future.

The primary resources that this alignment draws on are (Pennings 2001: 241):

- hard-to-copy technologies

- organisational routines (such as budgeting, research and development arrangements, templates for organising work and control and planning routines)

- culture and socialisation processes

- relational competencies that allow the organisation to combine its unique resource with those of other firms, particularly those belonging to its value chain.

Today's business environment is so fast-moving that structures can no longer be regarded as products cast in stone. Research indicates that reorganising, regardless of size or type of organisation, now tends to be an incremental process rather than sudden and irregular leaps from one design of structure to another, and that in the UK fundamental restructuring is occurring on average once every three years or so (see, for example ,Whittington 2002; Whittington and Mayer 2002; CIPD 2004b).

NETWORK AND PARTNERSHIP FORMS

Organising through co-operative alliances, networks, cellular structures and other such flexible arrangement is now common in public and private sectors and can effectively create clusters of separate small businesses that are held together by a strong company brand. Keywords are partnership, trust and mutual dependency. Such alliances enable partners to access new knowledge that each on their own could not produce, to rapidly share it, and to apply it through their core competences to innovation in goods, processes, products and services. These more flexible ways of organising need great skill in order to ensure enough, but not excessive, formal controls to monitor exchanges of competence or capital assets (Koenig and Van Wijk 2001: 126). Without that, participating organisations' core competences and knowledge can be poached and competitors can gain a unique means of assessing a partner's strengths and weaknesses (Hamel 1991).

The skill must extend to binding together people who, in the increasing number of multi-employer situations, work side by side in a single workplace yet are contracted and paid by different employers (Rubery *et al* 2002). It concerns, in other words, enhancing an organisation's 'structural capital', meaning the way in which its work is organised, including 'the physical working arrangements and the interrelationships between individuals, units and teams, both inside and outside the organisation' (Baron 2006).

Reviewing research and practice across Europe, Whittington and Mayer (2002) examined various frameworks for organisations working in conditions of rapid change and identified a need for a mix of stable and fluid features, of which five seem crucial:

- clear formal structures and reporting relationships

- clear, standardised performance metrics across the organisation

- consistent, standardised compensation policies across the organisation

- the propensity to organise in small, performance-oriented units

- a culture of change within the organisation.

Managers should therefore organise people in ways that give them clarity about what is expected from them and how it will be measured, but avoid tight controlling systems that inhibit use of discretion and creativity. Once again context is all. Each organisation must find its own best way of organising activity and of managing its employment system, helped by flexible HR strategies and a mix of psychological contracts to suit its workforce profile.

ORGANISING THE L&D FUNCTION

WHAT DECIDES THE SHAPE?

REFLECTION

As an introduction to this section, imagine that you have been asked to review an organisation's current L&D function in order to decide whether its shape needs to change – or, if there is no formal pattern to L&D activity overall at present, how such activity should be organised. What kinds of analysis should you carry out initially? Suggestions follow below.

The main kinds of analysis needed to guide organisation or reorganisation of an L&D function include:

- analysing the external environment to identify big issues that have implications for L&D in the business

- analysing internal organisational context and major organisational issues, to identify where the L&D process could add most value. Key here will be vision, values and business goals of top management related to the L&D investment; the L&D roles and responsibilities of management (especially line management) and their general competence, commitment and discretion related to these; and HR structure, strategies and practices that have a bearing on L&D activity

- assessing the way in which L&D activity is currently organised in the business and the reasons for its present structural arrangements

- identifying any weaknesses in the current relationship between corporate structure, HR structure (if there is one) and the organisation of the L&D function. If managers carry significant L&D responsibilities, is that role included in their business targets, job descriptions and appraisals? If the L&D function is part of a wider HR function, how effectively does that relationship work? What aids and constraints does it provide for L&D strategy and activity?

- identifying key players in the organisation whose support is needed if L&D initiatives are to succeed, and their attitudes towards the function

- identifying those with whom the L&D function should form business partnerships, and those (for example union learning representatives) who could act as 'learning champions' in the workplace

- assessing resources available for L&D activity – including financial, material, human and reputational.

Such analysis can lead to a radical rethink in order to create more flexible forms that can give better value.

WHAT ARE THE OPTIONS?

Three of the most common options at present for structuring an L&D function are to devolve significant L&D responsibility to line management, to outsource some or all L&D work, or for the function to become part of an HR 'three-legged stool'. To explain these options:

The line-managed function

With this model, line managers are handed the main responsibility for L&D activity in their workplaces, leaving only a small core of it to be handled on a corporate basis at centre whether by L&D specialists or in some other way (by the HR function, by external strategic advisers, by a senior executive, and so on). Hutchinson and her colleagues (2007) identify from their extensive research a number of drivers of this devolution:

- to improve the quality of L&D, because line managers are usually in a better position than specialist HR staff to understand both organisational and individual needs

- the strong relationship that research indicates exists between effective coaching and guidance by line managers and employee satisfaction, commitment and motivation, which in turn can lead to employees going the extra mile for the business

- the fact that line managers are usually the gatekeepers to formal training opportunities. They play a leading role in the performance management process and even where their discretionary power related to financial rewards is limited, they often have considerable freedom to use L&D opportunities as a way of recognising and encouraging good performance

- the importance of the line managers' role in promoting knowledge-sharing and collaborative problem-solving and the developmental nature of those processes

- the increasing use by organisations of HR shared service centres (see below), requiring certain L&D responsibilities – for example, career development – to be shared between individuals and their line managers.

In Chapter 6 I have already discussed the support, incentives, training and development that line managers need if they are to have the competence and commitment to fulfil their L&D tasks. It is sufficient to draw attention here to five essentials if any devolution of L&D responsibility to the line is to be effective:

- *Vision and strategy* – There must be a clear L&D corporate vision and strategy that is in line with overall HR and business goals and strategy, and corporate leadership's active and regularly communicated commitment to a high-quality line-managed L&D function.

- *Objectives* – There must be strategic L&D objectives that can be carried through by divisional and unit managers into straightforward, practical plans for implementation.

- *Systems, processes and resources* – There must be company-wide systems and processes, plus the necessary resources, to ensure that all who carry L&D roles and responsibilities have a clear understanding of their tasks and the support, recognition and discretionary power to carry them out effectively.

- *Performance management* – There must be a performance management process that ensures effective training, appraisal, recognition and continuing development of those carrying L&D responsibilities.

- *Learning culture in the workplace* – There should be a workplace culture conducive to the integration of learning and work, and support for employees in self-managed learning and continuing personal development.

Failure to meet these demanding requirements often explains why devolution is unsuccessful. Lynch (2003), for example, found in her study of three large retail stores that store managers responsible for people management tended to neglect 'softer' policies in order to meet the hard budgetary and performance targets that were their real bottom line. HR policies outside those targets were subject to few tangible measurements and were less closely monitored by the centre, so tended to be taken less seriously by pressured managers. The case is of particular relevance now, because the pressures it highlights are increasing. In their research Worrall and Cooper (2006) found that over a mere five-year period from 2000 to 2005 the pressures caused by often multi-faceted organisational change resulted in significant loss of loyalty and morale in a high proportion of managers, and that for many their sense of job security and well-being had 'plummeted'. The decline was worst in the public sector where the pace and weight of change was highest (see Chapter 10). Managers' work had also intensified with many reporting that they felt overloaded and had neither the time nor resources to do their job to the standard they felt was needed. Worrall and Cooper concluded:

> Despite the HR rhetoric of empowerment and job involvement, most UK managers feel their participation in decision-making and objective-setting has reduced, that they are not listened to and they are subject to more top-down control, typically through performance management systems. Many also say they feel more controlled and subject to greater scrutiny and surveillance.

Outsourcing

Outsourcing can provide economies of knowledge and of scale, enabling an organisation to keep abreast of the latest research and innovations and to take advantage of high-level expertise, research facilities, technology and networks that would otherwise be beyond its reach (Ulrich 2007).

Outsourcing of HR services is most common in large and especially multinational organisations, with an increasing number of credible specialised firms now competing for single-process contracts – particularly to take on payroll and recruitment work – and a few global providers like Accenture, ACS, Convergys and IBM (*ibid*) handling the much rarer multi-process contracts. In HR, single-process outsourcing is far more common than multi-process outsourcing not just because of lack of high-calibre external providers but because organisations seem now to be thinking more strategically about how best to structure their HR function (Palmer 2008).

Partial outsourcing is the most common form in the L&D field. Typically it involves operational training delivery and administrative back-up, although sometimes it can extend to the use of external agencies to help design, deliver and evaluate high-level specialist programmes. It must never mean that the L&D function loses control over the work, however. The client must agree critical parameters of the work with the contractor and then monitor and exercise overall control over the contract's operation. Handled well, the partnership can result in lower costs and improved results of a service, while leaving the organisation's core L&D team freer to work as strategic partners in the business. Sometimes the team may also provide a revenue-generating consultancy service to external clients. Handled badly, outsourcing can become the catalyst for a slide to a fragmented function or to one that eventually disappears.

AVAYA'S OUTSOURCED TRAINING FUNCTION

An example of successful outsourcing of an entire training function is Accenture's 2001–2007 contract with leading telecommunications company Avaya to deliver training in the 51 countries in which Avaya has a presence. Accenture produced around 40% cost reduction coupled with a higher volume of training, and relieved Avaya of the task of delivering courses to customers, distributors and other business partners (Arkin 2006).

The Accenture website explains how the contract enabled Avaya to transform its learning function, Avaya University, in support of its plans to grow and improve market share through an aggressive schedule of new product launches. The University's transformation has helped Avaya to meet its strategic goals

and drive high performance for its employees, business partners and customers. Like the partnership described in Chapter 8 that was forged between an internal front-line management development project team and an external consultancy firm, working with Accenture greatly enhanced L&D skills at Avaya. According to its vice-president Suellen Roth (Arkin 2006: 21):

> We are also learning how to improve continually the velocity, quality, delivery, customer perception and employee perception of training.

Sources: Arkin, A. (2006) *People Management Guide*, February; *http://www.accenture.com/Global/ Outsourcing/Business_Process_ Outsourcing/Accenture_ Learning/ Client_Successes/AvayaOutsourcing. htm* [accessed 17 July 2008]

The HR 'three-legged stool'

The HR three-legged stool model and variants of it are in growing although not yet widespread use, being mainly found in large, multi-unit organisations. The CIPD research cited at the start of this chapter found that of the 80% of organisations that had changed their HR function since 2003, 57% had introduced some form of the model. Typical reasons were (Gifford 2007):

- to enable more business-focused and strategically-oriented HR work overall

- to ensure more cost-efficient transactional HR work that also enables employees to become more self-reliant

- to free up HR business partners and specialists to concentrate on transformational, value-adding activity

- to devolve more HR work to line managers and gain their commitment to it.

Since in most cases the L&D function is likely to be either an integral part of the HR function or closely (whether or not effectively) associated with it, such research findings have direct implications for the organisation, impact and operation of L&D activity.

The three-legged stool model is widely attributed to Dave Ulrich (1997) but he himself sees it as a form of organising that has emerged from many different sources (Arkin 2007c). The three 'legs' are service centres, business partners and centres of expertise, although as Figure 13 shows Ulrich has suggested a fourth 'operational executor' (OE) leg where work may be falling between the cracks of the other three. As one example of an OE's utility Ulrich cites the case of an

FIGURE 13 The HR three- (or four-) legged stool

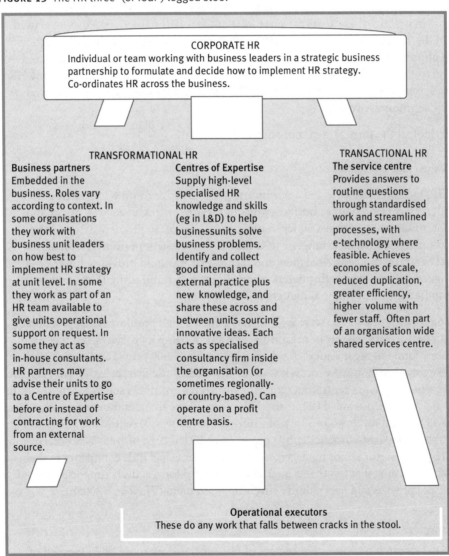

CORPORATE HR
Individual or team working with business leaders in a strategic business partnership to formulate and decide how to implement HR strategy. Co-ordinates HR across the business.

TRANSFORMATIONAL HR

Business partners
Embedded in the business. Roles vary according to context. In some organisations they work with business unit leaders on how best to implement HR strategy at unit level. In some they work as part of an HR team available to give units operational support on request. In some they act as in-house consultants. HR partners may advise their units to go to a Centre of Expertise before or instead of contracting for work from an external source.

Centres of Expertise
Supply high-level specialised HR knowledge and skills (eg in L&D) to help businessunits solve business problems. Identify and collect good internal and external practice plus new knowledge, and share these across and between units sourcing innovative ideas. Each acts as specialised consultancy firm inside the organisation (or sometimes regionally- or country-based). Can operate on a profit centre basis.

TRANSACTIONAL HR

The service centre
Provides answers to routine questions through standardised work and streamlined processes, with e-technology where feasible. Achieves economies of scale, reduced duplication, greater efficiency, higher volume with fewer staff. Often part of an organisation wide shared services centre.

Operational executors
These do any work that falls between cracks in the stool.

Source: Drawn from information in Ulrich, D. (2007); Arkin, A. (2007b, c)

employee who discusses with her line manager and the business unit's HR business partner options for career progression and draws up with them a portfolio of L&D experiences relevant to her career plan or aspirations. The OE then helps her to put the plan into practice by identifying appropriate specific programmes or internal job opportunities (Arkin 2007c).

The Prison Service website provides an example of the restructuring of HR services along three-legged stool lines (*http//www.welcometothefrontline.co.uk* [accessed 16 July 2008]). It describes one of the largest and most complex HR transformation projects in central government.

Given the complexity of the interactions evident in Figure 13 it is unsurprising that in practice there are great variations in the way the three-legged stool is used. Of the 787 respondents to the CIPD's 2007 survey on the changing HR function (Gifford 2007), 81% reported that their organisations had recently restructured, but of those, only 18% had adopted the three-legged stool model in full. Most HR structures seemed to consist of single HR teams comprising generalists, specialists and administrative staff.

To look at the three legs in more detail:

Shared and HR service centres

CIPD research has detected a significant trend to move routine transactional HR services from within business units to service centres, usually in-house and not infrequently within a wider shared service centre (Reilly 2007). Part of the rationale for such an arrangement is that it can free senior HR professionals to act as strategic business partners and part is that it should provide a lower-cost, higher-volume service through pooling HR expertise and using IT systems to handle routine procedural matters (CIPD 2004c).

The concept of a shared service centre has gained a high profile over the past decade as a non-traditional way of organising a variety of company services, but they are rarely found in organisations employing fewer than 5,000 people and almost all that do exist are in-house, a process known as 'insourcing' (Reilly *et al* 2007). For example, the Prison Service's centre, operating mainly from a greenfield site in Newport, South Wales, delivers not only HR but also Finance and Procurement transactional services to 48,000 employees and 130 establishments. Shared service centres are now central to public sector cost-efficiency efforts but research by law firm Browne Jacobson covering 178 public sector senior managers found respondents had little confidence in their value, claiming that less than a quarter of their workforce actively supported shared service projects and over a third actively opposed them (*The Times* 2008b).

Centres of HR expertise and business partners

CIPD research indicates that centres of HR expertise are more often focused on specialised L&D work than on any other type of specialised HR activity (Reilly *et al*

2007). L&D centres of expertise tend to operate in parallel with an L&D business partnership process, organised most commonly in one of three ways:

- a central team of professionals whose members move out into the business to work with internal clients and customers on a variety of L&D projects

- a small strategic and co-ordinating core located at the centre, with the rest of the L&D staff permanently outposted across the organisation working within its strategic business units (SBUs) – another type of business partnership

- an L&D team acting as an internal consultancy (which sometimes also offers services to external clients on a commercial basis), with line managers holding their own L&D budgets which they can use to purchase services from the L&D team and/or external providers. A small central L&D function holds a corporate budget to cover organisation-wide training and learning activity and to meet contingencies with major L&D implications – for example, relating to new legislation, downsizing, or a forthcoming acquisition or merger.

Each of these three structural forms requires exceptional collaboration between L&D staff in the centre of expertise, L&D business partners at corporate and local levels and the business unit managers. The basic challenge is one of 'fit': how best to strike a balance between central and localised needs. If L&D strategy in an organisation has to stretch too far in attempting to meet local needs, the result can be that every SBU pursues its own L&D practices regardless of corporate L&D strategy while the L&D team becomes fragmented with a lack of central co-ordination. If SBUs feel that their local needs are poorly served, the L&D team loses credibility and clients. Either way, the function can become vulnerable to restructuring or closure.

Where are we now?

To conclude this discussion of the HR three-legged stool and other HR structural forms, what is the present state of play?

Findings from a CIPD HR survey reported in 2003 covering over 1,000 organisations of all types and sectors in England and Northern Ireland showed senior HR and development professionals to be significantly upbeat about their functions. Most felt that a corner had at last been turned. They saw the shape and content of HR to be expanding, with outsourcing and insourced shared service centres playing a positive part in a move that was making HR business partners significant strategic players (CIPD 2003c). However, the survey also indicated some serious problems preventing the effective transfer to line management of a core of people management responsibilities, and so threatening the successful operation of the three-legged stool.

Those problems remain. In 2005 an important report was published on the organisation of HR for the future (Ashton *et al* 2005). The authors predicted that in the next five years there would have to be a major transformation of HR into a leaner, more analytical and network-based function if it was to survive. In a web article the authors warned against HR professionals being preoccupied with the organising along 'Ulrich' lines. Instead they should get a clear focus on what was needed to support organisational performance today while also helping to develop capabilities for the future. Although in what they called 'first tier' (transforming) functions there was evidence of strategic thinking and effective business partnering, in 'second tier' functions too many were doing too much HR process work. These faced reduction of services and marginalisation (*http://www.humanresourcesmagazine.com.au/ articles/c0/0c02cec0.asp* [accessed 29 July 2008]).

Other research supports these authors' findings. Reilly (2006) found that both structural cracks and overlap were occurring in some three-legged stool structures. Many of the problems arose from lack of role clarity and accountability especially in business partner work. There were also boundary management problems caused by the frequent difficulty of separating transactional from centres of expertise work, and by conflicting expectations between HR and the line about who should handle operational people management and development matters (Reilly 2006).

In the same year a global survey of 1,400 organisations, carried out by Mercer Human Resource Consulting, showed that although half had been transforming their HR functions over the past five to 10 years the function had remained essentially administrative and transactional in its focus despite improvements in technology and service delivery. The biggest barrier to HR gaining the desired strategic focus was lack of line management capability to manage their people. Unskilled HR staff and a poor business perception of the value that HR could bring to the organisation were also significant problems (Scott 2007). The same kind of perception was reported in 2008 by DDI, a 35-year-old international consultancy firm based in Pittsburgh, USA, which conducts regular global surveys of senior HR and business executives in countries across the world. Although 47% of almost 1,500 HR professionals responding to its 2008/9 Global Leadership Forecast survey claimed that the CEO often involved them as a strategic partner, only 30% of CEOs in another DDI study saw it that way, reporting a limited confidence in their HR staff (Howard and Wellins 2008: 3).

Responses to the CIPD's 2007 survey on changing HR functions (Gifford 2007) and to its 2007 annual L&D survey (CIPD 2007a) confirmed the continuing difficulties being encountered in effectively transferring HR responsibilities – including those relating to L&D work – to the line, due especially to:

- line managers' priorities

- lack of appropriate line manager skills

- insufficient time for line managers to do the work.

Other contributory factors were failure of managers' bosses to encourage them to tackle people management issues, and technical problems with self-service (Gifford 2007).

It seems logical to conclude that although the HR function (including L&D) doubled the proportion of its time spent on strategic activities between 2003 and 2007, line management problems together with difficulties in managing the 'fragmentation inherent in the three-legged model' and with self-service technology have all combined to limit restructuring's success (Reilly 2007: 45). It is clear too that the role of business partner needs more clarification. Many in such a role find themselves underprepared or inadequately skilled for the role, and cite 'being strategic' as a major problem. Often the problem arises because they are drawn into irrelevant activity, experiencing tension between responding to corporate and business unit needs and operating largely to immediate and short-term management agenda, sometimes out of their own preference (Gifford 2007).

More detailed information about the challenges and areas of success being experienced as HR functions continue to be restructured can be found in the 2007 CIPD survey and its research report (Gifford 2007; Reilly *et al* 2007). In Chapter 13 I will look in detail at business partner challenges confronting L&D professionals.

REFLECTION

Consider the way in which the L&D function is structured in your own organisation and identify which of the structural forms discussed in this section it most resembles. How far do you think its structure is appropriate given the outcomes set for the function?

THE L&D FUNCTION: FRAGMENTATION OR INTEGRATION?

Contrary to the generally optimistic views expressed in the CIPD's 2003 HR survey by its respondents, at London Business School in the same year Lynda Gratton (2003b) saw a worrying fragmentation taking place, largely due to the 'bloated, introverted state that many functions had reached'. A similar judgement had already been passed in 2002 by the Audit Commission on the state of HR in local government. Here is another case that shows the difference that can exist between rhetoric and reality, this time the reality of the relationship between training and the wider personnel function.

A 'CINDERELLA' PUBLIC SECTOR TRAINING FUNCTION

Researchers studying the effectiveness of a training function in a large public sector used a comprehensive blended methodology to ensure that reliable information was obtained from those managing the personnel and training functions and from their organisational customers.

Stewart and Harris found that HR was structured in a traditional way, with training part of a personnel function that was headed by a generalist. Training activity and those responsible for it held a significantly lower status than elsewhere in the personnel function. Training itself was characterised by a traditional approach dominated by courses held and managed at centre.

Some responsibility for personnel and training had been devolved, and the staff who worked in line departments were independent of the centre, often combining their HR role with other resource management duties. At centre,

little attention seemed to be paid to training issues. The impression was of training operating independently of personnel matters, mainly because of a disinterest by personnel generalists in getting involved. Some of them were more concerned with the efficient use of the organisation's training centre than with establishing the most effective approach for a given need. Overall there were few signs of a professional partnership or of shared professional values between the personnel and training staff.

The researchers concluded that in this organisation training was the Cinderella of the HR function. They commented that this is not an uncommon scenario and that the relationship between personnel and training generally seems likely to continue for some time to be 'fractured rather than integrated'.

Source: Stewart, J. and Harris, L. (2003) *People Management*, 25 September

Gratton posed some awkward questions about fragmented functions of the kind this case example describes (2003b):

- Why not outsource the lower value end to low cost providers?

- And the top value end to strategic consulting firms?

- And the employee-facing part to line managers?

And there's the rub: why not indeed? That answer has already led to the downsizing and sometimes the disappearance of once-powerful, stable HR functions, and of training departments also. They have been found wanting in a business environment where many companies, after decades of cost-cutting and human asset stripping to improve short-term performance, seem at last to be appreciating the need to build human and social capital. Looking to their training and development staff for the expertise to help here, too many look in vain. A few years ago companies were spending an estimated 36% of revenues on pay, benefits, training and other expenses related to their workforces. Asked in one survey where the spend was going to, only 16% of financial directors seemed to have any real idea (Rogers 2004). A similar picture has been produced subsequently by each of the CIPD's annual Training/L&D surveys between 2006 and 2008. All have indicated that despite an extraordinary increase in coaching and the popularity of in-house training (all carrying heavy if often indirect costs for the business) very few organisations are even attempting to measure outcomes, let alone provide a business case for the investment (CIPD 2008a). I will be discussing ways of measuring the organisation's L&D investment in Chapter 14 but it has to be emphasised here that if an L&D function cannot and does not communicate convincingly to the business what value it provides, it can expect to be dismantled.

In this section I have identified a number of challenges to traditional concepts of how to organise an L&D function whether it is stand alone or part of a wider HR unit. The many options available confirm the point made at the start of the chapter about the growing irrelevance of a concept of structure as a fixed state or infrequently redesigned product. Rigid structures cannot deliver the kind of demanding L&D agenda now common across all employment sectors. Continuous organising, fluid relationships and fuzzy organisational boundaries are the way forward. Judging by the results of research covered in this chapter alone, this requires very different kinds of skills from those possessed by many L&D practitioners today.

All of this raises significant challenges for L&D professionals. They must be able to operate outside the protective walls of a specialist function as they help to produce initiatives that, while focused adequately on corporate goals, can also meet local needs. They must be skilled in 'relationship management' (Miles and Snow 1995: 11) and contribute to the building and sustaining of a relational type of psychological contract between organisation and employees in order to build trust and commitment to a common purpose. Finally, they must be credible business partners (discussed in detail in Chapter 13) or they have no hope of influencing the leaders, managers and HR colleagues whose strategies and actions strongly shape internal organisational context.

REFLECTION

Consider the 'awkward questions' Gratton raised about fragmented HR functions. How far do you think they apply to HR activity in your own organisation (or one which you know about)?

DETERMINING L&D ROLES

ROLE AND ROLE-HOLDER

The same forces that influence the organisation of the L&D function also shape L&D roles. In both cases radical changes are now taking place. First, though, what do we mean by 'role'? One dictionary definition is (Allen 1990):

> Role: an actor's part … a person's or thing's characteristic or expected function.

This is a useful way of thinking about 'role' because of the emphasis on playing a part, on interacting in a particular way with others, as well as on functions to be performed. It also highlights the concept of dynamism. Every actor differs in his or her interpretation of a given part and makes of it something unique, as well as fulfilling its formal requirements. These related ideas of a given and a developed element are emphasised in much of the published research about training roles.

Morgan (1997: 169) illuminates the ways in which roles can be affected by role holders' attempts to maintain or increase their own status, self-respect and political influence at the expense of those of others. He describes how people can identify with and protect the responsibilities and objectives associated with their specific role, work group, department, or project team, to the point where they 'value achievement of these responsibilities and objectives over and above the achievement of wider organizational goals'.

Fascinating though it would be to extend this discussion by moving into sociological theory in more depth, there is no space here to do so. Suffice to agree with Morgan that 'the potential complexity of organizational politics is mind-boggling, even before we take account of the personalities and personality clashes that usually bring roles and their conflict to life'.

CHANGING TYPOLOGIES

Turning to the formal roles that L&D practitioners occupy: for a surprisingly long time the typology (that is to say, classification framework) produced by Pettigrew and colleagues in 1982 remained a meaningful reflection of the range of activity in which trainers have been involved across different organisational settings. Even today, many trainers identify with its descriptors. Of the five roles – change agent, provider, training manager, role in transition and 'passive provider' – the last often strikes a particular chord. This is the practitioner who performs a purely reactive role, operating at a low level of activity and influence. He or she provides services and systems when asked but never challenges what or how things are done or suggests any better approaches (Pettigrew *et al* 1982: 8).

However, such a typology can no longer adequately reflect a shifting reality and a world that goes beyond the bounds of 'training' into the broader territory of learning and knowledge productivity. New roles have been identified over the past two decades, often using such terms as 'strategic facilitators' and 'internal consultants'. Now, even these descriptions may be falling out of date. As Alex Wilson, group HR director at BT (Morton and Wilson 2003) pointed out, in many organisations managers are being trained to take on specialist development roles themselves, so that they can act as 'people development consultants' who work with their teams to make sure that people 'make the best of themselves'. Line experts or external agencies can also take over roles of administrative expert and even strategic partner.

A SUGGESTED TYPOLOGY

Drawing on Morton and Wilson's (2003) suggestions but also reflecting on material covered in the previous section, I have produced a future-oriented typology of L&D roles, shown in Table 14. It would only be in the larger organisations, of course, that it would be appropriate to have all these roles and the body of work that they encompass, and in smaller companies many of the roles may have to be performed by a single individual. But I suggest that the roles in Table 14 cover most of the work being carried out in the L&D field today, and show the synergistic relationship that should link its key areas of activity.

TABLE 14 A suggested typology of L&D roles

Role	Major focus of role
Professional adviser	Strategic business partner, working to achieve tailored, value-adding solutions to meet clients' needs. Helps the organisation to prepare for change and supports increased external strategic alliance activity.
Knowledge architect	Senior strategic adviser on training and learning processes and solutions to aid knowledge creation, sharing, transfer and application to add value.
Brand manager	Shapes and maintains a clear and consistent brand image for all L&D activity and ensures that L&D staff are engaging with and motivating those who use their services. Manages the training/L&D function.
Commercial lead	Creates revenue streams from the organisation's L&D processes and products, selling them to internal and external customers.
Learning specialist	Expert with specialised skills in design, delivery and evaluation of learning events and processes.
Administrator	Supports L&D activity at all levels.

To say something about each of the professional roles shown in Table 14:

Professional adviser

This was a term used by PriceWaterhouseCooper (Arkin 2001) to describe their senior, most highly qualified L&D staff who worked in their HR shared professional services centre. An alternative term would be 'consultant' or 'business partner', but both are in such common use that they have little real meaning. Advisers should be able to operate alone or in teams, self-managing or leading others. They must be deeply informed not only about the L&D field but about all areas of the business. They must also ensure that the projects for which they are responsible are delivered on time and to specification, making appropriate use of service-level agreements (identifying how the relationship will work through responsibilities, timescales and measurement criteria based on the specific services to be provided).

Knowledge architect

This could be part of the professional adviser role or a distinctive role in itself. It reflects and emphasises the unique importance of 'knowledge management' work for the L&D field. The term is borrowed from Lank (2002) to describe those senior strategic people who are able to provide advice, skills and solutions related to 'knowledge management'. They would be deeply informed in how people use and share knowledge and information, and in the creation and enhancement of collective and individual learning processes supported and stimulated by information and communication technology (ICT).

Brand manager

If L&D activity, however fragmented it may be in an organisation, is to survive as a meaningful collective programme for an organisation, then it must have a clear brand with which L&D mission, values and code of behaviour are consistently associated. The brand manager would be the prime mover here, responsible for managing and marketing the L&D function within and beyond the organisation. A related task would be to ensure that those belonging to the L&D professional team, however far-flung they may be, share a collective identity and work effectively as a team, holding and putting into practice a set of values that represent the way that the function should behave towards clients and customers in and outside the organisation.

Commercial lead

This role would require entrepreneurial flair, product development and marketing skills, and financial expertise, although not necessarily specialist L&D qualifications. In many organisations now, helped especially by web-based technology, there is a trend to convert the fruits of L&D activity and experience within the organisation into knowledge-based commodities with external commercial appeal.

Learning specialist

This role would involve specialist training, learning and development functional tasks but acquires a new dimension with the rapid growth of innovative ICT. Learning specialists would need to work closely with all other types of L&D role-holders as their work would have to support and inform elements of each.

This typology is only tentative, intended to stimulate reflection and debate. L&D professionals need to take the lead in proposing new shapes for their function and new roles for themselves. Standing still is not an option if they want to avoid the fate that has overtaken many old-style HR functions (Gratton 2003b):

> a Humpty Dumpty, fallen from the wall and shattered into fragments on the hard pavement below.

LEADING AND MANAGING THE L&D FUNCTION

REFLECTION

Build a vision, strip out non-core activities, develop new ways to assess and develop skills and learning capability in the organisation ...

Reflecting on Rogers' (2004) advice,

how far do you think it has been met by the L&D function in your own organisation (or one you know about), and can you identify any 'new ways' that it would be valuable to adopt?

THE EFFECTIVE FUNCTION

Responsibility for an L&D function in an organisation can take many forms depending on how that function is structured, its size and scope. In this section I have no particular functional model in mind, nor in the space available is it possible to provide any detailed technical or operational guidelines. My concern is simply to draw attention to the fact that where an L&D professional is responsible for the work of a team, no matter how small, to carry out L&D work for an organisation, that professional must not only possess a high level of L&D expertise. He or she must also be a skilled leader and manager, and must achieve a function that (drawing broadly on Gratton 2003c):

- *takes a strategically focused, holistic approach to L&D activity.* A variety of L&D initiatives may be being pursued across an organisation, but all should be framed by an accurate overall picture of L&D activity in the organisation and a clear strategic framework (see Chapter 12). Fragmentation must not mean disintegration.

- *translates policies into practice through realistic plans.* Project teams, service-level agreements and business partnerships all have a part to play here, and the L&D manager must have the expertise to plan, direct, organise and control the processes that they involve. Yet although he or she will be accountable for their outcomes to whoever at senior management level carries final responsibility for L&D in the organisation, skilled delegation is crucial. Recalling the principles embedded in the 'people and performance' framework discussed in Chapter 6, the emphasis should be on giving maximum discretion possible in the particular situation to competent and committed L&D staff to exercise their skills as they judge best.

- *keeps the best and scraps the rest.* L&D strategies, processes and initiatives need to be regularly monitored so that they can be changed or abandoned when it is clear that they are no longer fulfilling a useful purpose. Value for money and achieving added value should be the guiding principles here – both to be explained in detail in Chapter 14.

Four tasks lie at the core of the L&D manager's role:

- people leadership and management

- professional and career development

- managing the budget

- managing marketing and data bases.

PEOPLE LEADERSHIP AND MANAGEMENT

As already explained, innovative structural forms offer a way of combining a strategic core and a strong L&D brand with flexibility, adaptability and knowledge productivity for the L&D function. For this to work, however, there must be high-quality leadership and management of those with L&D responsibilities wherever they are located in the organisation – and outside it. Putting Lynda Gratton's ideas into an L&D context, what any L&D manager must ensure is four kinds of integration (Gratton 2003b):

- '*Operational integration*' around an attractive L&D brand, utilising new technology where possible. Unipart has done this through its corporate university, and this way of branding a company's investment in the learning and development of its people is becoming increasingly popular, despite the considerable investment it involves in establishing, maintaining and publicising (see *http://www.managementskills.co.uk/articles/univer.htm* [accessed 21 August 2008]). But however small and unsophisticated an L&D function may be it must still demonstrate that it has a strong and engaging purpose – a Big Idea – that pulls together clusters of localised L&D activity into a coherent whole, aligned with business goals and serving as well as helping to shape needs from corporate to individual levels.

- '*Performance integration*', through a clear sense in the L&D function of what it wants to achieve, of the streams of projects and processes that it needs to pursue in order to meet its goals, and of its current progress in each together with measures to establish outcomes. Performance integration as described here is about co-ordinated project management and interlocking activities all focused on an organisation-wide L&D goal that supports the goals of the business. It is also about the effective performance management of L&D practitioners.

- '*Professional integration*', described by Gratton as 'the capacity of the whole team to move into collective action through shared bonds of friendship and reciprocity'. This is to do with binding L&D specialists together as a professional group. When they are working on a variety of projects for or across an organisation, there is a danger that they will become professionally isolated. They may then lose their identity, threatening the corporate L&D brand. The L&D leader must therefore ensure regular opportunities to meet, whether virtually or face-to-face, in order to refresh their knowledge of the function's progress in supporting the aims of the business and of the different initiatives that they are all engaged in to that end, to review their own professional development, and for purposes of social interaction. New technology can be a major aid to this process, with intranets and portals having an important part to play in the establishment and integration of virtual L&D teams.

- '*Intellectual integration*', through a shared knowledge base. This kind of integration is about accessing, sharing and building on best practice in L&D whether within or outside the organisation in order to increase the power of its impact both within the L&D team and across the organisation. The Local Government Association's initiative described in the following case example is a case in point.

SHARING KNOWLEDGE: IDeA

CASE EXAMPLE

The Improvement and Development Agency (IDeA) is a not-for-profit organisation owned by the Local Government Association and acting as local government's in-house HR consultancy. It provides information about best practice throughout the sector, and offers a peer review service whereby a team of experienced people will review an authority's practices in a challenging but supportive manner. Amongst its many initiatives IDeA provides access to virtual communities of practice and discussion forums, and a database of professional networks.

IDeA's knowledge team gathers and displays on its website information, ideas and case studies supplied by local authorities who wish to share their knowledge about good practice and improved performance with others across local government. Many lessons learnt are shared throughout the sector and fed into national policy development.

Pickard (2002) described the work of an IDeA consultant with Ipswich Council in a pioneering organisation development and learning programme involving councillors and officers. During the programme maintenance engineers who were experts at project management were brought in to teach the rest of the council, typifying an approach to learning that sees it as a matter of exchanging knowledge in ways that actively involve all participants in the teaching and learning process. Such initiatives aim to shift control over learning from trainers to learners, directing attention away from a preoccupation with controlling training budgets to helping people learn and grow (*ibid*).

Sources: Pickard, J. (2002) *People Management*, 21 March; IDeA website at *http://www.idea.gov.uk/idk/core/page.do?pageId=1* [accessed 15 July 2008]

PROFESSIONAL DEVELOPMENT AND CAREER PLANNING

In career planning for L&D staff it is important to pay attention to the needs of all the function's staff, not just those likely to be moving up or out, and including support staff. This will make an important statement about how the entire team forms a community of practice, and about how they can develop within as well as beyond the boundaries and levels of their present positions. It will give impetus to building a learning culture and relational psychological contracts within the L&D function. The principles that apply to the development of staff working in the L&D function should also be applied wherever feasible to the development of others with L&D responsibilities, especially line managers to whom, as noted earlier, L&D tasks are increasingly being devolved but who often find their L&D responsibilities a burdensome addition to already pressurised workloads.

Constraints on time and financial resource mean that self-development is the most reliable way for L&D staff to drive their careers forward. It is of particular importance for the increasing number of those who, although wanting to pursue a career in the L&D field, are working initially as junior HR generalists in organisations that structure their HR function along 'three-legged stool' lines. However, research has shown that often they cannot break out into work involving relationship management, business understanding and specialist expertise and so face major obstacles to their career progress (Reilly *et al* 2007).

In 2008 Orion Partners consultancy studied 20 large organisations that have moved to the HR three-legged stool model. None had a comprehensive career development structure for HR staff although some offered features such as job rotation. Junior HR personnel therefore faced almost insuperable barriers in trying to make the leap either into specialised work (including L&D) in centres of expertise or into business partner roles. For their part, such organisations often have to import talent to fill business partner roles, with the result that yet another barrier confronts HR staff trying to make the structured moves that could enable them to move up the career ladder (Pickard 2008; Orion Partners 2008). Claus (2007) identified the likely consequences for HR practitioners generally (including those in L&D work) if the shared service centre trend continues:

* few working in-house, and more acting as 'external vendors' of HR services

* for those who stay in-house, a premium being placed on process/project management skills and on certain areas of highly specialised HR expertise.

Choosing and using professional qualifications and standards

Appropriate qualifications are not only vital to L&D practitioners' career development. Just as important, they stand as a guarantee that they are fit to practise, and that they, alongside others in the HR professional community, are committed to a vision and set of values that fundamentally shape their conduct and their professional identity. But what is 'appropriate' in the L&D context? Websites for the main bodies that now offer L&D qualifications both within the National Qualifications Framework and outside it are given at the end of the chapter. Here, it is sufficient to comment briefly on the CIPD, since it is the oldest and largest professional HR body of its kind in Europe, was granted chartered status in 2001 and has produced professional standards at certificate, advanced certificate and postgraduate levels that cover the whole spectrum of HR work and include at postgraduate level a suite of L&D Standards. All its qualifications form part of the current (2008) National Qualification Framework and are cross-mapped to S/NVQs where relevant for accreditation purposes.

The CIPD is criticised by many who work in, or wish to enter, education, training and learning positions on two grounds:

* It does not offer a stand alone professional qualification for those wishing to specialise in education/training/L&D.

* It does not allow those who already possess diploma-level qualifications in the education, training and learning field (DTLL, PGCE, master's awards of a relevant kind, and so on) full exemption from the CIPD-accredited routes to professional membership.

Its stance on these criticisms explains the way in which, in the CIPD's current (2001) Standards, those relating to L&D work are linked both to the wider HR area and to the business. It is that:

* In today's organisations more than ever before a broad base of business and people management knowledge and competence is essential to effectiveness and credibility in the L&D field as in all other HR fields.

- L&D is an integral part of HR work more widely. Therefore its professionals, alongside other HR professionals, should be committed to work to the vision, purpose and set of values that frame the CIPD's body of professional standards.

However, the Institute's professional standards, routes to membership and qualification portfolio are being reviewed through a wide-ranging consultative process at the time of writing (mid-2008), so nothing is set in stone.

REFLECTION

Reflecting on the material in this part of the chapter, what recommendations would you make about career development for L&D staff working in or for your organisation, and what do you consider should be the main priorities here?

MANAGING THE BUDGET

Financial management is a big issue now for L&D managers and project leaders, especially with the wide variety of funding sources available. Funding from whatever source is usually quite tightly tied to targets, with funders and sponsors having high expectations of accountability and unique accounting procedures. Service-level agreements are common also, and they too require a precise identification of costs and expected returns (see Karten 2001 for an explanation). In whatever context, the L&D budget is therefore a crucial tool and its core purpose is always the same: to identify what is being or to be spent, under what headings, why, and with what intended and actual outcomes.

A budget's format and coverage should make it possible to quickly identify changing trends in L&D activity from one financial period to the next, and to highlight areas of activity that, cost-wise, are problematic. Where priority needs cannot be met within planned budgetary limits, a business case must be put forward for obtaining more money or for meeting needs through a changed pattern of activity. A good L&D budget will identify the annual running costs of the L&D function (personnel, overheads and administrative) together with L&D activity areas, the significant costs associated with them and their projected returns. Returns can flow from L&D commercial enterprise, from line managers with devolved budgets who decide to purchase the function's services, from external funders, and from reduction in measurable costs that can be confidently traced to the success of L&D initiatives (reduced turnover rates, improved production rates, increased sales and so on).

There is no one best way to produce an L&D budget whether for a company, an L&D function or a single L&D project. It is a practical document and has to be adapted to context. It must clarify in a format and language that suits its envisaged audience the costs of the L&D investment, how and why they vary from costs in the previous budget period, how they are going to be recouped, and what if any gaps there are between finance available and needed. Those gaps will then become the subject for discussion. In sum: the budget is core to financial accounting but it also informs options for action and aids decisions about the L&D function's operation and the organisation's L&D investment. Budgeting is a crucial responsibility of any L&D manager.

MANAGING MARKETING AND DATA BASES

Competent marketing of an organisation's L&D brand is essential in order to raise awareness within and outside the organisation of what L&D offers and the unique difference it can make to the business and to individuals. Equal emphasis, though, must be placed on the need for collaborative working with stakeholders since without their active support for the L&D function its aspirations cannot be realised. Branding will then be seen as no more than a glib public relations exercise. Marketing the L&D function in this sense is not to do with glossy brochures or expensive public relations efforts. It is to do with developing the right kind of products and services for clients and customers, and involving them throughout in that process. Any L&D marketing plan therefore needs to clarify:

- how the L&D function fits into the organisation's value chain and serves the organisation's vision and goals

- how L&D specialists will work with internal customers in order to identify their L&D needs, relate them to overall business needs, and agree on how best to respond to them

- how the L&D function will offer the most appropriate and cost-effective L&D products, services and processes for the organisation

- how L&D plans will be collaboratively implemented, monitored and evaluated across the organisation.

The success of marketing depends significantly on having an accurate, up-to-date and appropriate information system, but that is essential for far more than marketing purposes alone. A good database will capture the organisation's skills base, aid the identification of training and learning needs, supply evidence of L&D activity, provide details of when, where, why, for whom and for what purposes that activity has been undertaken, and act as a centralised source of up-to-date knowledge, experience, practices and ideas. It should also make clear what links are being made with other HR policies and practices.

In a multi-site organisation, L&D records will probably be kept at each site but there must also be a centralised data base, and with progress in information and communication technology, the potential tensions between two systems should be much reduced. Failure to adequately reconcile the local with the central in the interests of a unified system can give rise to any or all of the following problems:

- L&D activity across the organisation will not be adequately identified and monitored, leading to the possibility of irrelevant, costly, or needlessly duplicated initiatives.

- There will be no integration of L&D and personnel records held in different parts of the organisation, thus hampering achievement of consistency of overall human resource policy-making.

- There will be insufficient attention to core organisation-wide L&D needs.

- The organisation will lack adequate evidence to show that all its L&D activity is legally compliant and ethical.

- There will be no central store of knowledge to show outcomes of L&D activity initiatives across the organisation, and this will impair the quality of the L&D planning process.

- Individuals' records of training (and associated data on any problems in their performance during or after training) may get lost when they move from one part of the organisation to another, or from one organisational level to another.

- There will be a lack of coherent organisational policies on qualification structures, career and succession planning.

The importance of an L&D database that is fit for purpose and that meshes well with wider HR information systems cannot be overemphasised. In its report into the 1997 rail crash in Southall in which seven people lost their lives, the Health and Safety Commission extensively criticised the training function. One of the most disturbing deficiencies that the report highlighted was a failure to maintain and pass on drivers' records, so that key performance errors which training should have remedied were not always identified. Another was a 'surprising' absence of any unified record system (Cooper 2000b). Despite the Commission's many recommendations, that 'surprising absence' evidently continued, since in subsequent major train crashes in England (notably Paddington) similar training records failures were identified.

AN L&D RESOURCE MANAGEMENT CYCLE

To conclude this section on leading and managing an L&D function, in Figure 14 I have adapted the learning cycle first produced by Kolb *et al* (1974) to produce a resource management process for the L&D function.

FIGURE 14 The cycle of L&D resource management

Put into practice

Implement L&D plans, monitoring and evaluating their costs, including costs of recording and marketing them. Use simple and effective costing methods. Agree well in advance who is to be responsible for identifying, recording and monitoring costs, and what budgetary and costing systems are to be used.

Generate creative options and make decisions

Work with business partners to generate creative options in order to decide on the most effective and efficient way of choosing and using L&D resources. Use benchmarking and best practice to identify types of resources, financial management and record systems that could be imported into the organisation to better meet L&D needs, or to improve/expand L&D resources and their utilisation.

Observe and reflect on practice

Look at the current corporate L&D budget (or, if none is available, some equivalent figures that show the costs of running the L&D function and carrying out L&D activity across the organisation). Look also at any unit L&D budgets. Establish what L&D activity is identified, and what it costs. Identify all key tangible and intangible L&D resources available, how and by whom they are being used, recorded and marketed, and at what cost benefit. Improve format and presentation of budgets where this is clearly needed.

Analyse

Analyse this information by reference to key contextual factors in order to establish whether all resources are being used efficiently to meet key L&D needs.

CONCLUSION

You should by now have a broad-based understanding of key issues effecting the organisation and management of the L&D function, and feel confident in tackling the review questions on this chapter that are provided in Appendix 3.

The chapter's four sections have covered the following main ground:

- the nature of the changing structural arrangements evident in many organisations today; some implications for L&D practitioners working in a context where organising and re-organising takes place regularly

- key influences on the ways in which L&D functions are organised in different settings, and various options for its shape; the significance of incorporation into an 'HR three-legged stool' and the threats as well as opportunities that such a move can offer to L&D staff

- two opposite directions in which L&D functions are moving in today's fast-changing and turbulent business environment: some towards further fragmentation and possibly to disintegration, others towards a new kind of integration with real strategic and commercial thrust

- the pressures and opportunities that newer structural forms

for the function are placing on L&D practitioners, who should take the lead in proposing relevant and innovative roles for themselves if they are to move forward; a suggested new typology of L&D roles

- the need for L&D managers to lead and develop as well as manage the function's staff and bind together all who operate under an organisation's L&D brand; the skills this requires both in the leadership and management of people and in the management of financial, material and reputational resources; an L&D resource management cycle.

EXLPORE FURTHER

FURTHER INFORMATION SOURCES

Hayes, A. (2007) *Training: The qualifications that count*. 6 August. Online article available at http://www.trainingzone. co.uk/cgi-bin/item.cgi?id=171238 [accessed 21 August 2008]

Wilson, J. P. (ed.) (1999) *Human Resource Development: Learning and training for individuals and organizations*. London: Kogan Page. Chapters 22 and 23 – managing and marketing the HRD function

Reid, M. A., Barrington, H. and Brown, M. (2004) *Human Resource Development: Beyond training interventions*, 3rd edition. London: CIPD. Chapter 6: The HRD function

CIPD podcast, 4 December 2007. *The changing face of the HR function*. Available online at: http://www.cipd.co.uk/podcasts [accessed 4 August 2008]

http://www.cipd.co.uk/subjects/ training/general/cstngtrain. htm?IsSrchRes=1 [accessed 18 July 2008]. CIPD factsheet on how to calculate the cost of developing and delivering training programmes

Websites with information on L&D national occupational standards, professional standards, qualifications and awarding bodies:

http://www.ento.co.uk/ standards/landd/index.php/ [accessed 18 July 2008]. Website for the national L&D occupational standards and qualification structure

http://www.cipd.co.uk/mandq/ standards/prac/sgpd/ [accessed 18 July 2008]. Website for the Chartered Institute of Personnel and Development's professional standards.

http//www.itol.org/ [accessed 17 July 2008]. Website of the Institute of Training and Occupational Learning

http://www.capita-ld.co.uk/ training-courses/Institute+of+ Training+and+Organisational+L earning.htm/ [accessed 17 July 2008]. Website of the Institute of Training and Organisational Learning

http://www.trainingfoundation. com/ [accessed 1 August 2008]. Website of the Training Foundation

CHAPTER 12

Producing and Implementing L&D Strategy

INTRODUCTION

Strategy identifies the route to be taken over a defined timescale in reaching a specified goal. In the CIPD's 2008 annual L&D Survey respondents were asked how L&D could best make its contribution to organisational effectiveness in the future. The highest proportion of respondents by far – 35% – identified 'a clear L&D strategy aligned to business needs/strategy/organisational development' (Sloman 2008b). The purpose of this chapter is to encourage reflection on strategy as a field of research and practice, and to explore ways of ensuring that L&D activity in an organisation has a strategic orientation, underpinned by a sound planning process.

It may seem perverse that a chapter about such a vital subject should be one of the shortest in the book. The reason is simple: as I explained in the Preface 'being strategic' in HR terms means using professional expertise, business understanding and a proactive approach to help managers and other employees to solve major current problems and to prepare for future challenges. In that sense the entire book so far has had a strategic focus, so much of this chapter's content is either a drawing together or an expansion of issues discussed earlier at different points. Many readers are perhaps unlikely to be in a position yet to help develop corporate L&D strategy for their organisations. For those who are, there are more specialised texts to guide them in tasks whose complexity I can only briefly outline here. All, however, should be able to look critically at corporate business and HR strategies that frame their work in order to understand how those have been developed, and with what impact and L&D implications at their organisational level. That rationale explains the content of this chapter.

The first of the four sections introduces some key research findings relating to the strategic integration of L&D activity, and the second explores their practical implications.

The third focuses on ways of enhancing the strategy process, again drawing on research evidence. The chapter concludes with lessons for HR/L&D professionals and an illustrative case study.

ISSUES OF INTEGRATION

PROBLEMS IN ACHIEVING 'FIT'

It is a classic principle in the HR literature that any HR strategy should achieve horizontal and vertical integration. Applied to L&D strategy this means

- *horizontal integration* – integrating L&D activity with other HR practices so that there is consistency across the whole HR area (as shown in Figure 2 in Chapter 1), with all its activity supporting HR goals

- *vertical integration* – integrating L&D strategy with business strategy at corporate and business unit levels and aiding performance management, learning and development at operational and individual levels.

Table 15 provides a picture of a fully integrated L&D function.

The table is, of course, an idealised picture. The integrating principles are clear but the practice is difficult and sometimes the task proves impossible. There has been much discussion about the problems of integration (also referred to as 'alignment' or 'fit') in the HR literature, notably by Karen Legge (1995). The following points indicate the challenges involved for an L&D function.

Horizontal integration

- When adjustments or changes are needed to any aspect of L&D practices, consequent adjustments need to be made to other HR practices. Likewise L&D activity should give continuing support to HR practices so that there is overall consistency. But if those practices are of poor quality, irrelevant or failing to motivate employees, to align L&D activity with them will only compound those problems and put barriers in the way of L&D's effectiveness.

- Smooth integration of L&D with other HR practices is in any case rare. We saw in the previous chapter the pessimistic observations of Stewart and Harris (2003) following their study of an HR function in local government in the UK. Hirsh and Tamkin's (2005) case-based research identified a similar problem.

TABLE 15 Building L&D into the business

Strategic level	L&D's strategic focus is on	L&D must	Crucial processes for L&D	L&D specialist/ manager needs to
1 Corporate	• formulating L&D mission, goals and strategy to achieve corporate goals • influencing and developing strategic thinking and planning	• 'fit' with wider HR strategy • be aligned with corporate strategy • help to secure appropriate balance between corporate goals for survival and for advancement • produce L&D strategy that is capable of implementation at level 2	• collaboratively developing mission and goals for L&D • strategic planning and thinking • influencing key stakeholders • adding value through L&D activity	• have board-level position/access and skills • be proactive as well as reactive • have deep knowledge of competitive environment • fully understand the value chain and strategic assets of the business • speak the language and logic of the business • work in business partnerships
2 Business unit/ managerial	• developing L&D policies and systems in line with strategic needs of the business unit • ensuring achievement of business targets • influencing and developing strategic thinking, organisational capacity and human capability	• 'fit' with wider HR policies and systems • be aligned with business unit policy • have a clear plan within the overall business plan, with agreed evaluation measures • ensure feedback on policies to level 1	• working with HR and business unit managers to produce policies and plans for acquisition, retention, growth/redeployment of workforce • developing key performance indicators • strategic thinking and business planning • adding value through L&D activity	• work in business partnership with managers and others • have collaborative relationships with other HR specialists • have deep knowledge of competitive environment of company and of business units • fully understand how strategic assets can be developed • speak the language and logic of the business units
3 Operational	• ensuring that individual and team performance targets are met • improving acquisition, quality and motivation of people for the business	• adapt to the needs of the business and the needs and aspirations of people • ensure that L&D activity is expertly carried out and appropriately evaluated • ensure feedback of outcomes to level 2	• working with teams and individuals to implement business plans for L&D • appraisal, personal development planning to achieve targets and improve core competencies and capabilities	• work in partnership with internal and external stakeholders • have effective and efficient systems and procedures • have a deep knowledge of the culture of the workforce • be expert and continuously self-developing

They found that many HR strategies deal largely with HR processes rather than with workforce capability. It requires a shared base of knowledge about learning needs identified at individual and team level in order to adequately link workforce planning and capability issues and then align both with business needs. They found that often HR business partners could not be relied on to understand the learning needs of the business. In consequence the shared knowledge base was lacking and the necessary linkage between HR strategy and training and development strategy tended to be weak (Hirsh and Tamkin 2005).

- Such cases indicate lack of joined-up thinking in the HR area and explain L&D's frequent status as poor relation in the HR family. Yet if there is no attempt at horizontal integration the threats to the L&D function are obvious: silo mentalities, fragmented activity and a consequent failure to add value either to the business or to individuals.

- In some organisations L&D is a standalone function in the business. How then can it be horizontally aligned? In such cases – not uncommon in smaller firms – the L&D professional (who may be an HR generalist or an L&D consultant rather than an in-house L&D specialist) should make every attempt to convince the organisation's management of the need for first priority to be given to establishing a framework of HR policy and action. The professional should be able to offer advice on what that framework might be and to play a leading role in its implementation.

Vertical integration

- The command to 'align L&D strategy with business strategy' begs some awkward questions about the type of strategy in mind: corporate or divisional? Short- or long-term? Of high quality, or merely any strategy – good or bad – that is formally in place at the time? Answers to those questions must be found before taking any steps to align L&D activity with business strategy, or the last state will be worse than the first. Again, though, that is easier said than done and explains why L&D activity can often fail to add value even when it is vertically integrated.

- Vertical integration requires strong L&D business partnerships, yet from evidence cited in the previous chapter it seems that relatively few HR professionals (including those in the L&D field) are as yet occupying genuinely strategic partner roles.

- As Chapter 11 also showed, barriers to effective business partnership with line management often arise because of constraints and ambiguities inherent in the HR function's structure. The way in which HR activity as a whole is organised in the business can significantly aid or hinder L&D activity from being aligned effectively with the organisation's strategic goals.

TIGHT AND LOOSE COUPLING WITH BUSINESS STRATEGY

HR strategy's purpose is to provide a framework for applying people management and development practices to achieve business outcomes. Given the difficulties involved in achieving 'fit' in the L&D field, what is the way forward? Research findings suggest that there are two different approaches in use: tight and loose coupling.

The tight-coupled approach

Tight-coupled models involved a close interconnection between different types of business strategy and organisational structure on the one hand, and of HR activity on the other. The type and content of selection, appraisal, reward and developmental policies should, in this view, follow the specific type of business strategy and organisational structure.

So-called 'hard' tight-coupled models come predominantly from the Michigan School of Business management theory in the USA. The approach advocated by HR writers such as Galbraith and Nathanson (1978) and Fombrun, Tichy and Devanna (1984) appeals through its surface rationality and its practical detail. However, it depends for its success on a relevant, clear and detailed business strategy that is agreed by all stakeholders, that remains fairly stable through time, and that consistently guides action throughout the organisation. In today's fast-moving and complex business world such conditions are increasingly unlikely to be present. Even where strategy is appropriate and has the commitment of most of the parties for much of the time, many contingencies can throw it out of line – together with any HR strategies that are tied to its coat-tails.

The loose-coupled approach

Chris Hendry (1995) urged HR professionals to develop a deep knowledge of the business, its attributes and its environment, and to work with management on flexible HR strategies that best fit current needs and can be quickly adapted to meet new contingencies. This 'loose-coupled' approach relies on HR practitioners, working in business partnerships, to operate pragmatically. They must produce HR plans for business units that respond to their needs while being in line with the overall goals and drivers of the business rather than lining up with every element of business strategy.

The aim of loose-coupling is to expand organisational capacity through well-contextualised practices. Such capacity is produced by organisational structure and culture, routines and procedures, budgetary controls and corrective actions, business processes and organisational networks. Research has shown that it can be enhanced by many HR practices, especially in the L&D field (Huselid 1995; Patterson *et al* 1997; Terry and Purcell 1997; Scarbrough and Swan 1999; Guest and King 2001). However, loose-coupling calls for great skill. I have described in Chapter 6 the differing ways in which Tesco's corporate HR policy and strategy was implemented in four of its stores, in some cases producing effective loose-coupling, in others not. The HR practices that worked best were flexible and had a robust link with the 'Big Idea' and its values. They were implemented by front-line managers who gave their teams significant opportunity to use the kind of discretionary behaviour in their jobs that would improve store performance (Purcell *et al* 2003: 28–31). Where that discretion is not delegated, or is not used to the benefit of the business, even the best HR strategies will come unstuck at business unit level.

The HR 'three-legged stool' described in Chapter 11 represents an attempt to organise HR (including L&D) in ways that achieve a mix of tight- and loose-coupling. I discussed there some of its successes and failures. The CIPD has produced a practical tool to help users understand the strategy process in their organisations and to build or implement HR strategy at their organisational level. The tool first takes the user through what are described as the main 'building blocks' in the strategy process. It then helps the user to diagnose HR priorities, develop an appropriate HR strategy, and identify ways to implement it (CIPD 2005e)

REFLECTION

Reflecting on what you know about HR strategy in your organisation (or one with which you are familiar), do you think it is linked strongly or weakly to the business? And on what evidence are you relying to inform your assessment? Downloading and using the CIPD's practical tool will provide you with a structured approach to this **Reflection** (*http://www.cipd.co.uk/ subjects/corpstrtgy/general/tools.htm* [accessed 31 July 2008]).

PUTTING THEORY INTO PRACTICE

ACHIEVING L&D STRATEGIC INTEGRATION

Chapter 11 cited research into the changing HR function that has highlighted the importance for HR and L&D of moving from being merely a service provider to occupying a full business partner role. The CIPD has produced another online practical tool to help L&D practitioners understand the alignment process and to strategically integrate their activity at no matter what organisational level they are working (CIPD 2008f). It provides a structured approach to ensuring that L&D activities in an organisation are aligned with the organisation's strategic goals. It shows users how to:

- examine the strategic priorities of their organisations

- assess the extent to which current L&D processes are focused on what is important for organisational success

- assess the extent to which internal alignment of learning processes is achieved, through engaging in constructive dialogue with a range of organisational stakeholders

- identify the extent to which there may be skill gaps that need to be addressed by those who take responsibility for L&D in their organisations

- take forward key actions to enhance L&D practice relating to alignment.

LIMITATIONS OF TEXTBOOK APPROACHES

The logic of the practical tools and textbook approaches to L&D strategic integration is clear. Typically it involves six stages, summarised in Table 16.

The systematic, structured approach shown in Table 16 can work in practice, and Figure 15 provides one illustration of this. It outlines the system used at a large acute hospitals trust during the 1990s. I have called it Wesdale Trust, although that is not its real name.

However the scenario shown in Table 16 and Figure 15 is exceptionally difficult to achieve. It depends on HR/L&D strategy being given full support by top management, on robust HR/L&D business partnerships with leaders and managers, on high-quality strategic thinking, and on an expert HR/L&D service. It also relies on a relatively stable business environment. In many organisations such an advantageous situation simply does not exist. It is relevant here to add that at Wesdale Trust fundamental problems whose seeds were sown in the 1990s subsequently developed. They were caused by a combination of flawed strategic and financial management of the trust, the impact of the private finance initiative on beds and services, and external community, political and regional planning issues. HR strategy became increasingly difficult to hold in place and ultimately Wesdale was forced to merge with another trust, further complicating its problems and leading to radical staffing and policy changes across the whole new organisation.

Often an ineffective alignment of HR (and L&D) with the business is the result of a naïve understanding by its professionals of their organisation's strategy process. I have already mentioned in Chapter 7 Wright *et al*'s 2004 survey of HR professionals responsible for corporate HR strategies in nine multinational companies. It is worth drawing attention to their research again here because it produced disturbing findings about the mindsets and cognitions that can govern HR decision-making. All respondents were in high-profile positions in organisations where the importance of effective people management was well understood. They were actively attempting to integrate their HR activities to support the business, yet in formulating strategy the majority started with HR and worked outwards to link to the business, an approach the authors saw as typifying the 'inside-out mindset that continues to plague many HR organizations' (Wright *et al* 2004: 43). Many had no deep, formal knowledge of the competitive issues facing their organisations, and their HR strategies appeared to be the product of

TABLE 16 The textbook approach to L&D strategy and plan

---

1 Allocate responsibility for L&D strategy-development
Decide who is going to be involved in producing the strategy and in drawing up plans for its implementation in the organisation. The person or group responsible then carries out the tasks below.

2 Clarify organisational mission
Identify the espoused purpose of the organisation and its long-term goals.

3 Explore core organisational identity and values
Carry out internal and external stakeholder analysis to clarify:

- the organisation's identity/brand as it seems to be perceived by employees and external stakeholders
- its vision and values, and whether or not they are shared across the organisation. Values espoused at the top but not reflected in actions and behaviours in the organisation (whether at the top itself or elsewhere) will hinder the implementation of any strategy that professes to be based on those values
- the basic needs it exists to meet, its ultimate clients and any current barriers preventing it from meeting those needs
- anything that makes the L&D function distinctive in the organisation, either in positive or negative ways.

4 Carry out SWOT or PESTLE analysis to identify the strategic issues facing the organisation
Draw on professional and business knowledge to analyse the above data in order to diagnose the strategic issues faced by the organisation. Then prioritise these, for example in terms of:

- issues to keep an eye on for the future – they do not need immediate action but may throw up problems or opportunities at some later point in time
- issues that the organisation can handle within its ongoing plans and activity and so need no new strategies to tackle them
- issues that are relevant to the L&D area – these will provide the frame for the next step.

5 Agree an L&D strategy
Agree on L&D goals and strategy to add value to the organisation as well as to employees. Long-term goals for the function should be set, and then a strategy for the shorter term to guide progress towards them. ('Long' and 'shorter' are relative terms. For a small firm 'long term' may only be a couple of years, for a large organisation considerably longer.) This stage involves generating options in order to produce a high-quality and feasible strategy.

6 Produce strategic plan
The plan takes each area outlined in the strategy and identifies what is to be done to convert it into action. It specifies activity, for whom it will apply, the financial, human and material resources it requires, and who will be accountable for its delivery. Often activity is expressed as projects, with project leaders drawn variously from the L&D, HR and line management functions.

'an exercise of standing where they are and reaching out to the business' (*ibid*: 37). The researchers concluded that a 'paradigmatic shift' was vital if the HR executives were to build their HR strategies 'outside-in', from the starting-point of the business.

FIGURE 15 Linking training and development to the strategic and business planning cycle of an acute hospitals trust

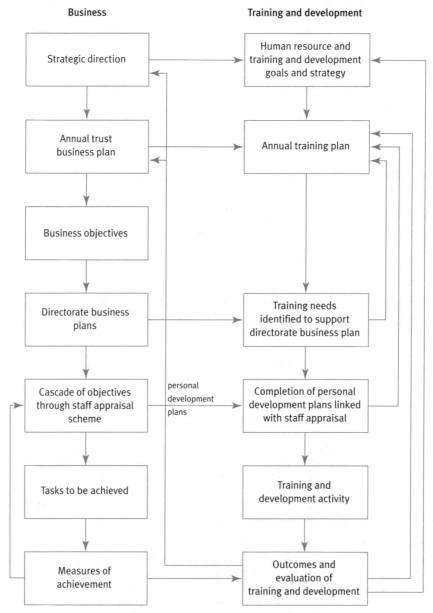

In the UK, the CIPD's 2007 Learning and Development survey (CIPD 2007a) revealed that although about a third of the organisations surveyed involved or consulted their learning, training and development managers at initial strategic planning stages, two thirds only involved them once the strategic decisions had been made. This suggests that senior decision-makers in many, perhaps most, organisations 'simply don't think the views of those in L&D are necessary or valuable when they're developing strategy' (Jennings 2007).

Problems of bounded rationality

To return to the problems associated with the strategic management of the business: the classical view of the strategy process rests on two assumptions:

- that decision-makers have a common purpose and are driven by a shared economic logic when making strategic decisions: all seek to maximise economic rewards and minimise costs for the business

- that decision-makers systematically 'collect and sort information about alternative potential solutions, compare each solution against predetermined criteria to assess degree of fit, arrange solutions in order of preference and make an optimizing choice which they then equally systematically draw up plans to implement' (Miller *et al* 1999: 44).

In reality, as Simon memorably identified (1945), all decision-making is severely limited by the bounded economic rationality of the players involved. In organisational life as more widely decisions are not 'arrived at by a step by step process which is both logical and linear' (Miller *et al* 1999: 44). An organisation is not a unitary system, with the players coming together naturally in pursuit of a common goal. It is a pluralist system, where economic rationality often breaks down in the confusion caused by conflicting interests and by diverse perceptions as to 'what matters here' and how to tackle it.

The concept of bounded rationality does not refer to people behaving irrationally in the broad sense of that word. Quite the reverse: for most of the time, most people are, by their own lights, very logical in their behaviour. What it means is that the reasoning underpinning their behaviour is influenced by many non-economic arguments and by 'human frailties and demands from both within and outside the organization' (Miller *et al* 1999: 45). Some of the factors that militate against a purely 'rational' approach include confused, excessive, incomplete or unreliable data, incompetent processing or communicating of information, pressures of time, human emotions, and differences in individuals' cognitive processes, mental maps and reasoning capacity (Simon 1955; Cyert and March 1963). The decision-making process is further distorted by the power-play that becomes intense the more the issues under discussion are controversial and important for the organisation.

As I have explained in some detail in Chapter 7, the dominant decision-making model for the training profession has long been the systematic training cycle, grounded in an economic logic. In real life, the operation of a bounded rationality often causes that logic to fail as stakeholders' perceptions and needs related to 'what matters here' and how to tackle it come into conflict. Many L&D practitioners cannot resolve such conflict because they lack the necessary understanding of the strategy process and do not possess the necessary business knowledge, political, negotiating and networking skills (Harrison 1996, 1997: 54–63, 2000; Holton III and Naquin 2005; Pfeffer 2005).

The strategic management process is further complicated by the fact that in any organisation some members have the automatic right to sit at the strategy table, others are excluded from it and many have little or no access to or influence over those who make the big strategic decisions that relate to their field – a fate that often typifies L&D professionals' position, even when there is an HR director at board level.

Strategy's 'silent killers'

Following more than a decade of research into US-based companies, Beer and Eisenstat (2000) identified that failure of strategy to achieve its intended outcomes was primarily due to six 'silent killers' – so called because they are rarely publicly acknowledged or explicitly addressed. They fall into three categories (*ibid*: 32–3):

- *Quality of direction*
    - top-down or laissez-faire senior management style
    - unclear strategy and conflicting priorities
    - an ineffective senior management team
- *Quality of learning*
    - poor vertical communication
- *Quality of implementation*
    - poor co-ordination across functions, businesses or borders
    - inadequate skills and development of leaders and managers at all organisational levels.

The killers relate to L&D strategy as much as to any other type. Blocked vertical communication is particularly damaging in its effects on the ability to produce, implement and refine strategy – in short, in the barriers it places in the path of learning. In some of the organisations studied by Beer and Eisenstat strategic planning documents were very detailed about long-term technology trends, customer behaviour and the company's environment, but (*ibid*: 33):

> They failed to communicate downward a coherent story showing why the changing world outside the organization demanded new ways of working together. Employees never heard how the strategy affected priorities nor received any guidelines showing the relative priorities of projects. How could [they decide] which of their activities would be most helpful in making the business successful?

They concluded that poor leadership, teamwork and strategic direction were the key causes of poor-quality strategies and ineffective implementation, not employees' commitment or functional competence.

REFLECTION

Reflecting on the three 'killers' identified under 'Quality of direction', how might these be tackled in an organisation? Beer and Eisenstat (2000) have provided their recommendations for transforming 'killers' into 'capabilities' in their article, which can be downloaded using EBSCO or a similar journal search engine. Other suggestions follow this **Reflection**.

DEVELOPING AN EFFECTIVE STRATEGY PROCESS

THE IMPORTANCE OF PROCESS

Wright *et al* (2004: 45) made six recommendations to tackle the frequent failure of even the most senior HR professionals to achieve the necessary 'outside-in' approach to HR strategy development. Adapted to an L&D context these are as follows:

1   Develop a formal process for involving line managers in the development of L&D strategy.

2   Create formal mechanisms to track developments in the external environment as part of the process (scenario planning is recommended for this purpose).

3   'Begin with the assumption that everything the current L&D function is doing is either wrong or does not exist' (in order to destroy any skilled incompetence and produce fresh insights about how to add value to the business).

4   Identify the key business and HR metrics related to success of the business and ensure that these are understood and used by L&D staff in their work (something that was emphasised in the 'Procon' case in Chapter 8, and that I will explain in further detail in Chapter 14).

5   Develop (or promote) an L&D strategy that uses those metrics to drive L&D activity linked to business outcomes.

6   Remember that any strategy is a process, not a document, intervention, or event.

That final point has been explained in Chapter 11 and cannot be overemphasised here. In classic textbook approaches to HR/L&D strategy the main discussion tends to be of strategy as a product, with the result that the main emphasis is on how to perform the functional tasks involved in developing that product. Yet in over 10 years of research into business strategy in US organisations Beer and Eisenstat, like Wright *et al* and many other earlier and subsequent researchers, found that the 'killers' in the strategy arena are overwhelmingly to do with the human processes involved in 'strategising'.

ELEMENTS OF THE STRATEGY PROCESS

A useful notion of the strategy process is to understand it as having four interacting elements or stages: situation analysis, strategic thinking, strategic decision-making and strategic planning (Day 1990).

The strategy group

Understood in this way, the starting-point for developing L&D strategy should still be that shown in Table 16, but the priority should be to choose as members of the strategy team those who can be relied on to produce a high quality of strategic thinking, analysis and decision-making rather than selection determined by organisational rank and status. Ginsberg (1994) emphasised the importance of bringing to the strategy table a heterogeneous group – that is to say, people drawn from a wide variety of backgrounds, ideally from outside as well as from within the organisation and from different organisational levels. Beer and Eisenstat (2000) found that a major problem in strategy development was its domination by leaders and others in the organisation who brought with them outdated assumptions, values and skills formed in their company's traditional business – in other words a homogenous group comprising individuals with like minds, like status, like experience and like views of the business and its environment.

In smaller organisations there may be only a single individual advising top management on L&D strategy – not necessarily an L&D specialist and sometimes an externally-sourced individual or agency (Investors in People and Train to Gain offer relevant services, as I have explained in Chapter 2). In larger organisations the core group will probably be small, perhaps consisting of the head of L&D services and the HR director or a similar arrangement. Whoever carries the strategy responsibility, they should have proven ability and experience to 'think outside the box' in order to convincingly challenge accepted views and values, generate innovative options, and counteract any damaging influence on strategy and plans for its implementation of the kind of 'skilled incompetence' that the Northern Rock case in Chapter 5 illustrated.

Situation analysis and strategic thinking

Situation analysis involves SWOT, PESTLE or similar analysis, clarifying organisational mission, identifying its current strategic priorities, and establishing the current L&D investment, its purpose and the value it is adding to the business. High-level *strategic thinking* is then needed to generate strategic options for the L&D function before choosing the optimum strategy to adopt for the time-frame agreed. A heterogeneous group of lateral thinkers will bring the necessary variety of perspectives to these stages of the strategy process.

Scenario planning has proven value here. Its purpose is to confront uncertainty by first producing as clear an understanding as possible of the forces likely to shape the organisation's (and the L&D function's) environment in the future, and then by generating a variety of strongly contrasting options for a way forward for both, over the required time-frame. The following case example outlines how it operates.

CASE EXAMPLE

SCENARIO PLANNING TO AID THE STRATEGY PROCESS

Scenario planning involves challenging customary patterns of thinking and logic in order to imagine innovative routes forward. For it to work, the members of the strategy group must be drawn (or be able to draw on) a wide social and knowledge network in order to bring varying and sufficiently sharply contrasting mindsets and bodies of knowledge to bear on both analysis and thinking. By considering more information and a broader range of viewpoints than a homogenous group would do, its members are more likely to define their business and L&D environment comprehensively and creatively, generate lateral thinking and produce a set of clearly differentiated choices for future paths (Ginsberg 1994). Through a thorough exploration of these multiple perspectives, a strategy and plan for L&D can be agreed that has a built-in adaptability to future contingencies and sufficient loose-coupling from current business strategy.

Scenario planning has another value: in developing strategic thinking and planning skills at business unit level. It is used for both purposes at BUPA, where it has proved particularly effective in developing operational managers, especially those who have risen through the ranks because they are good at delivering in the short term, and now need to bring a longer-term perspective to their work and planning (Arkin 2007).

Despite this double value, Peter Reilly (cited in Arkin 2007: 27) in his work as director for HR research and consultancy at the Institute for Employment Studies found little evidence of its use in the HR world. He blames this largely on the decentralisation of much HR work to individual business units and the loss of most HR planning specialists through downsizing during the 1990s. The result has been that most of such units are preoccupied with short-term thinking and rarely consider what their future workforce requirements might be – the very problem that BUPA has found scenario planning well equipped to tackle (Ibid).

Strategic decision-making and planning

Strategic decision-making requires choice of the strategy to be taken, agreement on its specific objectives, and determination of the resource requirements if these are to be achieved. Once again a heterogeneous group is more likely than a homogenous group to be effective here, because it will be more likely to rely on negotiation, compromise and the reaching of consensus in decision-making. It will also tend to encourage greater use of monitoring of strategy's progress once it is implemented, and of re-evaluation as each strategic milestone is reached.

Strategic planning is the final and arguably the most crucial stage of the strategy process. Terry Leay, Tesco's chief executive, commenting on reasons for the store's astonishing success, has explained (Rankine 2004):

> We don't stand out by our strategy. It's the execution that has been better.

Effective execution is the hallmark of any sound L&D strategy, and it is here that so many strategies fall apart. One commentator, reviewing HR research findings, concluded that there is now a greatly increased awareness in businesses about the difference that good people management could make but that (Baron 2000: 31):

> It appears that we do not yet know enough about translating strategic intentions into implementation and action, or why a particular course of action might prove successful in one situation but not in another.

Many potential implementation problems should have been picked up at previous stages of the strategy process, especially if scenario planning has been used. If they have been intelligently debated then, there is a far better chance at this point that a sound L&D plan will be developed. However, if the strategy on which L&D implementation plans are based is either misunderstood or unsupported by employees, those plans will fail.

Maitland (2007) observed that although much research links high levels of employee engagement to superior business performance, most of it focuses on the extent to which employees are affectively engaged (that is, are proud of their company). Yet it is equally important to assess their cognitive engagement – whether they support the company's strategy and the direction it is taking. One lesson here is that at the planning stage there must be certainty that the strategy for which implementation plans are being drawn up will gain cognitive engagement. The planning process should provide the opportunity before any plans are finalised to reflect on the proposed strategy once more, reviewing all the evidence available about its likely reception by the workforce and any clear barriers to its success. Altering the route at this point is far better than risking failure of the whole journey.

Another lesson is that once plans are put into action there must be monitoring to track progress so that no serious disconnection occurs between strategy's intent and its realisation. I mentioned in Chapter 1 that HR researchers often find a 'major disconnect' between the espoused and the real. Sometimes, this can be because claimed HR 'strategies' are no more than 'reconstructions after the fact': action has preceded thought rather than followed it, and what are now on record as 'strategies' were actually little more than accidents (Pettigrew *et al* 2002b: 12). More often, though, it is due either to unrealistic strategies or to imperfect planning of their implementation.

REFLECTION

An organisation's L&D manager complains that although she produces drafts for an L&D strategy that fully supports business goals and strategy, and provides logical arguments to underpin her proposals, she still doesn't seem to be a strategic player in the organisation and often finds herself having to try to implement an L&D strategy which she finds unsatisfactory. 'Where am I failing and what should I do?' she asks you.

Reflecting on research evidence and other material in the chapter so far, what advice would you give her?

L&D STRATEGISING: LESSONS FOR THE PROFESSIONALS

MOVING FORWARD

It should by now be clear that many of the problems related to L&D strategy and its implementation are built into the strategy process. Many, however, could be avoided by a better relationship between HR professionals and front-line managers whose actions have such a direct effect on the skills, motivation and discretionary behaviour of employees. What, then, should those professionals do (whether or not they are L&D specialists) to ensure that there is a sound, feasible and engaging L&D strategy to guide L&D activity in their organisations?

- Analyse, diagnose, produce contextualised goals and plans, and work with business partners in setting a clear path for L&D as a key business process. A pragmatic approach is essential too. Where stakeholder interests vary widely HR professionals should identify at the start the likely aids and barriers to effective collaboration. They must either possess or have access to the L&D expertise as well as the business knowledge, the creativity, political and interpersonal skills to promote and help to implement value-adding L&D strategy.

- Be proactive and achieve excellence in L&D services, products and processes. Build a springboard for increasing credibility and political power in the business at all organisational levels by developing a proven record of achievement that is rooted in a real knowledge of the business, the big issues that confront it, and strong partnerships with those who manage it.

- Keep in touch with strategy on the ground. Throughout the organisation people's perceptions, actions and influence related to L&D strategy will vary, sometimes widely. Such variations will affect its implementation in each workplace. Whether it is HR generalists or L&D specialists who are responsible for ensuring successful implementation they must regularly communicate L&D strategy's purpose, monitor the progress of L&D plans and help to train, motivate and support front-line managers who carry L&D roles.

- Treat strategy as a process, not a product. Much strategy emerges in an ongoing manner from individual and collective learning and from new threats and opportunities arising for the business. Such contingencies will require adjustments, sometimes radical, to be made to the strategic route originally agreed. Occasionally they will mean it has to be abandoned. As we saw in Chapter 11, in today's business environment a continuous strategising process makes more sense that a reliance on strategy and plans as products fixed at one point in time and resistant to change thereafter.

The final case in this chapter concerns an innovative approach that combines an effective mix of tight- and loose-coupled L&D strategic integration. It illustrates, too, an approach to L&D in the business that has been directly shaped by the way in which the umbrella HR function is structured.

CASE EXAMPLE

LEARNING AND DEVELOPMENT: A STRATEGIC FUNCTION AT WESTPAC BANK, NEW ZEALAND

The L&D centre of expertise

Westpac is New Zealand's largest bank, and was launched as a brand in 1996 from a merger of Westpac and Trust banks to form WestpacTrust, later changed to Westpac. The two banks' high-cost, fragmented and heavily staffed training units were combined and restructured to create what was named the 'Development Centre'. It was to be run as a business adding strategic value to the bank, and in effect was an L&D centre of expertise. This called for a major shift in attitudes throughout the company from regarding learning as something gained by going on a course to understanding it as an integral part of work, with the crucial questions for all employees to be: 'How and where do we learn, and how does this support my business objectives?'

By 2000 most of the Centre's products and services were being promoted through, or used by, HR portfolio managers and their teams of HR consultants. They worked with line managers to whom many routine responsibilities had been devolved. The Centre held strategic accountability for learning and training, with agreed criteria against which to measure itself including spend per employee, cost per training day and goals for training delivery through formal and informal learning. Benchmarking was used to establish these goals and to guide the creation of an infrastructure for training administration.

In the early days of the merged organisation the Centre played a vital role in aiding the change process and creating a sense of direction for employees. A range of planning and monitoring tools helped people to understand how their roles had changed, what skills they had and what they needed, and how to track the progress of their learning and development.

Through time new L&D standards were produced to reinforce the Centre's brand and ensure that its staff provided excellence, innovation and a coherent approach in their service to its customers. The Centre was customer-facing in two senses: providing a service for internal customers, and helping them to provide an enhanced service to the bank's external customers.

L&D strategising

The Centre was linked to the business at corporate strategic level so that the bank could develop the corporate and individual capabilities required to achieve the WestpacTrust vision of 'a great New Zealand company'. The link was provided by a 'virtual' strategic learning advisory team (SLAT) that was formed as a decision-making and policy body. Its brief was to look at issues in the context of the wider organisation and to give key stakeholders, mostly executives and senior managers, the opportunity and vehicle to contribute to the strategic direction of learning and training. SLAT's membership changed through time to deal with specific strategic issues that required a corporate perspective and response.

SLAT helped the Centre to develop strategic partnerships with other key business functions including strategic planning and finance so that it could play its part in the bank's decision-making

processes as well as creating performance support tools for staff. This led to better forecasting of corporate capability requirements, smoother implementation of changes in products or procedures, and better integration of training into mainstream business decisions, projects and processes.

L&D planning

L&D planning and monitoring was informed by a computerised system feeding into the HR information system, downloading into a central bank system where financial information could be added. This enabled the Centre to contribute to balanced scorecard measurement and reporting. An insourcing policy was formed with key suppliers that in effect enlisted them as part of the bank's development team. This ensured better management of staff costs, access to a unique range of skills, and access also to new knowledge from around the world that led to innovative learning processes and products.

Ultimately the Centre was negotiating and monitoring all supplier agreements and working with business unit heads to identify how to share training staff, resources and information to reduce duplication and costs. A universal 'training estimator tool' was produced to enable a broad-brush preview of training requirements that could be updated every six months. This linked to the bank's performance management framework, and also linked skills requirements to development solutions.

Sources: Simmons, C. and Valentine, E. (2000); the company's website at: *http://westpac.co.nz* [accessed 25 September 2004]

This case example shows how L&D can be linked to the business through a type of HR three-legged stool structure where HR business partners, supported by an L&D centre of expertise, achieve vertical 'fit' of L&D at business unit level. The centre is an influential strategic player at corporate level, also forming alliances with external agencies.

Such an approach relies on HR professionals being fully versed in all the core fields of HR and possessing a deep understanding of their organisation, the big strategic issues it faces and key learning needs at all organisational levels. It requires HR generalists to work closely with L&D specialists and with heads of business units, while L&D specialists must have the high-level business knowledge and credibility, the specialist expertise and the consultancy skills needed to operate a complex internal and external partnership network. This is a demanding set of requirements and I have already referred in the chapter to some of the research evidence indicating that few HR or L&D practitioners as yet have the ability to meet such challenges. When that ability is present, cases like Westpac and Procon Manufacturing in Chapter 8 demonstrate the added value that strategically-oriented L&D activity can achieve for the business and for its employees.

CONCLUSION

By now you should have a sound general understanding of different ways in which a strategy and strategic plan for an organisation can be produced and implemented, together with barriers and aids to the strategy and planning processes. You should also feel confident in tackling the review questions contained in Appendix 3.

The main themes in this four-section chapter have concerned:

- the pressures on HR and L&D functions in today's business environment which make it more essential than ever for their professionals to be able to link their activity to business strategy and to convince stakeholders of its value

- problems surrounding horizontal and vertical alignment of L&D strategy;

tight- and loose-coupled approaches to improving 'fit'

- textbook approaches to achieving L&D's strategic integration and their practical limitations – weak links between L&D and other HR functions, lack of 'outside-in' strategic thinking, bounded rationality and six 'silent killers' of strategy

- research evidence suggesting how to improve the strategy process; the gap between strategy and its implementation and problems of the HR profession in tackling this

- four practical suggestions to help L&D professionals ensure effective and continuous L&D strategising in their organisations; case example of an innovative L&D function.

EXLPORE FURTHER

FURTHER INFORMATION SOURCES

Hirsh, W. and Tamkin, P. (2005) *Planning Training for Your Business*. Institute of Employment Studies, Report 422. London: IES. Informative online article also available at http://www.employment-studies.co.uk:80/pubs/summary.php?id=422 [accessed 4 August 2008]

Mayo A. (2004) *Creating a Learning and Development Strategy: The HR partner's guide to developing people*, 2nd edition. London: CIPD.

http://www.idea.gov.uk/idk/core/page.do?pageId=5676619 [accessed 29 July 2008]. Local authority website for those producing HR strategies for workforce development linked to key national targets. A common approach places heavy reliance on working in partnership and using scenario planning. Note especially East Riding of Yorkshire's case study.

CHAPTER 13

Developing L&D Business Partnerships

INTRODUCTION

The purpose of this chapter is to explore the concept of 'business partnership' applied to L&D professionals, and to examine what is involved in its practice.

Since 1987 when Dave Ulrich first used it in a strategic HR context the term 'business partner' has come into widespread use but it has now drifted across so many levels and types of work that its meaning has become almost lost. In the Ministry of Defence, for example, there are at least three categories of HR business partner: those who cover a whole business unit or area and support its leadership team; specialist experts, including L&D, providing similar support; and those carrying out operational or administrative work that 'can't easily be swept up into shared services' (Arkin 2007b: 24). While this may be in line with Ulrich's more recent description of business partnership as an overriding feature of all the key roles that HR professionals play in organisations (*ibid*: 27), in practice it can cause considerable role ambiguity.

The first of the chapter's four sections explores issues to do with L&D business partnerships, using the metaphor of the game and the implications for L&D practitioners of playing 'on side'. The second section moves to the metaphor of the dance to examine various forms of learning partnership, and the third discusses issues of power, politics and ethics in partnerships. The final section incorporates a case study to illustrate good practice in L&D partnerships that cross the organisation's boundaries.

PARTNERSHIP: MEANINGS AND METAPHORS

HR 'PARTNERSHIPS': A CRITICAL VIEW

Collaborative capability is essential to an organisation's effective functioning in an environment characterised by structural forms that lay stress on co-operative arrangements, and in work environments that increasingly rely on teamwork, cross-functional and cross-boundary working. However for some, to apply the business partnership concept in relation to HR work is unacceptable because 'it implies we are working alongside our line management colleagues, but on a separate track, rather than … being an integral part of the business' (quoted in Pickard 2005). A similar concern was expressed in an article written over a decade ago by US authors Beatty and Schneier (1997). They used the metaphor of 'the game' to urge all HR professionals to focus on scoring 'by making things happen', warning that unless they moved from being merely partners in teams supporting business strategy to being proactive in finding ways of adding real value to the business they risked being 'excised through downsizing, delayering, and especially through outsourcing' – a prophecy that has subsequently come true for many.

Finally, some fear that an obsession with strategic business partnership is bringing about 'the shrinking of the employee champion role', leaving vulnerable 'the long-standing ethical agenda at the heart of HR work' (Francis and Keegan 2005) at a time when an increasingly tough economic outlook makes that agenda essential to defend (Moir 2008).

These comments relating to the HR business partnership role provide an essential backcloth to the discussion in this section, which revolves around an unpicking of the definition with which it opened.

REFLECTION

Reflecting on doubts just described about the relevance of the concept of strategic business partnerships for those in HR roles, how far, if at all do you share them – and why?

(You can use the online EBSCO search engine to access both Pickard's and Schneier's articles if you need a fuller explanation of the criticisms.)

SHARING THE RISKS AND BENEFITS

To appreciate the basic meaning of partnership a dictionary definition is revealing (Pearsall and Trumble 1996):

> Partner: a person who shares or takes part with another or others, especially in a business firm with shared risks and profits; a player on the same side in a game; a companion in dancing.

Who in business terms takes the biggest risks in return for some of the biggest gains? In privately owned enterprises the owner-manager carries the main burden of risk and in Chapter 10 we have already seen the dynamic relationship that exists between L&D activity and the direction and lifecycle of small and medium-sized firms. In respect of limited companies the shareholders would argue that they take the major risks and deserve proportionately substantial returns. To this end big shareholders are increasingly using their stake in businesses to influence its strategic direction, and (as seen in Chapter 9) they and other stakeholders are also shaping the ways in which many organisations interpret their corporate social and ethical responsibilities. Although most L&D professionals do not deal directly with shareholders, the latters' influence can directly affect the company's L&D agenda and investment. Often it forces a focus on early payback, to the detriment of all but short-term training for proficiency. This is where the politics of L&D's bottom line frequently begin.

The Government, responsible for protecting the public interest, makes a huge financial investment in the public sector and sets demanding targets in order to secure the benefits it wants to see in return for risking taxpayers' money in this way. Its skills strategy covers all types of organisation and is supported by innumerable funded initiatives, again tied to targets that make clear the benefits to the economy and society at large that are expected to follow that funding. It now seems clear that unless employers invest more heavily of their own accord in what Government considers to be appropriate skills training, some form of legislation will be introduced to achieve that end. Better, then, for L&D professionals to help their organisations to forge voluntary skills partnerships with official agencies that bring benefits to the business than be forced into skills strategies that (on the evidence of the Industrial Training Board system in the 1970s) may for many result in no noticeable increase in workforce proficiency. Chapters 2 and 3 identified ways of promoting such partnership.

Owner-managers, shareholders, the Government – going into the organisation, who else by a similar line of reasoning are L&D business partners? Clearly the directors because they set the goals and strategy for the business and are publicly and legally accountable for its results. Clearly too the managers. They carry the formal responsibility of ensuring that business targets are achieved at their organisational levels, and they receive rewards or penalties in line with the extent to which they discharge that responsibility effectively. It is at this point that the second part of the dictionary definition becomes significant: a player on the same side.

PLAYING THE GAME: STRATEGIC BUSINESS PARTNERSHIPS

I have already referred to Beatty and Schneier's argument (1997) that playing the game as no more than a team member is not enough for HR practitioners to add value to the business. They must 'score wins' as well. To play 'on side' in a business partnership means that the L&D partner needs to:

- aim for the same goals as those of the business. Setting up separate goalposts for L&D is a counterproductive exercise. There must be a clear even if loose-coupled alignment of L&D activity with business strategy

- score wins for the business. L&D practitioners must not just preach 'added value'. They must get results.

The next chapter explains in detail ways of achieving added value. Here, it is more relevant to emphasise the importance of L&D practitioners working with partners to define an agreed set of outcomes for L&D activity to achieve, and then being able to ensure delivery. There are two levels of partnership here: top-level, where the partners are those who sponsor L&D strategy; and middle-level, where the partners are managers and team leaders who have the main responsibility for implementation.

Partnership at the corporate level

A major study (O'Driscoll *et al* 2005, cited by Jennings 2007) found that the IMB Global Chief Executive Officers (CEOs) and their senior managers covered in the survey did not require direct evidence to substantiate their belief in the business value of L&D activity. Effective L&D business partnerships at that level resulted in learning strategies being embedded into business strategies at the outset and L&D professionals being influential in deciding how to implement them. In such partnerships (as was illustrated in the case in Chapter 8) responsibility for successes and failures in achieving expectations is shared, helping to inform future planning. This emphasis on the importance of shared expectations has received further support in CIPD-sponsored research, whose practical implications I will discuss in the next chapter (Anderson 2007). Here, it is sufficient to say that it also is an element in the Institute's L&D Business Partnership model pictured in Figure 16 (CIPD 2006a: 5).

L&D business partnerships

Strategic business partnerships between L&D professionals and senior managers may still be relatively rare but strategically-focused partnerships at middle management level are increasingly expected. Although the L&D role of line managers is rapidly expanding, survey evidence suggests that the bulk of responsibility for determining L&D needs still rests with LD specialists (CIPD 2008a: 12–13). It is therefore essential for those specialists to forge a relationship with the line that produces a shared and accurate perception of needs and priorities for action. The case in Chapter 8 spelt out this message in detail, explaining the many processual skills that are required if the outcomes that the sponsors of L&D strategy want and expect are to be realised.

As I have stressed often in this book, an organisation is a pluralist, not a unitary system, containing many and often conflicting values and interests. The intent behind L&D strategy often fails to translate into effective action because

FIGURE 16 A Learning and Development business partnership model

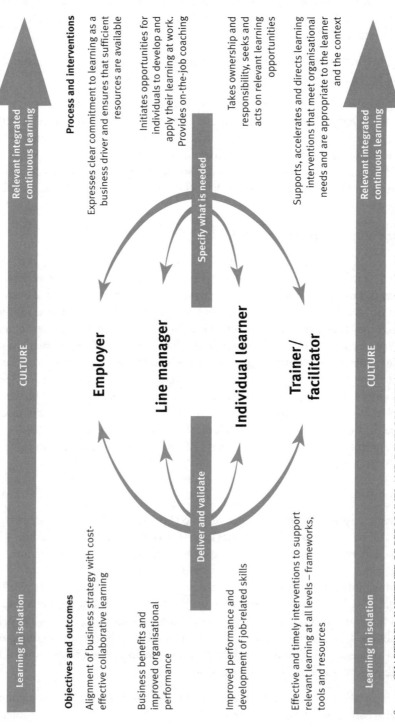

Source: CHARTERED INSTITUTE OF PERSONNEL AND DEVELOPMENT (2006a), p 5. Reproduced with permission.

management is not committed to that strategy, or does not understand it, or lacks the competence to carry it out. Often too there is little organisational incentive or support given to line managers in their L&D roles. Just as worrying are the barriers that can prevent collaboration between L&D specialists and other HR colleagues, since without the support of wider HR policies and practices even the best-designed learning event has little chance of making its desired impact.

To achieve a shared perception of needs in any kind of L&D business partnership thus requires a high level of relational and negotiating skills, and I will discuss these further shortly. Crucially it also demands an evidence-based approach. Pfeffer and Sutton (2006a: 26–7) explain this as basically about developing a mindset that 'embraces learning and enquiry'. Their proposals relate to HR generally (see Chapter 1). Here, I adapt them to fit an L&D context:

- Know what the literature says about L&D practices and use it to design more effective L&D processes and initiatives.

- Base decisions on facts, rather than 'belief, ideology, casual benchmarking, what they want or hope for, what they have done in the past, what they seem to be good or experienced at doing …'.

- Be committed to obtaining data from appropriate sources and to acting on the data even if analysis revealing 'what is really going on here' produces uncomfortable insights that are not what management or the L&D function expect (as was the case, for example, in the pre-programme survey carried out at Procon UK's Birmingham site, outlined in Chapter 8).

- Use data to determine where the greatest improvement opportunities are.

- Run many small L&D experiments to gather information on how well things are working, and to test different learning approaches. Provided that people perceive that they are free to make mistakes, with both success and failure feeding into the learning process, the results can be not only to discover what does or could work best in particular scenarios, but to generate a spirit of enquiry and learning that is of value for the business and enhances individuals' learning capability.

REFLECTION

Reflecting on any L&D business partnership with which you are familiar, to what extent and for what reasons do you judge it to be successful or unsuccessful in achieving its stated purpose?

COMPANIONS IN DANCING

DRAWING IN THE LEARNERS

Business partnership alone cannot achieve the objectives of any L&D strategy for the simple reason – emphasised in Chapters 4 and 5 – that learning is a property of the individual and is strongly shaped by social processes in the workplace. It cannot be bent to the purposes of others without the agreement of its owner, and learning plans also risk failure when they ignore the influence of workplace culture on employees' values and levels of organisational commitment. Learners must be convinced that they have something to win if they are to invest their own learning whose value for themselves they cannot perceive.

These considerations direct attention to the definition of partnership as a dance, highlighting themes of companionship, harmony and trust. The concept of learning partnerships emphasises the sharing of the risks and gains inherent in any learning process through a sensitivity and responsiveness to individual needs and the respect for diversity already discussed in Chapter 9. Individual differences should enrich the process. Each dancer should be able to express themselves in their unique way, while responding with others to the basic rhythm of the dance.

In learning partnerships harmony is often difficult to achieve. Reporting on a two-year study of management training and development in Britain and six major continental European countries, for example, the authors referred to management education in Britain as an 'uneasy dance' between employers and employees, with both sides seeing the advantages in being partners but with each having a different dancing style (Mabey and Ramirez 2004).

DANCING ACROSS BOUNDARIES

A study of HR in globalising firms showed that international HR executives working in situations across countries where increasingly they have to share information and work in virtual teams need process and political skills as much as technical knowledge. They have to be strong personal networkers with a capacity for and tolerance of the ambiguities and uncertainties inherent in new business situations, resource negotiators, appreciative of cultural differences and showing respect for them. Such skills are as important as being 'strategic thinkers' (Brewster et al 2002: 18).

Similar challenges face L&D professionals who form learning partnerships across the organisation's boundaries. Such an extension of the L&D dance is important for two reasons. First, it ensures the entry of those on whom the organisation depends for the ultimate quality of its products and service. Second, it brings into the dance skills, knowledge, networks and ways of perceiving and understanding the business environment that can add value for the business. Supplier development programmes are a case in point. Many are driven purely by a training rationale, focusing on the improvement of skills to perform given tasks and carry out prescribed processes. Some, however, go deeper and seek through a partnership dance to produce double-loop learning – the kind of learning that involves questioning why problems occur in the first place and challenging the continued utility of long-standing systems and processes. Such programmes encourage participants to identify underlying causes instead of only their surface symptoms. They are therefore based on an adult-to-adult relationship. Questioning by suppliers of the client firm's way of doing things is a risky venture, but where there is sufficient trust and openness it can produce new ways of learning together, and valuable innovations for both client and supplier organisations (Batchelor *et al* 1995).

There are other kinds of boundaries across which L&D partnership should extend. Consider, for example, those who are often disadvantaged in L&D strategies: part-time and temporary workers. Failure to integrate them into organisations' L&D systems has given rise to concern at government level (White 1996). Often, such workers have less access than permanent full-time workers to:

- upskilling through training, growth in the job and increased responsibility

- performance management processes that combine appraisal reviews, target-setting, performance feedback and merit pay

- increasing personal discretion in tasks.

Where managers and L&D practitioners work together to raise the status of hitherto undervalued stakeholders in the business through various forms of training and learning process, the whole organisation can gain as these partners are enabled to join fully in the L&D dance.

One common form of cross-boundary learning partnership is that created by an alliance between an organisation and an academic institution. The following case illustrates the kind of challenge that this kind of dance can involve for partners.

PARTNERSHIP IN L&D EVALUATION

CASE EXAMPLE

A 2004 research paper by Valerie Stead describes the design, development and implementation of a business-focused collaborative model of evaluation that aimed to provide a link between training evaluation research and practice, academia and industry. The evaluation related to an organisational development intervention and was designed around key principles identified by a global company, Zetex plc, and academics at Lancaster University, drawing on Zetex practice and current evaluation research.

The experience gained from implementing the model showed that partnership working is problematic and complex, often having to be based on compromise between partners who have differing aims and values. It demonstrated the importance of explicitly addressing partnership issues on the basis of joint ownership, rather than assuming that decisions will be agreeable to both partners or effective in enabling learning. Stead concluded:

> The case study demonstrates the need for explicit and challenging management of any collaborative evaluation process that includes clarification of exactly what is involved for partner organizations and the consequent implications at strategic and operational levels. At a practical and micro-level, the study showed a need for greater interaction and regular feedback between partners, and at the point of intervention with participants, to ensure that tools and processes in place are effective and providing added value and contribution to the existing learning processes.
>
> Source: Stead, V. (2004)

ISSUES OF WORKPLACE CULTURE

The case example shows that for a collaborative evaluation model to make its intended impact on learning at the organisational level, partners need to identify whether it and the evaluation tools it deploys are consistent with prevailing organisational values about learning. For example, the CIPD's 2008 annual L&D survey revealed the importance that the great majority of its respondents attached to the building of workplace cultures where continuous learning is facilitated and accepted as an integral part of the everyday work process. Yet it also revealed the difficulties they faced in their attempts to do so, especially in relation to the partnerships they needed to forge with their line managers (CIPD 2008a). At this point a closer look at 'culture' is required.

Culture affects behaviour by providing people with a 'toolkit' of material such as symbols, stories, procedures, habits and skills which, if reinforced by time and circumstance, become a set of general cultural 'capacities'. They draw on these capacities when making choices about which actions to take, which initiatives to support (Swidler 1986). Ghoshal and Bartlett (1994) claimed corporate culture to be perhaps an organisation's most inimitable and therefore uniquely valuable resource. They proposed that organisational context has a direct implication for firm performance, and that it is general managers who are the main shapers of context. Many researchers were subsequently to argue along similar lines. In the UK nearly a decade later, for example, Purcell and his colleagues (2003) produced almost identical views.

Culture is dynamic. It is also different at different levels and locations, and some claim that all cultures are local, being created by the behaviour of local managers and their teams (Buckingham 2001: 40). So there can be multiple cultures in an organisation, some of which may work in opposition to the primary culture that leadership is trying to embed. This, in turn, can weaken any sense of a collective identity and thereby loosen ties of loyalty and of engagement with the organisation's purpose and goals. I will say more about the relationship between identity and engagement in the next chapter. Suffice to observe here that some organisations introduce initiatives such as cross-functional project teams to strengthen collective ties but find these do not achieve that objective because the thread of commonality is too fragile.

Such considerations return us to the three fundamental influences on the context in which an organisation's members learn and perform from day to day: leadership, management and HR practices. They need to interrelate in ways that engender a strong sense of an organisational community committed to a common purpose. But that is no easy task, particularly where strategy's implementation may differ across business units. Differences in front-line managers' competence, use of discretionary power, and ability to balance local against corporate needs all have differentiating effects on workplace culture (Purcell *et al* 2003).

As I explained towards the end of Chapter 5, at present whether in the UK or more widely across Europe there are relatively few signs that L&D professionals, let alone line managers, are actively promoting learning cultures in their organisations. The European research detailed in that chapter showed that even in self-styled learning-oriented organisations L&D professionals rarely appear to be taking a proactive stance and that few managers and their employees seem to be involved in the kind of new learning tasks and innovative learning processes that would typify such a culture (Tjepkema 2002: 172). Such findings are in line with earlier studies in suggesting that more often than not the true motives for changes in L&D orientation are to do with reducing training budgets and scaling down central training departments rather than with the emergence of any new learning philosophy (Raper *et al* 1997). They suggest that where learning cultures are concerned there is a big gap between aspirations and reality. L&D professionals should be taking a lead in finding ways to tackle it if they are to succeed in their partnership dance.

REFLECTION

Consider two different workplaces in an organisation with which you are familiar. How would you describe the culture of each, and to what extent do these workplace cultures support or conflict with the primary organisation culture that top management is trying to develop?

POWER, POLITICS AND ETHICS

It should by now be evident that if the term 'partner' seems to imply a cosy relationship, this is misleading. Business and learning partnerships both involve

resolving differences and reconciling diverse interests and values. They require
unlearning in order that new, mutual learning can develop. They call for partners
to demonstrate skill and courage in challenging each other's assumptions about the
nature of business, organisational and L&D issues and in questioning their own
and others' customary ways of thinking and behaving. All of this moves partnership
skills into the territory of the emotional, the social and the intellectual.

ISSUES OF POWER AND POLITICS

Within organisations issues of power and conflict are bound to complicate the
task of collaboration. Power is a property that exists in any human society, and
politics is the way it is commonly expressed (Torrington and Weightman 1985). In
an organisation there are three sources of power that an L&D practitioner should
consider when developing business partnerships. They can act as constraints or as
opportunities depending largely on the practitioner's skills in achieving conflict
resolution.

- *Resource* – 'Power accrues to those parts of the organization that can control
  the flow of resources, especially if these are scarce and critical for organizational
  functioning' (Miller *et al* 1999: 46). Resources in this sense can be of any kind –
  financial and non-financial, material and intangible, resources of time, space and
  expertise. They constitute means to an end. Resource management is not simply
  a set of tasks. It is a political process. Resource starvation in the L&D field is
  common. It is one of the many reasons why political and partnership skills must
  be a crucial part of any L&D professional's armoury.

- *Position* – This refers to the power derived from formal position, its
  accompanying status and the knowledge and information to which it gives
  access. Since knowledge is vital to decision-making at all levels, positions that act
  as gateways to information and to knowledge networks constitute a formidable
  power source. The formal positions bestowed on those who carry the main
  responsibility for the L&D function in an organisation will always be a strong
  indication of the value that key players place on the L&D investment.

- *Expertise* – Expert power is that which is derived from a uniquely valued area of
  knowledge or competence. One well-known study of a French tobacco company
  revealed that maintenance workers, despite their lowly position, had exclusive
  possession of expert and essential knowledge. Through this power source
  they were able to gain and maintain control over production processes and so
  negotiate to their advantage (Crozier 1964).

When strains arise in an L&D partnership players may use their sources of power
to protect or pursue their interests. Conflict is natural in any pluralist society. Used
effectively it can bring new ideas, innovation and progress. Handled without skill,
it can lead to the breakdown of relationships. Morgan (1997: 205–9) identifies a
range of typical responses by individuals to conflict situations:

- avoidance – tries to avoid conflict, but when it arises tries to stifle or postpone it, or at least ensure that there is no direct confrontation

- compromise – seeks compromise by negotiation and by making deals

- competition – tries to win, either by exploiting rivalries or by exercise of power

- submission – usually gives way, either because of a belief that conflict is counterproductive or because it is clear from the start that winning is impossible

- accommodation – encourages the other party/parties to put the reasons for conflict on the table, so that they can be resolved

- collaboration – seeks to work together to find solutions that build on differences and that help each of the parties involved to win something.

The first instinct of most L&D professionals new to their roles would probably be to favour the collaborative approach. After all, they have been educated to espouse values of co-operation, of openness and of mutual benefit. However, the more experienced could not be blamed for responding more cautiously. Collaboration is not easy to achieve in some organisational contexts, and the more powerful the players the more politicised the game becomes. Politics is the art of achieving the possible. Sometimes collaboration will not work: it may be better to go for compromise through negotiation in order to preserve all players' commitment and to move the game forward. Sometimes it will be wiser to abandon a chosen course altogether in the interests of making progress on another front.

Where collaboration is the obvious course to take, one important way forward is to employ principles of Appreciative Inquiry (Cooperrider and Srivastva 1987). 'AI' is a method intended originally to achieve whole system change, but now often used in organisations to build teams and achieve conflict resolution. It focuses not on identifying problems blocking progress in a situation but on discovering strengths that the parties bring to the table, encouraging them to produce a 'dream' of what those strengths could achieve, and helping them to 'design' a project that will enable the dream to be realised. AI is informed by social constructivist theory (discussed in Chapter 4) and works on the belief that in a working relationship individuals can and will co-create an effective future when the relationship has at its heart a spirit of positive inquiry. The conversations that it involves are processes to achieve unlearning and new learning. They (Finegold *et al* 2002: 235):

> serve to build trust and strengthen relationships allowing for the disruption of old patterns of thinking. This opens a pathway for new insights, new hope, and therefore new possibilities. We are better able to reach for these new possibilities when we are mindful of the successes we have had and of the strengths in our system.

THE ETHICAL APPROACH TO PARTNERSHIP

In previous chapters I have emphasised the need for visionary leadership and facilitative, ethical management if organisational members are to work together in pursuit of a common business purpose. Lynda Gratton (2003a) takes these points further. In her concern with the balance to be struck in an organisation between accountabilities, obligations and trust she argues for a truly democratic enterprise. Among the tenets she proposes are four that go to the heart of any L&D partnership:

- There is an adult relationship between the parties.

- Individuals are able to develop their natures and express their diverse qualities.

- The freedom of some is not gained at the expense of others.

- Individuals acknowledge accountabilities and obligations both to themselves and to their community.

What is at issue here is ethical behaviour informed by principles of good citizenship (Hosmer 1994). It is when ethics enters into the matter that the appropriateness of the dance metaphor to describe L&D partnerships becomes most evident. There is no context in which an L&D professional should behave in ways that seek to exploit or undermine any learners. Vulnerabilities in individuals or groups must never be used by L&D partners to gain advantage for themselves or for more powerful players.

Harrison and Smith (2001) have described the kind of behaviour that 'good citizenship' involves as the exercise of *practical judgement*, a term suggested by Aristotle's concept of '*phronēsis*' and one that is most easily explained as being to do with applying the wisdom born of experience in ways appropriate to the particular situation and respectful of the values of others. The literature suggests that three types of intelligence may have relevance here: emotional, social and spiritual.

Emotional and social intelligence

The concept of emotional intelligence (EI) and social intelligence (SI) have been popularised by Daniel Goleman (1998, 2006). EI is summarised in basic terms as (Jack Mayer, quoted by Pickard 1999: 495):

> the understanding of emotion. The ability to perceive, to integrate, to understand and reflectively manage one's own and other people's feelings.

Clarke (2006, cited in *People Management* 2007b) identifies three major types of EI models:

- personality models, conceptualising EI as consisting of five elements that contain between them a range of emotional dispositions and competencies: self-awareness, motivation, self-regulation, empathy, and adeptness in relationships

- mixed models, incorporating aspects of personality as well as abilities to perceive and manage emotions

- the ability model, taking a narrower view of EI and comprising a set of four cognitive abilities that involve capacity to identify, reason with and use emotions effectively.

Clarke points out that despite there being little evidence in research to indicate that the first two models have much validity, they are in widespread use as the base of EI training. There are also concerns about how EI can be clarified sufficiently to enable it to be assessed in some meaningful way, especially when so much depends either on self-reporting or on the uncertainties of 360-degree feedback (Smewing 2004). However, Clarke confirms that recent research is giving some support to the ability model, suggesting that there may be a clear link between its set of emotional abilities, transformational leadership and the quality of individuals' social relationships. Goleman (2006) has built on this research to develop his concept of social intelligence.

'Spiritual' intelligence

Some go further, proposing the concept of 'spiritual intelligence'. Zohar and Drake (2000) explain this as the ultimate intelligence, because it represents an individual's deep, intuitive sense of meaning. They observe that when the immediate environment is uncertain, people need an inner security in order to be flexible, adaptable, imaginative, spontaneous, innovative, inspirational. 'Spiritual intelligence' can supply that security.

All of these concepts may resist close definition, but each draws attention in its own way to partnership as a process calling for more than technical and strategic skills. Learning is the most intimate and individualised of human processes that organisational leaders, managers and L&D specialists try to shape to their purposes. The oft-declared shift from a preoccupation with training to a concern that individuals take charge of their own learning is born at least in part from the realisation that every individual has personal sensitivities, emotions, needs, beliefs and insecurities that require care and respect in the handling if he or she is to become committed to any wider learning agenda than his or her own.

For L&D professionals the skills and styles needed in business partnerships are not skin deep or easily acquired. Reflecting on the concepts of practical judgement, emotional, social and spiritual intelligence is not sentimentalism or wacky thinking. It is a way of exploring the nature of some essential but hard to express dimensions of partnership.

THE PARTNERSHIP DANCE

The various elements of establishing and maintaining effective business partnerships in L&D can be summarised by identifying the major steps in the process. In real life, of course, these steps are rarely taken in sequence. They constitute a set of movements often performed almost simultaneously so that the partnership dance can progress:

Partner others: build effective working relationships inside and outside the business so that L&D strategies work on the ground and new initiatives gain the support they need.

Achieve results: promote L&D activity that supports the business and the learners and work with others to monitor and evaluate its outcomes.

Raise awareness: ensure that all potential partners understand the importance of the big L&D issues facing the organisation and the valuable part they can play in tackling them.

Travel around: establish a proactive and visible presence in the business, deepening your business knowledge and cementing crucial relationships.

Never be complacent: use partnerships as a vehicle for your own learning as well as that of others, stimulating your professional development and generating innovative L&D processes and initiatives.

Ensure ethical practice. Respect the values of others, create trust and build on an inclusive approach to diversity to produce rich learning experiences, with access for all employees to opportunities to develop their performance and potential.

Recognise the importance of context. Unless it is favourable people cannot or will not use their learning and skills for the benefit of the business. To take a lead in promoting learning cultures in the workplace, first identify any potential barriers and decide how best to tackle them.

Finally, here is a case example to incorporate principles discussed in this chapter.

CASE EXAMPLE

WORKING WITH CLIENTS TO DESIGN AND DELIVER LEARNING: THE HEMSLEY FRASER PROCESS

At Hemsley Fraser Group Ltd (HF), an international L&D consultancy firm, the provision of services to clients is organised around a number of interactive core processes underpinned by four principles:

- precision in identifying and responding to client needs (learner and organisational)

- ensuring that learning achieved through a project will be transferred to the workplace and contribute to business results

- provision of a service that has built-in quality and innovation

- provision of a service underpinned by a body of professional knowledge related to workplace learning and development.

At the heart of the HF process model lies faculty management, an overarching process that builds in quality, continuous improvement and innovation throughout the relationship with the client.

Faculty management

The title given to this process signals the professional knowledge and expertise and the educational ethos that HF consultants bring to their relationship with clients. It ensures the roll-out of a learning programme to a consistent quality standard. A 'head of faculty' and a team of 'learning consultants' are selected for each such project, their choice being based on:

- capacity – the scale and pace of the project

- type of client organisation – its sector, culture, geographical location and so on

- characteristics of the learners who will be involved and the nature of their work

- subject matter and nature of the delivery (for example a leadership programme, a modular programme, an action learning process)

The faculty management process frames a cycle of interactive 'plan, set up, manage and evaluate' processes to deliver the service required. Each involves the use of a set of customised HF tools.

The design process

Faculty management is closely integrated with the HF design process, which is organised around key phases, starting with capture of information that is gathered by HF sales and learning consultants, using a collaborative tool. Initial meetings with the client lead to the production of a scoping document that provides the framework for the design of the learning event, process or initiative required. Once it has been discussed and agreed with the client, detailed design and learning materials are produced.

The whole design process is structured to ensure:

- that the learning provision is backed up by quality standards and incorporates leading-edge thinking

- that an 'audit trail' is produced, showing how the final design has been rooted in a shared understanding between the client and the HF learning consultants regarding organisational context, characteristics of the audience, the desired links between the learning event or programme and business goals

- a basis from which informed decisions can be made about about improvements and innovations to future learning provision, and which can underpin the evaluation process.

Source: With acknowledgements to Hemsley Fraser Group Limited

CONCLUSION

You should by now have a clear understanding of what an L&D business partnership involves, in terms of its purpose, its partnerships and its skills. You should also be able to tackle competently the review questions contained in Appendix 3.

Main themes in the chapter's four sections have been:

- the importance of understanding partnership as a process involving a fair distribution amongst partners of the risks and benefits involved in working towards a shared purpose; the need for L&D practitioners to achieve partners' shared expectations concerning what those risks and benefits are likely to be

- insights gained by applying to L&D partnerships the metaphors of both the game and the dance. The 'game' emphasises the need to play on side, scoring wins

for the business. The 'dance' points to the need to achieve harmony through diversity and a constructive approach to the resolution of conflict. It highlights the benefits as well as the challenges of extending L&D partnerships across a variety of boundaries

- the need for a favourable workplace context if the aims of any kind of L&D partnership are to be achieved; the fundamental influence exercised over context by corporate and front-line leadership, management style and actions and HR practices. The need for L&D professionals to take a strong lead in promoting and helping to build workplace learning cultures

- power, politics and ethical issues involved in partnerships, and the 'soft' skills that L&D practitioners require in order to respond effectively to them. Seven steps in the L&D partnership process.

FURTHER INFORMATION SOURCES

CIPD (2006a) *The Changing Role of the Trainer: Building a learning culture in your organisation.* Online interactive tool, available at: http://www.cipd.co.uk/subjects/lrnanddev/general/_chngrltrnr [accessed 12 July 2008]

Ulrich, D. and Beatty, D. (2001) 'From players to partners: extending the HR playing field', *Human Resource Management*, Vol.40, No.4: 293–307

EXLPORE FURTHER

CHAPTER 14

Adding Value

INTRODUCTION

The purpose of this chapter is to explain how L&D activity can add value to an organisation. To add value is to make a difference where it matters most. In the context of this chapter it means producing outcomes that enable the organisation to respond better than it could before to challenges and threats, and to do so at a cost – in the widest sense of that word – that is considerably less than the value of those outcomes. In the turbulent economic conditions that are building up across the world at the time of writing (mid-2008) adding value to the business and thereby also contributing to the job security of those who work for it could hardly be a more vital – or a more demanding – task for L&D practitioners.

The chapter has five sections. The first distinguishes between achieving 'best value' and 'added value' – a distinction too often missed. The next explains the organisation's 'value chain' and how value chain analysis can aid L&D activity. The final three use an 'align, engage and measure' framework as a further aid to fulfilling L&D's value-adding potential.

REFLECTION

Taking your own or some other organisation with which you are familiar, consider how you would decide where and how L&D activity could add greatest value to that organisation.

CLARIFYING 'ADDED VALUE'

'BEST VALUE' AND 'ADDED VALUE': WHAT IS THE DIFFERENCE?

'Best value' is often confused with 'added value' but in reality the two are quite distinct. Identifying best value involves establishing how far a service or function in an organisation provides good value for money compared with 'best in class'. Take, for example, the four criteria that the Audit Commission has used to assess local authority services (Gorman 2000):

- *Challenge* – Why is the service carried out at all?

- *Consult* – What do customers think about our service and the level of performance?

- *Compare* – How does our performance compare against the best of the public and private sector?

- *Compete* – Can the service be delivered more effectively by alternative providers?

The Commission concluded in 2002 that most local authority HR functions gave poor value for money. However, it does not follow that they failed to add any value to their organisations. To determine that would have involved applying a fourth criterion: in what, if any, ways has our HR service enhanced our authority's capability to achieve its goals? The CIPD's (2007d) 'Value of learning' tool, discussed in Chapter 12, makes a meaningful attempt to identify the 'value' of L&D's contribution to the business in ways that are likely to yield relevant information about both best value and added value of that contribution.

A key process in assessing best value is *benchmarking*. It also has a significant part to play in planning how to add value. It involves finding a particular standard, whether internal or external, and using it as a continuous marker for a strategy, process or initiative. It is not merely a technique for copying. It involves making internal, competitive or functional comparisons in order to inform decisions about how to enhance performance. The key to its utility, however, is to use it as an informational aid, viewing the insights that it yields in the context of the particular organisation in order to decide whether and where they are relevant. What is best practice in one organisation or function may be quite inappropriate for another – and any practice that can be copied is, of course, no longer unique to an organisation and will therefore lose competitive value.

THE VALUE CHAIN MODEL

THE RESOURCE-BASED VIEW OF THE FIRM

One of the best-known models to aid value-adding activity is Porter's (1980) Value Chain. To understand its conceptual base it has to be seen in the broader context of strategic management and competitive advantage.

In the literature of business strategy a central theme since the 1980s has been that an organisation's competitive performance is determined not only by its relative position in the industry but also by the ability of its strategic management to understand and mobilise the potential offered by the organisation's internal resources and capabilities. A key strand of the literature explores how internal capabilities can be generated, combined, utilised and sustained in order to bestow competitive advantage (Barney 1991). This so-called 'resource-based view' highlights the asset value of the organisation's base of human capital, which has the potential to produce and apply valuable organisational capabilities (Selznick 1957; Penrose 1959; Wernerfelt 1984; Barney 1991). Those capabilities represent the capacity for a team of resources to perform some task or activity (Grant 1991). 'Resources' comprise know-how that can be traded, financial and physical assets, human and social capital, and so on.

A firm's resources become valuable when they enable it to exploit opportunities and reduce threats. They do this by (Barney 1991):

- meeting or creating a market need

- having uniqueness (scarcity value) and sustainability

- being hard to copy (because their basic components interact in complex and non-linear ways to generate value for the organisation)

- being path-dependent (that is to say, so deeply embedded in the fabric of the organisation through their development over time that they cannot be poached by competitors).

The impact that resources and capabilities actually achieve is mediated by many variables, notably by the outcomes of policy decisions in the business and by the firm's strategic position in its industry at any given time – its 'positional capability' that broadly decides the potential of the firm for growth and profitability (Porter 1985). Porter devised a 'Five Forces' model to help strategic managers to analyse that capability. He produced his Value Chain model to aid analysis of the firm's internal environment in order to decide where and how most value could be added to the firm.

THE VALUE CHAIN OF THE FIRM

A firm's value chain consists of five linked primary activities that convert inputs into outputs (Porter 1980):

- inbound logistics (referring to the control and regulation of the flow of goods, materials, staff, and so on, coming into the business)

- operations

- outbound logistics (referring to the control and regulation of outputs from the business)

- marketing and sales

- service.

'Support activities' are those that underpin these five primary activities. These include (Balderson 2005: 92):

- management of the administrative infrastructure

- HR policies and practices

- research and development

- procurement.

Value can be added at each stage of the chain's primary activities and by enhancing support activities, but the greatest value-adding potential can lie in improving the operation of the linkages between the value chain's primary activities. This is because those linkages are strongly influenced by intangibles: organisational culture, tacit knowledge and organisational capabilities embedded in the social fabric of the organisation such as leadership, trust, talent, mindsets and innovation (Younger et al 2007; Holbeche 2007). Because these intangibles are path-dependent they are unique and difficult to copy.

An organisation can also expand its value chain by increasing the scope of its business or by partnering others. It can link to the value chains of the organisation's network of clients, suppliers, partners and regulators, to each of their value chains, and so on until the organisation has achieved a total, sometimes global, 'value system' (Porter 1985; Swart and Kinnie 2007). Although not directly employed by the organisation, some of these external groups will possess skills, knowledge and networks that have high strategic value for the organisation. It is to gain their engagement with the primary organisation's purpose and goals that the organisation will often extend to them its HR practices to do with communicating its corporate values and ethos, training, innovation and facilitating knowledge-sharing (Baron 2007a). Here is a brief case in point.

CASE EXAMPLE

ADDING VALUE THROUGH CO-OPERATIVE RELATIONSHIPS: THE FIVE PARTNERS MODEL

In the 1990s France Telecom developed global strategies for competitiveness in telecommunications. Its structure was geared to sharing and accessing resources with partner organisations, and was based on what came to be called the 'Five Partners Model'.

This model is 'a means of organizing economic activity among partner organizations through cooperative relationships in a business network' (D'Cruz *et al* 1994: 59). It is based on a five-way partnership consisting of the flagship firm (usually a multinational), key suppliers, key customers, competitors, and the non-business infrastructure. Partners yield the strategic leadership role to the flagship firm and undertake much of the responsibility to execute and operationalise the network's strategy. The non-business infrastructure is so called because it provides human and technological capital essential to the successful functioning of the partnership.

The model focuses on 'forging linkages with other organizations which have advantages in other parts of the value chain'. It also emphasises the value of behaviours often not considered in competitive strategies – trust, relationship stability and longevity, and shared inter-organisational purpose (*ibid*: 61). It therefore responds directly to the increasing trend for organisations to make progress through collaborative as well as competitive strategies.

Source: D'Cruz, J. R. and Rugman A. M. (1994)

Porter's value chain model is enduringly popular. It has great logical appeal, it simplifies complex concepts without losing their core meaning, and it is grounded in the language and operation of the business. Some, though, believe it has become outdated in a world which, by contrast to the 1980s, lacks relatively stable market structures and clear organisational boundaries, where business drivers can include both collaboration and competition, low cost and high quality, and where digitalisation, globalisation and deregulation in both private and public sectors may call for new strategic frameworks and different analytic and business design tools (Downes and Mui 1998). Some feel, too, that it is more relevant to the private than to the public sector when the latter's distinctive features (noted in Chapter 10) are taken into account.

THE VALUE CHAIN MODEL AND THE L&D DOMAIN

Whatever the criticisms of the value chain model, for the L&D professional seeking to form a clear picture of how to 'add value' its great virtue is its focus on end results. Its outside-in thinking consistently draws attention to 'what we are here to do', highlighting the many points at which the knowledge, competencies and engagement of employees can make a critical difference to the value chain's operation and thereby to its ultimate outputs.

Indeed in today's business world there is one sense in which the value chain model can be claimed to be uniquely relevant for L&D professionals, and that is through the potential of the value chain to become 'a domain of integrated learning' (Nevis *et al* 1995: 74). It has been described as such because the work involved in each major activity along the chain can also become a 'sub-system for learning experiments' that lead to continuous improvement and to innovation through new knowledge acquisition, knowledge sharing, and knowledge utilisation at different points in the chain. In a globalised and fast-moving knowledge economy the individual and collective capability to learn rapidly, co-create value with customers and generate and apply new knowledge in the business is essential to organisational survival (Senge 1990; Huber 1991; Nonaka 1994; Prahalad and Ramaswamy 2002).

A 'domain of integrated learning' is hard to achieve. We have seen (Chapters 4 and 5) that learning within workplace communities of practice does not always operate to the benefit of the business. For it to do so management must understand and be committed to learning as an integral part of the production or service process, so that 'work' and 'learning' become fused, with the behaviours that define each being one and the same (Zuboff 1988). For this to happen there must be a culture and a style of management that gains employees' commitment to the organisation's purpose and goals, and the competencies to facilitate, manage and work effectively in a continuous learning environment. There must also be a genuinely inclusive approach to learning, whereby knowledge embedded in the grass roots of the organisational community is accessed and shared (Harrison 2000). Each of these requirements poses formidable challenges that much research evidence shows the L&D profession is slow to meet.

Reflection on the value chain model suggests the following value-adding tasks for L&D professionals:

- Organise the L&D function to focus continually on adding value rather than merely on training evaluation or on 'best value' (Chapter 11 explains some structural options).

- Identify within the L&D function and in the wider organisation any obstacles that prevent L&D activity from adding value. Assess particularly where in the organisation's value chain there are barriers and gaps to prevent it becoming a 'domain of integrated learning'.

- Work with organisational leaders, local managers, team leaders and HR partners to address obstacles, barriers and gaps through L&D policies and practices that, carefully tailored to organisational context, are most likely to achieve a 'happy balance' between adding value to the organisation and to individuals (Holbeche 2007).

REFLECTION

The first **Reflection** in this chapter focused on a specific organisation of your choice. Now take that same organisation and try to identify its value chain. Consider where and how along the chain L&D activity might add the greatest value.

ALIGN, ENGAGE AND MEASURE: ALIGNING THE PEOPLE

An HR framework to assess added value, and one that can be used either in conjunction with the Value Chain model or as an alternative to it, has been suggested by Green (1999). It involves three processes:

- *align* – point people in the right direction

- *engage* – develop their belief and commitment to the organisation's purpose and direction

- *measure* – provide the data that demonstrate the improved results you achieve.

In this and the following two sections I will explain these three processes and relate each to the L&D domain.

POINTING PEOPLE IN THE RIGHT DIRECTION

In the context of adding value, 'aligning people' means pointing them in the direction of the organisation's purpose and corporate goals. To contribute to this alignment L&D practitioners must ensure that their own activity is vertically integrated. It must continuously interact with the cycle of business change to provide a service that is relevant to the business, its vision and its goals. Of course the L&D function too needs its vision and goals, but these must be related to those of the business, not exist in some separate dimension.

A popular method of aligning people with the organisation's goals is the balanced scorecard (Purcell *et al* 2003). It works well in conjunction with the Value Chain model, being based on similar outside-in thinking and having its focus on maximising internal assets to add value to the business. Kaplan and Norton's prototype (1996) highlights an integrated set of measurements to link customers, internal processes, employees and systems to long-term financial success. It relates these measures to each other and to the firm's strategic objectives by grouping them around four perspectives: financial, internal business process, customer, and learning and growth (a measure which some have expanded to incorporate innovation).

TABLE 17 Identifying L&D targets and measures for Procon UK's Birmingham site using a balanced scorecard approach

Scorecard area	Business target	L&D target/s
Financial	Ensure that efficiency gains are achieved and driven through every aspect of the organisation while getting work out on time, every time, to company standards	Put managers at all levels through Lean Manufacturing Programme to ensure that they understand lean manufacturing principles and practices and use them to manage their workplaces to standard
Customer	Maintain world-class standards of customer experience, continuous improvement and quality	Put senior management and the entire workforce through the Leadership Programme focused on the company's Five Values and related standards. Put all middle and front-line managers through management development programme to transform organisational culture and manage workplaces to world-class standards
Internal business	Update and introduce new business processes and procedures to ensure continuous monitoring of KPIs	L&D staff work with HR staff and other business partners to embed new performance management system. Ensure that all managers and other employees have PDPs and that these are actioned and monitored regularly
Learning and Growth/Innovation	L&D investment to link firmly to corporate outcomes and produce added value for the business as well as individuals	L&D strategy to be driven by 'outside-in' thinking. Use informal as well as formal evaluation data to influence strategic decision-making in the business, not just in the L&D domain. All L&D staff to understand how to achieve added value, and demonstrate high engagement levels

Building on Balderson's example (2005: 97), the development needs of individuals and employee groups can also be related to how well equipped they are to meet targets and measurements in all four areas of the scorecard. Going back to the narrative in Chapter 8, if Procon UK (Birmingham) had used the balanced scorecard for its key L&D targets it might have looked as shown in Table 17.

That Table demonstrates the use of the scorecard involves linking employees' everyday actions to company-wide strategic objectives. This has a direct impact on the performance management process, which must be aligned with business objectives in order to give the required strategic thrust to appraisal discussions and to personal development plans.

Some scorecards are tailored specifically to the HR area. That produced by Huselid *et al* (2001) links HR to measures that senior executives and managers will value, and claims to demonstrate how to manage the HR architecture as a strategic asset. Mayo's (2001) 'Human Capital Monitor' aims to capture the extent to which people are adding value for stakeholders and to enable every employee to be linked to one or more areas of value.

However, no method is foolproof. Kaplan and Norton pointed out (2001) that a scorecard will only provide an effective strategic framework for employees' actions if management communicates with and educates employees about business strategy. Neely's (2007) research findings suggest that although the scorecard method is a good starting-point for improving performance, it can lead to an obsession with measurement and to defensive behaviour. He proposes that all such methods should be used primarily as vehicles for learning, encouraging people to think broadly about what success constitutes for their organisation and hence decide what should be measured.

ALIGNING THE PEOPLE: TASKS FOR L&D PROFESSIONALS

From this section we can conclude that in this first step towards adding value L&D professionals should be:

- learning how to track emerging trends in both markets and technologies relevant for the organisation, and then assessing the implications of these trends for the business and for its L&D activity (Dougherty 1999: 183)

- helping to communicate the organisation's vision, values, goals and business strategy through a variety of formal and informal learning processes

- working with HR and business partners to identify and tackle any barriers that are preventing people from using their skills and knowledge in support of business goals and targets

- raising awareness in senior executives, team leaders and managers of the ways in which approaches like the balanced scorecard can help them to 'point people in the right direction'

- equipping people across the organisation with the competence to use such approaches as vehicles for learning, continuous improvement and innovation.

ENGAGING THE PEOPLE

WHAT IS 'ENGAGEMENT'?

Aligning people with the organisation's goals is the essential first step towards achieving added value, because without that alignment there will be no clarity about shared purpose and goals with which people can engage. Engagement is the second step, and one in which once again it is the organisation's leadership and management who must play the major role, with L&D professionals working to support them. So what exactly is meant by 'employee engagement'?

Employee engagement refers to employees' willingness and capability to 'go the extra mile' in working for the organisation and its goals. Engagement means, literally, interlocked, and this term captures the active and intense nature of engagement. Survey data suggest that highly engaged employees put in more discretionary effort than those whose engagement levels are average to low, and that two thirds of such employees plan to stay with their organisation (Johnson 2004). Research by the CIPD, Gallup and the Institute of Employment Studies (IES) all points to the conclusion that a high level of employee engagement adds value to the business through its direct link with organisational outcomes such as customer service, productivity and financial performance and through its positive correlation with turnover (Sappal 2004). That correlation is illustrated in the following example.

EVOTEC OA1, 2002–3

CASE EXAMPLE

Evotec OA1 is a pharmaceutical 'discovery' company. In 2002 its staff turnover had reached an unacceptable high of 26%. HR staff, working with external consultants, carried out a staff survey and organised focus groups. The role of the consultants was of particular importance in obtaining honest feedback by guaranteeing staff confidentiality for views that they expressed. When data from the two exercises were analysed it became clear that three issues needed major attention:

- *Career development* – Feedback showed the high value that employees placed on career development. Acting on this, a more structured career path was introduced and was linked to an appropriately changed performance appraisal system

- *Leadership and management behaviour* – Standards here were found to be very mixed. HR's analysis of results by department enabled identification of high and low scorers. High scorers 'talked to their employees, who in turn knew what was expected of them and were therefore more engaged and productive'. Recognition of these scorers boosted their motivation and satisfaction, and reinforced their behaviour. Low scorers were often highly capable in their technical roles but lacked management competence. Coaching and training courses helped to remedy that lack

- *Valuing employees* – Feedback here led to the introduction of more flexible benefits, since these proved to be highly valued by most employees.

As a result of these three sets of initiatives employee engagement with the organisation increased,

and turnover dramatically reduced from around 26% in 2002 to 12% in 2003.

Source: Sappal, P. (2004)
People Management, 9 December

WHAT DRIVES ENGAGEMENT?

Engagement is today's Holy Grail – a tantalising vision that is rarely achieved to the levels the employer requires. Its main drivers are to do with the quality of employees' relationships with leaders, managers and co-workers, the type and design of their work, their opportunities for autonomy and development and the extent to which they are aligned with the organisation's goals. However, prescriptions to achieve this complex mix vary, and some raise more questions than they claim to answer. To draw on just four sets of research findings:

- Research by the IES (Sappal 2004) into employees' feelings about their work and organisation and their engagement levels found that in the organisations surveyed levels of engagement were highest where employees felt valued and involved.

- In-company research and a model developed by management at Sears Roebuck and publicised by Harvard Business School authors have led many to believe there is a strong correlation between employee satisfaction and engagement (Rucci *et al* 1998).

- Case-based research by Pass (2005) illustrates the positive impact on motivation and engagement that can be achieved by managers who provide an effective balance of relationships, respect and recognition in the workplace.

- Findings from an electronically conducted nationwide survey of employee attitudes and engagement, using a stratified sample of 2,000 employees from across Great Britain, has indicated that engagement is most strongly influenced by (Truss *et al* 2006):

  - an employer that listens, so employees can feed their views upwards

  - employees who feel well informed and understand how their work contributes to the whole

  - managers who are committed to the organisation and show respect for employees.

Looking at the research methodologies here, it is clear that not all are likely to have produced reliable findings, or findings from which generalisations can safely be made. Putting that aside, however, there are some common threads that run through all the findings, and there are three human phenomena in particular that emerge as having some claimed or evident link with engagement levels: motivation, satisfaction and commitment.

MOTIVATION, SATISFACTION AND COMMITMENT

Engagement and these three phenomena are often confused, yet they are in reality different and it is arguable in at least one case – that of employee satisfaction – whether any confidence should be placed in claims for its correlation with engagement.

Employee satisfaction refers to the extent to which employees feel and express pride in their organisation, its products, brands and services, and believe that that they have fulfilling and relevant opportunities for career development.

There is a quite widespread belief that there is a correlation between high employee satisfaction and high levels of employee engagement (Matthewman and Matignon 2004). One story that has influenced this is that of Sears Roebuck's employee-customer-profit chain linking 'a compelling place to work' to 'a compelling place to shop' and thence to 'a compelling place to invest'. Its stated rationale is that 'if you keep your employees satisfied, they will ensure that your customers remain satisfied, and your customers in turn will ensure and improve your corporate profits' (Rucci *et al* 1998). The Sears model has been used successfully in a number of UK organisations, including Nationwide.

However, the *Harvard Business Review* article (Rucci *et al* 1998) that evaluates Sears' model makes it clear that at Sears the strapline 'employee satisfaction' was a simplistic overview of a far more complex reality – a skilful integration of business processes, HR and L&D practices and a performance management system that together worked to continuously align, engage and measure people in the business to achieve added value for Sears.

There is in fact no convincing evidence that employee satisfaction in the strict sense of that term leads to employee engagement. In some situations it contributes to it (as at Sears), but in others it does not. In others again it is engagement that boosts satisfaction. People may feel well treated and well rewarded, but if they do not understand the organisation's goals, are not committed to the organisation or are not motivated and enabled to 'go the extra mile', engagement will not occur.

Employee motivation refers to the extent to which individuals want and are stimulated to act in the organisation's interests. Emmott (2006) emphasised the importance of distinguishing engagement from motivation, because the latter 'has echoes of a world where people were thought to need incentives such as discipline, performance bonuses – or fear – to persuade them to work hard'. He reflected that lessons learned from managing customer relations are increasingly being applied to understanding employees who, too, 'have a choice about how far they are willing to be engaged'. Another way of saying, perhaps, that you can take a horse to water but you can't make it drink …

The fact remains that if employees are to become engaged they must have that will to be so. Motivation has to be achieved somehow, but in Chapter 6 we saw how mysterious and little understood that process is, going as it does to the heart of human psychology and behaviour. A unique interplay of internal and external factors shapes and continuously changes each individual's motivation in the workplace, with organisational context being one major contributory factor.

Employee commitment refers to individuals' loyalty to their organisation, its values and its goals, so there is a clearer kind of link here with engagement. In the discussion on 'Building commitment' in Chapter 6 we saw that many research studies point to the dominating influence of four factors on commitment levels:

- the quality of leadership

- the development opportunities provided for employees

- the amount of empowerment (ie discretion) given to employees to carry out their job effectively

- supervisors' people management skills.

Attempts to raise levels of employee commitment in order to improve employees' engagement are complicated by the fact that commitment comprises a mix of attitudes and behaviour. Like motivation it differs in every individual and is not a stable state. Commitment profiles vary across sectors and between large and small organisations. Within an organisation they vary across occupational groups and across the age spectrum, and – as we have seen in Chapter 9 – they are particularly influenced by the extent to which the individual's psychological contract with the employer is relational or transactional. Commitment levels can also change dramatically through time, being particularly volatile when there are new pressures on the employment relationship and major changes in the operation of organisations (Swailes 2002). Commitment therefore needs some kind of stable organisational anchor. For many commentators this is what a strong organisational identity provides.

ISSUES OF ORGANISATIONAL IDENTITY

One conclusion from the CIPD-sponsored research into employee engagement (Truss *et al* 2006) was that organisational culture has a direct impact on engagement, and that therefore HR professionals must facilitate the building of supportive and engaging cultures. Holbeche (2007) takes a similar line and it is not new. In the resource-based view of the firm it has long been argued that when organisational culture is unique, cohering and sustainable it can be an important source of competitive advantage (Barney 1986; Fiol 1991).

An organisation's identity lies at the heart of its culture. For if (as we saw in the previous chapter) organisational culture can be described as representing 'the way we do things here', organisational identity answers the question 'who are we?' It has been defined as (Weick and Westley 1999: 197):

> What members perceive as central, enduring, and unique or distinctive about their organization and believe others share as well.

Fiol, a leading US academic, explains organisational identity as 'essentially social in nature and situated in context' and as the source of a person's 'sense of oneness or belongingness with an organization'. Its significance for employee commitment and engagement is therefore clear. The current high levels of interest with 'employer branding' as a way to attract and retain talent (Younger *et al* 2007) and to raise engagement levels reflects the belief that the stronger the identification of employees with the organisational brand – or identity – the stronger will be their commitment to a common purpose and a shared future, and therefore the higher will be their engagement with the organisation's goals. Fiol continues (2001: 692):

> Organizational identities have been described as narratives that provide a sense of organizational continuity (Hauerwas 1983; Rappaport 1993). An identity story "allows the organization to draw coherence from its past and establish direction for the future" (Kimberly 1987: 233). To the extent that people share an identity story (Hogg and Terry 2000) an organization has a relatively homogeneous organizational identity. Strong dominant identities that are simple, clear, highly focused, and consensual often characterize successful startup organizations.

Sometimes, though – and especially in today's world where boundaries between organisations are blurred through outsourcing, supply chain relationships, strategic alliances and other partnership networks – there can be mixed perceptions as to what is central, distinctive and enduring about an organisation. Employees then become exposed to not one but a number of organisational identities. To take two examples (Pratt and Foreman 2000):

- Employees of an organisation that provides services for client companies can become more influenced by the management of those companies than by their own management.

- Within an organisation employees may be torn between conflicting perceptions of the organisation's identity expressed by powerful external stakeholders who are increasingly intervening in organisations' affairs.

Such an emergence of multiple organisational identities would seem to threaten employees' loyalty to their organisation and therefore their commitment, thereby ultimately reducing their engagement levels. However, there is a more positive possibility (Pratt and Foreman 2000: 37):

> If a firm can gain sustainable advantage over its rivals through having a single identity that is rare and difficult to imitate, does it not seem logical that a firm that is characterized by multiple identities would be even more difficult for its rivals to imitate?

The authors cited complex industries such as healthcare and highly diversified firms where multiple identities are likely to exist but do not necessarily reduce engagement levels.

REFLECTION

Consider whether your own organisation seems to have a single powerful identity, or multiple identities. What kind of evidence have you to support your views on this, and in what ways do you think 'organisational identity' affects commitment levels in your organisation?

Fiol (2001: 693) could see the advantages of a single dominant organisational identity but also the downside. Sometimes it can 'severely constrain organizational interpretations, actions, and potential for change'. The very fact that people are bound strongly together in relation to that identity and its history can entrench them in behaviours that no longer serve the interests of the business. In a world of almost continuous change such a barrier to an organisation's adaptive capability can threaten the survival of the business:

> Nothing about what we do in organizations or how we do it at any given moment is likely to provide a sustainable advantage … Rather, identities may need to be continuously fluid. … The glue that holds them together may not always be a stable, fully elaborated culture, since this can lead to core rigidities. Rather, organizational members' deep identification with what they value and with the outcomes they wish to produce may bring coherence.

Therefore Fiol, like Pratt and Foreman (2000), was not convinced that multiple organisational identities necessarily threaten employee engagement. What is likely to matter most in today's highly unpredictable business environment is to gain employees' commitment not by focusing on 'who we are' (a single, powerful and enduring organisational identity) but rather on 'why we do what we do' (Fiol 2001: 697). The kind of employee commitment this can attract will favour rather than oppose the adoption of new adaptive behaviour, because it links to a set of values and outcomes that are core to the organisation no matter how many its identities or how often it may have to change identity through time. Fiol (*ibid*) quotes the example of General Electric, whose culture and multiple identities have changed radically since the 1980s, yet 'whose members' identification with an unwavering sense of excellence and devotion to a set of outcomes have remained unchanged at the core'.

At this point, looking back at the 'Big Idea' section in Chapter 6, we can see that Purcell and his colleagues (2003) advanced virtually the same views as a result of their UK-based research studies. To repeat part of that section, and to italicise salient phrases:

> A major finding from the Bath research is the power of the 'Big Idea' as the primary source of shared organisational purpose. It refers to a clear mission, unique to each organisation and underpinned by values and a culture expressing *what the organisation stands for and is trying to achieve*, that draws all organisational functions and members together in a shared purpose.

> By acting as this kind of glue, the Big Idea gives a collective focus to individuals' work and learning and to the application of their skills. *L&D activity plays its part in this process of connecting when it demonstrates and enacts the organisation's core values*, whether in formal training courses, on the job learning, mentoring, coaching or any other more informal learning processes.

In sum, therefore, while the main drivers to engagement are becoming reasonably clear the human processes related in some way to it – satisfaction, motivation and commitment – remain opaque. The precise nature and cause of the link they have with engagement may never be fully clear, but research is suggesting in relation to commitment, at least, some hopeful possibilities. Organisational identity is becoming a key issue, and here, given the high turbulence levels in the business environment, it is the ability to manage multiple rather than single identities that may provide the key to developing and sustaining high levels of commitment coupled with high individual and organisational adaptive capability.

ENGAGING THE PEOPLE: TASKS FOR L&D PROFESSIONALS

From this section, and adapting some advice from Dougherty (1999) made in a rather different context, we can conclude that in this second step towards adding value L&D professionals can help to enhance engagement levels in an organisation by:

- 'within the umbrella of organizational identity as value', using L&D events and processes to help people and business units to define themselves in terms of how they can contribute to value creation (Dougherty 1999: 183)

- helping to develop a common language of 'adding value' that 'can bridge the departmental thought worlds' (*ibid*), using L&D events and processes to demonstrate and enact what the organisation stands for and is trying to achieve

- helping to develop systematic patterns of thinking and acting in employees that will enable and stimulate them to use value-adding tools and techniques effectively (*ibid*)

- helping employees to work faster and smarter in their jobs and become skilled at self-managed continuous learning, thereby increasing the organisation's adaptive capability

- monitoring regularly how far and in what ways L&D activity is successful in engaging people with the organisation's values and goals. Climate surveys and audits such as those supplied by Investors in People give snapshots of a current situation, function or activity across the organisation in order to compare what is happening with what should be happening, and to identify any action needed. Audits are of most value when they are conducted at regular intervals through time, enabling trends to be identified and acted upon (Adamson and Caple 1996; Harrison 1999).

MEASURING THE DATA

RESEARCH FINDINGS

In Chapter 7 I noted the poor state of training evaluation across the world. A similar picture is evident in the broader field of measuring L&D's value-adding impact and potential. Consider the following research findings:

- A report produced in 2004 by consultancy firm Empower indicated that nearly half of FTSE-500 companies do not measure engagement, and those that do fail to link it to business aims (Higginbottom 2004).

- The CIPD's annual L&D surveys consistently show that demonstrating the value of L&D is a key challenge for the profession. In the 2006 L&D survey (CIPD 2006d) four fifths of respondents felt that their activities delivered greater value to the business than they could prove, yet only 36% sought to capture the effect of their activity on the bottom line, and even fewer (18%) attempted to assess return on investment. The 2007 L&D survey showed that less than 50% of respondents' organisations had an established method for evaluating the impact of L&D (Jennings 2007: 15). The 2008 survey revealed that although 56% of respondents anticipated more emphasis on monitoring, measurement and evaluation of training effectiveness during the coming five years – the second highest-rated kind of change anticipated – only 21% spent most of their time in such activity currently. This contrasted with 49% who were preoccupied with planning and managing L&D activity, and 46% with training delivery (CIPD 2008a).

One of the issues here is the need for more use of a pay-forward approach to measurement.

PAY-BACK AND PAY-FORWARD MEASURES

A pay-back approach to measurement assesses return on a past investment in financial or comparable quantitative terms. Typically in the L&D domain it involves measuring the impact of training outcomes on business variables like turnover, profit, increase in sales, conversion of leads to sales – what accountants call the 'direct return' achieved by the training investment (Lee 1996). It is used where cost, efficiency and short-term bottom-line results of L&D (and mainly of training) are the major concerns of the training function and/or its clients.

A 'pay-forward' assessment is future-oriented and is typically used to describe benefits that cannot be expressed directly in financial terms – Lee (1996) gives the examples of cultural/behavioural change, increased staff identification with business objectives and observed changes in individual or team behaviour and adds:

> The key is that investment in training is made not to produce an end in itself, but rather to improve the organisation's ability to learn and change. Hence the notion that the benefits are projected into the future.

The aim, then, is to add value. It typically involves L&D working with business partners and sponsors to generate options in order to decide which is likely to achieve the greatest balance of benefits for the business and its employees. With pay-forward assessment far more than financial considerations alone are at issue (Lee 1996: 31). If agreement on how to spend the L&D investment is reached at the start then once the investment is made and L&D activity is under way the vital measurement question becomes not 'What did it cost?' but 'Did it achieve what we agreed it should achieve? If so, let's build on that. If not, let's tackle the causes.' We saw this pay-forward approach illustrated in the long management development programme described in Chapter 8.

A 2007 CIPD research project offers a similar perspective on how to measure the value of learning, its findings persuasively suggesting that senior decision-makers now have only a 'limited interest' in return on investment measures, preferring the use of 'expectation' measures of value (Anderson 2007). These involve collecting hard and soft data from key stakeholders in order to assess how far benefits anticipated from the learning investment have been realised. The Institute has produced an online tool to enable the application of this 'return on expectations' approach (CIPD 2007d).

Both Lee (1996) and Wintermantel and Mattimore (1997) link the measures used to demonstrate the organisational contribution of training or HR to the role that these respective functions actually carry in an organisation. The two typologies are very similar, but where Lee refers to levels of 'organisational maturity' of the function Wintermantel and Mattimore refer to its 'mission'. In Table 18 I have adapted their HR classification system to fit the L&D domain.

THE RELEVANCE OF HUMAN CAPITAL REPORTING

Under the UK Companies Act, all company reports must include a business review incorporating information 'to the extent necessary for the understanding of the business' (Baron 2007b). This presents a real opportunity for HR professionals – including those in the L&D field – to demonstrate to external as well as internal stakeholders the value that their activity adds to the business. Sadly but perhaps predictably – given the proviso 'to the extent necessary' – evidence to date shows

TABLE 18 Aligning measures with mission

Mission: providing (L&D) services in response to requests
The 'servant' role associated with this mission typifies many training functions. It explains why commonly used L&D measures and metrics relate to the frequency and urgency with which the function responds to customer requests, the cost of its administrative systems and easily quantified training inputs, and so on.

Mission: optimising (L&D) resources, processes and systems
Where training/L&D functions have moved beyond the servant role to one where the major indicator of success is the extent to which they manage to do more with less – a typical scenario now in the public sector – relevant measures include the training cost per employee, attendance rates on training courses, use of e-technology to reduce training times and expand training numbers, and so on. The authors refer to the role here as 'expendable servant' because, perversely, the more successful the function is in achieving its mission, the smaller and more vulnerable to closure or outsourcing it is likely to become (Wintermantel and Mattimore 1997: 338).

Mission: Building competitive advantage by helping create productive organisations
Those L&D professionals able to follow this mission have an 'expert consultant' role and should be using more strategically-focused measures incorporating a pay-forward rather than a pay-back approach. The guiding measure of their success is to prove themselves expert consultants who 'help managers build capable and committed organizations' (*ibid*).

Mission: Shaping business' future success
L&D professionals with this mission have a strategic business partner role. Appropriate measures of impact therefore include contribution to defining the strategic direction of the business, helping to facilitate or generate good ideas for the business that otherwise might not have developed, creating added organisational value through unique, innovative L&D planning, design, delivery and evaluation processes for the external as well as internal market, and so on.

Mission: Leading in the building of knowledge-productive organisations
This is a variation of the mission that the authors propose for HR more widely ('the creation, preservation and utilization of human and intellectual capital'). It is a mission that we know is rarely followed, but to which L&D professionals operating in a knowledge economy should aspire. Key measures of impact here would relate to the organisation's value chain as a domain of integrated learning, to the rate of continuous improvement and innovation achieved through the effective generation, sharing and application of new knowledge from the organisation's grass roots upwards, and to the accessibility and sustainability of valuable tacit skills and knowledge across the business.

Source: Adapted from Wintermantel, R. E. and Mattimore, K. L. (1997)

that far from there having been a surge in meaningful HR capital reporting, financial measures still dominate (Phillips 2007b).

Although a CIPD study found that most investors are only interested in information indicating the top team's strategic capability, it also indicated that business analysts would value information on employees and how they are managed provided this is linked clearly to business outcomes (CIPD 2007e). To do this within the space constraints of a company report is challenging but possible. It poses at least four requirements:

- The HR professionals must have high credibility and influence in the business. Without that, they will not be able to persuade top management to include a specific HR section in the company report, let alone information within that on L&D.

- Their external reports must be brief – focused only on what has added/will add greatest value to the company – and accurate, therefore likely to generate trust.

- There must be a balance between data explaining the contribution of employees in the context of the organisation's unique position and data enabling comparisons to be made with other organisations (Baron 2007b).

- The data must be expressed in terms of business outcomes and refer to key performance indicators that are in use throughout the business, not merely in the HR/L&D domain. For example, merely identifying L&D inputs such as 'a major management development programme' and a KPI such as 'achieved high levels of participants' satisfaction with programme design and delivery' will not interest investors or analysts since these give no hint of value added to the business.

The CIPD's ongoing Human Capital Reporting project publishes an annual report on the development and use by companies represented on its HC Champions' Panel of data and measures to demonstrate the contribution of human capital to their bottom line. Not all the seven companies in its first report mentioned development data – a fact significant in itself. Equally significant was the fact that of those that did, several only reported on training inputs – number of training events, training days per employee, and so on – and not on outcomes for the business (CIPD 2006e). However, the reports do produce some measurement frameworks and methods that, although mostly in their early stages of use, could be adapted to an L&D context. Take the following case.

CASE EXAMPLE

CENTRICA AND STANDARD CHARTERED BANK: INTERNAL REPORTING ON HUMAN CAPITAL

Centrica, the energy company, has adopted seven 'must ask' questions as the foundation for its people measurement methodology to guide internal reporting on human capital:

- What is the business unit strategic agenda? Three months? Six months? 12 months? Beyond?

- What are the key people issues driving/blocking the strategic agenda?

- For each people issue, what would be a successful outcome? Ie what would 'good' look like?

- What information do we need to show that we achieved 'good'? How often? How detailed? How accurate? How should it be used to drive actions?

- Where will the data come from?

- How will the information be analysed/presented?

- Who is going to drive this?

Standard Chartered Bank uses a balanced scorecard to report across the organisation. They summarise their reporting as follows:

- Reports on the health of the business and areas for future strategic focus enables the business to spot early warning signals ...This helps with the prioritisation of resources and investment.

- Tracks progress on key areas or programmes where internal and/or external stakeholders have interest, for example diversity trends

- Provides rigorous metrics to underpin key strategic processes eg resourcing skills and talent reviews

- Creates internal benchmarks by comparing markers and other business units

- Demonstrates the contribution of the HR function in the journey to become a more strategic player in the organisation

- Allows planning and measurement of the impact of initiatives developed as a result of the data.

Source: Reproduced from CIPD (2006e), pp12, 13. With permission.

These companies' focus on internal reporting makes a vital point: before there can be any meaningful external reporting on L&D value-adding activity there must be adequate internal measurement systems (Brown 2004). That is the essential starting point.

MEASURING WHAT MATTERS

Questions like those used at Centrica are relevant to the measurement of L&D's impact on added organisational value because they reflect a set of principles that should always drive that measurement. These were also reflected in the case study recounted in Chapter 8:

- Put measurement into perspective. 'There is no truly objective measure of either HR resource or efficiency ... because ... the analysis of even highly quantifiable measures ... requires subjective, judgmental interpretation' (Walker 1992: 336).

- Use measurement to make substantive improvements. An overemphasis on measurement can be counterproductive by leading to attempts to score well. Its rightful purpose is to lead to improvements (Walker 1992). There needs to be 'a shift from measurement as a system of control to measurement as a system of learning', especially when using scorecards for measurement purposes (Neely 2007: 16).

- Use measures that demonstrate and test the linkage between L&D activity and specific business outcomes. It is pointless to attempt to make a direct

correlation between an organisation's bottom-line financial performance and
its L&D practice since L&D activity does not achieve its most value-adding
organisational impact on its own but with the support of – and in alignment
with – a cluster of HR practices carefully tailored to organisation context
(Purcell *et al* 2003).

- Focus adequately on the future. By definition 'learning and development'
  incorporates more activity focused on the longer term than on the immediate.
  Measures restricted to identifying short-term financial returns will miss much of
  the added value achieved by L&D activity.

TASKS FOR L&D PROFESSIONALS

From this section we can conclude that in this third and final step towards adding
value to the organisation, key tasks for L&D professionals include:

- using the business's operating and financial review systems rather than any
  unique to the L&D function to make explicit L&D's value-adding strategies and
  targets, to communicate these to business partners, and to measure L&D activity
  – a point urged by Charles Handy in relation to all HR work (Scott 2005) and
  one that, again, was emphasised in the case narrative in Chapter 8

- presenting to business sponsors insights into issues related to adding value not
  on an ad hoc or crisis basis but regularly so that it will become part of their
  ongoing conversations about the priorities of the business (Gratton 2005)

- before any decisions are made on how to 'spend' the L&D investment, sharing
  with business partners and sponsors a clear picture of the initial state of affairs,
  then envisaging how various options would be likely to change that picture and
  how such change could be measured

- expressing learning expectations in terms of clear, feasible value-adding
  goals. For example, a goal to do with 'improving managerial effectiveness'
  is too imprecise. In what ways do partners and sponsors want managers to
  improve? How do they expect managers to act and perform once training and
  development has taken place? What would they know and be able to do, and
  how would they behave then as distinct from now?

- agreeing with partners and sponsors on the path to follow in order to achieve
  agreed outcomes, and on how and when to measure progress along that path
  (making use of strategic milestones and business KPIs and metrics)

- agreeing also on what must happen in the workplace if that path is to be taken.
  For example, learning driven by new technology cannot achieve its aims in a
  workplace where there are no skills to use it, no infrastructure to support it,
  no willingness on management's side to exploit its full potential or a fear of new
  technology amongst the workforce

- producing a pragmatic mix of quantitative measurement methods for hard objectives, and for softer objectives a range of techniques to capture their essence – for example, behaviourally anchored rating-scales, surveys, benchmarking and observation to ensure cross-checks on value and outcomes

- ensuring that measures are broad and flexible enough to capture the essence of L&D activity without interfering overmuch in operations. 'Measure everything' is not a natural law: it is a dangerous and time-consuming obsession.

CONCLUSION

By now you should have a sound understanding of the concept of adding value, and should be able to identify the kind of added value that L&D activity is producing or could produce for an organisation. You should also feel confident to tackle the review questions contained in Appendix 3.

The main ground covered by the chapter's five sections has been:

- the distinction between providing 'best value' and adding value

- Porter's Value Chain model, its relevance for the L&D domain, and three tasks that it suggests for L&D professionals seeking to add value through their activity

- Green's 'Align, engage and measure' value-adding framework :

  - *aligning the people*: how the balanced scorecard can direct people's attention to the organisation's purpose and align them with its goals; five tasks for L&D practitioners to aid this alignment and to encourage the use of scorecard approaches as vehicles for learning, continuous improvement and innovation

  - *engaging the people*: the meaning of the engagement and its main drivers; the complex and dynamic interrelationship of engagement, satisfaction, motivation and commitment; the importance of organisational identity in relation to employee engagement and the organisation's adaptive capability; five tasks for L&D practitioners to enhance engagement

  - *measuring the data*: the importance of measuring only what matters and of distinguishing between pay-back and pay-forward assessments; matching measurement approaches to the L&D function's role and mission in the organisation; principles to guide the measurement process; eight tasks for L&D professionals seeking to achieve clear, credible and business-relevant measures and metrics to assess how far L&D activity achieves the value that stakeholders intended and expected.

EXLPORE FURTHER

FURTHER INFORMATION SOURCES

CIPD (2006f) *Reflections on Employee Engagement*. Change Agenda. London: CIPD. Online version also available at: http:// www.cipd.co.uk/ researchinsights [accessed 7 March 2008]

http://www.balancedscorecard. org/basics/bsc1.html [accessed 6 March 2008]

CIPD podcast, 1 March 2007. *How do you get employees to go the extra mile? Are private* sector employees more engaged than those in the public sector? And how can you measure engagement? Available at: http://www.cipd.co.uk/podcasts [accessed 25 March 2008]

CIPD podcast, 1 September 2007. *The value of learning.* Available at: http://www.cipd.co.uk/ podcasts [accessed 25 March 2008]

PART 4

Building for the future

CHAPTER 15

Tackling Challenges of Change

INTRODUCTION

In Part 4 of the book the focus is on building organisational capacity and adaptability for the future. The subject matter of the first three chapters concerns ways in which L&D processes can aid those tasks. The fourth reflects on major themes that have emerged from the book to identify challenges that they signal for the L&D profession.

In 1982 Pettigrew and his colleagues identified the 'change agent' as a key training role. Today, with the speed of technological innovation and volatile economic conditions across the world, helping organisations and individuals to tackle challenges of change has become core to the work of the L&D profession, which faces its own challenges too. The L&D function becomes particularly vulnerable when the organisation is threatened. Its budget is often the first to be cut and immediate problems facing the business tend to dominate its agenda, raising the risk of rushing into quick fixes that later come unstuck.

Major organisational change usually requires a shift in workplace culture and new patterns of social organisation. Ideally these should be planned well in advance but today the speed and unpredictability of external events call for ever faster responses at all organisational levels. L&D professionals must therefore be able to rapidly carry out what Starkey and McKinlay (1993: 2) described as 'deep analysis rather than superficial prescription' to provide timely and informed advice and initiatives that will aid the business and those who work for it.

This five-part chapter does not detail change management techniques. Its purpose is to explore challenges of change and their implications for L&D activity. The first section covers common reasons for the widespread failure of change initiatives and identifies various approaches to guide change management. The following three explain how Lewin's widely-known three-stage change cycle can be put to practical use, and the final section suggests tasks for L&D professionals at each of its stages.

REFLECTION

If major change had to be introduced in your organisation, or one with which you are familiar, what do you think would be the main barriers that would stand in its way, and how might L&D activity enable some of those barriers to be tackled?

MANAGING ORGANISATIONAL CHANGE

WHY DO CHANGE INITIATIVES FAIL?

A 2003 survey by the CIPD of more than 800 CEOs, HR directors and managers from private and public sector organisations confirmed the broad scope and far-reaching challenges of reorganisations today, but also indicated that 40% of these initiatives fail to achieve their objectives (CIPD 2003d). Hamlin (2002) found in his review of 1990s' research studies that many change initiatives failed so badly that their unintended consequences 'seriously damage the organization and the people within it'. A major cause was failure to appreciate both the complexity of process issues associated with organisational change and the difficulty of managing them successfully, coupled with a frequent lack of change management expertise (Hamlin 2001: 19). While much attention is usually paid to hard measures of change like cost-reduction and increased accountability, far less is paid to 'softer' outcomes such as faster decision-making, more flexibility and greater participation. Assessment of the psychological and behavioural impact of change on employees and its implications for the organisation is also often ignored (Hamlin *et al* 2001: 77).

At the heart of what he called 'this vicious circle' of failure in the management of change Hamlin (2002: 105) saw:

> a perceived lack of sufficient evidence-based or research-informed professional practice on the part both of line managers, trainers, developers and other HR professionals.

His proposals to improve L&D professionals' change management capability therefore placed a strong emphasis on:

- the need for careful choice of theoretical approaches, models and concepts to inform and shape their decision-making and practice

- the importance of developing a strong research culture in their work. They should build into their activity the time to assess why particular aspects of managing change have failed or succeeded, in order to help them build new theories informed by their own professional practice.

Hamlin (2001) identified a widespread lack of awareness of the vital contribution that the L&D function can make to change management, in terms both of helping people to acquire the necessary new knowledge, skills and behaviours and of ensuring the optimum use across the organisation of existing know-how. He attributed this not only to low credibility of many L&D professionals but also to an often unfavourable management climate. Keep and Mayhew (1994: ii) directed attention to another important contextual factor – lack of sophisticated personnel management systems – and context had been highlighted too in earlier research by Goodman and Dean (1982: 268). The majority of L&D-led organisational change initiatives that they examined had become 'deinstitutionalized' over time because of a failure to develop the structures and management environment needed to embed them.

The evaluation problem

The influence of contextual as well of individual factors on the quality and outcomes of change management initiatives points strongly to the need for their careful planning and evaluation, yet Hamlin and Davies (2001: 55) found evaluating strategies for change to be 'one of the most under-reported issues in the British management literature' with very few longitudinal studies carried out in different organisational contexts. Skinner (2004) came to a similar conclusion. In her extensive desk research and her case-based study she found that decisions to go ahead with many change initiatives were based essentially on:

> the unquestioned belief that there would be a benefit to the organisation from introducing these particular change initiatives [which] reduced any perceived need to incorporate planned evaluation – those responsible for their initiation already 'knew' that their effect would be positive.

Typical reasons for lack of formal evaluation included:

- a perceived difficulty of measurement, with managers feeling that the literature offered them only limited help

- reluctance to break new evaluative ground

- failure to plan for evaluation at the start of the whole change management process

- a tendency for management to base decisions on gut feeling and personal informal assessment.

Another important reason lies in divergent views in the social sciences about how to conduct research into organisational change. One view is that such change is essentially driven by the top. The other is that it emerges primarily from the bottom up, being determined by previous actions taken especially by individuals (Hollis 1994; Hatton 2001). When research studies draw on different methodologies and the concepts used have differing bases, there is little likelihood of reaching shared understanding. As Hatton (2001: 107) remarked:

> Studies jump alarmingly from individuals (e.g. motivation at work, job satisfaction), to groups (e.g. dynamics, organizational culture), to organizations (e.g. organizational theory, strategy and marketing) and even to nations (as in the continuing debate over the management of public services, ... Assembling data at one level of analysis (or organization), and using it to draw conclusions in another, is simply nonsensical.

KEYS TO SUCCESSFUL ORGANISATIONAL CHANGE INITIATIVES

If change programmes rest on a slim and unreliable evidence base it is unsurprising that so many fail. This makes it all the more important for those involved in the planning and management of change to be aware of those research findings likely to provide valid guidelines for their work. In this connection a CIPD survey has identified six features that seem to characterise successful reorganisations, several linking directly to the role of HR professionals (CIPD 2004b):

- *Holistic organisation-wide change* – This involves planning and implementing cohesive programmes of complementary changes in organisation structures, business processes and supporting systems. The survey found that while changes in leadership, culture, business processes and enabling technologies were a common focus of reorganisation, wider complementary changes to – for example – career and reward structures were less frequent. The approach was usually piecemeal instead of holistic.

- *Effective project management* – The use of formal project management techniques and skills offers the likelihood of a greater level of success than using other practices, both in delivering reorganisations to time and cost and in achieving planned outcomes regarding organisational efficiency and effectiveness. However, more than half the organisations surveyed by the CIPD did not possess the necessary project management skills.

- *Employee involvement* – HR professionals have a key responsibility to ensure that this is meaningful, not tokenist, and that it takes place in the context of rigorous project management and clearly defined milestones.

- *Effective leadership* – The approach adopted by the executive team in planning and leading change is a fundamental determinant of success – a point to which I will return regularly in this chapter.

- *Extensive communication with external stakeholders* – This is essential in order to obtain and provide relevant information regarding the change initiative.

- *Internal and external experience* – The survey showed that reorganisation planning benefited from inputs from people within and outside the organisation possessing extensive experience of reorganisation programmes. The experience was particularly valuable when it had been gained in different kinds and sectors of organisations, thus providing varied perspectives on ways forward.

THEORETICAL FRAMEWORKS TO GUIDE THE CHANGE PROCESS

There are innumerable theoretical frameworks to guide the change process. Amongst the best known are the McKinsey seven-S framework – a holistic approach to determine how the company will operate (Peters and Waterman 1982), Kotter's (1996) eight-step model, Kübler-Ross's (1969) seven-stage 'grief' cycle and Lewin's (1951) three-stage 'unfreeze, transition, refreeze' cycle. Hendry (1995) identified two typical approaches, programmatic and critical path, to achieving one of the most difficult of all organisational change tasks – changing culture. The programmatic approach assumes that behaviour can be altered by a planned experience or set of experiences, whereas critical path adopts a more incremental, long-term approach that recognises the need for a sustained change process in order to prevent the regressive tendency that so often causes culture change to fail. The following case provides an example of the critical path approach.

CASE EXAMPLE

CULTURE CHANGE AT CAMDEN COUNCIL

In 2007 Camden Council gained external recognition as one of the top 10 high-performing councils in England and Wales. Three years previously it had faced an unusual challenge – the need for major change in order to sustain its excellent reputation. The problem was that excellence was costing too much to achieve, and that strong service departments needed to offer a more joined-up service to customers.

The decision was made at that point to change the Council's culture through a set of organisational values titled Camden's 'Ways of Working', reflecting:

- focusing on customers

- working together

- individuals taking personal responsibility

- doing things in better, cheaper ways

By 2007, in the view of Mike Cooke, director of organisational development, the new values had become embedded across the organisation, with recruitment, induction and performance all operating in the context of 'Ways of Working'. The change had not been achieved by any single major culture change initiative but by a gradual and incremental process. Cooke explained:

> We set about systematically, quietly and persistently weaving our Ways of Working into our business processes and everyday life.

He said that the journey had not been smooth but ultimately it had been successful, with the Council delivering a major efficiency programme in 2007, Council Tax frozen for the first time, and an employee survey yielding, at the height of organisational uncertainty, some of the best results seen at Camden. The HR team had also 'reinvented' itself, modernising its service in line with customer feedback and achieving £1 million savings in 2007.

Lessons learnt from the change process were:

- All organisational members need to make a conscious decision to behave differently (and so must be persuaded of the need for organisational and individual change).

- A big formal change programme is not necessary; change can be achieved by 'subtle, quiet and persistent changes'.

- HR staff working together as a united team is vital to the success of change.

Source: Cooke, M. (2008)
People Management, 1 May

Lewin's three-stage change process

Lewin (1951) saw organisations as dynamic systems that make progress through continuous adaptation to their environments. He believed that in order for people to change there has to be a disturbance – whether immediate or incremental – that is powerful enough to tip them into action and achieve the 'unfreezing' of old habits, attitudes and values standing in the way of change. He developed 'force-field analysis' as a technique to decide when the time is ripe for organisational change and how it should be achieved. It involves identifying the relative strengths of forces likely to support or oppose change, and of those likely to stay neutral until a crucial tipping point for change is reached. Such analysis is crucial to the success of the planning of change. It can sometimes suggest that change should not be introduced at the present time, or that a gradual approach is the wisest way forward – an approach taken in the case example I have just outlined.

Following the unfreezing stage there has to be a transition period that allows people time to come to practical terms with change, acquiring the skills, understanding and values that will help them to move forward competently and with confidence in their new or changed roles and tasks. The final stage – refreezing – marks the point at which a different way of life in the organisation has taken root, with changed norms of behaviour and performance, and systems in place to encourage, support and reward them. Refreezing is never complete, nor should it be: it is best understood as marking the end of one stage in the organisation's life-cycle and the start of another. Burack (1991: 94–5) recommended a combination of programmatic and critical path approaches to move an organisation through this three-stage process.

Kemp (2001: 263), reflecting on his own attempts to establish an integrated HRD approach in financial services, found that 'using someone else's model is simply using yesterday's solution out of context'. He concluded that there is no 'right' way of bringing about organisational change: context, and diagnosis of the fundamental drivers of change, are the crucial factors to consider. His points, of course, are valid. However, Lewin's conceptual framework is in widespread use in organisations and has been praised by Edgar Schein (1995) as 'fundamentally necessary in trying to explain various phenomena I had observed, and I found that it lent itself very well to refinement and elaboration'. Why reinvent the wheel? I therefore use it to frame the rest of the chapter. In so doing I cannot avoid over-simplification. For an explanation of its true power and value and a fascinating account of how to use it in a graduate class context I recommend Schein's web-based paper referred to above.

ACHIEVING ORGANISATIONAL CHANGE: THE UNFREEZING PROCESS

THE ROLE OF CORPORATE LEADERSHIP

In today's organisations many corporate leaders are having to drive a more or less continuous organising process to achieve enough flexibility to 'get on with the business' while also 'creating new business'. There must be accompanying changes in strategy as current stocks and resources within the firm are redeployed and/or new ones are acquired (Whittington and Mayer 2002). Success in speedily achieving the necessary unlearning and new learning that such innovation requires is vital, because organisations have only short periods in which they can maintain competitive advantage before strategic assets lose their relevance (Kirjavainen 2001: 189).

The first stage of Lewin's change process involves motivating people to accept the need for change, and engaging them in the change process. It requires the identification and analysis of reasons for change and the generation and evaluation of options for ways forward. Old features of the organisation's culture have to be 'unlocked', unlearning has to occur and new 'internal behavioural benchmarks' should begin to emerge (Burack 1991). It is essential to take people management issues fully into account at this planning stage. No matter how rapidly change may have to be introduced, expectations should be managed by giving employees early warning and full information about what is proposed, and consulting with them in order to get their reactions and suggestions and fully involve them in the whole change process (CIPD 2005f). The more adaptable to change the workforce is already, the more fruitful that involvement will be, and this is yet another factor that, in today's turbulent economic conditions, argues for a continuing investment by organisations in the development of workplace learning cultures and of the capability and commitment at all levels to manage and sustain them.

Senge (1996) saw corporate leaders as the social architects of their organisations, needing to work with a broad-based group whose membership stretches beyond the traditional elite of senior managers in order to produce innovative policies, strategies and structures for the future. The key is not 'getting the right strategy' but:

- fostering strategic thinking to gain insights into the nature of the complexity facing the organisation and to formulate concepts and plans for coping with it (Mason and Mitroff 1981: 16)

- ensuring learning processes that will help everyone to gain a better understanding of the current organisational reality and to suggest new possibilities for shaping the future (Senge 1996: 296).

Senge's advice reflects the constructivist approach to learning that takes full account not only of what should be done – systems, networks and rule-following – but of what is really happening here, why, and what those involved feel and think about it (Beckett 1999: 86). Beckett suggests that this kind of learning can be promoted through workplace processes like mentoring, coaching and team-based projects because they focus on a shared organisational vision. However, in the particular situation much will depend on individual readiness to learn and on people's enthusiasm to join in shared learning efforts. Many theories of adult learning point to the conclusion that people are pragmatic in their approach to learning, doing so only when convinced it is in their own interests. The most important requirement, therefore, is for employees to believe that the learning and change asked of them will lead them as well as their organisation 'to a better state' (West 2002: 201).

MANAGING CHANGE AS 'LEARNING'

In Schein's (1995) view 'change' is better defined as 'learning' and planned change as 'managed learning'. It is essential when planning any major change to first identify and understand the dominant assumptions in the organisation about learning and whether those assumptions need to change (Nevis *et al* 1995). As Bohn observed (1994), many organisations become proficient at only one or a few methods of learning before management assumes that there is nothing more to learn. There is then a tendency to 'lock in' present methods by specifying rigid procedures that can deskill the workforce – the phenomenon of 'skilled incompetence' that was explained in Chapter 5.

There is a broad consensus in the literature that learning and knowledge processes must change substantially as organisations move from operating in relatively stable to increasingly unstable environmental conditions. When an organisation can achieve relatively unchanging goals by a strategy of continuous improvement, single-loop, adaptive learning will usually suffice, since it will produce an understanding of the gaps with competitors that relate to productivity, quality or operational flexibility and cost, and of how to steadily close those gaps (Senge 1990). However, when the task is requiring fast and innovative responses to unfamiliar and major challenges, this puts a premium on double-loop learning, where the very goals, norms and assumptions of the organisation itself have to be questioned if the organisation is to survive, let alone make progress (Argyris 1996).

Double-loop learning requires leaders at all organisational levels to be open to questioning of their own thinking, policies and actions. Initially this is likely to produce confusion, defensiveness and a general state of 'muddling through'. This should not automatically be dismissed by leaders and managers as the result of 'inertia, incompetence or ignorance'. In some circumstances – especially when fundamental unlearning has to be achieved – it may be a necessary condition that, together with leadership that generates a shared purpose across the organisation, stimulates creative thinking and ultimately leads to a strategy for the future which all stakeholders endorse (Stacey, 1995: 484). It can protect against the institutional inertia that is common in a hitherto overprotected stable environment.

PROMOTING UNLEARNING

A CIPD (2003d) report on reorganising revealed that although comparatively few respondents reported use of seminars, media reports, external consultants and organisation peers to stimulate their own and others' thinking about how to reorganise, many intended to make greater use of learning from external sources in the future, especially through benchmarking other organisations.

However, the most important requirement is for corporate leaders to create consultative and decision-making processes that can bring to the surface and challenge prevailing mental models, while also ensuring that all parties are committed to ultimately producing a vision that will unify and engage all organisational members. This highlights the need for the kind of ongoing leadership development that will build an executive team that (Tushman and Nadler 1996):

* possesses the technical, social and conceptual skills to accomplish diverse tasks and recognises the need for changing roles and tasks at top level as new challenges emerge for the organisation

* has effective problem-solving processes. 'Once the decisions are made, the executive team must implement [them] with a single voice' (*ibid*: 154)

* provides clear corporate direction for change and infuses the change programme with energy and value. The executive team must work actively on articulating vision, on energising the organisation, and on encouraging required behaviours by providing the necessary resources and rewards and building supportive organisational structures and processes.

The implementation of change depends for its success on collaborative relationships and complementary skills at all leadership levels. It is particularly reliant on managers and HR professionals who have broadly based perspectives and relationships and foster supportive organisational norms and values. Front-line managers play crucial roles here (Purcell and Hutchinson 2007).

The case that follows describes a major restructuring programme to which the organisation's HR function is attempting to make a powerful contribution informed by a new vision.

HR'S CHANGE STRATEGY AT THE BBC

The British Broadcasting Corporation (BBC) employs 23,027 people worldwide. In 2007 its director-general announced a contentious new six-year strategy for the troubled corporation – one of 'delivering creative future'. A major trigger for the strategy was the need to achieve extensive cost-savings to compensate for a £2 billion budget shortfall. Amongst other measures it is likely to involve the closure of 2,500 positions, the creation of around 700 new jobs, most to be filled internally, and the selling off of Television Centre in west London, estimated value £200 million and currently the base for thousands of employees (Phillips 2007c).

For Kelly, director of BBC People, the Corporation's strategic HR division, the new strategy means 'rebalancing' the workforce during a period of radical change and working in line with a new vision for employees. The vision, which resulted from eight months' work by HR staff and extensive interviews with senior managers, has five themes:

* *Collective leadership* – ensuring that everyone understands the new strategy and direction and can relate it to their own area of work

* *Skills and talent for a changing BBC* – equipping the workforce with the skills they will need for a future that, with the emergence of new technology and multimedia platforms, will be very different from the past. This will require retraining, reskilling and redeploying

* *Reward for performance* – involving what Kelly (quoted by Phillips 2007c: 15) calls more 'agile' working patterns needed to 'take costs out of the business to reinvest in services and content'

* *Changing how we work* – requiring the engagement of employees and unions with the new practices, so that old working practices will not be imported into new state of the art facilities in Glasgow and Salford

* *Getting the basics right* – focusing on giving managers the tools and techniques to manage people in a flexible way. 'The basics are as important as strategy' (Kelly, ibid).

Source: Phillips, L. (2007c)
People Management, 1 November

BBC People is no stranger to controversy. In 2006 it outsourced many of its services to Centrica on a 10-year contract, primarily to cut costs. In February 2007 the Corporation was threatened by an all-out stoppage of union members in BBC TV News followed by three days of action by 100 staff in a technical department affected by the rota changes. The strike was only averted at the last minute, after a protracted period of negotiations with the unions and referral of the redeployment plan to ACAS. The threat of strike action resurfaced at the end of 2007 when the

Corporation's plans for its 'Delivering creative future' strategy were announced. In May 2008 the Corporation was heavily criticised for financial mismanagement resulting in a £36 million overspend on its websites budgets. In Chapter 10 I outlined some of the radical organisational change programmes, with their associated HR initiatives, now being pursued across the public sector – notably in the NHS and in local government. The same generic challenges that they confront face the BBC's change programme also. Will that programme, and within it the new HR strategy, succeed in moving beyond the 'unfreezing' stage?

ACHIEVING ORGANISATIONAL CHANGE: THE TRANSITION PERIOD

This second stage of Lewin's three-stage process involves changing what needs to be changed and consolidating new directions. Communication must help to boost employees' morale and belief in the change by raising awareness of growing successes in restructuring the organisation and in shifting culture, values and behaviours. New forms of communication and behaviour should also begin to take root (Burack 1991).

TASKS FOR THE EXECUTIVE TEAM

While old values and behaviours are being replaced by new ones that will take time to become habitual, the organisation's executive team has four crucial tasks in order to ensure that the momentum of change is sustained without any damaging regression to old ways of behaving and performing (Tushman and Nadler 1996):

- Develop and communicate a clear image of the organisation's strategy and core values, and the role of innovation in meeting the organisation's strategy.

- Be a role model for all organisational members. Words and action must go together, not contradict one another.

- Use informal and formal rewards to reinforce innovation.

- Communicate organisational history that provides key crises, events, organisational myths and heroes to shape and reinforce new values and behaviour – or create and regularly communicate a new history as the change process unfolds.

 REFLECTION

For a fuller appreciation of that fourth point you should go back to the discussion of 'issues of organisational identity' in Chapter 14 and consider its implications in the context of this section.

CHALLENGES OF CROSS-BOUNDARY WORKING

One of the main tasks of leaders, managers and HR professionals in reframing an organisation to become more innovative and adaptable to future change is to build a culture of working with customers, forming teams, appreciating the relationships among functions and businesses well enough to shift them as necessary, and developing an ongoing sense of how well they are doing. Dougherty (1999: 186) calls this 'high cross-value development' because it is about cutting across all internal boundaries, as well as reaching out across external ones, in order to co-create value throughout the value chain of the business. However, the collaborative behaviours that such development requires can be difficult to achieve, as the following case illustrates.

CLOSED NETWORKS OR STRUCTURAL HOLES?

CASE EXAMPLE

Gargiulo and Benassi (2000) used concepts of network closure and structural holes to explore views of managers working in a special unit within the Italian subsidiary of a leading multinational computer firm that was undergoing major organisational change. The study was complex. This, and the small size of the sample, means caution should be exercised in generalising from the findings. Nevertheless the following insights that it produced have particular interest at this point in the chapter.

Closed networks – that is to say, groups characterised by close, cohesive ties (Coleman 1990) – were typically brought about through years of collaborative working within the same organisational units. A shared organisational history bound people together, prompted them to exchange advice and services, and allowed for repeated exchanges that promoted strong relationships. Closed networks had organisational value in supporting the emergence and the enforcement of the norms

that could secure co-operative behaviour and protect individuals against the risk of defection.

On the other hand networks containing 'structural holes' (Burt 1992, 1997) tended to have the opposite effects. Such teams were characterised by 'dispersed ties' – that is to say, by relationships that had to be formed between team members and parties outside the team's (and often the organisation's) boundaries in order to achieve the team's mission.

Over time the strength of the 'normative environment' developed in a closed network (work team) could bring disadvantages to its members, isolating them increasingly from the outside world. Also a sudden rise in uncertainty triggered by large-scale change could lead them to retreat further into the perceived safety of their cohesive network, thereby reducing both their and the wider organisation's ability to respond positively to change. By contrast a group whose network was rich in structural holes was by its nature better able to promote innovation and advance by exploring new opportunities and importing new information.

Whether managers preferred the safety of highly cohesive teams to the flexibility of teams with 'structural holes' seemed to depend to an extent on the stage each manager had reached in his or her career. Those new in role were likely to prefer a small, cohesive core of supportive contacts in order to legitimise their authority and establish their identity, but that advantage could become a liability at later stages of the managerial career. At that point many experienced a need to develop a range of different contacts across network boundaries in order to be help them cope effectively with the increased diversity and challenges of their management responsibilities.

The researchers concluded that although each kind of team can produce some benefits for the organisation and for team members, closed teams are more likely to suffer from a poor ability to adapt to significant environmental changes. Networks rich in structural holes have more potential to promote adaptability, the generation of new knowledge, and innovation.

Source: Gargiulo, M. and Benassi, M. (2000)

BUILDING ADAPTABLE TEAMS

Gargiulo and Benassi were studying a cluster of 'communities of practice', so it is unsurprising that the case contains strong echoes of some conclusions reached in Chapter 5 concerning unlearning, adaptive and generative learning in such communities. One crucial insight provided by their research is that although organisations facing more of less continuous change are increasingly looking to cross-functional teamworking to achieve adaptability, that outcome is unlikely to occur where some teams have become very tight-knit and inward-looking (something, of course, that open systems theory long ago made clear – Cyert and March 1963).

The study also suggests that where a team is highly cohesive, simply instructing or expecting it to collaborate across boundaries may prove counterproductive, driving team members yet further into the perceived safety of their silo and often securing the co-operation of key players (senior managers, for example) in so doing. When even one team in an organisation fails to commit to the task of cross-boundary working, the success of the whole organisational change process may be at risk. The risk will increase where some teams do not commit to forming collaborative relationships with agencies and individuals in the organisation's external value chain (as discussed in Chapter 14).

How can a productive balance of cohesion and adaptability in teams be achieved in an organisation undergoing major change? Tushman and Nadler's (1996) research into innovative organisations suggests the importance of establishing and embedding in all organisational routines, systems and practices (especially in the performance management system) the following norms:

- informality, enabling the exercise of discretionary behaviour and the formation of cross-boundary social as well as work ties

- high work standards and performance expectations

- flexible decision-making, problem-solving and conflict resolution patterns

- strong informal linkages across the organisation and across its boundaries.

Their findings suggest that practices likely to promote powerful cross-functional linkages include (Tushman and Nadler 1996: 143):

- *teams, committees or task forces,* bringing together individuals from diverse areas to work on common opportunities or problems

- *project managers* working to achieve integration and co-ordination for new developments

- *formal meetings* providing a regularly scheduled setting for individuals from different areas to share information and trade ideas. They also build informal relationships that facilitate cross-organisation problem-solving and collaboration.

REFLECTION

Reflecting on any L&D function with which you are familiar, how far do you see that function to be working in a silo, or on the other hand to be characterised by structural holes that enhance adaptability? In either case, why has the function developed in that way?

ACHIEVING ORGANISATIONAL CHANGE: 'REFREEZING'

This third stage of Lewin's change process involves reinforcing new values so that they become internalised in individuals, and embedding a new culture through 'a growing nucleus of organizational processes, relationships, leadership styles, analysis approaches and rituals' (Burack 1991: 94–5).

ENSURING CONSISTENCY AND EQUITY

At this stage it is vital to ensure a general consistency and equity in the way changed HR processes of recruitment, appraisal, rewards, development and disengagement are administered (Tushman and Nadler 1996). The CIPD (2003d) survey highlighted two particularly important leadership contributions for HR professionals here:

- *A reorganisation process centred on project and people management* – Gaining performance improvement from reorganisation requires skilled management of both the project and people aspects of the process. The survey found that this capability was not widespread, but that where HR professionals had formal managerial roles in reorganisations and performed effectively in them there did appear to be an improvement in employee-related factors such as morale.

- *People management system-wide design* – A large proportion of respondents recognised that managing holistic, system-wide change in people management practice was important, yet in reality piecemeal change seemed the norm. Changes that should have been made to reward structures and career systems in order to ensure effective and durable implementation of change programmes were particularly neglected.

Another requirement (illustrated in the Procon UK case in Chapter 8) is to develop a performance management system that clarifies the relative effort to be given to different goals and tasks at team and individual levels. At this point it is vital to monitor the effects of change on employees' well-being and morale, since much research now points to the negative impact that the pace and nature of organisational change is having on loyalty and retention rates and on managers' ability to carry out their increasing responsibilities effectively.

In Chapter 11 I mentioned research findings produced by Worrall and Cooper (2006) that concerned the impact of change on employee well-being. To elaborate briefly here: they commented on the unprecedented weight and multi-faceted nature of organisational change since 2000 and its gathering pace – most notably in the public sector and in public listed companies. They found a 'clear relationship' between the type of organisational change experienced and the incidence and severity of psychological symptoms amongst managers (*ibid*: 38) and their data suggested that change makes a far more negative impact on the health of managers (especially at junior levels) than of directors, the latter being less than half as likely to assess their own health as poor. Worrall and Cooper emphasised the variety of factors likely to be at play here, but concluded that with more managers being confronted by more types of change than ever before, many are now struggling to cope. They doubted the sustainability of change at current organisational levels. They also doubted the feasibility of the multi-faceted form that it is so often taking.

Perhaps most worrying are two features which, they observed, often related as much to HR managers as to line managers (Worrall and Cooper 2006: 38):

> Many managers feel these systems (of control and surveillance) have been imposed on them: that they have little say in setting targets and objectives, many of which are

seen as unreasonable and unattainable. Too many managers think their workloads are unmanageable within their contracted hours.

[There is a] sharp and systematic difference of views between the boardroom and the rest of the organisation, where two groups of managers seem to be living in different worlds.

Such research findings raise the likelihood that the most severe problems of organisational change may often occur not during the 'unfreeze' and 'transition' stages but during 'refreezing'. As I have already noted, refreezing is not, despite that term, a fixed state but a continuing process. It is therefore essential for leaders and HR professionals in particular to maintain a watching brief over that process right across the organisation to ensure that the momentum of change is not lost, and that plans are being implemented without damage to employees' health, well-being, morale and engagement with the change process.

Looking back over this summary of the three-stage change process in action, it is useful to reflect on the wise advice given well over two decades ago by Michael Thomas (1985), then a principal consultant with PA Consulting Services. It proves, once again, that in the literature and practice of HR and L&D there is little, if anything, new under the sun:

● Give special attention in a change situation to the 'key opinion formers' – those who 'by virtue of role, personality or history have undue leverage on the opinions and behaviour of others'. These are the people whom it is essential to get 'alongside' to champion the cause of change.

● Follow up, or if necessary precede, any high-impact communication campaign with real change to those structures and systems, policies and practices that threaten contradictory messages.

● Use every opportunity to reinforce the new values formally and informally.

● Try to keep to a small number of values, preferably one, and make operational compromises accordingly.

CHANGE AGENT TASKS FOR L&D PROFESSIONALS

CHANGE MANAGEMENT PROBLEMS

In an environment of constant change the ability to mobilise people to deliver change is essential. In the PricewaterhouseCoopers 11th Annual Global CEO Survey (PWC 2008) that I will also discuss in the next chapter, most of the 1,300 chief executive officer respondents reported confidence in their leadership teams' competence to drive change but did not see those teams' efforts reflected in the results their companies achieved. They put much of the blame for that on senior

FIGURE 17 Learning and development to aid and stimulate organisational change

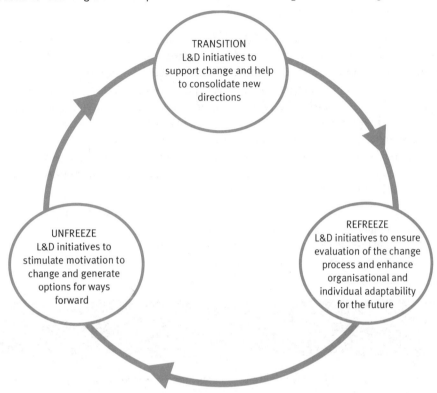

and middle management, on organisational barriers, poor communications and on internal politics. 50% of respondents said that lack of motivation on the part of middle managers was a major obstacle, while nearly as many blamed lack of change-management skills and experience at more senior levels.

Working with other HR colleagues, L&D professionals should be able to play a major part in tackling such change management problems. For consistency I will discuss their roles and tasks here by reference to Lewin's three-stage process. Figure 17 provides an overview.

AIDING 'UNFREEZING'

The main role for L&D professionals at this first stage is one of diagnosing, understanding and making sense of the organisation and the challenges that require it to change, and of helping to formulate appropriate change strategies (Hamlin and Davies 2001). They should play a key part in communicating to employees the need for change, in promoting unlearning and new learning, and in gaining commitment to the change. The organisation's purpose and driving goals that form the framework for major change must be understood and supported by all organisational members if that change is to succeed. Planned L&D can support 'unfreezing' by a variety of methods including workshops, roadshows, team briefings and training events.

The most demanding tasks for the L&D function, however, will be to create awareness of the need for leadership and management development, and to play a leading part in those processes. In the unfreezing stage they should help to enhance strategic thinking and leadership across the organisation, especially amongst its leaders at all levels, in order that assessment of L&D needs can be closely integrated with wider thinking about competitive strategy, organisational strategy and the business environment (Hamlin and Davies 2001: 53). For this to happen L&D professionals must have the necessary status and credibility with management and the executive team – something that research suggests few at present possess. Hamlin and Davies (2001: 42) urge them to:

> be conversant with current theory and practice concerning strategic thinking, organizational change and the role of the change agent. This means they need to understand theory in order to apply and evaluate it in practice [and] they need to evaluate their own effectiveness as change agents.

REFLECTION

Reflecting on your own organisation or some other with which you are familiar, try to find or suggest an example to show how L&D professionals, working with HR colleagues and in wider business partnerships, can play a leading role in unfreezing an organisation and moving it towards the transition stage of change.

EASING THE TRANSITION PERIOD

The key role for the L&D change agent at the transitional stage of change is to implement effectively change strategies for which they have full or partial responsibility. 'Effectively' in this sense means in accordance with strategic intent, and in ways that bring benefits to both the employer and employees (Hamlin and Davies 2001).

A major task is to help to build appropriate workplace learning cultures. I have discussed this demanding area at length in Chapter 5 so will not go over that ground again. Suffice to note here that in the 2008 CIPD Learning and Development survey (CIPD 2008a) 62% of respondents reported efforts to develop a learning and development culture in their organisation. In view of L&D functions' current poor record across Europe in that connection (Tjepkema *et al* 2002) it will be important in future surveys to track the outcomes of those efforts.

The training of front-line managers/team leaders (FLMs) should form a central plank of any attempt to change workplace culture, and the Procon UK case in Chapter 8 illustrates the kind of obstacles – as well as aids – that such training can confront. FLMs carry responsibility for organising and managing people, ensuring the quality and profitability of products or services, improving safety, and controlling costs. These tasks require them to possess a considerable knowledge of the commercial, economic and customer-care aspects of a business as well as the mastery of people management and development skills. The competencies and disposition needed to perform well in their roles are specific to their particular organisational context (Warr and Bird 1968). Training must therefore be tailored to that context.

That is a demanding task in itself, but training must also take account of FLMs' past experience. Many programmes ignore the needs of those who have been moved into team leader roles because of their successful experience of supervising sections or individuals, often in hierarchical organisation structures. They are likely to have little understanding of the difference between that kind of management and the team leadership that their new roles require. One factor that the traditional hierarchical supervisor can easily overlook is the danger of a team that is too cohesive. Gargiulo and Benassi's research (2000), outlined in an earlier case example, identified some of the problems here. The following case looks at team behaviour and adaptability in the context of changing organisational structures.

DEVELOPING COLLABORATIVE TEAMS

CASE EXAMPLE

The structural context

Although cross-functional teams have improved new product processes in many organisations, not all work equally well, nor are all equally collaborative. Jassawalla and Sashittal's study (1999) of high technology-based industrial organisations showed that collaborative behaviours seldom result merely from changing an organisation's structure from one that is hierarchical to a matrix or project-driven design. Some teams do transform, adopt co-operative behaviours and produce valuable improvements and

innovation for the organisation, but others produce barriers to change caused by problems of interpersonal interaction and of committing to a common agenda.

Companies X and Y instituted cross-functional teams primarily to accelerate new product development. They failed, however, to nurture the learning and development that must occur before teams eventually exhibit collaborative behaviours. They assumed that their functionally divided, hierarchical organisation with its linear workflows would 'instantly and painlessly' transform new product development processes. In fact, participants did not commit emotionally to making co-operation happen and so teams at companies X and Y became little more than microcosms of the divisiveness that existed in the larger organisation. The lack of a sense of ownership, and the suspicion about others' intentions and competence, prevented the development of a shared vision. Management's attempts to resolve these problems by intensifying its control mechanisms over groups simply worsened the situation, leading to apathy, low commitment, and a lack of trust and co-operation.

Building collaborative behaviours

Collaborative behaviours developed when participants were helped to reach agreement on a common agenda, and where they could openly share concerns and power. These behaviours emerged more from opportunities to experiment and learn in work environments that promoted risk-taking and tolerated failure, than from management directives.

Source: Jassawalla, A. R. and Sashittal, H. C. (1999)

The findings from Jassawalla and Sashittal's research in many ways match later findings that emerged from the Bath University researchers' 'Black box' studies (Purcell *et al* 2003) already described in Chapter 6. However, we also know from research that it is no easy task to build 'environments that promote risk-taking and tolerate failure'. It requires a culture of learning in the workplace that L&D professionals are increasingly seeking to develop yet which are still quite rarely found (Tjepkema *et al* 2002; CIPD 2008a). Some of the learning methods, especially work-based, that can be effective in tackling the problems described in the case example are:

- cross-functional business improvement groups to tackle fundamental business problems

- virtual learning centres: an Internet-based learning resource allowing employees to access data on business initiatives and engage in discussions with other staff members on these

- cross-functional mentoring, shadowing and job rotation

- regular cross-functional team reviews of team work and team processes

- newsletters and other initiatives to publicise and encourage cross-functional learning achievements

- training events (including outdoor development programmes) to promote cross-functional leadership, learning and working.

'REFREEZING' – MOVING ON

During the refreezing stage a key role for the L&D change agent is to step back and critically evaluate the effectiveness of their own contribution, and to draw lessons by reflecting upon their own professional practice (Hamlin and Davies 2001). Lessons learnt will often point the way to improving the pace and direction of change, revealing unexpected new needs. Such critical reflection should be a regular process since as I have already emphasised 'refreezing' should be seen as a continuing journey, with organisations having to face regular change in order to survive in uncertain environmental conditions.

In this third, ongoing, stage four key tasks for L&D professionals are:

- to monitor the ways in which new management systems and business processes are being operated, ensuring that there are the skills to design and use them in ways that enable decision-making to be pushed down to the levels where quick responses can be made to competitive forces – and ensuring too that managers appreciate that this is a crucial task (Hamlin *et al* 2001)

- to assess how far those with cross-functional roles, in which influence and persuasion are more relevant than the exercise of direct control and authority, are demonstrating the skills to operate in those roles (Hamlin *et al* 2001)

- to continue to raise the awareness of senior management and FLMs of the need for a workplace environment that facilitates individual and team learning and adaptability, and to help them acquire the skills and commitment to do this (Hamlin *et al* 2001)

- to give managers support in carrying the burden of implementing change initiatives, and to raise awareness with HR colleagues and with business leaders of any evident strains that may be adversely affecting managers' well-being, morale and ability to cope with the increased pressures on them and on their teams (Worrall and Cooper 2006).

The final case in this chapter shows the valuable lessons that can be gained from reflective practice. The researcher is not an L&D specialist but a senior manager who has significant L&D responsibilities as part of her role. The case is located in the voluntary sector where, as was seen in Chapter 10, organisations are experiencing continuous and radical change but where most lack the specialist expertise needed to appreciate or tackle effectively the major people management challenges that accompany that change.

RESEARCHING CHANGE IN A MERGED ORGANISATION

In 2007 a new charity, formed through a merger of two smaller voluntary organisations, was established in the south of England to aid lone-parent families. In the newly formed organisation it was essential to grow membership, by providing the kind of products and services that lone parents want and need, and by recruiting new lone-parent family members. For that to happen, a number of departments outside as well as within the charity's Membership and Development department needed to work collaboratively. However, that was a challenge because following the merger – as is so often the case in such organisations – staff from the two previously autonomous small charities were still working like two organisations instead of one, with new roles and responsibilities not yet clear and a new organisational culture not yet formed.

The charity's new head of membership development decided to investigate the problems and challenges by carrying out an electronic questionnaire survey of all staff and semi-structured face-to-face interviews with key managers. She focused her investigation on two major perspectives (Leeming 2008):

- markets – exploring the internal collaboration required in order to provide the products and services members need and to recruit new members

- people – exploring barriers and opportunities to achieving effective cross-team working required in order to develop membership for the charity.

Findings from her research that are particularly relevant for this section of the chapter were that:

- Respondents did not think that at the present time organisational members were working together effectively to achieve shared organisational goals.

- Respondents were willing to engage in more cross-team working, as long as they could be convinced that this would be mutually beneficial for teams and was focused on a specific goal.

- Respondents saw a need for clear leadership from the top to promote and develop effective cross-team working.

The respondents made three key proposals:

- The Membership Development team should hold staff and management team meetings to raise internal awareness of the importance and benefits of recruiting members.

- The Membership Development team should produce an internal 'toolkit' to provide other teams with all they needed to understand and promote membership. It should work with those teams to develop effective promotional material and easy joining mechanisms.

- The head of membership development should discuss

with the new chief executive ways in which membership and cross-team working could be promoted from the top. (At the time the research was carried out a chief executive for the charity had yet to be appointed).

Subsequently Leeming used her investigation as the basis for an Open University dissertation. As part of that she had to reflect critically on her research, using a structured process. Amongst the insights she gained from this reflective practice were the following (Leeming 2008: 47–9):

> One key lesson that I have learnt from this process is that my views of what are causing problems and difficulties in my area of work do not necessarily reflect the whole picture. [I have realised that] there is a lot more that I could have done, as a manager and leader, to help build understanding of what membership is within the charity, and made it easier for teams to participate in its development. Until I embarked on this project, I had assumed that the research would support my view that the key challenges are outside my department. This lesson – of taking a broader view and having a more open mind – is one that I intend to apply to future situations.
>
> Another useful lesson is that using [theoretical] frameworks can help to identify the nature of a problem ... and provide a clear way of investigating possible solutions in a way that can challenge my own thinking.

Source: Leeming, J. (2008)

This case highlights four points that, because they echo key themes that have emerged in this chapter, can stand as a final summary of major issues in the management of change:

- As a senior manager at the new charity, Leeming saw cross-functional teamworking as an invaluable aid to organisational change. However, her research revealed that staff needed to be convinced that it had a specific and meaningful purpose, and that it offered benefits to them as well as to the charity. They looked to the charity's leadership to produce and communicate the necessary unifying vision.

- At the charity, success in establishing a fully integrated new organisation largely depends on the ability of senior managers like Leeming 'to understand and articulate the nature of environmental change to the wider organization' and convey that picture in a manner which all employees understand and accept, so that there is a shared impression of the current reality (West 2002).

- That, in turn, requires the development of an organisational culture where managers fully accept their responsibility to help their teams to learn new skills and knowledge, and to enable individuals to gain the confidence and the perceived right to challenge any 'skilled incompetence' that is preventing progress.

- In Chapter 5 reflective practice was described as a way of ensuring that people become willing and motivated to subject their own 'taken-for-granteds' and activities to serious scrutiny in order to learn from them and if necessary change (Johnston and Badley 1996: 10). It was also noted there that reflective practice does not happen naturally – it has to be carefully developed. Reflective practice gave Leeming unique insights into her own management values, attitudes and approach and inspired her to apply those insights to her managerial activity at the charity.

CONCLUSION

In this chapter the purpose has been to explore challenges of change and major implications for L&D activity in an organisational context. You should now have a sound understanding of why change initiatives so often fail, and of the skills and dispositions needed to ensure that leaders, managers and HR/L&D professionals work effectively together to improve adaptive capability in the organisation and to tackle successfully challenges of change. You should also be confident in tackling the review questions for this chapter, contained in Appendix 3.

The main ground covered by the chapter's five sections has been:

- the increasingly rapid rate of economic and technological change now affecting all organisations and the consequent heightened importance of the L&D professional's change agent role

- an exploration of reasons for the failure of change initiatives; the need to provide a strong base of evidence for any proposed change programme; the need for more research evaluating the planning, outcomes and durability of change initiatives

- some popular theoretical frameworks to guide change management, and the rationale

for using Lewin's three-stage process as the framework for the chapter

- Stage 1: Unfreezing – The role of corporate and front-line leadership in creating awareness of the need for change, and in involving organisational members in generating options for ways forward; the importance of managing change as 'learning', and ways of achieving this

- Stage 2: Transition – Tasks for the executive team in order to guide the organisation through the transitional process when new directions, behaviours and culture are being introduced; challenges of cross-boundary working, and ways of developing teams that will be adaptable to future change as organisations are forced into ever more frequent cycles of reorganising and strategising

- Stage 3: Refreezing – The need for ensuring consistency and equity in HR policies and practices to embed organisational change; the importance of monitoring, evaluating and reflecting on the ongoing outcomes of change across the organisation and putting to use insights gained

- change agent tasks and skills for L&D professionals in relation to these three stages.

FURTHER INFORMATION SOURCES

Burnes, B. (2004) *Managing Change*. London: Prentice Hall

Hamlin, B., Keep, J. and Ash, K. (2001) *Organisational Change and Development: A reflective guide for managers, trainers and developers*. London: Financial Times/Pitman Publishing

Molloy, E. and Whittington, R. (2005) *HR: Making Change Happen*. Research Report. London: CIPD. Provides tools, tips, case studies and a '7 Cs' model for influencing and aiding organisational change

Tomkinson, B. (2005) 'Organizational change'. In

J. Wilson (ed.) *Human Resource Development: Learning and training for individuals and organizations*, 2nd edition. London: Kogan Page; pp44–57

White, M., Hill, S., Mills, C. and Smeaton, D. (2004) *Managing To Change? British Workplaces and the Future of Work*. Basingstoke: Palgrave Macmillan

CIPD podcast, 30 April 2008. *Learning and development – equipping people for change*. Available online at: http://www.cipd.co.uk/podcasts [accessed 25 May 2008]

EXLPORE FURTHER

CHAPTER 16

Promoting Talent and Career Development

INTRODUCTION

The purpose of this chapter is to explain what is involved in developing talent and careers in organisations, and to explore the contribution made by these processes to building organisational commitment and capacity for the future.

It is common in today's organisations to find that a former preoccupation with succession and career planning has given way to a concern to identify and prepare key talent for the future in a fast-changing business environment. The phrase 'talent management' has come into popular use since 1997 when American consultancy McKinsey referred to the 'war for talent' as a critical driver of corporate performance. That model controversially focused on an elite of high-flying individuals, but as I briefly noted in Chapter 1 the scenario for many organisations, especially those that are globally based, is now far more complex, and for all organisations there is a strong strategic imperative to manage their talent effectively. This does not mean that career planning is dead, but it does add another dimension to the task.

The chapter has five sections. The first two explore concepts of talent and careers in changing times and review research evidence pointing to key issues and trends. The third focuses on the need to integrate talent and career management with other areas of HR strategy and with business goals, identifying the particular importance of achieving consistency and inclusivity. The fourth section concerns ways in which managers and L&D practitioners can support individuals in a self-managed approach to career development. The final section proposes an agenda for L&D professionals related to promoting the development of talent and access to career pathways both for employees and for many in the wider community.

REFLECTION

To set the scene for what follows, reflect on your own career aspirations: to what extent do you find that your organisation offers support in pursuing them?

CAREERS IN CHANGING TIMES

THE SHIFTING CONCEPT OF 'CAREERS'

Schein (1978: vii) observed that career development marks the point at which the shifting needs of an organisation's people confront the shifting nature of its work. The challenge it embodies is to match the needs of the organisation with those of the people who work for it, from their entry into the organisation to their departure. The concept of mutual commitment lies at its heart.

The CIPD's career management guide draws on HR research evidence in emphasising the important role that a career management system can play in enhancing organisational performance through improving levels of employee trust, retention and engagement with the organisation's purpose and goals. It concludes that (King 2004):

> By developing able and motivated employees and giving them an environment in which they can excel, effective career management should, in conjunction with other factors, enable the business to achieve superior performance in terms of labour productivity, cost-effective investment in HR, quality, innovation and customer satisfaction.

Traditionally, the concept of 'career' has been one of upward movement but few organisations today can guarantee job security and regular promotion opportunities. In many, waves of de-layering have produced flatter structures and leaner workforces. The concept of the 'portfolio career' is increasingly common, and in a knowledge economy many organisations find it more difficult to attract and retain valued knowledge workers, increasing their preoccupation with 'talent'. Such trends raise the question of whether, in reality, the traditional concept of a 'career' is in the throes of collapse. Crawshaw (2006) speculates that:

> The dynamics of career management may be changing towards short-term careers with limited promotional opportunities and an emphasis on employability.

Research evidence

Some of the most reliable research evidence available suggests that both the optimistic prescriptions of textbooks and guides and the negative pictures presented by those fearing the death of the traditional career system are simplistic.

The relationship between employee and employer regarding career management is both more complex and more positive than many suppose. Consider the following findings:

- In their survey of the changing employment relationship Sparrow and Cooper (2003) identified that while the psychological contract between employers and employees is not being breached in the dramatic way that many suppose, there is a clear switch in emphasis from organisations to individuals as drivers of change in the employment relationship and that a process of negotiation lies at the heart of modern careers. Some may want a relational type of psychological contract, others a more transactional type, but one way and another individuals appear to be taking more control in the negotiating process.

- Research carried out on a major scale in the ESRC's *Future of Work* Programme (White *et al* 2004) showed that the trend to flatter organisations seemed at last to have slowed down and to some extent to have been reversed. Two out of three had offered career ladders to most employees, and sectors that historically had not done so were becoming involved in organisational career management, opening up new career routes for their employees.

- The five-yearly Workplace Employment Relations Surveys (WERS), referred to in Chapter 6, provide the most reliable and comprehensive source of information about changing trends, practices and employer/employee perceptions of life at work in the UK today. The 2004 survey covered 37% of all workplaces in Britain and 91% of all those in employment. Its data showed an overall increase in employee satisfaction derived from a sense of achievement from work (from 64% in 1998 to 70% in 2004), and this seemed mainly due to improvements in job security as well as to an improved climate of employment relations. The data offered insights into several areas of HR practice that have a direct bearing on career development:

  - Recruitment and selection, performance appraisal and training: these can open doors to career pathways, as well as help to increase employees' commitment to the organisation and satisfaction with their work.

  - Flexible work arrangements: with changing demographics and social trends these are now an important factor in career choice and in career advance.

  - Managers' attitudes to work–life balance and employees' perceptions of those attitudes: with changing demographics work–life balance has become another key factor affecting access to career opportunities and to career advancement.

Table 19 summarises some of the key findings from WERS 2004 (Kersley *et al* 2005) relating to these three areas.

- Clarke and Patrickson (2008) confirmed from their literature review that although changing career patterns and the erosion of job security have led to a growing emphasis on employability as a basis for career and employment

TABLE 19 Workplace practices in 2004 with relevance to career development and employees' feelings of job satisfaction and security

Recruitment and selection
68% of managers said they treated internal and external applicants equally; around one fifth gave preference to the former, only 10% to the latter. Private sector workplaces were more likely to favour internal applicants.

Performance appraisal
78% of managers (73% in 1998) said they undertook appraisals, but not always regularly and not for all employees.

In 65% of workplaces (compared to 48% in 1998) at least 60% of non-managerial employees were regularly appraised.

Training
84% of managers (73% in 1998) had provided off-the-job training for some experienced core workers in the previous year. In 27% of workplaces such workers had spent at least five days on average in training in the previous year.

64% of all employees had off-the-job training (42% in 1998).

66% (69% in 1998) of workplaces had trained at least some staff to be functionally flexible, but the proportion training all rather than just some of their core employees to be functionally flexible had declined from 15% to 7%.

Nearly half of workplaces had trained at least some core employees in teamworking, communication or problem-solving skills in the previous year, but only 8% of all workplaces involved at least 60% of their non-managerial employees in problem-solving groups, mostly the smaller workplaces.

Flexible work arrangements
This was one of the main areas of change. A substantial increase in availability of part-time working, home-working, flexitime, job-sharing, term-time working, parental leave and annualised hours (although flexitime was still only offered in 26% of workplaces).

Flexible arrangements were offered mainly in larger organisations, in the public sector and in unionised workplaces.

Work–life balance
Data indicated increased managerial understanding of employees' responsibilities outside work since 1998.

BUT it also seems that employees did not perceive such a change in attitudes and were often unaware of what was available to them.

More managers in the private sector (69%) and in non-unionised workplaces than in the public sector (47%) and in unionised workplaces felt it was up to individuals to balance work and family responsibilities.

More employees in the public than in the private sector (61% compared to 56%) found managers were understanding of their responsibilities outside work.

Employees in unionised workplaces were less likely to perceive their managers were understanding of their non-work responsibilities than those in non-unionised workplaces (55% compared to 61%).

Source: Based on information from Kersley, B., Alpin, C., Forth, J., Bryson, A., Bewley, H., Dix, G. and Oxenbridge, S. (2005)

success, there has been no widespread transfer of responsibility for employability from organisation to individual. There is still an expectation that organisations will manage careers through job-specific training and development. Likewise Lips-Wiersma and Hall (2007) found in their small-scale case-based research that in the organisation that they studied more responsibility was being transferred to individuals as drivers of their careers, but that the organisation had become more, not less, actively involved in career development and management although not in the traditional top-down way. The involvement was more in the nature of:

> a kind of 'organizational dance,' a highly interactive mutual influence process, in which both parties are at once the agent and the target of career influence.

- 'More', however, is a relative term. The CIPD's 2003 careers survey showed that whilst HR professionals wanted to improve career development across all employees in their organisations, only a third believed that senior managers were fully committed to this. In practice most effort was perceived to be focused on relatively small groups of senior or high-potential employees – in other words, on HIPOs (CIPD 2003e). Tower Perrin's *Global Workforce Study*, reported in 2008 and the latest then in the firm's regular surveys, found that although respondents wanted chances to improve their skills and develop their careers only 27% felt that there were excellent career opportunities in their organisation. At the same time only 14% of UK employees surveyed were fully 'engaged' – that is to say, 'inspired to contribute as much as they can to business success and to apply themselves to the goals of their organisation' (Harding 2008). This suggests the importance of ensuring that no groups of employees are overlooked in terms of development opportunities, provided that there is also a workplace environment in which all are enabled to fully contribute to business success and can see the value of doing so (*ibid*).

- Another strand of research findings relates to an increasingly prominent issue: that of employee well-being. Data in WERS 2004 highlighted stress in the workplace as a significant problem for many employees now (Kersley *et al* 2005). Worrall and Cooper (2006) found in their research already mentioned in Chapters 11 and 15 that the effect on all employees of organisational change has reached 'epidemic proportions' but that its impact on managers was particularly severe, having increased from 83% in 2000 to 90% in 2005, with a peak of over 97% in public listed companies and the public sector. The fact that change is now taking a variety of forms is increasing the stress that it involves. Well over half the managers in their survey cited a 'triad' of forms – cost reduction, use of contract staff and culture change – as having increased by between 10% and 16% by 2005, and absence levels were significantly higher in those organisations where the 'triad' of changes had been used than where they had not. Many seemed unable to cope with the increased workloads and psychological pressures that change brought for them in its wake. Gilbreath (2008) urges the importance of job training, mentoring programmes and succession planning being accompanied by the maintenance of a psychologically and physically healthy work environment in order to enhance employee loyalty and aid retention of valued employees.

Three conclusions can be drawn from all these research findings:

- The main drivers for improving employees' access to career routes – whether vertical or horizontal in kind – are to attract, develop and retain more 'talent' and, overall, a more engaged, more flexibly skilled and more adaptive workforce. These drivers are increasingly powerful in today's turbulent business environment.

- Despite difficult times, most organisations are now offering their employees improved opportunities for skills development, career progression and associated inducements, and they are not restricting these opportunities to the management level. There are significantly more opportunities for non-managerial employees in Britain to gain access to satisfying work and enhanced skills than there were at the start of this century. However, the progress made is relative. The proportion of employees who are fully satisfied with the career opportunities to which they have access at work still appears to be quite small.

- While organisations are demonstrating more concern to provide effective career management systems, the main responsibility for operating such systems falls on the shoulders of middle managers and of HR staff, and the increasing pressures on them of more or less continuous and complex organisational change raises doubts about their ability to cope. Many need better training, reward and reorganisation of stressful workloads if they are to become fully committed and competent in the career management tasks they are expected to perform.

REFLECTION

Reflecting on the research findings outlined in this section, what insights do they provide for you in connection with your own organisation's approach to careers management – or that of any organisation with which you are familiar?

THE RISE OF TALENT MANAGEMENT

In line with these changing perspectives on career planning and management I have already referred briefly to an issue that has steadily gained in prominence: talent management.

RESEARCH FINDINGS

In 2008 the Boston Consulting Group and World Federation of Personnel Management Associations conducted a survey of over 4,700 executives in 83 nations, asking them to state their top future people challenges and how they expected to tackle them. Managing talent emerged as the most important, involving the development and retention of the best employees and using techniques of talent management that included improved leadership development and managing work–life balance (Strack and Krinks 2008). Such findings are now quite common (see, for example, Blass 2007; Guthridge and Lawson 2008).

In PricewaterhouseCoopers' 11th annual Global CEO Survey, 2008 (PwC 2008) nearly 90% of the 1,300 chief executive respondents reported that their concerns over people and talent were as great as those about recession and regulation. In a competitive and uncertain environment they saw it as imperative to be able to identify the right talent with the agility needed to drive value in challenging conditions. Their views reflect lessons learnt from the early 1990s when, under similar economic pressures to today's, many businesses cut back dramatically on their graduate intake. When the economy recovered they found to their cost that competitors who had nurtured 'talent' during the lean years were now reaping the benefit.

THE DRIVERS OF TALENT MANAGEMENT

This emphasis across the world on attracting, retaining and developing talented people is a reaction to the combination of a number of factors:

- People with talent and leadership potential are becoming scarcer because of the greater complexity of businesses and the more demanding expectations of employees (Strack and Krinks 2008).

- Changing demographic patterns mean that there are now more employees approaching retirement than entering the workforce. People are also having fewer children. Strack and Krinks (2008) have found in their global HR research that dealing effectively with 'talent' as well as other implications of a rapidly ageing workforce was the fourth highest priority overall, but of much greater concern in Canada, the USA and much of Europe than in Japan, where executives have been grappling with the problem for years.

- The 'talented' in younger generations have different needs now, and in consequence are renegotiating the psychological contracts with their employer. They are highly mobile, quick to move if their organisation is not meeting their expectations and increasingly concerned with non-financial issues to do, for example, with work–life balance and corporate social and ethical responsibility. The PricewaterhouseCoopers' 2008 Survey already mentioned (PWC 2008) showed that CEOs are recognising that existing and new generations of employees' needs and demands are evolving, and that employers must work hard to earn their loyalty. More than 60% of respondents believed that they needed to change their current talent strategy.

DEFINING AND MANAGING 'TALENT'

Strack and Krinks (2008) found that although senior managers involved in their research saw talent management as a strategic priority, over half of their line managers were resistant to its processes. One problem was a confusion over meanings, given the conflicting views and differing practices in organisations (the researchers identified 18 dimensions affecting talent management's operational impact). To take two recent definitions, drawn from a year's CIPD-sponsored research carried out by a team at Nottingham Business School (Tansley *et al* 2007: xi):

> *Talent* consists of those individuals who can make a difference to organisational performance, either through their immediate contribution or in the longer term by demonstrating the highest levels of potential.

> *Talent management*: the systematic attraction, identification, development, engagement/retention and deployment of those individuals with high potential who are of particular value to an organisation.

The researchers stressed that 'talent' varies considerably in its meaning from one organisation to the next, variously referring to (Brittain 2007):

- *High potentials* – 'HIPOs', high performers earmarked for promotion. They typically represent 2% to 10% of managers in organisations.

- *Key talent* – they have business-specific technical knowledge or skills (known as 'technical key talent') or they possess special know-how (known as 'individual key talent') such as having unique relationships with clients. They may stay in their roles longer than HIPOs, and some may never become future leaders, but they are crucial to the success of the organisation and have unique skills that are difficult to replace. Key talent typically represents 5% to 10% of all employees.

It is therefore crucial to clarify in the particular organisation what is considered 'talent' and why its effective management matters to the business, since without a common understanding and acceptance of its purpose and how it will operate, no talent strategy can succeed. However, in giving 'talent' special consideration there is a risk of alienating other employees who do not have the same rewarding career trajectory to look forward to, yet who provide the organisation's bedrock of capability. One way of tackling the issue is to call everyone 'talent', as is the practice at newspaper group Metro. Its director of talent explained the reasoning here (Warren 2006: 26):

- Everyone can perform better with the right training, development and learning.

- Each individual is unique and has the potential to contribute something that others cannot.

Yet even Metro runs special talent projects and puts potential managers on a tailored managers' course. The dilemma therefore remains: because many, perhaps most, organisations rely heavily on between 2% and 10% of their employees for uniquely valuable skills and knowledge that can help secure the business's future, they must find some way of attracting, developing and motivating 'talent', and of retaining it long enough to justify the original investment in it, without reducing the affective commitment of the rest of the workforce.

Specialist knowledge workers

The specialist knowledge workers who are of particular significance in today's knowledge economy all represent 'key talent' and some will also be HIPOs. Swart and colleagues' study (2003) of six UK-based research and technology organisations confirmed that work in knowledge-intensive firms (KIFs) poses major challenges to widely held beliefs about how such organisations should be managed. Knowledge workers formed a high proportion of employees in the KIFs studied and were uniquely important to their success. They wanted to work on interesting projects making good use of their high-level knowledge and skills. Given their importance to KIFs, special care had to be devoted to crafting HR policies to do with their recruitment, development, reward and retention. But it was also essential to find ways of ensuring the transfer of knowledge between separate project teams, and of resolving the potential tension between knowledge workers' competing loyalties – to the team, their organisation more widely, their clients and their professions (Swart *et al* 2003: 69–71).

People management practices are key here, but Swart *et al*'s research findings suggested that they are likely to work best when they evolve naturally from the organisation's culture and its structural arrangements, rather than being imposed from the top down. This, of course, raises a big question mark over the relevance and value of formal management roles in such organisations. As Harrison and Kessels observe (2003: 49):

> Management, after all, was the product of the Industrial Revolution. In a new kind of economy where knowledge is the key asset, we have to ask whether some new conceptualisation should replace the old.

Focus and fit

Wendy Hirsh sees both talent management and overall employee development as important, but advises keeping the former clear and focused to ensure cost-benefit and to prevent talent management gaining the reputation in the organisation of being no more than a set of HR initiatives that never really deliver (cited in Warren 2006: 26):

> Business fit is the issue. ... It is about thinking about the critical talent pools you need to identify for roles in the business.

The NDA case overleaf is an example of one approach that appears to have struck

THE NUCLEAR DECOMMISSIONING AUTHORITY (NDA)

The NDA places great stress on an inclusive approach to talent management. It produced a capability framework that maps core behaviours against business challenges. Discussions also took place with managers to produce a plan identifying organisational strengths and weaknesses. Staff used an online tool to identify their skills against the framework, and had discussions with their managers about the results and about how these relate to the organisational plan. This consultative process covered all managers and specialists and so naturally took care of HIPOs by ensuring that they had appropriate development plans.

Evaluation of this talent programme showed that it had gained employees' support because of its clear link to business strategy, its emphasis on behavioural as well as technical skills and its consultative process. It brought home to managers the fact that they had a responsibility to manage talent, while making clear to employees their own responsibility to develop their talents.

Source: Caplan, J. and Reay, D. (2008)
People Management, 17 April

a successful balance between meeting the needs of 'talent' while opening up developmental opportunities for everyone and ensuring business fit.

EMPLOYER BRANDING

Talent management needs to be linked positively to the employer's brand, both for consistency and so that it can enhance the organisation's image in the labour market. Carrington (2007: 36) explains:

> It was the talent war in the mid-1990s that encouraged professional firms in the US to look more closely at what made them distinct as employers and then to think of their employment proposition as a brand similar to their corporate or customer brands.

The employer brand represents the deal that the organisation offers to its people. It has been described as the driver of the talent agenda, helping to define what makes the employer stand out from competitors as the employer of choice for scarce talent (*ibid*). It is not the same as the organisation's customer brand, but there should be synergy between the two. For example Marks & Spencer has 10 brand statements that include making employees feel valued and proud to work for the company, rewarding them well by comparison with competitors and keeping them informed on the company's progress. This employer brand is underpinned by core values of quality, value, service, innovation and trust that represent its customer brand (Carrington 2007: 37).

Achieving consistency between what is offered to customers and what is offered to employees is no easy task, especially when value statements like 'loyalty' and 'trust' are virtually impossible to measure and can be regarded by employees as little more than empty rhetoric. Recruiting only those who espouse the brand values and fit the brand image can also be discriminatory, can work against diversity by promoting a culture of 'sameness' – an issue already discussed in Chapter 9 – and can encourage manipulative behaviour on the part of employees (Carrington 2007b).

REFLECTION

Reflecting on any organisation known to you either from personal experience or from the literature, how far does its approach to attracting and retaining 'talent' reflect any of the approaches identified in this section, and what seem to be the outcomes of that approach for 'the rest' of its employees?

STRATEGIC INTEGRATION OF TALENT AND CAREER MANAGEMENT

BUILDING VERTICAL INTEGRATION

If an organisation is to manage effectively both its 'talent' and its careers system there must be clear direction from the top and integration of talent and career development policies with business and HR policies. In other words there must be a coherent, strategically-oriented process rather than simply a knee-jerk response to each changing situation:

At corporate level talent and career management should be part of business strategy and planning and the direct responsibility of senior management. Only in this way can there be full commitment to developing an integrated policy to apply throughout the organisation, and to ensuring that policy is implemented. In larger organisations a central integrative body is usually needed in order to develop company-wide policy, systems and procedures for talent and career development. Evaluation can then reveal whether the system is achieving its success criteria, and whether chosen development programmes and other activities are providing the most mutually beneficial growth paths for individuals and for the organisation. This is particularly important when the organisation is undergoing fundamental restructuring leading to changed employment policies. The integration of international talent and career development planning into a company's business and HR strategies is another major challenge and a field of study in its own right, with 'boundaryless organisations' and globalised careers becoming a common feature for middle as well as senior managers. I will say more about this in the next chapter.

PricewaterhouseCoopers' 11th annual Global CEO Survey, referred to earlier (PwC 2008), found that CEOs were looking to various methods within their organisations to both attract and retain talent. 73% of respondents were increasing the remuneration they offered, but they were also using imaginative methods including:

- creating a more flexible working environment (76%)

- hiring and developing people from more diverse pools of talent (67%)

- collaborating with networks of external specialists (66%).

The 'overwhelming majority' of CEOs believed that the answer was to train and develop the people within their organisation. However, in the companies surveyed by Saratoga (the PwC HR benchmarking platform), only 39% of the executive-level jobs that fell vacant were awarded to the internal successors who had previously been designated to fill them; also very few were measuring the direct impact that people were having on the companies' business objectives or measuring the success of these internal programmes. These two findings may go far to explain why so many line managers seem resistant to talent management processes (Strack and Krinks 2008).

At business unit level responsibility for developing talent and for career planning and management should form part of the managerial role, and in order to emphasise its importance it should be a key result area on which managers are appraised, and for which they are trained and given meaningful recognition. The skills that they need to acquire relate to job design, career coaching and counselling, succession planning, appraisal, the giving of feedback and personal development planning. They should be able to arrange job movements, including inter-unit co-operative arrangements such as transfers, secondments, special projects and other assignments.

Given this demanding list of requirements and the increasing pressure that regular waves of organisational change are already placing on line managers (Chapter 15), it is perhaps unsurprising that in a 2008 Hewitt Talent Survey half of the HR managers in the 240 firms surveyed said their organisations had lost out on business opportunities because talented employees had not been effectively managed. 60% found that their managers lacked the necessary skills, and 84% reported that managers did not have the time to devote to talent management (Scott 2008b). Clearly many, perhaps most, line managers need support and advice from their HR functions to ensure more effective talent management. However the PricewaterhouseCoopers 2008 global survey found that few such functions were perceived to be sufficiently effective in their approach. Only 43% of respondents believed that their HR teams could handle any change required to compete for talent, and 40% were unable to answer this question at all (PWC 2008).

At individual level there should be a process that involves individual and manager in exchanging information about wants and expectations, and in negotiating ways in which the individual's work and career can be progressed to meet their and the organisation's needs. Again there are clear implications for HR professionals in terms of the training, development and support from HR practices that they should be able to provide as aids to the process.

ACHIEVING CONSISTENCY

Some of the most intractable problems in developing career paths in an organisation are to do with achieving consistency in two senses: from one occupational or professional group to the next, and between pathways for 'talent' and 'the rest'.

In the public sector the complexity of the occupational structure makes consistency very difficult. Each group has its own historical patterns of recruitment, training, pay, and terms and conditions of service. Many have their own negotiating rights. In Chapter 10 I have explained the radical modernisation agenda facing all public sector organisations. One of the central planks of HR strategy in the NHS relates to a new approach to career planning, with the Skills Escalator playing a crucial role in opening up career pathways for all staff at every level. That model provides one that could usefully be applied in many other organisational settings, but as I noted in Chapter 10 its implementation in the NHS is proving problematic in the face of financial pressures.

Opportunities for career development are used to attract and retain scarce talent but I have explained earlier that they can be divisive. There is also a fundamental conflict of interest between 'talent' and its employer (Baron 2004):

- 'Talented' individuals want up-to-date skills that will enable them to move easily out of one firm into another in pursuit of attractive career moves. The employer, on the other hand, does not wish to lose them by investing heavily in their self-managed strategy only to see competitors poach them at a critical point.

- Valued specialist workers want to hang on to their unique knowledge, since it is their negotiating tool and key source of employability. The employer, on the other hand, needs to find ways of inducing them to share their knowledge so that it can be put to the organisation's use.

What, then, is the way forward here? First, there must be clarity about what the organisation wants from its 'talent', and a sound understanding of what such employees can contribute to the business as well as of what they want from their employment there. Wants and needs must then be carefully balanced in order to find an approach to talent development that works in the interest of the parties without creating damaging effects elsewhere in the organisation. Here is another case demonstrating an effective approach, this time at Centrica, the energy company.

CASE EXAMPLE

TALENT AND CAREER MANAGEMENT AT CENTRICA

All employees are included in Centrica's talent management strategy but there is a specific talent review process for its management cadre of around 1,000 employees called 'Centricans'.

Early in every year up to a day is spent by every business unit and functions such as HR and Finance in reviewing the potential of individuals, using information gained from a variety of sources including assessment centres (discussed later in this chapter). At a mid-year review all this information is fed into an annual performance review process where staff are advised of their 'potential' rating and discuss any development needs they seem to have. Twice annually the group HR director meets executive colleagues to assess which employees are ready for a move in the next six months and to review progress of those who had been due to move in the previous six months.

The overall measure used to determine the success of this process is the extent to which the company proves able to fill its vacancies from internal rather than external sources. However, 'robust processes' are also in place for all other employees, including succession planning and the company's customer and engineering academies. As the group HR director explained:

Everybody has a value in this company. If our front-line operators are not helping our customers, or engineers are not out there servicing people's central heating systems, then we don't have a business. Those people are critical and some of them have gone a long way up the management cadre. That is something that as an organisation we are proud of.

Source: Warren, C. (2006)
People Management, 23 March

AN INTEGRATING FRAMEWORK

It is essential for talent management, HR practices and business success to be linked in a consistent way, and for line managers – as those whose commitment is key to strategy's successful implementation – to be centrally involved from the start in the whole process of developing a talent management strategy and ensuring its horizontal and vertical integration. Many frameworks have been suggested, and Figure 18 incorporates thinking from the kind of research studies mentioned in this chapter together with some specific suggestions by Boudreau and Ramstad (2005) and Dave Ulrich (2008). To briefly explain these:

Boudreau and Ramstad's HR BRidge® Decision Framework has three main parameters: impact, effectiveness and efficiency:

- *Impact* – This requires identifying where the company's key talent is – not just HIPOs, but also those employees whose unique skills make a critical difference to the organisation's success. They cite as an example their work with Federal Express in the Asia-Pacific region, where although most HR and business leaders identified pilots (the traditional HIPOs) as key talent, in fact it was the FedEx couriers and dispatchers who could be more important as a focus of talent management, because their jobs were less engineered than those of pilots yet in certain contexts they had unique chances to make a significant impact on business success by improving punctuality and customer satisfaction.

- *Effectiveness* – This requires HR practices that will ensure that key talent is fully capable, motivated and is supported in having the opportunity to apply their talent appropriately and effectively in their work.

- *Efficiency* – This requires identifying the most cost-efficient methods of investing in 'talent' – an important consideration to ensure a careful focus on delivery of talent management plans.

Ulrich (2008) defines talent in a general sense as comprising 'Competence, Commitment and Contribution', stressing the need to ensure all three. Talent strategy and the HR practices associated with it should attract, retain, motivate and develop the particular kind of talent an organisation needs in ways that build commitment, ensure competence, and result in a contribution that the business finds valuable and that the individual regards as personally meaningful.

INTEGRATING DIVERSITY WITH TALENT AND CAREER MANAGEMENT

As Figure 18 shows, a big issue in talent and career management is how to achieve an inclusive approach, and particularly how to open up career paths to those for whom, traditionally, access has either been barred or has been very difficult to achieve – including minority groups in the organisation, whether in full-time or part-time positions, those with low levels of educational attainment and poor basic skills, and those who need to take breaks from working in the organisation at crucial points in their career. European companies tend to be more progressive than those based in the UK in career-break policies that are sensitive to the stress factors involved in combining a full-time career with childbearing or eldercare, for example, and to the adverse affects on productivity and performance that can result.

The UK Labour Government has pushed hard for employers to increase such policies in order to enhance lifelong learning opportunities, and earlier in the chapter we have seen that according to data from WERS 2004 (Kersley *et al* 2005) managers generally seem more aware of the importance of work–life balance issues. That survey also revealed, however, that in most employees' eyes their managers' treatment of it has not significantly changed since the late 1990s. There is a clear need for better communication of the organisation's policies here, and for more consistency in their implementation in the workplace.

Another important diversity issue is the frequent failure of an organisation's managerial population, especially at senior executive level, to reflect its client base.

FIGURE 18 An integrated and inclusive career and talent management system

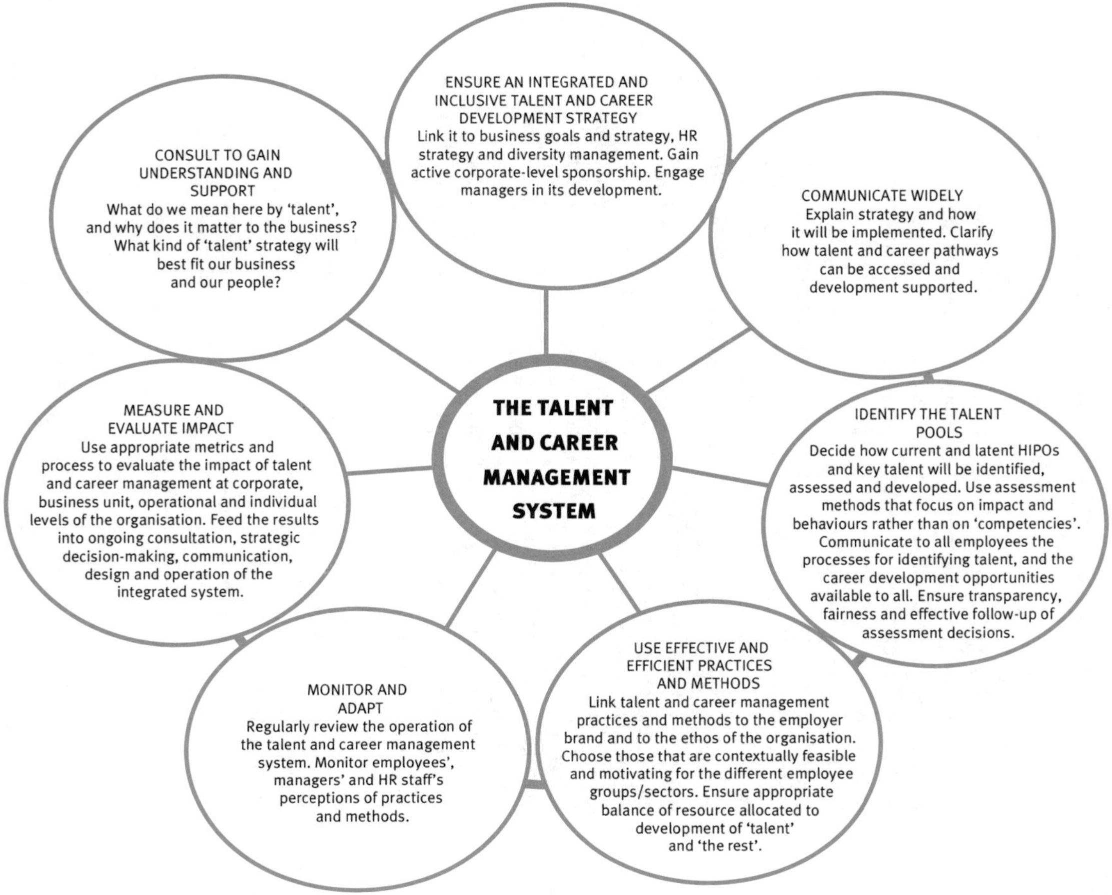

THE TALENT AND CAREER MANAGEMENT SYSTEM

COMMUNICATE WIDELY
Explain strategy and how it will be implemented. Clarify how talent and career pathways can be accessed and development supported.

IDENTIFY THE TALENT POOLS
Decide how current and latent HIPOs and key talent will be identified, assessed and developed. Use assessment methods that focus on impact and behaviours rather than on 'competencies'. Communicate to all employees the processes for identifying talent, and the career development opportunities available to all. Ensure transparency, fairness and effective follow-up of assessment decisions.

USE EFFECTIVE AND EFFICIENT PRACTICES AND METHODS
Link talent and career management practices and methods to the employer brand and to the ethos of the organisation. Choose those that are contextually feasible and motivating for the different employee groups/sectors. Ensure appropriate balance of resource allocated to development of 'talent' and 'the rest'.

MONITOR AND ADAPT
Regularly review the operation of the talent and career management system. Monitor employees', managers' and HR staff's perceptions of practices and methods.

MEASURE AND EVALUATE IMPACT
Use appropriate metrics and process to evaluate the impact of talent and career management at corporate, business unit, operational and individual levels of the organisation. Feed the results into ongoing consultation, strategic decision-making, communication, design and operation of the integrated system.

CONSULT TO GAIN UNDERSTANDING AND SUPPORT
What do we mean here by 'talent', and why does it matter to the business? What kind of 'talent' strategy will best fit our business and our people?

ENSURE AN INTEGRATED AND INCLUSIVE TALENT AND CAREER DEVELOPMENT STRATEGY
Link it to business goals and strategy, HR strategy and diversity management. Gain active corporate-level sponsorship. Engage managers in its development.

This causes failure to understand the company's customers and so leads to failure to provide them with the service they expect, want or need. The following example is a case in point, and also explains how Shell, the company in question, successfully tackled it.

CASE EXAMPLE

SHELL'S DIVERSITY AND INCLUSIVENESS STANDARD

Top leaders at Shell, the Anglo-Dutch oil giant, have traditionally been predominantly white, male and either British or Dutch, but by the end of 2004 local nationals were filling nearly 80% of the top jobs in the company's country operations, and almost 10% of senior corporate leaders were women.

The company attributes much of this achievement to its 'diversity and inclusiveness standard' launched in 2001. It requires every Shell company to develop a systematic approach to diversity management, to value personal and cultural differences, and to promote a workplace free of harassment and discrimination.

The standard is part of a wider framework that includes global targets to increase the proportion of women and local nationals in leadership positions. An annual talent review incorporates diversity, and an assurance

process requires senior business leaders to confirm their compliance with the standard or explain why they have not done so. This measurement of performance has made a big difference, although progress has not always been easy, especially within the dominant groups who used to hold the bulk of senior roles. One approach here has been to get them involved in the process and ensure that they fully understand its business case: that Shell is a multinational company and needs talent that reflects the markets in which it operates.

Another key to success is the integration of diversity and talent management by having those responsible work closely together at global level. In many of the group's other businesses the same person is responsible for both areas.

Source: Arkin, A. (2005)
People Management, 14 July

To summarise this section of the chapter: without strategic integration that starts at corporate level, all that will result from talent and career planning at unit or operational levels of the organisation is a proliferation of initiatives without any overall coherence. Employees are likely to find their expectations frustrated as action that has been promised fails to materialise or does not deliver the expected outcomes. Lack of an inclusive approach is likely to lead to reduced organisational commitment and low morale, both because of perceptions of unfairness and because those not identified as 'talent' may find access to career development opportunities effectively impossible.

Two requirements follow from this:

- Employees should receive clear and consistent messages about talent and career development opportunities.

- There should be close collaboration between HR professionals and line managers and between those managers and employees reporting to them in order to find talent and career development solutions that strengthen each individual's effective commitment to the organisation.

REFLECTION

How far does there seem to be an inclusive and integrative approach to talent and career management in your organisation, and where, if at all, would you recommend changes to be made?

SUPPORTING SELF-MANAGED DEVELOPMENT

THE CAREER LIFE-CYCLE

An integrated talent and career management system should stimulate and support a process of continuous development through which all employees have opportunities to acquire new skills, expand their experience and develop their potential. At the individual level many will need help in making the most of their opportunities. Gilley and Eggland (1989: 72) identified four questions to which each individual continuously seeks answers during their career. They remain valid today:

- Who am I (in terms of abilities and potential)?

- How am I viewed by others?

- What are my career options?

- How can I achieve my career goals?

These questions are of special relevance at key career transition points, the three most common being:

- the first point at which, when working in an organisation, career development opportunities become accessible

- the plateau reached when little if any further upward career movement is likely

- the approach to exiting from the organisation.

To take each in turn:

Opening up access to career development opportunities

This first transition point is one with which government skills strategy has now a particular concern, as I have explained in Chapters 2 and 3. The push to improve basic skills levels across the economy, raise levels of educational participation, reduce wastage rates during educational programmes, and lower barriers that have traditionally prevented many groups and individuals in society from gaining access to meaningful career paths – all of these factors are now helping to put career development on the map for the hitherto disadvantaged. The kind of L&D activity that can open career doors for many such individuals and groups includes:

- a motivating induction process, supported by mentoring and personal development plans whose implementation is actively supported by the new recruit's manager and other relevant staff. The induction period should also act as the first stage of career development with an organisation. Its aim therefore should be to build recruits' effective commitment to the organisation as well as to help them gain or improve learning strategies and skills that will equip them to take up career development opportunities as and when these arise

- a learning programme that includes a short period of core competence training or coaching followed by an extended period of familiarisation and practice in the basics of the organisation's business.

Motivating those on a career plateau

For employees who are in the later stages of their career and/or feel that they are stagnating, availability of career counselling, joint planning and job redesign can all help to boost their effective commitment and in some cases to reorientate them to expanded or different tasks or stimulating external opportunities. Offering employees training to become coaches or mentors is another way of utilising their skills and accumulated experience to the benefit of others, and of aiding their access to rewarding new roles.

Supporting those approaching exit from the organisation

When restructuring, downsizing or mergers lead to the loss of sections of a workforce, and also when individuals reach the time when they are likely to retire from the organisation, it is vital to have strategies in place to ease their exit and to maintain the effective commitment of those who are staying on. Too often in such situations it is 'talent' that leaves, while those who stay fall prey to loss of focus and motivation and ultimately to reduced performance. Strategies should incorporate plans to deal with such contingencies. Ad hoc initiatives are of little value. What is needed is a comprehensive approach that embraces those who leave, those who stay and those who have to manage the change process, incorporating the following kind of L&D help:

- appropriate L&D before the changes take place, to ease their path

- support and opportunities for those leaving the organisation

- initiatives to equip those staying in the organisation to handle new roles and tasks

- initiatives to sustain effective commitment and continuing development in those who are staying on.

All initiatives and processes to ease the passage through critical career transition points should be incorporated into an organisation's talent and career management strategy from the start, providing a framework with guidelines on blending on-the-job developmental methods with formal development experiences. It should identify what approaches should be used for what purposes at each career stage.

Development centres

Development centres (DCs) have an important part to play in aiding the identification of career needs and talent potential and in providing data to inform subsequent personal development planning. They should not be confused with assessment centres, although both share a similar methodology. An *assessment centre* is used primarily to inform decisions about selection, promotion or some other form of employee redeployment. A *development centre* is most appropriately used to diagnose individual training needs, facilitate self-development or form part of an organisational career management system (Rodger and Mabey 1987). With both approaches (which are sometimes incorporated in a physical centre) participants take part in a variety of job simulations, tests and exercises, with observers who assess their performance against a number of pre-determined, job-related dimensions.

DCs bring not only current and potential skills to the surface but also personal values and motivation, providing a valuable opportunity for individuals to clarify what kind of career paths they want and seem best equipped to follow. Iles and Mabey (1993), commenting on a range of empirical studies, found that DCs, psychometric tests with feedback and career review with superiors were particularly well viewed because (when effectively conducted) they:

- focused on the future as much as on the past and present

- promoted reflection and insight as well as measurement of skills or competencies

- provided two-way, collaborative processes

- were transparent, with participants able to see clear evidence for assessments

- were realistic, not only on account of the methodology used but also because managers were involved as assessors and because of the focus on the actual career criteria and activities used in the organisation.

Following DC participation each individual should have a personal development plan agreed with their manager, opportunities to develop, and support from colleagues, superiors and internal development staff.

To assess their true utility, the outcome of DCs should be followed up through time, with evaluation that captures the views of participants, of DC observers and of participants' managers in the workplace. Cost-benefit analysis also needs to be conducted, since DCs are expensive to design, to pilot and to operate and require careful selection and training of observers. Yet although DCs are in increasing use by organisations Neary and Lucks (2005) found only a sparse research literature on their impact. The few evaluative studies that do exist show development following participation in a DC is a significant weakness in organisations using this methodology. This finding also emerged from their own study conducted in a large financial services organisation. The study confirmed that workplace support and development planning was essential in two ways to the effective transfer of learning from a DC and the continuing development of DC participants:

- the extent to which DC participants subsequently reported valuable learning on the DC directly correlated with the extent to which they had undertaken development activities after the event

- the extent to which they could undertake such activities was primarily determined by the support they received in the post-DC work environment.

Yet again, organisational context is all.

SUPPORTING SELF-DEVELOPMENT

Self-development encourages active ownership of their career development by the individual, whether or not they opt for an entirely self-managed career process. The process requires an informed and objective assessment of the kind of skills and experience that will be relevant for the future, together with access to appropriate developmental opportunities such as:

- personal and career development workshops and seminars to encourage individuals to take responsibility for their careers

- resource centres giving access to a variety of facilities for self-directed and e-based learning at the company's expense, although in the employee's time. Such centres can offer occupational guides, educational references, e-based self-assessment questionnaires and other diagnostic instruments to help people consider their career interests, values and competence, together with e-based educational and training programmes

- access to career and counselling services of local colleges and universities and to their vocational and non-vocational courses.

L&D practitioners' contribution to self-managed career development

L&D practitioners have a range of tasks to perform in promoting and gaining support for a self-managed approach by employees to their development:

- *raising awareness of the centrality of self-development to the effective operation of the organisation's talent and career management system* – This is the vital link to make, and it needs to be identified early on in the talent and career management planning cycle.

- *ensuring an effective personal development planning process* – Personal development plans (PDPs) as outcomes of appraisal discussions are widely used in organisations but (as seen in the Procon UK case in Chapter 8) often their implementation is only partial. When training appraisers and appraisees, L&D practitioners should explain why self-development matters and how it can be promoted through effective personal development planning. They should also monitor the progress of PDP implementation and take appropriate action either themselves or through others to remedy any problems that are occurring.

- *focusing on learning styles and skills* – While bearing in mind that learning styles inventories are not scientific instruments but are best used as aids to discussion about ways in which individuals feel they learn best, L&D practitioners should raise awareness across the organisation of the ways in which individual learning style and skills influence the effectiveness of the self-development process. Raising managers' awareness is particularly important, and one way in which this can be done is to draw attention to learning styles when discussing the learning needs of individuals and teams reporting to them.

- *resourcing the self-development process* – L&D practitioners should advise their organisations on the affordability, feasibility and benefits of resources that can encourage and support employees' self-development. Nike, for example, has transformed its entire L&D function to enable employees to self-manage their learning. It has moved from being almost entirely classroom-based to offering a range of development practices such as coaching, learning groups, e-learning and project work (*People Management* 2008d: 11). Such practices have major implications not only for L&D budgets but for the workloads of L&D and line management staff who carry the main responsibility for organising, facilitating and evaluating them. They will have to be carefully calculated, with piloting often essential before introducing them fully into the workplace.

REFLECTION

At this point you may like to return to Chapter 8 and re-read the Procon case study there to remind yourself of problems encountered by some participants in the FLM development programme in relation to the new personal development process. The adverse effects these problems had on their motivation and their continuing development following the programme were very similar to those identified in Neary and Lucks' research.

TALENT AND CAREER MANAGEMENT: THE L&D AGENDA

Reflecting on the research evidence and other material in this chapter, a clear agenda has emerged for L&D professionals in relation to enhancing talent and career management in their organisations. It can be summarised as:

- promoting the business case and individual benefits of coherent organisational talent and career management system, well aligned with business goals and integrated within HR strategy

- producing and working with management and HR colleagues to introduce innovative, value-adding initiatives to help drive the talent and career development processes

- working to achieve an inclusive talent and career system for all employees

- taking a lead in building learning cultures that encourage and support a self-managed approach to career development

- providing relevant support for line managers to enable and motivate them to carry out their talent and career management tasks.

There is another L&D agenda whose reach goes beyond the organisation into wider society. Chapter 3 explained the Government's vision of life-long learning, and the funded educational and training initiatives that it is producing to support that vision. There is an important task here for L&D professionals not only in promoting equality of opportunity and access to career development for all employees in their organisations but also in promoting similar activity in the local community. The development of a meaningful career – in the broad sense of a rewarding and stimulating job and of the opportunity for continuing personal and professional or occupational development of every individual – is something to which all members of society should be able to aspire, and which they should be supported in trying to achieve.

REFLECTION

Imagine that you have a free hand to change talent and career management system in your organisation (or the part of it with which you are most familiar). What major changes might you make, or what kind of new system might you propose? Alternatively, if you would keep the system as it is, why would this be?

CONCLUSION

You should by now have a clear understanding of principles that underpin an effective talent and career management system in an organisation, and understand the contribution it can make to raising employees' commitment to the organisation and to motivating them in ways that should ultimately improve organisational as well as individual performance. You should also be able to tackle competently the review questions in Appendix 3.

In the five sections of the chapter the following have been the main issues covered:

- what research reveals about the concepts of 'career' and of 'talent' in today's organisations; evidence indicating that an increasing number of organisations are now opening up opportunities for more satisfying work and internal career pathways to non-managerial as well as managerial employees

- the importance of ensuring a career and talent management system that is aligned with other areas of HR strategy and integrated at corporate, business unit and individual levels of the organisation

- ways of achieving a balanced and inclusive talent and career management system

- processes and practices to aid individuals in their career path through an organisation, sustaining their affective commitment at key tension points and supporting and encouraging their control over their own career development; key tasks for HR professionals, including L&D practitioners

- a wider agenda for L&D professionals, promoting talent and career development beyond the organisation's boundaries.

FURTHER INFORMATION SOURCES

EXLPORE FURTHER

Chartered Institute of Personnel and Development (2008g) *Talent Management: Design, implementation and evaluation*. Toolkit. London: CIPD. Online version also available at: http://www.cipd.co.uk/tools [accessed 21 August 2008]

Michaels, E., Handfield-Jones, H. and Axelrod, B. (2008) *The War for Talent*. Boston, MA: Harvard Business School Press

Sturges, J., Guest, D., Conway, N. and Davey, K. M. (2002) 'A longitudinal study of the relationship between career management and organisational commitment among graduates in the first ten years at work', *Journal of Organisational Behaviour*, Vol.23, No.6: 731–48

CIPD podcast, 26 March 2008. *Employer branding*. Available online at: http://www.cipd.co.uk/podcasts [accessed 4 August 2008]

CIPD podcast, 2 October 2008. *Strategies for attracting and retaining talent*. Available online at: http://www.cipd.co.uk/podcasts [accessed 8 October 2008]

CHAPTER 17

Developing Leaders and Managers

INTRODUCTION

In 2007 Roffey Park's annual *Management Agenda* survey, covering 479 UK managers, found that 70% identified leadership as the most pressing business issue they faced, its data suggesting that organisations that develop leaders are twice as likely to over-perform against financial expectations as those that do not (Sinclair *et al* 2008). Such findings are becoming common and help to provide the rationale for this chapter: to explore how an organisation's leadership and management development (LMD) processes can help to build its future capability as well as aiding the achievement of excellent performance in a current situation.

For Kotter (1996), in the USA, leaders and managers are distinct in their roles and functions: management is to do with planning and organising, leadership to do with creating, coping with change and helping to adapt to a turbulent world. In Kotter's view the biggest leadership challenge in an organisation is that of transforming people's behaviour through changing their feelings. That is why emotional intelligence plays an important part in the successful performance of leadership roles. In the UK Boydell and his colleagues (2004) take a similar view: management is about implementation, order, efficiency and effectiveness, whereas leadership is more concerned with future direction in uncertain conditions. Management may be sufficient in conditions of relative stability. It is not enough in conditions of 'complexity, unpredictability and rapid rates of change'.

Yet while leadership and management are distinct there is an overlap between them, as there is between both and 'talent' as discussed in the previous chapter. Development in these three areas therefore needs to be an integrated process, set in its organisational context and shaped by the particular challenges facing an organisation. Because of its strategic importance it should be a core component of any corporate HR strategy.

In the space of one chapter it is only possible to provide an overview of some key issues related to LMD. The chapter has six sections. In the first I explore roles and tasks of corporate leaders, managers and first-line team leaders. In the second I outline some key research studies and surveys related to LMD in the UK and competitor countries, assessing in the third section how much reliance to place on this largely critical body of findings. The fourth section suggests guidelines for an effective LMD system, and the fifth provides a short critique of some of the most popular LMD methods. In the final section I suggest crucial tasks for HR/L&D professionals related to LMD in their organisations.

THE LEADERSHIP PIPELINE

WHAT IS 'LEADERSHIP'?

The debate in response to this question is extensive, but what is important here is to note the general consensus on the contextual and relational nature of leadership. This points to a need for each organisation to produce its own definition and ensure that it is understood and agreed across the business to be meaningful. There is nothing new in this contextualised view of leadership, and the very brief historical outline that follows indicates how much of our thinking today represents little more than old wine in new bottles.

By the 1950s in the UK alone over 100 studies had been carried out on 'leadership traits' yet only 5% of those identified appeared to be common to all leaders and they were so generalised as to be of little use as aids to selection or development. Subsequently, and largely due to the efforts of social scientists in the Human Relations and Organisational Psychology schools in the USA, much research was carried out on the effectiveness of different styles of leadership, ranging from those tending towards the authoritarian, or structuring, to those tending towards the democratic, or supportive. They too failed to provide evidence that any one style was associated with high productivity in all or even in most organisational situations (McGregor 1960; Likert 1961).

Contingency theorists, strongly influenced by the growth of systems theory in the 1960s and 1970s in both the USA and Europe, sought to find key variables that influenced leadership. Fiedler (1965), for example, concentrated in his research on the relationship between the leader and the group, and on the structure of the task that the group had to perform. Whilst more practical and specific than previous approaches to leadership in organisations, this kind of thinking was often expressed in such complex terms as to make it frustrating for the practising manager whose concern was to know what to *do* rather than how to *think* about leadership. The most important criticism of such theories is that they directed insufficient attention to the environment – a weakness remedied by what Handy (1976) called the 'best fit' approach. He found that leadership is most effective when there is a good fit between:

- the preferred leadership style and characteristics of the leader

- the leadership style preferred by the followers and their own characteristics

- the aims, technology and nature of the work that the group have to carry out

- the organisational setting or context in which leader, group and work are situated.

Since then continuing research into leadership has produced a mass of research findings, claims and counterclaims. Yet in essence there is a negligible difference between core views expressed by the gurus of the 1970s and today. Holbeche, for example, writes in 2008:

> Leadership is increasingly defined not as what the leader is or does but rather as a process that engenders and is the result of relationships – relationships that focus on the interactions of both leaders and collaborators instead of focusing on only the competencies of the leaders.

Ulrich and Brockbank (2005) argue that leadership competencies should be diagnosed from their results and their organisational impact, not from some idealised competency template. Again, the emphasis on impact is not new. However, it is assuming central importance now in a field of practice that still favours leadership development focused on competency frameworks despite growing doubts that competencies provide any real prediction of productivity (Alimo-Metcalf and Bradley 2008). I will return to that issue later, but consider at this point the following case.

NORWICH UNION'S APPROACH TO LEADERSHIP

CASE EXAMPLE

The following is the guidance provided by Norwich Union to its future leaders.

When we look for leadership we look for ...

- evidence in the outcomes your leadership produces (not your rank, role, experience, psychometric profile)

- performance over time across outcomes we value: sustained performance (not a one-hit wonder)

- learning agility, achieving outcomes in the face of change (not being stuck in one way of doing things)

- authenticity that increases your impact on outcomes – being yourself more, playing to your strengths, with skill (not acting a role)

- followers who are engaged in the outcomes we value and excited to exceptional performance (not subordinates who comply)

- behaviours in line with our values (not outcomes at any cost).

Source: Holbeche (2008) *Impact*: Quarterly update on CIPD Policy and Research. August, p.7. Reproduced with permission

Note, in this case example, the lack of any mention of leadership competencies and instead the emphasis on engagement and outcomes. These interlinked themes emerge strongly in much current research, which is highlighting the importance of embedding in the culture of the organisation those leadership behaviours that promote employees' engagement with business goals. Alimo-Metcalf and colleagues in their studies have found that (Alimo-Metcalf and Bradley 2008: 41):

> People find the model of engaging leadership instantly appealing ... but ... one of the greatest frustrations for staff is when this form of leadership is not reflected in the style of those at the top of the organisation, and is consequently at variance with the dominant culture.

And so we return full circle to the central issues highlighted decades ago: leadership as a collective capacity and a relational process, fundamentally influenced by, and related to, organisational context and therefore directly shaped by the style, actions and culture set at corporate level.

WHO ARE THE LEADERS AND THE MANAGERS?

Whether we look at the latest HR research findings, at the radical change agenda facing the public and not-for-profit sectors or at the highly competitive environment in which all private sector organisations now operate, there is an overwhelming need for effective leaders at all organisational levels. Those levels vary in number and type from one organisation to the next. For the purposes of this chapter I will use a generalised classification system to describe what is often called the 'leadership pipeline' (DDI/CIPD 2007) as follows:

- *Corporate leadership – the top level –* managing directors, chief executive officers and non-executive officers, responsible for setting and executing corporate strategy

- *Operational leadership – the middle level –* functional and business unit heads in charge of a department or geographical area; middle managers with leadership responsibilities

- *First line leadership – the first level –* team leaders and others with people leadership responsibilities – for example, those in charge of short-term projects or programmes.

To look in more detail at these three levels:

Corporate leaders

Leaders at corporate level are accountable for the results of an organisation and their brand has a major influence on shareholder confidence. They have the prime responsibility for developing a language and organisational identity that binds everything together, directing people's attention to 'what really matters here' and inspiring them to move forward collectively. In organisations with this top leadership capability, every member feels a strong loyalty to the goal of preserving, extending or perfecting the corporate mission. All can therefore be trusted to make decisions in the organisation's interests (Elfring and Volberda 2001: 273). Non-executive chairs and directors are a part of corporate leadership, and in the UK the Higgs Review (2003) and the subsequent Tyson Report (2003) have been instrumental in directing attention to their needs for appraisal, development and effective leadership and how those needs can be tackled.

A broad-based body of research from the 1990s on has confirmed the importance of corporate leadership tasks (see for example in Starkey *et al* 1996). The following have all been discussed at different points in this book so far, so none should come now as a surprise:

- building and sustaining a shared vision and high ethical values that provide a compelling, engaging picture of a desired future, while also communicating an accurate picture of current reality. As far back as 1938 Chester Barnard identified this task as one of inculcating in all organisational members a belief in a common purpose. Vaill (1996) described the process it involves as 'purposing', achieved through a continuous stream of actions that result in inducing clarity, consensus and commitment regarding the organisation's basic purpose

- achieving an organisational culture and a quality of life in the organisation that will generate the sustained commitment of internal and external stakeholders to corporate goals – a task that has assumed increased importance in today's pressured workplaces and with talent whose expectations (especially in the younger generation) in this respect can be demanding

- leading a regular organising process that enables the organisation to be flexible, fast-moving, knowledge-productive and proactive in its environment

- working with a broad-based group in a continuous strategising process to identify and communicate long-term goals and strategic direction for the organisation, and to determine and oversee the courses of action and allocation of resources necessary for achieving those goals

- building and maintaining a learning culture across the organisation. As often observed in this book, this responsibility, which is shared with leaders at the other organisational levels, is one of the most difficult and most rarely achieved. In a turbulent business environment the focus should be on generative learning – which is about creating new ideas, new assets for the organisation – as well as adaptive learning, which is about coping with current tasks and workloads. That task involves promoting and managing the development of strategically valuable knowledge, and continuously bringing to the surface and challenging prevailing mental models in order that the necessary unlearning can occur and new ways forward can be found.

REFLECTION

To what extent does corporate leadership in your own organisation seem to successfully tackle the tasks discussed in this section? Where do you see the greatest barriers and aids to effective corporate leadership to lie?

Operational leaders and managers

At this level and the one below there is increasing difficulty in separating 'leadership' from 'management' because the tasks involved in each considerably overlap. De-layering and decentralisation involve devolution of problem-solving and decision-making and often result in supervisors having to take on new team leadership roles. An increasing number of those who have occupied traditional middle management positions now find themselves in charge of semi-autonomous business units and therefore involved for the first time in the strategy process and with substantial leadership responsibilities. Their strategic role can have a direct impact on the performance of the organisation, especially in those flattened structures where innovation and market-sensitivity are essential to the advancement of the business in its competitive environment (Floyd and Wooldridge 1994; Hedlund 1994). Finally, professionals such as clinical directors in the health service are frequently having to take on expanded managerial and leadership responsibilities, some of a strategic nature (Harrison and Miller 1999).

With a new emphasis on partnership rather than control and on processes that will add value, managers still have to manage. However, those planning their development must find answers to searching questions concerning how they should manage, with whom they should collaborate as they manage, how they should behave in order to achieve the desired outcome, and how those with leadership potential should be developed at this key transition stage.

Operational-level leaders and managers have to use a range of skills that cannot easily be categorised but that must be integrated in their practice. Such skills have been termed 'overarching competencies' since by their nature they go far beyond the functional, explaining why effective management is more than just the sum of its parts (Burgoyne 1989). In a report on management training and development across Europe, Mabey and Ramirez (2004) confirmed the vital role performed by managers in creating high-performing workplaces, with their importance most marked in the following respects:

- making critical decisions about opportunities afforded by communication and information technology

- ensuring the success of organisational change

- creating a culture of life-long learning for all employees, particularly those traditionally disadvantaged.

To this list at least one more task must now be added: managers' role in ensuring engaged and healthy employees. Recent research has identified core behaviours here under four broad headings (CIPD 2008h):

- managing emotions and having integrity

- managing and communicating existing and future work

- managing difficult situations

- managing the individual within the team.

Most leadership activity at the middle level of the organisation is further complicated by the fact that it is undertaken through complex webs of social and political interaction and has to operate across many internal and often external boundaries. Overall it involves a continuous process of adaptation to changing pressures and challenges. As Partridge observed from his research (1989: 205):

> Managerial work across all levels ... is characterized by pace, brevity, variety and fragmentation ... It is hectic and fragmented, requiring the ability to shift continuously from relationship to relationship, from topic to topic, from problem to problem.

It is unsurprising that in the kind of work environment described in Chapter 15 most managers feel under ever more pressure, with some finding it almost impossible to cope (Worrall and Cooper 2006). Organisational leaders and HR practices should help them to achieve a greater level of well-being themselves so that they can better handle the task of promoting the health, well-being and engagement of those reporting to them.

Front-line leaders and managers

As explained in Chapter 6, the 'Black box' research carried out at Bath University has produced many insights into the leadership tasks of front-line managers. Their reports contain cases illustrating aids and constraints on the effective performance of those tasks, and showing these managers' direct influence over the amount and exercise of employees' discretionary power (Purcell *et al* 2003; Hutchinson and Purcell 2003; Pass 2005; Purcell and Hutchinson 2007).

Ghoshal and Bartlett (1994) argued that it is a primary task of leaders and managers to create a context in which their organisation can collectively achieve high performance. They proposed that such a context should have as its key dimensions discipline, stretch, trust and support, since a focus on these qualities would release the skills, motivation and commitment of all employees and direct them to achieving organisational goals. They saw the task of business unit managers as especially vital where fundamental organisational change must be achieved and where entrepeneurial behaviour is needed at all levels in order to move forward. They identified from case-based research the ways in which employees' behaviour is powerfully influenced by the actions of their leaders, especially those at the front line (Bartlett and Ghoshal 1993).

REFLECTION

Reflecting on any group of front-line or operational leaders in your organisation, what seem to be their leadership tasks, and what help do they receive in developing the knowledge, skills and behaviours needed to perform them?

HOW EFFECTIVE IS LMD?

INTERNATIONAL RESEARCH FINDINGS

Over the past two decades or so a large body of research conducted into LMD in the UK and abroad has consistently identified that all is not well in the field, and that the UK continues to lag behind in LMD practice and effectiveness. To take a sample of the more recent findings:

● In 2004 Mabey and Ramirez reported from their extensive research that the UK was falling significantly behind other countries in developing its managers despite progress made since the mid-1980s in national policy and qualification frameworks. It also relied far more than any European country except Denmark on a qualifications-based approach to management development (MD), and like most countries it made little use of e-learning. Less than half the organisations they studied appeared to have an MD policy statement although most had a clear business strategy. On average the HR contribution to that strategy was 'moderate at best'. The UK, along with France, had the least faith in HRM as delivering competitive advantage and was much less likely than other countries to adopt a strategic approach to it. Unsurprisingly, therefore, firms in the UK were found to be comparatively weak in taking a thoughtful, long-term and consistent approach to the creation of a management cadre. Management training was often non-strategic, piecemeal and rarely evaluated.

- Mabey and Ramirez (2004) also found it not uncommon for development programmes to be politicised by being used to reinforce instead of challenge the leadership and management status quo. Opportunities for development were frequently offered in order to secure loyalty to the present culture rather than to run the risk of upsetting it. Such behaviour puts barriers in the way of employees' self-development, often now a central part of LMD programmes and processes. Its extent and focus can be significantly influenced by those who 'do the empowering' rather than being freely chosen by those being 'empowered' (Dispenza, 1996: 245). Such findings point to the need for corporate leaders to recognise the changed attitudes and values that an LMD programme is likely to produce, and for them to actively facilitate and support appropriate outcomes (Mabey and Ramirez 2004). Where cultural change is essential it should be explictly targeted by LMD strategy, and its evaluation should be planned from the start (as it was in the Procon UK FLM programme described in Chapter 8). If the 'renewal' in an organisation's leadership and management that is offered by an LMD strategy is resisted by those who hold the most powerful positions in the organisation it is unlikely that such renewal will take place.

- In 2005 the CIPD's annual Training and Development survey found that 65% of its senior HR/L&D respondents believed that there was a shortage of effective leaders in the UK (CIPD 2005g). Most of their organisations were providing leadership development but 31% of the respondents did not feel that this was very effective. 47% also reported that employees were not keen to learn leadership skills. A joint DDI and CIPD survey into UK global comparisons of leadership, also conducted in 2005, revealed the same sense of urgency and similar critical views (DDI/CIPD 2005: 17). Its authors concluded:

  - Leaders in the UK often lacked the necessary support from their superiors to help them develop in a planned fashion both from job experiences and more formal training activities.

  - In consequence they tended to arrive in leadership positions less well prepared than their counterparts elsewhere, and to inspire less confidence in their ability to execute strategies successfully.

  - Although succession processes were usually in place the plans did not always focus on early identification of potential, tended to lack transparency, and had less effective outcomes than elsewhere in the world.

  - HR professionals seemed busy rather than effective in their LMD activity and leaders were mutually critical rather than being mutually supportive, with little sharing of experiences or coaching through daily challenges of the job.

- In 2007 a Harvard Business School/Hay Group research project looked at more than 120 senior teams in 11 countries. The researchers found that the effective teams had enormous potential to contribute to their organisation, but that only one in five of those studied was outstanding, while a third were mediocre and

42% were poor. Conditions required for effective functioning included a clearly defined top team, an interdependency of members who were committed to its purpose, and a clear and challenging reason for the team to exist. Three key 'enablers' were organisational support (reward, education and information), team coaching and a sound structure with clear norms of conduct (Wageman *et al* 2008).

- In its 2008 annual L&D survey the CIPD found that 90% of its senior HR professional respondents saw a need for their organisations to focus on developing leadership skills in order to meet business objectives in the next two years (CIPD 2008a). In the same year DDI, the international consultancy firm already mentioned in Chapter 11, reported that in its research across thousands of global organisations over a 10-year period it had found 'a steady decline in the confidence we have in our leaders to drive future business success', with more than half of those organisations expecting it to be increasingly difficult to find competent leadership for the future (*http://www.ddiworld.com/products_services/ bn_strengtheningtheleadershippipeline.asp* [accessed 8 August 2008]).

KEY FAILINGS IN LMD

In DDI's 2008 *Global Leadership Forecast* based on data covering nearly 1,500 HR professionals and over 12,000 leaders from 76 countries the authors examined why confidence in leaders continues to decline despite a heightened focus on developing leadership talent. Their conclusions can be read online but in summary identified five major failings that other research such as that outlined above confirms (Howard and Wellins 2008):

- *Lack of appropriate leadership development strategies*
  Only 41% of leaders, compared to 53% two years previously, reported their satisfaction with the ways in which their organisations helped them to develop their leadership capabilities. All major world regions showed similar rates of decline in satisfaction levels.

- *Poor implementation of leadership development programmes*
  Only just over half of organisations on average were taking the necessary actions to ensure effective implementation. The most striking weakness related to evaluation, with very few organisations even attempting to measure the outcome of their investment.

- *Lack of effective succession planning*
  Less than half of organisations had succession plans at any level and typically around 37% of succession candidates failed. Nearly half failed to provide any development for leaders at transition stages and almost all ignored the first-line leader level.

- *Neglect of multinational leaders*
  Only 29% of organisations had processes to develop their multinational leaders

and in most global regions the multinational leaders were considered lower-quality than other leaders.

- *Poor partnership between HR and corporate leaders*
Leaders had little confidence in the abilities of their HR professionals and in the UK the latter expressed the lowest confidence of any HR professionals across the world in their leaders overall, particularly in their first-line managers.

The problem of evaluation

The issue of evaluation of LMD strategies and programmes has been regularly highlighted by research and forms part of the wider problem of lack of adequate and reliable evaluation of L&D initiatives generally that has been noted throughout this book. The Institute of Executive Development and the Danish Leadership Institute (2004) found that 'despite utilising a variety of metrics to track the effectiveness of leadership development solutions, a full 63% of organisations reported that they "never" evaluate leadership development in terms of return on investment' (Osbaldeston 2005: 28). The task was admittedly difficult, including the need to create a common language defining value, gain access to appropriate business data, and find matched samples to contrast against leader development participants. Nevertheless that cannot fully explain why so little evaluation was carried out, and why the evaluation that was done relied largely on sources of individual assessment by participants and their line managers (*ibid*):

> Organisational sources, such as improvements in organisational culture, employee attitudes and business performance, remain problematical and are certainly cited less frequently.

In their review of a decade of MD research carried out by Mabey and an international consortium Mabey and Terry (2007) commented:

> We were … struck by the fact that most organisations give little time to anything more than rudimentary evaluation of management development, but continue to pour immense resources into it.

The problem of complacency

Well over 20 years ago, in 1985, a damning report on management training and development in the UK was published and became highly influential in directing government's attention to the need for a greater and more effective investment nationally and locally in LMD. I mentioned this report – *Challenge to Complacency* (Coopers and Lybrand) – at the start of my first book on training and development, to draw attention to the dangers inherent in 'a combination of complacent, ill-informed and sceptical attitudes to training at all organizational levels, including that of personnel practitioners themselves' (Harrison 1988: 2).

If findings such as those recently reported by the Institute of Leadership and Management (ILM) in 2008 are to be believed, little has changed over the years, whether in the UK or across the Western world.

CHINESE MANAGERS: A REVELATORY PICTURE

In China companies with global aspirations face an enormous task in building locally sourced talent, with a big dearth in the supply of qualified professionals and managers who can work effectively in global environments (Farrell and Grant 2005). Mercer, a global consultancy, outsourcing and investment firm, has identified three important leadership and management groups (Wilson 2008):

- *Current leaders* – Many of these were brought up during the Cultural Revolution when education was sporadic and centralised planning was the norm. They are not always strong strategists or innovators, being more comfortable with a command-and-control style of management. Their strengths lie in endurance and in engaging those who work with them.

- *Potential leaders from a younger generation* – Their main developmental needs are for business, entrepreneurial and people management skills.

- *Middle managers* – This group is well educated but has generally received little formal management training, is driven to succeed and tends to see as its core strengths team leadership and teamwork, organisational agility and relationship management. Its younger membership (around 30–34 years old) has quite a high turnover, causing lack of stability in the leadership pipeline.

In the West, there is a common perception of Chinese managers as coming from a communist background, lacking an understanding of business, and operating in an authoritarian sweatshop economy. However, a 2008 Global Management Challenge conducted by the Institute of Labour Management (ILM), in the words of its website, 'paints a picture of Chinese managers who are hugely underestimated by their complacent Western counterparts and who are launching a serious challenge to established Western business and management practices'.

The ILM survey covered around 325 managers in the UK, USA, France and China. It was just a scoping exercise to provide the basis for more in-depth research and was based only on telephone interviews. Nevertheless its findings are quite revelatory. The Chinese respondents conveyed a self-image of themselves as customer-oriented, safety-focused and honest, with a high concern for their impact on the environment, deep respect for rules, modest about what they know and with a hunger for learning. They were also found to be better educated and to receive more in-house training than their Western counterparts.

Like the Chinese, Western managers were largely satisfied with the standard of managers in their country, but whereas Chinese managers were 'by far the most focused on improving performance and processes' over

65% of Western managers felt that there were no management weaknesses in their business that could hold back development. They also saw Chinese managers simplistically as driving their workers hard to get work done on time, suggesting that strategies adopted in the West to compete with China may be misconceived. The researchers commented that:

> [Chinese managers] were far more ambitious than those in the West; although we seem happy with the current state of our management

capacity, they are not and are doing something about it.

The ILM's Chief Executive concluded that:

> Success breeds complacency and there are signs from the research that decades of economic success and prosperity have made managers in the West complacent.

Sources: Wilson, B. (2008) *People Management*, 7 August; *http://www.i-l-m.com/research-and-comment/3428.aspx* [accessed 10 August 2008]

ASSESSING THE EVIDENCE

RESEARCH PROBLEMS

In Chapter 1 I devoted some space to discussing the importance of evidence-based practice in the HR field. The theme has recurred regularly and here it needs attention once more.

Hamlin (2002) observes that much MD practice in the UK lacks a convincing evidence base concerning conditions prevailing in particular organisational contexts, and that despite much qualitative research on managerial work in the management literature, little has been used to inform MD. In practice and theory it is over-reliant on findings from US research and even when British research is influential, it is mainly concerned with the effectiveness of top managers as opposed to senior, middle and junior managers. There is likewise little agreement, even amongst US researchers, on what constitutes 'leadership', specifically, and most studies exclude leadership roles of middle, junior and first-line supervisory managers (a deficiency that researchers like Purcell and his team at Bath University have sought to remedy).

Hamlin also found much MD to be based on 'inappropriate or obsolete models of management' (*ibid*: 99), with programmes often drawing primarily on the views of classical theorists and current management 'gurus' and failing to achieve the desired return on investment because of lack of clarity about what managers actually do in the particular organisation. Beard and Irvine (2005: 385) came to a similar conclusion. They found that 'management is not a clear and precise term on which MTD can be based'.

Beard and Irvine (2005) highlighted another issue making the evaluation of management training and development programmes problematic: the fact that they can serve as an instrument of control exercised by senior management over those in lesser positions. When that is their real function it is hard to ensure their objective evaluation, whether by trainers or participants, since any criticism can be seen as challenging the organisation's values (as set down by top management) and as acting in a way that identifies the critic as 'not part of the team' (*ibid*: 394).

KEY FINDINGS

Factors with a direct bearing on the validity and reliability of any research include the following:

- the research question and the assumptions underlying it

- the conceptual basis of the research and the appropriateness and rigour of its methodology, including the size, type and representative nature of samples chosen for study

- the original expectations of the researchers concerning the research's likely outcomes, compared with their eventual findings

- the values and expectations of the research's sponsors and the influence exercised by those sponsors over the research.

It is not possible to undertake here any scrutiny of the research questions and methodology underpinning the studies summarised in the chapter's second section, but two points should be immediately obvious:

- All the studies have been produced by individuals or bodies who, in one way or another, have a vested interest in emphasising the importance and need for leadership and management development. In some cases the interest has a commercial base. In others it is more to do with influencing or supporting government skills and educational policy or HR professional and educational standards. Vested interests can produce bias. Of course to a degree any research is vulnerable to that accusation. What matters is not the possibility of bias but the extent to which researchers demonstrate their awareness of it and take appropriate measures in their methodology, data collection and analysis to counteract it. So in the case of these research studies and surveys it would be important to probe this issue.

- On the positive front, a striking feature of the studies I have outlined is the degree of consistency between their findings, regardless of who has undertaken them, the samples surveyed and the research methodologies employed. It is also significant that most of the research has been conducted regularly through time with the researchers using the same kind of databases from one occasion to the next and therefore being able to build up a picture of trends, practices and impact through time rather than merely producing snapshots fixed in a particular moment.

It therefore seems reasonable on balance to accept the general picture presented by the research findings I have identified in the second section, negative although that is. On a variety of counts some of the most reliable recommendations are likely to be those that have emerged from the work of the international consortium researching management development in Europe between 2000 and 2007 under Chris Mabey's leadership. The researchers accumulated strong statistical evidence across organisations of varying size and sectors in six countries that 25% of variance in organisational performance was explained by three interlinked factors. The other studies I have cited confirm their importance:

- a strategic approach to HRM, ensuring its integration with business strategy

- a thoughtful, long-term approach to developing managerial capability

- a belief by line managers that their employer is taking management development seriously.

The researchers found that on their own, neither MD systems and procedures nor the amount and diversity of training improved organisational performance significantly. It appeared to be 'a properly aligned, and therefore distinctive and idiosyncratic, management development approach' that was the key and that therefore represented a 'core capability' for the organisation (Mabey and Terry 2007).

REFLECTION

At this point you may find it helpful to re-read the Procon UK case study in Chapter 8 to see how the Birmingham site approached the planning and design of its major programme for front-line managers. You should pay particular attention to the three factors just discussed above.

PUTTING FINDINGS INTO PRACTICE

THE STARTING-POINT

Where should an organisation begin, then, with its LMD system? Differing perspectives about the purpose of LMD and differing views about how an organisation should be managed make it essential to first find answers to the following questions (Beard and Irvine 2005):

FIGURE 19 Principles to guide leadership and management development

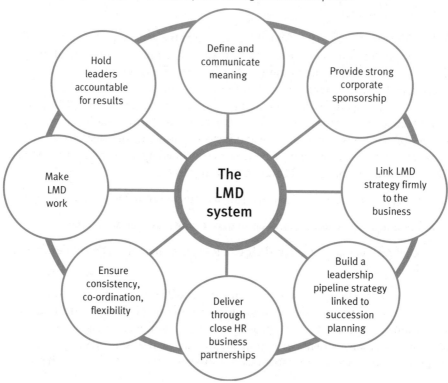

- What do we mean by 'leadership' and 'management' in this organisation?

- What is the culture of our organisation – or what shift in culture do we want our LMD strategy to help us achieve?

- What are the best methods of developing individuals in the leadership and management skills and behaviours needed at key transition points in the leadership pipeline?

- How can we evaluate our LMD effectively, both in terms of whether training and learning needs were accurately identified and of the impact of that activity on the business and on individuals?

Figure 19 takes this as the starting-point for the development of an effective LMD system and continues to draw on research evidence throughout the cycle of activity it proposes. The eight guiding principles identified in the cycle are explained below.

1 DEFINE AND COMMUNICATE MEANING

Define and communicate to all employees what is required of the organisation's leaders and managers at each organisational level and the processes to be used for identifying and developing them. In view of the lack of clarity surrounding the meaning of 'leadership' and 'management' and of what those roles involve in practice, this is the essential first stage. There should be a strong focus on understanding organisational context and the challenges the particular organisation faces, in order to set an appropriate direction for the LMD system.

2 PROVIDE STRONG CORPORATE SPONSORSHIP

The board, including non-executive directors, and the CE should be the business sponsors of LMD strategy and should be actively involved in its processes and its implementation. They should communicate its purpose clearly and persuasively across the organisation, ensure its effective implementation and role-model the behaviours and qualities that it aims to develop. Since many top teams are ineffective, a key requirement is to incorporate their own development in LMD strategy and its execution. Furthermore the essential leadership task of creating an 'engaging' culture must start with the CE and the top team. Attempting to create such a culture through interventions only at the lower levels 'may well create more problems than it alleviates' (Alimo-Metcalf and Bradley 2008: 41).

3 LINK LMD STRATEGY FIRMLY TO THE BUSINESS

LMD should be linked directly to the business through an outside-in strategy that begins and ends with business outcomes and achieves an appropriate balance in relation to organisational and personal development needs. In the words of Fulmer and Bleak (2007) in their online review of a wealth of European research into LMD, there should be a:

> leadership development architecture ... integrated and linked to the strategy and needs of the business in order to increase the potential for real impact and then communicated widely to engender support.

It is vital to incorporate the development of international and multi-national managers in LMD strategy. Neglect of their needs was a key weakness noted in DDI's 2008 *Global Leadership Forecast* (Howard and Wellins 2008), despite the rapid increase in the numbers and importance of this leadership and management sector for all types and sizes of organisation and the fact that graduates are increasingly including international experience in their list of 'wants' from employers of choice (Harris and Dickmann 2005; Dickmann *et al* 2006). As Wilson (2008: 6) observes:

> The need to find ways of creating managers with international mindsets who can deliver solutions in a globally competitive environment is one of the biggest drivers in the quest for excellent international management development today.

4 BUILD A 'LEADERSHIP PIPELINE' STRATEGY LINKED TO SUCCESSION PLANNING

Strategy should be integrated to encompass the development of leaders, managers and individual talent – as discussed in the previous chapter – at each transition point in the leadership pipeline and in preparation for entry to it. Few leaders report making transitions effectively, especially at the lower levels (Paese and Wellins 2006). Relatively few individuals will reach, or may even aspire to reach, corporate level, but the essence of an integrated strategy is that it should secure the best leaders at every organisational level while offering motivating choices and appropriate development opportunities and resources at the key transition stages (DDI and CIPD 2007).

Although most organisations today are more preoccupied with talent management than with succession planning that does not mean that the latter should be abandoned. Indeed, it was emphasised in the previous chapter that such planning is one of the special set of skills that managers at business unit level need to possess in order to fulfil their talent management responsibilities effectively. It does, though, mean that the traditional model of succession planning only for the most senior roles is now increasingly outmoded. Planning now frequently covers key roles at all levels and aims to develop a broad pool of current and of latent leadership talent, as well as buying in new talent from time to time (Holbech 2008: 24). It is also about sideways developmental moves as well as upward progression (CIPD 2005h: 29–30).

5 DELIVER THROUGH CLOSE HR BUSINESS PARTNERSHIPS

Ineffective HR business partnerships comprise a major area of weakness in LMD strategy and practice today, taking us back to Chapters 11, 12 and 13 where the issues involved have been examined in detail. All HR professionals must work closely with their corporate and operational leaders to cultivate leadership and management talent at all organisational levels, developing potential for the future as well as enhancing current performance. Key tasks are (DDI and CIPD 2007):

- Identify the skills, knowledge, experience and personality attributes needed to ensure excellent leaders in the particular organisation and its culture.

- Identify those with the strongest leadership potential and focus resources and attention particularly on them.

- Ensure accurate methods of assessing the readiness of leaders and potential leaders to move into and up the leadership pipeline so that valid promotion and development decisions can be made.

The second of these two elements may seem controversial, since it raises the prospect of excluding many from the possibility of leadership development who might otherwise prove in time to have the talent and commitment required. In reality, as seen in Chapter 16, this need not be the case. The following example explains why.

INCLUSIVE LEADERSHIP DEVELOPMENT AT TESCO

There is a firm belief at Tesco in the need for a collective, inclusive approach to leadership development and the company has always sought to grow its own leaders, rejecting the idea of selecting senior managers purely from an elite group. The great majority of those at corporate level have come up through the ranks. The consistent success of the business has been demonstrated in several research studies to be significantly due to the quality of corporate leadership and the vision and values that it communicates and enacts, tight links between business and HR strategies and practices, and an integrated approach to leadership development at all levels (Purcell *et al* 2003; Hutchinson and Purcell 2003).

However, the company also believes in the need to regularly identify talent. It does this through having lists of people with potential for promotion drawn up regularly from store level upwards, with a senior team at that level selecting for special development or promotion on the basis of three criteria:

- those who always improve the business for customers
- those who take people with them
- those who live the company's values.

The approach to leadership is part of an integrated staff development strategy that starts with opening up educational and learning opportunities for new recruits and on the shop floor.

In May 2007 it was announced that Tesco was to pilot a Foundation Degree in Retail, to be developed through a partnership with a number of external academic institutions, Skillsmart (the retail sector's Sector Skills Council) and a learning specialist consultancy. Tesco would recruit students in employment with diverse educational backgrounds, looking for a combination of experienced retail professionals and new entrants to the sector.

The programme aims to provide a work-based higher-education route for students who would not have traditionally progressed to university at 18 or would be unlikely for various reasons to move into higher education. Following successful piloting it will be available to the whole retail sector to help establish consistent, national learning provision that can aid organisations' workforce and personal development strategy.

The Foundation Degree is to form part of a suite of qualifications, alongside the Retail Apprenticeship Level 2 programme that started in 2004 at Tesco. The aim is that over the next five years all store employees will be able to enhance their education with Tesco regardless of their level or age.

Sources: Purcell, J. *et al* (2003); Hutchinson, S. and Purcell, J. (2003); *http://www.trainingpressreleases. com/newsstory.asp?NewsID=2845* [accessed 11 August 2008]

6 ENSURE CONSISTENCY, CO-ORDINATION AND FLEXIBILITY

There should be co-ordinated standards, practices and metrics used in LMD across the organisation, and they should be consistent with those used in the business, in its performance management system and in its other HR practices and procedures. The aim should be mutual reinforcement, with any necessary changes to secure this being made before any LMD development programmes begin.

Such programmes and other initiatives should all focus on the strategic goals of the LMD system, but should be flexible enough to enable local business unit needs for LMD to be addressed and for personal development plans and methods to be tailored to individual needs and preferences.

7 MAKE LMD WORK

A wide range of methods is used to develop leaders and managers (see next section), yet often there is what a DDI/CIPD global survey in 2005 (p.17) referred to as 'a mismatch between common practice in leadership development and what actually works'. The survey showed that despite HR professionals in the UK rating special projects outside the job, expatriate assignments and coaching by both internal and external coaches highest in a list of methods, 'formal workshops still dominate common practice by far' (*ibid*: 9). This criticism of ill-chosen LMD media and methods recurs in research, underlining the importance of HR professionals – especially those with specialised L&D expertise – paying more informed attention to the mix of activities that are best suited to develop the skills, knowledge and behaviours needed in their organisation's leaders and managers (see below).

8 HOLD LEADERS ACCOUNTABLE FOR RESULTS

This is vital, and at corporate level the investment in LMD and its primary outcomes for the business and its employees should form part of the organisation's annual report. Where a balanced scorecard is used (as explained in Chapter 14) this should be a key entry. Fulmer and Bleak (2007) found that competency frameworks are in widespread use in companies' LMD systems, setting behavioural standards for leaders and managers and with pay influenced by performance against them, but that even their outcomes are often not measured.

REFLECTION

Reflecting on your own organisation (or one with which you are familiar) which of the eight principles discussed in this section seem/s to pose the greatest challenges, and why?

WHAT KIND OF DEVELOPMENT?

ORGANISATIONALLY-BASED LMD

Following their research into the development of directors Mumford and his colleagues contend that the possession of a management qualification is of little relevance – what promotes the most effective learning is day-to-day work-based experience and appropriate role models (Mumford *et al* 1987; Mumford and Gold 2004). They and many others argue that LMD should be organisationally-based, although with a clear strategic focus. New tasks and methods can be supported, and sometimes initiated, by changes in business processes and unlearning and relearning can take root when supported by organisational systems. Methods should also be of a kind that will stimulate the required changes in values, attitudes and behaviour (Lippitt 1983: 38):

> The most meaningful aspect of personal change resulting from a management development process is the examination and alteration of attitudes within the organisation. Reinforcement will need to be related to meaningful renewal systems.

Work-based learning methods

Work-based learning can be stimulated in many ways including project work, self-development, action learning, coaching and mentoring, competency-focused, 360-degree and other types of appraisal, developmental job rotations, rewards and recognition and talent management. Such learning is becoming increasingly popular as a way of developing high-potential managers into future leaders, especially in international LMD where a favoured method is a blended approach that provides more hands-on learning through international assignments, with the chief executive and the senior management team giving strong support. The assignments have a unique value when they produce greater diversity in multinational organisations, especially in the top team which often reflects only the nationality of the parent company. To quote Wilson (2008: 6):

> If potential senior managers are exposed to working practices and operations in different countries, there is a greater chance that they will fulfil their potential, and multicultural boards will be in greater evidence.

When relying primarily or entirely on the work-based learning route to develop the organisation's current leaders and managers and secure its stock for the future, careful thought must be given to how that learning can be sufficiently strategically focused and to the evaluation of its outcomes for the business as well as for individuals. It is essential to incorporate developmental methods that encourage lateral thinking and double-loop learning, since without those correctives work-based learning can result in narrow mindsets and skilled incompetence (Argyris 1986). L&D practitioners can help to enhance strategic understanding and capability in LMD participants through:

- processes and methods to develop 'thinking performers' at all levels and to ensure skilled use of the organisation's strategic processes and routines (for example, through informational processes to do with environmental scanning, scenario-building, the identification of strategic issues, and the generation of wide-ranging strategic options)

- processes and initiatives to continuously improve the cognitive abilities and emotional intelligence of strategic managers and teams. This is particularly important at middle management level where strategic orientation may be critical for organisational performance yet where many feel ill-equipped to deal with their newly acquired strategic roles (Floyd and Wooldridge 1994)

- processes and initiatives to improve skills related to the implementation of strategy – for example, skills in setting and monitoring plans and targets, and in evaluating their impact in the workplace

- the stimulation of the search for strategically valuable knowledge throughout the organisation through work-based learning processes.

The development of front-line leaders and latent leadership and management potential should have a strong focus on:

- learning activity that incorporates and helps to embed strong organisational values that show clearly those leadership behaviours expected and those not permitted

- skills training related to team leadership and team management

- career development and access to meaningful career paths. Without that, employees' commitment levels drop, especially if coupled with little or no sense of support from their managers

- learning activity that induces and reinforces good working relationships with their managers and that helps them to achieve an effective work–life balance themselves – thereby enabling them to cope better with the pressures surrounding their work – and to better promote the well-being of those for whom they are responsible. Mabey and Terry (2007), whose international research I noted earlier, found that much MD stresses the importance of collaboration yet focuses in its methods solely on the individual. They also warned against a frequent 'obsession' in MD schemes with 'getting it right' and against learning from 'getting it wrong'.

In connection with the last point, Grant (2005) emphasised the importance of organisational cultures that encourage 'constructive dissent' rather than 'destructive consent' – that is to say, allow challenges to leaders where followers think the latter are wrong, provided that this is done in a the spirit of treating errors as opportunities and using them to promote collective learning. As noted earlier in the chapter, in workplaces where a command-control management culture is deeply embedded this kind of encouragement will be extremely hard to develop – sometimes, sadly, impossible. Where that is the case it is the responsibility of HR professionals to identify to top management the threats that such failure pose to the LMD system, and to determine with business leaders how the necessary shift in culture can be achieved.

Competency frameworks

Development centres, a methodology described in the previous chapter, are widely used in LMD programmes. So too are competency frameworks which are often used as the basis for such centres on the grounds that they provide a clear set of performance criteria at all organisational levels, and express in measurable ways the expected outcomes of achieving those criteria, thereby offering an inclusive and objective approach to assessment and development. Competencies in this sense are a set of character features, knowledge and skills, attitudes, motives and traits that comprise the profile of a leader or of a manager and enable an individual to perform effectively in the role. A competency framework provides a template against which teams as well as individuals can be developed, since no individual will have more than a few of the competencies needed for superior organisational performance (Miller *et al* 2001).

I have mentioned earlier in the chapter that competency frameworks used as the basis for LMD are of suspect relevance yet are widely used in the field. Hamlin (2002) found the UK's government-inspired 'competency' approach to MD, which has been spearheaded by the Management Charter Initiative, to be very poorly supported by convincing evidence. He identified a string of academics who have questioned the soundness of the research base and methods used to derive the generic competencies on which the MCI's competency framework is based. To summarise some of the main weaknesses of competency-based LMD:

- Competency frameworks are expensive to design, install and monitor and need to be expertly administered.

- They encourage a focus on 'sameness' and can therefore disadvantage diversity (a criticism explored in Chapter 9).

- They carry the assumption that selected individuals can be 'trained' into leadership and will then provide good leadership for others (Boydell *et al* 2004). This ignores the collective and relational nature of the leadership process.

- They rarely discriminate enough between leadership and management roles and needs.

- They assume that a number of discrete components can adequately describe critical features of a role, and that those components will remain relatively constant and standardised through time. Mintzberg (1973, 2004), on the other hand, has produced a mass of data pointing to the high level of variability in management roles, emphasising managers' often simultaneous pursuit of a variety of objectives in changing ways according to their judgement in the particular situation. He has repeatedly portrayed managers' work as highly contextualised, requiring managers to have significant discretion in deciding how best to operate, what tasks to tackle and how.

- Even where there are attempts to formalise and link both individual and organisational competencies to organisations' strategic priorities and their HR systems, tight-coupling runs the danger of supporting current strategy and practices regardless of their quality (Alvarez 1996). It can reinforce narrow managerial perspectives that stifle questioning and prevent unlearning, thus leading to a skilled incompetence that hinders change (Argyris 1986).

Holbeche tends towards optimism in noting an increased concern by practitioners to ensure the validity of a competency-based approach to leadership development, with a greater focus on 'the organisational capabilities that appear to underpin corporate agility' and therefore an emphasis on 'leaders who can lead beyond the short term, transform culture, stimulate innovation and also drive a successful business agenda' (Holbeche 2008: 6). Be that as it may, if a competency-based approach to LMD is used, competencies should be analysed in the context of the particular organisation and be agreed as meaningful and relevant by the key parties involved in and affected by its LMD strategy. The Investors in People Leadership and Management framework and the CIPD's professional Leadership and Management standards make a point of their flexibility in this respect.

These varied views and findings about LMD competency frameworks suggest three conclusions:

- Leaders and managers do need training and development in their many functional tasks, but there is a danger that reliance on functionally-based competency frameworks as the basis for the LMD system may ignore the higher-level capacities and holistic skills that are crucial to success in their roles. They may also ignore or underplay the situational and collective nature of leadership by an excessive focus on individual competencies.

- In the short term and in the more stable organisations a competency-based approach to management development can produce useful results, enabling the linking of performance criteria, development activity and performance outcomes at individual and organisational levels. It is essential, though, to carry out internal research in order to identify organisation-specific competencies and gain ownership and commitment in the organisation to the competency framework that is ultimately produced (Woodall and Winstanley 1998).

- An alternative approach to LMD should be considered in those organisations where the future is highly uncertain, where leaders and managers are already facing complex, unfamiliar problems, or where there can be no certainty as to the exact nature and interrelationship of the competencies needed to deal with them.

QUALIFICATION-LED LMD

The UK strongly favours a qualification-led approach to LMD and in 2004 national occupational standards were launched (being reviewed at the time of writing, mid-2008), with related S/NVQs in management and leadership. The Chartered Management Institute, one of the leading awarding bodies, offers a range of qualifications linked to the Scottish and National Qualification Framework (also currently under review). The CIPD's professional Leadership and Management Standards, also cross-mapped to the national framework, form part of its master's-level professional diploma. Another popular kitemark is the Institute of Leadership and Management's Level 3 Diploma for first-line managers (*http://www.i-l-m.com/* [accessed 10 August 2008]) used to accredit the Procon UK FLM training programme described in Chapter 8.

However, qualification programmes based on national occupational standards are often not the most relevant way for an organisation to tackle its leadership and management development needs, because although those standards are useful in describing what managers do, they do not define what a manager *is* (Beard and Irvine 2005: 385). When considering what part formal training and education programmes should play in an LMDP, the real question to ask is not 'Why do we not have enough qualified managers?' but 'Will qualification make our managers more effective?' (Chambers 1990).

In contrast to the UK's qualification-led approach, the Master of Business Administration route to MD is virtually ignored in Japan and Germany, yet as a sector their managers are highly regarded. However, in both those countries, as in China, recruits have a high standard of educational attainment by the time they enter employment. Most well-educated Germans do not join a large company until 27 years of age because they tend to have followed an apprenticeship after school and then pursued a degree and often a higher degree in subjects such as engineering, law or economics. In Japan and in Britain, the average age for joining such a company is 22, but in Japan the potential manager will study law or engineering at a top university, and after entry to a large firm will go through a rigorous process of job rotation, private study and classroom learning which can last for up to 15 years before being promoted to the first level of management.

In France, the route to management in a larger organisation is either through business or engineering at one of the Grandes Ecoles, or through some other educational pathway leading to the same kind of functional qualifications as in Japan and Germany. In France, too, the law requires all firms to spend a small percentage of the wage bill on continuing education and training, and corporations with more than about 2,000 employees spend significantly more than the legally required minimum, investing about one third in management training. Such investment is common across most of mainland Europe and the USA, but not in the UK.

Where, as in the UK, many of those promoted into management positions have a poor basic education this can lead to low levels of ability to cope with new technologies, to manage and develop people, and to think and act strategically. Therefore in many UK organisations it is relevant and important for educational programmes to supplement ongoing work-based learning in the LMD system. Such programmes can incorporate a variety of work-based scenarios in their design but because they take participants out of their daily work environment they can broaden their vision, challenge their customary ways of thinking and behaving in the organisation, and expand their intellectual capacity. They offer a safe environment in which individuals can identify and reflect on their personal weaknesses and strengths and explore problematic scenarios in a variety of organisational settings. They have an important role in stimulating and aiding the unlearning that is essential to enable new mindsets and behaviours to develop (Harrison and Miller 1999; Harrison 2005).

REFLECTION

Imagine that a manager who has been converted by the works of Alan Mumford says to you forcefully:

Management development? No two ways about it – learning from the job, in the workplace is the only real way.

Give us a good job pathway and plenty of role models and mentoring – and you'll find our development takes care of itself.

What reply do you think you should give, and why?

TASKS FOR HR/L&D PROFESSIONALS

SEVEN AREAS OF IMPACT

From research evidence and other material covered in this chapter it can be concluded that HR professionals – including those in the L&D field – have an important contribution to make to an organisation's LMD system in seven key areas:

● LMD strategy must be integrated with talent and career management and other areas of HR strategy overall in order to achieve consistency across the processes of LMD planning, recruitment, selection, appraisal, rewards and development. This argues for the HR function to have a central involvement in planning and managing the LMD system, but it is essential to avoid that system being dominated by HR staff or it will not gain management's ownership.

● Business units as well as the centre must be actively involved in planning, operating and evaluating the LMD system, so that it is both 'owned' by units and well integrated across the organisation. This calls for considerable skill on the part of HR professionals especially. The danger of loosening central control is that divisions/units will take too much power into their own hands, and end by doing things their own way according to their own workplace cultures. The danger of putting central control into the hands of an HR or L&D function is that its specialists may hold insufficient power, and be seen as 'outside' the real management system of the organisation.

- HR professionals must be proactive in interpreting business priorities and in translating these into well resourced and well understood LMD policies and practices (Mabey and Ramirez 2004). This will require a thorough knowledge of the business, its goals and strategy as well as expertise in LMD systems and processes. They must also work with current and potential participants in LMD programmes to gain their views and experiences, using these to inform LMD planning and evaluation.

- LMD strategy is likely in most organisations to involve a need for major cultural change, another point emphasised regularly in research. HR professionals must work with business leaders to decide how to achieve that change and to put plans into action.

- Operational leaders and managers must be trained in how to train and develop others and in how to execute LMD strategy in their workplaces. Research also points to the need for greatly enhanced effectiveness in top teams (Wageman *et al* 2008) indicating a need for LMD at that level – a particularly sensitive and challenging task requiring senior HR professionals to both raise awareness and propose convincing ways forward.

- For any formal LMD programme to make an impact on organisational performance it must encompass a critical mass – something that emerged as a problematic issue at Procon UK, whose front-line management programme was described in Chapter 8. It must also be founded on transparent, relevant and fair principles that are translated into practice consistently throughout the organisation.

- There must be measurement of key outcomes of LMD strategy, and monitoring and evaluation of the operation of the whole LMD system. This is a primary task for L&D professionals, again working in business partnerships.

REFLECTION

Reflecting on the material covered in this chapter and taking any relevant experience of your own also into account, what do you consider should be the main features of your organisation's approach to developing its leaders and managers? And are there any improvements that you could suggest to the operation of its leadership pipeline?

CONCLUSION

You should by now have a sound basic understanding of the differences and overlaps between leadership and management roles in an organisation, and have developed useful insights at a practical level into different approaches to LMD that are common across organisations. You should also be able to tackle the review questions for this chapter, found in Appendix 3.

In the chapter's six sections the following main issues have been discussed:

- an organisation's 'leadership pipeline' and the key roles and tasks that it incorporates relating to corporate, operational and front-line leaders

- international research findings on LMD's effectiveness in the UK and other countries; five major failings emerging from research, and the particular problems of sparse evaluation and of management complacency

- lack of a convincing evidence base for much LMD practice in the UK, and how to interpret the research findings

- eight principles suggested by research to guide the development of an integrated and inclusive LMD strategy and system, and ensure its effective implementation

- a critical appraisal of organisationally-based and qualification-based approaches to LMD; the importance of grounding LMD methods in an organisation's specific needs and challenges whilst also ensuring a strong educational base for management and leadership; the need to choose a mix of learning media and methods to suit organisational context and learners' needs and preferences

- seven areas where HR/L&D professionals should be contributing to the organisation's LMD strategy and system.

EXLPORE FURTHER

FURTHER INFORMATION SOURCES

Alimo-Metcalf, B. and Alban-Metcalf, J. (2008) *Engaging Leadership: Creating organisations that maximise the potential of their people*. Research Insight. London: CIPD. Online version also available at: http://www.cipd.co.uk/ researchinsights [accessed 8 October 2008]

Hill, R. and Stewart, J. (eds) (2007) *Management Development: Perspectives from research and practice*. London: Routledge

Jones, P. and Holton, V. (2006) 'Teams today: taking the strain', *The Ashridge Journal*, Spring. Available online at http://www.ashridge.org.uk/ Website/ Content.nsf/FileLibrary/AA394 15FC3209CE6802571A30071E A59/$file/ComplexTeams.pdf [accessed 12 August 2008]

http://www.trainingjournal.com/news/749.html [accessed 10 August 2008]. Details of The Work Foundation's research programme, *Leading for High Performance*, a three-year study commenced in 2006

http://www.investorsinpeople.co.uk/Standard/Introducing/Pages/Whatis.aspx [accessed 10 August 2008]. Information about the Investors in People Standard, which features Leadership and Management as one of its four key strategies for improving organisational and individual performance

http://www.management-standards.org.uk/ [accessed 10 August 2008]. Details of the national occupational standards (under review, 2008), with related S/NVQs in management and leadership

http://www.managers.org.uk/content_1.aspx?id=10:63&id=10:7 [accessed 10 August 2008]. Details of the CMI's leadership and management qualifications and their relationship to Scottish and national qualification frameworks

http://www.discussionleader.hbsp.com/hmu/managing-people/ *Why some teams succeed (and so many don't)* [accessed 12 August 2008]. Lively and informative 'Harvard Management Update' by Professor Richard Hackman

CIPD podcast, 3 June 2008. *The future of global HR*. Available online at: http://www.cipd.co.uk/podcasts [accessed 9 October 2008]

CIPD podcast, 27 June 2008. *HR and Leadership*. Available online at: http://www.cipd.co.uk/podcasts [accessed 9 October 2008]

CHAPTER 18

Pulling the Threads Together: Challenges for the Profession

INTRODUCTION

Learning and development (L&D) in organisations has been exposed to a remarkable pace of change in recent years, much of it due to increasingly turbulent external conditions that have raised needs within businesses for new goals, new strategies, new ways of working and sometimes a new conception of their role in society.

For an exhaustive global account of the changed world of L&D I recommend a report produced by the Training Journal and Institute for Employment Studies (TJ and IES 2008). The purpose of this final chapter is different. It is to reflect on some of the big issues raised in this book and to suggest challenges now facing the L&D scholarly and practitioner profession.

A DEMAND-LED NATIONAL SKILLS STRATEGY?

Looking first at national skills and educational strategy, Chapters 2 and 3 have shown that the intended demand-led approach is supported by a wide range of ambitious initiatives, but that it is questionable whether the sustained funding and partnerships required in order to achieve national targets can be achieved. There is no doubting Prime Minister Gordon Brown's determination to unlock potential and talent and to meet the doubling in demand by 2020 for skilled jobs worldwide required by Leitch (2006). Nor is his sincerity in question in seeking to open up access for all to lifelong learning opportunities and to give particular support to the most disadvantaged in society. But as Riddell (2008) points out:

> He is strong on the analysis and goals … less persuasive on the implications, notably for the scale and scope of the State at a time of much slower public spending growth for at least the next five to six years.

Since that statement was made the UK's financial situation has dramatically deteriorated following a worldwide banking crisis unprecedented since the 1930s. How much of national skills strategy and, indeed, of the public and third sector reforms described in Chapter 10 can be sustained must now be uncertain.

INCREASED INVESTMENT IN TRAINING?

Investment in formal training, as distinct from the many other forms of planned learning and development in organisations, is relatively easy to measure. According to information provided by the Learning and Skills Council's National Employers Skills Survey (LSC 2008) companies invested £38.6 billion during 2007, up 16% from 2005, and since 2005 the average spend per head had risen to £1,750, in real terms an increase of 10%. There was also an increase in the proportion (67%) of employers providing training, almost half now holding a training plan and over a third a training budget. Other positive findings showed fewer employers reporting skills gaps and a 3% drop in the number of vacancies caused by skills shortage.

As much material in this book has shown, it is not the figures that are at issue here but quite what they signify.

Certainly coverage of training has improved. The 2004 Workplace Employment Relations Survey (Kersley *et al* 2006) revealed that many more employees at the lower levels of the firm are now enjoying training and learning opportunities than hitherto. Yet we have seen that in the UK too many organisations still give disproportionate attention to the learning needs and aspirations of senior staff and 'talent', and that even their training and development often falls far short of even the adequate. If this is the case for the favoured few, what then of the remaining many? What, especially, of the needs, rights and concerns of the particularly disadvantaged?

At the bottom of the organisational pile are those who still labour in unfulfilling jobs, without any prospect of advancement and for little extrinsic reward. In Chapter 6 the cook-freeze centre case was enough to demonstrate that sending such employees on a course to give them basic skill qualifications may attract official funding but is likely for the individuals concerned to provide no benefits, may in fact make the last position worse than the first because, with no way of using such qualifications and no way out of dead-end jobs, what is the point of training anyway?

In Chapter 9 many L&D issues related to equality and inclusivity were discussed, but here the needs of just one other widely disadvantaged group can be recalled: older workers. Despite the UK's 2006 legislation outlawing age discrimination in employment, research data show that older people have experienced an absolute and relative decline in job satisfaction over the past decade – a decline that seems mainly due to employers doing less to develop their potential once they reach around middle age, and training provision overall remaining heavily skewed towards younger workers (Turner 2004; Turner 2005; CIPD/CMI 2005; Philpott 2006). Why is this? The CIPD's Chief Economist suggests one cause (Philpott 2006):

> A false stereotype that older people don't want or can't benefit from training, labelling them as technophobes unable to adapt to 'the new economy'. At worst, this can become a self-fulfilling prophecy – older workers may find it harder to adapt to new technology precisely because they have fewer opportunities to do so.

It is a common view, too, that training is wasted on those about to retire yet this is another mistaken assumption. With greater longevity many want as well as need to work longer. Providing them with L&D opportunities would 'enable them to raise their overall performance over an extended working life while also substantially improving their job satisfaction' (*ibid*). Development alone, of course, will not be enough. There are other big issues here, to do with reward, with health and safety, with balanced working lives and with ensuring more flexible working arrangements not least for those with carer responsibilities (Clake 2005).

A SHIFT FROM TRAINING TO LEARNING?

A central issue discussed in the book relates to the claimed shift in organisations from training to learning. The rich body of adult learning theory that was developed in the USA and UK during the early years of the twentieth century especially made relatively little impact on training practice in organisations. Now, however, it is being mined afresh and expanded by academics located across the world. Its increased accessibility to practitioners via the Internet and reports, summaries and practical tools disseminated by professional bodies like the CIPD in the UK has done much to clarify its business value.

In addition to the extensive discussion of this issue in Chapter 4 it is relevant to recall the importance of a culture of work-based learning for any real shift of the kind claimed to occur. In this connection many organisations now are seeking to build delivery capacity by creating teams of in-house coaches, and action learning, project activity and mutual feedback are increasingly being used at the most senior organisational level to supplement off-the-job training (Sloman 2007c). The business value of focusing on work-based learning rather than only on formal accredited training is also beginning to be understood at government level in the UK, especially with the reform of national occupational standards and vocational qualifications and with the launch in England in 2008 of a government-backed consultation on informal adult learning (Chapters 3 and 5).

However Stern and Sommerlad (1999: 1) observed that the complex theoretical base relating to workplace learning makes for a 'rich but confusing field of inquiry', an observation confirmed by Clarke (2004, 2005) whose research review was cited in Chapter 5. Looking specifically at management development, in the workplaces that Woodall investigated she found a recognition of on-the-job learning as a powerful contributor but little attention being focused on how it could be facilitated or effectively assessed (Woodall 2000: 27). On the broader front Chapter 3 identified some disturbing evidence of poor workplace learning practice in the UK. There has been recent progress but that still leaves the organisation, provision and assessment of such learning in most UK organisations in need of much improvement. This places at least one big question mark against the claim of any substantial shift from 'training' to 'learning'.

A STRATEGICALLY-FOCUSED PROFESSION?

In his travels to explore trends across the world Sloman (2007c) formed the view that a common language in training seems to be developing worldwide, with trainers sharing similar concerns and tackling similar strategic issues no matter in which country or kind of organisation they work. All those he met were seeking to provide value-adding initiatives tailored to context and aligned with the business. All were aware of the need to build effective partnerships with stakeholders, respond to the needs and strengths of learners and achieve a good balance between satisfying short- and longer-term business priorities. Even in China, where business training and development needs are immense, he found that those needs differed essentially in scale rather than in kind (Sloman 2007d). Gerhart and Fang (2005) also found evidence pointing to a growing convergence in HR challenges and HR practitioners' responses to them across the world, and concluded from their rigorous analysis of relevant data that – contrary to prevailing belief in much of the international HRM literature – organisational differences may explain more variance than country differences in culture.

In 2008 the Boston Consulting group and the World Federation of Personnel Management Association, reporting on their survey of over 4,700 executives in 83 nations, found a striking similarity in the top future people challenges that were identified. Each has a strong L&D focus (Krinks and Strack 2008: 20):

- developing and retaining the best employees, including improved leadership development and managing work–life balance

- anticipating and managing change and cultural transformation

- enabling the organisation to work effectively by becoming a learning organisation and transforming HR into a strategic partner.

In a globalised knowledge economy it is unsurprising that a common language of training should develop, together with a convergence in the type of issues that trainers are striving to help their organisations resolve. However, each chapter in this book has provided evidence to indicate that gaining recognition as a strategic player remains an aspiration rather than an achievement for much of the L&D profession. There are always outstanding achievements. They regularly feature in national training awards and in the various '100 Best Companies to Work For' league tables. But elsewhere there are too many examples of L&D functions that add little or no value at any level because their activity is unsupported by a convincing business case, does not rest on secure business and learning partnerships, is poorly implemented or is little if at all measured or evaluated.

I identified at the start of Chapter 1 some indicators that L&D has now become widely recognised for its potential to make a major contribution to the business, and that its scope extends far beyond the training field. Yet while the potential is clear, material subsequently covered in the book has gone far to confirm the disappointing verdict expressed by two experts and also cited in that first chapter (Wain 2008a: 25):

> One senses little real movement over the past decade – worrying given the extraordinary developments that have happened in the wider business and economic world.

> If the past is indeed a foreign country, it is less because we did things differently there than because we used different terminology.

My reflection on four of a number of claims commonly made about L&D that have been discussed during the course of this book leads naturally into an assessment of the major challenges that now confront the L&D profession.

SIX MAJOR CHALLENGES

HONOURING THE ETHICAL AGENDA

First, the agenda for the L&D profession has an ethical dimension that should be of greater concern than any mere list of 'challenges'. Today, as seen in Chapter 9, powerful external forces are putting pressure on organisations to work to a triple rather than just to a single bottom line – one that acknowledges not only economic accountability and affordability but also diversity and equity. It is a matter of what

Adam Smith termed 'prudence' rather than of 'benevolence' that in organisations there should be 'good' leadership and management that goes about its business in a manner respectful of certain values and achieves equality and inclusivity in the workplace (Harrison and Smith 2001). Likewise if work is to become 'the new classroom' where learning leads to continuous improvement and regular innovation in products, services and processes, there must be a sense in the organisation of a learning community that embraces diverse value systems (Rana 2002).

In the UK more than elsewhere in the world a mass of anti-discrimination legislation is reaching deep into organisations with its tentacles, causing in reaction a strong focus on compliance-based rather than values-based diversity training. Although people may be persuaded or forced into compliance no one can be made to value others as they do themselves. Respectful behaviour stems from internal values and it is values-based programmes that can bring people face to face with their fundamental assumptions about those who are 'different'. As a case example in Chapter 9 showed, they can enable participants to stand in others' shoes for a while and experience emotionally something of what it is like to be on the other side of that divide. They can act, therefore, as a catalyst for behavioural change.

There has never been a greater need for such change, or for equality of access to lifelong learning opportunities, because as Klaus Schwab (2007) observed, although organisations today are increasingly flat the same is not true of the social world in which they are located:

> Globalisation does create winners and losers. . . . The gap between those able to ride the wave of globalisation, especially because they are knowledge- and creativity-oriented, and those left behind is becoming wider at global, national, corporate and individual levels.

ACTING ON EVIDENCE

Many writers cited in the book have emphasised the need for evidence-based L&D practice. However, it should be clear by now that the search for 'evidence' contains many traps for the unwary, for it is no longer the case, in the field of learning and development, that we lack information. Rather it is the case that we are overwhelmed by it and too often are at a loss to know how to convert it into useful knowledge.

I mentioned in Chapter 1 the major disconnect that researchers often find between the espoused and the real in HR strategy and practice. Establishing its causes can be problematic, often because a mass of information can block their enquiry. Some of the gatekeepers to that information will be reluctant to release it. Others may release so much that it will be virtually impossible to sort out what is meaningful – a favourite ploy of Sir Humphrey, the devious civil servant in the British television series, 'Yes, Minister', to ensure that his boss lived in a state of permanent bewilderment as he tried, usually in vain, to understand 'what is really going on here'.

Often, though, no human agency is to blame, simply a process of accumulation. Even a glance at the number of website references appearing in every chapter of this book and in its index should make clear that e-technology, the rapid growth of virtual communities, the ceaseless flow of data from seemingly unlimited sources, the pressure on academics to generate and publish ever more 'research' to satisfy the demands of their institutions and of national assessment – all this is producing a rising sea of information in which some feel they are drowning. For the individual the challenge is not so much to 'find out' as to understand how to select from this deluge what is of most relevance, and then to collate, to analyse and finally to transform it into a personal stock of 'knowledge' that can guide future research and practice. And here, the warning of Mattinson (2006) could not be more relevant:

> Accurate and insightful ... research depends not just on reliable fieldwork but also on thoughtful and experienced analysis that sets the findings in a proper context and interprets them accordingly. Too often the analysis is carried out with an eye on the headline, not an eye on the truth.

Cynical? No, just realistic. We have seen in Chapter 15 that the majority of organisational change programmes fail because they are founded on an inadequate evidence base and because there is too little monitoring and evaluation of their outcomes at critical stages. We have also seen in Chapter 17 that despite over two decades of high investment in leadership and management training and development, practice is still deficient with little apparent concern to apply lessons from research, to align plans with business goals and to evaluate impact. And management complacency, highlighted as a central problem as far back as the 1980s, still presents an obstacle to progress.

So the need is not for cynical professionals, but for those who understand the research process and its pitfalls, who are well-versed in sound theory and how to apply it in practice, and who can be relied on to provide well-informed and honest advice. Hamlin (2002: 107) concedes that an evidence-based approach to HRD is unlikely to be able to emulate the original model of 'evidence-based medicine'. Best efforts may have to be limited to assessing findings drawn from good-quality empirical research. At worst, they may have to be satisfied by building into their everyday practice a questioning approach. But at a minimum they must be 'research-informed', meaning (Hamlin 2002: 98):

> The conscientious and explicit use of research findings and the research process to inform, shape, measure and evaluate professional practice.

BREAKING NEW GROUND

The need for research-informed practice is undeniable, but it is important not to become over-cautious, attempting nothing unless it has a secure evidence base. Space must be allowed for the exercise of entrepreneurial flair. In a field where old recipes to which practitioners continue to cling are often irrelevant to needs in a rapidly changing world there must be willingness to take risks in the interests of progress. Time and resources should be set aside to mount small experiments with little or no evidence base in order to test out a hunch that may prove to be inspired, to conduct some purely exploratory research that rests on untested methodologies, or to pilot some innovative proposal. Gary Hamel (quoted in Roberts 2006) sees HR professionals as central to management innovation, needing to help organisations break out of conventional patterns of behaviour. To do this they need to become 'inventors and innovators'.

Experimentation requires sponsors who are willing to make an investment that will not always pay off. Failure has a value if it identifies pitfalls that otherwise would have gone unnoticed, and if it is treated as a source of learning that can improve the quality of future L&D decision-making. The risk-assessment calculations involved here are fine and require there to be strong bonds of trust between business leaders and the L&D professionals involved. Those professionals will need to have earned respect for their specialist expertise, their consistent delivery of value-creating initiatives and their deep understanding of the organisation and its business. Another message to have come through strongly in this book is that relatively few appear as yet to have earned such credibility. L&D business partnerships, in consequence, are often weak or fail.

ENHANCING ENGAGEMENT AND BUILDING SOCIAL AND STRUCTURAL CAPITAL

I have placed the case of Procon UK, recounted in Chapter 8, at the heart of this book because it is an example of what can be achieved when there is visionary leadership at corporate level and strong strategically-focused L&D partnerships. It is a core challenge for all L&D professionals to encourage, enable and support leadership and people management and development in the workplace that will raise the commitment of organisational members and partners to corporate goals and their ability to 'go the extra mile' to achieve them.

Such engagement cannot be gained without mutual trust. Investment in L&D strategies and practices that brings powerful benefits to all the parties, not just to 'the business', is of critical importance in the trust-building task. As noted in Chapter 1, trust is also crucial as both a source and an outcome of social capital, defined (OECD 2001: 41) as

> networks together with shared norms, values and understandings that facilitate co-operation within or among groups.

In the UK, Kinnie and colleagues (2006) in their research into knowledge-intensive firms in the professional services sector have drawn attention to the importance of effective interaction between various forms of 'human capital', broadly defined, in relation to organisational performance. One of those forms – social capital – was discussed in Chapter 1 and has featured throughout much of the book thereafter. Another – structural capital – refers to the outcome of the structuring process examined in Chapter 11. The close relationship that exists between the two has a significance that goes beyond individual organisations, as Klaus Schwab (2007), founder and executive chairman of the World Economic Forum, explained:

> We are witnessing profound decay in the structures we have historically used to manage our world. ... Power is moving from the centre to the periphery. Vertical command and control structures are eroding and are being replaced by horizontal networks of social communities and collaboration. Unprecedented integration and interconnectedness have created a true global neighbourhood.

He emphasises the 'revolution' that this represents, the core challenge now being:

> how we will reinvent ourselves, our social relations and our power structures within this flat world ...

Returning to the context of the individual organisation, this underlines the importance of discovering new ways to build mutually reinforcing social and structural capital. The task has become more daunting in an 'interconnected' world where organisational boundaries are increasingly blurred, organisational networks are more complex, and collaborative working through far-flung virtual communities is a regular requirement because interconnectedness at one level can mean disconnection at another. As Schwab again explained, in those many organisations where there is now a wide physical separation of local units from the centre, there has been a corresponding weakening of the old informal relationships, fostered by close proximity of employer and employees, from which strong bonds of trust could customarily be developed. In Chapter 10 this kind of damaging disconnection was noted particularly in relation to organisations in the public sector.

In his great philosophical work *The Theory of Moral Sentiments* (1759) Adam Smith emphasised the folly of those 'in the system' who imagine that human beings can be manipulated 'with as much ease as the hand arranges the different pieces upon a chessboard', when in reality:

> In the great chessboard of human society, every single piece has a principle of motion of its own, altogether different from that which the legislator might choose to impress upon it.

Building social and structural capital in the chessboards of many of today's organisations is one of the most important tasks to which L&D professionals must contribute. It is one of particular challenge in the many organisations where, as research cited in Chapters 5 and 6 has shown, work-based learning processes that could be directed to the task are instead focused only on immediate proficiency needs.

LINKING THE SCHOLARLY AND PRACTITIONER FIELDS

The field that is still referred to by many academics as human resource development (HRD) rather than L&D continues to expand into a significant domain of study in its own right. One indicator of this is the growth of rigorous empirical research. Another is the development of critical HRD inquiry. Although sometimes giving the impression of being carried out for its own sake rather than to advance understanding, it is making a vital contribution to the field's conceptual and philosophical base, challenging those who take too much for granted its core assumptions and values (Sambrook 2004; Elliott and Turnbull 2005; Valentin 2006; Rigg *et al* 2007).

A related indicator is the incidence of postgraduate programmes and their popularity in the market, but here the signs are less reassuring. The website *http://www.b.shuttle.de/wifo/l&w-pro/=index.htm* links to a directory of around 80 master's-level programmes offered in 15 European countries covering the broad area of learning and work related to HRD and/or vocational education and training in fairly equal proportions. Few feature HRD as a subject in its own right; it is more usually found as a component of broader subjects, especially HRM. While an integrated approach is logical it is also important for HRD to gain recognition as a field with its own specialist knowledge and expertise. Since 2004 when the directory last appeared there has been little growth in HRD academic programmes, in contrast to the areas of VET, education and organisation/work where there has been much change and innovation.

On another indicator, the number of academic journals devoted to HRD is only expanding slowly. In the UK there are many training and development magazines and periodicals for practitioners but few HRD refereed journals. More, but still relatively few, are published in the USA. In both countries as across the world HRM remains the dominant area for publications. The story is similar in the textbook arena.

On the other hand there are some strong international publishing and research links between institutions as well as individuals in the HRD field. For example the EURESFORM network (which provides a framework for the mutual recognition of learning outcomes in HRD across Europe) and the UK's University Forum for HRD (which encompasses around 25 member institutions conducting research and providing postgraduate HRD programmes) collaborates with the US-based Academy of HRD in running the refereed journal, *Human Resource Development International* and in organising research conferences.

On balance the signs of HRD's scholarly development are mixed but promising. The greater challenge lies in forging stronger links with the field of practice, which seems relatively little influenced by academic outputs. Salas and Cannon-Bowers (2001: 472) argued from their survey of training research over the previous decade that 'things have progressed dramatically in terms of both the science and practice of training'. The material in this book indicates that their claim is optimistic. Looking at the literature on links between training and the business and on evaluation of training alone – both core tasks for any L&D practitioner – it is clear that there is now an extensive body of research and that much of it has produced conceptual frameworks offering real practical utility. But it also raises the question, why do practitioners not make better use of them?

One reason appears to be the lack of synergy across multiple research strands. If research is to make a greater impact on the development of the L&D profession there needs to be more integrative commentary that pulls together and reflects on key theory, concepts and models. Too much academic output at present cries out for Occam's razor to slice away spurious arguments and theories. Gary Hamel voices a common lament that applies as much to research in the L&D field as to management research generally (Roberts 2006: 31):

> Management research is largely disconnected from the world of practice. Business professors turn out a lot of articles in academic journals. But if you ask the average executive what difference management research has made to the way they run their company most of them don't have any kind of answer.

Axelsson (1998, cited by Hamlin *et al* 2001: 290) reached a similar conclusion after his 'wide-ranging and historical study of the management research literature' over the past two decades:

> The field has been left wide open for consultants and different charlatans to influence managers with their fashionable models of organization and management. ... After nearly a hundred years of research on organization and management, the practical knowledge in the field seems to be back almost on the same scientific level as when the research started. This is a sad development compared with the many other fields where research has been more cumulative and its results are continually enriching and improving practical knowledge.

One obvious remedy is an expansion of partnerships between the academic and the practitioner worlds. In the USA the Academy of HRD has long been promoting this, and the task is being greatly aided in the UK by the University Forum for HRD and by sponsoring bodies like the CIPD which (as many references in this book identify) is dedicated to promoting academically rigorous research that can also make a positive impact on professional practice.

THE CHALLENGE OF CONTEXT

Throughout the book context, in one shape or the other, has been an outstanding theme. The practical tools, the guides and prescriptions, the complex diagrams found everywhere in the literature and the websites too often project a systematic, 'best practice' approach that belies the need to adapt aspirational strategies and plans to the messiness and uncertainties of the real-life context. As Woodall and her colleagues observed (Woodall *et al* 2002):

> 'Managing' learning in organisations is less about adhering to formal procedures of instruction and increasingly about creating the environmental conditions (including building trust, fostering networks and working with a range of stakeholders) within which learning can take place.

Writing this chapter in the closing months of 2008 as countries across the world face the destructive effects of skilled incompetence in their financial institutions, the need to understand the power of context has become all too clear. A complacency stemming from two decades of prosperity, near-full employment and inadequate regulation of the banking system led in the UK to 'excessive and irresponsible risk-taking' (Gordon Brown, quoted by Webster *et al* 2008). In the USA it caused the collapse of Lehman Brothers' bank. Others that had seemed hitherto impregnable quickly followed, triggering a worldwide panic that led to the bankruptcy of one small country – Iceland – and left others teetering on the verge of chaos. Within a month The *Times* (2008c) in a leading article was forecasting 'a self-reinforcing spiral of collapsing investment, job losses and recession'. Seen in retrospect it is clear that the fall of Northern Rock in the UK during the summer of 2007 (Chapter 5) was no isolated failure. It was an early warning sign of a far greater, widespread malaise in the world's interconnected banking system.

Bringing the discussion back to the level of L&D in organisations, it will require all the skills that L&D professionals possess – and many that as yet they do not – to demonstrate in these recessionary times that they can produce efficient, innovative strategies whose outcomes justify investment by the business and whose benefits will also extend to those individuals in greatest need of them.

Internal organisational context, like the external context that shapes it, cannot be changed overnight, not least because it is shaped powerfully by the past. Organisations that have developed high adaptive capability cope well with situations demanding change, but elsewhere the weight of history can be heavy. Embedded structures, routines and procedures, a culture and organisational identity forged over years, reinforcing myths, stories and symbols, skilled incompetence – all can combine to pull back both leaders and followers as they struggle to understand and respond to new challenges.

The 'context' challenge for L&D professionals is twofold: they must carefully tailor their activity and processes to internal and external context. They must also help to build and often to change workplace culture – a task that for many commentators constitutes L&D practitioners' primary role, giving them the potential to become 'centrepiece players on the organizational stage' (Hamlin 2002: 115). Again, there is a dual task here: to contribute to the effectiveness of change processes, but also to act as catalysts for change, proposing L&D initiatives and processes that, through transforming employees' competence, confidence and aspirations, can make possible new goals for themselves and their organisation.

THE FINAL CHALLENGE

The last and greatest challenge is one of leadership. Rarely in recent times has it been more needed, whether in L&D functions, in work organisations, in society, in governments or in nations. It was 'appalling failures of leadership' and 'spectacular' mismanagement of banks in the UK that bore much of the responsibility for the scale of the crisis that unfolded there during 2007–8 (The *Times* 2008d), leaving it uncertain today that Britain can escape a depression that lasts not for months but for years (Conway 2008). The same failures were embedded in the global banking system, the restoration of confidence made the more difficult because everywhere there was, as one commentator remarked, 'a collective contagious madness' that signified (MacIntyre 2008):

> as much a psychological crisis as a financial one … it is [at a deep level] about emotions and feeling that have little to do with reason, percentages, profit or loss.

What counts most in any crisis is effective leadership. In threatening times when the survival of businesses and of jobs are all at risk L&D professionals must do more than find an 'evidence base' to justify their advice and actions. They must be able to inspire confidence and shared purpose not only through timely and relevant L&D strategies but through the exercise of the same leadership qualities in their own field that they should be helping to develop in their organisations' leadership pipeline (Chapter 17).

A fundamental responsibility of leadership is to critically consider the norms and assumptions that lie at the heart of taken-for-granted strategies and practices. I opened this book with a quotation from Dickens. It is apt near its close to cite the reflection of a poet, Janette Turner Hospital (2001) from another country (Australia) and our own age:

> When we learn that we are too ignorant to formulate intelligible questions we learn a great deal. We begin to cross the divide, to think with 'forked brain', to become a different self, one which is no longer at ease in the old dispensation. From that moment, we understand how very strange our own unexamined assumptions are and, like T. S. Eliot's Magi, we begin to feel foreign in our own country.

The acknowledgement of the need to 'think with forked brain', the realisation of how little we know, how much more we need to discover, and the determination to constantly unlearn in order to learn afresh – these are the hallmarks both of leadership and of the true learning and development professional. They call for two virtues that go to the heart of all this book's matter – wisdom and humility: the wisdom to search for the fundamental questions to ask, and the humility to realise that some may never be possible to answer. These are the ancient virtues proclaimed by Socrates, whose voice still speaks to us down the ages:

> The highest form of human excellence is to question oneself and others. … All I know is that I know nothing.

Appendices

The CIPD's Learning and Development Generalist Standard and Performance Indicators (CIPD 2005a): links to the text

PERFORMANCE INDICATOR 1: INTEGRATING LEARNING AND DEVELOPMENT ACTIVITY AND ORGANISATIONAL NEEDS

Practitioners must be able to explain and critically evaluate the organisation's business environment and internal context, and must be able to co-operate with learning and development stakeholders in producing and integrating learning and development policy, strategy and plans, in order to integrate their activity with wider personnel and business policy.

All chapters

PERFORMANCE INDICATOR 2: PROVIDING A VALUE-ADDING LEARNING AND DEVELOPMENT FUNCTION

Practitioners must be able to advise on how to achieve a well-managed, appropriately staffed and value-adding learning and development function.

Chapters 1, 7, 8, 10, 11, 12, 13, 14, 18

PERFORMANCE INDICATOR 3: CONTRIBUTING TO THE RECRUITMENT AND PERFORMANCE MANAGEMENT PROCESSES

Practitioners must be able to contribute to learning and development that will aid the processes of recruitment and performance management.

Chapters 1, 6, 9, 10, 12, 13, 16, 17, 18

PERFORMANCE INDICATOR 4: CONTRIBUTING TO THE RETENTION OF EMPLOYEES

Practitioners must be able to contribute to learning and development that will help the organisation retain the people it needs for the future.

Chapters 1, 6, 10, 12, 13, 15, 16, 17, 18

PERFORMANCE INDICATOR 5: CONTRIBUTING TO BUILDING ORGANISATIONAL CAPACITY AND FACILITATING CHANGE

Practitioners must be able to contribute to learning and development that will expand or change the organisation's overall capacity and capability and will help to introduce and embed organisational change.

All chapters

PERFORMANCE INDICATOR 6: STIMULATING STRATEGIC AWARENESS AND THE DEVELOPMENT OF KNOWLEDGE

Practitioners must be able to promote learning that will stimulate strategic awareness, and will develop and help to disseminate organisationally valuable knowledge.

Chapters 1, 4, 5, 13, 15, 17, 18

PERFORMANCE INDICATOR 7: DESIGNING AND DELIVERING LEARNING PROCESSES AND ACTIVITY

Practitioners must be able to contribute to the design and provision of effective and inclusive learning processes and activity, using new technology as appropriate.

Chapters 1, 4, 5, 7, 8, 9, 13, 18

PERFORMANCE INDICATOR 8: EVALUATING AND ASSESSING LEARNING AND DEVELOPMENT OUTCOMES AND INVESTMENT

Practitioners must be able to evaluate learning outcomes, and help to assess the returns on the organisation's past and planned investment in learning and development.

Chapters 1, 7, 8, 12, 13, 14, 18

PERFORMANCE INDICATOR 9: ACHIEVING ETHICAL PRACTICE

Practitioners must be able to identify and promote learning and development processes and practices that meet or exceed legal, mandatory and ethical requirements.

Chapters 1, 5, 9, 13, 18

CIPD Research Resources

Website

http://www.cipd.co.uk/research provides an overview of the CIPD's research projects and publications. Alternatively after http://www.cipd.co.uk/ type the headings in the list below (omitting any word spaces) to go straight to the resources described.

Research insights (previously known as Change Agendas)

Analyse current thinking on topical HR issues. Provide interim information on major research projects.

Guides

Offer practical insights into key people management and development issues.

Surveys

Provide benchmarking data and analysis of current issues and emerging trends.

Event reports

Provide write-ups of CIPD events focused on research and policy.

Research reports

Give details of priced reports in the Research section of the CIPD Bookstore.

Also:

Practical tools and activities (Member resource)

Interactive tools developed from CIPD research.

Factsheets

Introductory guidance on a variety of HR issues; provide starting-point for further research.

Podcasts

Regularly updated, including exclusive speaker interviews and conference highlights.

Public policy

CIPD responses to government consultations on proposals affecting employment law and people management and development.

Company profiles (Member resource)

Over 660 online full-text company profiles.

Journals (Member resource)

Access through EBSCO covers 320 online full-text HR, business and management journals.

Communities (Member resource)

Useful way to network, find out information and exchange views, ideas and experiences.

Helping people learn

Interactive web area for CIPD research, to support, accelerate and direct learning towards organisational needs.

Chapter Review Questions and Advice for Students

The questions that follow typify those set by the CIPD and a number of higher education institutions for students taking Learning and Development at postgraduate level, whether as a generalist subject in its own right or as part of a wider human resource paper. Each is intended to take about six or seven minutes to answer. Here is some advice to help you tackle them successfully in an examination context:

1 Take time at the start of the examination to read carefully through each question and identify its specific requirements. You must respond clearly to those in order to pass.

2 Where a mini-case scenario is included in the question, note its key features and tailor your answer to those. Contextualised responses are vital.

3 Differentiate between what is stated as fact and what is indicated as assumption in a question. Your diagnosis of issues and related advice must rest on a convincing evidence base.

4 Quality counts more than quantity. On average, CIPD students produce about one handwritten A4 page in answering questions like these. Some write more yet fail because their answers are poorly informed, irrelevant or lack the evaluative thrust that is essential at postgraduate level. Others write less yet gain a pass because all the content is well-focused, reflective and well justified.

5 Remember that no script can be perfect. As in examinations, so in life – one or two weaknesses rarely kill, so even when you feel you have answered a question badly, disregard that and *press on*!

CHAPTERS 1 AND 18: LEARNING AND DEVELOPMENT IN ORGANISATIONS TODAY

- Identify some major challenges facing learning and development as an organisational process today, and assess the impact that *one* of these challenges is having on the L&D function in your organisation or one with which you are familiar.

- The HR profession is increasingly being urged to practise more evidence-based management. What practical steps could you take to ensure that your own L&D work has a strong base of evidence to support it, and why should you take them?

CHAPTER 2: NATIONAL SKILLS STRATEGY

- Identify *up to three* factors in the external environment of UK-based organisations that have major implications for the learning and development of employees, and assess the impact of these factors on your own organisation.

- In its 2001 skills strategy the UK government emphasised the importance of national workforce development. Identify one funded initiative that could aid workforce development in your organisation (or one with which you are familiar) and explain why it would be of value.

CHAPTER 3: REFORMING VOCATIONAL EDUCATION AND TRAINING

- A further education (FE) college, like most in the FE sector, is struggling to ensure the required 'demand-led' provision in the face of a big increase in student numbers, high staff turnover and a general strain on financial, material and human resources. As the college's first L&D manager, what kind of L&D activity would you propose for the college in order to improve this situation, and why?

- Official reports have uncovered many weaknesses in the management of workplace learning in organisations. What criteria would you use to assess its management in a particular organisation, and why?

CHAPTER 4: UNDERSTANDING LEARNING AND THE LEARNERS

- There is much talk of a shift in organisations from 'trainers' to 'learners'. Draw on research to identify and justify major steps to take in an organisation if such a shift is actually to take place and be sustained.

- What does published research suggest is one of the most powerful ways in which people learn, and how would you use that approach in a training programme or situation of your choice?

CHAPTER 5: PROMOTING WORKPLACE LEARNING AND KNOWLEDGE

- An organisation's top management wants to promote knowledge-sharing at all levels by making major use of new information and communication technology (ICT). Outline and justify what its L&D section could do to ensure the success of this strategy.

- Strong 'workplace learning cultures' are fairly rare, both in the UK and across Europe. If, as an organisation's L&D manager, you wished to promote such a culture, what priorities would you focus on as a start, and why?

CHAPTER 6: ENHANCING PERFORMANCE MANAGEMENT

- Drawing on your knowledge of good organisational practice, identify and justify key steps you would recommend in order to make a performance appraisal process effective from the organisation's viewpoint and fair to appraisees.

- Top management in an organisation has decided to introduce coaching as a key L&D process for the development of its middle management. Draw on research to advise on how to ensure that coaching is carried out to high and consistent standards.

CHAPTER 7: A SIX-STAGE TRAINING CYCLE FOR CO-CREATING VALUE

- One of your HR colleagues says to you:
  'I've just read that it's out of date to base the design of learning events on the systematic training model. What do you think?'
  Provide an informed reply.

- Over a coffee, a colleague training professional says to you:
  'Training evaluation is still the big problem, of course – and far from Kirkpatrick being any help there, I think his model must take much of the blame for the poor or non-existent evaluation that is done in most organisations. We need a completely new approach.'
  To what extent do you agree or disagree with these claims, and why?

CHAPTER 8: THE SIX-STAGE CYCLE IN ACTION – A CASE STUDY

- You want to propose a training programme to improve team leaders' managerial competence in an organisation undermined by ineffective team leadership at all levels. Justify what you should include in your business case in order to make it as convincing as possible.

- You are an HRD consultant in discussion with the HR director of a chain of retail stores. He tells you that the store sales assistant are loyal and hard-working, but that many are poor at customer service. He wants you to provide an exciting, motivational company-wide training programme that will 'sprinkle them all with magic dust' to transform customer service across the chain. What response will you give to this request, and why?

CHAPTER 9: ACHIEVING ETHICAL PRACTICE

- Reply helpfully to the following message you have just received from an L&D colleague who works in another organisation:
  'Many of our managers still don't understand some of the dramatic implications of the age discrimination legislation. Last year we put them all through a two-day awareness-raising course run by an external legal expert, but clearly that's not been enough. What do you think I should do next, and why?'

- An L&D manager wants her team of five to have a practical understanding of their ethical responsibilities as trainers and developers of people at all levels in the organisation. Explain and justify major steps that she could take to build that understanding.

CHAPTER 10: THE L&D AGENDA IN DIFFERENT SECTORAL SETTINGS

- An L&D professional has been asked to present to her top management her ideas for a leadership development strategy for their small but expanding organisation that operates in an unpredictable business environment. Justify key points to make in her presentation.

- As an L&D consultant advising a medium-sized charity on the training and development of its staff, both volunteers and employees, what priorities for action would you suggest, and why? (You may expand this case scenario with further factual detail if you wish, but it must be consistent with the outline given here.)

CHAPTER 11: SHAPING AND MANAGING THE L&D FUNCTION

- A large organisation has been restructured to become flatter and more project-driven. Some of the 'personnel' and 'training' staff who previously worked in separate units, in virtual isolation from each other, have been brought together to form a slimmer, integrated 'HR services department'. Justify learning objectives to be achieved by a short course that must begin to develop all these staff into an effective team of 'HR and learning consultants'.

- Assess some advantages and disadvantages for an L&D function of becoming part of an in-house HR 'three-legged stool' structure to serve the organisation.

CHAPTER 12: PRODUCING AND IMPLEMENTING L&D STRATEGY

- It is quite common in organisations to find impressive L&D strategies that fail at the implementation stage. What would you recommend – and why – to ensure that L&D strategy in an organisation is put into practice effectively?

- Assess whether L&D activity in your organisation, or one with which you are familiar, has achieved vertical and horizontal integration, identifying reasons for its high or low level of 'fit'.

CHAPTER 13: DEVELOPING L&D PARTNERSHIPS

- Draw on contemporary research and/or current practice to suggest the crucial skills L&D practitioners need in order to perform well as business partners, and how these might be acquired.

- Why do you think many L&D practitioners have problems in forming and sustaining effective business partnerships at middle-management level, and what suggestions would you make to improve such a situation?

CHAPTER 14: ADDING VALUE

- Explain the key factors in your organisation that EITHER support OR work against a value-adding L&D function.

- Explain and justify criteria that an L&D professional should use in order to decide how best to add value to the business for which he or she works.

CHAPTER 15: TACKLING CHALLENGES OF CHANGE

- You have to design a programme to train managers in the management of culture change. What core skills would you aim to develop in them, and why?

- Organisations operating in turbulent environments usually cannot offer their employees much job security yet still need to build committed and adaptable workforces. Outline and justify the kind of contribution learning and development processes can make to meet that need.

CHAPTER 16: PROMOTING TALENT AND CAREER DEVELOPMENT

- Draw on research to justify the kind of talent/career development practices that can attract specialist knowledge workers to an organisation and retain them long enough for them to provide real value for the firm.

- A medium-sized firm is growing rapidly. It operates in a tough and unpredictable business environment. Most of its employees are long-serving but it is increasingly having to recruit from outside to fill new specialist and managerial positions. What overall career development strategy would you suggest, and why, in order to build a high-calibre workforce for the future?

CHAPTER 17: DEVELOPING LEADERS AND MANAGERS

- Most long-serving voluntary non-executive directors on a housing association's board object to the chair's proposal that each should have an annual appraisal

NVET in the Devolved Administrations

AN INTRODUCTION: HOW THE UNITED KINGDOM IS RUN

Scotland, Wales and Northern Ireland are governed by devolved bodies, but each in a different way. Scotland has a parliament with legislative powers, the National Assembly of Wales has powers over secondary but not over primary legislation, and although Northern Ireland's assembly has legislative powers, following the Northern Ireland Act of 1998 its executive must contain representatives of both the two main communities in the province (Catholic and Protestant), so the assembly operates in a power-sharing fashion rather than by majority vote (Bogdanor 2006: 32). The Scottish Parliament and to a degree the National Assembly of Wales are becoming 'supreme authorities over their respective domestic affairs', with the English Parliament having 'little more than a vague right of supervision' over the Scottish Parliament (*ibid*).

England contains 85% of the UK's population and its Parliament at Westminster still exercises a real power to make laws affecting every aspect of the country's domestic affairs. However, the population's human rights, which traditionally have been determined by Parliament, are in future likely to be derived from the European Convention on Human Rights which the Human Rights Act has made part of English law (*ibid*).

Bogdanor summarises this confusing system thus (2006: 36):

> Westminster ... has been transformed into a parliament for England, a federal parliament for Scotland and Northern Ireland, and a parliament for primary legislation for Wales.

TRAINING AND SKILLS ISSUES

In the UK training and skills are a devolved issue, but qualifications approved in Wales, Scotland and Northern Ireland can also be offered in England (with a few exceptions). Following the Leitch Review (2006) the Devolved Administrations in Northern Ireland, Scotland and Wales have been asked to consider the Review's recommended policy framework in the context of differing circumstances in those countries and their contribution for delivering world-class, economically valuable skills. What follows is an outline of their various statements of broad intent.

WALES

http://www.learning.wales.gov.uk/topics/ [accessed 13 April 2008]

To quote from the above website:

> The Welsh Assembly Government wants Wales to be a learning country, where high quality, lifelong learning liberates talent, extends opportunities, empowers communities, provides the better jobs and skills that people need to prosper in the new economy and creates a sustainable future for Wales.

A single Department for Children, Education, Lifelong Learning and Skills contributes to the Welsh Assembly Government's vision of better public services. The department operates through four groups, which are responsible for policy, planning, funding, and monitoring services in their respective areas: the Children and Schools Group, the Qualifications and Curriculum Group (covering content of the school curriculum and the regulation of qualifications), the Lifelong Learning and Skills Group (covering post-16 education and training and development of 14–19 Pathways) and the Higher Learning Group (covering higher education, student support, practitioner development and Welsh educational interests in Europe and beyond). In January 2008 the Deputy Minister for Skills launched a consultation document on the Welsh Assembly Government's proposals for a Learning and Skills (Wales) Measure 2008. On the education front, a revised curriculum for 3- to 19-year-olds in Wales should be implemented from September 2008.

NORTHERN IRELAND

http://www.delni.gov.uk/index/successthroughskills.htm [accessed 13 April 2008]

A 'Success through Skills' strategy provides the overarching framework for the development of skills in Northern Ireland. The lead on developing workforce skills is taken by the Department for Employment and Learning (DELNI) working closely with the industrial development agency for the region, Invest Northern Ireland. DELNI's aim is 'to promote learning and skills, to prepare people for work and to support the economy'. Objectives, customers and key areas for action are identified on the website (*http://www.investni.gov.uk*) [accessed 13 April 2008]) as:

Objectives

To promote economic, social and personal development through high-quality learning, research and skills training; and to help people into employment and promote good employment practices.

Customers

The two main groups are:

- individuals who are seeking to improve their levels of skills and qualifications or who require support and guidance to progress towards employment, including self-employment

- businesses in both the public and private sectors.

Key areas of activity

- enhancing the provision of learning and skills, including entrepreneurship, enterprise, management and leadership

- increasing the level of research and development, creativity and innovation in the Northern Ireland economy

- helping individuals to acquire jobs, including self-employment, and improving the linkages between employment programmes and skills development

- the development and maintenance of the framework of employment rights and responsibilities.

The department also receives advice on a range of policy and operational issues from the NI Skills Task Force, the Northern Ireland Higher Education Council (NIHEC) and other partners and stakeholders. Sector Skills Councils operate in Northern Ireland as in England. As there, the National Training Awards (NTA) provide a framework for benchmarking the training of organisations and individuals, and the Investors in People Standard is a key vehicle for business-focused training and individual as well as organisational development.

SCOTLAND

http://www.scotland.gov.uk/Topics/Education [accessed 13 April 2008]

The Scottish administration (Scottish Nationalist Party) was formed after elections in May 2007. It states on its website above that:

> The Government wants to ensure that everybody has access to learning opportunities that can help them achieve their full potential – giving children and young people the best possible start in life as they move from school to university and college or into the workforce, providing employability and adaptability throughout life.

The Scottish Parliament has complete responsibility for devising and implementing education and employment strategies, and for the delivery system. In June 2007 the Cabinet Secretary for Skills and Lifelong Learning announced that the new government would develop Scotland's skills strategy as part of its 'first 100 days' commitments. 'Skills for Scotland' was then launched as the government's response to Leitch.

In a statement to the Scottish Parliament on 12 September 2007 the Cabinet Secretary explained that it was not the new government's intention to implement the Leitch review as it stands, since whereas the Leitch focus is on growing the number of qualifications, the focus in Scotland must be about supply and importantly use of those skills. The government agreed with the need to improve skills levels but did not agree that 'simply injecting more skills into the labour market will have the economic effect that we seek'. Furthermore, whereas Leitch 'wants to subsidise employers to badge skills that people already have', the intention in Scotland is 'to focus on developing further skills and more importantly use of skills, as the Scottish Chamber of Commerce reminded us. This is widely recognised as a desirable key difference'. Further details of the government's proposed strategy and objectives can be found at *http://www.scotland.gov.uk/News/ This-Week/Speeches/skills-strategy/* [accessed 13 April 2008].

References

Adamson, P. and Caple, J. (1996) 'The training and development audit evolves: is your training and development budget wasted?', *Journal of European International Training*, Vol.20, No.5: 3–12

Adult Learning Inspectorate (2004) Annual Report of the Chief Inspector, 2003–04. Coventry: ALI

Ahmed, M. (2008) 'New era dawns at home of the Internet', *The Times*, 29 September: 3

Alimo-Metcalf, B. and Alban-Metcalf, J. (2008) *Engaging Leadership: Creating organisations that maximise the potential of their people*. Research Insight. London: CIPD. Online version also available at: http://www.cipd.co.uk/researchinsights [accessed 8 October 2008]

Alimo-Metcalf, B. and Bradley, M. (2008) 'Cast in a new light', *People Management*, Vol.14, No.2, 24 January: 38–41

Allen, R. E. (1990) *The Concise Oxford Dictionary of Current English*, 8th edition. Oxford: Clarendon Press

Allinson, C. W. and Hayes, J. (1996) 'The cognitive style index: a measure of intuition – analysis for organizational research', *Journal of Management Studies*, Vol.33, No.1: 119–35

Alred, G., Garvey, B. and Smith, R. (1998) *The Mentoring Pocket Book*. Alresford: Management Pocket Books Series

Alvarez, J. L. (1996) 'Are we asking too much of managers?', *Financial Times*, 12 July: 13

Andalo, D. (2007) 'Insider dealing', *The Guardian*, 21 March: 7

Anderson, L. (2006) *Online learning comes of age*. 20 March. http://www.ft.com/cms/s/2/2a38ddoe-b5b1-11da-9cbb-0000779e2340.html [accessed 13 August 2008]

Anderson, V. (2007) *The Value of Learning – A new model of value and evaluation*. Change Agenda. London: CIPD. Online version also available at: http://www.cipd.co.uk/subjects/lrnanddev/evaluation [accessed 12 July 2008]

Applebaum, E., Bailey, T. and Berg, P. (2000) *Manufacturing Advantage: Why high performance work systems pay off*. Ithaca, NY: Cornell University Press

Aragon-Sanchez, A., Barba-Aragon, I. and Sanz-Valle, R. (2003) 'Effects of training on business results', *International Journal of Human Resource Management*, Vol.14, No.6: 956–80

Argyris, C. (1957) *Personality and Organization*. New York: Harper & Row

Argyris, C. (1977) 'Double-loop learning in organizations', *Harvard Business Review*, Vol.55 No.5: 115–25

Argyris, C. (1982) *Reasoning, Learning and Action*. San Francisco, CA: Jossey-Bass

Argyris, C. (1986) 'Skilled incompetence', *Harvard Business Review*, Vol.54, No.5: 74–9

Argyris, C. and Schon, D. A. (1974) *Theory in Practice: Increasing professional effectiveness*. San Francisco, CA: Jossey-Bass

Argyris, C. and Schon, D. A. (1978) *Organizational Learning: A theory of action perspective*. Reading, MA: Addison Wesley

Argyris, C. and Schon, D. A. (1996) *Organizational Learning II: Theory, method and practice*. New York: Addison Wesley

Arkin, A. (2001) 'Central intelligence', *People Management*, Vol.7, No.23, 2 November: 38–41

Arkin, A. (2005) 'Hidden talents', *People Management*, Vol.11, No.14, 14 July: 26–30.

Arkin, A. (2006) 'School's out', *People Management Guide: Outsourcing*. Vol.12, No.4, February: 20–1

Arkin, A. (2007a) 'Force for good?', *People Management*, Vol.13, No.3, 8 February: 26–9

Arkin, A. (2007b) 'Street smart', *People Management*, Vol.13, No.7, 5 April: 24–7

Arkin, A. (2007c) 'In the hot seat', *People Management*, Vol.13, No.13, 28 June: 28–32

Arkin, A. (2007d) 'The generation game', *People Management*, Vol.13, No.23, 29 November: 24–7

Armstrong, M. and Baron, A. (2004) *Performance Management: Action and impact*. London: CIPD

Arney, E. (2006) 'Distinguish between coaches and managers', *People Management*, Vol.12, No.25, 28 December: 48

Ashton, C., Haffenden, M. and Lambert, A. (2005) *The Future of HR: Creating the fit for purpose function*. London: CRF Publishing. Online article on the report also available at: http://www.humanresourcesmagazine.com.au/articles/co/ oco2ceco.asp [accessed 29 July 2008]

Ashton, D. N. (2004) 'The impact of organisational structure and practices on learning in the workplace', *International Journal of Training and Development*, Vol.8, No.1: 43–53

Audit Scotland (2005) *How Government Works: Leadership development*. Edinburgh: Audit Scotland

Augustine, St (1964) *Confessions*, tr. R. S. Pine-Coffin. London: Penguin Classics

Axelsson, R. (1998) 'Towards an evidence based health care management', *International Journal of Health Planning and Management*, Vol.13: 307–17

Bacon, N. and Hoque, K. (2005) 'HRM in the SME sector: valuable employees and coercive networks', *International Journal of Human Resource Management*, Vol.16, No.11: 1976–99

Bailey, T. (1993) *Discretionary Effort and the Organization of Work: Employee participation and work reform since Hawthorne*. Mimeo. Columbia University: Teachers College

Baird, J.-A. (2007) 'Who is really qualified to assess assessment?', *EducationGuardian*, 11 December: 8

Bajer, J. (2001) 'Same old seasoned greetings', *People Management*, Vol.7, No.24, 6 December: 27

Balderson, S. (2005) 'Strategy and human resource development'. In J. Wilson (ed.) *Human Resource Development: Learning and training for individuals and organizations*, 2nd edition. London: Kogan Page; pp83–97

Barnard, C. I. (1938) *The Functions of the Executive*. Cambridge, MA: Harvard University Press

Barney, J. (1986) 'Organizational culture: can it be a source of sustained competitive advantage?', *Academy of Management Review*, Vol.11, No.3: 656–65

Barney, J. (1991) 'Firm resources and sustained competitive advantage', *Journal of Management*, Vol.17, No.1: 99–120

Baron, A. (2000) 'Advance beyond intuition', *People Management*, Vol.6, No.15, 20 July: 30–1

Baron, A. (2004) 'Get to know those in the know', *People Management*, Vol.10, No.14, 15 July: 25

Baron, A. (2006) 'Structural capital', *Impact:* Quarterly update on CIPD Policy and Research. Issue 16, 1 August. London: CIPD; p.14

Baron, A. (2007a) 'Managing across boundaries', *Impact:* Quarterly update on CIPD Policy and Research. Issue 20, August. London: CIPD; p.27

Baron, A. (2007b) 'Demonstrating the impact of people on business', *Impact:* Quarterly update on CIPD Policy and Research. Issue 21, November. London: CIPD; p.11

Bartel, A. (2000) 'Human resource management and performance in the service sector: the case of bank branches', *NBER Working Paper Series*. Cambridge, MA: National Bureau of Economic Research

Bartlett, C. A. and Ghoshal, S. (1993) 'Beyond the M-form: toward a managerial theory of the firm', *Strategic Management Journal*, (Winter Special) Issue, Vol.14: 23–46

Bass, B. M. and Vaughan, J. A. (1967) *Training in Industry: The management of learning*. London: Tavistock Publications

Batchelor, J., Donnelly, R. and Morris, D. (1995) 'Learning networks within supply chains', Working paper, Coventry Business School. Coventry: Coventry University

Beard, C. and Irvine, D. (2005) 'Management training and development: problems, paradoxes and perspectives'. In J. P. Wilson (ed.) *Human Resource Development: Learning and training for individuals and organizations*, 2nd edition. London: Kogan Page; pp380–403

Beatty, R. W. and Schneier, C. E. (1997) 'New HR roles to impact organizational performance: from "partners" to "players"', *Human Resources Management*, Vol.36, No.1: 29–37

Becker, B. and Gerhart, B. (1996) 'The impact of human resource practices on organizational performance: progress and prospects', *Academy of Management Journal*, Vol.39, No.4: 779–801

Becker, G. (1975) *Human Capital: A theoretical and empirical analysis with special reference to education*, 2nd edition. New York: Columbia University Press

Beckett, D. (1999) 'Past the guru and up the garden path: the new organic management learning'. In D. Boud and J. Garrick (eds) *Understanding Learning at Work*. London: Routledge; pp83–97

Beer, M. and Eisenstat, R. A. (2000) 'The silent killers of strategy implementation and learning', *Sloan Management Review*, Vol.41, No.4: 29–40

Bennett, R. (2007) 'Banking really can be a charitable business', *The Times*, 29 January: 52

Bettis, R. A. and Hitt, M. A. (1995) 'The new competitive landscape', *Strategic Management Journal*, Vol.16, (Summer Special) Issue 5: 7–19

Billett, S. (1998) Understanding workplace learning: cognitive and sociocultural perspectives. In D. Boud (ed) *Current Issues and New Agendas in Workplace Learning*. Adelaide: National Centre for Vocational Education Research. pp47–68.

Billett, S., Barker, M. and Hernon-Tinning, B. (2004) 'Participatory practices at work', *Pedagogy, Culture and Society*, Vol.12, No.2: 233–58

Bizhelp News 24 (2007) 'Small Business News: could you be missing out on Government training initiatives?', *BizHelp24*, No.188, 7 June. Available online at http//www.bizhelp24. com/news/jun-07-missing-training-188.php – 52k, go to 'SmallBiz' portal [accessed 8 May 2008]

Blass, A. (2007) *Talent Management: Maximising talent for business performance*. Executive Summary. London: Chartered Management Institute. Online version also available at: http://www.managers.org.uk/listing_1.aspx?id=10:106&id=10:9 [accessed 4 August 2008]

Block, P. (2008) 'Recent broadcasting scandals highlight need for training', *People Management*, Vol.14, No.19, 18 September: 18

Bloom, B. S., Engelhart, M. D., Furst, E. J., Hill, W. H. and Krathwolh, D. R. (1956) *Taxonomy of Educational Objectives*. London: Longmans, Green

Blunkett, D. (2000) 'How partnerships can aid failing schools', *Daily Telegraph*, 15 March; 22

Boaden, R., Marchington, M., Hyde, P., Harris, C., Sparrow, P., Pass, S., Carroll, M. and Cortvriend, P. (2008) *Improving Health through Human Resource Management: The process of engagement and alignment*. London: CIPD. Online Research Insight also available at: http//www.cipd.co.uk/research [accessed 9 May 2008]

Bober, C. F. and Bartlett, K. R. (2004) 'The utilization of training program evaluation in corporate universities', *Human Resource Development Quarterly*, Vol.15, No.4: 363–88

Bogdanor, V. (2006) 'Tomorrow's government', *Royal Society of Arts Journal*, April: 32–7

Bohn, R. E. (1994) 'Measuring and managing technological knowledge', *Sloan Management Review*, Vol.36, No.1: 61–73

Borrill, C., West, M. A., Chapiro, D. and Rees, A. (2000) 'Team working and effectiveness in health care', *British Journal of Healthcare*, Vol.6, No.8: 364–71

Boud, D., Cohen, R. and Walker, D. (1993) 'Understanding learning from experience'. In D. Boud, R. Cohen and D. Walker (eds) *Using Experience for Learning*. Bucks: SRHE and The Open University Press; pp1–17

Boudreau, J. and Ramstad, P. (2005) 'Talentship ahoy', *People Management*, Vol.11, No.20, 13 October: 33–5

Bowen, D. E. and Ostroff, C. (2004) 'Understanding HRM-firm performance linkages: the role of the "strength" of the HRM system', *Academy of Management Review*, Vol.29, No.2: 203–21

Boyatzis, R. E. (2008) 'Competencies in the 21st century', *Journal of Management Development*, Vol.27, No.1:5–12

Boydell, T., Burgoyne, J. and Pedler, M. (2004) 'Suggested development', *People Management*, Vol.10, No.4, 26 February: 32–4

Boydell, T. (1971) *A Guide to the Identification of Training Needs*. London: BACIE

Brewster, C., Harris, H. and Sparrow, P. (2002) *Globalising HR*: Executive Briefing. London: CIPD

Bright, B. (1996) 'Reflecting on "reflective practice"', *Studies in the Education of Adults*, Vol.28, No.2: 162–84

Brittain, S. (2007) 'How to manage key talent', *People Management*, Vol.13, No.12, 14 June: 46–7

Brockett, J. (2006) 'NHS sees learning as marginal activity run by "eggheads", claims policy chief', *People Management*, Vol.12, No.14, 13 July: 13

Brockett, J. (2008a) 'Top firms pledge to hire more JobCentre candidates', *People Management*, Vol.14, No.2, 24 January: 19

Brockett, J. (2008b) 'HR's role in "McA-levels"', *People Management*, Vol.14, No.3, 7 February: 9

Brockett, J. (2008c) 'Equality bill won't close pay gap, experts warn', *People Management*, Vol.14, No.14, 10 July: 9

Brook, L. and Graham, J. (2005) 'More than words', *People Management*, Vol.11, No.23, 24 November: 7

Brookes, M. (2007) 'Measures of success', *SocietyGuardian*, 21 November: 1, 2

Brooks, W. and Hulme, K. (2007) 'Five key principles that guarantee business results', *Training and Management Development Methods*, Vol.21, No.2: 23–37

Brown, A., Charlwood, A., Forde, C. and Spencer, D. (2007) *Changes in Human Resource Management and Job Satisfaction 1998–2004: Evidence from the Workplace Employment Relations Survey*. Ian Beardwell Prizewinning Research paper presented at CIPD Standards Conference, University of Keele, 26, 27 June

Brown, D. (2004) 'Capital vetters', *People Management*, Vol.10, No.19, 30 September: 38–41

Brown, J. S. and Duguid, P. (1991) 'Organisational learning and communities-of-practice: towards a unified view of working, learning and innovation', *Organization Science*, Vol.2, No.1: 40–57

Browne, A. (2006) 'No school, no job for record numbers', *The Times*, 11 December: 1

Bruce, I. (2004) 'Think tank', *SocietyGuardian*, 7 April: 9

Bryson, A., Forth, J. and Kirby, S. (2005) 'High-involvement management practices, trade union representation and workplace performance in Britain', *Scottish Journal of Political Economy*, Vol.52, No.3: 451–91

Buckingham, M. (2001) 'What a waste', *People Management*, Vol.7, No.20, 11 October: 36–40

Burack, E. H. (1991) 'Changing the company culture – the role of human resource development', *Long Range Planning*, Vol.24, No.1: 88–95

Burgoyne, J. (1989) *Management Development: Context and strategies*. Aldershot: Gower

Burgoyne, J. (1999) *Develop Yourself, Your Career and Your Organisation*. London: Lemos & Crane

Burnes, B. (2004) *Managing Change*. London: Prentice Hall

Burt, R. S. (1992) *Structural Holes. The social structure of competition*. Cambridge, MA: Harvard University Press

Burt, R. S. (1997) 'The contingent value of social capital', *Administrative Science Quarterly*, Vol.42, No.2: 339–65

Business in the Community (2007) *Benchmarking Responsible Business Practice: The corporate responsibility index*. London: BITC. Online version also available at: http/www.bitc.org.uk/crindex [accessed 5 July 2008]

Butler, E. (1999) 'Technologising equity: the politics and practices of work-related learning'. In D. Boud and J. Garrick (eds) *Understanding Learning at Work*. London: Routledge; pp132–50

Butler, S. (2007) 'How the M&S boss turned green and decided that his Bentley just had to go', *The Times*, 25 June: 50

Butterfield, K. D., Trevino, L. K. and Weaver, G. R. (2000) 'Moral awareness in business: influences of issue-related and social-context factors', *Human Relations*, Vol.53, No.7: 981–1018

Cabinet Office (1999) *Modernising Government:* White Paper. Norwich: The Stationery Office. Online version also available at: http://www.archive.official-documents.co.uk/document/ cm43/4310/4310-00.htm [accessed 14 May 2008]

Cabinet Office (2007) *Policy Review: Public Services. January 2007*. Cabinet Office: Prime Minister's Strategy Unit. Online presentation available at: http://archive.cabinetoffice.gov. uk/policy_review/documents/public_services.pdf [accessed 8 May 2008]

Cannell, M. (2007) *Training: A short history*. Fact Sheet. Available online at: http://www.cipd.co.uk/subjects/lrnanddev/general/thistory.htm?IsSrchRes=1 [accessed 16 April 2008]

Caplan, J. and Reay, D. (2008) 'Why an inclusive talent strategy leads to business success', *People Management*, Vol.14, No.8, 17 April: 16

Cappelli, P. and Neumark, D. (2001) 'Do "high performance" work practices improve establishment-level outcomes?', *Industrial and Labour Relations Review*, Vol.54, Issue 4: 737–75

Carrington, L. (2005) 'The third way', *People Management*, Vol.11, No.10, 19 May: 25–8

Carrington, L. (2007a) 'The skills equation', *People Management*, Vol.13, No.17, 23 August: 24–8

Carrington, L. (2007b) 'Designs on the dotted line', *People Management*, Vol.13, No.21, 18 October: 36–9

Cartwright, J. (2007) 'The London Library', *The Author*, Autumn: 112

Catalanello, R. F. and Kirkpatrick, D. L. (1967) 'Evaluating training programs: the state of the art', *Training and Development Journal*, Vol.2, No.5: 2–9

Caulkin, S. (2003) *People and public services: Why central targets miss the mark*. Change Agenda. London: CIPD. Online version also available at: http://www.cipd.co.uk/research/rsrchplcypubs/researchinsights [accessed 8 May 2008]

Caulkin, S. (2007) 'Too many chiefs?', *Royal Society of Arts Journal*, February: 36–40

CHA (2008) *Worthwhile Work: A CHA Report*. London: CHA. Online version also available at: http://zookri.com/Portals/6/reports/worthwhile%20work.pdf [accessed 16 July 2008]

Chambers, C. (1990) 'Self reliant', *Times Higher Education Supplement*, 6 April: 26

Chartered Institute of Personnel and Development and Chartered Management Institute (2005) *Tackling age discrimination in the workplace: creating a new age for all*. London: CIPD. Online version also available at: http://www.cipd.co.uk/onlineinfodocuments/surveys [accessed 25 July 2008]

Chartered Institute of Personnel and Development and KPMG (2007) *Labour Market Outlook*: Quarterly Survey Report, Spring 2007. London: CIPD. Online version also available at: http://cipd.co.uk/surveys [accessed 12 April 2008]

Chartered Institute of Personnel and Development (2001) *Performance through People – the new people management*. Change Agenda. London: CIPD. Online version also available at: http://www.cipd.co.uk/research/rsrchplcypubs/ researchinsights [accessed 3 April 2008]

Chartered Institute of Personnel and Development (2003a) *Evaluating human capital*. Research summary. London: CIPD. Online version also available at: http://www.cipd.co.uk/research/_summaries.htm [accessed 28 July 2008]

Chartered Institute of Personnel and Development (2003b) *Organising for success in the twenty-first century: a starting point for change*. Research summary. London: CIPD. Online version also available at: http://www.cipd.co.uk/research/_summaries.htm [accessed 28 July 2008]

Chartered Institute of Personnel and Development (2003c) *Where we are, where we're heading*. Survey Report. London: CIPD. Online version also available at: http://www.cipd.co.uk/surveys [accessed 18 July 2008]

Chartered Institute of Personnel and Development (2003d) *Re-organising for success: CEOs' and HR's perceptions*. Survey Report. London: CIPD. Online version also available at http://www.cipd.co.uk/onlineinfodocuments/surveys [accessed 29 May 2008]

Chartered Institute of Personnel and Development (2003e) *Managing employee careers: Issues, trends and prospects*. Survey Report. London: CIPD. Online version also available at: http://www.cipd.co.uk/surveys [accessed 29 September 2008]

Chartered Institute of Personnel and Development (2004a) *Towards a unified e-learning strategy:CIPD response to the Department for Education and Skills*. London: CIPD. Online version also available at: http://www.cipd.co.uk/ about/_unielrnstrg.htm [accessed 15 March 2008]

Chartered Institute of Personnel and Development (2004b) *Re-organising for success: A survey of HR's role in change*. London: CIPD. Online version also available at: http://www.cipd.co.uk/surveys [accessed 18 July 2008]

Chartered Institute of Personnel and Development (2004c) *Business Partnering – A new direction for HR*. A Guide. London: CIPD. Online version also available at: http://www.cipd. co.uk/subjects/corpstrtgy/general/ busprtnrnewdir.htm [accessed 10 July 2008]

Chartered Institute of Personnel and Development (2005a) 'The Learning and Development Generalist Standard'. In *CIPD Practitioner-Level Professional Standards*. London: CIPD; pp81–8. Online version also available at: http://www.cipd.co.uk/about/profstands/ professional-standards-full-document.htm?IsSrchRes=1 [accessed 25 July 2008]

Chartered Institute of Personnel and Development (2005b) *CIPD Practitioner-Level Professional Standards*. London: CIPD. Online version also available at: http://www.cipd.co.uk/about/profstands/ [accessed 25 March 2008]

Chartered Institute of Personnel and Development (2005c) *People and performance: designing the HR processes for maximum performance delivery*. Practical tool. London: CIPD. Available online at http://www.cipd.co.uk/tools [accessed 30 March 2008]

Chartered Institute of Personnel and Development (2005d) *The Public Policy Agenda: Public policy perspectives*. London: CIPD

Chartered Institute of Personnel and Development (2005e) *HR Strategy: Creating the framework for successful people management*. Practical tool. Available online at: http:// www.cipd.co.uk/subjects/corpstrtgy/general/tools.htm [accessed 31 July 2008]

Chartered Institute of Personnel and Development (2005f) *Managing Change: the role of the psychological contract*. London: CIPD. Online version also available at: http://www.cipd.co.uk/research/rsrchplcypubs/researchinsights.htm [accessed 23 August 2008]

Chartered Institute of Personnel and Development (2005g) *Training and Development*. Annual Survey Report. London: CIPD. Online version also available at: http://www.cipd.co.uk/surveys/ [accessed 9 August 2008]

Chartered Institute of Personnel and Development (2005h) *Developing managers for business performance*: *Managing the return on your investment in management development*. Practical tool. London: CIPD. Online version also available at: http://www.cipd.co.uk/onlineinfodocuments/toolacts [accessed 24 August 2008]

Chartered Institute of Personnel and Development (2006a) *The changing role of the trainer: building a learning culture in your organisation*. Practical tool. London: CIPD. Online version also available at: http://www.cipd.co.uk/subjects/lrnanddev/general/_chngrltrnr [accessed 12 July 2008]

Chartered Institute of Personnel and Development (2006b) *Large Employers and Apprenticeship Training*. Research Report. London: CIPD

Chartered Institute of Personnel and Development (2006c) *Improving Health through Human Resource Management: A starting point for change*. Change Agenda. London: CIPD. Online version also available at: http://www.cipd.co.uk/research/rsrchplcypubs/researchinsights [accessed 11 May 2008]

Chartered Institute of Personnel and Development (2006d) *Learning and Development*. Annual Survey Report. London: CIPD. Online version also available at: http://www.cipd.co.uk/subjects/lrnanddev/general [accessed 2 February 2008]

Chartered Institute of Personnel and Development (2006e) *Human capital evaluation: getting started*. Human Capital Panel Report. London: CIPD. Spring. Online version also available at: www.cipd.co.uk/subjects/corpstrtgy/hmncapital/_hmcpevgtst.htm [accessed 8 March 2008]

Chartered Institute of Personnel and Development (2006f) *Reflections on Employee Engagement*. Change Agenda. London: CIPD. Online version also available at: http://www.cipd.co.uk/researchinsights [accessed 7 March 2008]

Chartered Institute of Personnel and Development (2007a) *Learning and Development*. Annual Survey Report. London: CIPD. Online version also available at: http://www.cipd.co.uk/onlineinfodocuments/surveys [accessed 25 July 2008]

Chartered Institute of Personnel and Development (2007b) *Coaching in organisations*. Research Insight. London: CIPD. Online version also available at: http://www.cipd.co.uk/research/ [accessed 28 March 2008]

Chartered Institute of Personnel and Development (2007c) *Reward Management*. Annual Survey Report. London: CIPD. Online version also available at: http://www.cipd.co.uk/subjects/pay/_rewrdmansurv [accessed 3 April 2008]

Chartered Institute of Personnel and Development (2007d) *Value of Learning: Assessing and reporting on the value of learning to your organisation*. Practical tool. London: CIPD. Online version also available at: http://www.cipd.co.uk/subjects/lrnanddev/evaluation [accessed 4 March 2008]

Chartered Institute of Personnel and Development (2007e) *Investors' Views of Human Capital*. Research Insight. London: CIPD. Online version also available at: http://www.cipd.co.uk/researchinsights [accessed 2 February 2008]

Chartered Institute of Personnel and Development (2008a) *Learning and Development*. Annual Survey Report. London: CIPD. Online version also available at: http://www.cipd.co.uk/surveys/ [accessed 8 May 2008]

Chartered Institute of Personnel and Development (2008b) *Reward Management*. Annual Survey Report. London: CIPD. Online version also available at: http://www.cipd.co.uk/subjects/pay/_rewrdmansurv [accessed 3 April 2008]

Chartered Institute of Personnel and Development (2008c) *Code of Professional Conduct and Disciplinary Procedures*. London: CIPD. Online version also available at: http://www.cipd.co.uk/about/profco.htm?IsSrchRes=1 [accessed 7 July 2008]

Chartered Institute of Personnel and Development (2008d) *The Psychological Contract:* Factsheet. Online version available at: http://www.cipd.co.uk/ subjects/empreltns/ psycntrct/psycontr.htm?IsSrchRes=1. [accessed 7 July 2008]

Chartered Institute of Personnel and Development (2008e) *Managing Diversity and the Business Case*. Research Report. London: CIPD. Summary available online at: http://www. cipd.co.uk/Bookstore/research.htm [accessed 7 August 2008]

Chartered Institute of Personnel and Development (2008f) *Aligning learning to strategic priorities*. Practical tool. London: CIPD. Online version also available at: http://www.cipd. co.uk/tools [accessed 31 July 2008]

Chartered Institute of Personnel and Development (2008g) *Talent Management: Design, implementation and evaluation*. Practical tool. London: CIPD. Online version also available at: http://www.cipd.co.uk/tools [accessed 20 August 2008]

Chartered Institute of Personnel and Development (2008h) *Line management behaviour and stress at work: updated advice for HR*. London: CIPD. Online version also available at: http://www.cipd.co.uk/subjects/health/_strswrkhr.htm [accessed 23 August 2008]

Child, J. (1988) 'On organizations in their sectors', *Organization Studies*, Vol.9, No.1: 1–32

Chynoweth, C. (2007) 'War games', *People Management*, Vol.13, No.19, 20 September: 46–8

Chynoweth, C. (2008) 'To the test', *People Management*, Vol.14, No.2, 24 January: 42–3

Clake, R. (2005) *Flexible Working: The implementation challenge*. Guide. London: CIPD. Online version also available at: http://www.cipd.co.uk/research/rsrchplcypubs/guides. htm?IsSrchRes=1 [accessed 25 July 2008]

Clarke, M. and Patrickson, M. (2008) 'The new covenant of employability', *Employee Relations*, Vol.30, No.2: 121–41

Clarke, N. (2004) 'HRD and the challenges of assessing learning in the workplace', *International Journal of Training and Development*, Vol.8, No.2: 140–56

Clarke, N. (2005) 'Workplace learning environment and its relationship with learning outcomes in healthcare organizations', *Human Resource Development International*, Vol.8, Issue 2: 185–205

Claus, L. (2007) 'Get a virtual grip', *People Management*, Vol.13, No.17, 23 August: 38–9

CM 7228 (2007) *The Government Response to the House of Lords Select Committee on Economic Affairs' Fifth Report of Session 2006–07 on Apprenticeships*. October. Norwich: The Stationery Office. Online version also available at: http://www.official-documents.gov. uk/document/cm72/7228/7228.pdf [accessed 28 April 2008]

Coffield, F. (2002) 'Britain's continuing failure to train: the birth pangs of a new policy', *Journal of Education Policy*, Vol.17, No.4: 483–97

Coffield, F. (2007) 'Running ever faster down the wrong road: an alternative future for education and skills', *Inaugural Lecture to the Association of Colleges*. Online version available at: http//www.ioe.ac.uk/schools/leid/lss/FCInauguralLectureDec06.doc [accessed 4 May 2008]

Coffield, F., Moseley, D., Hall, E. and Ecclestone, K. (2004) *Should we be using learning styles? What research has to say to practice*. London: Learning and Skills Research Centre. Online version also available at: http://www.lsda.org.uk/files/ PDF/1540.pdf [accessed 25 March 2008]

Cohen, W. M. and Levinthal, D. A. (1990) 'Absorptive capacity: a new perspective on learning and innovation', *Administrative Science Quarterly*, Vol.35, No.1: 28–52

Coleman, J. S. (1990) *Foundations of Social Theory*. Cambridge, MA: Harvard University Press

Collier, J. and Esteban, R. (2007) 'Corporate social responsibility and employee commitment', *Business Ethics: A European Review*, Vol.16, No.1: 19–33

Collins, A. (1997) 'Cognitive apprenticeship and educational technology'. In L. Idol and B. F. Jones (eds) *Educational Values and Cognitive Instruction: Implications for reform*. Hillsdale, NJ: Lawrence Erlbaum Associates; pp121–38

Conway, E. (2008) 'Panic stations', *Daily Telegraph*, 11 October: 1, 2

Cooke, M. (2008) 'Close up: how I made a difference at work', *People Management*, Vol.14, No.8, 1 May: 40

Cooper, C. (2000a) 'The Met fails inspection on race and recruitment', *People Management*, Vol.6, No.2, 20 January: 11

Cooper, C. (2000b) 'Southall rail crash report orders review of training', *People Management*, Vol.6, No.5, 2 March: 17

Cooper, C. (2003) 'Hooked on ethics', *People Management*, Vol.9, No.14, 10 July: 30–2

Cooperrider, D. L. and Srivastva, S. (1987) 'Appreciative inquiry in organizational life'. In W. Pasmore and R. Woodman (eds) *Research in Organization Change and Development*. 1. Greenwich, CT: JAI Press; pp129–69

Coopers and Lybrand Associates (1985) *A Challenge to Complacency: Changing attitudes to training. A report to the Manpower Services Commission and the National Economic Development Office*. Sheffield: MSC

Cottee, P. (2006) 'Free to feel good', *People Management*, Vol.12, No.1, 12 January: 34–6

Coulson-Thomas, C. (2001) 'Fashion victim', *People Management*, Vol.7, No.17, 30 August: 51

Cox, A. and McBride, A. (2007) 'What goes up', *People Management*, Vol.13, No.10, 17 May: 36–8

Crawshaw, J. (2006) 'Justice source and justice content: evaluating the fairness of organisational career management practices', *Human Resource Management Journal*, Vol.16, No.1: 98–120

Croner Reward and Chartered Institute of Personnel and Development (2007) *Personnel Rewards Survey 2007*. Surrey: Wolters Kluwer UK Ltd or email info@croner.co.uk

Crozier, M. (1964) *The Bureaucratic Phenomenon*. London: Tavistock

Cunningham, I. (2004) 'Back to reality?', *People Management*, Vol.10, No.7, 8 April: 37–8

Curtis, P. (2008) 'Exam chief: rival to A-level in disarray', *The Guardian*, 17 April: 1, 2

Cyert, R. M. and March, J. G. (1963) *A Behavioural Theory of the Firm*. Englewood Cliffs, NJ: Prentice Hall Inc.

Czerny, A. (2005) 'HR aid for small charities', *People Management*, Vol.11, No.3, 10 February: 8

Daft, R. L. and Weick, K. E. (1984) 'Toward a model of organizations as interpretation systems', *Academy of Management Review*, Vol.9, No.2: 284–95

Darling, J., Darling, P. and Elliott, J. (1999) *The Changing Role of the Trainer*. London: Institute of Personnel and Development

Day, G. S. (1990) *Market Driven Strategy: Processes for creating value*. New York: Free Press

D'Cruz, J. R. and Rugman, A. M. (1994) 'The five partners model: France Telecom, Alcatel, and the global telecommunications industry', *European Management Journal*, Vol.12, No.1: 59–66

De Menezes, L. M. and Wood, S. (2006) 'The reality of flexible work systems in Britain', *International Journal of Human Resource Management*, Vol.17, No.1: 106–38

Dearing, R. (1997) *Higher Education in the Learning Society. Report of the National Committee of Inquiry into Higher Education*. London: Her Majesty's Stationery Office

Department for Children, Schools and Families (2008) *Secondary National Strategy*. Online version only, available at: http//www.standards.dfes.gov/uk/secondary/keystage3 [accessed 4 May 2008]

Department for Children, Schools and Families and Department for Innovation, Universities and Skills (2008a) *Raising Expectations: Enabling the system to deliver*. White Paper. Norwich: The Stationery Office. Online version also available at: http://www.dcsf.gov.uk/publications/keydocuments.shtml [accessed 20 April 2008]

Department for Children, Schools and Families and Department for Innovation, Universities and Skills (2008b) *World Class Apprenticeships: Unlocking talent, building skills – the Government's strategy for the future of Apprenticeships in England*. Sheffield: DIUS. Online version also available at: http//www.dius.gov/uk/publications/index.htm [accessed 4 May 2008]

Department for Children, Schools and Families and Department for Innovation, Universities and Skills (2008c) *Draft Apprenticeships Bill*. CM 7452. Norwich: The Stationery Office. Also available online at: http://www.dius.gov.uk/consultations/documents/apprenticeship_bill.pdf [accessed 24 July 2008]

Department for Communities and Local Government (2006) *Strong and prosperous local communities: Local Government White Paper*. Norwich: HMSO. Online version also available at: http://www.communities.gov.uk/publications/localgovernment/strongprosperous [accessed 13 May 2008]

Department for Education and Employment (1997) *Excellence in Schools*. White Paper. Online summary available at: http://www.literacytrust.org.uk/Policy/excellence.html [accessed 4 May 2008]

Department for Education and Employment (1998) *The Learning Age*. Green Paper. Norwich: The Stationery Office. Online version also available at: http://www.lifelonglearning.dfee.gov.uk/greenpaper/index.htm [accessed 16 April 2008]

Department for Education and Employment (2001) *Skills for Life*. London: HMSO. Online version also available at: http://www.dfes.gov.uk/readwriteplus/ [accessed 4 May 2008]

Department for Education and Skills (2002) *Success For All: Reforming further education and training: Our vision for the future*. Nottingham: DfES. Online summary also available at: http://www.globalgateway.org.uk/pdf/PZ-Success-2002.pdf [accessed 4 May 2008]

Department for Education and Skills (2003a) *21st Century Skills: Realising our potential: individuals, employers, nation*. White Paper. Norwich: The Stationery Office. Online version also available at: http://www.dfes.gov.uk/ skillsstrategy/uploads/documents/21st%20Century%20Skills.pdf [accessed 16 April 2008]

Department for Education and Skills (2003b) *The Future of Higher Education*. White Paper. Norwich: The Stationery Office. Online version also available at: http://www.dfes.gov.uk/hegateway/uploads/ [accessed 28 April 2008]

Department for Education and Skills (2004) *Five-Year Strategy for Children and Learners – Putting people at the heart of public services*. Norwich: The Stationery Office. Online version also available at: http://www.dfes.gov.uk/14-19/documents/5YearStrategy-14-19.d [accessed 4 May 2008]

Department for Education and Skills (2005a) *Skills: Getting on in business, getting on at work*. White Paper. Norwich: The Stationery Office. Online version also available at: http://www.dfes.gov.uk/publications/skillsgettingon/ [accessed 10 April 2008]

Department for Education and Skills (2005b) *14–19 Education and Skills*. White Paper. Norwich: The Stationery Office. Online version also available at: http://www.dcsf.gov.uk/publications/keydocuments.shtml [accessed 4 May 2008]

Department for Education and Skills (2005c) *Higher Standards, Better Schools for all – more choice for parents and pupils*. White Paper. Norwich: The Stationery Office. Online version also available at: http://www.dcsf.gov.uk/publications/keydocuments.shtml [accessed 4 May 2008]

Department for Education and Skills (2006a) *Further Education: Raising skills, Improving life chances*. White Paper. Norwich: The Stationery Office. Online version also available at: http://www.dfes.gov.uk/furthereducation/ [accessed 27 April 2008]

Department for Education and Skills (2006b) *Widening participation in Higher Education*. Nottingham: DfES. Online version also available at: http://www.dfes.gov.uk/hegateway/uploads/ [accessed 28 April 2008]

Department for Education and Skills (2007) *Raising Expectations: Staying in education and training post-16*. Green Paper. Norwich: The Stationery Office. Online version available at: http://www.dcsf.gov.uk/publications/keydocuments.shtml [accessed 29 July 2008]

Department for Innovation, Universities and Skills (2007) *World Class Skills: Implementing the Leitch Review of Skills in England*. Norwich: The Stationery Office. Online version also available at: http://www.dius.gov.uk/publications/worldclassskills [accessed 4 May 2008]

Department for Innovation, Universities and Skills (2008) *Higher Education at Work – High Skills: High Value*. Available online until July 2008 at: http://www.dius.gov.uk/consultations [accessed 8 May 2008]

Department of Health (2003) *Delivering the HR in the NHS Plan 2003*. Annual Report. London: DoH. Online version also available at: http://www.dh.gov.uk/en/Publicationsandstatistics/Publications/PublicationsPolicyAndGuidance/DH_4055864 [accessed 21 August 2008]

Department of Health Workforce Directorate (2006) *A National Framework to Support Local Workforce Strategy Development: A guide for HR Directors in the NHS and Social Care*. London: DH Publications. Online version also available at: http://www.dh.gov.uk/en/Publicationsandstatistics/Publications/PublicationsLibrary/ [accessed 21 August 2008]

Department of Health Workforce Directorate/NHS Partners/Manchester University (2006) *HR High Impact Changes – An evidence based resource*. London: DH Publications. Online version also available at: http://www.dh.gov.uk/en/Publicationsandstatistics/Publications/PublicationsLibrary/ [accessed 21 August 2008]

Development Dimensions International and The Chartered Institute of Personnel and Development (2005) *UK Global Comparisons Leadership Forecast 2005–2006: Best practices for tomorrow's global leaders*. Survey Report. London: CIPD. Online version also available at: http://www.cipd.co.uk/onlineinfodocuments/surveys [accessed 10 August 2008]

Development Dimensions International and The Chartered Institute of Personnel and Development (2007) *Leadership Transitions: maximising HR's contribution*. Research insight. London: CIPD. Online version also available at: http://www.cipd.co.uk/research/rsrchplcypubs/researchinsights [accessed 10 August 2008]

Dewey, J. (1916) *Democracy and Education*. New York: Macmillan

Dewey, J. (1938, republished 1997) *Experience and Education*. New York: Simon & Schuster

Dickmann, M., Harris, H. and Wilson, F. (2006) 'A wing and a prayer', *People Management*, Vol.12, No.1, 12 January: 39–41

Dietrich, H., Koch, S. and Stops, M. (2004) *Ausbildung muss sich lohnen – auch für die Betriebe*. IAB-Kurzbericht: Nr.6/2004

DiMaggio, P. J. and Powell, W. W. (1991) 'Introduction'. In W. W. Powell and P. J. DiMaggio (eds) *The New Institutionalism in Organizational Analysis*. Chicago: University of Chicago Press

Dispenza, V. (1996) 'Empowering students: a pragmatic philosophical approach to management education', *Management Learning*, Vol.27, No.2: 239–51

Dougherty, D. (1999) 'Organizing for innovation'. In S. R. Clegg, C. Hardy and W. R. Nord (eds) *Managing Organizations: Current issues*. London: Sage; pp174–89

Douglas, D. (2004) 'Ethical challenges of an increasingly diverse workforce: the paradox of change', *Human Resource Development International*, Vol.7, No.2: 197–210

Downes, L. and Mui, C. (1998) *Unleashing the Killer App: Digital Strategies for Market Dominance*. Boston, MA: Harvard Business School Press

Drucker, P. (1993) *Post-Capitalist Society*. Oxford: Butterworth-Heinemann

Drummond, J. (2004) 'A matter of principle', *People Management*, Vol.10, No.12, 17 June: 42

Duncan, G. (2007) 'Ageing population brings grave problems', *The Times*, 25 June: 41

Durman, P. (2003) 'Tip of the iceberg', *Sunday Times*, 26 October: 3, 5

Education Reform Act (1988) *An Act to amend the law relating to education*. London: the Parliamentary Bookshop. Online version also available at: http//www.opsi.gov.uk/acts/acts1988/UKpga_19880040_en_1 [accessed 21 July 2008]

Eisenhardt, K. M. and Santos, F. M. (2002) 'Knowledge-based view: a new theory of strategy?' In A. Pettigrew, H. Thomas and R. Whittington (eds) *Handbook of Strategy and Management*. London: Sage; pp139–64

Elfring, T. and Volberda, H. W. (2001) 'Multiple futures of strategy synthesis: shifting boundaries, dynamic capabilities and strategy configurations'. In H. W. Volberda and T. Elfring (eds) *Rethinking Strategy*. London:Sage; pp245–85

Elliott, C. and Turnbull, S. (eds) (2005) *Critical Thinking in Human Resource Development*. London: Routledge

Ely, R. and Thomas, D. (2001) 'Cultural diversity at work: the effects of diversity perspectives on work group processes and outcomes', *Administrative Science Quarterly*, Vol.46, No.2: 229–75

Emmott, M. (2006) 'Going the extra mile', *Impact:* Quarterly update on CIPD Policy and Research. Issue 16, August. London: CIPD; pp4–5

Employment Department Group (1991) *A strategy for skills: Guidance from the Secretary of State for Employment on Training, Vocational Education and Enterprise*. London: Department of Employment

Eraut, M. J., Alderton, G. C. and Senker, P. (1998) *Development of knowledge and skills in employment*. Final Report on a research project funded by 'The Learning Society' programme of the Economic and Social Research Council. Cheltenham: ESRC

European Union Commission (2003) 'Commission recommendation of 6 May 2003 concerning the definition of micro, small- and medium-sized enterprises', *Official Journal of the European Union*, L124/36. 20 May. Available online at: http://www.berr.gov.uk/files/file25591.pdf Go to File 25591 [accessed 8 May 2008]

Evans, K., Hodkinson, P., Rainbird, H. and Unwin, L. (2006) *Improving Workplace Learning*. London: Routledge

Evans, R. (2007) 'Telly vision', *People Management*, Vol.13, No.6, 22 March: 24–9

Evans, W. R. and Davis, W. D. (2005) 'High-performance work systems and organizational performance: the mediating role of internal social structure', *Journal of Management*, Vol.31, No.5: 758–75

Facteau, J. A., Dobbins, G. H., Russell, J. E. A., Ladd, R. T. and Kudisch, J. A. (1995) 'The influence of general perceptions of the training environment on pretraining motivation and perceived training transfer', *Journal of Management*, Vol.21, No.1: 1–25

Fairbairns, J. (1991) 'Plugging the gap in training needs analysis', *Personnel Management*, Vol.23, No.2, February: 43–5.

Farrell, D. and Grant, A. J. (2005) 'China's looming talent shortage', *The McKinsey Quarterly, The On-line Journal*, No.4, 20 October: 1–7. Available online at: http://www.mckinseyquarterly.com/home [accessed 11 October 2008]

Felstead, A., Gallie, D., Green, F. and Zhou, Y. (2007) *Skills at work 1986–2006*. Oxford/Cardiff: SKOPE/ESRC. Online version also available at: http//www.skope.ox.ac.uk [accessed 12 April 2008]

Fennell, E. (2007) 'Jobless helped to get a foot in the door', *The Times*, 4 December: 52

Fennell, E. (2008) 'Opportunities for the jobless as teamwork cuts skills gap', *The Times*, 28 January: 44

Fiedler, F. (1965) 'Engineer the job to fit the manager', *Harvard Business Review*, Vol.43, No.5: 115–22

Field, J. (2000) *Lifelong Learning and the New Educational Order*. Stoke on Trent: Trentham Books

File On 4 (2007) *Apprenticeships and the Skills Gap*. BBC Radio 4. 20 February, 8.00 to 9.00pm. Transcript available at: http://news.bbc.co.uk/1/shared/bsp/hi/pdfs/20_02_07_fo4_ski.pdf [accessed 28 April 2008]

Finegold, M. A., Holland, B. M. and Lingham, T. (2002) 'Appreciative inquiry and public dialogue: an approach to community change', *Public Organization Review*, Vol.2, No.3: 235–52

Fiol, C. M. (1991) 'Managing culture as a competitive resource: an identity-based view of sustainable competitive advantage', *Journal of Management*, Vol.17, No.1: 191–211

Fiol, C. M. (2001) 'Revisiting an identity-based view of competitive advantage', *Journal of Management*, Vol.27, No.6: 691–700

Fitzgerald, R., Taylor, R. and LaValle, I. (2003) *National Adult Learning Survey 2002*. Research Report 415. London: Department for Education and Skills

Fleetwood, S. and Hesketh, A. (2006) 'HRM-performance research: under-theorized and lacking explanatory power', *International Journal of Human Resource Management*, Vol.17, No.12: 1977–93

Floyd, S. W. and Wooldridge, B. (1992) 'Middle management involvement in strategy and its association with strategic type: a research note', *Strategic Management Journal*, Vol.13, No.2: 153–67

Floyd, S. W. and Wooldridge, B. (1994) 'Dinosaurs or dynamos? Recognizing middle management's strategic role', *Academy of Management Executive*, Vol.8, No.4: 47–57

Fombrun, C., Tichy, N. M. and Devanna, M. A. (eds) (1984) *Strategic Human Resource Management*. New York: Wiley

Forth, J., Bewley, H. and Bryson, A. (2006) *Small and Medium-sized Enterprises: Findings from the 2004 Workplace Employment Relations Survey*. Available online at: http//www.niesr.ac.uk/pibs, then go to 'Display by category – View all reports' [accessed 29 April 2008]

Foster, A. (2005) *Realising the Potential: a review of the future role of further education colleges*. Online version also available at: http//www.dfes.gov.uk/furthereducation/index [accessed 28 April 2008]

Foster, C. and Harris, L. (2004) *'Easy to say but difficult to do' – managerial perspectives on implementing diversity in retailing*. Ian Beardwell prizewinning research paper presented at the CIPD Professional Standards Conference, Keele University, 28–30 June. Nottingham: Nottingham Business School, Nottingham Trent University (CD-ROM)

Francis, H. and Keegan, A. (2005) 'Slippery slope: reclaiming the role of employee champion', *People Management*, Vol.11, No. 13, 30 June: 26–31

Frean, A. (2008a) 'You want fries with that? No, just a brighter future', *The Times*, 29 January: 10

Frean, A. (2008b) 'Row over plans to recycle 24,000 failing teachers', *The Times*, 2 May: 1

Freeman, R. and Gilbert, D. (1988) *Corporate Strategy and the Search for Ethics*. Englewood Cliffs, NJ: Prentice Hall

Fulmer, R. M. and Bleak, J. L. (2007) 'Strategic Leadership Part 1: Applying lessons learned from research about strategic leadership development', *Graziadio Business Report*, Vol.10, Issue 2. Online journal available at: http://gbr.pepperdine.edu/072/leadership.html [accessed 10 August 2008]

Further Education and Training Act (2007) London: The Parliamentary Bookshop. Online version available at: http://www.opsi.gov.uk/acts.htm [accessed 4 May 2008]

Gagne, R. M. (1967) *Learning and Individual Differences*. Columbus, OH: Merrill

Galbraith, J. R. and Nathanson, D. (1978) *Strategy Implementation*. St Paul, MN: West Publishing

Gargiulo, M. and Benassi, M. (2000) 'Trapped in your own net? Network cohesion, structural holes, and the adaptation of social capital', *Organization Science*, Vol.11, No.2: 183–96

Garrick, J. (1999) 'The dominant discourses of learning at work'. In D. Boud and J. Garrick (eds) *Understanding Learning at Work*. London: Routledge; pp 216–29

Garvey, B. (2004) 'Call a rose by any other name and perhaps it's a bramble?', *International Journal of Development and Learning in Organizations*, Vol.18, No.2: 6–8

Gerhart, B. and Fang, M. (2005) 'National culture and human resource management: assumptions and evidence', *International Journal of Human Resource Management*, Vol.16, No.6: 971–86

Gershon, P. (2004) *Releasing resources for the frontline: Independent Review of Public Sector Efficiency*. Norwich: The Stationery Office. Online version also available at: http://www.hm-treasury.gov.uk/spending_review [accessed 9 May 2008]

Ghoshal, S. and Bartlett, C. A. (1994) 'Linking organizational context and managerial action: the dimension of quality of management', *Strategic Management Journal*, Vol.15, (Summer Special) Issue 5: 91–112

Gibb, A. (1997) 'Small firms' training and competitiveness: building upon the small business as a learning organisation', *International Small Business Journal*, Vol.15, No.3: 13–29

Gifford, J. (2007) *The changing HR function*. Survey report, September. London: CIPD. Online version also available at: http://www.cipd.co.uk/surveys [accessed 21 July 2008]

Gilbreath, B. (2008) 'Creating career-conducive organizations: a primary intervention approach', *Advances in Developing Human Resources*, Vol.10, No.1: 8–31

Gillard, D. (2007) *Education in England: A brief history*. Online version only, available at: http//www.dg.dial.pipex.com/history/ [accessed 26 April 2008]

Gilley, J. W. and Eggland, S. A. (1989) *Principles of Human Resource Development*. Maidenhead: Addison Wesley

Ginsberg, A. (1994) 'Minding the competition: from mapping to mastery', *Strategic Management Journal*, Vol.15, (Winter Special) Issue 8: 153–74

Gioai, D. A. and Poole, P. P. (1984) 'Scripts in organizational behaviour', *Academy of Management Review*, Vol.9, No.3: 449–59

Gioai, D. A. and Sims, H. P. (1986) 'Introduction: social cognition in organizations'. In D. A. Gioia, H. P. Sims and Associates (eds) *The Thinking Organization*. San Francisco CA: Jossey Bass; pp1–19

Gittleman, M., Horrigan, M. and Joyce, M. (1998) '"Flexible" workplace practices: evidence from a nationally representative survey', *Industrial and Labour Relations Review*, Vol.52, No.1: 99–115

Glover, C. (2002a) 'Good for the soul', *People Management*, Vol.8, No.14, 11 July: 29–31

Glover, C. (2002b) 'A common good', *People Management*, Vol.8, No.20, 10 October: 38–9

Goleman, D. (1998) *Working with Emotional Intelligence*. London: Bloomsbury

Goleman, D. (2000) 'Leadership that gets results', *Harvard Business Review*, Vol.78, No.2: 78–90

Goleman, D. (2006) *Social Intelligence: The new science of social relationships*. London: Hutchinson

Gonczi, A. (1999) 'Competency-based learning: a dubious past – an assured future?'. In D. Boud and J. Garrick (eds) *Understanding Learning at Work*. London: Routledge; pp180–95

Goodman, P. S. and Dean, J. W. (1982) 'Creating long-term organization change'. In Goodman, P. S. (ed.) *Change in Organizations*. San Francisco: Jossey-Bass

Gorman, T. (2000) 'C's the opportunity', *People Management*, Vol.6, No.7, 30 March: 57

Grant, K. (2005) 'Public opinion', *The Times Public Agenda*, 8 March: 9

Grant, R. M. (1991) *Contemporary Strategy Analysis: Concepts, Techniques, Applications*. Oxford: Blackwell

Gratton, L. (2003a) 'Paradise Club', *People Management*, Vol.9, No.23, 20 November: 35–7

Gratton, L. (2003b) 'The Humpty Dumpty effect', *People Management*, Vol.9, No.9, 11 May: 18

Gratton, L. (2003c) 'The HR matrix reloaded', *People Management*, Vol.9, No.12, 1 June: 21

Gratton, L. (2005) 'Terms of engagement', *People Management*, Vol.11, No.7, 7 April: 20

Gray, D. E. (2007) 'Facilitating management learning developing critical reflection through reflective tools', *Management Learning*, Vol.38, No.5: 495–517

Gredler, M. E. (1997) *Learning and Instruction: Theory into practice*, 3rd edition. Englewood Cliffs, NJ: Prentice Hall

Green, K. (1999) 'Offensive thinking', *People Management*, Vol.5, No.8, 22 April: 27

Greeno, J. (1997) 'On claims that answer the wrong questions', *Educational Researcher*, Vol.26, No.1: 5–17

Greeno, J., Moore, J. and Smith, D. (1993) 'Transfer of situated learning'. In D. K. Detterman and R. J. Sternberg (eds) *Transfer on Trial: Intelligence, Cognition and Instruction*. Norwood, NJ: Ablex; pp99–167

Gribben, R. (2008) 'Tesco wins apprentices red-tape fight', *Daily Telegraph: jobs.telegraph. co.uk*, 24 July: 1

Griffiths, J. (2004) 'NHS teamwork is called into question', *People Management*, Vol.10, No.13, 30 June: 12

Griffiths, S. (2007) 'Diplomas – a cut above A-levels?', *Sunday Times*, 28 October: 11

Guardian (2004) 'Education reform: a new school consensus', *Guardian*, leader, 18 February: 23

Guest, D. and King, Z. (2001) 'Personnel's paradox', *People Management*, Vol.7, No.19, 27 September: 24–9

Guest, D. E., Michie, J., Sheehan, M. and Conway, N.(2000) *Employment Relations, HRM and Business Performance: An analysis of the 1998 Workplace Employee Relations Survey*. London: IPD

Guest, D. E, Michie, J., Conway, N. and Sheehan, M. (2003) 'Human resource management and performance in the UK', *British Journal of Industrial Relations*, Vol. 41, Issue 2: 291–314

Guinan, G. (2008) 'Be seen to be green to avoid belief claims', *People Management*, Vol.14, No.3, 7 February: 19

Guthridge, M. and Lawson, E. (2008) 'Divide and survive', *People Management*, Vol.14, No.19, 18 September: 40–4

Hall, D. T. (1984) 'Human resource development and organisational effectiveness'. In D. Fombrun, N. M. Tichy and M. A. Devanna (eds) *Strategic Human Resource Management*. New York: Wiley; pp159–81

Hall, G. (2004) 'Work in progress', *People Management*, Vol.10, No.19, 30 September: 25

Hall, L. (2005) 'IT support', *People Management*, Vol.11, No.6, 24 March: 34–7

Hall, L. (2006) 'Inside job', *People Management*, Vol.12, No.16, 10 August: 34–6

Hall, R. (1996) 'Supply chain management – the challenges for the 21st century'. *Paper presented to the CIPS Conference at Durham University Business School*, 9 May. Durham: Durham University Business School

Halpin, T. (2006a) 'Town halls to take over coasting state schools', *The Times*, 13 April: 1, 2

Halpin, T. (2006b) 'Evening classes to double charges', *The Times*, 28 March: 1

Hamblin, A. C. (1974) *Evaluation and Control of Training*. Maidenhead: McGraw-Hill

Hamel, G. (1991) 'Competition for competence and inter-partner learning within international strategic alliances', *Strategic Management Journal*, Vol.12, Summer: 83–103

Hames, T. (2004) 'A one-size exam won't pass', *The Times*, 19 October: 17

Hamlin, B. (2002) 'Towards evidence-based HRD practice'. In J. McGoldrick., J. Stewart and S. Watson (eds) *Understanding Human Resource Development: A research-based approach*. London: Routledge; pp93–121

Hamlin, B., Keep, J. and Ash, K. (2001) *Organisational Change and Development: A reflective guide for managers, trainers and developers*. London: Financial Times/Pitman Publishing

Hamlin, R. G. (2001) 'A review and synthesis of context and practice'. In B. Hamlin, J. Keep and K. Ash (eds) *Organisational Change and Development: A reflective guide for managers, trainers and developers*. London: Financial Times/Pitman Publishing; pp13–38

Hamlin, R. G. and Davies, G. (2001) 'Managers, trainers and developers as change agents'. In B. Hamlin, J. Keep and K. Ash (eds) *Organisational Change and Development: A reflective guide for managers, trainers and developers*. London: Financial Times/Pitman Publishing; pp39–60

Handy, C. B. (1976/1985) *Understanding Organizations*, 3rd edition. Harmondsworth: Penguin

Harding, S. (2008) 'Engaging your staff is more important than the war for talent', *People Management*, Vol.14, No.16, 7 August: 16

Harlow, T. and Smith, A. (2003) 'Necessary measures', *People Management*, Vol.9, No.23, 20 November: 48

Harris, H. and Dickmann, M. (2005) *International Management Development*. Guide. London: CIPD. Online version also available at: http://www.cipd.co.uk/guides/ [accessed 12 August 2008]

Harris, S. G. (1994) 'Organizational culture and individual sensemaking: a schema based perspective', *Organization Science*, Vol.5, No.3: 309–21

Harrison, J. and Lord, P. (1992) 'Investors in People and the accreditation of training in SMEs'. In *Proceedings of the 15th National Small Firms Policy and Research Conference, Southampton*. Northern Ireland Small Business Institute, United Kingdom Enterprise Management Research Association. November

Harrison, R. (1996) 'Action Learning: route or barrier to the learning organization?', *Employee Counselling Today, The Journal of Workplace Learning*, Vol.8, No.6: 27–38

Harrison, R. (1988) *Training and Development*. London: Institute of Personnel Management

Harrison, R. (1997) *Employee Development*, 3rd edition. London: Institute of Personnel and Development

Harrison, R. (1999) *The Training and Development Audit: An eight-step audit to measure, assess and enhance the performance of your organisation's training and development*. Cambridge: Cambridge Strategy Publications

Harrison, R. (2000) 'Learning, knowledge productivity and strategic progress', *International Journal of Training and Development*, Vol.4, No.4: 244–58

Harrison, R. (2005) *Learning and Development*, 4th edition. London: CIPD

Harrison, R. and Kessels, J. (2003) *Human Resource Development in a Knowledge Economy: An organisational view*. Basingstoke: Palgrave Macmillan

Harrison, R. and Miller, S. (1999) 'The contribution of clinical directors to the strategic capability of the organization', *British Journal of Management*, Vol.10, No.1: 23–39

Harrison, R. and Smith, R. (2001) 'Practical judgement: its implications for knowledge development and strategic capability'. In B. Hellgren and J. Lowstedt (eds) *Management in the Thought-Full Enterprise. A socio-cognitive approach to the organization of human resources*. Bergen: Fagbokforlaget; pp195–213

Hatton, A. (2001) 'The complexity-clarity paradox'. In B. Hamlin, J. Keep and K. Ash (eds*) Organisational Change and Development: A reflective guide for managers, trainers and developers*. London: Financial Times/Pitman Publishing; pp101–34

Hauerwas, S. (1983) *The Peaceable Kingdom*. Notre Dame, IN: University of Notre Dame Press

Hayes, A. (2007) *Training: The qualifications that count*. 6 August. Online article available at: http://www.trainingzone.co.uk/cgi-bin/item.cgi?id=171238 [accessed 21 August 2008]

Hedlund, G. (1994) 'A model of knowledge management and the N-Form corporation', *Strategic Management Journal*, (Summer Special) Issue, Vol.15: 73–90

Hendry, C. (1995) *Human Resource Management: A strategic approach to employment*. London: Butterworth-Heinemann

Hendry, C., Jones, A., Arthur, M. B. and Pettigrew, A. M. (1991) 'Human resource development in small to medium sized enterprises'. *Research Paper No.88*. Sheffield: Employment Department

Hertzberg, F. (1966) *Work and the Nature of Man*. London: Staples Press

Higginbottom, K. (2004) 'Firms ignoring staff opinion', *People Management*, Vol.10, No.5, 11 March: 7

Higgs, D. (2003) *Review of the role and effectiveness of non-executive directors*. London: Department of Trade and Industry. Online version also available at: http://www.berr.gov.uk/bbf/corp-governance/higgs-tyson/page23342.html [accessed 11 August 2008]

Higher Education Act (2004) London: The Parliamentary Bookshop. Online version also available at: http://www.opsi.gov.uk/acts.htm [accessed 4 May 2008]

Hill, R. (2002) 'Researching HRD in SMEs'. In J. McGoldrick, J. D. Stewart and S. Watson *Understanding Human Resource Development: A research-based approach*. London: Routledge; pp122–145

Hill, R. (2004) 'Why HRD in small organisations may have become a neglected field of study'. In J. Stewart and G. Beaver (eds) *HRD in Small Organisations: Research and practice*. London: Routledge; pp8–25

Hill, R. and Stewart, J. (eds) (2007) *Management Development: Perspectives from research and practice*. London: Routledge

Hills, H. and Francis, P. (1999) 'Interaction learning', *People Management*, Vol.5, No.14, 15 July: 48–9

Hirsh, W. and Tamkin, P. (2005) *Planning Training for your Business*. Report 422. London: Institute for Employment Studies. Online summary also available at: http://www.employment-studies.co.uk/pubs/summary.php?id=422 [accessed 4 August 2008]

Hirsh, W., Carter, A., Gifford, J., Strebler, M. and Baldwin, S. (2008) *What Customers Want From HR: The views of line managers, senior managers and employees on HR services and the HR function*. Report 453. London: Institute for Employment Studies. Online summary also available at: http://www.employment-studies.co.uk/ – follow link to 'Publications' [accessed 11 October 2008]

Hirst, L. (2008) 'Upskill challenge', *People Management*, Vol.14, No.2, 24 January: 9

Hiscock, D. (2004) 'The only way is up', *People Management*, Vol.10, No.14, 15 July: 37–9

HM Treasury (2004) *2004 Spending Review – Stability, Security and Opportunity for All: Investing for Britain's long-term future. New Public Spending Plans 2005–2008. CM 6237.* Norwich: The Stationery Office. Online version available at: http//www.hm-treasury.gov.uk [accessed 9 May 2008]

Hodkinson, H. and Hodkinson, P. (2004) 'Rethinking the concept of community of practice in relation to schoolteachers' workplace learning', *International Journal of Training and Development*, Vol.8, No.1: 21–31

Hogg, M. A. and Terry, D. J. (2000) 'Social identity and self-categorization processes in organizational contexts', *Academy of Management Review*, Vol.25, No.1: 121–40

Holbeche, L. (2007) 'Building high performance – the key role for HR', *Impact:* Quarterly update on CIPD Policy and Research. Issue 20, August. London: CIPD; pp10–11

Holbeche, L. (2008) 'Realising leadership development potential', *Impact:* Quarterly update on CIPD Policy and Research. Issue 24, August: 6–9. Online version also available at: http://www.cipd.co.uk/research/rsrchplcypubs/_impact.htm [accessed 12 August 2008]

Hollis, M. (1994) *The Philosophy of Social Science: An introduction.* Cambridge: Cambridge University Press

Holmes, B., Tangney, B., Fitzgibbon, A. and Savage, T. (2001) 'Communal constructivism: students constructing learning for as well as with others'. In *Proceedings of 12th Society for Information Technology and Teacher Education International Conference.* Orlando: Florida, 5–10 March

Holt, D. G. and Willard-Holt, C. (2000) 'Let's get real: students solving authentic corporate problems', *Phi Delta Kappan*, Vol.82, No.3, November: 243–46

Holton III, E. F. and Naquin, S. (2005) 'A critical analysis of HRD evaluation models from a decision-making perspective', *Human Resource Development Quarterly*, Vol.16, No.2: 257–80

Honey, P. and Mumford, A. (1992) *A Manual of Learning Styles*, 3rd edition. Maidenhead: Honey

Hope, K. (2004) 'Back to basics', *People Management*, Vol.10, No.15, 29 July: 14–15

Hosmer, L. T. (1994) 'Strategic planning as if ethics mattered', *Strategic Management Journal*, Vol.15, (Summer Special) Issue: 17–34

Hospital, J. T. (2001) *Strangers in a Strange Land*. Talk on Radio 4. 18 August: 7.45–8.00 pm

Houldsworth, E. (2007) 'In the same boat', *People Management*, Vol.13, No.2, 25 January: 35–6

Houldsworth, E. and Jirasinghe, D. (2006) *Managing and Measuring Employee Performance.* London: Kogan Page

Howard, A. and Wellins, R. S. (2008) *Overcoming the shortfalls in developing leaders: Executive Summary of DDI Global Leadership Forecast 2008/2009.* London: Development Dimensions International. Online version also available at: http://www.ddiworld.com/whatsnew/default.asp?id=928 [accessed 9 August 2008]

Howe, M. (2008a) 'Coaching at the crossroads – is it enough to position coaching activities with line managers?' In CIPD (ed.) *Reflections on the 2008 Learning and Development*

Survey: latest trends in learning, training and development. London: CIPD; pp17–19. Online version also available at: http://www.cipd.co.uk/subjects/lrnanddev/general/_reftrendtd. htm?IsSrchRes=1 [accessed 12 July 2008]

Howe, M. (2008b) 'Putting down routes', *People Management*, Vol.14, No.6, 20 March: 34–6

Huber, G. P. (1991) 'Organizational learning: the contributing processes and literatures', *Organization Science*, Vol.1, No.3: 85–115

Huff, A. S. (1982) 'Industry influences on strategy reformulation', *Strategic Management Journal*, Vol.3, Issue 2: 119–31

Hunt, C. (2005) 'Reflective practice'. In J. P. Wilson (ed.) *Human Resource Development: Learning and training for individuals and organizations*, 2nd edition. London: Kogan Page; pp234–51

Huselid, M. A. (1995) 'The impact of human resource management: an agenda for the 1990s', *International Journal of Human Resource Management*, Vol.1, No.1: 17–43

Huselid, M. A., Becker, B. E. and Ulrich, D. (2001) *The HR Scorecard: Linking People, Strategy and Performance*. Boston, MA: Harvard Business School Press

Hutchinson, S. and Purcell, J. (2003) *Bringing Policies to Life: The vital role of front-line managers in people management*. London: CIPD

Hutchinson, S., Purcell, J. and Winkler, V. (2007) 'Golden Gate', *People Management*, Vol.13, No.8, 19 April: 39–40

Huysman, M. and De Wit, D. (2002) *Knowledge Sharing in Practice*. Dordrecht: Kluwer Academic Publishers

Hyde, P., Boaden, R., Cortvriend, P., Harris, C., Marchington, M., Pass, S., Sparrow, P. and Sibbald, B. (2006) *Improving health through human resource management: a starting-point for change*. Change Agenda. London:CIPD. Online summary also available at: http://www. cipd.co.uk/subjects/hrpract/general/_imphlthhrm.htm [accessed 20 August 2008]

Iles, P. and Mabey, C. (1993) 'Managerial career development programmes: effectiveness, availability and acceptability', *British Journal of Management*, Vol.4, No.3: 103–11

Improvement and Development Agency and Local Government Employers (2008) *Briefing note: the new Comprehensive Area Assessment process and the workforce*. London: Local Government Association. Online version also available at: http//www.lge.gov.uk/ge/ aio/124464 [accessed 13 May 2008]

Institute of Executive Development and The Danish Leadership Institute (2004) *Leadership Development in European Organisations. Challenges and best practices*. Available online at: http://www.mannaz.com/Mail.asp?MailID=54&TopicID=495&L=2 [accessed 10 August 2008]

Institute of Leadership and Management (2008) *The Global Management Challenge: China vs the World*. Online report available at: http://www.i-l-m.com/research-and-comment/3428. aspx [accessed 10 August 2008]

Institute of Personnel and Development (1999) *First IPD National Training Survey*. London: CIPD

Jackson, L. (1989) 'Transforming managerial performance – a competency approach'. In *Proceedings of Institute of Personnel Management National Conference, Harrogate*. London: Institute of Personnel Management. October

Jackson, S. E. and Schuler, R. S. (1995) 'Understanding human resource management in the context of organizations and their environments', *Annual Review of Psychology*, Vol.46, No.1: 237–64

Jackson, T. (2000) *Career Development*. London: Institute of Personnel and Development

Jarvis, J., Lane, D. A. and Fillery-Travis, A. (2006) *The Case for Coaching*. London, CIPD

Jassawalla, A. R. and Sashittal, H. C. (1999) 'Building collaborative cross-functional new product teams', *Academy of Management Executive*, Vol.13, No.3: 50–63

Jennings, C. (2007) 'Integrating learning and development into wider organisational strategy'. In *Latest trends in learning, training and development: reflections on the 2007 L&D Survey*. London: CIPD; pp13–17. Online version also available at: http://www.cipd.co.uk/subjects/lrnanddev/general [accessed 2 February 2008]

Johnson, D. (2000) 'Scandal of our failing schools', *Daily Telegraph*, 11 March: 22

Johnson, M. (2004) *The New Rules of Engagement*. London: CIPD

Johnson, R. (2006) 'Singular focus', *People Management*, Vol.12, No.18, 14 September: 36–8

Johnston, R. and Badley, G. (1996) 'The competent reflective practitioner', *Innovation and Learning in Education*, Vol.2, No.1: 4–10

Jones, K. (2003) *Education in Britain: 1944 to the present*. Cambridge: Polity Press

Jones, P. and Holton, V. (2006) 'Teams today: taking the strain', *The Ashridge Journal*, Spring. Available online at: www.ashridge.org.uk/Website/Content.nsf/wFAR/Publications [Accessed 12 August 2008]

Jones, R. A. and Goss, D. M. (1991) 'The role of training strategy in reducing skills shortages: some evidence from a survey of small firms', *Personnel Review*, Vol.20, No.2: 24–30

Joy-Matthews, J., Megginson, D. and Surtees, M. (2004) *Human Resource Development*, 3rd edition. London: Kogan Page

Kant, I. (1781; Rev. 1999) *The Critics of Reason*. London: Cambridge University Press

Kaplan, R. and Norton, D. (2001) 'Marked impact', *People Management*, Vol.7, No.21, 25 November: 52–7

Kaplan, R. S. and Norton, D. P. (1996) *Translating Strategy into Action: The balanced scorecard*. Boston, MA: Harvard Business School Press

Karten, N. (2001) *Service level agreements: clarifying the concept*. Article available to download from http///www.nkarten.com/sla.html [accessed 18 July 2008]

Kazmier, L. J. (1964) *Principles of Management: A program for self-instruction*. New York: McGraw-Hill

Keep, E. (2006) 'Live and learn', *People Management*, Vol.12, No.15, 27 July: 7

Keep E. and Mayhew, K. (1994) *Scoping Paper for the 'What Makes Training Pay' Project*. London: Institute of Personnel and Development

Keep, J. (2001) 'To restructure or not? Reflections on an NHS healthcare Trust'. In B. Hamlin, J. Keep and K. Ash (eds) *Organisational Change and Development: A reflective guide for managers, trainers and developers*. London: Financial Times/Pitman Publishing; pp210–15

Kelly, G. (1955) *The Psychology of Personal Constructs*. New York: Norton

Kemp, N. (2001) 'Establishing an integrated HRFD approach to financial services'. In B. Hamlin, J. Keep and K. Ash (eds) *Organisational Change and Development: A reflective guide for managers, trainers and developers*. London: Financial Times/Pitman Publishing; pp258–63

Kersley, B., Alpin, C., Forth, J., Bryson, A., Bewley, H., Dix, G. and Oxenbridge, S. (2006) *Inside the Workplace: First Findings from the 2004 Workplace Employment Relations Survey*. London: Department of Trade and Industry/Economic and Social Research Council/Advisory, Conciliation and Arbitration Service/Policy Studies Institute. Also available at: http://www.berr.gov.uk/employment/research-evaluation/wers-2004/ [accessed 1 April 2008]

Kersten, A. (2000) 'Diversity management: dialogue, dialectics and diversion', *Journal of Organisational Change Management*, Vol.13, No.3: 235–48

Kessels, J. (1993) *Towards Design Standards for Curriculum Consistency in Corporate Education*. Dissertation. Hulshorst, Netherlands: Foundation for Corporate Education

Kessels, J. and Harrison, R. (1998) 'External consistency: the key to success in management development programmes?', *Management Learning*, Vol.29, No.1: 39–68

Kessels, J. W. M. (1996) 'Knowledge productivity and the corporate curriculum'. In J. F. Schreinemakers (ed.) *Knowledge Management, Organization, Competence and Methodology*. Würzburg: Ergon Verlag; pp168–74

Kim, J. S. (2005) 'The effects of a constructivist teaching approach on student academic achievement, self-concept, and learning strategies', *Asia Pacific Education Review*, Vol.6, No.1: 7–19

Kimberly, J. R. (1987) 'The study of organization: toward a biographical perspective'. In J. W. Lorsch (ed.) *Handbook of Organizational Behaviour*. Englewood Cliffs, NJ: Prentice Hall

King, Z. (2004) *Career Management: A CIPD guide*. London: Chartered Institute of Personnel and Development

Kingston, P. (2007a) 'Short changed', *People Management*, Vol.13, No.16, 9 August: 28–31

Kingston, P. (2007b) 'Long-term investment', *EducationGuardian Supplement on 14–19 reforms*, 6 March: 1

Kingston, P. (2007c) 'The end of colleges as we know them?', *EducationGuardian*, 11 December: 3

Kingston, P. (2007d) 'Halfway house', *The Guardian*, 8 May: 8

Kinnie, N., Swart, J., Lund, M., Morris, S., Snell, S. and Kang, S-C. (2006) *Managing People and Knowledge in Professional Service Firms*. London: CIPD

Kirjavainen, P. (2001) 'Strategic learning in a knowledge-intensive organisation'. In H. W. Volberda and T. Elfring (eds) *Rethinking Strategy*. London: Sage; pp172–90

Kirkpatrick, D. L. (1975) *Evaluating Training Programs*. Madison, Wisconsin: American Society for Training and Development

Kitching, J. (2007) 'Regulating employment relations through workplace learning: a study of small employers', *Human Resource Management Journal*, Vol.17, No.1: 42–57

Kitson, A. and Campbell, R. (2008) *The Ethical Organisation*, 2nd edition. Basingstoke: Palgrave Macmillan

Knowles, M. S. (1973) *The Adult Learner. A neglected species*. Houston: Gulf Publishing

Koenig, C. and Van Wijk, G. (2001) 'Managing beyond boundaries: the dynamics of trust in alliances'. In H. W. Volberda and T. Elfring (eds) *Rethinking Strategy*. London: Sage; pp116–27

Kolb, D. A. (1984) *Experiential Learning*. Englewood Cliffs, NJ: Prentice Hall

Kolb, D. A., Rubin, I. M. and McIntyre, J. M. (1974) *Organizational Psychology: An experiential approach*. Englewood Cliffs, NJ: Prentice Hall

Kotter, J. P. (1996) *Leading Change*. Boston MA: Harvard Business School Press

Krinks, P. and Strack, R. (2008) 'The talent crunch', *People Management*, Vol.14, No.13, 26 June: 30–1

Kübler-Ross, E. (1969) *On Death and Dying*. New York: Macmillan

Lank, E. (2002) 'Head to head', *People Management*, Vol.8, No.4, 21 February: 46–9

Larsen, H. H. (1994) 'Key issues in training and development'. In C. Brewster and A. Hegewisch (eds) *Policy and Practice in European Human Resource Management: The Price Waterhouse Cranfield Survey*. London: Routledge; pp107–21

Laukkanen, M. (1996) 'Environmental upheaval and management thinking: a longitudinal single-case study'. *Article presented at European Institute for Advanced Studies in Management, 4th International Workshop on Managerial and Organisational Cognition: Management in the thought-full enterprise*, 29–30 August. Stockholm: Stockholm School of Economics and Linköping University

Lave, J. and Wenger, E. (1991) *Situated Learning: Legitimate peripheral participation*. Cambridge: Cambridge University Press

Learning and Skills Council (2004) *Widening Adult Participation: Policy and Strategy*. Coventry: Learning and Skills Council, Skills and Education Network

Learning and Skills Council (2008) *The National Employers Skills Survey 2007*. Coventry: LSC. Online version also available at: http://readingroom.lsc.gov.uk/lsc/National/nat-nessurvey2007mainreport-may08.pdf [accessed 15 August 2008]

Leckie, D. (2005) 'Active duty', *People Management*, Vol.11, No.7, 7 April: 18–19

Leckie, D. and Fraser, J. (2007) 'Stay on the safe side of new law', *People Management*, Vol.13, No.16, 9 August: 20

Lee, G. and Pick, L. (2004) 'How to buy coaching', *People Management*, Vol.10, No.5, 11 March: 50–1

Lee, R. (1996) 'The "pay-forward" view of training', *People Management*, Vol.2, No.3, 8 February: 30–2

Leeming, J. (2008) *An investigation into how cross-functional team working could contribute towards membership development within a newly merged charity*. Unpublished dissertation. Milton Keynes: The Open University

Legge, K. (1995) *Human Resource Management: Rhetorics and realities*. London: Macmillan

Leitch, S. (2006) *Review of Skills: Prosperity for All in the Global Economy – World-Class Skills. Final Report*. Norwich: Her Majesty's Stationery Office. Online version also available at: http//www.hm-treasury.gov.uk/leitch [accessed 12 April 2008]

Levinthal, D. A. and March, J. G. (1993) 'The myopia of learning', *Strategic Management Journal*, Vol.14 (Winter Special) Issue 8: 95–112

Lewin, K. (1951) *Field Theory in Social Science*. London: Tavistock

Likert, R. (1961) *New Patterns of Management*. New York: McGraw-Hill

Lippitt, G. (1983) 'Management development as the key to organisational renewal', *Journal of Management Development*, Vol.1, No.2: 36–9

Lips-Wiersma, M. and Hall, D. (2007) 'Organizational career development is not dead: a case study on managing the new career during organizational change', *Journal of Organizational Behaviour*, Vol.28, No.6: 771–92

Lloyd, C. and Payne, J. (2005) 'High performance work organisation: a driver for the high skills vision?', *SKOPE Issues Paper 6*. Coventry: SKOPE, University of Warwick. October. Online version also available at: http//www.skope.ox.ac.uk [accessed 12 April 2008]

Lockett, J. (1992) *Effective Performance Management: A strategic guide to getting the best from people*. London: Kogan Page

Lye, G. and Kay, J. (2006) 'How business can change the world', *Royal Society of Arts Journal*, June: 54–6

Lymer, A. (1996) 'Educational impacts of the World Wide Web', *Account*, Vol.8, No.1: 9–10

Lynch, S. (2003) 'Is it safe to hand HR tasks over to non-experts?', *People Management*, Vol.9, No.18, 11 September: 56

Mabey, C. and Ramirez, M. (2004) *Developing Managers: A European Perspective: A survey of management training and development in the United Kingdom, France, Germany, Spain, Denmark, Norway and Romania*. London: Chartered Management Institute. Online version also available at: http://www.managers.org.uk/listing_1.aspx?id=10:106&id=10:9 [accessed 12 August 2008]

Mabey, C. and Terry, R. (2007) 'The manager in the mirror', *People Management*, Vol.13, No.14, 12 July: 38–40

MacDuffie, J. P. (1995) 'Human resource bundles and manufacturing performance: organizational logic and flexible production systems in the world auto industry', *Industrial and Labor Relations Review*, Vol.48, No.2: 197–221

Machin, J. L. J. (1981) 'The expectation approach'. In J. L. J. Machin, R. Stewart and C. Hales (eds) *Towards Managerial Effectiveness: Applied research perspectives on the managerial task*. Farnborough: Gower

Macintyre, B. (2008) 'Be confident: two and two still make four', *The Times*, 9 October: 27

Mackinnon, I. (2004) 'Make the grade', *People Management*, Vol.10, No.20, 14 October: 50

Mager, R F. (1984) *Preparing Instructional Objectives*. California: Fearon

Mahony, C. (2007) 'A collective bargain', *People Management*, Vol.13, No.18, 6 September: 36–7

Maitland, R. (2007) 'Support for company strategy is essential to employee engagement', *People Management*, Vol.13, No.5, 8 March: 48

Manwaring, T. and Wood, S. (1985) 'The ghost in the labour process: job redesign'. In D. Knight (ed.) *Critical Perspectives on the Labour Process*. Aldershot: Gower

Marchington, M. and Wilkinson, A. (2008) *Human Resource Management at Work: People Management and Development*, 4th edition. London: CIPD

Marsick, V. (1994) 'Trends in managerial reinvention: creating a learning map', *Management Learning*, Vol.25, No.1: 11–33

Marton, F. and Ramsden, P. (1988) 'What does it take to improve learning?' In P. Ramsden (ed.) *Improving Learning: New perspectives*. London: Kogan Page

Mason, G. (2002) 'High skills utilisation under mass higher education: graduate employment in service industries in Britain', *Journal of Education and Work*, Vol.15, No.4: 427–56

Mason, R. and Mitroff, I. (1981) *Challenging Strategic Planning Assumptions*. New York: John Wiley & Sons

Matthewman, J. and Matignon, F. (2004) *Human Capital Reporting: An internal perspective*. London: CIPD

Matthews, J. H. and Candy, P. C. (1999) 'New dimensions in the dynamics of learning and knowledge'. In D. Boud and J. Garrick (eds) *Understanding Learning at Work*. London: Routledge; pp47–64

Mattin, D. (2005) 'So much to learn from continental neighbours', *The Times Focus Report – Skills for Business*, 29 November: 5

Mattinson, D. (2006) 'Gordon Brown is in the lead – go figure', *The Times*, 23 October: 21

Mayo, A. (2001) *The Human Value of the Enterprise: Valuing people as assets – measuring, managing, monitoring*. London: Nicholas Brealey Publishing

Mayo, A. (2004) *Creating a Learning and Development Strategy: The HR partner's guide to developing people*, 2nd edition. London: CIPD

McGoldrick, J., Stewart, J. and Watson, S. (eds) (2002) *Understanding Human Resource Development: A research-based approach*. London: Routledge

McGregor, D. (1960) *The Human Side of Enterprise*. Maidenhead: McGraw-Hill

McPherson, M. (2005) 'E-learning: a guide to principles and practice'. In J. P. Wilson (ed.) *Human Resource Development: Learning and training for individuals and organizations*, 2nd edition. London: Kogan Page; pp318–41

Merali, Y. (1999) 'Informed decisions', *People Management*, Vol.5, No.12, 17 June: 59–62

Mezirow, J. A. (1985) 'A critical theory of self-directed learning'. In S. Brookfield (ed.) *Self-Directed Learning: From theory to practice*. San Francisco, CA: Jossey-Bass

Michaels, E., Handfield-Jones, H. and Axelrod, B. (2008) *The War for Talent*. Boston, MA: Harvard Business School Press

Miles, R. and Snow, C. (1995) 'The new network firm: a spherical structure built on a human investment philosophy', *Organizational Dynamics*, Vol.23, No.4: 5–18

Miller, L., Rankin, N. and Neathey, F. (2001) *Competency Frameworks in UK Organisations*. Research Report. London: CIPD

Miller, R. and Stewart, J. (1999) 'Opened university', *People Management*, Vol.5, No.12, 17 June: 42–5

Miller, S., Hickson, D. J. and Wilson, D. C. (1999) 'Decision-making in organizations'. In S. R. Clegg, C. Hardy and W. R. Nord (eds) *Managing Organizations: Current Issues*. London: Sage; pp43–62

Mintzberg, H. (1973) *The Nature of Managerial Work*. New York: Harper & Row

Mintzberg, H. (2004) *Managers Not MBAs*. London: Financial Times/Prentice Hall

Mohrman, S. A. and Lawler III, E. E. (1999) 'The new human resources management: creating the strategic business partnership'. In R. S. Schuler and S. E. Jackson (eds) *Strategic Human Resource Management*. Oxford: Blackwell; pp433–47

Moir, S. (2008) 'Why HR can be the people's profession in trying times', *People Management*, Vol.14, No.14, 10 July: 19

Molloy, E. and Whittington, R. (2005) *HR: Making Change Happen*. Research Report. London: CIPD

Moore, C. (2007) 'Dame Suzi prepares to drag charities into the "modern world"', *Daily Telegraph*, 10 November: 26

Morgan, G. (1997) *Images of Organization*, 2nd edition. London: Sage

Morris, J. (1991) 'Action Learning: the long haul'. In J. Prior (ed.) *Handbook of Training and Development*. Aldershot: Gower; pp611–28

Morris, J. and Farrell, C. (2007) 'The "post-bureaucratic" public sector organization. New organizational forms and HRM in ten UK public sector organizations', *International Journal of Human Resource Management*, Vol.18, No.9: 1575–88

Morton, B. and Wilson, A. (2003) 'Double vision', *People Management*, Vol.9, No.20, 9 October: 37–8

Moxon, G. R. (1943) *The Functions of a Personnel Department*. London: Institute of Personnel Management

Mumford, A. and Gold, J. (2004) *Management Development: Strategies for action*, 4th edition. London: CIPD

Mumford, A., Robinson, G. and Stradling, D. (1987) *Developing Directors: The learning processes*. Sheffield: Manpower Services Commission

Nadler, L. (1970) *Developing Human Resources*. Houston: Gulf

Nadler, L. (1992) 'HRD – where has it been, where is it going?', *Studies in Continuing Education*, Vol.14, No.2: 104–14

Nafukho, F. M., Hairston, N. R. and Brooks, K. (2004) 'Human capital theory: implications for human resource development', *Human Resource Development International*, Vol.7, No.4: 545–51

Neary, P. and Lucks, S. (2005) 'How external factors help staff to get the most out of development centres', *People Management*, Vol.11, No.9, 5 May: 44

Neely, A. (2007) 'The search for meaningful measures', *Management Services*, Vol.51, No.2: 14–17

Nelson, R. and Winter, S. (1982) *An Evolutionary Theory of Organizational Change*. Cambridge MA: Harvard University Press

Nevis, E. C., Di Bella, A. J. and Gould, J. M. (1995) 'Understanding organizations as learning systems', *Sloan Management Review*, Vol.36, No.2: 73–85

Nonaka, I. (1991) 'The knowledge-creating company', *Harvard Business Review*, Vol.69, No.6: 96–104

Nonaka, I. (1994) 'A dynamic theory of organizational knowledge creation', *Organization Science*, Vol.5, No.1: 14–37

Nonaka, I. and Takeuchi, H. (1995) *The Knowledge-Creating Company*. Oxford: Oxford University Press

O'Connell, G. (2008) 'Crystal clear', *People Management*, Vol.14, No.4, 6 March: 40–2

O'Driscoll, T., Sugrue, B. and Vona, M. K. (2005) 'The C-level and the value of learning', *Training and Development*, Vol.59, No.10: 70–5

Onions, C. T. (ed.) (1973) *The Shorter Oxford English Dictionary*, 3rd edition. Oxford: Oxford University Press

Opie, R. (2008) 'The "four camps" of employee skills'. In CIPD (ed.) *Reflections on the 2008 Learning and Development Survey: latest trends in learning, training and development*. London: CIPD; pp5–7. Online version also available at: http://www.cipd.co.uk/onlineinfodocuments/surveys [accessed 8 May 2008]

Organisation for Economic Co-Operation and Development (2001) *The Well-being of Nations: The role of human and social capital*. Paris: OECD

Orion Partners (2008) *Facing up to the Future – meeting the challenge of changing HR career paths*. London: Orion Partners LLP or contact partners@orion-partners.co.uk

Orr, J. E. (1990) 'Sharing knowledge, celebrating identity: community memory in a service culture'. In D. S. Middleton and D. Edwards (eds) *Collective Remembering*. Newbury Park, SA: Sage; pp169–98

Osbaldeston, M. (2005) 'Developing your leaders'. In CIPD (ed.) *Reflections on the 2005 Training and Development Survey: latest trends in learning, training and development*. London: CIPD; pp26–9. Online version also available at: http://www.cipd.co.uk/onlineinfodocuments/surveys/ [accessed 12 August 2008]

Ostapski, A. S., Oliver, J. and Gonzales, G. T. (1996) 'The legal and ethical components of executive decision-making: a course for business managers', *Journal of Business Ethics*, Vol.15: 571–9

Overell, S. (2005) 'Get wise: the value of diversity', *Royal Society of Arts Journal*, April: 48–52

Paese, M. and Wellins, R. S. (2006) *Leaders in Transition: Stepping up, not off*. London: Development Dimensions International. Online version also available at: http://www.ddiworld.com/whatsnew/default.asp?id=928 [accessed 9 August 2008]

Paine, L. S. (1994) 'Managing for organizational integrity', *Harvard Business Review*, Vol.72, No.2: 106–17

Palmer, R. (2005) 'The identification of learning needs'. In J. Wilson (ed.) *Human Resource Development: Learning and training for individuals and organizations*, 2nd edition. London: Kogan Page; pp138–55

Palmer, T. (2008) 'Tortoise beats hare', *People Management Guide: HR Outsourcing*. March: 4–7

Pan, S. L. (1999) 'Knowledge management at Buckman Laboratories'. In H. Scarbrough and J. Swan (eds) *Case Studies in Knowledge Management*. London: Institute of Personnel and Development; pp76–84

Parr, J. P. (2005) 'The adult learner: theory into practice'. In J. P. Wilson (ed.) *Human Resource Development: Learning and training for individuals and organizations*, 2nd edition. London: Kogan Page; pp220–33

Partridge, B. (1989) 'The problem of supervision'. In K. Sisson (ed.) *Personnel Management in Britain*. Oxford: Blackwell; pp203–21

Partridge, C. (2006) 'No ragged-trousered philanthropists these', *The Times*, 21 November: 55

Pass, S. (2005) *Missing links in the 'causal chain' between HR practices and organisational performance*. Ian Beardwell Prizewinning Research Paper, presented at CIPD Professional Standards Conference, University of Keele, 27–29 June

Passmore, J. (2003) 'Goal-orientated coaching', *The Occupational Psychologist: Special Issue – Coaching Psychology*. No.49, August: 30–3

Patterson, M. G., West, M. A., Lawthom, R. and Nickell, S. (1997) *Impact of People Management Practices on Business Performance*. London: Institute of Personnel and Development

Pavlov, J. P. (1927) *Conditioned Reflexes*. Oxford: OUP

Pearsall, J. and Trumble, B. (eds) (1996) *The Oxford English Reference Dictionary*, 2nd edition. Oxford: Oxford University Press

Pedler, M. and Boutall, J. (1992) *Action Learning for Change: A resource book for managers and other professionals*. Eastwood Park, Avon: NHS Training Directorate

Pedler, M., Burgoyne, J. and Boydell, T. (1997) *The Learning Company: A strategy for sustainable development*, 2nd edition. London: McGraw-Hill

Pennings, J. M. (2001) 'Configurations and the firm in current strategic management'. In H. W. Volberda and T. Elfring (eds) *Rethinking Strategy*. London: Sage; pp240–4

Penrose, E. T. (1959) *The Theory of the Growth of the Firm*. Oxford: Blackwell

People Management (2002) 'World Bank fails to "set an example on corruption"', *People Management, Letters page*, Vol.8, No.21, 24 October: 26

People Management (2006a) 'Less will be more for tomorrow's NHS workforce, says report', *People Management, News in Brief*, Vol.12, No.8, 20 April: 12

People Management (2006b) 'The success of NGOs hinges on their people – but HR is neglected in the sector', *People Management, Study Notes*, Vol.12, No.6, 23 March: 44

People Management (2007a) 'MPs condemn NHS workforce planning', *People Management, News*, Vol.13, No.7, 5 April: 10

People Management (2007b) 'Research Forum: Be selective when choosing emotional intelligence training', *People Management*, Vol.13, No.9, 3 May: 9

People Management (2008a) 'Don't underestimate the value of NVQs', *People Management, Letters*, Vol.14, No.5, 6 March: 6

People Management (2008b) 'Culture change focus of equalities bill', *People Management, News section*, Vol.14, No.11, 29 May: 9

People Management (2008c) 'NHS staff feel undervalued, reveals survey', *People Management, News*, Vol.14, No.8, 17 April: 11

People Management (2008d) 'Just do it – yourself', *People Management, News*, Vol.14, No.8, 1 May: 11

Performance and Innovation Unit (2001) *In Demand: Adult skills for the 21st century, Part 1*. Printed copies available from strateg@cabinet-office.x.gsi.gov.uk. Online version also available at: http://www.cabinetoffice.gov.uk/strategy/work_areas/workforce_development.aspx [accessed 16 April 2008]

Peters, T. and Waterman, R. (1982) *In Search of Excellence*. New York: Harper & Row

Pettigrew, A. M., Arthur, M. B. and Hendry, C. (1990) 'Training and human resource management in small to medium-sized enterprises: a critical review of the literature and a model for future research'. *Research Paper No. 56*. Sheffield: Employment Department

Pettigrew, A., Thomas, H. and Whittington, R. (2002a) 'Strategic management: the strengths and limitations of a field'. In A. Pettigrew., H. Thomas and R. Whittington (eds) *Handbook of Strategy and Management*. London: Sage; pp3–30

Pettigrew, A., Thomas, H. and Whittington, R. (eds) (2002b) *Handbook of Strategy and Management*. London: Sage

Pettigrew, A. M., Jones, G. R. and Reason, P. W. (1982) *Training and Development Roles in their Organisational Setting*. Sheffield: Manpower Services Commission

Pfeffer, J. (2005) 'Changing mental models: HR's most important task', *Human Resource Management*, Vol.44, No.2: 123–8

Pfeffer, J. and Sutton, R. I. (2006a) 'A matter of fact', *People Management*, Vol.13, No.22, 28 September: 24–30

Pfeffer, J. and Sutton, R. I. (2006b) *Hard Facts, Dangerous Half-Truths and Total Nonsense*. Cambridge, MA: Harvard Business School Press

Phillips, L. (2006) 'Surveying the damage', *People Management*, Vol.12, No.18, 14 September: 16–17

Phillips, L. (2007a) 'Can apprenticeships close the UK skills gap?', *People Management*, Vol.13, No.24, 29 November: 14–15

Phillips, L. (2007b) 'It starts to add up', *People Management*, Vol.13, No.18, 6 September: 17

Phillips, L. (2007c) 'BBC sets out creative restructuring plans', *People Management*, Vol.13, No.22, 1 November: 14–15

Phillips, L. (2008) 'Apprentices' equivalent of Ucas is on its way', *People Management*, Vol.14, No.1, 10 January: 14

Philpott, J. (2003) 'The great stakeholder debate', *People Management*, Vol.9, No.16, 7 August: 20

Philpott, J. (2004) 'Work audit – employer training for adult workers: who are the European Champions?', *Impact:* Quarterly update on CIPD Policy and Research. Issue 9, November. London: CIPD: pp32–6

Philpott, J. (2006) 'After Turner – how to manage the Methuselah generation', *Impact:* Quarterly update on CIPD Policy and Research. Issue 14, February. London: CIPD: pp20–3

Piaget, J. (1950) *The Psychology of Intelligence*. London: Routledge & Kegan Paul

Pickard, J. (1999) 'Sense and sensitivity', *People Management*, Vol.5, No.21, 28 October: 48–56

Pickard, J. (2002) 'An ideal solution', *People Management*, Vol.8, No.6, 21 March: 33–4

Pickard, J. (2003a) 'Joint effort', *People Management*, Vol.9, No.15, 24 July: 33–5

Pickard, J. (2003b) 'A clearer provision', *People Management*, Vol.9, No.12, 12 June: 28–34

Pickard, J. (2005) 'Part, not partner', *People Management*, Vol.11, No.21, 27 October: 49–50

Pickard, J. (2006a) 'Suits ewe', *People Management*, Vol.12, No.12, 15 June: 36–7

Pickard, J. (2006b) 'On the critical list', *People Management*, Vol.12, No.17, 31 August: 24–9

Pickard, J. (2007) 'Tried and tested', *People Management*, Vol.13, No.22, 1 November: 32–5

Pickard, J. (2008) 'HR careers hit a new glass ceiling', *People Management*, Vol.14, No.12, 12 June: 12–13

Pilbeam, S. and Corbridge, M. (2002) *People Resourcing – HRM in practice*. London: Financial Times/Prentice Hall

Pinnington, A. H. and Bayraktaroglu, S. (2007) 'Ethical leadership in employee development'. In A. Pinnington, T. Macklin and T. Campbell (eds) *Human Resource Management: Ethics and Employment*. Oxford: Oxford University Press; pp190–208

Plummer, J. (2004) 'Charities need to get tough', *The Times, Public Agenda*, 30 November: 5

Poell, R. (2005) 'Learning organizations and communities of practice: a critical evaluation'. In J. P. Wilson (ed.) *Human Resource Development: Learning and training for individuals and organizations*, 2nd edition. London: Kogan Page; pp99–110

Poell, R. F. and Tijmensen, E. C. M. (1998) 'Using learning projects to work towards a learning organisation: two cases from professional work'. In R. F. Poell and G. E. Chivers (eds) *Continuing Professional Development in Europe: Theoretical views, fields of application and national policies*. Sheffield: University of Sheffield; pp43–57

Polanyi, M. (1966) *The Tacit Dimension*. New York: Doubleday

Porac, J., Thomas, H. and Fuller, C. B. (1989) 'Competitive groups as cognitive communities: the case of the Scottish knitwear manufacturers', *Journal of Management Studies*, Vol.26, No.4: 397–416

Porter, M. E. (1980) *Competitive Strategy: Techniques for analyzing industries and competitors*. New York: Free Press (Republished with a new introduction, 1998)

Porter, M. E. (1985) *Competitive Advantage*. New York: Free Press

Prahalad, C. K. and Ramaswamy, V. (2002) 'The co-creation connection', *Strategy and Business*, Issue 27, 2nd quarter: 50–61

Pratt, M. G. and Foreman, P. O. (2000) 'Classifying managerial responses to multiple organizational identities', *Academy of Management Review*, Vol.25, No.1: 18–42

PricewaterhouseCoopers (2008) *11th Annual Global CEO Survey: Key HR issues arising*. Available online at: http://www.pwc.com/extweb/insights.nsf/docid/15D1A76FC7C2E94580 25741E004EDF86 [accessed 6 August 2008]

Prowse, M. (1995) 'Adam Smith and the virtue of capitalism', *Financial Times*, 16 January: 14

Purcell, J. and Hutchinson, S. (2007) 'Front-line managers as agents in the HRM-performance causal chain: theory, analysis and evidence', *Human Resource Management Journal*, Vol.17, No.1: 3–20

Purcell, J., Kinnie, N., Hutchinson, S., Rayton, B. and Swart, J. (2003) *Understanding the People and Performance Link: Unlocking the black box*. London: CIPD

Putnam, R. (2000) *Bowling Alone: The collapse and revival of American community*. New York: Simon & Schuster

Qualifications and Curriculum Authority (2004) *A Framework for Achievement (FfA): recognising qualifications and skills in the 21st century*. Stakeholder consultation. London: QCA. Online version also available at: http//www.qca.org.uk/ffa/ [accessed 29 April 2008]

Rainbird, H., Munro, A. and Holly, L. (2004) 'Exploring the concept of employer demand for skills and qualifications: case studies from the public sector'. In C. Warhurst, I. Grugulis and E. Keep (eds) *The Skills that Matter*. Houndmills, Basingstoke: Palgrave Macmillan; pp91–108

Ram, M. (2000) 'Investors in People in small firms: case study evidence from the business services sector', *Personnel Review*, Vol.29 Issue 1/2: 69–87

Rana, E. (2002) 'A class above the rest', *People Management*, Vol.8, No.9, 2 May: 15

Rana, E. (2003) 'Council appraisals discriminate', *People Management*, Vol.9, No.2, 23 January: 11

Rankine, K. (2004) 'Putting customers first helped store come from behind in High St stakes', *Daily Telegraph*, 21 April: 6

Raper, P., Ashton, D., Felstead, A. and Storey, K. (1997) 'Toward the learning organisation? Explaining current trends in training practice in the UK', *International Journal of Training and Development*, Vol.1, No.1: 9–21

Rappaport, J. (1993) 'Narrative studies, personal stories, and identity transformation in the mutual help context', *Journal of Applied Behavioural Science*, Vol.29, No.2: 239–56

Ray, T. (2002) 'Managing Japanese organizational knowledge creation: the difference'. In S. Little, P. Quintas and T. Ray (eds) *Managing Knowledge: An essential reader*. London: Sage; pp102–38

Reid, M. A., Barrington, H. and Brown, M. (2004) *Human Resource Development: Beyond training interventions*, 3rd edition. London: CIPD

Reilly, P. (2006) 'Falling between stools?', *People Management*, Vol.12, No.23, 23 November: 37

Reilly, P. (2007) 'Facing up to the facts', *People Management*, Vol.13, No.19, 20 September: 43–5

Reilly, P., Tamkin, P. and Broughton, A. (2007) *The Changing HR Function: Transforming HR?* London: CIPD. Online summary also available at: http://www.cipd.co.uk/Bookstore/_catalogue/CorporateAndHRStrategy/9781843981978.htm [accessed 21 August 2008]

Revans, R. W. (1982) *The Origins and Growth of Action Learning*. Bromley: Chartwell-Bratt

Reynolds, J. (2002) 'Method and madness', *People Management*, Vol.8, No.7, 4 April: 42–3

Richards, J. (2006) 'Working where money isn't everything', *The Times Public Agenda*, 10 October: 8

Riddell, P. (2008) 'A must-read report on the problems that face us all', *The Times*, 12 February: 22

Rigg, C., Stewart, J. and Trehan, K. (eds) (2007) *Critical Human Resource Development: Beyond orthodoxy*. London: Financial Times/Prentice Hall

Roberts, A. (2006) 'Nouveau stratagem', *People Management*, Vol.12, No.15, 27 July: 30–1

Rodger, D. and Mabey, C. (1987) 'BT's leap forward from assessment centres', *Personnel Management*, Vol.19, No.7: 32–5

Roe, P., Wiseman, J. and Costello, M. (2006) *Perceptions and Use of NVQs:A survey of employers in England*. Research Report No.714. Nottingham: DfES publications. Online version also available at: http//www/dfes.go.uk/research [accessed 29 April 2008]

Rogers, M. S. (2004) 'Power to the people managers', *People Management*, Vol.10, No.18, 16 September: 25

Rubery, J., Earnshaw, J., Marchington, M., Cooke, F. and Vincent, S. (2002) 'Changing organisational forms and the employment relationship', *Journal of Management Studies*, Vol.39, No.5: 645–72

Rucci, A. J., Kirn, S. P. and Quinn, R. T. (1998) 'The employee-customer-profit chain at Sears', *Harvard Business Review*, Vol.76, No.1: 99–109

Russ-Eft, D. and Preskill, H. (2005) 'In search of the Holy Grail: return on investment evaluation in human resource development', *Advances in Developing Human Resources*, Vol.7, No.1: 71–85

Salas, E. and Cannon-Bowers, J. A. (2001) 'The science of training: a decade of progress', *Annual Review of Psychology*, Vol.52, No.1: 471–89

Sambrook, S. (2004) 'A "critical" time for HRD?', *Journal of European Industrial Training*, Vol.28, No.8/9: 611–24

Sambrook, S. and Stewart, J. (eds) (2007) *Human Resource Development in the Public Sector: The case of health and social care*. London: Routledge

Sampson, H. (1992) 'Vorsprung Durch Training: How the Germans do it', *Human Resources*, Spring, Issue 5: 41–3

Sanchez, R. (1995) 'Strategic flexibility in product competition', *Strategic Management Journal*, Vol.16, No.5: 135–59

Santos, A. and Stuart, M. (2003) 'Employee perceptions and their influence on training effectiveness', *Human Resource Management Journal*, Vol.13, No.1: 27–45

Sappal, P. (2004) 'Long engagement', *People Management*, Vol.10, No.24, 9 December: 31–3

Scarbrough, H. (1998) 'Path(ological) dependency? Core competencies from an organizational perspective', *British Journal of Management*, Vol.9, No.3: 219–32

Scarbrough, H. and Swan, J. (eds) (1999) *Case Studies in Knowledge Management*. London: Institute of Personnel and Development

Schein, E. (1995) 'Kurt Lewin's change theory in the field and in the classroom: notes toward a model of managed learning'. *Online article* available at: http://www.a2zpsychology.com/articles/kurt_lewin's_change_theory.htm [accessed 29 May 2008]

Schein, E. H. (1978) *Career Dynamics: Matching individual and organizational needs*. Reading, MA: Addison Wesley

Schendel, D. and Hofer, C. (1979) *Strategic Management: A new view of business policy and planning*. Boston, MA: Little, Brown

Schon, D. A. (1983) *The Reflective Practitioner: How professionals think in action*. New York: Basic Books

School Standards and Framework Act (1998) London: The Parliamentary Bookshop. Online version also available at: http://www.opsi.gov.uk/acts.htm [accessed 4 May 2008]

Schuck, G. (1996) 'Intelligent technology, intelligent workers: a new pedagogy for the high-tech workplace'. In K. Starkey (ed.) *How Organizations Learn*. London: International Thomson Business Press; pp199–213

Schultz, T. W. (1961) 'Investment in human capital', *American Economic Review*, Vol.51, No.1: 1–17

Schwab, K. (2007) 'New order needed for a flatter world', *The Times*, 22 January: 41

Scott, A. (2005) 'HR's "bold" mission for unique value', *People Management*, Vol.11, No.22, 10 November: 9

Scott, A. (2007) 'Is HR still admin-focused?', *People Management*, Vol.13, No.14, 12 July: 13

Scott, A. (2008a) 'Latest news: Learning providers to be rated on performance', *PM Online*, 30 June. Available online at: http://www.peoplemanagement.co.uk/pm/articles/2008/06/learning-providers-to-be-rated-on-performance.htm [accessed 28 July 2008]

Scott, A. (2008b) 'Managers "don't have the time to develop talent"', *People Management*, Vol.14, No.17, 21 August: 10

Selznick, P. (1957) *Leadership in Administration*. New York: Harper & Row

Senge, P. M. (1990) *The Fifth Discipline: The art and practice of the learning organization*. New York: Doubleday

Senge, P. M. (1996) 'The leader's new work: building learning organizations'. In K. Starkey (ed.) *How Organizations Learn*. London: International Thomson Business Press; pp288–315

Seymour, W. D. (1959) *Operator Training in Industry*. London: Institute of Personnel Management

Sharkie, R. (2003) 'Knowledge creation and its place in the development of sustainable competitive advantage', *Knowledge Management*, Vol.7, No.1: 20–31

Shepherd, C. (2008) 'How we can face up to the challenges of "Learning 2.0"?', *People Management*, Vol.14, No.7, 3 April: 49

Shields, J. (2007) *Managing Employee Performance and Reward – Concepts, practices and strategies*. Cambridge: Cambridge University Press

Simmons, C. and Valentine, E. (2000) 'Good mixers', *People Management*, Vol.6, No.7, 30 March: 48–50

Simms, J. (2006) 'Put into practice', *People Management*, Vol.12, No.4, 23 February: 30–3

Simms, J. (2007) 'Direct action: HR goes green', *People Management*, Vol.13, No.15, 26 July: 36–9

Simon, H. A. (1945) *Administrative Behaviour*, 2nd edition. New York: Free Press

Simon, H. A. (1955) 'A behavioural model of rational choice', *Quarterly Journal of Economics*, Vol.69: 99–118

Sinclair, A., Robertson-Smith, G. and Hennessy, J. (2008) *Management Agenda 2008*. Horsham: Roffey Park Institute. Outline available online at: http://www.roffeypark.com/whatweoffer/Research/reports/Pages/managementagenda2008.aspx [accessed 12 August 2008]

Skapinker, M. (2002) *Knowledge Management*. Change Agenda. London: CIPD

Skinner, B. F. (1953) *Science and Human Behaviour*. London: Macmillan

Skinner, D. (2004) 'Evaluation and change management: rhetoric and reality', *Human Resource Management Journal*, Vol.14, No.3: 5–19

Sloman, M. (2007a) 'Skills at work', *Impact:* Quarterly update on CIPD Policy and Research. Issue 20, August. London: CIPD; pp6–9

Sloman, M. (2007b) *The Changing World of the Trainer: Emerging good practice*. London: CIPD

Sloman, M. (2007c) 'World standard', *People Management*, Vol.13, No.6, 22 March: 38–40

Sloman, M. (2007d) 'Chinese puzzle', *People Management*, Vol.13, No.1, 11 January: 38–43

Sloman, M. (2008a) 'Learning and development – from top-down to support and challenge'. In CIPD (ed.) *Reflections on the 2008 Learning and Development Survey: latest trends in learning, training and development*. London: CIPD; pp9–11. Online version also available at: http://www.cipd.co.uk/onlineinfodocuments/surveys [accessed 8 May 2008]

Sloman, M. (2008b) 'Strategic alignment – establishing expectations'. *Impact:* Quarterly update on CIPD Policy and Research. Issue 23, May: 16–17. Online version also available at: http://www.cipd.co.uk/research/rsrchplcypubs/_impact.htm [accessed 1 August 2008]

Small Business Service (2001) *Small Firms: Big Business. A Review of Small and Medium-Sized Enterprises in the UK*. London: HMSO

Smedley, T. (2008) 'Learning from the past?', *People Management*, Vol.14, No.15, 24 July: 18–22

Smethurst, S. (2005) 'Training providers criticised over lack of awareness', *People Management*, Vol.11, No.13, 30 June: 12

Smethurst, S. (2007) 'Keep the faith', *People Management*, Vol.13, No.4, 22 February: 33–4

Smewing, C. (2004) 'Feeling the way', *People Management*, Vol.10, No.21, 28 October: 66

Smith, A. (1759) *The Theory of Moral Sentiments*. London: A. Millar. For (imperfect) copy filmed from the Kress Library, see also books.google.co.uk/books, search for 'Adam Smith' [accessed 9 October 2008]

Smith, P. J. and Sadler-Smith, E. (2006) *Learning in Organizations: Complexities and diversities*. London: Routledge

Snell, S. (2005) 'Bilateral thinking', *People Management*, Vol.1, No.10, 13 October: 40–2

Solomon, N. (1999) 'Culture and difference in workplace learning'. In D. Boud and J. Garrick (eds) *Understanding Learning at Work*. London: Routledge; pp119–31

Sparrow, P and Cooper, C. (2003) *The Employment Relationship: Key challenges for HR*. Oxford: Butterworth-Heinemann

Sparrow, P. and Hiltrop, J.-M. (1994) *European Human Resource Management in Transition*. Hemel Hempstead: Prentice Hall

Sparrow, P. R. (1999) 'Is human resource management in crisis?' In R. S. Schuler and S. E. Jackson (eds) *Strategic Human Resource Management*. Oxford: Blackwell; pp416–32

Spitzer, D. R. (2005) 'Learning effectiveness measurement: a new approach for measuring and managing learning to achieve business results', *Advances in Developing Human Resources*, Vol.7, No.1: 55–70

Stacey, R. D. (1995) 'The science of complexity: an alternative perspective for strategic change processes', *Strategic Management Journal*, Vol.16, No.6: 477–95

Starkey, K. (1996) 'Executive tourism: the dynamics of strategic leadership in the MNC'. In K. Starkey (ed.) *How Organizations Learn*. London: International Thomson Business Press; pp368–80

Starkey, K. and McKinlay, A. (1993) *Strategy and the Human Resource: Ford and the Search for Competitive Advantage*. Oxford: Blackwell

Stead, V. (2004) 'Business-focused evaluation: a case study of a collaborative model', *Human Resource Development International*, Vol.7, No.1: 39–56

Steare, R. (2006) 'How to create an ethical culture', *People Management*, Vol.12, No.3, 9 February: 46–7

Stern, E. and Sommerlad, E. (1999) *Workplace Learning, Culture and Performance*. London: Institute of Personnel and Development

Sternberg, R. J. (1994) 'PRSVL: an integrative framework for understanding mind in context'. In R. J. Sternberg and R. K. Wagner (eds) *Mind in Context: Interactionist perspectives on human intelligence*. Cambridge: Cambridge University Press; pp218–32

Stevens, C. (1985) 'Assessment centres: the British experience', *Personnel Management*, Vol.17, No.7: 28–31

Stevens, J. (2000) *High Performance Working Is for Everyone*. London: Institute of Personnel and Development/International Labour Organisation

Stevens, J. and Ashton, D. (1999) 'Underperformance appraisal', *People Management*, Vol.5, No.14, 15 July: 31–2

Stewart, J. and Beaver, G. (eds) (2004) *HRD in Small Organisations: Research and practice*. London: Routledge

Stewart, J. and Harris, L. (2003) 'HRD and HRM: an uneasy relationship', *People Management*, Vol.9, No.19, 25 September: 58

Stewart, J. and Tansley, C. (2002) *Training in the Knowledge Economy*. London: CIPD

Stone, A. (2006) 'The new office: smaller, but its scope is huge'. *Sunday Times 'Business Agility' supplement*, 26 February: 21–4

Stone, A. (2007) 'Clean up in business by being responsible', *Sunday Times: Companies that Count 2007*, 6 May: 13

Stone, I., Braidford, P. and Houston, M. (2006) *Insights from studying the 2004 Sunday Times' 50 Best SMEs to Work For. Report prepared for the Small Business Council*. Durham: Durham Business School. Internet only. http//www.berr.gov.uk – go to 'Reports and Publication' then search 'Small firms'. [accessed 3 May 2008]

Storey, J. (1994) *New Wave Manufacturing Strategies: Organizational and human resource management dimensions*. London: Chapman

Storey, J. (1992) *Developments in the Management of Human Resources*. Oxford: Blackwell

Strack, R. and Krinks, P. (2008) 'The talent crunch', *People Management*, Vol.14, No.13, 26 June: 30–1

Strategy Unit (2002) *In Demand: Adult skills for the 21st century, Part 2*. Available from strategy@cabinet-office.x.gsi.gov.uk. Online version also available at: http://www.cabinetoffice.gov.uk/strategy/work_areas/workforce_development.aspx [accessed 16 April 2008]

Sturges, J., Guest, D., Conway, N. and Davey, K. M. (2002) 'A longitudinal study of the relationship between career management and organisational commitment among graduates in the first ten years at work', *Journal of Organisational Behaviour*, Vol.23, No.6: 731–48

Styhre, A. and Josephson, P.-E. (2007) 'Coaching the site manager: effects on learning and managerial practice', *Construction Management and Economics*, Vol.25, No.12: 1295–1304

Sung, J., Raddon, A. and Ashton, D. (2006) *Skills Abroad: A comparative assessment of international policy approaches to skills leading to the development of policy recommendations for the UK*. Research Report 16. May. South Yorkshire: Sector Skills Development Agency. Online version also available at: http//www.skillsforbusiness.org.uk [accessed 29 April 2008]

Swailes, S. (2002) 'Organisational commitment: a critique of the construct and measures', *International Journal of Management Reviews*, Vol.4, No.2: 155–78

Swart, J. and Kinnie, N. (2007) *Managing Across Boundaries: Human resource management beyond the firm*. London: CIPD

Swart, J., Kinnie, N. and Purcell, J. (2003) *People and Performance in Knowledge-Intensive Firms: A comparison of six research and technology organisations*. London: CIPD

Swidler, A. (1986) 'Culture in action: symbols and strategies', *American Sociological Review*, Vol.5: 273–86

Tamkin, P. (2005) *Measuring the Contribution of Skills to Business Performance: A Summary for Employers*. Nottingham: DfES Publications. Online version also available at: http://www.employment-studies.co.uk/pdflibrary/rw39.pdf [accessed 12 April 2008]

Tansley, C., Turner, P. A., Foster, C., Harris, L. M., Sempik, A., Stewart, J. and Williams, H. (2007) *Talent: Strategy, Management and Measurement*. Research into Practice. London: CIPD. Summary available online at: http://www.cipd.co.uk/Bookstore/research.htm [accessed 7 August 2008]

Taylor, F. W. (1947) *Scientific Management*. New York: Harper & Row

Taylor, H. (1991) 'The systematic training model: corn circles in search of a spaceship?', *Management Education and Development*, Vol.22, part 4: 258–78

Temple, M. (2007) 'Whose department?', *People Management*, Vol.13, No.12, 14 June: 7

Tennant, M. (1999) 'Is learning transferable?' In D. Boud and J. Garrick (eds) *Understanding Learning at Work*. London: Routledge; pp165–79

Terry, M. and Purcell, J. (1997) 'Return to slender', *People Management*, Vol.3, No.21, 23 October: 46–48, 51

The Times (2006a) 'A class apart', *The Times*, leader, 28 March: 19

The Times (2006b) 'Sector needs to "get smart"', *The Times, Public Agenda*, 31 January: 4

The Times (2007) 'Up with School', *The Times,* leader, 12 January: 14

The Times (2008a) 'New contract alarms charities', *The Times, Public Agenda*, 5 February: 8

The Times (2008b) 'Shared services: economies of wishful thinking', *The Times, Public Agenda*, 13 May: 8

The Times (2008c) 'Beyond boom and bust', *The Times*, leader, 10 October: 2

The Times (2008d) 'Confidence boost', *The Times*, leader, 9 October: 2

Thomas, M. (1985) 'In search of culture: holy grail or gravy train?', *Personnel Management*, Vol.17, No.9, September: 24–7

Tjepkema, S. (2002) 'Conclusions from case studies and survey'. In S. Tjepkema, J. Stewart, S. Sambrook, M. Mulder, H.Ter Horst and J. Scheerens (eds) *HRD and Learning Organisations in Europe*. London: Routledge; pp156–77

Tjepkema, S. (2003) *The learning infrastructure of self-managing work teams*. PhD. thesis. The Netherlands: Twente University

Tjepkema, S., Ter Horst, H. and Mulder, M. (2002) 'Learning organisations and HRD'. In S. Tjepkema, J. Stewart, S. Sambrook, M. Mulder, H. Ter Horst and J. Scheerens (eds) *HRD and Learning Organisations in Europe*. London: Routledge; pp6–19

Tomkinson, B. (2005) 'Organizational change'. In J. Wilson (ed.) *Human Resource Development: Learning and training for individuals and organizations*, 2nd edition. London: Kogan Page; pp44–57

Tomlinson, M. (2004) *14–19 Curriculum and Qualifications Reform. Final Report of the Working Group on 14–19 Reform*. Nottingham: DfES. Online version also available at: http://image.guardian.co.uk/sys-files/Education/documents/2004/10/18/Tomreport.pdf [accessed 4 May 2008]

Torrington, D. and Weightman, J. (1985) *The Business of Management*. London: Prentice Hall

Training Journal and Institute for Employment Studies (2008) *Learning and Development 2020. Interim Findings – February 2008*. University of Sussex, Brighton: IES. Online version also available at: http//www.employment-studies.co.uk [accessed 2 August 2008]

Trevino, L. K. and Weaver, G. R. (2001) 'Organizational justice and ethics program "follow-through": influences on employees' harmful and helpful behavior', *Business Ethics Quarterly*, Vol.11, No.4: 651–71

Trist, E. and Bamforth, K. (1951) 'Some social and psychological consequences of the longwall method of coal-getting', *Human Relations*, Vol.4: 3–38

Truss, C. and Gratton, L. (1994) 'Strategic human resource management: a conceptual approach', *International Journal of Human Resource Management*, Vol.5, No.3: 663–86

Truss, K., Soane, E., Edwards, C. Y. L., Wisdom, K., Croll, A. and Burnett, J. (2006) *Working Life: Employee attitudes and engagement 2006*. Research Report. London: CIPD

Tulip, S. (2006) 'Lighting the way', *People Management*, Vol.12, No.18, 14 September: 44–5

Turner, A. (2004) *Pensions: Challenges and Choices: The First Report of the Pensions Commission*. London: The Stationery Office

Turner, A. (2005) *A New Pensions Settlement for the 21st Century: The Second Report of the Pensions Commission*. London: The Stationery Office

Tushman, M. and Nadler, D. (1996) 'Organizing for innovation'. In K. Starkey (ed.) *How Organizations Learn*. London: International Thomson Business Press; pp135–55

Tyson, L. (2003) *The Tyson Report on the Recruitment and Development of Non-executive Directors*. London: London Business School. Online version also available at: http://www.london.edu/facultyresearch.html?url=http://facultyresearch.london.edu/detpub.asp?id=7803 [accessed 11 August 2008]

Ulrich, D. (1987) 'Organizational capability as a competitive advantage: human resource professionals as strategic partners', *Human Resource Planning*, Vol.10, No.4: 169–84

Ulrich, D. (1997) *Human Resource Champions: The next agenda for adding value and delivering results*. Boston, MA: Harvard Business School Press

Ulrich, D. (2007) 'The new HR organization', *Workforce Management*, Vol.86, No.21: 40–4

Ulrich, D. (2008) 'Not-so-standard deviation', *People Management*, Vol.14, No.16, 7 August: 32–3

Ulrich, D. and Beatty, D. (2001) 'From players to partners: extending the HR playing field', *Human Resource Management*, Vol.40, No.4: 293–307

Ulrich, D. and Brockbank, W. (2005) *The HR Value Proposition*. Boston, MA: Harvard Press

Vaill, P. B. (1996) 'Purposing of high-performing systems'. In K. Starkey (ed.) *How Organizations Learn*. London: International Thomson Business Press; pp60–81

Valentin, C. (2006) 'Researching human resource development: emergence of a critical approach to HRD enquiry', *International Journal of Training and Development*, Vol.10, No.1: 17–29

Van Luijk, H. (1994) 'Business ethics: the field and its importance'. In B. Harvey (ed.) *Business Ethics: A European approach*. Hemel Hempstead: Prentice Hall International (UK); pp12–31

Vere, D. (2005) *Fit for Business: Building a strategic HR function in the public sector*. Research Report. London: CIPD. Online summary also available at: http://www.cipd.co.uk/research/ [accessed 13 May 2008]

Vere, D. and Butler, L. (2007) *Fit for Business: Transforming HR in the public sector*. Research Report. London: CIPD. Online summary also available at: http://www.cipd.co.uk/research/ [accessed 13 May 2008]

Von Krogh, G., Roos, J. and Slocum, K. (1994) 'An essay on corporate epistemology', *Strategic Management Journal*, Vol.15, (Summer Special) Issue 5: 53–71

Vroom, V. H. and Deci, E. L. (eds) (1970) *Management and Motivation: Selected readings*. Harmondsworth: Penguin

Vygotsky, L. S. (1978) *Mind in Society: The development of higher psychological processes*. Cambridge, MA: Harvard University Press

Wageman, R., Nunes, D., Burruss, J. and Hackman, R. (2008) *Senior Leadership Teams: What it takes to make them great*. Boston, MA: Harvard Business Press. Outline available online at: http://blog.theleadershipsphere.com.au/ the_leadership_sphere/2008/01/senior-leadersh. html [accessed 12 August 2008]

Wain, D. (2008a) 'Method acting', *People Management*, Vol.14, No.4, 21 February: 25–7

Wain, D. (2008b) 'Why the end of the blend is not in sight for learning', *People Management*, Vol.14, No.12, 12 June: 21

Walker, B. A. (1994) 'Valuing differences: the concept and a model'. In C. Mabey and P. Iles. (eds) *Managing Learning*. London: The Open University and Routledge; pp211–23

Walker, D. (2007) 'Power of three', *Royal Society of Arts Journal*, February: 56–9

Walker, J. (1992) *Human Resource Strategy*. New York: McGraw-Hill

Wallace, M. (1990) 'Can Action Learning live up to its reputation?', *Management Education and Development*, Vol.21, Part 2: 90

Ward, L. (2004) 'Drive to tackle failures focuses on key skills', *Guardian*, 18 February: 4

Warnock, Baroness (2006) 'The foundations of global morality'. Lecture at the Royal Society of Arts. *RSA Journal*, April: 24–31

Warr, P. B. and Bird, M. W. (1968) *Identifying Supervisory Training Needs*. Training Information Paper No.2. London: HMSO

Warr, P., Bird, M. W. and Rackham, N. (1970) *Evaluation of Management Training*. Aldershot: Gower

Warren, C. (2006) 'Curtain call', *People Management*, Vol.12, No.6, 23 March: 25–9

Webster, P., Charter, D. and Hosking, P. (2008) 'World must follow my example, says Brown', *The Times*, 10 October: 1

Webster, P. (2008) 'Learn more skills or face losing benefit, jobless will be told', *The Times*, 29 January: 11

Weick, K. E. and Westley, F. (1999) 'Organizational learning: affirming an oxymoron'. In S. R. Clegg, C. Hardy and W. R. Nord (eds) *Managing Organizations: Current Issues*. London: Sage; pp190–208

Wenger, E., McDermott, R. and Snyder, W. M. (2002) *Cultivating Communities of Practice*. Boston, MA: Harvard Business School Press

Wernerfelt, B. (1984) 'A resource-based view of the firm', *Strategic Management Journal*, Vol.5, No.2: 171–80

West, M. A., Borrill, C. and Dawson, J. (2002) 'The link between the management of employees and patient mortality in acute hospitals', *International Journal of Human Resource Management*, Vol.13, No.8: 1299–1310

West, P. (2002) 'Learning to change, changing to learn: case studies in the automotive sector'. In J. McGoldrick, J. Stewart. and S. Watson (eds) *Understanding Human Resource Development: A research-based approach*. London: Routledge; pp182–203

Westwood, A. (2001) 'Drawing a line – who is going to train our workforce?' In D. Wilson, E. Lank, A. Westwood, E. Keep, C. Leadbeater and M. Sloman *The Future of Learning for Work: Executive Briefing*. London: CIPD; pp17–22

White, J. (2008) 'Education is not an experiment, Mr Balls', *Daily Telegraph*, 19 April: 22

White, M. (1996) 'Flexible response', *People Management*, Vol.2, No.6, 21 March: 33

White, M., Hill, S., Mills, C. and Smeaton, D. (2004) *Managing To Change? British Workplaces and the Future of Work*. Basingstoke: Palgrave Macmillan

Whittaker, M. (2003) 'Cinderella treatment', *People Management*, Vol.8, No.1, 9 January: 27–30

Whittington, R. (2002) 'Corporate structure: from policy to practice'. In A. Pettigrew, H. Thomas and R. Whittington (eds) *Handbook of Strategy and Management*. London: Sage; pp113–38

Whittington, R. and Mayer, M. (2002) *Organising for Success in the Twenty-First Century: A starting-point for change*. Research Report. London: CIPD. Summary available at: http://www.cipd.co.uk/subjects/corpstrtgy/orgdevelmt/org4succ.htm [accessed 18 July 2008]

Whittington, R., Pettigrew, A. and Thomas, H. (2002) 'Conclusion: doing more in strategy research'. In A. Pettigrew, H. Thomas and R. Whittington (eds) *Handbook of Strategy and Management*. London: Sage; pp475–88

Wilson, B. (2008) 'Hidden dragons', *People Management*, Vol.14, No.16, 7 August: 18–23

Wilson, F. (2006) 'HR expanding its horizons'. *Impact*: Quarterly update on CIPD Policy and Research. Issue 14, February. London: CIPD; pp6–7

Wilson, J. P. (ed.) (1999) *Human Resource Development: Learning and training for individuals and organizations*. London: Kogan Page

Wilson, J. P. (ed.) (2005) *Human Resource Development: Learning and training for individuals and organizations*, 2nd edition. London: Kogan Page

Wilson, J. P. and Cattell, A. (2005) 'Knowledge management'. In J. P. Wilson (ed.) *Human Resource Development: Learning and training for individuals and organizations*, 2nd edition. London: Kogan Page.

Wiltshire (2005) 'Fundamentals of adult learning'. In J. P. Wilson (ed.) *Human Resource Development: Learning and training for individuals and organizations*, 2nd edition. London: Kogan Page; pp201–19

Wintermantel, R. E. and Mattimore, K. L. (1997) 'In the changing world of human resources: matching measures to mission', *Human Resource Management*, Vol.36, No.3: 337–42

Wintour, P. (2008a) 'Business to fund 30,000 new places in university shake-up', *The Guardian*, 14 April: 2

Wintour, P. (2008b) 'Man with a mission to open universities to the many', *The Guardian*, 14 April: 12

Wood, S. and De Menezes, L. (1998) 'High commitment management in the UK: evidence from the Workplace Industrial Relations Survey and Employers Manpower and Skills Practices Survey', *Human Relations*, Vol.51, No.4: 485–515

Woodall, J. (2000) 'Corporate support for work-based management development', *Human Resource Management Journal*, Vol.10, No.1: 18–32

Woodall, J. and Winstanley, D. (1998) *Management Development: Strategy and Practice*. Oxford: Blackwell

Woodall, J., Alker, A., Macneil, C. and Shaw, S. (2002) 'Convergence and divergence in HRD: research and practice across Europe'. In J. McGoldrick, J. Stewart. and S. Watson (eds) *Understanding Human Resource Development: A research-based approach*. London: Routledge; pp339–54

Workplace Employment Relations Survey (2004) London: Department of Trade and Industry/ Economic and Social Research Council/Advisory, Conciliation and Arbitration Service/ Policy Studies Institute. Also available at: http://www.berr.gov.uk/employment/research-evaluation/wers-2004/ [accessed 1 April 2008]

Worrall, L. and Cooper, C. (2006) 'Short changed', *People Management*, Vol.2, No.13, 29 June: 36–8

Wright, P. M., Snell, S. A. and Jacobsen, P. H. H. (2004) 'Current approaches to HR strategies: inside-out versus outside-in', *Human Resource Planning*, Vol.27, No.4: 36–46

Younger, J., Smallwood, N. and Ulrich, D. (2007) 'Developing your organization's brand as a talent developer', *Human Resource Planning*, Vol.30, No.2: 21–9

Zacharias, L. (2003) 'Small change', *People Management*, Vol.9, No.9, 1 May: 24–7

Zemke, R. (1985) 'The Honeywell studies: how managers learn to manage', *Training,* August: 50–1

Zohar, D. and Drake, J. (2000) 'On the whole', *People Management*, Vol.6, No.8, 13 April: 55

Zuboff, S. (1998) *In the Age of the Smart Machine.* New York: Basic Books

Subject Index

Author Index

The CIPD would like to thank the following members of the CIPD Publishing editorial board for their help and advice:

- Caroline Hook, Huddersfield University Business School
- Edwina Hollings, Staffordshire University Business School
- Pauline Dibben, Sheffield University Business School
- Simon Gurevitz, University of Westminster Business School
- Barbara Maiden, University of Wolverhampton Business School
- Wendy Yellowley and Marilyn Farmer, Buckinghamshire New University School of Business and Management